MW00424963

Compliments of Hamilton and Sargent

A Story *of* Mystery *and* Tragedy *on the* Gilded Age Frontier

Maura Jane Farrelly

University of Nebraska Press
Lincoln

The University of Nebraska Press is part of a land-grant institution with campuses and programs on the past, present, and future homelands of the Pawnee, Ponca, Otoe-Missouria, Omaha, Dakota, Lakota, Kaw, Cheyenne, and Arapaho Peoples, as well as those of the relocated Ho-Chunk, Sac and Fox, and Iowa Peoples.

Library of Congress Cataloging-in-Publication Data
Names: Farrelly, Maura Jane, author.
Title: Compliments of Hamilton and Sargent: a story of mystery and tragedy on the Gilded Age frontier / Maura Jane Farrelly.
Description: Lincoln: University of Nebraska Press, [2024] | Includes bibliographical references and index.
Identifiers: LCCN 2023037531
ISBN 9781496237057 (paperback)
ISBN 9781496239273 (epub)
ISBN 9781496239280 (pdf)
Subjects: LCSH: Sargent, John Dudley, 1861–1913. | Hamilton, Robert Ray, 1851–1890. | Sargent, Edith Drake. | Frontier and pioneer life—Wyoming—Jackson Hole. | Jackson Hole (Wyo.)—Biography. | Scandals—New York (State)—New York—History. | New York (N.Y.)—Biography. | BISAC: HISTORY / United States / 19th Century | LANGUAGE ARTS & DISCIPLINES / Journalism
Classification: LCC F767.T28 F37 2024 | DDC 978.7/55030922 [B]—dc23/eng/20240312
LC record available at https://lccn.loc.gov/2023037531

Set in Emigre Filosofia by A. Shahan.

For my mother, Kathleen Swift Farrelly

And for my father, Eugene Vincent Farrelly

Contents

Illustrations

Acknowledgments

This book could not have been written without the assistance of Kenneth and Lenore Diem. The oral interviews they conducted in the 1970s and the extensive document collection they gathered and then donated to the American Heritage Center at the University of Wyoming were vital to my research. I am particularly grateful to Lenore for putting me in touch with Kenneth's assistant, Celeste Havener, who shared additional documents with me that are not a part of the AHC collection.

At the American Heritage Center, I was fortunate to work with Ginny Kilander, Molly Marcusse, and John Waggener. I thank them for their assistance. The same goes for Robin Everett, Carl Hallberg, and Kathy Marquis at the Wyoming State Archives; Kasi White at the University of Wyoming's Chisum Special Collections Library; Nora Dewitt-Hoeger at the Jackson Hole Historical Society and Museum; Anne Foster at the Yellowstone Heritage and Research Center; Heidi Stringham at the Utah State Archives; Joseph Van Nostrand at the County Clerk Records Office in New York City; Jocelyn Wilk at Columbia University's Rare Book and Manuscript Library; and Elayne Watts at the Washington County Courthouse in Machias, Maine.

Stephen Nicholas, Jereme Frank, and Ken Laustsen at the Maine Forest Service helped me understand the timber industry in that state. My conversations with Nigel Bark from the New York State Office of Mental Health assisted me in devising a way to discuss Edith Sargent's health history, even though the OMH was legally obliged to deny me access to her medical records. Rex Lawson and Jim Cardoza provided me with useful information about player pianos and travel trunks; Gyla Gonzalez told me that "Mitchelana" was "Muchilena"; Aimee Slater helped me find the rest of "Mrs. Eva Hamilton's Story"; and in an old house he was restoring on Campobello Island, New Brunswick, Tim Smith showed me that my instincts were correct about the phrase "Compliments of."

Much of my research was funded with grants I received from the Theodore and Jane Norman Fund at Brandeis University and the University of Wyoming–National Park Service AMK Ranch Research Station in Grand Teton National Park. The Norman Fund also provided me with a generous subvention that enabled the University of Nebraska Press to price this book affordably.

Michael Dillon and Bonnie Robinson at the UW-NPS research station have been enthusiastic supporters of this project. Bonnie put me in touch with Gordon Richman, who put me in touch with Ann Seacrest, who was able to tell me what happened to Beatrice Ray Hamilton. I am grateful to Ann and her husband, Kent, for their hospitality and for sharing their family with me. I am also grateful to Bill Fessel, who taught me a lot about his mother, Catherine Winthrop Sargent.

Before I discovered this project, my research focus was on colonial and early American religious history. I knew little about the Gilded Age or the American West, and I am grateful to my colleague at Brandeis Jerome Tharaud, along with Hal Corbett, Katie Curtiss, and Chris Slay, for telling me who and what to read.

Harriet Corbett lent me her copyediting skills, as did Beth Beighlie, Moira Davenport, Jennifer Ford Davis, Alison Donohue-Harding, Glen Heiss, and Sam Winch. Terrell Austin, Jack Davis, Mark Feeney, Eileen McNamara, Dona Nicholas, and Sybil Schlesinger read the manuscript or the book proposal and offered me valuable advice. My former students Donnie Weisse and Anna Zeitz did the same—as did Clark Whitehorn and Taylor Gilreath at the University of Nebraska Press. Clark was the first editor to make me feel like this project was worthwhile. My nieces, Anna and Elise Vinick and Bridget Farrelly, helped me with the tedious but vital work of index creation. They are part of a circle of family and friends who have been listening to me prattle on about Ray, Jack, and Edith for years now, and I am grateful to them all: Laura Anrud, Dale Archer, Graham Austin, Tucker Austin, Eson Kim Avent, Nino Badridze, Bryan Barks, Tommy Bass, Denise Bennett, Moe Brown, Kim Chater, Donna Decatrel, Amber, Brother Gene, Father Gene, Jack, and Meg Farrelly, Craig Foucht, Luis Guevara, Ann Lambert, Stephanie Lynn, Megan

McOsker, James Pritchard, Chris Riley, Ann Rindone, Chris Rodgers, Leslie Turner, Peter and Sam Vinick, Tammy Waltzman, and—as always—Charley Simmons.

The person who was my greatest supporter and my most helpful sounding board was my mother, Kathleen Swift Farrelly, to whom this book is dedicated, along with my extraordinary father. Mom listened to every tale from every archive, kept track of every character, and read every word I wrote—four times—including the nearly sixty thousand words I ultimately threw out.

I wanted my mother more than anyone to hold this book in her hands. It never occurred to me that she would not. But in December 2022 my mother was diagnosed with stage 4 pancreatic cancer, a disease that I already knew takes no prisoners. She died on October 2, 2023, the day before I received the copyedited manuscript from Emily Shelton. I got Kari Andresen's stunning cover one week later.

My mother is my ballast and my muse. The nearly ten months she gave us beyond her diagnosis ravaged her body and were her final gift. They allowed me to wrap my head around what was coming and to say everything I needed to say to her. Mom, I will never look back on my life with you wishing I had told you what you are to me. I know that you know I love you forever.

Author's Note

For the sake of consistency, I have chosen to capital-
ize "Black," "White," and "Indigenous" whenever I
have used those words as a racial or ethnic category.

Compliments of
Hamilton and Sargent

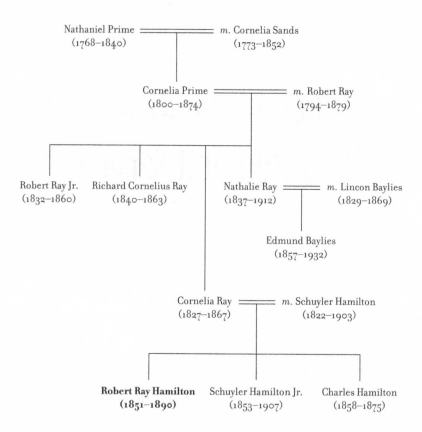

Nathaniel Prime ══════ m. Cornelia Sands
(1768–1840)   (1773–1852)

Cornelia Prime ══════ m. Robert Ray
(1800–1874)   (1794–1879)

Robert Ray Jr.   Richard Cornelius Ray   Nathalie Ray ══════ m. Lincon Baylies
(1832–1860)   (1840–1863)   (1837–1912)   (1829–1869)

Edmund Baylies
(1857–1932)

Cornelia Ray ══════ m. Schuyler Hamilton
(1827–1867)   (1822–1903)

Robert Ray Hamilton   Schuyler Hamilton Jr.   Charles Hamilton
(1851–1890)   (1853–1907)   (1858–1875)

Relevant Rays and Primes.

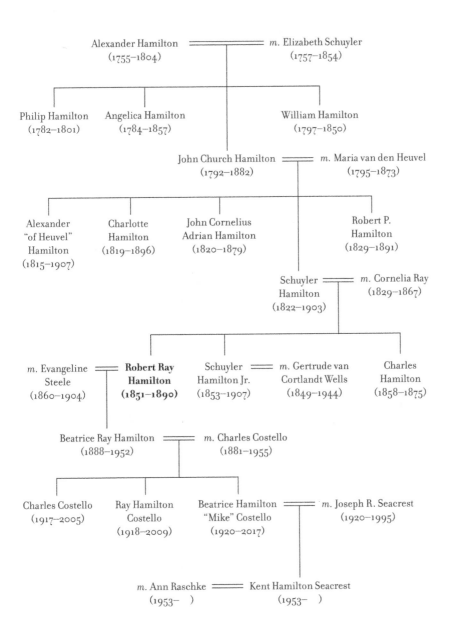

Relevant Hamiltons.

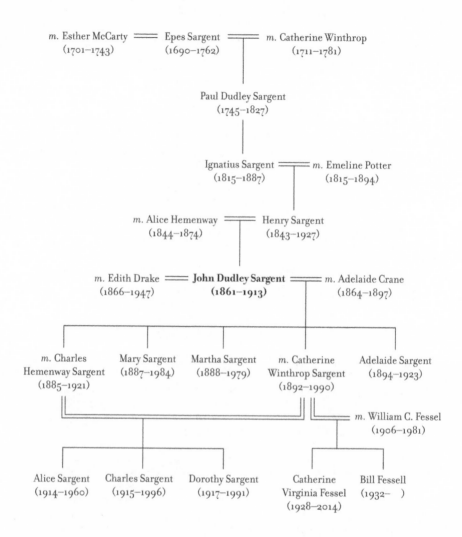

m. Esther McCarty ══ Epes Sargent ══ m. Catherine Winthrop
(1701–1743)   (1690–1762)   (1711–1781)

Paul Dudley Sargent
(1745–1827)

Ignatius Sargent ══ m. Emeline Potter
(1815–1887)   (1815–1894)

m. Alice Hemenway ══ Henry Sargent
(1844–1874)   (1843–1927)

m. Edith Drake ══ **John Dudley Sargent** ══ m. Adelaide Crane
(1866–1947)   **(1861–1913)**   (1864–1897)

m. Charles   Mary Sargent   Martha Sargent   m. Catherine   Adelaide Sargent
Hemenway Sargent   (1887–1984)   (1888–1979)   Winthrop Sargent   (1894–1923)
(1885–1921)   (1892–1990)

══ m. William C. Fessel
(1906–1981)

Alice Sargent   Charles Sargent   Dorothy Sargent   Catherine   Bill Fessell
(1914–1960)   (1915–1996)   (1917–1991)   Virginia Fessel   (1932–   )
                                                         (1928–2014)

Jack's Sargent family.

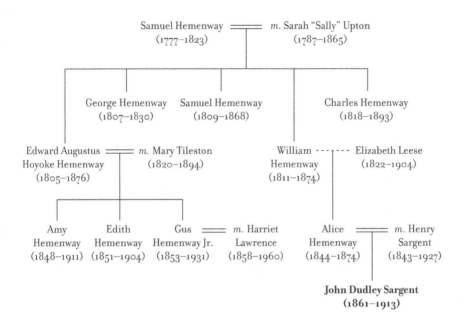

Samuel Hemenway
(1777–1823)
    m. Sarah "Sally" Upton
(1787–1865)

George Hemenway
(1807–1830)
    Samuel Hemenway
(1809–1868)
    Charles Hemenway
(1818–1893)

Edward Augustus
Hoyoke Hemenway
(1805–1876)
    m. Mary Tileston
(1820–1894)
    William
Hemenway
(1811–1874)
    Elizabeth Leese
(1822–1904)

Amy
Hemenway
(1848–1911)
    Edith
Hemenway
(1851–1904)
    Gus
Hemenway Jr.
(1853–1931)
    m. Harriet
Lawrence
(1858–1960)
    Alice
Hemenway
(1844–1874)
    m. Henry
Sargent
(1843–1927)

John Dudley Sargent
(1861–1913)

Jack's Hemenway family.

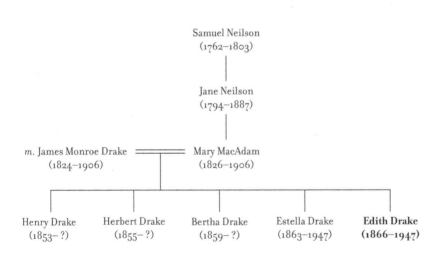

Samuel Neilson
(1762–1803)

Jane Neilson
(1794–1887)

m. James Monroe Drake
(1824–1906)
    Mary MacAdam
(1826–1906)

Henry Drake
(1853– ?)
    Herbert Drake
(1855– ?)
    Bertha Drake
(1859– ?)
    Estella Drake
(1863–1947)
    Edith Drake
(1866–1947)

Edith's family.

Prologue

Stories

I wrote this book because of a photograph my mother found in her parents' house after my grandmother died. A lone woman in silhouette stands outside a rough-hewn log cabin, playing a violin in the shadow of the Teton Mountains. A Victrola is situated in the grass in front of her, suggesting the music she's creating is not without accompaniment. Her hair is piled on top of her head. She wears a loose Garibaldi blouse, popularized in the 1860s by the leader of the Italian unification movement, and a slim, high-waisted skirt known as a "Rainy Daisy" that debuted in the 1890s. It had a higher-than-usual hemline, so that active women could wear it while hiking or playing tennis and not have to worry about tripping over themselves or having the skirt get wet.[1] On the back of the photograph, in her tight script, my grandmother had written the name "Edith Sargent."

Curious about who this woman was, I did what all good scholars do when faced with a question about the past: I hopped on Google. After narrowing my search, combining Edith's name with words like "violin" and "Wyoming," I finally discovered a letter to the editor in the online archives of the *New York Times*. It was written in August 1913 by a woman named Edith Sargent who took great exception to the way the *Times* had covered the death of her husband.

According to the newspaper, John Dudley Sargent had been a "recluse." He'd killed himself earlier that summer in the valley between the Gros Ventre and Teton Mountains known then as Jackson's Hole. "I am here to state as a loyal, loving wife that the man was incapable of committing murder," Edith angrily told the newspaper's editor. "He was never unbalanced except by melancholia, which does not prompt people to murder their chums."[2]

In its coverage of John Dudley Sargent's death, the *Times* had res-urrected rumors about his relationship with a man named Robert Ray Hamilton. "The stories to which Mrs. Sargent objects originated among ranchers in Jackson's Hole who did not like Sargent and Hamilton," the paper explained in an effort to give Edith's letter some context. "The stories had to do with the death of Hamilton and the first wife of Sargent. They were to the effect that Sargent knew more about Hamilton's death in October 1890 than was ever brought out by official investigators."[3]

The *Times* reminded its readers that Robert Ray Hamilton had been a state lawmaker from the Murray Hill district of Manhattan before he died. He was "the son of Gen. Schuyler Hamilton of this city," it noted—meaning he was the great-grandson of Alexander Hamilton, the nation's first treasury secretary. Ray Hamilton had also been "the central figure in a scandal in 1889," the *Times* recalled, "in which a woman by the name of Eva Mann and a purchased baby figured."[4]

Thus began my journey down the rabbit hole and into the den of other people's secrets that became the setting for this book. The secrets I uncov-ered soon involved more than just murder, suicide, baby-selling, and a founding father's family. They also involved bigamy, blackmail, debt, rape, incest, guillotining, *corpse-skinning*, child abuse, mental illness, and (not to be outdone by any of that) elk-poaching.

Suffice to say there were days when I found myself wondering whether this story was one I had any right to pursue and tell.

The older I get, the more comfortable I become with the reality that people are complicated, and that the most interesting people often have secrets, lives that are characterized to a greater or lesser degree by mys-tery or deliberate obfuscation. Teaching and writing about history has also helped me come to terms with this truth. Historians will rarely admit it, but archival research is often voyeuristic. Almost all of us go into an archive hoping to find something we were never meant to see, some-thing that was meant for some other set of eyes and is available to us now only because the person who created it or for whom it was intended is no longer alive to protect it from the prying eyes of others.

This book is a story about the secrets that shaped the lives of three Americans in the late nineteenth century: Robert Ray Hamilton, John Dudley Sargent, and Edith Drake Sargent. Exposed secrets are usually humiliating, and humiliation is what drove Ray, Jack, and Edith—independently from one another—to leave their lives in the eastern United States and settle in Wyoming, a wild and isolated region along the last remnants of America's frontier.

Ray hoped to free himself from a messy marriage that had attracted quite a bit of press attention in New York City. Jack was tired of being passed around by wealthy family members in New England who were more interested in business and philanthropy than they were in raising him. And Edith went west after a reporter for the *Boston Globe* discovered she'd had a romantic relationship with an infamous criminal in Paris who'd generated headlines all around the world.[5]

When they settled in Wyoming, Ray, Jack, and Edith were doing what generations of Americans before them had done, starting with those Puritans who left England in 1630 and founded the city of Boston along the shores of Massachusetts Bay: they were moving west, to what they believed to be an unsettled and uncivilized part of the world, because they hoped that doing so would make it possible for the humiliations and persecutions of their old lives to be forgotten.

In the case of Ray, Jack, and Edith, however, the strategy did not work. They were not forgotten—not in their own time and, to some extent, not even in ours. Robert Ray Hamilton is memorialized on a plaque at Riverside Drive and Seventy-Sixth Street in Manhattan that reduces his life and career to the scandal over his marriage. Jack is the subject of a folk opera called *Marymere*, which was showcased at the Brooklyn Academy of Music in January 2020, shortly before all live performances were shut down because of COVID-19. Just about any travel guide to Grand Teton National Park will tell you that Signal Mountain within the park was named for the "signal" fire set by the search party that found Ray Hamilton's body in the Snake River in 1890. And a historical marker on what used to be John Dudley Sargent's homestead—now a biological research center in the middle of Grand Teton National Park—calls Jack the "undesirable offspring" of a prominent East Coast family (the same family that produced the portrait painter John Singer Sargent). It also echoes the newspaper coverage Edith found so objectionable when it informs visitors Jack was "suspected of murdering his first wife and his partner, Hamilton."[6]

Meanwhile, Edith herself is a bit of a cult figure in Jackson Hole. I had no idea who she was when my mother showed me her picture, but many long-time residents of Jackson, Wyoming, would have recognized her instantly. The Chamber of Commerce there has used her image to promote tourism in the region (that is almost certainly the disappointingly mundane reason my grandmother had the photograph on the cover of this book in her possession). Edith Sargent is a character in a musical titled *Petticoat Rules*, which has been staged several times over the last twenty years by the Off the Square Theater Company in Jackson. And graduate students working at the biological research center on what used to be Jack Sargent's homestead have a tradition of grabbing bear spray and heading out into the woods to find Edith's "violin tree," a now-dead white bark pine that Edith is said to have climbed—sometimes naked—during the years she lived on the homestead so that she could privately play her violin and "gobble peanuts," according to one particularly amusing version of the story.[7]

The stories of Ray, Jack, and Edith and the secrets that defined their lives reveal truths about what it means to be a human being that transcend time and culture, even as they also caution us that "the past is a foreign country," to quote the British novelist L. P. Hartley. "They do things differently there."[8]

So many elements of the modern American experience—not just the elements that depend upon science and technology, but also the ones that depend upon collective agreements, formal and informal, to bestow meaning and power upon people and things—had to evolve into what they are: the existence of a single, national currency, for instance, or the connotation of a word. When Judge James Kent described Alexander Hamilton's legal argument as "pathetic" in 1805, after Ray Hamilton's great-grandfather had argued a libel case before the New York State Supreme Court in what turned out to be the final months of his life, he meant the observation as a compliment. Hamilton's appeal was "a master Piece of Pathetic, impassioned, & sublime Eloquence," Kent wrote. "I never heard him so great."[9] Clearly, two centuries ago, the ability to arouse pity was not a mark of inadequacy or weakness, as it often is now. There is much to be learned about our own times simply by contemplating this point.

Part of a historian's job is to be a docent or a diplomat. We guide our contemporaries through the foreign country that is the past, encouraging them to develop relationships with that country's culture and advising them on how to do so. Such a task requires us to emphasize to ourselves and our readers the ways in which the past is different and why. We are obliged to be vigilant about not falling into the trap of assuming that the manners, values, rules, and habits governing our lives today are the same ones that governed the lives of those who came before us—not even when the people we're contemplating inhabited the same landscapes we inhabit, swimming in the same lakes, gazing at the same mountains, navigating the same roads, and walking the same city streets.

Indeed, being a historical diplomat in the modern era sometimes requires us to recognize the extent to which the very landscape we inhabit has changed from what it once was—and how those changes, then, have reflected and shaped our values and goals. Human beings have always worked to alter their landscapes to make those landscapes conform to their wants and needs. Our ability to change our environment has expanded greatly in the last 150 years, a truth that crops up periodically throughout the course of this book. In fact, it was concerns about the scope and permanence of our ability to change the land that prompted federal officials to create America's first national park in 1872, eighteen years before John Dudley Sargent settled with his family fewer than twenty miles south of that park and invited Robert Ray Hamilton to join him there. Together the men planned to operate a hunting lodge that would entice visitors out of Yellowstone and down to the Tetons, where they could marvel at the glory and grandeur of that magnificent range.[10]

This, then, brings us to the other part of a historian's job, which is to recognize that even though the past is a foreign country, some impulses are shared by human beings across culture and time. People were awestruck by the Tetons long before we existed. If we are careful, they will still be awestruck by those mountains long after we are gone. There is something comforting about this truth—that we are rarely, if ever, the first people in the world to desire the things we desire, fear the things we fear, hate the things we hate, and love the things we love.

The world Ray, Jack, and Edith inhabited would seem foreign to us today in some significant and important ways, were it possible for us to be whisked back to the 1880s, when Jack brought his first wife, Adelaide Crane, to Wyoming from their shared hometown of Machias, Maine, or to 1906, when Edith posed with her violin for photographer Sumner Matteson under a lean-to, next to a Victrola, and before Mount Moran. Yet who among us hasn't taken a selfie in front of a stunning landscape or with a brand-new toy? The popularity of social media sites testifies to the fact that there is nothing foreign about the desire to be seen by others with the things that move us.

Ray, Jack, Edith, and all of the people who influenced their lives should not feel foreign to us, even if the rules, customs, and beliefs that governed them do. The passions that animated these people are the same passions that animate many of us today; the demons that haunted them are some of the same demons. And, actually, even their world should feel mildly familiar at times to modern-day readers. The decades that followed the Civil War were when America as we know it today started to take shape. The past may be a foreign country, but the dawn of the twentieth century is more like Canada or Mexico than Azerbaijan.

This book is about more than just secrets and the efforts of people to have their humiliations be forgotten. It's also a history of Gilded Age America, East and West—one where the routes traveled are determined by the lives of three people who were shaped in big and small ways by the history being discussed.

To understand Ray, Jack, and Edith and the secrets that defined them, the book has to interrogate the world they inhabited, the history that shaped them and the developments they witnessed and participated in that shape the lives of Americans today. All of our lives are a bit like a room that has been illuminated with a seemingly simple flick of the switch—which is to say there is nothing "simple" about our lives at all. There is a massive and complicated grid behind many of the decisions we make, and as with electricity, the source of our decisions sometimes lies very far away from us.

Ray, Jack, and Edith were early casualties of a revolution in transportation and communication technology that now touches the lives of many of us. The internet has opened up a vast wilderness of ideas and information to exploration and settlement. In so doing it has given our past actions an artificial kind of permanence, empowering strangers to discover those actions anew, years and sometimes even decades after we have moved on from them. In this sense, the internet has closed a kind of "frontier" that many of us didn't know was there—and mattered—until it was gone.[11]

The year Ray fled his scandal-laden life in New York and joined Jack and his first wife, Addie, on their homestead in Wyoming was the year the frontier famously "closed." After reviewing population data from the 1890 census, Robert Porter, head of the U.S. Census Bureau, announced his agency would no longer be using "westward expansion" as a rubric for tracking population growth. His reason was that there was no unsettled space left in the continental United States for the country's population to expand west into. "At present, the unsettled area has been so broken into by isolated bodies of settlement," Porter wrote—almost as if he were staring directly at the remote valley in northwestern Wyoming where Jack and his family had moved just a few years earlier—"that there can hardly be said to be a frontier line" left in the United States. All previous understandings of the population's "westward movement can not, therefore, any longer have a place in the census reports."[12]

Porter's announcement prompted a young historian from the University of Wisconsin named Frederick Jackson Turner to formulate an argument about the development of American cultural identity known as the "Frontier Thesis." The rugged, isolated, and untamed nature of life on the frontier, Turner argued in 1893, had shaped the character of America's people. Even when it was just an idea—a place people thought they might someday visit or move to, though they never did—the frontier shaped Americans' understanding of themselves; it turned them into fiercely independent people who believed it was their right to control their own destinies. The West was a place where Americans could go to reinvent themselves, a region wild enough to be unencumbered by the traditions, institutions, and reputations that always make it difficult for anyone to start over.[13] Put differently, the frontier made it possible for Americans to be forgotten.

Turner's Frontier Thesis continues to animate our cultural conceptions of the American West, even as Turner, himself, has been rightly criticized for ignoring the role of the federal government in promoting the settlement of the West, exaggerating the extent to which individuals relied upon only themselves for their survival, and failing to adequately consider the experiences of women, Indigenous Americans, and racial and ethnic minorities.[14] Turner's Frontier Thesis remains powerful not because it was a thoroughgoing explanation of every component of American cultural identity, but because the young historian was right to recognize that something significant was happening in his country at the dawn of the twentieth century. Something was being lost.

It wasn't just that population density in the West had risen to greater than two settled people per square mile, which was what the Census Bureau meant when it said the frontier had closed. It was also that the region was accessible now by train and telegraph. A journey from New York to Idaho that used to take two to three months could, by 1890, be done in three to four days. Messages that used to take weeks to be delivered could now be conveyed in a matter of minutes. Many of the people using telegraph services in the West were reporters for the Associated Press, a wire service that aimed to spread news and information *about* any part of the country *to* any part of the country, using a network of newspapers that all subscribed to its reports. The first AP journalist killed in the line of duty was a reporter who covered the Battle of Little Bighorn in southeastern Montana, three years before Jack Sargent moved to the Wyoming Territory and worked for the Union Pacific Railroad in Cheyenne.[15]

Civil service reforms implemented by Congress in the 1880s made the delivery system adopted by the U.S. Postal Service more efficient and reliable. By 1895 there were more than 1,200 post offices in Montana, Idaho, and Wyoming, four times as many as there had been twenty years earlier. Jack Sargent's first wife, Addie, planned on opening a post office at their ranch shortly before she died unexpectedly in 1897. She was going to call it "Hamilton P.O.," according to her husband, in memory of Ray. Once a letter made it to the post office in Cheyenne, it could be delivered to New York in just fifty-four hours. That's about as long as it takes a letter to go from Cheyenne to New York today.[16]

Word traveled fast after the closing of the frontier. This truth was one that Ray, Jack, and Edith were all forced to confront in various ways. It's the reason newspapers were able to remind readers of their humiliating stories years and even decades after those humiliations first happened. And it is the reason Ray, Jack, and Edith were never entirely forgotten.

In 1891, on the back of a photograph of the Tetons taken from his lodge along Jackson Lake, John Dudley Sargent wrote the words "Compliments of Hamilton + Sargent." It was a phrase you'd often find on postcards in the late nineteenth century. Business owners looking to advertise their products and services would have it printed onto cards that featured attractive images—a colorful tulip or morning glory, perhaps, or a cute little girl in a meadow, picking flowers. The cards were designed to be collected, the idea being that the image had been provided to the card collector by the business: "Compliments of Reynolds Brothers Fine Shoes," for example, or "Compliments of C. S. Price, Druggist."[17]

The lodge where the photograph was taken was something Ray and Jack had built together. Their intention had been to host wealthy vacationers from the East Coast, people who were willing to pay good money to awake to the same view Jack awoke to almost every summer morning for twenty-three years.

Today the Grand Teton Lodge Company charges visitors as much as $600 a night to have that morning view, suggesting that Ray and Jack were not wrong to think they might be able to make money off the grandeur of the Tetons, half a century before America's fifth-most-visited national park was created. Jack planned on turning the photograph into postcards, which he would then use to market his ranch to people in Boston and New York who, he knew, would recognize his last name and that of his deceased friend who had not been forgotten.[18]

More so than railroads, telegraphs, the closing of the American frontier, or baby-selling, corpse-skinning, bigamy, incest, and elk-poaching, this story is about people—their eccentricities, their naivete, their loneliness, their corruptibility, their eagerness to find or assume the worst in one another, and their longing for peace, beauty, anonymity, nobility, and love.

I bring it to you, compliments of Hamilton and Sargent.

Revolutionary Legacies

Evacuation Day used to be a riotous affair in New York City. Celebrated on November 25, the holiday marked the anniversary of the British army's retreat from Manhattan, nearly three months after the Treaty of Paris had been signed, and the Revolutionary War was completely over. New York had been a hotbed of Loyalist sentiment, occupied by British troops almost from the very beginning. In the negotiations that ended the war, England had demanded it be given enough time to safely relocate nearly thirty-five thousand supporters of the king who'd either lived in New York at the start of the war or moved into the city at some point during the conflict. Loyalists made up more than half of New York's civilian population, and many Patriots were being terribly ungracious winners, breaking into Loyalists' homes and smearing their furniture and dishes with whale blubber and excrement.[1]

You'd never know there had been so many Loyalists in New York, however, to look at the way the city's residents celebrated Evacuation Day in the decades that followed the British retreat. This "glorious day," as the famous diarist George Templeton Strong once called it, was for many years the most important holiday on New York's social calendar. It was an opportunity for the city's residents to "kick up our heels all day at our leisure," according to Strong. New York's schools were typically closed for the holiday. In 1836, however, administrators at Columbia College made the mistake of trying to hold classes on Evacuation Day, prompting sixteen-year-old Strong to declare the decision a "diabolical outrage." He and his peers all played hooky, rather than condone Columbia's gaffe and miss out on the fun.[2]

There were fireworks on the East River, parties in Fraunces Tavern, military drills on the Bowling Green, and parades—which included "wandering gypsies" and an "albino lady" for some reason in the 1830s—up

Broadway, past the Trinity churchyard where Alexander Hamilton was buried in 1804, and on to City Hall. "Why the New Yorkers celebrate this evacuation day annually, I don't know," one perplexed visitor from Maine observed in 1834. "Isn't it as well to forget that an enemy once had possession of your city?"[3]

As it turned out, many New Yorkers did eventually forget that their city had once been occupied by British troops. Interest in Evacuation Day waned in the 1860s, when the growing casualties of the Civil War gave Americans few reasons to celebrate. By November 1882 only the city's Irish immigrants, who seethed with resentment at all things British, seemed to care anymore that ninety-nine years earlier, the English army had left Manhattan with its collective tail between its legs. Most New Yorkers preferred to spend late November *inside*, quietly celebrating a holiday that Abraham Lincoln had declared in the midst of the Civil War. That holiday, Thanksgiving, wasn't a rollicking party, nor was it a celebration that belonged only or even especially to New Yorkers.[4]

The centennial year of New York's liberation needed to be different, however. The complacency and ignorance the city's residents had lapsed into about Evacuation Day was not acceptable in the year 1883. Philadelphia's residents had hosted an entire World's Fair in 1876 to mark the centennial of the signing of the Declaration of Independence in their city.[5] Philadelphia had a substantial claim to the young country's history, of course—but New York had been important to America's founding, too. And the men who comprised the Joint Committee on the Centennial Celebration of the Evacuation of New York by the British were determined to make sure every American knew that.

The committee was a mix of "old" and "new" New York—though it was mostly made up of the new. Its members came primarily from the ranks of the rich entrepreneurs whose business aplomb and often nonexistent scruples had made New York the epicenter of what Mark Twain and Charles Dudley Warner called "the Gilded Age," a period in America's history when the problems of political corruption, income inequality, labor unrest, and financial instability were masked by the wonders of technological development and the opulent spending of "robber barons" who had leveraged their personal and financial connections to create artificial monopolies that guaranteed them truly fantastic accumulations of wealth.

For every John Schuyler, whose great-grandfather Philip Schuyler had been in the Continental Congress, or Rutherfurd Stuyvesant, whose great-grandfather Lewis Morris had signed the Declaration of Independence, there was a Cornelius Vanderbilt II, Cyrus W. Field, or William E. Dodge Jr. serving on the committee.[6] None of these men could stake an ancestral claim to the American independence movement—but they all knew how to make money.

William Dodge was president of the Phelps Dodge Corporation, which had made a fortune in the 1870s, wiring America's cities and fueling the country's industrial revolution with copper and coal from its mines in New Mexico and Arizona. Cyrus Field had used substantial subsidies from the American and British governments to found the Atlantic Telegraph Company in 1856. Two years later that company laid the first telegraph line across the Atlantic Ocean, allowing Queen Victoria in London to send a greeting to President James Buchanan in Washington DC in fewer than six minutes.[7]

Cornelius Vanderbilt II was the favorite grandson of the "Commodore," who'd famously made his fortune in the 1830s off of steamships and then made his fortune again in the 1850s off of railroads. Cornelius II was the Vanderbilt who commissioned "the Breakers," the grandest of all the "cottages" along the famous Cliff Walk in Newport, Rhode Island. Today the villa is a museum. Visitors to the Breakers can gaze at Cornelius II's violet eyes and thick dark hair, thanks to a John Singer Sargent painting the museum acquired in 2009. Sargent was the most sought-after portrait painter of his generation, charging his clients $5,000 per painting—or about $150,000 in today's money. Only the very wealthy could afford to sit for John Singer Sargent. Members of the Vanderbilt family sat for him at least a dozen times.[8]

All of the committee's members were "gentlemen interested in the history of our city." Not all of them were gentlemen *directly connected* to the city's history, however—at least not yet. Many of them were just rich guys whose families had recently joined New York's social scene. They were on the committee because they wanted to make sure they were part of the celebration.

Evacuation Day was supposed to be about more than just seeing and being seen, however. The purpose of the holiday was to "hold in grateful memory the illustrious men who secured the independence of the States through their counsel and arms."[9] The newly wealthy members of the celebration committee, therefore, took special pains to ensure that people like John Schuyler and Rutherfurd Stuyvesant weren't the only descendants of historically famous New Yorkers involved in the festivities.

Among the events the committee planned was a "banquet for representatives of the old families" of New York. It was to be held on November 26 at the Hotel Brunswick, a stately building on Madison Square that had been designed ten years earlier by the prominent American architect H. H. Richardson. Richardson's unmistakable style—known today as "Richardson Romanesque"—can be seen in the Allegheny County Courthouse in Pittsburgh, the Museum of Natural History in New York, the Glessner House Museum in Chicago, and Trinity Church on Copley Square in Boston. Architectural enthusiasts, however, should not look for any Richardson Romanesque along the boundaries of Madison Square today. The Hotel Brunswick closed down not long after it hosted the Evacuation Day dinner for several dozen descendants of New York's revolutionary leaders. The building remained empty until 1904, when it was finally torn down and replaced by the unremarkable structure that's on the corner of Fifth Avenue and Twenty-Sixth Street today.[10]

Delmonico's Restaurant across the street, however, which was thought by many people to be the finest restaurant in the United States, continued its operations long after the Hotel Brunswick closed, until 1923, when the pressures of Prohibition finally killed it. Delmonico's was where the *other* great banquet celebrating the centennial of Evacuation Day was held on November 26, 1883. This dinner was sponsored by New York's Chamber of Commerce, and all the great scions of industry, banking, and trade were invited: J. P. Morgan, Jay Gould, John D. Rockefeller—and 225 other people. The purpose of the Delmonico's banquet was not to honor the heroes of the War for Independence whose names had made it into the history books; rather, it was to remind Americans that "the liberality and patriotism of the merchants of New York [had] contributed in no small measure to the triumph of the American Revolution."[11]

Although he had only recently returned from a two-month-long hunting and fishing expedition to Yellowstone National Park, President Chester Arthur made sure he got up to New York for the banquet at Delmonico's. He never made it across to the street to the dinner at the Hotel Brunswick. "You gentlemen have abundant right to share in this celebration," Arthur assured the businessmen who had assembled for the dinner, "for you are . . . the successors of those patriotic merchants who so signally held up the national cause." "I am proud to meet you," the president of the United States told the moneymakers in the room. He then expressed his faith that Morgan, Rockefeller, Gould, and their ilk were "ready to give your support to every measure which is calculated to promote the honor and credit and glory of the nation."[12]

The two different Evacuation Day banquets nicely captured a transition the northeastern United States was going through in the 1880s. Prior to the Civil War, America's economy had been primarily agricultural, its landscape of manufactured goods dominated by imports from Europe. The country did have a handful of wealthy men; John Jacob Astor had made more than $20 million off of Oregonian fur, Manhattan real estate, and Turkish opium by the time he died in 1848 (today a fortune that size would have the buying power of about $591 million).[13] Astor was unusual, however. In the mid-nineteenth century, most Americans were farmers, not businessmen, and the wealth that any rich American had tended to be modest compared to that of John Jacob Astor and those who were to come.

In 1858 just seventy men in the United States could claim to be millionaires, and their influence on the country's political, legal, and cultural landscapes was limited.[14] For the bulk of the nineteenth century, power in America was derived from heritage, not wealth. It resided among the "old families" of the nation, according to Massachusetts senator Henry Cabot Lodge, people who "represented several generations of education and standing in the community" and "had traditions running back not infrequently to the first white settlement" in any given state.

Looking back on his life in 1913, Lodge recalled that when he had been a young man in the early 1870s, the powerful people in Boston, Philadelphia, and New York had had "ancestors who filled the pulpits or sat upon the bench." Those ancestors had "fought in the Revolution, helped to make the state and national constitutions . . . been members of the House or Senate in the early days of the republic, and won success as merchants, lawyers, or men of letters."[15]

By the turn of the twentieth century, all of that had changed. The families Lodge spoke of had been "pushed out of sight, if not actually driven against the conventional wall" by wealthy and ruthless speculators: immigrants like Andrew Carnegie, who'd made his initial fortune buying and selling freight stock and engaging in practices that are now illegal and considered to be "insider trading"; or native-born Americans who were descended not from judges, ministers, or "men of letters" but from con artists like William Avery Rockefeller, who'd traded horses and sold patent medicines in upstate New York before his son, John Davison, recognized that the stuff refineries were literally throwing away after they'd distilled kerosene from oil—namely, tar, paraffin, and gasoline—could be used to make roads, lubricate machines, and fuel the fires that were distilling the oil in the first place.[16]

"The money-maker, the speculator, and the financier were a class as familiar to ancient Rome as they are at this moment to New York," Henry Cabot Lodge conceded. But "that which differentiates our own time is the rapidity with which wealth has been amassed and the size of the fortunes which have been gathered." "The persons who now fill society," the New England senator continued, "are for the most part the modern, very modern plutocrats who are widely different from their modest predecessors." The newly rich had no interest in tracing their roots to a revolutionary soldier or a signer of the Constitution. John D. Rockefeller had once bragged to a group of genealogists that he had "no desire to trace myself back to the nobility." When Lodge was a boy in the 1850s, "the man who, rising from the ranks, had made a fortune and wished to establish himself, sought entrance to the society of the old families, and hoped, and sometimes endeavored, to marry his children among them." Now, though, "to the modern and recent plutocrat, the old American family means nothing. He knows naught of the history or traditions of his State and Country, and cares less. . . . He wants his children to marry money, and for that reason, he prefers the children of other plutocrats, no matter how new."[17]

Of course Henry Cabot Lodge's observations came with a healthy dose of sour grapes. The phrase "Cabots and Lodges" is a synecdoche in American parlance, a part that stands for a whole—in this case, the whole group of "old families" who lost their power and prestige to the wealthy industrial upstarts who came on the scene in the last quarter of the nineteenth century. The senator traced his lineage on both sides to colonial leaders in seventeenth-century Massachusetts. The Cabots and Lodges were part of a group the physician, poet, and novelist Oliver Wendell Holmes Sr. called the "Brahmin Caste of New England," a term he derived from the caste system in Hinduism that divides human beings into groups on the basis of the karma they've inherited from their actions in previous lives. The Brahmin caste is the highest caste, the order from which Hindu priests and intellectuals come.[18]

Holmes insisted Brahmins were the "harmless, inoffensive, untitled aristocracy" of the United States. Their wealth was solid, but modest, tied up in investments that yielded comfortable, but not ostentatious lifestyles. They had "fine old houses and city lots that have risen in the market"; their names were "written in the stock-books of all the dividend-paying companies" and could frequently be found in "some college catalogue or other," either because a scholarship or lecture series had been funded by a Brahmin, or because a building had been constructed with money donated by a Brahmin. That was the other thing about Brahmin families— they felt an obligation to give back.[19]

Oliver Wendell Holmes didn't mention it, but Brahmin family names could be found on many of the maps in his native New England, as well: Winthrop, Maine, for instance, which had been founded in 1771 and named after the family of one of the state's early colonial governors, John Winthrop. Or Dudley, Massachusetts, a town on the Connecticut line, which shares its name with several early judges and lawmakers in the Bay State's history. Or Sargent Street in Boston, Brookline, Cambridge, Holyoke, Melrose, Needham, Newton, North Andover, and Revere, Massachusetts; Norwick, Vermont; Belmont, Hinsdale, Northfield, and Suncook, New Hampshire; Hartford, Connecticut; Warwick, Rhode Island; and Winter Harbor, Maine. The Sargents had been *all over* colonial New England, and they had the maps to prove it.[20]

Brahmins weren't confined just to the six states that made up Yankeeland, either. New York and Philadelphia had their "old families," too. In New York they were sometimes called "Knickerbockers," a term taken from Washington Irving's satirical and irreverent novel *A History of New York*.[21] Edith Wharton, the first woman to receive the Pulitzer Prize, came from a Knickerbocker family. Her father, George Jones, was descended from some of the original Dutch colonists who'd settled New Amsterdam in 1625.

In the 1850s two of George's spinster aunts, Mary and Rebecca Jones, famously started competing with one another over who could construct the bigger mansion, one woman building on Fifth Avenue and the other in the Hudson River Valley. The frenzy is believed to have been the origin of the phrase "keeping up with the Joneses," and although it was all over before Edith Jones was born in 1862, the future author of *The Age of Innocence* was always a little embarrassed by the stories of her aunts' shameless behavior. Old families, after all, were supposed to have more subtlety than that. As she got older, Wharton lamented that extravagant displays were starting to become more common in her own time, particularly among the newly rich. Writing to a friend in 1883, Wharton echoed Henry Cabot Lodge when she observed with dismay that "New York social life has become more obviously based on money."[22]

It wasn't Delmonico's, but the Hotel Brunswick was still a grand place to have a banquet. The building was seven stories tall and took up the entire block on Fifth Avenue between Twenty-Sixth and Twenty-Seventh Streets. A popular travel guide described the hotel's main dining room as "one of the most charming hotel dining-halls in this country." It was one floor up from the street, long and narrow, with colorful frescoes "amply" lit by ten large windows that ran along the room's eastern wall. In the evening guests dined by the light of gas candelabras that were mounted on ornamental "jardinères"—or flower stands—situated throughout the room. In the center of the dining room there was a fountain, landscaped with lush vegetation, which must have been particularly inviting to diners during the dark and cold winter months.[23]

The Evacuation Day dinner took place in the Brunswick's ballroom.

A large, oval-shaped table—big enough, incredibly, to seat eighty-three people—was brought into the room for the affair. Terrapin, canvasback duck, wild turkey, and port were among the delicacies served. Diamond-back terrapins are tiny turtles, measuring just six inches across and weighing an average of fifteen ounces. They used to be an extremely expensive menu item; served with butter and a sherry-based sauce, one serving of terrapin at an American restaurant in the 1880s cost the equivalent of about $95 in 2019. At one point in 1890, the average restaurant price for terrapin soared to an astonishing $6 per dish—the equivalent today of about $170. To put this in perspective, the average menu price for lobster in 2019 was just $35.[24]

Flowers for the banquet were supplied by Charles Klunder, a florist from Germany who was believed by many to have the "finest and choicest array of cut flowers to be found in the city." His nurseries along the Hudson River in Ossining—which consisted of seventy-five greenhouses Klunder had spent more than $50,000 renovating in the 1860s, when the United States was at war with itself—were of "national prominence" and "famous far and wide for their ornamental scenery and beauty."[25]

The china was provided by Davis Collamore & Company, a high-end importer of French, English, and German porcelain. The souvenir menus and place cards were designed by stationers from Tiffany's. Music for the evening was provided by Lander's Band, a twelve-piece orchestra represented by the Phipps Musical and Lyceum Bureau, New York's first talent agency. The bureau had opened its doors four years earlier in 1879, just two years after the first modern advertising agency in the United States, the J. Walter Thompson Company, had begun to manipulate consumer demand for a host of household goods. James Walter Thompson recognized in 1877 that with the right words and images, Americans could be made to believe they desperately needed toothpaste—sold for the first time in 1873—or that there was a meaningful difference between Pears soap and its upstart competitor, Ivory, because one bar was clear, and the other one floated.[26]

James Phipps believed these same methods could be used to generate demand for actors and musicians. Under his management Lander's Band became one of the most sought-after musical ensembles in all of New York, playing at the private parties and fundraisers of the some of the wealthiest and most connected people in the city, including Caroline Astor, who hosted an annual ball at the mansion she shared with John Jacob Astor's grandson, William, on Fifth Avenue and Thirty-Fourth Street.[27]

Lina Astor was known throughout the city as simply "Mrs. Astor," but to Ward McAllister, the self-appointed arbiter of high society and all good taste in Gilded Age New York, she was "Mystic Rose," the flower mentioned in the final cantos of Dante's *Paradiso* upon which the souls of all the saints rest in a hierarchical order ordained by God. McAllister famously claimed there were just four hundred people in the entire city (the capacity, conveniently enough, of Lina Astor's ballroom) who were equipped to determine the manners and relations of everyone in New York who had an education or came from money. "If you go outside that number," McAllister declared in 1888, "you strike people who are either not at ease in a ballroom or else make others feel not at ease." His self-consciously pretentious list ultimately served as the inspiration for O. Henry's now-famous collection of short stories *The Four Million*, where the author used heartbreaking tales like "The Cop and the Anthem" and "The Gift of the Magi" to argue that the lives of all New Yorkers mattered, regardless of whether they had ever set foot in a ballroom.[28]

Lina Astor's nephew, William Schermerhorn, was among the eighty-three men who attended the Evacuation Day banquet at the Hotel Brunswick. Lina had married into one of America's wealthiest families, but she'd been born into one of America's oldest. Like Edith Jones Wharton, Caroline Webster Schermerhorn Astor was a Knickerbocker. Several Schermerhorns had served in the Albany County Militia or on New York's Committee of Safety during the American Revolution, which is why Lina's nephew was a guest at the banquet. Had the members of the centennial celebration committee been remotely interested in including women in their celebration, Mrs. Astor certainly would have been invited—perhaps to join her nephew, or, more likely, to represent the Schermerhorn family entirely on her own. Lina Astor was *that* important. But the banquet was as much about contemporary New York politics as it was about the city's history, and while some Americans in the late nineteenth century had begun to challenge the notion that women had no place in politics, the business and intellectual leaders of Gilded

Age New York had not yet accepted that female political engagement was appropriate or needed. Mrs. Astor, therefore, spent the evening of November 26, 1883, in her mansion on Fifth Avenue, alone.

In addition to William Schermerhorn, the banquet's guest list included John King, a merchant from Jamaica, Queens, whose grandfather Rufus had served in the Continental Congress; Horatio Gallatin, a retired chemistry professor from New York University, whose grandfather Albert had served in the administrations of Adams, Jefferson, Madison, and Monroe; and Theodore Roosevelt, a twenty-five-year-old Columbia Law School dropout who'd recently been elected to the New York State Legislature and whose great-great-uncle Isaac had represented New York at the Constitutional Convention.[29]

Roosevelt wasn't the only state lawmaker who attended the banquet. His Republican colleague in the New York Assembly Robert Ray Hamilton attended as well. "Ray," as he was known to his family and friends, had been chosen by the descendants of Alexander Hamilton to represent their family at the Evacuation Day dinner. His father, Schuyler, was a retired army general who'd made a name for himself in the Mexican and Civil Wars. His grandfather John Church Hamilton was the fourth son of Alexander and Elizabeth Schuyler Hamilton. John was eleven years old when his father died. He went to his grave insisting that his father had been "assassinated" by Aaron Burr when Burr shot Hamilton in a duel in July 1804.[30]

The Hamilton family had been through a lot in the years since the Revolutionary War. As fans of Lin-Manuel Miranda's Tony Award–winning musical know, Alexander Hamilton had an extramarital affair with the wife of a political rival in the 1790s. That affair blew up into a very public extortion scandal that threatened his career and deeply embarrassed his wife, Eliza. The couple's oldest son, Philip, was killed in a duel in 1801, three years before Alexander died the same way. Philip's sister, Angelica, was devastated by her brother's death and struggled with mental illness for her entire adult life.[31]

John Church Hamilton seems to have suffered from some of the same fidelity issues that afflicted his father. He had several "alienation of affection" lawsuits brought against him after he'd married his wife, Maria Van den Heuvel, in 1814. Alienation of affection statutes were eliminated by the various state legislatures in the mid-twentieth century. In John Church Hamilton's lifetime, however, these laws were a way for the families of wealthy young women who'd been seduced by cads to receive compensation for the damage done to their reputations. In New York the fact that a man like John Church Hamilton was already married was no defense against the charge of seduction.[32]

John's oldest son, Alexander, also found it difficult to stay faithful to his wife, though early dementia may have played a role in his infidelity. This Alexander Hamilton, who adopted his mother's maiden name to distinguish himself professionally from his famous grandfather, had "long been considered eccentric by his neighbors," according to the *New York Times*. When he was in his seventies, "Alexander Hamilton of Heuvel," as he was known, threatened publicly to kill his wife before moving in with his mistress, a married woman in her thirties with whom he had become "infatuated" (to use the *Times*'s word) after meeting her at a dinner for Civil War veterans. Alexander's wife eventually got a court to declare him insane, giving her attorney the power to freeze his assets until he came home.[33]

Alexander's brother, John Cornelius Adrian Hamilton, had a gambling problem that got him into quite a bit of trouble during the Mexican War. Already notorious for his "unfair play at cards," J. C. A. Hamilton was accused in 1847 of breaking into several civilian homes in Mexico, including one where four women whose husbands were off fighting in Santa Anna's army were living on their own, without the protection of a man. The women, according to newspaper reports, were robbed and "outraged."[34]

Military leaders took the allegations seriously, since the Mexican War was already unpopular with many people back home. This was the war Henry David Thoreau famously refused to support with his taxes, calling it an "invasion" that would inevitably lead to the expansion of hereditary, race-based slavery. Allegations that American soldiers were robbing and raping civilians fanned the flames of antislavery sentiment that were already burning robustly in Philadelphia and Boston.[35]

General William Worth ordered an investigation, and the soldier-with-the-famous-grandfather deserted, along with several of his peers. The men were eventually captured, and two of them were court martialed and executed. J. C. A. Hamilton's life was spared. The reason may have been that he was innocent; he'd angered a lot of people with his dishonest card-playing, after all, and one of his victims may have decided to get even with him by circulating false rumors that he had raped and robbed four women. Had the military tried him, however, there would have been some powerful optics for the army's leaders to consider. It would not have looked good to have the grandson of America's first treasury secretary put to death. It's also possible J. C. A. Hamilton was spared because of the heroism of his younger brother, Schuyler—father of the man who represented the Hamilton family at the Evacuation Day dinner. On the day J.C.A. was captured, Schuyler Hamilton was lying in a hospital bed, recovering from a punctured lung he'd received after a lance pierced his back at the Battle of Mil Flores in August 1847.[36]

John Cornelius Adrian Hamilton did not return to New York after the Mexican War was over—or if he did, he didn't stay long. He and his wife made their way out to the newly formed state of Wisconsin, where they lived for a time with J.C.A.'s uncle, William Stephen Hamilton, who'd been seven years old when Aaron Burr shot and killed his father.

William was an incorrigible and unrepentant West Point dropout who'd ended up in southern Wisconsin after he took a federal contract in the late 1820s to drive seven hundred head of cattle across the state of Illinois (a rather remarkable feat for a young man who'd been born and raised in New York City; supposedly, just one steer died along the way). He never married, though there were rumors that he and his nephew's wife had had an affair. He fought as a volunteer in the Black Hawk War of 1832, shot a man while serving in Wisconsin's territorial assembly in 1843, and had a reputation, according to one *sympathetic* biographer, as a "good-for-nothing rogue, a derelict, and an adventurous scion who contributed nothing to the prestige of his family."[37]

There was one other Hamilton in the first two generations that followed Alexander who didn't fit in, and his life was tinged with sadness and shrouded in quite a bit of mystery. His name was Robert P. Hamilton.

He was born in June 1828, the ninth of fourteen children. Alexander of Heuvel, John Cornelius Adrian, and Schuyler Hamilton were his older brothers; John Church Hamilton and Maria Van den Heuvel were his parents; William Stephen Hamilton was his uncle; Alexander Hamilton was his grandfather; and Robert Ray Hamilton was his nephew.

No biography of Robert P. Hamilton has ever been written, and very little is known about him. There is nothing in the Hamilton Family Papers at Columbia University's library that indicates what the "P" in his middle name stood for. It's not even clear how Cuyler Reynolds, a genealogist who published a history of the Hamilton family in 1914, knew that Robert had been born in 1828—though Reynolds does mention that Robert's younger sister, Adelaide, was still alive at the time he wrote his book, so perhaps he got that detail from her.

Reynolds's book provides a good bit of information about all of the adult sons—and most of the adult daughters—of John Church Hamilton, except for Robert P. About him Reynolds says only that he was born in New York and that he "died, Mitchelana, Honduras, Central America, unmarried, January 10, 1891."[38]

"Mitchelana" was probably Muchilena, a tiny beach town on Honduras's Atlantic coast, about 120 miles north of Tegucigalpa, the capital city. Why Robert P. Hamilton moved to Muchilena is unknown, but by the time he died there at the age of sixty-two, he had been living in Central America for nearly four decades. Robert first moved to the region in the early 1850s, settling initially in San Juan del Sur, on Nicaragua's Pacific coast. A few years later, he moved to the country's Atlantic side and spent at least fifteen years there, living near the mouth of the Prinzipolka River.[39] For his first two decades in Nicaragua, Robert had very little contact with his family.

It wasn't until 1874, when Robert P. Hamilton was well into his forties, that he began to correspond with his family again—and, even then, the correspondence was limited mostly to his sister, Charlotte. Over the years Robert had exchanged a few letters with his older brother, Schuyler. Those exchanges, he told his sister, had been "principally upon business matters." Although he was "much interested in hearing from home and a word about home was of more value to me than many dollars," Charlotte's letter to him was "the first communication I have received as to the position of the family and its different members . . . after a silence of nearly twenty years."[40]

Charlotte's reasons for writing to Robert were not good. Their mother had died a few months earlier after a long illness. Her passing hit Robert hard, but Charlotte's letter did give him an occasion to feel some joy. "I thank you sincerely for the kind message you sent me of my dear father's Love," he told her. "For years I have waited to receive it, and I trust I shall henceforth be worthy of it. May God bless him and spare him to you all for some time to come."[41]

Charlotte, it turned out, was being more gracious than truthful. Eight and a half years after she reestablished contact with her brother— following the death of John Church Hamilton in July 1882—Robert P. learned his father had disinherited him. He fought the will, but lost his case. In August 1883, however, three months before the Evacuation Day dinner at the Hotel Brunswick, the curiously repudiated middle child of John Church Hamilton traveled from Nicaragua to New Orleans to receive a one-time payment from his father's estate that his siblings had elected to give him. The person they sent to New Orleans to deliver the money was the same person they chose to represent the dignity and honor of the Hamilton family at the Evacuation Day dinner: Alexander Hamilton's thirty-two-year-old great-grandson, Robert Ray Hamilton.[42]

Ray was the oldest of three sons born to Schuyler Hamilton and his wife, Cornelia Ray. The Hamiltons and Rays had a long history together. Cornelia's paternal grandfather, Cornelius Ray, had been an early investor in the Bank of the United States, an idea Alexander Hamilton convinced the first U.S. Congress to sign onto in 1791. The bank was part of Hamilton's plan to stabilize the new country's economy, pay off its war debts, and promote the development of manufacturing.[43]

Cornelia's other grandfather was Nathaniel Prime, founder of one of the very first investment banks in New York City. Born in Massachusetts in 1768, Prime spent his youth working as a private coachman for a wealthy merchant in Boston. In 1795 he moved to New York, made some good investments with the money he'd saved, and opened a business that helped other investors do the same. When the New York Stock and Exchange Board was formed in 1817, its members made Nathaniel Prime their first president.[44]

As wealthy and successful as he was, Prime seems to have been haunted by demons that could not be chased away by money and power. Writing in his diary one evening in 1840, George Templeton Strong—the college student who'd resented Columbia's decision to hold classes on Evacuation Day—observed that Nathaniel Prime had chosen a rather odd way to celebrate the revolutionary-era holiday the day before. "Prime went to his room at two o'clock, and appears to have taken up and read his prayer book," Strong wrote on November 26. "Then he went before the glass, cut his throat coolly and steadily from ear to ear, replaced the razor in its case, then walked into the next room and there fell." He was seventy-two years old.[45]

Prime's great-grandson, Robert Ray Hamilton, was different, however. He exhibited none of the incorrigibility or darkness that could be found on both sides of his family. He was attractive, intelligent, and accomplished—a true standard-bearer for the next generation of Hamiltons, Rays, and Primes. Like his grandfather John Church Hamilton, he had "glossy black hair" and "shiny black eyes." Newspapers described him as "honest" and "noble," with a "kindly face," a "graceful form," and "noticeably large and perfect" front teeth. He walked with a bit of a limp, thanks to a poorly set broken leg he'd acquired after falling from his horse as a teenager. But that limp did not prevent him from mucking around in the marshes of New Jersey, Michigan, and Long Island, where he liked to hunt ducks with his friends.[46]

In 1872 Ray's classmates at Columbia College chose him as their valedictorian. Three years later, after graduating from law school, he hung out his shingle with Hamilton Fish Jr., a classmate from Columbia whose father, Hamilton Fish Sr., was the U.S. secretary of state. Ray's annual income from his law work would soon exceed $18,000 (about $512,000 today). To put this income in perspective, a survey completed in 1875 by a government-run agency in Massachusetts found that American men working in "occupations involving chiefly mental and literary qualifications" earned an average of just $1,016 per year.[47]

Ray was a guest at many of the most exclusive weddings and charity parties that attracted the attention of reporters in Gilded Age New York.

He belonged to several tony hunt clubs, and not long after the Evacuation Day dinner, he was invited to join the Union League, a private men's club that met in a mansion on Fifth Avenue, five blocks away from Lina Astor's ballroom. Ray Hamilton had not yet made it into Ward McAllister's Four Hundred—but he was young, and he still had time.[48]

Ray's intelligence and kindness were apparent to his friends and family very early on. From the time he was a toddler, he had been close to his maternal grandfather—his namesake, Robert Ray. In a nod to that relationship, Ray's father, Schuyler, took the step of asking him in 1864, when he was just thirteen years old, to consider dropping "Hamilton" from his name and going simply by "Robert Ray," since his grandfather had no surviving sons. The older Robert Ray's first son, Robert Jr., had died of an unknown illness in 1860, shortly after completing medical school. His second son, Richard Cornelius, had died three years later, in the middle of the Civil War, while stationed in Mississippi with Schuyler Hamilton's army unit.

"Mr. Ray has always been kind and liberal to me," Schuyler wrote to his father, after his father-in-law had given him a loan of $25,000. "I have determined, therefore, as his family by the male line is extinct, to use my influence with my son Ray . . . to take his grandfather's name, and thus continue the name of a family who have in public & private life done good to the community in which they have lived and been honored and loved."[49]

Young Robert Ray Hamilton considered his father's request, but ultimately chose to keep his historically famous last name. His relationship with his maternal grandfather remained close, however. When the older Robert Ray died in 1879, he named the grandson who'd been named after him as his heir, splitting his estate between Ray Hamilton and his only surviving child, Nathalie Ray Baylies (Cornelia, Ray's mother and Robert's daughter, had died twelve years earlier). Ray and his Aunt Nathalie became the joint owners of several properties in Manhattan. Twenty-eight-year-old Robert Ray Hamilton also inherited an annuity. He was already making a pretty penny as an attorney. His grandfather's annuity promised to add another $40,000 a year to that income for the rest of his life—slightly more than $1 million in today's money.[50]

For good reason, everyone in Ray's family had high hopes for him. That's why they chose him to represent them at the Evacuation Day dinner on November 26, 1883. Certainly none of the men sitting around the oval table that evening, savoring the terrapin and duck that had been prepared for them by the Brunswick's chefs, ever could have imagined that in eight years' time, Ray's family members would be begging New York's aldermen not to honor him with a memorial fountain—or that they would be working actively to hide his remains and his personal papers from the prying eyes of people in his own time and generations to come.[51]

2

Blueberries and Timber

On a pleasantly cool morning in the summer of 1860, Augustus Hemenway Sr. left his house on Beacon Hill in Boston and traveled seven and
a half hours by train and horse-drawn carriage to Litchfield, Connecticut, where he promptly checked himself into the Spring Hill House for
Nervous Invalids, the first private sanitarium in the United States. He
did not come out for the next thirteen years.[1]

"During this long period of seclusion," one newspaper noted after
Gus had rejoined society, "the great civil war broke out and was extin-
guished, specie disappeared, a new currency was born, new channels
of trade were opened, and new methods of business evolved." Augustus
Hemenway had missed a lot. He'd missed the deaths of more than seven
hundred thousand Americans and the demise of the brutal labor system
that had sustained his country's economy for more than two centuries.
He'd also missed the rise of a new political party (the Republican) and
the first impeachment of an American president (Andrew Johnson); the
constitutional extension of the franchise to Black American men; the
frenzy that followed the drilling of the first oil well in Titusville, Pennsylvania; the completion of the transcontinental railroad and its crucial
companion, the transcontinental telegraph; the destruction of the cities
of Chicago and Boston by fire; the widescale adoption of the Hoe "lightning" printing press by newspapers across the country; the Sand Creek
Massacre of the Cheyenne and Arapaho people and the escalation of the
Indian Wars in the American West; and the inauguration of the federal
Homestead Acts that led to the settlement of the West by thousands of
White—and some Black—Americans who ultimately "closed" the frontier
in 1890, fourteen years after Augustus Hemenway died.[2]

America as we know it today began to take shape in the 1860s and 1870s,
during the years Gus spent in seclusion under the care of Dr. Henry Buel,

a Yale-trained physician who specialized in mental disorders. And all of it, according to the *New York Sun*, had "swept by him unnoticed, while to his friends, Hemenway appeared to be hopelessly insane."[3]

Edward Augustus Holyoke Hemenway probably came by his nervous proclivities honestly. His mother, Sarah, was considered by many people in her life to be eccentric and a little bit impulsive. In 1818, in a fit of unhappiness, she divorced her husband, Samuel Hemenway, a doctor who'd trained with Edward Augustus Holyoke, founder of the Massachusetts Medical Society and the most esteemed physician in all of antebellum New England.[4] Sally fled the home she shared with Samuel in the middle of the night, eventually moving in with her brother and his family in what was then Steuben, Massachusetts, which soon became Steuben, Maine, thanks to the Missouri Compromise of 1820. That was the congressional deal that brought Missouri into the union as a slave-holding state after Massachusetts agreed to allow the District of Maine to separate from the commonwealth and become an autonomous state where slavery was outlawed.

"'Tis reported by your father that I am crazy," Sally Hemenway wrote to her thirteen-year-old son, Gus, after she'd left not just her husband but also four of her five sons behind in Boston. Only Charles, who'd been born a few weeks earlier, came with her when she left the Hemenway home. "I have had enough said and done to me to make half a dozen silly women crazy," Sally told her son in vague terms that seemed to suggest she recognized how extreme her actions might appear to those observing them from the outside. If she were a little erratic or emotionally unstable after being married to Dr. Hemenway for fifteen years, Sally hoped she was "not past cure." Nevertheless, she would not be returning to her husband; of that much she was certain. "Your father says he is all the Friend I have in the world," she informed her oldest son. "Let him show it by a uniform conduct and by being what a Father ought to be to his children."[5]

Reading over her correspondence with Augustus, one does get the impression that Sarah Upton Hemenway may have suffered from something similar to what medical experts today call "bipolar disorder"—or, if not that, then at the very least that she was subjected to quite a bit of gaslighting by family and friends, enough to occasionally dull her otherwise vibrant and adventurous personality. In some letters to Gus, Sally is brimming with excitement about life, telling her son she rode nonstop on horseback for seventeen miles, traversing the distance in fewer than three hours (meaning she had to have done the entire ride at a trot), before hopping off her steed to pick raspberries, which she then turned into wine and jelly that same afternoon, presumably after trotting another seventeen miles home.[6]

In other letters Sally is plagued by self-doubt. "I feel a little depressed sometimes, but with my usual fortitude endevour to drive it off," she told her son after spending the day with friends. "Perhaps it be said that I am self-willed; I think I am not. I am willing to be advised by those who are older and more experienced than myself, and for whatever I am to blame am ready to accuse myself." Nevertheless, she could not "see where I am to blame, except if I believe what everybody has said to me."[7]

Sally didn't share with her son the details of her problem-plagued marriage, but Augustus Hemenway had eyes of his own and a mind that was increasingly able to comprehend the faults and frailties of the adults around him as he matured and grew. He shared his mother's sense of discretion when it came to Samuel Hemenway, but in a letter he wrote to his fiancée in 1840, Gus did hint at a history of alcoholism in his family. His memories of his father, he told Mary Tileston, were "not grateful ones." Standing over Samuel's open grave in 1823, listening to "the dry rattle that tells that earth was mixing with earth," eighteen-year-old Gus was "forced to draw my hat over my face to conceal the bitter, bitter tears that fell over the recollection of his life . . . a life that promised much of joy and happiness, but where error was permitted to enter, which wrecked it on the shoals of intemperance."[8]

Shortly after Sally left her husband, thirteen-year-old Gus took a job at a dry goods store on Cornhill Street, where Boston's massive and controversially "brutalist" City Hall building stands today. His mother had arranged for him to live with the family who owned the store, earning his keep by sweeping the floors and stocking the shelves. Gus's younger brother, George, moved in with Sally's half-sister, Polly. Samuel and William, who were nine and seven years old, respectively, lived with their paternal grandfather in Groton, Massachusetts, for nearly two years, until their mother was financially stable enough to have them join her in Maine.[9]

"I know I am capable of getting a living for myself and assisting my children," Sally wrote to Gus shortly after she'd moved out of the poorhouse in Salem, Massachusetts, where she lived with her infant son for several weeks after leaving her husband. From her perch in Washington County, Maine, Sarah Upton Hemenway started a business. Initially she made hats and clothing for her neighbors. That endeavor quickly evolved into a trade partnership between herself and her teenaged son, whereby he procured luxury items from the international ports in Boston and Salem—things like cigars, gingham, lemons, and silk umbrellas—and she sold the goods to people living along the remote and fractal coastline of northeastern Maine.[10]

By the time she died in 1865, Sally Hemenway's months in the poorhouse were a remote memory. She owned a large clapboard house in the town of Machias, "considered the handsomest in eastern Maine," according to one newspaper, where she lived with her adult son, William, his daughter, Alice, and Alice's young son, John Dudley Sargent. Alice had grown up in the house and given birth to her son there. She moved back in with her grandmother and father after her husband, Henry Sargent, left his family and moved to California.[11]

Sally also owned stock in the Assabet Manufacturing Company, a mill in Maynard, Massachusetts, that made most of the woolen uniforms and blankets for the Union Army during the Civil War. When her estate was finally settled, Sally's assets were worth more than $17,000, not counting the house in Machias. In 2019 that kind of money had the buying power of nearly half a million dollars.[12]

It was an impressive sum for a woman, especially a mother of five who'd divorced her husband in the early years of the nineteenth century. It paled in comparison, however, to the fortune Sally's oldest son was able to accumulate, with the help of his brothers, William and Charles. Sarah Upton Hemenway, it turned out, had given her son more than just a disposition that was prone to nervousness. She'd also given him business sense and an instinct for trade. By the time Gus died in 1876, three years after he'd ended his thirteen-year-long sojourn at the Spring Hill House for Nervous Invalids, he, too, had become quite financially comfortable. Indeed, Edward Augustus Holyoke Hemenway Sr. was believed by many newspaper editors to be "the wealthiest man in America."[13]

Trade had been the engine driving New England's economy for many decades by the time Sally and Gus started their partnership in 1819. The region's cold weather and rocky soil made it difficult, if not impossible for farmers there to grow large quantities of wheat and corn, as they did in colonies like Pennsylvania and New Jersey, or tobacco and rice, as they did in Maryland, Virginia, and the Carolinas. New England was not without its advantages, however. It had some excellent natural harbors. Two of the ten deepest in all of British colonial America were in Massachusetts, and in an age before dredging, the natural depth of a harbor was the primary factor that determined its usefulness.[14]

Massachusetts quickly became a hub for brokers like Sally and Gus, people who bought goods that had been produced in one place and sold them to consumers who lived someplace else.[15] Not everyone in the state was a merchant, however. Properly speaking, Massachusetts's economy wasn't "agricultural," since its residents weren't growing most of the nonmanufactured commodities they sold in the market. But they were *harvesting* those commodities. Specifically they harvested fish from Massachusetts and Cape Cod Bays and timber from the state's extreme northern regions along the Kennebec, Penobscot, and Machias Rivers, in the area Sally Hemenway ultimately called home—the area known then as the District of Maine.

Lawmakers were eager to increase the sales tax revenue coming from Maine's timberlands after the Revolutionary War. Alexander Hamilton would eventually convince Congress to assume the states' war debts, but in 1783, when the Treaty of Paris was signed, no one knew federal lawmakers were going to do that. Massachusetts's leaders were on the hook for more than $6 million in debt certificates they'd issued to people who'd supplied food, clothing, blankets, horses, and arms to the government during the conflict—more than any other state except South Carolina. Shays's Rebellion in 1786 made it clear that new taxes were not going to be popular with a group of people who'd just fought a war over the issue of taxation. To replenish Massachusetts's depleted coffers, lawmakers were going to have to increase the revenue generated by taxes already in place.[16]

The problem with relying upon timber to do that was that in 1783, 80 percent of the land in Maine was publicly owned. If lawmakers wanted to realize the economic potential of Maine's dense, coniferous forests, they were going to have to get that land into private hands—not *settled*, necessarily, since settlers (and especially their grazing cattle and sheep) took up space that could be used to grow more trees. But they needed to get the land *owned*.[17]

It took a while, but the strategy Massachusetts's leaders devised for doing this worked. Today 94 percent of the land is Maine is privately owned, although almost none of it has been developed; in fact, Maine is the most heavily forested state in the entire country, with about 90 percent of its landscape covered by trees. More than half of the land area in Maine is divided into units known as "unorganized townships." UTS, as Mainers now call them, don't have any municipal government. People living in a UT are supervised, serviced, and taxed directly by the state—though pointedly (and perhaps ironically, given that Massachusetts's lawmakers designed this system just one year after the Revolutionary War was over), the full-time residents of Maine's 429 UTS don't have any representatives in their state's legislature. They are shamelessly subject to taxation without representation, and the effect of that has been that few people choose to live in a UT, making Maine the least densely populated state east of the Mississippi River and the most "rural" state in the entire country, according to the U.S. Census Bureau.[18]

This is exactly how Massachusetts's lawmakers wanted it back in 1784, when they hired surveyors to bundle Maine's timberlands into hundreds of unorganized townships before selling the land to private investors. There was a reason people who chose to live full-time in a UT would not be given representation in their state's legislature. Lawmakers didn't want a whole bunch of people moving into Maine's northern woods. UTS were an important part of the plan Massachusetts's early leaders devised for getting Maine's public lands into private hands, without necessarily boosting the District's population and replacing its forests with subsistence farms that would never generate the kind of revenue timber could.[19]

UTS were also an important part of the business plan Gus Hemenway devised, enabling him to accumulate an estate worth nearly $35 million by the time he died in 1876. It was an astonishingly large sum that had the buying power today of more than $840 million and was not subject to federal income tax (except briefly during the Civil War), since that tax did not exist until the Sixteenth Amendment was ratified in 1913.[20]

Gus's business relied upon markets he tapped and even helped to create in the Caribbean and South America. His supply chain began, however, on an unorganized township in Washington County, Maine, where his mother lived with his younger brother, William, and William's grandson, John Dudley Sargent, a bookish child with a deep love of music who would one day move very far away from the Pine Tree State in an effort to make a name for himself.

The sun rises first in Washington County, Maine. It's as far east as you can go and still be in the continental United States. If you visit the region today, it's a good idea to get an international plan for your cell phone, since you'll be pinging off TELUS towers in New Brunswick, Canada, for much of the time you're there. Washington County has the smallest population of all of Maine's coastal counties, and American cellular service providers haven't exactly been scrambling to build a reliable communication infrastructure there.[21]

Nearly 70 percent of the wild blueberries harvested in the United States come from Washington County—and if you think all blueberries taste the same, you've never had a fistful of wild ones. Wild or "lowbush" blueberries are sweeter than their larger, cultivated "highbush" cousins, which can be grown just about anywhere. Lowbush blueberries, strictly speaking, can't be "grown" at all. They're rhizomes, which means the most farmers can do is create the conditions that encourage existing plants to spread. One of those conditions is the highly acidic environment that was created in New England and southeastern Canada more than ten thousand years ago, when migrating glaciers dragged much of the region's topsoil out to sea and ground the remaining rocks into coarse granite sand. Those ancient glaciers are the reason this tiny northeastern corner of the United States is covered with blankets of crimson, tangerine, and gold every September, as the wild blueberry barrens go through their annual ritual of autumnal senescence, rivaling—and maybe even eclipsing—the evergreen-dominated forests for their brilliance and beauty.[22]

Twenty percent of the residents of Washington County live below the poverty line. That statistic puts it ahead of many counties in the American South, but it still makes it one of the poorest counties in the northeastern United States. Only Philadelphia, the Bronx, and Brooklyn (all urban) have higher percentages of their residents living in official poverty. One-third of the households in Washington County survive on less than $25,000 a year, and half of those households have an annual income of less than $15,000. Lobster harvesting, blueberry raking, and clam digging are the primary sources of income here—and none of that grueling seasonal work pays very much.[23]

Still, this part of Maine has seen better days. Every August hundreds of people from across New England travel to Washington County to eat pie and listen to music during the county's Wild Blueberry Festival. As they drive through towns like Cherryfield, Columbia Falls, Dennysville, and Machias, these visitors pass by dozens of Greek Revival, Second Empire, Queen Anne, and Colonial Revival mansions, most of them built sometime between 1850 and 1900, and many of them now in varying stages of disrepair.[24] These houses testify to the reality that there was a time in Washington County's history when some of the residents, at least, were doing more than just getting by. Indeed, there was a time in the county's history when the economy was booming.

That booming period was when Gus Hemenway and his family members were there. Gus never actually lived in Washington County, the way his mother and brother did. But he did own an entire unorganized township there: UT 36, which goes by the same name today and consists of 23,040 acres on the western edge of the county, about thirty-five miles straight north from the coast, that were mapped out and bundled into a UT in 1784.[25]

It's not clear when Gus acquired the township. William, who helped to manage his brother's business affairs while Gus was at the Spring Hill House for Nervous Invalids, may have been the one who bought it.

The surviving records indicate only that in 1846, much of UT 36 was still owned by the state of Maine, but that by 1868—eight years into Gus's thirteen-year-long confinement—the entire township was owned by Augustus Hemenway, and William Hemenway was milling timber from it at a steam-powered sawmill he operated along the Machias River.[26]

Some of the timber William milled stayed in Washington County, which by 1850 had become the epicenter of America's shipbuilding industry. Some of the timber was shipped down to Cuba, where the people working on Gus's plantation along the Sagua la Grande River used the wood to fuel the fires that boiled the plantation's saccharum grasses into sugar and molasses. Many of Gus's Cuban workers were enslaved—a dirty little secret about the New Englander's business dealings that strangely never received any attention from the press, even though abolitionist publishers like William Lloyd Garrison delighted in exposing Yankees who were tainted by slavery. Whether the enslaved workers Gus used were actually owned by him, or merely rented, is not clear from the surviving records of his business.[27]

Some of the timber William milled was sent to urban centers like Boston, New York, and Philadelphia, where it was used to build housing for the large number of immigrants coming into those cities. And some of the timber was ground into wood pulp and sold to papermakers throughout New England, who first started using wood, instead of cotton rags, to make their product in the mid-1860s and really ramped up their commitment to this method of papermaking after 1870, when the *Boston Herald* and the *New York World* became the first English-language newspapers in the United States to print their articles entirely on paper made from wood.[28]

In the 1820s, during Maine's first decade as an independent state, Americans had been consuming an average of 5.4 billion board feet of lumber every year. By 1873, when Gus Hemenway finally left the Spring Hill House for Nervous Invalids, that number had risen to 44.5 billion board feet.[29] Cotton may have been "king" in the United States during the first half of the nineteenth century, but in the years that followed the Civil War, lumber was the commodity that wore the crown. The 1860s and 1870s were a good time to be owning a timber-laden UT in Washington County, Maine. And, as people like Gus's nephew,

Jack Sargent, knew, those years were a great time to be growing up in a timber family in the place where the sun shone first on the United States of America.

Not a whole lot is known about Gus Hemenway's younger brothers. William and Charles were the youngest of the five Hemenway boys, born in 1811 and 1818, respectively. During the thirteen years Gus spent at Henry Buel's sanitarium, these two brothers managed his business affairs, along with Gus's father-in-law, Thomas Tileston. Charles did not yet have a family, so he took on the bulk of the travel responsibilities, going back and forth between and among Gus's offices in Boston, New York, Havana, and Valparaiso, Chile. Charles bought and sold anything he could find a market for: copper, silver, salmon, lard, even Jesuits' bark, which grew in the Andes Mountains and was greatly valued by people in the American South, since it could be steeped to make a tea that was high in quinine and helpful in the treatment of malaria.[30]

William, in turn, managed Gus's timber interests in Maine, since he lived there with Sally and was caring for Gus's first trade partner as she grew older. William's responsibilities included more than just the timbering of UT 36 and the milling of all the trees that came from it. Gus was also the sole owner of at least six different ships by 1860 that needed to be maintained: a schooner and a brigantine, which he used for coastal travel and trade between Machias and New York, and four barques, each of which was capable of carrying as much as 800 tons of cargo between the United States and Chile.[31]

William and Charles were still children in 1823 when their older brother started traveling to Cuba and Brazil for a merchant in Boston named George W. Bangs. Bangs allowed Gus to cut some deals of his own during these trips, and by 1840, the year he got married, the man who had learned the art of trade from his mother was generating profits that were "almost colossal," according to one Boston-area newspaper. "It seems as if every enterprise he engages in turns out well," the paper's correspondent gushed. Two other reporters claimed that Gus was a businessman of "untiring activity" who had "few equals and no superiors." He possessed an "extraordinary aptitude for business" and had "advanced with rapid strides."[32]

To what extent Gus's fabulous wealth was a result of decisions made by him—as opposed to decisions made by his brothers, William and Charles, during the years of his confinement—is unknown. Most of the records from Gus's company were stored in a warehouse in San Francisco that was destroyed during the earthquake of 1906.[33] The records kept in that facility might have been salvageable, except that they were, understandably, not a priority for the rescue workers who responded to that disaster. What wasn't lost to the earthquake's fires was lost to the rains that followed.

The only information we have on Gus's company, therefore, comes from documents that were kept by family members. Those documents, which are now stored in a museum archive in Rowley, Massachusetts, make it clear that by the time Gus Hemenway died, sugar, lumber, and silver had become the only commodities his company was trading in; there were no more small-time dealings in things like lard or Jesuits' bark. Gus or his brothers had also made a number of real estate investments in Boston and New York that were paying out handsomely.[34]

Gus was the one who made the decision to buy his company's sugar plantation in Cuba. He finalized the purchase of that property in 1840, the year he married Mary Tileston.[35] What the records in Rowley don't tell us, however, is whether it was Gus or Charles who decided to purchase the two silver mines Gus owned near Valparaiso, Chile. Those records also don't tell us whether it was Gus or William who recognized the value of UT 36 in Washington County, Maine.

In February 1860, just a few months before Gus entered Buel's sanitarium, one newspaper claimed the businessman had a fortune of nearly $3 million—hardly a paltry sum (recall that there were only seventy millionaires in the entire country at the time) but also not nearly the $35 million Gus was worth sixteen years later, when he died. The *New York Herald* reported that Gus had accumulated $2,652,400—a surprisingly specific sum—before he began his extended medical sabbatical. Several other newspapers across the country, drawing upon reports they'd received from the various wire services they subscribed to, told their readers Gus's estate was worth $5 million before he "became a lunatic" and absconded from society.[36]

The numbers didn't match, but they also weren't wildly different from one another. Taken together and contrasted with the value of Gus's estate when it was probated in 1877, the newspaper reports do suggest strongly that Gus's business grew and generated quite a bit of revenue during the years when he was not involved in any of the business's dealings. The editors of the *Boston Herald* certainly thought this was the case. "Augustus Hemenway walked into his office on Lewis Wharf and resumed his place as if he had been absent only a few weeks," the paper reported after Gus had returned home to Boston. "He reviewed the business transactions of his house during the 13 years of his absence and was satisfied with the result, as well he might, for his business had grown to such proportions as to make him one of the richest men in America."[37]

The editors of the *Herald* didn't state it in straightforward terms, but they clearly believed that Augustus Hemenway Sr. had his brothers to thank for his fabulous wealth. They weren't alone in thinking that way. Gus's grandnephew, John Dudley Sargent, also thought that Augustus Hemenway had not done it all on his own. Specifically, he considered his maternal grandfather, William Hemenway, to have been essential to Gus's success.

Jack Sargent was born a little more than a year after Gus checked himself into Henry Buel's sanitarium. He was a child, therefore, during the years of Gus's absence from the family. That didn't keep him from forming opinions, however, about what had happened during the time when Gus was gone. His grandfather had been the "richest lumberman in Maine," according to Jack, until 1874, when Gus returned from the Spring Hill House for Nervous Invalids and "took [William Hemenway's] pet township away from him." William was "heartbroken" by his older brother's decision. "He drank himself to death in three weeks," Jack recalled in 1899—and William wasn't Gus's only casualty. Two months later, according to Jack, "my mother died because her father did."[38]

Most physicians will tell you it takes longer than three weeks for a person to drink himself to death. Jack's understanding of his grandfather's passing was almost certainly incomplete, in no small part because he was only twelve when it happened. Perhaps William Hemenway went on a real bender one night and died of acute alcohol poisoning. Or perhaps he'd been overdrinking for quite a while by the time Gus took the management of UT 36 away from him. We know that mental illness ran in his family, after all—as did alcoholism.[39]

One thing Jack Sargent seems to have gotten right in his understanding of what happened to his grandfather is that William and Gus Hemenway did have a major disagreement after Gus checked out of Henry Buel's sanitarium in November 1873. The surviving documentary evidence is frustratingly sparse, but Gus referred to the disagreement in a letter he wrote to his wife, Mary. His words to her confirm Jack Sargent's recollection twenty-five years later that Gus took the management of UT 36 away from William, and that William was very depressed about that decision. More than that, Gus's words also confirm Jack's understanding of the situation as having involved a great deal of money.

"Please write to William at Machias and cheer him up," Gus wrote to Mary in September of 1874, after he'd gone to Wales to examine a piece of smelting equipment. "My arrangements now take nearly all the business from his shoulders, as well as the responsibility, and he only wants cheerful intercourse and encouragement to make him as well as ever."[40]

Gus's remarks don't suggest he was harboring any anger toward his younger brother. Referring to an estate in Milton, Massachusetts, that Mary had purchased during the years her husband was gone, Gus wrote he was "sorry [William] did not make a longer visit to the Old Farm, and I shall get him up there again this fall." Part of Gus's motivation, however, was that he believed time away from Washington County would help his brother understand why he'd taken the management of UT 36 away from him. "These little breaks in his tedium of life open his ideas and widen his mind," Gus informed Mary, "and they break up its present morbid condition caused by his probably <u>now</u> seeing that following <u>his</u> ideas, rather than <u>my orders</u> to him have made a difference of half a million dollars, a serious thing to him, if not to myself."[41]

Half a million dollars. In 1874 that amount of money was the equivalent of about $11.3 million today. Jack Sargent's understanding of the situation did not mirror his uncle's in many important ways—but in one way, at least, his recollection of the affair was the same. "In 1873 A. Hemenway, the rich brother merchant who went insane, in twelve years recovered his mind, found his brother, William, and got one-half million of his estate," Jack wrote in a set of laconic and disjoined letters he asked his attorney to keep for him in 1899. These letters may have been the beginning of a memoir Jack would try more deliberately to write several years later.[42]

From this brief and uncontextualized recollection, it's not clear whether Jack thought the $500,000 (in cash or property?) belonged to Gus himself or to his grandfather; the antecedent for "his" when Jack says Gus got "one-half million of his estate" is frustratingly vague. Did Jack believe Gus returned from Henry Buel's sanitarium and took possession of property that had been managed by William, but had always belonged to him? Or did he believe Gus took something that properly belonged to William after he returned? We will never know. Either way Jack definitely believed that Gus Hemenway had committed an injustice against his grandfather.[43]

It's unlikely the orders Gus gave to William (and which William apparently ignored) were issued while Gus was living at the sanitarium. All of the newspapers that reported on Gus's return to society in 1873 insisted he had "passed his time in quiet amusement" while he was a patient. "He glanced at the daily newspapers, but would never allow the word business to be mentioned in his presence." Jacob Bigelow, a neighbor and friend who visited Gus during the early years of his confinement, didn't think Gus had the mental capacity to do any work while he was at the sanitarium. "It seemed to me his memory did not retain impressions," Bigelow reported to Mary Hemenway after he'd spent the afternoon with Gus in August 1862.[44]

What ignored orders, then, did Gus give to William during the short period between November 1873, when Gus returned from the sanitarium, and October 1874, when William died, that cost Gus so much money? Alas, thanks to the San Francisco earthquake, we will never know. But there's a reality about life in the timber industry that may point to an answer. That reality is fire.

Fire was the great fear of anyone in the nineteenth century who was heavily invested in timber—especially if the wood he was invested in happened to be pine, fir, or spruce. Coniferous trees are full of resin, which is why they're great for shipbuilding. Resin makes them resistant to rot. It also makes them extremely flammable. High-resin wood is flammable when it sits in a yard, waiting to be milled or shipped. It's flammable when it's been felled and sits in the woods, waiting to be floated down a river toward the coast. And it's flammable when it's still alive and growing in the dense forests of northern Maine.[45]

Often the fires that cost nineteenth-century lumbermen money happened naturally. Just one random spark of lightning during a time of drought was all it took to set the woods aflame. Sometimes, however, the fires that cost men money were no accident. "A lecture after the Kearney style was listened to by a portion of the citizens last night," Gus's agent in Machias informed his trustees in August 1878, two years after Gus had died. Denis Kearney was a labor organizer from Ireland who arrived in the United States in 1868 and quickly became infamous for advocating violence and the destruction of property as a way to advance workers' rights. He did most of his organizing in California and reserved his worst invective for Chinese immigrants who, he believed, drove wages down. But Kearney also delivered several lectures in New England in the 1870s, including one at Faneuil Hall in Boston just a couple of weeks before J. H. Bailey wrote to Gus's trustees.[46]

James Henry Bailey believed that Kearney's ideas were influencing some of the men who worked for Gus's company (an important reminder that the fantastic wealth Sally Hemenway's son amassed had not been accumulated without some degree of exploitation). "A fire started among the lumber piles on Phenix Mill Wharf at 3 am," Bailey informed Gus's trustees before telling them about the "Kearny style" lecture. "The place and time in which it started leave no doubt in my mind, but that it is the work of an incendiary, inasmuch as it has been wet for two or three days past and it rained hard last evening."[47]

Gus's trustees had already decided to get out of the lumber business by the time Bailey wrote to them about the fire. Unloading the Hemenway holdings in Washington County proved to be difficult, however. In October 1880, more than four years after Gus's death, James Bailey finally received an offer on what remained of the millionaire's estate in northeastern Maine: the mill in Machias that William Hemenway had operated; the wharf in Machias that William had had built in the mid-1860s; and all of the land in UT 36.[48] The offer came from a couple of locals named John Ames and Cornelius Sullivan. They were willing to pay $70,000 for the properties. It was a pretty good deal, in the estimation of J. H. Bailey. "I think it is as well as you could do with the properties at present, if you decide it best to close it out now," he advised. "A trade on these terms could, I think, be closed up in a week's time."[49]

In 1880, $70,000 for that much property wasn't a lot of money. Even if it weren't in good shape, the steam-powered sawmill William Hemenway had operated for his brother would have been worth at least $30,000. The wharf was worth ten or twelve thousand. And in the early 1880s, high-quality timberland in coastal Maine had a retail value of about $2.50 an acre. That meant the 23,040 acres comprising UT 36 would have been worth nearly $58,000, had the township still been a prime piece of timberland when Ames and Sullivan offered to buy it.[50] By 1880, however, it almost certainly was not.

There are a couple of reasons why Gus's township might have declined in value. First, it's possible—and even likely—that William Hemenway had overtimbered the property. Clear-cutting was common in an age before state and federal regulators started mandating forest management. Ninety percent of Maine may be forested today, but in 1872, the year before Gus Hemenway left Henry Buel's sanitarium, just 53 percent of the state's landscape was still covered with trees.[51] Many of Maine's barren acres were in Washington County—that's one of the reasons so many wild blueberry bushes started growing there. In addition to acidic, sandy soil, wild blueberries need lots of open space and sunlight to spread.

But William Hemenway's clear-cutting would not have been unusual at the time, making it unlikely that overtimbering was the source of his disagreement with his brother. A more reasonable explanation for the disagreement is the *other* reason the value of UT 36 may have dropped: fire. If some of the trees remaining on the township had been destroyed by fires set by disgruntled workers, that destruction would explain not only why the value of the land had dropped, but also why Gus Hemenway believed his brother's management decisions had cost him $500,000. The drop in land value, after all, would have been miniscule compared to the value of the timber that was lost.

It's impossible to determine with any degree of certainty what the retail value of an acre's worth of timber would have been in late nineteenth-century Maine. So much of that value was dependent upon not just the prices for raw and milled timber but also the kind of trees that were growing on a particular acre of land—pine or spruce, for instance, versus maple or ash. The density of the tree canopy was relevant as well. Tree canopy can vary widely from one decade to another, thanks to droughts and insect infestations. The age of the trees was also important; older trees are bigger and therefore more valuable.

This is what we know, however: the timber found on Gus Hemenway's township was of unusually high quality (suggesting that whoever bought the township in the 1860s—William, perhaps?—knew what he was doing). In 1884, a few years after Gus's trustees sold UT 36, the *Lewiston Journal* reported on a fire that had destroyed several thousand acres in Washington County, after two men looking to clear the underbrush from a field of wild blueberries lost control of the blaze they'd intentionally set. Several townships were touched by the fire, and among them, "Township 36 contained by far the most valuable timber," according to the *Journal*. The paper's unnamed correspondent was "amazed by the enormous size of the trees and the density of the growth" he saw on UT 36. "The timber that stood on these tracts was more valuable than any crop of blueberries could possibly be," he noted, "and great indignation is felt by the people here."[52]

We also know this: a typical acre of natural, uncultivated forest in Maine today has enough mature trees on it to yield roughly eight thousand board feet of useable, unmilled timber, or what is known in the industry as "saw timber." This statistic assumes that most of the trees on the acre are at least a hundred years old, as the ones on UT 36 almost certainly were, judging from the description of the *Journal*'s correspondent. The statistic also assumes the canopy on the acre is neither unusually dense, nor unusually sparse. Sparse acres might yield no more than five thousand board feet of saw timber, while dense acres—like the ones the *Journal*'s correspondent said he observed on UT 36—could yield as much as nine thousand board feet.[53]

In 1877, when Gus's estate was appraised, he had more than ten million board feet of saw timber sitting in his mill yard in Machias. That saw timber had an estimated value of $90,000—or a little less than 1 cent per board foot. If we assume that the composition of Washington County's uncultivated forests in the 1870s was not radically different from the composition of the county's uncultivated forests today, we can estimate that every untimbered acre on UT 36 had about $80 worth of saw timber on it, judging from the report in the *Lewiston Journal*. A fire that destroyed six thousand untimbered acres, in other words, might have been enough to cost Gus Hemenway nearly half a million dollars—and that's not counting the additional value those lost trees would have had, had they not just been timbered, but also milled. Gus had some milled lumber sitting in his yard in Machias as well. The estimated value of that milled lumber was three times higher than the value of the saw timber.[54]

The summer before Ames and Sullivan made their offer to Gus's trustees, James Bailey had to send forty men to the northern edge of UT 36 to put down a fire that had been started there by "trespassers." The fire destroyed nearly one thousand acres of pine and spruce. It is not at all difficult to imagine, therefore, that there might have been a bigger conflagration on the property just a few years earlier, right after Gus returned from Henry Buel's sanitarium and started giving his brother orders.[55]

It's also not difficult to imagine that Gus might have felt entitled to pass judgment on the cause of that fire and blame his brother for it. It turns out Gus felt entitled to judge many of the decisions that were made while he was gone. Shortly after he got back to Boston, for example, after being gone for thirteen years, he questioned the necessity of a $102 visit to the dentist his wife had made at some point during his extended absence. He insisted his accountant find him the receipt, so he could determine for himself whether the expense had been warranted. This attention to detail, one reporter enthused, was a "specimen of his minute, methodical ways." It was also probably the reason Augustus Hemenway Sr. went insane—and it suggests he was the kind of micromanager who would not hesitate to blame his brother for a costly labor dispute that was so complex it continued to fester long after both brothers were dead.[56]

Gus's trustees took Ames and Sullivan up on their offer and got Augustus Hemenway's company out of the lumber business in Maine. A relationship between the Hemenway family and the state of Maine that had begun more than sixty years earlier with a controversial divorce and a remarkably successful business partnership between a mother and her teenaged son was finally brought to a close.

There were no members of Sally Hemenway's family left in Washington County by the time Gus's trustees sold UT 36 in 1881. Her last remaining family member—Sally's great-grandson, Jack Sargent, who'd been born in her home in 1861—had left the state two years earlier. He wasn't the grandson of the "richest lumberman in Maine" anymore. His mother and grandfather were both dead, and without his grandfather's "pet township" to look forward to managing or working on, Jack Sargent had nothing to keep him in the county that had been his great-grandmother's refuge.

In 1879, at the age of seventeen, John Dudley Sargent went west. He moved to the Wyoming Territory, where he eventually partnered up with a former state lawmaker from Manhattan named Robert Ray Hamilton. The two men built a hunting lodge together, which they planned on marketing to wealthy New Yorkers and New Englanders they knew back home. Their dream never became a reality, however. Instead, Ray and Jack both died tragically at the base of the Teton Mountains, nearly a quarter of a century apart.

The Fourth Estate

Richard Hoe knew he was going to change the way news got done, though he had no way of knowing just how much. The inventor never imagined he'd help to turn the news industry into a machine that thrived on scandal and misfortune and amplified humiliation to levels never before seen in human history. Certainly, that was not his intention. It's exactly what Richard Hoe did, however—as people like Evangeline Steele, who also went by the names Eva Mann and Lydia Parsons, one day learned.

Hoe came from a family of printers. His maternal uncle, Peter Smith, patented the iron-framed flat-bed printing press that was used to produce the first copies of the Book of Mormon in 1830. Ten years later Hoe's father, Robert, became the first printer in the United States to start using a cylinder to feed paper into a printing press, instead of the iron frame his brother-in-law had designed. Robert Hoe didn't invent the cylinder press; that title belonged to a printer from Germany. But he did popularize its use in the United States. Even more important, he taught his son, Richard, how to use one.

Cylinders were an important advancement in the field of printing. They enabled a printer to roll a sheet of paper onto an inked bed of type, instead of loading the sheet into a wooden or iron frame, pressing the framed paper onto the inked type, and then slowly removing the paper from the frame so that the entire process could be done all over again. A cylinder press like the one Robert Hoe adopted in 1840 could turn out 1,100 sheets of printed paper in a single hour—nearly three times the number of pages a frame-based press could produce. That output paled, however, in comparison to the output of the press Richard Hoe patented in 1847.[1]

The younger Hoe's great innovation was to put the type directly onto the cylinder, instead of a flat plate that had to be moved away from the cylinder each time a sheet of paper rolled onto it, so that the wet print wouldn't smear and the type could be reinked. When the *Philadelphia Public Ledger* became the first newspaper in the United States to start using a Hoe rotary printing press, its printers turned out an astounding eight thousand sheets of printed paper during the first hour of the machine's operation.[2]

The increase in productivity was stunning. Unfortunately for Richard Hoe, most newspapers in the United States didn't need that kind of output in the mid-nineteenth century. Nearly 90 percent of them were weeklies rather than dailies, and even most dailies didn't have the kind of subscription numbers that would justify buying what came to be known as a "lightning press." A typical metropolitan daily in the 1840s had fewer than two thousand subscribers and was no more than four pages long. The *Philadelphia Public Ledger* had enough readers to justify the $4,000 expense of a Hoe rotary printing press. So did the *Baltimore Sun* and the *New York Herald*, which boasted a readership of more than 11,500 people per day.[3] Most American newspapers gave Hoe's machine a pass, however, when it debuted. The less advanced presses they already owned suited their needs just fine.

Richard Hoe, therefore, turned his attention to Europe, where, six years earlier, the Scottish historian Thomas Carlyle had called newspapers the "fourth estate," by way of emphasizing their importance to the honest, if not always smooth functioning of government. France and the United Kingdom didn't have nearly as many newspapers as the United States did, but the papers they had enjoyed circulation numbers that were significantly higher. *News of the World*, for instance—the 168-year-old British tabloid that famously closed its doors in 2011 after its reporters were found to be hacking the phones of celebrities, crime victims, and members of the royal family—had a daily circulation of more than one hundred thousand readers in 1855.[4] With numbers like that, its publisher was very eager to acquire Richard Hoe's invention.

The handful of American papers that did embrace the lightning press were part of a phenomenon known as the "penny press." These papers were creatures of the city. They came on the scene in the 1830s and had

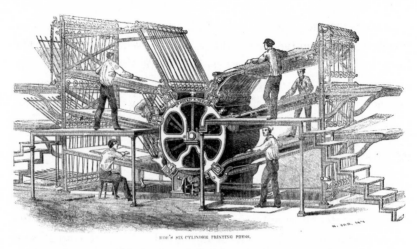

HOE'S SIX CYLINDER PRINTING PRESS.

An early version of Richard Hoe's "lightning press." *History of the Processes of Manufacture and Uses of Printing* (New York: Bradburn, 1864).

unusually large circulations. Cheaper than the older, more established newspapers they competed with, penny press papers cost exactly that—a penny—instead of the six cents per issue traditional newspapers charged. Penny press papers also didn't rely on subscriptions to get their product into readers' hands, the way traditional newspapers did. At six cents per paper, an annual subscription cost nearly $19—more than $500 in today's money. Many people in the mid-nineteenth century didn't have incomes large enough or stable enough to commit to an annual subscription, and even those who did have the money didn't always think the information conveyed to them by a traditional newspaper was worth the price (making them not unlike many Americans today).

A penny press paper was something you didn't need to subscribe to, however, in order to read it. You could buy one on a daily basis from a newsboy who stood on a street corner and shouted the headlines. Sometimes newsboys would hawk "extra" editions of newspapers they had sold earlier in the day, because something important or titillating had happened, and—lacking a Twitter feed or website to update its readers—the paper had used its Hoe rotary printing press to put out an amended edition. Hence the now famous if clichéd line used in movies ranging from *Citizen Kane* (1941) to *The Muppets Take Manhattan* (1984): "Extra! Extra! Read all about it!"

Americans *did* want to read all about it when it was conveyed to them by a reporter who wrote for the penny press. That was the other reason this kind of newspaper had so many readers. The information penny press papers relayed wasn't about ships that had come into port or legislation that was pending before lawmakers (topics that had been ubiquitous in American newspapers since the colonial days). Penny press papers *told stories*. They didn't simply relay information. And the stories they told—like all good stories—were filled with romance, betrayal, mystery, violence, and crime.[5]

This was one of the great contributions of the penny press to the history of American journalism. The reporters and editors working for newspapers like the *New York Herald*, the *Boston Herald*, the *Baltimore Sun*, and the *New York Sun* recognized the importance of storytelling to human understanding. It wasn't enough simply to convey the facts; indeed, one of the criticisms rightly laid at the feet of the penny press was that its reporters and editors felt no obligation to adhere to the facts when the facts got in the way of a good story. Storytelling was how people learned; it was how they came to understand, appreciate, and embody the differences between right and wrong and the values of their culture. "What Shakespeare did for the drama—what Milton did for religion—what Scott did for the novel, such shall I do for the daily newspaper," James Gordon Bennett, editor of the *New York Herald*, announced to his readers in 1836, during the first year of his newspaper's operation. The *New York Herald* went on to become one of the most widely read and financially successful newspapers in American history.[6]

The *Herald* regularly featured stories about suicides, murders, executions, and duels. Kentucky representative Richard M. Johnson's unconventional relationship with a mixed-race enslaved woman he had inherited from his father and with whom he had two fully acknowledged children was a particular object of fascination for the paper's writers. The woman, Julia Chinn, had died two years before the paper even started publishing. That didn't keep the *Herald* from presenting her to its readers as alive and socializing in Washington DC.[7]

Penny press papers didn't ignore the issues relating to commerce and politics that older, more traditional newspapers focused on. Actually, the *Herald* and its chief competitor, the *Sun*, were the first newspapers in New York to hire permanent correspondents in Washington DC.[8] But penny press papers didn't just publish a politician's speech or recite the bills he had sponsored in Congress, the way traditional newspapers did. Again, these papers were in the business of telling stories. Not only that, but as the *Herald*'s coverage of Representative Johnson's mixed-race family made clear, penny press papers were just as likely to report on a lawmaker's personal decisions as they were on his professional ones.

They were also just as likely to report on the accomplishments and failures of a Democrat like Johnson as they were those of a Whig like Massachusetts's Daniel Webster or Kentucky's Henry Clay.[9] That was the other thing that made penny press papers different from older, more traditional newspapers in the mid-nineteenth century: penny press papers were independent. They were not funded by political parties, and they weren't bound to represent the interests of political parties in their coverage.

Prior to the 1830s, almost no newspapers in the United States were independently funded. Although they all took in advertising revenue to supplement their incomes, that ad revenue was not how they paid their bills; the subscriptions they charged their readers weren't how they paid their bills, either. In fact subscriptions unto themselves have never been a powerful part of a newspaper's revenue stream. That's one of the reasons "pay walls" have proven to be a reliably unreliable way for newspapers to stay afloat in the internet age.[10]

To make ends meet, most newspapers in the nineteenth century relied on political parties or trade groups to sponsor them. They did so openly, often announcing the sponsorship in their mastheads. The *Quincy Whig*, the *Sonoma Democrat*, and the *Plattsburgh Republican* are three examples of the thousands of newspapers in nineteenth-century America that were sponsored by political parties. Many of these papers still exist today, and some of them have even retained their partisan names, although the news they now publish is ostensibly objective (even if their editorial pages sometimes represent the interests one party over the other).[11]

"We shall give no place . . . to political discussions of a merely partisan character," Arunah Shepherdson Abell announced in May 1837 when he launched the Baltimore *Sun*. "On political principles and questions involving the interests of honor of the whole country . . . our object will be that of the common good, without regard to that of sects, faction or parties."[12] Abell could make this pledge because just like the editors in New York he was emulating, he intended to fund the *Sun* primarily through the sale of ads. However, like those editors in New York, Abell was somewhat limited, in terms of the kinds of ads he could reasonably expect to run in the 1830s. The United States was not yet the manufacturing powerhouse it would one day become. The American landscape was not flooded yet with hundreds of domestically manufactured goods like soap or toothpaste or shortening that came in tins and crackers that came in boxes, many of these items quite similar to one another and all of them competing for consumers' attention.[13]

The age of consumption and the development of the kind of marketing techniques we think of today as "advertising" would not happen in the United States until after the Civil War. This meant that other than the inexpensive "want ads" individuals had been placing in newspapers since the colonial days, the editors of penny press papers had just two sources of ad revenue they could rely upon: (1) the manufacturers of what were known as "patent medicines," which were cheap elixirs made mostly of alcohol and opium that Americans used to alleviate a host of aches and pains; and (2) the purveyors of what were euphemistically referred to as "female remedies," which were pills, powders or surgical procedures that were said to help women "laboring under the suppression of their natural monthly illness."[14]

The moral implications of these ads (the second category included abortifacients, in case the nineteenth-century language was too opaque for modern-day readers) were part of the reason many traditional newspapers refused to rely on ads to pay their bills. In a rather shameless display of self-interested sanctimony, the publishers of several traditional newspapers in New York, Albany, Boston, Philadelphia, and Baltimore banded together in 1840 and launched what they called a "Moral War" against James Gordon Bennett and the New York *Herald*. In a series of coordinated editorials, the publishers called the *Herald*'s ads "vile," "monstrous," and "vulgar." They insisted the paper's articles were "a mass of trash" and "witless balderdash," and they claimed that Bennett, himself, was a "common bandit," a "daring infidel," and a "habitual liar."[15] The publishers threatened to stop reviewing productions at theaters that advertised in the *New York Herald*, and in each of their cities, they pressured the managers of the social clubs they belonged to not to carry the *Herald* in their reading rooms.

James Gordon Bennett responded to the assault by publishing the circulation numbers of all of the newspapers involved in the Moral War and then pointing out to his readers (and also to the publishers opposing him, since he knew they read his paper) that together, the newspapers still fell more than fourteen thousand issues short of the weekly circulation the *New York Herald* enjoyed all by itself. "The ascension of patronage of every kind, since the war began, has been greater than any we ever knew," Bennett bragged as he twisted the knife. His newspaper had something to sell that the American people wanted to buy. "Subscribers and advertisers pour in from all quarters," he claimed. "The attempt to dictate to the community against their own senses is a miserable failure."[16]

The advertising options available to penny press papers like the *New York Herald* and the *Baltimore Sun* may have been limited in the mid-nineteenth century, but the revenue they generated was enough to give those papers' publishers the ability and freedom to buy one of Richard Hoe's rotary printing presses as soon as the machine became available. A. S. Abell and James Gordon Bennett didn't have to ask anyone for permission to buy a lightning press. The papers sponsored by political parties and trade groups, however, had to convince the partisans paying the bills that a new press was worth the expense—and, by the time Hoe's invention debuted in 1847, the editors of traditional newspapers had more than just their low circulation numbers working against them every time they asked a political party for more money.

By the late 1840s, party leaders had begun to reevaluate their commitment to the funding of newspapers. They recognized that newspapers were becoming a less lucrative investment—not in terms of the money they made but in terms of the votes they generated. The U.S. Constitution says very little about who gets to vote. In fact, until 1870, when the Fifteenth Amendment declared that the right to vote could not be denied to any citizen on the basis of his race, the Constitution said nothing at all about voting requirements. It still leaves that determination mostly to the states. This is why some states give voters the option of casting their ballots early, and others do not; it's why some states require voters to present photo IDs and other states permanently disenfranchise convicted felons. And it's why former president Donald Trump lost every lawsuit he filed in 2020, when he claimed, incorrectly, that the U.S. Constitution did not permit states to change the way they voted in response to the COVID-19 pandemic.[17]

The Constitution gives states a great deal of freedom to define how and by whom the voting process gets done. At the time of the country's founding, nearly every state in the union had some kind of property requirement on voting. The thinking was that voters who owned property would have an interest in the stability and future of the government they were choosing to staff. They wouldn't elect candidates who promised to upend what was, in the 1790s, a young, fragile, and highly experimental form of government, because they would want that government to succeed.[18]

Property ownership meant a voter often had the financial security to be educated. That education, in turn, meant that most American voters in the early nineteenth century could read. This was why political parties had started sponsoring newspapers: they wanted to sway voters. As the great European observer of American society Alexis de Tocqueville remarked after he had visited the United States for the first time in 1831: "A newspaper is an advisor . . . that comes every day unbidden to talk to you briefly about public affairs. . . . Only a newspaper can deposit a thought in a thousand minds at once."[19]

But newspapers could deposit thoughts into the minds of voters only so long as a sizeable portion of those voters were literate—and as the country aged and grew more politically stable, and the states slowly started eliminating property requirements on voting (because, let's face it, those requirements were profoundly undemocratic), the literacy rates found among American voters started to drop.[20] This drop accelerated in the 1840s and 1850s, as thousands of impoverished immigrants poured into America's cities from Ireland, where three-quarters of the inhabitants were so illiterate, they couldn't even sign their own names. By 1850 at least a quarter of the residents of Baltimore, Philadelphia, New York, and Boston were immigrants *just* from Ireland, and every one of those immigrants who was male and at least twenty-one years old was eligible to vote.[21]

Until very recently there was no federal requirement that voters in the United States be citizens. The Constitution still doesn't require it, and not until 1996 did Congress pass a law mandating that a person be a citizen in order to cast a ballot. Granted, long before that law was passed, every American state had passed its own legislation barring noncitizens from voting. Nearly all of those state mandates were implemented in the twentieth century, however; in the nineteenth century noncitizens could vote. This meant that by 1856, when North Carolina became the final state to eliminate its property requirement on voting, every state in the union had adopted what was known as "universal, white manhood suffrage." Most of those poor Irish immigrant men could not read a single sentence in a newspaper, but they could vote.[22]

By the time Richard Hoe's rotary printing press came along, political parties just weren't getting the same bang for their buck out of newspapers anymore. They didn't abandon the papers right away, but they did become a lot more discriminating about the expenses they were willing to fund. Any editor who asked a party boss for the money to purchase a lightning press was likely to find his request fell on deaf ears. This was particularly true as the century progressed, and the cost of a lightning press went up.

Richard Hoe may have found a limited market for his invention at first, but he brought in enough revenue to do what all good inventors do: tweak and improve their inventions. He added an automatic inking mechanism to the machine. He worked with paper manufacturers to create rolls of paper that were five miles long and could be fed continuously into his press, and then he invented a way to cut that paper mechanically after it had been printed upon. He added more cylinders so his machine could print different pages at the same time. Finally, Hoe created a mechanism that folded each newspaper into a size that could be easily carried in the pouch of a news boy.[23]

The result was that a machine that had revolutionized the printing industry in 1847 by producing eight thousand sheets of printed paper in a single hour—seven times more than what any printing press before it had done—was able to produce, by the fiftieth anniversary of its debut, ninety-six thousand folded copies of an eight-page newspaper every hour. That's what the *New York World*'s brand-new eight-cylinder Hoe rotary printing press was able to produce when the newspaper's publisher, Joseph Pulitzer, had it installed in 1893. Pulitzer definitely needed that kind of power. The year before, the *World* had hit a circulation record of 374,000 copies per day.

By the Gilded Age, anyone who expected to run a successful newspaper needed to be using some version of a Hoe rotary printing press, regardless of whether the partisans funding the paper wanted to pay for it. There was simply no way to compete without one. The improvements Hoe made to his technology did not come cheap, however. A machine that had cost just $4,000 in the late 1840s—or about $110,000 in today's money—cost more than $80,000 by the early 1890s, the equivalent of about $3 million today.[24]

To be fair, Hoe's press wasn't the only reason news got expensive in the second half of the nineteenth century. The Civil War jacked up the costs of news production, even as it also increased the demand the American people had for news. About 2.5 percent of the population was killed by disease or combat during the Civil War—meaning that if the United States were to experience a comparable war today, roughly seven million Americans would die because of that war in the span of just four years.[25] The appetite people had for news during the Civil War was voracious, and many papers in the early 1860s determined that they needed to purchase a Hoe rotary printing press to meet that demand, even if the political parties funding them were unwilling to shoulder the expense.

The cost of disseminating news during a time of war was just one part of the story, however. There were also the costs of *gathering* the news. Individual newspapers spent between $60,000 and $100,000 each year on reporters they sent to battlefields across the South, an expense that did not include the five cents per word those reporters had to pay telegraph service providers every time they transmitted their stories back home. It's difficult to convert that expense into today's currency because of the skyrocketing inflation that came with the war, but the Civil War probably added the equivalent of between $1.3 million and $2.2 million a year in unanticipated expenses to a newspaper's costs, *if* that newspaper was fortunate enough to be able to afford to have its own reporters on the front line, which many were not.[26]

If a paper couldn't afford that expense, its publisher at the very least had to find the funds to subscribe to the Associated Press. The AP was a consortium of editors who agreed to share articles from their newspapers with the editors of other newspapers, in exchange for a fee. It had been around since 1846, but it was during the Civil War that the service really became important, since it supplied vital information to the readers of small-town newspapers that didn't have the financial resources to send their own reporters to Antietam or Chickamauga.[27]

By the end of the Civil War in 1865, most newspapers in the United States were still supported to some degree by political parties.[28] The expenses involved in wartime news production had changed the funding formula considerably, however. Many papers that were funded by political parties had turned to advertising during the war to supplement their revenue streams and meet their increased expenses, and they continued to do so after the war, particularly as the advertising options available to them expanded beyond just patent medicines and abortifacients.

Technology that became available shortly before, during, and after the Civil War radically altered the way Americans consumed a host of different products they'd been consuming for generations. Many of these innovations still play important roles in our lives today, although we don't necessarily think of them as "technology" anymore—paperboard boxes, for example, which made it possible for things like crackers and oats to be sold to consumers in small quantities off of shelves, instead of in bulk, out of barrels. Refrigerated boxcars were another innovation. They were unstable and unreliable when they first appeared on America's rails in 1857, but they became safer and better insulated after the war, in part because of changes that were experimented with during the war for some sad and rather gruesome reasons: families needed a way to get the bodies of their loved ones home to New Hampshire or Maine after they'd died on battlefields in Maryland or Georgia. These boxcars made it possible for stockyards in Chicago and St. Louis to slaughter cattle in the Midwest and sell the beef to consumers in Philadelphia and Baltimore weeks later, without bothering to can or cure the meat.[29]

Buying crackers in boxes or uncured meat that had been dead for three weeks was something Americans had never done before, however—and at first, they were very reluctant to do it. Nowadays we don't even think about whether a box of Wheat Thins is full of broken or worm-eaten crackers when we take the box off a shelf in a store. In the late nineteenth century, though, that was all Americans *could* think about when the National Biscuit Company—later known as Nabisco—started asking them to buy their crackers sight unseen, instead of the way they'd traditionally bought crackers, which was with a scoop from a barrel. Today when we pick up a package of ground beef at the grocery store, it probably doesn't occur to most of us to wonder when the animal(s) that meat came from died. But prior to the 1870s, if you were going to eat a piece of meat that wasn't cured, it was important for you to know when the animal it came from had been slaughtered, because otherwise you could die. As one early pioneer of the Chicago meatpacking industry recalled, "the idea of eating meat a week or more after it had been killed met with a nasty-nice horror" when businessmen like Gustavus Swift and Philip Armour started asking American consumers to do so in the early 1870s.[30]

There are many reasons why we don't ask ourselves these questions anymore, not the least of them being the many safety regulations that now govern our food processing industry, starting with the Pure Food and Drug Act of 1906. There are other, less monumental reasons for why these questions no longer occur to us, however, and one of those reasons is the fact that we've been trained by our lives in modern-day America not to ask such questions. The texts we've learned these lessons from are the thousands of advertisements we see every day—and many of the techniques used to teach us were tried for the first time on the pages of Gilded Age newspapers.[31]

Advertising agencies like the J. Walter Thompson Company, founded in New York in 1877, and Lord & Thomas, founded in Chicago in 1881, told manufacturers to use words like "natural," "old-fashioned," and "homemade" in their ad copy, to make consumers who felt overwhelmed by the rapid social and technological changes that followed the Civil War feel like they were being brought back to an earlier, less complicated time whenever they consumed a particular product. To get Americans to try a product for the first time, they promoted coupons, which proved to be an important part of the process whereby Americans were trained to trust meat that had been dead for several days. Agencies also helped manufacturers tap the potential of trademark legislation passed by Congress in 1881, advising manufacturers to design labels and containers—such as the iconic bottle that is the origin of the phrase "Coke bottle glasses"—that could be used to train people in an almost Pavlovian sense to associate the packaging with the product.[32]

It was a happy coincidence that the very point in history when news was starting to become more expensive to produce, and the partisan funding model that had governed traditional news production for decades had broken down, happened to overlap with a period in America's history when domestic manufacturing was booming and the creators of new products and new ways of consuming old products were desperate to teach Americans how and what to buy. The advertising-driven funding model that began with a few penny press papers in the late 1830s was embraced by nearly all newspapers in the country by 1900.[33] This development helped to make news more objective. Advertisers didn't care if a reader was a Republican or a Democrat, and most newspaper publishers didn't care, either (except when they ran for office themselves, as Joseph Pulitzer and William Randolph Hearst did in 1884 and 1902, respectively).

But this change to the funding model also led to a phenomenon in the history of American journalism known as "yellow journalism." The gossip and sensationalism that early editors like James Gordon Bennet and A. S. Abell had introduced in the 1830s and 1840s became the norm in American journalism in the 1880s and 1890s. Some papers engaged in it more than others; Hearst's *New York Journal* and Pulitzer's *New York World* are usually held up as the great exemplars. But even the staid *New York Times*, which prided itself on being a respectable newspaper that published only the news that was "fit" to be print, dabbled in the prurient from time to time.[34] It had to. The advertisers paying the paper's bills wanted their ads to be seen, and even "respectable" people enjoy stories about sex, passion, and intrigue every now and then.

Sex, passion, and intrigue were exactly what a young woman named

Evangeline Steele—a.k.a. Eva Mann—gave readers across the country in August 1889, when she got into a drunken argument with her husband and stabbed the wet nurse who'd been feeding the couple's infant daughter while the family vacationed in Atlantic City, New Jersey. That incident would generate headlines for the next twenty-five years, long after Eva, her husband, and the wet nurse were all dead. Indeed, to this very day, there's a historical marker on the Upper West Side of Manhattan that memorializes the incident, thanks to the continual newspaper coverage Eva's stabbing of Mary Ann Donnelly received well into the second decade of the twentieth century.

Using newspapers from Gilded Age America as a way to understand the past must always be done with some caution, since these newspapers often prioritized writing a good story over gathering all the facts. Still, "yellow" newspapers (which got their nickname from a popular comic strip character known as "the Yellow Kid") did have some standards. They didn't publish rank fiction as fact, the way penny press papers had done half a century earlier. In 1844, for example, the *New York Sun* ran a series of stories by a writer named Edgar Allen Poe about a gas-powered balloon journey that an intrepid traveler supposedly made across the Atlantic in an astounding three days. The accounts were a complete fabrication, and the author of *The Murders in the Rue Morgue*—published just three years earlier—clearly had no interest in being a mere recorder of events. Nevertheless, the *Sun* initially presented Poe's "balloon hoax" to its readers as fact. By the Gilded Age, newspapers didn't engage in that kind of deception anymore (although the *New York Journal*'s coverage of the Spanish-American War in 1898 was an exception that proved this rule).[35]

Editors and publishers like Joseph Pulitzer, William Randolph Hearst, Charles Anderson Dana, and James Gordon Bennett Jr. did manufacture news sometimes so that their reporters could cover it, creating what cultural critics in the twentieth century would later call a "pseudoevent." James Gordon Bennett Jr., for instance, sent one of his journalists to Africa to see if he could find a famous British explorer named David Livingstone who'd disappeared in 1869 while searching for the source of the Nile River. Henry Morton Stanley's article about his encounter with the lost explorer is the source of the now famous phrase, "Dr. Livingstone, I presume?"[36] In 1889 Joseph Pulitzer sent one of his reporters out to see if she could break the "record" set by the fictional character Phileas Fogg in Jules Verne's novel *Around the World in Eighty Days*. Two years earlier Elizabeth Cochrane (a.k.a. "Nellie Bly") had pretended to be insane so police would commit her to the Women's Lunatic Asylum on Blackwell's Island in New York City. There she investigated—and then later confirmed in her reports for the *World*—rumors about the deplorable conditions patients were being kept in at the asylum.[37]

But a pseudoevent wasn't the same as what the *Sun* had done in 1844, when it published a story about a balloon journey that never happened and presented it to readers as the truth. Henry Morton Stanley's article about David Livingstone almost certainly took some liberties with the truth (including, perhaps, his assertion that he greeted the lost explorer with those famous words). But Stanley did travel to Africa; he did find David Livingstone, who, it turned out, had witnessed the massacre of more than four hundred men, women, and children at a slave market along the Lualaba River shortly before he stopped corresponding with people he knew in England.[38] Nellie Bly may have embellished some of her accounts about riding camels in Yemen or being forced to take cold baths on Blackwell's Island, but she did in fact circumnavigate the globe, and she also spent time at the Women's Lunatic Asylum with doctors who thought she was insane.

Some real and important truths about the slave trade in Africa, the treatment of the mentally ill in New York, and the wonders of a transportation revolution that took place in the second half of the nineteenth century were revealed by the stories Henry Morton Stanley and Nellie Bly wrote. Stanley is now a controversial figure because of his early involvement in Belgium's exploitation of the Congo. His reports played a powerful role, however, in Britain's decision to finally end the slave trade in east Africa. In Bly's case her articles led to a grand jury investigation of the Women's Lunatic Asylum that resulted in a series of reforms, including a massive budgetary increase for the agency that administered the asylum.[39]

There was, in fact, a surprising emphasis among late nineteenth-century editors on the importance of accuracy to the accomplished practice of journalism—one that doesn't often get emphasized in popular

histories about the sensationalism of the Gilded Age, and one that reporters themselves sometimes chafed against, since so many of them, deep
in their hearts, really wanted to be novelists. A few of those reporters
did succeed in that endeavor.

Bylines were not a standard convention in the nineteenth century.
This was especially the case with self-consciously respectable newspapers like the *New York Times*, which eschewed the kind of celebrity
Joseph Pulitzer actively cultivated with reporters like Nellie Bly. "The
business of the paper must be absolutely impersonal," the *Times*'s publisher, Adolph Ochs, stressed in his newsroom. No editor or reporter
ever really "owned" a story. By the time an article got published, many
minds and hands had gone into producing it.[40]

It is often hard to determine, therefore, when scrolling through
archived editions of Gilded Age newspapers, who actually wrote a particular story. Still, the names of some of the writers who worked for these
papers should be familiar to anyone who has taken an introductory course
in American literature. Nowadays Theodore Dreiser is known for his
novels *Sister Carrie* (1900) and *An American Tragedy* (1925), rather than
the stories he wrote in the 1890s as a reporter for the *Chicago Daily Globe*.
Jack London is known for *The Call of the Wild* (1903) and *White Fang* (1906),
rather than the coverage he provided the *San Francisco Examiner* of the
Russo-Japanese War. Willa Cather's fame stems from her beautiful and
nostalgic novels *The Song of the Lark* (1915) and *My Ántonia* (1918), and
not from the theater reviews she did for the *Pittsburgh Leader* in 1897.[41]

Writing about a job interview he'd had at the offices of the New York
World in 1894, Theodore Dreiser recalled how he'd "looked about the
great room, as I waited patiently and delightedly, and saw on the walls at
intervals printed cards which read: *Accuracy! Accuracy! Accuracy!*" Clearly
it was a standard the yellow newspaper took seriously, and it was one the
twenty-three-year-old reporter from the Midwest valued, too. Nevertheless, when he failed to pass a test the newspaper's city desk editor
had given him as part of the interview process, Dreiser did wonder if
perhaps he'd taken the "accuracy" mantra a little too seriously. The editor
had sent him out to do a follow-up story on a fistfight between a socially
prominent attorney and a bar manager at the exclusive Hoffman House
hotel on Twenty-Fourth Street and Broadway. Dreiser couldn't get any

of the principal characters to talk to him, however. "I was afraid of these New York waiters and managers and society people," Dreiser recalled. "Suppose they complained of my tale and denounced me as a faker?"

Unable to confirm any elements of the story, the young reporter returned to the newsroom empty handed. But as he did, he "had a feeling I was turning aside an item by which, had I chosen to fake, I could have furthered myself." Dreiser had a sneaking suspicion that what the city desk editor had wanted from him was "not merely 'accuracy, accuracy, accuracy,' but a kind of flair for the ridiculous or the remarkable, though it had to be invented, so that the pages of the paper, and life itself, might not seem so dull."[42]

It was a delicate balance: how to write news that wasn't "fake" (Dreiser's word choice takes on new relevance in the twenty-first century . . .) but also wasn't boring. The key was to recognize that "fake" and "boring" were not absolute terms; there were gradations to both. "If you are invariably reliable in your statements, the public will forgive a moderate degree of dullness in your style," Edwin L. Shuman advised budding journalists in one of the first textbooks on reporting, *Steps into Journalism*, published in 1894. Alternatively, "if you have a simple, sensible, breezy style with a sparkle in it, the newspaper reader will forgive a good deal of inaccuracy in your matter." The one "unpardonable sin in journalism," according to Shuman, was "to be both stupid and inaccurate."[43]

So what did this advice mean in practical terms? It meant that reporters had to get the key facts in any story correct—the "who, what, how, when, and where," Theodore Dreiser recalled. But editors like Edwin Shuman wanted young reporters who aimed at achieving "sparkle" to know that the "trick of drawing upon the imagination for the non-essential parts of an article" was "certainly one of the most valuable secrets of the profession at its present state of development."[44]

If a reporter chose to describe a woman at the center of his story as a "handsome and refined brunette," when those who actually knew her thought she looked "more like a savage Indian than a civilized woman," that was perfectly fine—preferable over the truth, even—so long as the woman's name and what she had done (or had done to her) was correct. If a reporter told his readers that a wealthy and notorious homesteader living in the American West had been born in New York, when he'd really been born in Maine—or if a reporter said a millionaire's fortune was $5 million, when another newspaper had put it at just $2,652,400—those discrepancies could be forgiven, so long as they didn't alter the substance of the story. "Truth in essentials, imagination in non-essentials" was the rule all good reporters should follow, according to Edwin Shuman. "This rather doubtful *fin-du-siècle* sort of journalism is perhaps excusable as long as the imaginative writing is confined to non-essentials and is done by one who has in him at least the desire to represent the truth."[45]

The first time Evangeline Steele made it into the papers was on August 27, 1889, the day after she stabbed Mary Ann Donnelly—a "good-looking Irish woman," according to the *New York Times*—whom she had hired a few months earlier to breastfeed her eight-month-old daughter. Eva and her husband had recently returned to the East Coast after spending two months in California. They were vacationing at an inn along the boardwalk in Atlantic City, which had become a popular tourist destination for middle-class Philadelphians in the late 1850s, after a private developer built a rail line between one of New Jersey's barrier islands and the City of Brotherly Love. Prior to the mid-nineteenth century, "vacationing" was something middle-class Americans did not do; it was simply too expensive. The Atlantic City rail line was one of a number of innovations in the second half of the nineteenth century that made travel much more affordable for everyday Americans.[46]

Eva and her husband were not everyday Americans, however. While the police were investigating the scene of the stabbing, several pieces of jewelry worth more than $2,000 (about $57,000 in today's money) were taken from the apartment the couple had been renting. "The authorities and pawnbrokers throughout the country have been notified of the robbery," the *Times*'s reporter duly noted in his front-page story. The couple also didn't hail from Philadelphia; they lived in a house on West Fifteenth Street in Manhattan. But Eva had spent some time working for a theater group in Philadelphia in the early 1880s. That may have been when she developed a taste for the Jersey Shore.[47]

According to Eva's husband, the couple had been drinking quite heavily on the afternoon of the stabbing. They got into an argument, which Eva apparently blamed the wet nurse for. When the nurse walked into the room, Eva picked up a dagger her husband's father had acquired while soldiering in the Mexican War and—according to the *New York World*—slashed her husband, "cutting his trousers, but drawing no blood," before turning on the nurse.[48]

"You she devil," the newlywed supposedly yelled as she knocked over a piece of furniture and thrust her weapon into Mary Ann Donnelly's abdomen, "making a wound through which the intestines protruded." The term "she devil" was quite popular with Gilded Age writers; it was used in more than two hundred syndicated articles published *just* in 1889.[49]

The commotion caused by the argument drew the attention of a waiter downstairs. He ran to the apartment, kicked in the door, and found Mary Ann Donnelly "stretched on the floor in a pool of blood, and an infant was propped up on the bed." The nurse was still alive the next morning, when the papers in New York and Philadelphia went to press. Her condition, however, was precarious.[50]

In the days that followed, papers across the country—thanks to the AP—featured dozens of stories that purported to tell readers about the kind of woman Evangeline Steele was. "She is quite pretty," one reporter noted, "but absolutely devoid of the qualities which make decent women." Another reporter agreed that "she is a beautiful woman" but insisted she was "so haughty in her demeanor that she does not gain the liking of those who have to work for her." One article claimed she had assaulted her coachman with a deadly weapon in 1887, about a year and a half before she was married. Another reported she was "addicted to the use of strong stimulants" and had become a "confirmed slave to the morphine habit." One particularly bold writer even went so far as to imply—but never actually say—that ten years earlier, long before she'd gotten married and stabbed Mary Ann Donnelly, Evangeline Steele had worked as a prostitute in two high-end brothels in Newark, New Jersey.[51]

The young woman's family members, too, were subjected to the press's spotlight. Readers in Chattanooga, Tennessee; Independence, Kansas; St. Joseph, Missouri; and Montpelier, Vermont, read in their local papers that Eva's father, William, was a "wanderer" who "had a violent temper and placed very little value upon human life." Her brother George was in jail for attempted murder, and her brother Tom had been accused, but not convicted, of being a horse thief. Her sister, Alice (who, according to later court testimony, was actually her sister-in-law; the AP reporter had made one of those "forgivable" errors in the pursuit of "sparkle" that Edwin Shuman would later write about), "possessed a violent temper and was given to frequent quarrels."[52]

Only one reporter seemed genuinely interested in getting to know who Evangeline Steele really was. This reporter was important enough to snag an exclusive, jailhouse interview with her a few weeks after she was convicted of assault and sentenced to two years in the state penitentiary.[53] The reporter was also important enough to be the only person who ever had a byline attached to a story about Eva's stabbing of Mary Ann Donnelly.

"The sun came faintly in the high windows," Nellie Bly recalled, as she walked down the main corridor of the Trenton State Prison to interview Eva in her cell. The twenty-five-year-old journalist heard a low purr as she walked, "and looking down the corridor I saw seated along the spotless walls blue-clad women sewing," each one on her own machine. The scene was unremarkable in many ways. Except for the prison-issue dresses the women all wore, "they resembled nothing so much as a society sewing for charity purposes." As she got closer, however, Bly realized the women were not talking to one another, and that lack of conversation marked the group as undeniably different. After all, Bly observed, "no one ever saw a quiet sewing society."[54]

It was a cool afternoon in early October. In just five weeks' time, Bly would be leaving the United States to begin her now-famous journey around the world in seventy-three days. When she arrived at Eva's cell, she "looked in and saw a woman lying on a narrow cot. Her face was hidden in her hands, and she was crying bitterly." Bly walked into the room, introduced herself to the inmate, and told Eva she had come "to state justly and exactly what you choose to say to the world in your own defense."[55]

What followed Bly's interview was the only sympathetic rendering of Evangeline Steele to be published in any American newspaper for the rest of the woman's life. Not even when she died in 1904 did a newspaper show her an ounce of kindness. "Only one person mourned her death," the *Baltimore Sun* cattily observed after Eva had died in the charity ward of St. Vincent's Hospital in New York City—and that mourner, apparently, was too embarrassed to give his name to reporters. Eva's coffin was "a box of cheap, stained wood," according to the *Passaic Daily News*, and it was lowered into its final resting place "without the services of a clergyman." The *San Francisco Call* informed its readers that Eva was forty-seven years old when she died, "although owing to the lines which dissipation had left on her face, she seemed ten or fifteen years older."[56]

In contrast Nellie Bly told her readers Eva "looked much younger than I had expected." She had "a very sweet face and a most affectionate manner." There was "a pretty dimple in her round chin," and one that made an appearance on her cheek, as well, "when she forgets her troubles and remembers to smile." Eva wore a "simple blue gown," just like the women Bly had seen earlier at their sewing machines in the hallway. "Her bangs combed smoothly back and her soft, reddish-brown hair hanging in one braid down her back, she looked not more than twenty years old," according to Bly, although census records indicate that Eva was around thirty when she went to prison. Bly's description was the only one any paper ever gave of Evangeline Steele that did not insist her hair was blond.[57]

Eva told Bly she'd been born in Tunkhannock, Pennsylvania, a lumber town along the North Branch of the Susquehanna River in the northeastern part of the state. She claimed that her mother had died in childbirth, and her father had died from consumption a few years later. William and Lydia Steele adopted her when she was three years old—they'd had only boys—and "I never knew any other people but them."[58]

When she was fifteen, Eva was apprenticed to a milliner in Towanda, about fifty miles upriver from her hometown. There she met Walter Parsons, a man originally from Boston who worked for a railroad company. The two were married, even though Eva was only sixteen. "My folks and his folks fought it," she recalled. "I had one child, a daughter to Walter Parsons, and then things went so badly by others interfering that we separated." Nellie Bly pressed Eva for more information about her daughter, but Eva was reluctant to say too much more. "She is thirteen years old now. I have her at school, and she does not know anything about this. I don't want her to, and it is not right to drag Walter Parsons up, for he is married again."

Parsons was able to remarry because Eva's father had helped her secure a divorce in 1879. She got a job with a traveling burlesque company she refused to name, although Bly asked. Eva spent some time in Philadelphia before eventually moving to New York, where in 1885 she met the man who would become her second husband and the father of her infant daughter.[59]

The tale Eva told Nellie Bly about the relationship she had with this man was far from happy. She claimed he had gotten her pregnant twice before she finally gave birth, and each time he had given her $300 and "compelled me to consult a doctor." The third time she conceived, she kept the pregnancy hidden from him until it was too late for her to have an abortion. The father of her child still had not married her by the time she gave birth to her daughter in December 1888; indeed, he wasn't even with Eva on the day the child was born. A few weeks later, however, after he'd seen the child and Eva had threatened to leave him, he did finally ask her to marry him. "I said I would not," Eva told Nellie Bly. The man came from a wealthy family, and she was sure his father and brother would never accept her. "I would not marry him to take his people's abuse afterwards for having lived with him before we were married," Eva explained. The man persisted, however, and promised to take her on a trip to California if she agreed to marry him. "I loved him," Eva confessed to her interlocutor, "and with these promises I consented."[60]

At this point in Nellie Bly's front-page article, the story ends—quite literally, mid-sentence: "I went with Mrs. Swinton to . . . ," Eva says, referring to a friend who testified at her trial. The *World*'s editors then told readers the tale would be "continued in a later edition" of the newspaper. It was a shameless ploy, used by editors to entice people to buy more papers: "Extra, extra, read all about it!"[61] Anyone looking to learn what Eva had to say about the stabbing of Mary Ann Donnelly was going to have to find a newsboy and buy another edition of the *New York World* on October 9, 1889. There may have been as many as four editions of the paper on that particular day.

Unfortunately for anyone today looking to understand Eva's motivations, newspapers don't survive the test of time very well. The wood pulp paper the New York *World* started using in the 1870s is cheap and dry, and it begins to crumble after just a few years. This is why, in the

1940s, a number of university libraries partnered up with newspapers, the Library of Congress, and several commercial microform publishers to take pictures of old newspapers and store them on film. The goal was to capture a copy of at least one edition of every newspaper the librarians could get their hands on, going all the way back to the *New England Courant*, the newspaper Ben Franklin's older brother, James, published in the 1720s. It was a remarkable undertaking, given how many newspapers there were in early America—one that was made even more remarkable in the twenty-first century, when thousands of these films were digitized and made searchable.[62] But, again, the goal was to preserve just one copy of each day's newspaper. And the copy of the October 9, 1889, edition of the *New York World* that was preserved on film tells us that Evangeline Steele told Nellie Bly her husband had forced her to have two abortions—but it doesn't tell us what Eva told Bly about Mary Ann Donnelly.

Not every newspaper could afford to have a Nellie Bly, however—nor could every newspaper afford to print even one daily edition, let alone four. This is why papers in smaller cities and towns subscribed to the Associated Press, and it's why smaller papers, especially those that published weekly, rather than daily, sometimes took multiple stories they found on the AP wire and consolidated them into a single article. This is exactly what the *Salt Lake City Herald* did with Nellie Bly's jailhouse interview on October 10, 1889.

Eva had discharged Mary Ann Donnelly "several times," readers in the Utah Territory learned. Each time, Eva's husband "would always tell her not to go." The reason the young mother wanted the wet nurse gone was that she had found her husband "twice . . . in her room." "That is the secret of the fuss," Eva insisted—the reason she had quarreled with Mary Ann Donnelly. But Eva wanted Nellie Bly to know she did not stab the wet nurse. "I want to tell you that I never struck Nurse Donnelly," Eva solemnly declared. The nurse had been fine when Eva left the apartment to find the police after the two women fought. Eva had no idea what happened to Donnelly while she was gone or how the nurse had managed to get stabbed, but she felt certain the violence had something to do with the fact that "all my money and diamonds disappeared" from the apartment while she was off looking for the police.[63]

A guard arrived at the cell after Eva conveyed this part of her story. "Good-bye. I must go," the reporter told the prisoner as she was "invited outside and the iron-barred door was closed between us." Nellie Bly turned to Evangeline Steele: "I held her hands, her lips trembled, and her pretty blue round eyes filled with tears." Eva wanted Bly's readers to know she was alone. "'I have no friends,' she said huskily, holding my hand." Bly looked at the prisoner one last time, "and so with that, I took myself away."[64]

It was a classic bit of Nellie Bly reporting, written not by a dispassionate journalist, but by a human being who had clearly been moved by what she witnessed and heard. Bly never hesitated to insert herself into her stories; in fact, it was one of her hallmarks. At no point in her recounting of the jailhouse interview, however, did Nellie Bly ever explain to her readers why she had bothered to travel all the way to Trenton, New Jersey, to hear the story of an unremarkable woman from rural Pennsylvania who—let's face it—had *failed* to kill an even more unremarkable Irish immigrant whom she had hired to feed her daughter.

Bly didn't need to explain her interest in Evangeline Steele. The reason was apparent to everyone who read the headline, including even the editors of the *Salt Lake City Herald*, who lived and worked thousands of miles away from Atlantic City, but snapped the article up when they saw it come in over the AP Wire: "Mrs. Eva Hamilton's Story."

Eva's husband was Robert Ray Hamilton, a prominent lawmaker from New York, known to political, intellectual, and religious leaders throughout the country for his decency, honesty, and sense of honor. Ray's family members were looking to him to rescue the Hamilton name from a string of scandals and embarrassments that had been haunting the family for generations—ever since Ray's great-grandfather Alexander had had an affair with the wife of a political rival, almost exactly one hundred years before Evangeline Steele Hamilton stabbed Mary Ann Donnelly.

4

Charity Begins at Home

John Dudley Sargent was a Brahmin if ever there was one. His ties to America's colonial past ran deeper than those of most of the men invited to the Evacuation Day dinner at the Hotel Brunswick in New York in November 1883. Oliver Wendell Holmes Sr. proudly married his daughter, Amelia, off to a Sargent in 1869, less than a decade after he'd coined the term "Boston Brahmin." The Sargents were an old New England family, and they were just one group of Brahmins Jack could stake a claim to. His genealogy was top heavy, in fact, with men who had "filled the pulpits or sat on the bench."[1] If Henry Cabot Lodge had ever done John Dudley Sargent's genealogy, he'd have wept with envy.

Jack's father was a direct descendent of several early colonial governors. Henry Sargent's great-great-grandmother Catherine Winthrop Sargent was the great-granddaughter of John Winthrop, the Massachusetts governor whose famous "city upon a hill" speech, delivered aboard the *Arabella* as the Puritans sailed to Boston in 1630, set the tone for British colonial settlement and shaped Americans' collective understanding of themselves (rightly or wrongly) for centuries to come. Winthrop's image of the "model of Christian charity" America could be for the rest of the world popped up regularly in political speeches throughout the nineteenth and twentieth centuries, including those of Ronald Reagan in the 1980s.[2]

Catherine Winthrop Sargent's mother, Ann Dudley Winthrop, was the daughter of Governor Joseph Dudley and the sister of Paul Dudley, who had many important roles in the early history of Massachusetts, including that of chief justice of the colony's Supreme Judicial Court. When Paul Dudley died in 1751, he left a gift to Harvard, as Oliver Wendell Holmes noted many Brahmins did. That gift now funds the school's oldest endowed lecture series, hosted annually by Harvard Divinity School.

Administrators have had to get a bit creative in recent years with how they use Paul Dudley's money, since their Calvinist benefactor's values haven't aged well over time. According to the wonderfully descriptive mandates of Dudley's gift, every fourth lecture is supposed to focus on "detecting, convicting, and exposing the idolatry of the Romish church, their tyrannies, usurpations, damnable heresies, fatal errors, abominable superstitions, and other crying wickedness in their higher places." Nowadays that fourth lecture tends to focus on the benefits of Christian ecumenism. It's a stretch from the raging anti-Catholicism John Dudley Sargent's ancestor intended, but no descendant has ever stepped forward to complain about the change.[3]

Catherine Winthrop Sargent was the second wife of Epes Sargent, who served in Massachusetts's colonial assembly from 1744 until shortly before his death in 1762. Epes had fifteen children between his two wives, thirteen of whom made it to adulthood. They populated New England with hundreds of Sargents, quite a few of whom left their marks on not only the physical landscape of the region they called home—all those roads in New England that bear the name "Sargent"—but also on the legal, cultural, political, and religious landscapes of the United States.

Some of the more famous Sargents in American history (focusing *just* on the ones who traced their ancestry to Epes Sargent, as Jack did) include Judith Sargent Murray (1751–1820), the early feminist essayist and poet who helped to promote what is now known as Unitarian Universalism; Charles Sprague Sargent (1841–1926), who oversaw the creation of America's national forest system and directed Boston's Arnold Arboretum, the oldest public arboretum in North America; Fanny Sargent Osgood (1811–50), the poet whose flirtations with Edgar Allan Poe continue to fascinate historians and novelists today; and John Singer Sargent (1856–1925), a contemporary and distant cousin to John Dudley Sargent, who painted the violet-eyed portrait of Cornelius Vanderbilt II that hangs in the Breakers mansion in Newport, Rhode Island.[4]

"I was much gratified to have the pleasure of . . . looking through the names of the families who have the good fortune to have descended from such illustrious parentage," Jack's great-aunt Mary Sargent Smith wrote to him from her home in Cambridge, Massachusetts, after Jack had sent her an essay he'd written about Epes Sargent's descendants. Jack was the father of three children at this point in his life: a four-year-old son named Charles Hemenway, whom he and his wife called by his middle name, and two daughters, Mary, who was not quite two, and Martha, who was an infant. In the next five years, Jack would have two more daughters, the older of whom he would name after the distant grandmother who connected him to the founding of Boston, Catherine Winthrop Sargent.[5]

Having children had made Jack curious about his Brahmin past. To satisfy that curiosity, he'd collected some correspondence his grandfather Ignatius had had with various members of the family and used it to put together a genealogy that focused specifically on the Sargents who'd migrated from the north shore of Boston to the District of Maine. When Jack submitted his genealogical essay to the *Bangor Historical Magazine* in 1887, he insisted on having his grandfather listed as an author, although Ignatius Sargent was dead.[6]

"I am very much interested in tracing these varying branches," Jack's aunt told him after she read the essay. She planned on showing it to her neighbor, E. S. Dixwell (the "E. S." stood for "Epes Sargent"), who'd been the headmaster of the prestigious Boston Latin School from 1836 until 1851, when he left to start his own academy. "His mother was a Sargent," Mary wrote when explaining why she planned on showing the genealogy to her neighbor. "He is justly proud & grateful in looking back to the gifted & worthy who have come from that name."[7]

But even as she extolled the nobility of the Sargent family, using self-consciously elitist language that seemed to fly deliberately in the face of America's quaintly democratic sensibilities, Mary Sargent Smith still felt compelled to acknowledge that the family was not without its disappointments. "I suppose you have sometimes thought that in those who <u>should</u> have the rich inheritance [of the Sargent name], it is hard to trace the bright thread," she told her nephew. The comment was a thinly veiled reference to her brother's son, whom she knew had not been much of a father to Jack while he was growing up. Henry Sargent had moved to California when Jack was not yet two years old. He didn't return to New England until his son was well into his teens and his wife, Alice Hemenway, had died.[8]

"So many side threads are woven in that it seems sometimes hard to realize that the true stamp is not entirely lost," Aunt Mary conceded. Nevertheless, "side threads" could sometimes bring good qualities into a family, rather than bad, and she wanted Jack to know he was an example of that fact. "I fancy that the bright and lively musical nature & ready wit came to you not from Sargent or Winthrop or Dudley, but from that grandmother," she told him, referring to Sally Hemenway, in whose house Jack had spent the first thirteen years of his life.[9]

John Dudley Sargent was a living, breathing example of one of the major social transformations the United States went through in the latter part of the nineteenth century. The change he embodied was on display in the two different Evacuation Day dinners held in New York in 1883. It was the change Henry Cabot Lodge lamented in his memoir when he claimed that the authority certain families had had for generations was gone, undermined by a new understanding of power associated with vast quantities of money, rather than with the education and manners that came with being born into a "heritage."

Jack could stake a claim to both sides of the transition Henry Cabot Lodge bemoaned. On his father's side, there was plenty of history, and on his mother's side there was plenty of newly made money (even if his grandfather had lost $500,000 of it to a disagreement with Jack's uncle). His family's heritage and affluence would not prove to be helpful to Jack in the long run, however. During the years he spent in the American West, the man who was a Sargent, a Winthrop, a Dudley, and a Hemenway discovered he was incapable of leveraging the legacies his families gave him. At most he could only ever be haunted by them.

By his own account, Jack's parents did not have a happy, or even particularly close, marriage. His father, Henry, was the middle son of Ignatius and Emeline Potter Sargent. Ignatius owned a foundry and a mill in Machias, Maine. He was also a partial owner of at least four schooners and a brigantine that were registered in that coastal town.[10]

Ignatius's grandfather Paul Dudley Sargent—son of the family patriarch, Epes Sargent—had moved to the District of Maine in 1787 after being "ruined" by shipping losses during the Revolutionary War.[11] That's how Jack's branch of the Sargent family ended up in the Pine Tree State, and judging from Ignatius's property holdings, Washington County, Maine, turned out to a good place for the family to start over.

Henry Sargent was born in Machias sometime during the early months of 1844. Almost nothing is known about his childhood, except that he experienced the deaths of four siblings while he was growing up. When he was eighteen, Henry decided to fight for the Union Army. He left Machias and joined an infantry unit in Portland in June 1861, roughly two months after his son—the only child Henry Sargent would ever have—was conceived.[12]

It's possible Henry didn't know Alice Hemenway was pregnant when he left to join the army. Alice herself may not have understood what was going on with her body at that early point; she hadn't grown up on a farm, where the particulars of biology were impossible to miss, and she'd been raised by her father and grandmother—her mother, Elizabeth, had had almost nothing to do with her since her birth.[13] Who knows what Sally Hemenway did or did not tell her granddaughter about female reproduction? Sally, after all, had raised only boys.

Henry definitely knew Alice was pregnant by mid-July, however, when Alice's father, William Hemenway, tracked him down in Massachusetts after his infantry unit had left Maine to travel to Washington DC. Eighteen-year-old Henry Clay Sargent and seventeen-year-old Alice Bruce Hemenway were married in Boston on July 18, 1861. Henry continued on to the nation's capital and was eventually deployed to the Florida panhandle. He saw action in early October on Santa Rosa Island in the Gulf of Mexico, and by the end of that month, Henry was back in Machias on a disability discharge that had been secured through the influence of his wealthy father-in-law. His injury (or perhaps it was William Hemenway's money) was serious enough to keep him out of the military for the rest of the Civil War.[14]

The injury did not keep Henry Sargent in Machias, however. At some point in the family's development, a wanderlust "side thread" must have gotten woven into the great Sargent tapestry, because in the summer of 1863, several months before his son's second birthday, Henry Sargent left his family and moved to Sacramento, California. What he did out there is anyone's guess, but that winter of 1861–62 when his only child was born happened to be a significant one for Sacramento. It rained every day from December 9 to January 20, and the city was devastated by floods. There was plenty of work to be had, as California spent the next two decades raising the buildings in its capital city up on stilts, install-ing a levee system, and rerouting the American River.[15]

Alice Hemenway Sargent eventually grew tired of Henry's absenteeism. In 1871, just like her grandmother before her, she divorced her husband. Three years later—just a few weeks after her father died—the tuberculosis infection Alice had been struggling with for several years became intolerable. She traveled to Boston, hoping that the doctors at the New England Hospital for Women and Children would be able to help her. The hospital had been founded in 1862 by a protégé of Elizabeth Blackwell, the first woman to earn a medical degree in the United States, and all of the physicians working there were women. Alas, none of the doctors Alice encountered was able to help her. She died at the age of thirty on December 1, 1874, two weeks before her son's thirteenth birthday.[16]

Young Jack Sargent spent the next four and a half years going back and forth between Maine and Massachusetts, spending part of his time with his paternal grandfather, Ignatius Sargent, in Machias, and part of his time with relatives he had on his mother's side in the Boston area. Those relatives included his uncle Gus's wife, Mary Tileston Hemenway, and their children, Amy, Edith, and Augustus Jr., who were all about a decade older than Jack. His relations also included his grandmother Elizabeth Leese Tileston, Alice's mother, who lived ten miles south of Boston in the town of Dedham.

Elizabeth had never married William Hemenway, the father of her child. She was born in England in 1822 and later settled in New Brunswick, Canada. How exactly Elizabeth knew William is unclear. Sally Hemenway was not yet living with her son in 1843, when Elizabeth Leese became pregnant with William Hemenway's daughter. The twenty-nine-year-old bachelor was living in a boardinghouse in Machias when he and Elizabeth got together. The couple may have met in Machias, which is not far from the New Brunswick border, or they may have met in Bangor, roughly a hundred miles inland, which is where Elizabeth Leese gave birth to Alice Hemenway in the summer of 1844. She left the little girl with people she knew in Maine and moved in with her sister's family in Massachusetts sometime before 1850.[17]

That was when Sally Hemenway—who, again, had had only sons—learned that she had a granddaughter and that that granddaughter was being raised by people who weren't her relations. Sally insisted William travel to Bangor to retrieve the little girl and, according to Jack, raise her "openly acknowledged as his daughter." It may have been at this point that Elizabeth Leese resumed contact with William Hemenway, who eventually married a woman named Caroline Vinton and had a son and another daughter with her. That Elizabeth was in contact with William—and that the pair had a relatively amicable relationship—is made apparent by the fact that in 1862, just a few months after her grandson, Jack, was born, forty-year-old Elizabeth Leese, "a spinster," married forty-nine-year-old Jonathan Howard Tileston, a wealthy and eccentric widower from Dedham, Massachusetts. Tileston was the cousin of Mary Tileston Hemenway, William's sister-in-law through his brother Gus, who was tucked away at the Spring Hill House for Nervous Invalids when the marriage took place.[18]

The Hemenways may not have had the "heritage" the Sargents had, but by the time Jack came along in December 1861, they were starting to build a genealogy that was almost as convoluted and confusing as anything a Brahmin family might have been able to put together in the nineteenth century.

One person was not confused, however—and that person was Augustus Hemenway Sr. In spite of the thirteen years he'd spent away from his family, he knew exactly who all of the Hemenways were and how each person was related to him. When he modified his will in September 1875, roughly a year after his brother, William, had died, Gus arranged for his wife to receive a large, one-time payment from his estate in the event of his death. He left his only surviving brother, Charles Porter Hemenway, a nice sum, as well, and he asked that his estate give $10,000 in gold to Henry Buel, the doctor who'd attended him during his years of confinement.

Gus then arranged for everything else he owned to be put into a trust. The yearly earnings were to be distributed evenly among his wife and three children after the relevant taxes, fees, and debts had been settled, and several annuities had been paid out to extended family members whom Gus specifically named in his will. He left annuities to his brother Samuel's widow and each of their three daughters; he also left annuities to William's widow, Caroline, and their two children, Martha and Charles. Whatever it was that he and William had disagreed on, the costly dispute hadn't been rancorous enough to provoke Gus to penalize his brother's wife or the couple's children.[19]

Noticeably absent from Gus's will, however, was any mention of the fourteen-year-old grandnephew he had through his niece, Alice—a young boy who'd spent time in the Hemenways' home during and after the years of Gus's confinement and who, Gus knew, had lost the only guardians he'd ever known shortly before Gus revised his will. It's possible Gus's generosity simply didn't extend to Jack's generation. There's no way to know for sure, since Alice Hemenway was the only one of Gus's nieces and nephews who'd had a child by the time he modified his will, which means there is no one to compare Jack or his situation to. He was the only legitimate member of his generation of Hemenways.

Except that Jack wasn't exactly a "legitimate." Yes, his parents had been married, but his mother had been born out of wedlock. If Alice were still alive, would Gus have refused to recognize her as his niece, even as he provided annuities for all of her half-siblings and first cousins? Was Gus's failure to provide any money for his teenaged grandnephew an extension of his refusal to see Alice as a Hemenway, no matter how "openly acknowledged" she had been by William and Sally?

Again, it's hard to say. There are no existing versions of Gus's earlier wills, the ones he would have written before Alice died. We cannot know, therefore, if Gus named her as an heir while she was still alive. The final will we do have, however, makes it very clear Gus drew a distinction between children who were born to married parents and children who were not. At eleven different points, Gus used the phrase "lawful issue" to describe the beneficiaries and parameters of his trust: Amy, Edith, and Gus Jr. were his "lawful issue." His trust was to continue for twenty years after the death of his longest-lived "lawful issue," at which point it was to be dissolved and the proceeds evenly distributed among the "lawful issue" of his "lawful issue." If all of his legitimate grandchildren were dead by the time the trust was dissolved, then the proceeds were to be distributed to the "lawful issue" of the "lawful issue" of his "lawful issue."[20]

Marriage mattered to Gus, and he had no delusions about what it took to make a marriage work. "Young men and young women are perhaps too often prone to fancy a love for one another, when its base is not firmer than personal appearance," he wrote to Mary Tileston in November 1838, after the couple had gotten engaged and Gus had left Boston to travel to South America. A match based on physical attraction "too often fades into indifference, and if the parties even years after marriage feel any disappointment at each other's plans, views, prospects or fortune, their happiness is frequently wrecked forever and the dreadful story of domestic misery commences."[21]

Gus's head had not been turned by "the many ills 'the flesh is heir to,'" he assured his fiancée, in a letter that wasn't exactly *wrong* about the secrets to a long-lasting marriage but must have thrown some cold water onto any fantasies Mary Tileston may have had about her fiancé's passions or romantic proclivities. "Amiability, good nature, kindness, perseverance, decision, a constant employment of time, a sincere wish to improve, and a freedom from anything like self-importance or affectation" were the qualities Gus was looking for in a mate. The thirty-three-year-old businessman had asked Mary to marry him because he'd seen those qualities in her, and "when any two of the opposite sex see these traits in the other's mind, they cannot err in giving to each other their whole heart." "I fear, dear Mary, that you will think me a most inveterate sermonizer," Gus concluded in his unusual love letter, "but I would rather that every thought should be yours as it comes from me than that you should not know me as you ought."[22]

Gus was self-aware, at least. He *did* come across as preachy in the correspondence he shared with his wife. That preachiness was evident in the comments he made to her in 1874 about the mysterious disagreement he'd had with his brother, William. Recall that Gus took the management of UT 36 away from William, supposedly for his brother's own good. "He only wants cheerful intercourse and encouragement, to make him as well as ever," Gus flippantly concluded about the depression his brother fell into—a depression that turned out to be the cause of William's death. Gus told his wife he wanted William to visit the family's farm in Milton so that William could "widen his mind," which meant accepting responsibility for the disagreement between the two brothers.[23]

Gus's preachiness was also evident in the way he latched onto the therapy he'd received at Dr. Buel's sanitarium, believing it to be the only proper treatment for nervous disorders available in the late nineteenth century. "I do not think well of those large institutions for 100 or 300 persons, calling themselves 'Water Cures' or 'Retreats,'" he wrote to Mary after she'd told him that a servant in their home was suffering from a nervous malady. The young woman "would be sure to receive benefit by a temporary residence at Spring Hill under Dr. Buel's kind and very judicious treatment," Gus wrote. "If it has worked such a miracle with me, I do not see why it should not with others."[24]

Augustus Hemenway Sr. was capable of making some strong judgments about people, good or bad, even as he, himself, could easily have been judged—if not for leaving his family for thirteen years so he could convalesce on his own in a private sanitarium, then for leaving them *again* after he had checked out of that sanitarium and finally returned home. It probably wasn't the behavior Henry Buel recommended when he approved his patient's discharge, but once Gus was no longer under Buel's care, he dived right back into the obsessive business and travel habits that had sent him to the Spring Hill House for Nervous Invalids in the first place.

Gus returned to his family from his extended medical sojourn in November 1873, and by June 1874 he was writing to his wife and children from a friend's estate in France. He'd gone to Europe to commission several pieces of equipment for his silver mines in Chile and sugar plantations in Cuba. His plan was to stay in Europe until the fall and then sail back to Boston in early November, spending two weeks with his family before leaving them again to travel to Cuba. There were some problems with the equipment he'd ordered, however, so Gus stayed in Europe longer than he'd planned, heading straight to Havana from London in December 1874. He stayed in Cuba until March 1875, when he returned to Boston and, among other things, revised his will. He then left his family in November to sail to Europe and Cuba for a second—and final—time, dying on his plantation along the Sagua La Grande River on June 16, 1876, after suffering from an intestinal blockage for a number of weeks.[25]

The travel must have been devastating to Mary. Her oldest child, Amy, had been twelve years old when Gus left the family to spend thirteen years with Henry Buel; her youngest child, Gus Jr., had just turned seven. By the time Gus Sr. returned, all three of his children were adults. Mary had raised them on her own, without her husband, and remained devoted to him the entire time he was gone. "What a noble record of faithfulness and duty your life has been these many years of separation," her cousin Mary Ann Porter wrote to her after hearing from twenty-two-year-old Edith that Gus would soon be returning home. "I cannot express to you all I feel with regard to this happy change for you."[26]

Mary's friend Elizabeth Palmer Peabody also found it difficult to express her excitement, although she was not usually one to be at a loss for words. Sister-in-law to Nathaniel Hawthorne, Elizabeth Peabody had edited the *Dial*, the literary journal of the Transcendentalist movement that took New England by storm in the 1840s. Elizabeth Peabody had helped to make Ralph Waldo Emerson slightly more comprehensible; nevertheless, she didn't know what to say to Mary Hemenway when she learned Gus would soon be coming home. "I have no words to express my joy for you," she confessed. "What infinite happiness [Augustus Hemenway] must have in the possession of you as a wife, so faithful for better and for worse."[27]

Gus's own friends also recognized the remarkable nature of Mary's devotion to her husband. "You have had a rather long nap and made us all wait pretty well for your waking," Oliver Paine joked three weeks before Gus checked out of the Spring Hill House for Nervous Invalids. "Mary's faith that you would return seems never to have faltered, but I confess with blushes now that I gave you up more or less."[28]

No one imagined that Gus would leave his family so soon after being away from them for so long. But a person didn't become a multimillionaire in nineteenth-century America by paying a lot of attention to what other people thought. Gus clearly felt an obligation to provide for his family financially, but he didn't believe that obligation meant he had to have an actual presence in their lives. And he also didn't believe his financial obligations extended to family members like young Jack Sargent who were not "lawful issue."

Fortunately for Jack, Mary Hemenway and her children didn't seem to care too much about Gus's values after he was gone. Mary used her inheritance to pay for Jack to attend a private academy in Maine; this school may have been where he developed his rather large appetite for books. After Jack graduated in 1879, his cousin Gus Jr. financed his first trip to Cheyenne. The young millionaire also supported Jack for many years while he lived in Wyoming with his wife and five children.[29]

Young Gus's willingness to support his cousin's frontier life may have been an extension of a philanthropic impulse he developed not long after his father died. This impulse was almost certainly a rejection of the therapy the older Hemenway had received at Henry Buel's sanitarium. Buel believed that solitude and bed rest were the best way to deal with nervous disorders, but Gus Sr.'s frenetic behavior after he left the sanitarium suggested there were real limits to this approach. Young Gus, therefore, embraced a different approach to mental health when he inherited his father's fortune. That approach was exercise.

Augustus Hemenway Sr. wasn't the only American businessman with raw nerves in the Gilded Age. Many bankers, lawyers, and merchants struggled with psychosomatic ailments during this period—so many, in fact, that physicians started to think modernity might be making people sick. In words that are strikingly similar to what some psychologists suggest today about smartphones and social media sites and the impact they could be having on growing rates of anxiety and depression among teenagers and young adults, one prominent physician from Philadelphia blamed technology for the disorders he saw among his middle-class patients. The "racing speed which the telegraph and railway have introduced into commercial life," S. Weir Mitchell wrote in 1871, had brought "some great and growing evils" into the lives of men who made their livings through "intellectual exertion." Six years later advertisers like J. Walter Thompson started telling Americans they could cure these evils by consuming factory-made products that were "old-fashioned" and "homemade."[30]

The symptoms S. Weir Mitchell observed began as headaches and prolonged bouts of sleeplessness. They often evolved into a variety of digestive disorders that were severe enough to cause a man's death—as had happened to Augustus Hemenway Sr. in Cuba in the summer of 1876.[31]

Mitchell called the ailment "brain tire," and his solution was to get his patients up and moving. The great irony of brain tire, according to the physician, was that the men who suffered from it were actually "morbidly wide awake." Bed rest couldn't help a man who'd spent his day poring over account ledgers or filling out purchase orders; that kind of activity revved a brain up, and to be healthy, a man needed to find a way of turning his brain off, so it wouldn't "keep turning over and over the work of the day, the business or legal problem." "During active exertion of the body," Mitchell proclaimed, "the brain cannot be employed." Only exercise could "secure to [the brain] a state of repose which not even sleep is always competent to supply."[32]

Thomas Wentworth Higginson agreed. He was a Unitarian minister from Massachusetts and an early devotee of a movement within Protestantism known as "Muscular Christianity." Followers believed Protestantism had grown soft under the leadership of female Sunday School teachers, who stressed the "loving" and "forgiving" qualities of Jesus, while failing to present Christ as a force to be reckoned with in the world. Muscular Christianity aimed to "beef up" the faith, and its leaders recognized that the movement dovetailed nicely with the advice middle-class men were getting from their doctors.[33]

"Lock your brains into your safe at nightfall . . . and come with me to the Gymnasium," Thomas Higginson exhorted America's businessmen in an essay he wrote for the *Atlantic Monthly*. Gyms were cropping up all over the country, thanks to an organization known as the Young Men's Christian Association, a great promoter of Muscular Christianity. The YMCA built its first American gymnasium in New York City in 1869; gyms in Washington DC, San Francisco, Boston, and Chicago soon followed. Several colleges had also recently built gymnasiums on their campuses. Amherst opened a gym in 1860 after two seniors there died, reportedly from studying too much, and Yale and Princeton had opened gymnasiums on their campuses a few months earlier.[34]

The oldest college gymnasium in the country belonged to Harvard. Follen Gymnasium had opened its doors in 1826 and was the facility Young Augustus Hemenway Jr. had available to him in 1870, when he heard the founder of the Muscular Christianity movement, Thomas Hughes, speak on Harvard's campus. It must have been frustrating to Young Gus to hear Hughes speak of the "duty" students had to become "strong men, capable of enduring hardship" for Christ, given the condition of his school's gymnasium. It was one of the smallest buildings on campus, and calisthenics and rope climbing were the only opportunities for physical activity the building was capable of providing.[35]

Young Gus remembered that frustration when his father died and he came into a substantial amount of money. Three months after the funeral, he made a large donation to Harvard so that a state-of-the-art gymnasium could be built on his alma mater's campus. When it opened three years later, Hemenway Gymnasium was "the largest, best equipped, and most handsome gymnasium in the country," according to the *Harvard Crimson*. It had an indoor running track, a rowing room, and six bowling alleys. Several years later Gus Jr. provided the school with more money, so that a badminton court, several squash courts, and a basketball court that would later be frequented by a young law student from Hawaii named Barack Obama could be added.[36]

Harvard wasn't the only beneficiary of Gus Jr.'s philanthropic commitment to the therapeutic effects of exercise. The "parks movement" that took off in Boston in the late 1870s benefited, as well. That movement, which sought to preserve and cultivate green space in the city, was led by Frederick Law Olmsted, the designer of New York's Central Park, and Charles Sprague Sargent, the director of Harvard's Arnold Arboretum. In 1881 Olmsted moved his landscape architectural firm to Massachusetts so that he and Sargent could develop a chain of public parks in Boston that would include the Arboretum.[37]

Like John Dudley Sargent, Charles Sprague Sargent was a direct descendent of Epes Sargent, though he was descended from Epes's first wife, Esther McCarty, rather than Jack's distant grandmother Catherine Winthrop. The twelve parks Olmsted and Sargent designed were funded in large part by Augustus Hemenway Jr. and became known as the "Emerald Necklace," since they hung around what used to be the "neck" of the Shawmut Peninsula that jutted out into Boston Harbor and upon which the city of Boston had been founded.[38]

By the time the Emerald Necklace was created, the outline of the peninsular neck it hung on was known only to historians and cartographers, since the marshy area around the Shawmut Peninsula had been filled in with dirt to create more land for the growing number of factories and businesses in Boston. Concern about all that industrial growth and its impact on people and the landscape was what had animated the leaders of the parks movement. They believed the loss of Boston's greenspace was tragic, not only because the natural beauty that had been destroyed could never be replaced but also because walking and hiking in natural areas had therapeutic effects that helped to make modern life tolerable.[39]

"What we want to gain is tranquility and rest of mind," Olmsted wrote in 1870, in an essay that articulated the goals of landscape architecture. Parks were an effort to capture "the beauty of the fields, the meadow, the prairie . . . the green pastures and the still waters" in an urban environment where that kind of beauty could not exist without a deliberate effort to create and maintain it. While designing Prospect Park, Olmsted told a group of commissioners in Brooklyn that "a sense of enlarged freedom is to all, at all times, the most certain and most valuable gratification afforded by a park." A few years earlier, while working on a state park in the Yosemite Valley, he'd told California's lawmakers that "the occasional contemplation of natural scenes of an impressive character . . . is favorable to the health and vigor of men and especially to the health and vigor of their intellect."[40]

Young Augustus Hemenway Jr. must have been very excited—and maybe even envious—when his cousin Alice's teenaged son told him in 1879 that he planned to leave the cultivated environs of New England and go to the Wyoming Territory.[41] Wyoming, after all, had everything Frederick Law Olmsted had highlighted when he said nature could provide people with the "tranquility" and "rest of mind" that had eluded Young Gus's father for most of his son's childhood: prairies, fields, meadows, still waters, green pastures, and natural scenes that were so phenomenally impressive in terms of their expanse and verticality that a man's intellect was likely never to be the same again once he had experienced them.

Yet the Wyoming Territory was no walk in the park. It was rugged, wild, and still partially unmapped, a region with few roads, extreme weather conditions, and plenty of Indians who were hostile toward White encroachment on the land. Wyoming was the sort of place where only the truly "muscular" could survive, and where there were plenty of opportunities for a young college graduate to test his ability to "endure hardship," as the leader of the Muscular Christianity movement had called upon Gus Hemenway Jr. and his Harvard classmates to do.

When Jack Sargent told his cousin he planned to go to Wyoming, the young heir to one of the biggest fortunes in the country probably wanted to go, too. But Young Gus had responsibilities on the East Coast he had to attend to. He had just gotten engaged to Harriet Lawrence, a Boston socialite and an amateur ornithologist whose ardent interest in birds would one day provoke her to found the Massachusetts Audubon Society, the precursor to the National Audubon Society. Harriet had no interest in moving to Wyoming. There were glossy ibises and black terns in New England she had to protect. Those birds were being threatened by the ladies millinery industry, which was slaughtering them by the thousands for their feathers.[42]

Gus Hemenway Jr. had to stay put. But that didn't mean he couldn't finance his cousin's adventures and enjoy them vicariously, regardless of what his father might have thought of Jack Sargent's status within the Hemenway family.

The surviving historical records don't explain why Jack wanted to leave New England—but tellingly, his father had returned to Machias about a year before he left.[43] Having Henry Sargent back in his life after an absence of nearly fourteen years may have been difficult for Jack. If so he wouldn't have been the first teenage boy to leave home because of arguments with his father.

The records also don't tell us why Jack thought Wyoming, specifically, would give him what he needed. He wasn't alone in turning his eyes west, however; Congress had been trying to get the area beyond the Mississippi River settled by White people ever since Meriwether Lewis and William Clark had returned from their exploration of the Louisiana Purchase in 1806. Settlement by White Americans would cement the U.S. government's jurisdiction over the land and undermine any claims the French, the Spanish, the Mexicans, the English—or, most especially, the seminomadic Indigenous people already living within the territory—might be tempted to assert. Settlement would also facilitate the success of American democracy, which many people believed was deeply dependent upon property ownership. Remember that early on, men in most states had to own property in order to vote. Although those requirements were mostly gone by the time the Mexican War broke out in 1846, many lawmakers remained concerned about the impact poverty (particularly the extreme poverty that ran rampant among landless peasants in Europe and was starting to take root in the urban centers of the Northeast) could have on the democratic process. People who are poor, after all, have no vested interest in the stability of the existing political and cultural systems.[44]

With that in mind, federal officials took steps in the 1850s and 1860s to encourage men and women who were living in the increasingly congested Northeast to move west, where they could become landowners. First these officials negotiated treaties with native tribes on the plains in an effort to make the region safe for White settlement. They promised to maintain peace with the Sioux, the Blackfeet, the Gros Ventres, and the Cheyennes to the north and with the Apaches, the Kiowas, the Comanches, and the Arapahos to the south. They agreed to respect homeland boundaries that were said to have been carefully drawn in the tribes' best interests and to pay the tribes for land that would be open to White settlement because it was not within those boundaries. They promised to allow members of the tribes to continue to hunt on their ancestral lands, regardless of whether those lands were within the homeland boundaries as they had been drawn. They agreed to build schools and hospitals within the tribes' new homelands and to pay teachers and doctors to serve the tribes living there. And then famously, federal officials broke these treaties every time gold was found on a hillside or a railroad needed a particular corridor to lay its tracks, and they used the power of the U.S. Army to defend these treaty violations.[45]

In 1862 Congress passed the first of several "Homestead" laws that were designed to distribute the government's land to settlers in the West. For a small and very affordable fee, anyone who hadn't taken up arms against the U.S. government (meaning anyone who hadn't served in the Confederate Army) could acquire 160 acres of land. All he—or even she—had to do was live on the land for at least five years and "improve" it in some way, which generally involved building a house and a barn on the property and planting some crops.[46]

More than 1.6 million people became property owners in the American West because of the Homestead Acts. About 10 percent of all the land area in the continental United States was distributed to private land-owners through this legislation.[47] Jack Sargent was too young to make a claim when he first arrived in Wyoming; the law said a person had to be at least twenty-one years old, and he was only seventeen when he got off the train in Cheyenne. He found other things to do for the first few years he was out there. Jack was determined to become a homesteader, however, and although he had to fight a little harder than most people to prove he had met the requirements of the Homestead Act, John Dudley Sargent did eventually become the owner of an extraordinary piece of property along Jackson Lake in what is now Grand Teton National Park, thanks to this legislation that was passed a few months after he was born.

Many Mainers like Jack Sargent moved west in the decades that followed the Civil War. In 1870 the state's population actually dropped for the first time since the U.S. Census Bureau started gathering statistics in 1790. Until then Maine's population had consistently enjoyed double-digit growth rates, even during the decades when the area was still a part of Massachusetts and lawmakers were working actively to get the land there owned, but not settled.[48]

Maine's newspapers were full of stories in the 1870s about men and women who had scraped together the funds to go west and made their fortunes. The stories tended to focus on heavily forested states like Michigan, Wisconsin, Minnesota, Oregon, and Washington, where Mainers could use the skills they'd acquired in the Pine Tree State on fresh woodlands that hadn't been exhausted by decades of unmanaged timbering.[49] The Wyoming Territory wasn't typically mentioned as one of the places people from Maine went to; more than half the territory was open prairies, after all, rather than dense forests. But that may have been precisely the reason Jack Sargent went there. He may have wanted to go to a region where he knew he would not encounter other New Englanders. After four and a half years of being passed around by relatives who never expressed any desire to keep him, Jack wanted to go someplace where he could start over and be something more than just a poor and unwanted Sargent, Winthrop, Dudley, and Hemenway among many wealthy and highly accomplished others.

Jack knew he was too young to be a homesteader, however—and as the grandson of a man who had once been "the richest lumberman in

Maine," he didn't have much interest in migrating west on a shoestring budget. That's why he asked his cousin Gus for help. Over the next eighteen years, Augustus Hemenway Jr. would prove to be a reliable funding source for Jack. He'd regularly "grubstake" him money, making it possible for John Dudley Sargent to marry a hometown girl from Machias, bring her to Wyoming, and raise a family with her in the heart of the Teton range. Cousin Gus's personal philanthropy also made it possible for Jack to build a ten-room cabin along Jackson Lake that he heated with several Franklin stoves, stocked with hundreds of books, and, rather amazingly, furnished with a piano that was manufactured in Connecticut and made of solid, black walnut wood.[50]

It's not clear how Jack got that instrument—known as a "Symphony"—over the Teton Mountains. The nearest train station was nearly 150 miles away in Idaho, on the western side of the range, and there were no roads connecting the station to Jack's homestead, just old Indian trails that had been traveled for centuries. Trade magazines in the late nineteenth century were full of stories, however, about the extreme and exotic lengths musical instrument manufacturers would go to when delivering their products to customers. The New York–based Aeolian Company, for example, frequently employed camel trains to get its world-famous Pianola player piano to customers in Australia. The delivery system was not cheap—but if a person had the money, it could be done.[51]

Homesteaders in the American and Canadian West had a term for people like Jack Sargent, easterners who were supported by wealthy family members back home. They called them "remittance men," and the term wasn't meant to be a compliment. "'Remittance Men' are the wayward sons of wealthy men, who are sent to some frontier section of the country . . . and in this manner . . . quieted down from the experiences of a wild life," one western newspaper explained. "They are no good before their parents send them out to this country to get rid of them," another newspaper grumbled. "They can't make a living in a country where they are used to the ways, and yet they expect to make things go out here." Remittance men "are like to impress you with the fact that they are great businessmen," a third newspaper warned. "But bless you, they know no more about business than a Blackfoot Indian. They are only the black sheep . . . the poor fellows who kicked a bit over the dashboard at home and had to straightaway be sent to the frontier to be regenerated." Still, "all remittance men are not crooks or black sheep," one newspaper editor conceded. "Many are mighty good fellows, good sportsmen, and warm friends to those they like. There has simply been some unfortunate affair 'at home' which makes it a necessity for them to live apart from the family."[52]

John Dudley Sargent never relied exclusively on money he got from family members back home. He worked as a cowboy for a while when he first arrived in the West, and then he moved on to take a position with the Union Pacific Railroad in Cheyenne, a job he got through his uncle Daniel, Henry Sargent's older brother. Eventually Jack settled on his homestead in the Tetons. The reason he built such a large and luxurious cabin on the property was that he planned to make a living by operating a hunting lodge there; he recognized how exquisite the view from the eastern side of Jackson Lake was, and he anticipated affluent New Yorkers and Bostonians would want to take in that view.

Jack also never lived fully "apart" from his family on the East Coast. Winters in the Tetons are very harsh, and Jack and his family usually moved someplace else for the months of November through March. Most years, they went to Salt Lake City; at least one winter, however, Jack and his family went to New York, where Jack worked for the company Gus Hemenway Jr. had inherited from his father.[53]

But in the winter of 1896–97, Jack Sargent chose to stay on the homestead with his wife, Adelaide, and their five children. That winter would prove to be the reason Cousin Gus stopped "grubstaking" him money. It would be the reason Jack eventually married someone else: a wealthy and deranged violinist named Edith Drake, who had trained in Paris and was known to readers across the country as the source of her father's greatest heartbreak. And the winter of 1896–97 would also be the reason Jack Sargent was remembered well into the twentieth century by people in Jackson Hole as "the black sheep of a wealthy Maine shipbuilding and lumber family" who'd been "raised in luxury and great indulgence by his maternal grandmother" and "had a 'hunted' look—like he was afraid the devil would get him."[54]

5

Off with Their Heads

When you get off Interstate 80 at Exit 362 in Wyoming, you're left with no doubt that Cheyenne is still a railroad town. About a mile north of the interstate, along a road that goes through the city's historic district and straight to the state's capitol, there's a steep overpass that rises high above nearly thirty sets of active railroad tracks. On any given day, as many as eighty different trains pass through Cheyenne, most of them carrying coal to power plants in the Midwest. Appalachia's residents like to think of their region as "coal country," but twice as much coal is mined in Wyoming today as in Pennsylvania, West Virginia, and Kentucky combined.[1]

At the apex of the overpass, a red, white, and blue sign for the Union Pacific Railroad reminds travelers of Cheyenne's origins as that company's headquarters. At the base of the overpass, just off to the left, a brown and white sign for the Sand Creek Massacre Trail testifies to the reality that people lived in the area long before the UP was chartered by Congress in 1862 and given an exclusive right to build a railroad from the Missouri River to the Pacific Ocean, meeting up with a similar line being constructed eastward by the Central Pacific Railroad, incorporated one year earlier. In 1864 several dozen Cheyenne and Arapaho families fled north from Colorado, through the UP's future headquarters and on to what is now the Wind River Reservation in Central Wyoming. They were running away from the U.S. Army, which hadn't had its hands so full with the Civil War that it couldn't find the resources to kill and mutilate 230 Indians who were camped along the banks of a tributary of the Arkansas River.[2]

About thirty miles west of Cheyenne—again, just off Interstate 80—there's a granite monument rising 60 feet above Sherman Hill, which at 8,242 feet above sea level is the highest point along the original route the Transcontinental Railroad took from Omaha, Nebraska, to

San Francisco, California. Standing on Sherman Hill, looking out over the undulating plains of Albany County, people who've spent their lives on the East Coast can find it hard to develop a sense of perspective. In the East, after all, the horizons are broken up by mountains or trees. Here what appear at first to be pronghorn antelope are actually large, dinosaur-like pump jacks, extracting crude oil from the Cretaceous sandstone lying hundreds of feet below Wyoming's surface.[3] The true identities of the pumps become apparent only when what seemed to be tiny, cream-colored stones in the foreground start to move. *Those* are the antelope made famous by the old cowboy song.

The pyramid-shaped ashlar monument on Sherman Hill was designed by H. H. Richardson, the same guy who designed the Hotel Brunswick in New York, where Ray Hamilton dined on terrapin and duck while celebrating the centennial of Evacuation Day in 1883. Richardson designed the Union Pacific train depot in Cheyenne, as well—another fantastic example of "Richardson Romanesque." Today the depot is a museum and microbrewery.[4]

H. H. Richardson's monument honors two brothers, Oakes and Oliver Ames. Both wore their beards in the close-cropped, "chin curtain" style made popular by Abraham Lincoln—which is to say, without a moustache or neck hair.[5] Oakes was a U.S. representative from Massachusetts. Oliver was the president of the Union Pacific Railroad. In September 1872, a little more than two years after Leland Stanford drove a ceremonial "golden spike" into a crosstie in Utah, linking his Central Pacific Railroad to the Union Pacific Railroad Oliver Ames oversaw, the *New York Sun* broke a story about the construction company the UP had used to build its sections of the railway. That company had cheated the federal government out of millions of dollars, according to the *Sun*, and several members of Congress had known about the fraud and profited from it. One of those congressmen was Oakes Ames.

The name of the construction company was Crédit Mobilier, and no one affiliated with it had ever been anywhere near a construction site in his life. The company was created by Union Pacific executives—among them, Oliver Ames—two years after the UP had received its charter and gotten some very generous subsidies from Congress. Although Crédit Mobilier was separate from the Union Pacific Railroad, it was also heavily invested in it. The construction company owned stock in the railroad company, meaning the men who invested in Crédit Mobilier were invested in the Union Pacific, as well.

Conveniently, Crédit Mobilier got a no-bid contract from the UP to build all of the railroad's tracks going west out of Omaha. Because it wasn't really a construction company, however, Crédit Mobilier quickly subcontracted with smaller companies that knew how to find and transport the men and materials needed to get the work done. The money Crédit Mobilier charged Union Pacific to build the railroad was, of course, a lot more than the money it paid its subcontractors to construct the tracks. The route Crédit Mobilier insisted on taking was also not always the most efficient one. The Pacific Railroad Act of 1862 promised to give Union Pacific as much as $48,000 in government bonds and 6,400 acres in federal land for every mile of track the company completed (that amount of land was later doubled). The land grants included all of the mineral rights associated with the territory, which meant the UP could either sell its new property to mining companies and homesteaders, or it could mine the land itself. Given that the amount of land the UP received was tied to the miles of track it laid, Crédit Mobilier didn't get any pushback from Union Pacific when the route the construction company chose across Nebraska was nine miles longer than it needed to be.[6]

Congress didn't object to the route, either—or to the fact that Crédit Mobilier was charging Union Pacific nearly twice as much money as it was spending on subcontractors. That's because at least a dozen members of Congress were shareholders in Crédit Mobilier, thanks to Oakes Ames. The *Sun* noted that some of these congressmen had purchased stock in the company on the cheap, while others had received the stock from Ames as a gift. Either way the company's profits—which were in excess of 800 percent during some quarters—passed in the form of dividends to the lawmakers who were best positioned to question their legitimacy.[7]

Ames published a response to the *New York Sun*'s article in newspapers across the country. "Not a single share of the stock of that company was ever given to any member of Congress, directly or indirectly, by me or anyone else, to my knowledge," the congressman insisted—his qualifier at the end revealing more than he probably intended. Crédit Mobilier had been formed two years after the UP was chartered because the prospect of building a railroad across the western part of the United States "was in danger of breaking down." The railroad needed the kind of help Crédit Mobilier was able to provide. "I may have done wrong in my efforts to aid the national enterprise," he acknowledged in his letter's closing (placing yet another qualifier on his claims of innocence). "If so, I am unconscious of it. I have always regarded [the creation of Crédit Mobilier] as one of the most creditable and patriotic acts of my life."[8]

The scandal dominated the national conversation for months and is considered by historians today to be the first "modern" political scandal—a harbinger of the Teapot Dome scandal of the 1920s (also involving Wyoming); the Savings and Loan debacle of the 1980s; and the decision of several U.S. senators, including two from Georgia who were not reelected, to sell their investments in the hospitality industry after they were privately briefed on the impending economic consequences of COVID-19.[9] We'll never know if Oakes Ames would have suffered the same fate as Senators Kelly Loeffler and David Perdue of Georgia after their stock sales were exposed. Unlike them, he didn't come up for reelection. Oakes Ames was formally censured by his colleagues in the House of Representatives in February 1873. Three months later, at the age of sixty-nine, he had a massive stroke and died.

It's possible Ames might have weathered the storm. Other lawmakers who'd made money from Crédit Mobilier managed to get by unscathed. James Garfield, for instance, was consistently reelected by the people of Ohio to his position in the House of Representatives until November 1880—when voters made him the twentieth president of the United States. Ten years after Oakes Ames died, the Commonwealth of Massachusetts passed a resolution, commending him for his "enterprise, energy, and judgement" and declaring him innocent of all of the bribery and corruption charges levied against him. Four years earlier the board of directors of the Union Pacific Railroad had convinced the most celebrated architect in America at the time to design a monument honoring Oakes and Oliver Ames that would be seen by every traveler taking the train to California.[10]

Some of the rehabilitation the Ames brothers' legacy enjoyed may have been a consequence of just how important the Transcontinental Railroad was to America's development. According to Ames family lore, when Abraham Lincoln tapped Oakes in the middle of the Civil War to develop a plan for the Union Pacific Railroad, the president of the United States put his hand on the shoulder of the recently elected congressman from Massachusetts and said, "Ames, you take hold of this. The road must be built, and you are the man to do it." The story is probably apocryphal; it endures, however, because it reflects a belief Lincoln was absolutely committed to—namely, that the eastern half of the United States, which already had roughly thirty thousand miles of rail traversing it, *had* to be connected to the western half, which had no rail lines at all, but was starting to fill up with settlers. If the West were not connected to the East by a railroad, the North-South divide the president of the United States was dealing with would be just the first act in a dramatic performance about the splintering of America.[11]

The problem was that the U.S. government was fighting a civil war and didn't have the money to finance such a project entirely on its own. That's why it created a privately owned but publicly subsidized venture like the Union Pacific Railroad. The hope was that private investment money would join forces with government subsidies to get the tracks built, and the rewards for making a private investment in the UP would pour in later—from rail usage fees, matured government bonds, and the sale of land and mineral rights.

Alas, few private citizens were willing, at first, to invest in a venture like the Transcontinental Railroad, given the logistical challenges it faced. Those challenges included more than just the harsh and at times extremely mountainous terrain any western railroad was going to have to push through. There were also Indigenous Americans to contend with, many of whom lived on land the U.S. government had *already agreed* was formally theirs but that any railroad passing between Nebraska and California was going to have to use (and want to mine or sell later to homesteaders).

The Fort Laramie Treaty of 1851 acknowledged that the land in south-eastern Wyoming the Union Pacific Railroad ultimately passed through belonged to the Cheyenne and Arapaho people. When Colonel John

Chivington ordered his men in 1864 to slaughter those families who were camped along the banks of Sand Creek, he did so on Indian land. The U.S. government had tried in 1860 to renegotiate the treaty, but in what was a very familiar pattern by that point—dating back to the Treaty of New Echota in 1835, which forced the Cherokees out of northwest Georgia and into eastern Oklahoma—federal officials had engaged in the negotiations with people who were not authorized by the tribes to represent them.[12] Many Cheyennes and Arapahos, therefore, didn't recognize the renegotiated terms, and the U.S. Army's willingness to do the dirty work aside, anyone looking to invest in the Union Pacific Railroad would have been foolish not to consider the risks that came with building in Indian Country.

In theory this was why the Ames brothers had joined together with other people who wanted to see the Transcontinental Railroad built and founded the company known as Crédit Mobilier. Recall that Crédit Mobilier was more than just the construction company the UP had contracted with to build the rails; it was also an investor in the Union Pacific Railroad. Men who bought stock in Crédit Mobilier had provided funding to the public-private partnership that was created by the Pacific Railroad Act of 1862. Even if the Union Pacific Railroad failed, a man who had invested in it through Crédit Mobilier would still be able to walk away with something, since Crédit Mobilier was being paid the entire time by the UP. That was how Oakes Ames understood the reason for Crédit Mobilier's existence: as a way to encourage necessary investment in a high-risk venture like the Union Pacific Railroad.[13] It was why he could tell his constituents, with some degree of sincerity, that he believed founding the company was one of the "most creditable and patriotic acts" of his life.

Very few human beings see their motivations as being about bald-faced self-interest (even if that's exactly what they are). Few people see the motivations of the people they admire in those terms, either. To those who believed it was America's "manifest destiny" to spread European, Protestant values across the continent, the completion of the Transcontinental Railroad was an extraordinary and admirable thing. If it took a scheme like Crédit Mobilier to get it done, then so be it. It was just a shame Oakes Ames never lived to see the monument on Sherman Hill that was built in his honor.

Of course, the Union Pacific Railroad did eventually make money—a lot of money, for a lot of people. That's one other reason Oakes Ames's reputation was able to enjoy a vast degree of rehabilitation. Many of the people who were best situated to construct or maintain the dead congressman's reputation had also gotten rich off the circumstances that led to Ames's censure.

The UP was eventually purchased by Jay Gould, a ruthless financier who'd made his fortune in the late 1850s manipulating railroad stock for several lines in Pennsylvania and New York. Jay Gould *did* see his motivations as being entirely about self-interest. Shortly after he acquired a controlling share of the Union Pacific Railroad, he canceled all the contracts the company had had with independent mines in Wyoming, refusing to haul coal from any mine that wasn't operated directly by the UP. He also cut the pay Union Pacific had been giving its miners—immigrants, primarily, from Sweden, Ireland, Denmark, and Bohemia.

When workers at several UP mines went on strike, Gould replaced them with Chinese workers he brought in from Oregon. The resentment that action generated resulted in a nasty riot in September 1885 in the town of Rock Springs (located, like so many other things in southern Wyoming, just off Interstate 80). Nearly fifty Chinese men were burned to death in the fires that angry White miners set in that town. One year later Gould was said to have bragged with some degree of accuracy that he could "hire one half of the working class to kill the other half."[14]

Every time railroad stock changed hands, somebody made money, even if the stock were being sold at a loss, which is what happened when Jay Gould took over a controlling share of the Union Pacific Railroad. One of Robert Ray Hamilton's other, less historically famous great-grandfathers had discovered as much in the late eighteenth century, before depression got the best of him and he slit his throat. Recall that Nathaniel Prime had set himself up on Wall Street in 1796 as one of the nation's first "stock and commission brokers." He made a boatload of money helping New Yorkers purchase shares in banks and canals, which—along with the rivers and lakes they connected—were the primary method of commercial transit until the 1830s, when the railroads came along.[15]

There's a fantastic scene in Tom Wolfe's novel *The Bonfire of the Vanities* (1987) where the main character, Sherman McCoy, tries to explain to his daughter how he's able to afford the lavish lifestyle she enjoys. He gets himself into trouble when he tells her he buys and sells things called "bonds." The little girl doesn't understand what a bond is and mistakenly thinks her father is telling her he builds roads and schools. After an embarrassingly inadequate effort to clarify that he does not, in fact, *build anything*, Sherman McCoy finds that his passive-aggressive wife, Judy, wants to step in. "Just imagine that a bond is a slice of cake," Judy McCoy tells the couple's daughter. "You didn't bake the cake, but every time you hand somebody a slice of the cake, a tiny little bit comes off, like a little crumb, and you can keep that."[16]

Sherman is annoyed that his wife would describe his professional work as "collecting crumbs," but readers recognize that's exactly what he does—and it's what thousands of traders in stocks and bonds before him did, including the men in the 1860s and 1870s who helped James Garfield and Jay Gould invest in ventures like Crédit Mobilier or the Union Pacific Railroad. Collecting crumbs wasn't glamorous, but it could be quite lucrative, as the brokers who focused on the nineteenth-century railroad industry discovered.

One of the brokers who specialized in railroad stocks and bonds during the Gilded Age was a father of five, originally from Rhode Island, named James Monroe Drake. He'd been born in Providence in 1823 but moved to Manhattan as a child. In his late teens and early twenties, Drake apprenticed with Jacob Little, the Wall Street broker who helped Jay Gould manipulate the value of the Erie Railroad's stock.[17]

Jacob Little was the first trader in the United States to help his clients "sell short." Short-selling is a scheme whereby a speculator uses a broker to borrow stock from a company for a fee; he then sells the stock he's borrowed, agreeing to buy it back by a certain date and return it to the broker who lent it to him. The gamble is that if the stock has gone up in price by the time the speculator has to buy it back, he loses money. If the stock drops, though, and he's able to buy back what he borrowed at a lower price than he sold it for, the speculator keeps the profit. Short-sellers make money when the confidence investors have in a company plummets. That's why they aren't well liked by corporate executives; short-sellers seem to root rather unabashedly for executives to fail.[18]

Short-selling is how Jacob Little made his fortune—and it's how his protégé, James Monroe Drake, made his fortune, too. Following the example of his mentor, Drake specialized in railroads when he opened his own firm in the Drexel Building on the corner of Broad and Wall Streets in 1852. By 1872 James Drake had made enough money to become one of the first "cottagers" in Newport, Rhode Island, during the years when that town transitioned from being a favored vacation spot among moderately wealthy New England Brahmins to being an internationally recognized summer playground for Gilded Age millionaires, thanks in no small part to the attention Lina Astor's friend, Ward McAllister, lavished on Aquidneck Island.[19]

The name of Drake's Newport home was "Red Cross Cottage," a nod to the cruciform pattern within the brickwork of the house's main chimney. It still stands today, although part of the house has been turned into a separate condo or "in-law suite." Originally, the gothic mansion had eight bedrooms and sat on seven acres that looked out over Easton Bay. Immediately after he purchased the property, Drake made "great improvements upon the house," according to one local newspaper. He constructed a "new and elegant stable" for his family's horses; arranged to have the plumbing updated so that hot water could be pumped into all of the bathrooms; and laid out a carriageway that connected the cottage to Bellevue Avenue, where an ever-growing number of New York-based millionaires, many of them invested in railroads thanks to brokers like James Drake, was starting to build a collection of extravagant, European-style villas that now draw more than a million tourists to Newport every summer.[20]

Because he owned property in Rhode Island, James Drake was able to run for office in that state. He served briefly with no real distinction in the Rhode Island State Assembly in the mid-1870s. He was also prominent enough in New York's financial circles to make it into Moses King's *Handbook of Notable New Yorkers*, a glossy compendium of photographic portraits that showcased the careers of two thousand men who had "immortal names that were not born to die" in the estimation of the book's publisher.[21]

Much like Lina Astor's friend Ward McAllister, Moses King was a king-maker in Gilded Age New York. He had a "very extensive acquaintance with distinguished men of all walks of life," according to one newspaper, and his guides to the most important men in dozens of professions—not just in New York, but in Philadelphia and Boston, as well—were said to be "especially cherished" by foreign diplomats, who relied upon the guides as they sought to weave themselves into the cultural fabric of the American cities where they were stationed. Out of more than nine thousand attorneys practicing in New York, just two hundred had their photographs featured in Moses King's *Handbook*. Out of nearly six thousand doctors, just sixty had their visages in his tome.[22]

King's guides included actors, architects, detectives, engineers, jewelers, vintners, bakers, and chocolatiers—anyone, really, whom a person might need to know to safely navigate the shoals of New York's high society. In addition to James Monroe Drake, the list of movers and shakers in Moses King's silk-bound volume included men whose names are still recognizable today: Thomas Edison and Nikola Tesla, who were quaintly identified by King as "electricians"; Grover Cleveland; Theodore Roosevelt; John Philip Sousa; Joseph Pulitzer; Frederick Law Olmsted; and Oscar Hammerstein—not the famous librettist who gave us enduring musical favorites like *Oklahoma!* and *The Sound of Music* but his grandfather, a German-born composer and theater impresario who almost single-handedly turned the area around Longacre Square (or what is today known as Times Square) into the theater district, where Rodgers and Hammerstein's musical about lovesick homesteaders debuted in 1943.[23]

King's book also included two people who had direct connections to Robert Ray Hamilton: Elihu Root, who was Ray's attorney in the trials that followed Eva's stabbing of Mary Ann Donnelly in 1889 (Root would go on to become Teddy Roosevelt's secretary of state sixteen years later—suggesting that Moses King's instinct for identifying "notable" New Yorkers was a good one); and Edmund Baylies, Ray's first cousin, who was the oldest son of Nathalie Ray Baylies, the aunt with whom Ray shared his maternal grandfather's ample inheritance. Ed Baylies was also one of the four hundred New Yorkers Ward McAllister believed could comport themselves in a ballroom.[24]

James Monroe Drake and his wife, Mary MacAdam, kept good company, thanks to all the money he'd made helping his clients sell short. Early in their marriage, the couple lived on a large estate on Staten Island. Later, they moved to a brownstone on the West Side of Manhattan. They had five children together, all of whom made it to adulthood—a remarkable accomplishment in the second half of the nineteenth century, even among the rich. Their oldest child, Henry, was born in 1853. He was followed by Herbert in 1856. Bertha and Estella were born in 1859 and 1862, respectively. Finally, in the spring of 1866, the Drakes' youngest child, Edith, was born—and she would prove to be her family's greatest challenge.

Mary MacAdam came from a politically prominent Protestant family in Belfast, Ireland. Her maternal grandfather was a famous revolutionary named Samuel Neilson, who had owned and edited the *Northern Star*, the official newspaper of the Society of United Irishmen. The society, founded in 1792, was made up of Catholics and Presbyterians who wanted Ireland to be free and independent, beholden neither to England's Parliament nor the Anglican Church. To that end they famously launched a rebellion in 1798 that ended in the death of their leader, Theobald Wolfe Tone.[25]

Samuel Neilson spent three years in a Scottish prison before being exiled from Ireland in 1802. He went to New York, landing in December of that year, and started making plans to bring his wife and three children—including his eight-year-old daughter, Jane, who eventually became Mary MacAdam's mother and Edith Drake's grandmother—to the United States. Neilson also made plans to start republishing the *Northern Star*, so that the fight for Irish independence could continue.

Alas, Neilson's plans went awry when yellow fever struck New York City in the spring of 1803. He absconded to the countryside—a response to epidemics that was as common among affluent people in the nineteenth century as it is in the twenty-first. The virus that causes yellow fever was already in Samuel Neilson's blood, however, by the time he reached the village of Poughkeepsie. Edith Drake's famous great-grandfather died in August 1803 at the age of forty-three. Ten months later Robert Ray Hamilton's famous great-grandfather died, as well, not from an infection that had been caused by a mosquito bite, but from one that set in after his body was pierced by a lead ball, fired from a pistol.[26]

Samuel Neilson's family didn't forget who he was, however. "I am an Irish-Yankee daredevil," Edith Drake wrote to the editor of the *Los Angeles Times* in August 1913, more than a century after her great-grandfather had died. The newspaper was one of several that had resurrected uncharitable rumors about her husband, John Dudley Sargent, who'd died a few weeks earlier, and Edith was not happy. "We are lineal descendants of Sir Francis Drake and Samuel Nelson [*sic*], the Irish patriot," she said of herself and her siblings, staking an ancestral claim not only to a rebel but also to a pirate by way of warning the *Times*'s editor not to cross her on the pages of his newspaper. "My blood rises hot within me when charges so base are brought up against a dead man," she said of the nasty things ranchers in Jackson's Hole, Wyoming, had told the *Times* about her husband. "May God rest his weary soul—maligned as he always was by those who were jealous because he owned one of God's garden spots, while they dwelled in low valleys and swamps."[27]

The letter to the editor was not Edith's first byline. Twenty-five years earlier, when she was in her early twenties and still living in her parents' home on the West Side of Manhattan, Edith Drake submitted a rather raunchy joke to the *New York Evening World*'s "Midsummer Jokers" column and insisted that her name be published along with it. "A Boston girl got into a New York street car. Her ride was long. She fell asleep, her hand in her muff lying on the seat," Edith's joke began. "A young man full of Adam slipped his hand in the muff and tenderly held the contents until the owner awoke, and turning on her cold, calm intellectual eyes said: 'Sir! I am a Boston girl, and I give you just twenty minutes to take your hand out of my muff.'"[28]

Modern-day readers are not finding anything in the joke that would not also have been found by readers in 1888. The city of Boston's reputation for producing stiff and stodgy citizens with "cold, calm intellectual eyes" was not the sole source of the joke's humor:

> I heard the merry wag protest
> The muff between her haunches

Resembl'd most a mag-pye's nest
Between two lofty branches.

So ran the sixth stanza of a popular drinking song from the early eighteenth century called "The Crab-Tree." It told the story of a boy who'd
gotten caught up in an apple tree and could not get down before an unsus-
pecting maid, wearing no petticoat, started talking to herself and per-
forming handstands below him, entirely unaware of his presence.[29]

A "muff," in other words, had been much more than just a ladies' hand-
warmer for nearly two centuries by the time Edith Drake published her
joke in the *New York Evening World*. The ribald humor, in and of itself, was
not inappropriate for the times. Having the joke conveyed to a public
audience, however, by the daughter of a prominent broker and former
state lawmaker who played tennis in Newport and had his face featured
in Moses King's *Handbook of Notable New Yorkers* was a severe violation
of Gilded Age decorum.

James Monroe Drake's youngest child was a talented and loving, if
strange and sometimes troublesome, daughter. She enjoyed a good
joke or puzzle throughout her life. Years after she'd submitted her story
about the "Boston girl" to the *New York Evening World*, Edith put together
a list of riddles for her husband to consider, in a playful effort to distract him from the "melancholia" he sometimes slipped into during the
years of their marriage. "I planted a song-bird and something worn by
a horseman on the heel of his boot," she typed onto a sheet of paper one
summer evening while the couple sat with Jack's daughter, Catherine
Winthrop, in their cabin along Jackson Lake. "What came up?" Jack
got the answer right when he scrawled the word "larkspur" next to the
question. "I planted a sly little animal and something worn in boxing,"
Edith continued. "What came up?" The only logical answer was the one
Jack gave her: a "foxglove."[30]

In addition to having a sense of humor, Edith was a gifted musician.
She spent her teenaged years in France, studying the violin at the Paris
Conservatorie, where her friends described her as "brilliantly intelli-
gent," and her teachers were said to have "classed her as a genius." She

was also a voracious reader. Her library, which she took to Wyoming with her when she married John Dudley Sargent, was dominated by the adventure stories of Edgar Allan Poe, Alexandre Dumas, and Rudyard Kipling, who was about the same age as Edith and started making a name for himself not long after she returned from her musical studies in Europe in 1886.[31]

Edith's taste in literature may have been the reason she was prone to developing fantasies and crushes in her youth. Much to the dismay of her parents, she sometimes became obsessed with famous actors and musicians, prompting at least one of them, the comedian Francis Wilson, to call the police on her in 1889 because she kept dancing in the street in front of his house. According to Wilson's complaint, twenty-two-year-old Edith wrote to the actor incessantly and attended the comic opera he was starring in, *The Oolah*, for two months straight, always sitting in the front row.[32]

In 1904, nine years before she wrote to the *Los Angeles Times* to complain about its coverage of Jack Sargent's death, Edith submitted an essay to the *New York World* that was picked up by Joseph Pulitzer's other English-language newspaper, the *St. Louis Post-Dispatch*. She was thirty-eight years old and had not yet married John Dudley Sargent.[33] Like her letter to the editor in which she called herself an "Irish-Yankee daredevil" and accused her husband's enemies of living in "low valleys and swamps," Edith's essay was strident and a tad bizarre. It was rambling, disjointed, and at times risqué—far more so than the joke she'd submitted to the *Evening World* in 1888. Unlike the letter she would later write to the *Los Angeles Times*, Edith's essay didn't even seem to have a reason for being written. If there were a reason, she didn't identify it in the body of her piece.

The headline writer called the essay a "Cynical Plea for a Restless Man." Edith's overall message was that "love lives on imagination and seldom survives monotony." Men, she insisted, "reach out, by instinct, for new pastures." A wife, therefore, should strive to give her husband "all the variety he can stand," lest she find herself divorced a few years after getting married. "If you have to, turn into a female gorilla to tickle his fancy," Edith advised her readers (in words that undoubtedly made her Presbyterian mother blush). But do not fall into the trap of thinking marriage is forever. "Marriage is a mere merry-go-round now," Edith observed. "If it ceases to be merry, you pay your money and jump off."[34]

From her perch in 1904, Edith Drake predicted men might some-day choose to avoid getting married altogether. "When man discovers some substitute for woman, as he has for a horse," she mused, "we may hear of wifeless weddings and wireless wires sent to paperless papers." It was an observation that anticipated much more than just text mes-saging and websites like nytimes.com. Edith also seemed to predict a somewhat disturbing trend sociologists have charted among American men born in the 1980s and 1990s. These men are choosing not to date, form romantic relationships, or even have sex, in part because of the easy availability of online pornography.[35]

Why Edith chose to write her bizarre, if foresighted, rumination on marital relations and submit it to a newspaper is unclear, but the *Post-Dispatch*'s reason for publishing it is no mystery: Edith Drake was a celebrity—or at least she had been several years before her essay came out. "Mrs. Edith Drake McGibney, the writer of the article which follows, is the daughter of James M. Drake, a New York banker, whom she seri-ously offended 11 years ago," the newspaper reminded its readers. Edith had offended her father "by running away with and marrying Samuel D. McGibney, a young carpenter who at the time was said to be a racetrack frequenter. She was then 27 and he was 23 and poor. It was the social sensation of the day."[36]

John Dudley Sargent was not Edith Drake's first husband, in other words. She'd been married before they got together in 1906, and the *Post-Dispatch* was correct when it said Edith's first marriage had been "the social sensation of the day." It was a sensation, because that's exactly what newspaper publishers ensured it became.

The *Boston Globe* was the first newspaper to break the story of Edith's disappearance. "Her father is a millionaire, head of the banking house of Drake, Mastin & Company," the newspaper reported on July 5, 1893. "Her parents and friends are much alarmed. They have asked the police to help search for her, because, they say, her mind is affected somewhat." According to the *Globe*, "for some time prior to her disappearance," Edith had been "deeply infatuated with Samuel D. McGibney, a builder." He, in turn, had "professed the utmost affection for the girl, and they became engaged without the consent of her parents."[37]

For the next five years, newspapers across the country ran stories about the saga of Edith Drake and her carpenter husband. During the first month after her disappearance, the coverage was relentless. More than a hundred different articles were published in seventeen different states, all of them wondering whether Edith Drake, the "millionaire banker's daughter," had actually married Samuel McGibney, the "Scottish stage carpenter"—and, if so, what her father intended to do about it.

McGibney's sister told reporters her brother had married Edith in Long Island City, Queens. "They got a frame for the certificate and Edith walked through the street with it in her hand," Jessie McGibney claimed. "There was no secrecy about it. They wanted to get married and they were married."[38]

Jessie believed that James Monroe Drake opposed the marriage because Edith was his youngest child, and he just couldn't bear to let her go. "Edith plays beautifully on the violin, and that used to be a source of great pleasure to Mr. Drake," she told a group of reporters who came to her home on the Lower East Side of Manhattan. "Sam likes her playing, too, and she used to play for him a great deal. Then she fell in love with him and he fell in love with her, and after a while, she seemed to only care to play for Sam. That grieved Mr. Drake, because he seemed to think his daughter did not care for him as much as she had."[39]

James Drake had a different story. He strongly suspected that his daughter was "not mentally responsible," which is why he'd refused to give her $5,000 the year before, when she first told him she wanted to get married. "I have no objection to him as a carpenter, nor as a poor man," Drake said of Samuel McGibney in an exclusive interview with the *New York Evening World*. "I have opposed their marriage simply because she is not mentally fit. I should oppose her marriage to anyone else for the same reason."[40]

A few days after the *Boston Globe* ran its initial story, Edith showed up at the office of her father's attorney with a marriage certificate. That attorney, John Townsend, subsequently crafted a statement on behalf of the Drake family and released it to the press. "As this purely domestic trouble has found its way into the newspapers," Townsend began, "it is perhaps better for Mr. Drake that a correct version of it should reach the public eye." He confirmed that his client's daughter had married Samuel McGibney on July 6, 1893, then provided the press with some context. "Until about five years since, she has been a quiet, studious, and affectionate daughter," Townsend said of Edith. "Without apparent reason, she has, during these last few years, changed so much as to make her an object of solicitude to her mother." Mary MacAdam Drake had done her best to keep "much of the discomfort caused by [Edith] from the rest of the family, mainly her father." In the last year or so, however, Edith's behavior had become "so manifestly strange that it was impossible for her mother to protect her any longer."[41]

James Drake had consulted his attorney earlier that spring, after his wife shared some troubling stories with him about their daughter's behavior. "He gave me to understand that from what he had heard, it was unsafe for [Edith] to reside in his establishment," Townsend told the press. "The girl had made threats." Drake's attorney visited Edith himself and consulted several of her friends. On the basis of those interviews, he determined "there is no reasonable doubt that her mind is effected and that she requires treatment." He advised James Drake to have his daughter committed to an asylum, but Edith refused to go. Drake got a judge to order the commitment, and it was then that she ran away from home and married Samuel McGibney.[42]

"She is now married," Townsend told the press. "No further steps shall be taken by Mr. Drake." Legally, it was the responsibility of "her husband to look after her in the future." "I can assure her of one thing, however," Townsend continued. "She will receive no financial aid from her father while she is with her husband." The matter was "settled," according to the lawyer, and he hoped reporters would move on to the next, titillating story.[43]

Of course, the matter was far from settled. John Townsend may have thought he was putting every question to bed when he released his statement on behalf of the Drake family, but that statement had just raised a new question for the press to pursue: If Edith had been a quiet, studious, and affectionate daughter until five years earlier, what had happened late in 1887 or early in 1888 to cause her to go off the rails?

Once again it was the *Boston Globe* that broke the story. In a shocking article with the humiliating headline "Edith Drake's Lovers," the *Globe* informed its readers that "Miss Edith Drake, the banker's daughter, who loves a carpenter and ran away from home when her father wanted to put her in a sanitarium," was the author of a packet of letters "found among the belongings" of Enrico Pranzini, "a Levantine . . . possessed of some unknown and potent attraction for women."[44]

The letters had been used six years earlier by prosecuting attorneys in France, in a case they brought against Pranzini. The identity of the letter-writer had not been disclosed at the time; the jury was told only that she was "the daughter of a New York banker" and that she would be referred to as "Miss E." Miss E's letters convinced jurors that Enrico Pranzini was guilty of the charges brought against him. In August 1887 "he was guillotined in Paris for the dastardly murder of three people, of one of whom he had been the lover."[45]

Americans knew exactly who Enrico Pranzini was. His arrest and trial in Paris had dominated the front pages of newspapers in the spring and summer of 1887. The *New York Herald* was the first American paper to pick up the story. It reported in late March that Gutave Macé had been called out of retirement to help authorities in Paris investigate the murder of "three unfortunate women in the Rue Montaigne." Macé was the former chief of police in Paris. Excerpts from his celebrated memoir, *La Police Parisienne: Le Service De La Sureté*, had been translated into English by a London publisher the year before. The book was wildly popular with American readers; by the time Macé was asked to investigate the murders in the Rue Montaigne, it had already gone through two additional printings in the United States.[46]

Police were looking closely at an immigrant from Egypt named "Henri" Pranzini who knew one of the victims, a woman in her late forties by the name of Marie Regnault. The other two people who'd been killed were Regnault's housekeeper, Annette Gremeret, and Gremeret's twelve-year-old daughter, also named Marie. The crime scene was pretty brutal. Graphic drawings based on photographs taken in the morgue were run in several French publications. Young Marie Gremeret's head had nearly been severed from her body.

Law enforcement officials believed Pranzini had committed the murders, and they'd sent an investigator to Alexandria, Egypt, to interview his family. The retired chief inspector was not convinced, however, that the police had found their man. "It is likely that he was watching near by when the crime was committed, ready to give warning to the real assassin," Monsieur Macé told the *Herald*'s correspondent when asked whether he thought Pranzini had done the deed. His reasons for thinking this were that the victims' wounds were such that "it seems almost certain that the murderer was by profession a butcher, as the cuts were made in exactly the same way as they are at the slaughter-house at Villette."[47]

Pranzini was not a butcher. He was a gigolo—a male courtesan. Older women paid him to have sex with them (and to talk to them afterward). On his more romantic days, Pranzini may have seen himself as a modern-day Julien Sorel, the protagonist in Stendahl's famous coming-of-age novel *Le Rouge et Le Noir*. The novel, published in 1830, tells the story of an ambitious and intellectual young man, the son of a carpenter, who climbs the social ladder in Restoration France by sleeping with emotionally vulnerable women who are connected to titles and great wealth through their husbands and fathers. Sorel shoots one of his former lovers after she undermines his efforts to marry the daughter of a marquis. The woman doesn't die (at least not from her gunshot wound), which means Sorel isn't a murderer, and neither was Enrico Pranzini, at least according to what he told the authorities who arrested him in Marseilles after he'd used a watch that belonged to Marie Regnault to pay for a threesome with a couple of prostitutes.[48]

Enrico Pranzini was the thirty-year-old son of Gandolfo and Antoinetta Pranzini, a coal merchant and his wife who'd migrated to North Africa after the Revolution of 1848 brought a wave of violence to their native state of Tuscany. French reporters found Pranzini exotic, since he'd been raised in Egypt when it was still a part of the Ottoman Empire. He had a high forehead with a full head of hair; a clear, olive-toned complexion; light-brown eyes; and a close-cropped beard that was said to be "flecked with amber." He'd gone to an English school in Alexandria, worked as a translator for Russian army officers in Constantinople, and clerked at a hotel in Bombay. Pranzini spoke seven languages and could read and write three different alphabets: Latin, Arabic, and Greek. He was precisely the sort of man a talented and intelligent young woman with an active and artistic imagination might fall for. "Pranzini has an English air and the soft gracefulness of an Oriental," one newspaper in Paris reported. The prosecuting attorney who tried him for murder called him an "Oriental Don Juan."[49]

Newspapers in the United States were fascinated by Pranzini—but they were even more fascinated by the American girl whose letters formed the foundation of the case against him. According to the prosecution's theory, Pranzini had killed Marie Regnault so he could steal her jewels and sell them; that, in turn, would provide him with the money he needed to sail to New York, where—he'd been told by the American girl in her letters—he would be welcomed as a son-in-law by her mother, who'd had the opportunity to be charmed by him in Paris one year earlier.[50]

The problem for the press was that they knew very little about this American girl who fascinated them so much. "That the name of this lady . . . has not once been whispered is another singular feature of this celebrated case," the New York Times told its readers. The statement wasn't entirely accurate. One of Joseph Pulitzer's correspondents had, in fact, learned that some of Pranzini's letters were "signed Edith," and that information did make it into a story that ran on July 26, 1887. For the most part, however, French authorities and the American press did respect the anonymity of the young woman Pranzini had seduced. "It is a credit to the Paris detectives that they have maintained a strict silence regarding the identity of the deceived girl," the New York Times conceded.[51]

Reporters still found a way to give their stories the kind of "sparkle" that journalism textbook writer Edwin Shuman said would "forgive a good deal of inaccuracy in your matter." Readers in the United States learned that Pranzini's American conquest had arrived in Paris "a little over a year ago." She was "a young and beautiful girl, a resident of Fifth Avenue," who was "taken to Europe by her parents to spend the Christmas holidays." After doing the "grand tour," she'd settled with her family in Paris, "in a house on Victor Hugo Avenue," where her parents "gave balls and parties, received a great deal of company, visited many houses and were widely known for their refinement, amiability, and liberality."

During this time the young woman had many suitors: "Peers and peers' sons, dukes, and even princes were said to have sought her hand." She had no interest in any of them, however; instead, "she smiled them all away, and with a pretty shake of the head gave them to understand they would be welcome on any footing but that of an intended."[52]

The stories were mostly wrong. Edith had not gone to Paris for the holidays shortly before the murders in the Rue Montaigne. She'd spent years in that city, studying at the Paris Conservatorie, and had actually left Europe to return to the New York roughly a year before Marie Regnault and Annette and Marie Gremeret were killed. Her parents lived on the West Side of Manhattan, not Fifth Avenue. While her mother did spend some time with her when she lived in Paris, and her father may have occasionally visited her, too, Edith spent most of her teenaged years away at school, separated from everyone in her family except her sister Stella, who also studied in Europe. Edith was also just fourteen when she arrived in Paris, making it highly unlikely any aristocrat asked for her hand in marriage—at least not right away.[53]

Nevertheless, some of what the American newspapers reported was accurate. Specifically, the excerpts from Edith's letters that they published were accurate. Those letters were translated from English to French and read out loud in the courtroom during Pranzini's trial. They were recorded verbatim by a French reporter named Georges Grison. American editors then arranged to have Grison's notes translated back into English, and those notes were published in newspapers across the country.

Miss E.'s identity may have been a mystery to the public in the summer of 1887, but there was one young woman in New York who knew exactly who she was. One can only imagine what it must have been like for twenty-one-year-old Edith Drake to read her words of intimacy in the newspapers, knowing that thousands of other people were reading them, too:

"You are the only man, the only thing, I would be happy to possess," she wrote to Pranzini in one letter. "Your magnificent form is ever before my eyes. . . . For myself, I am yours body and soul when you wish."

"I was delighted to see that you possessed such grand power the evening when for the first time I touched your iron muscles," she wrote to him in another letter. "I don't care for those men who have flabby arms and women's muscles."

In a third letter Edith reminded Pranzini he had been her first. "God! When I think of how I gave myself to you immediately! My fatal destiny! You, who never wanted to believe that it was the first time in my life," she told him.

"Magnificent being," she wrote to him in a fourth letter. "At night, when all is tranquil and no sound but the nightingale is heard, I try to imagine that he who I love is beside me, near me, beside me, folded down upon my heart, where I rest my head and sleep the sleep of the happy and blest."[54]

Many more letters were included in Grison's transcript. They spoke of how much the writer's mother liked him and admired him. They spoke of why New York was a better city to live in than Paris—and how much her "sweet friend" would enjoy his life with her there, once he came to New York, met her father, and married her. These entreaties were the heart of the prosecution's case against Pranzini. In reading them one cannot help but wonder why Georges Onfroy de Bréville, the lead attorney in the case, bothered to share some of the more embarrassingly intimate details from the letters of *la jeune Américaine* with the court. Did jurors really need to know, for instance, that Enrico Pranzini had taken Edith's virginity in order to believe he had killed three people in order to join her in New York? Probably not. Bréville, however, seems to have seen himself as a bit of a courtroom comedian, and the laughs he enjoyed were often obtained at a woman's expense.

Georges Grison's transcript of the trial mentions *hilarité general* on several occasions. People laughed, he noted, at the prosecutor's response to a doctor who had examined Pranzini and testified he had "muscles of steel," rendering him more than capable of severing a twelve-year-old's head from her body with only a butcher's knife. "And behold," Bréville replied, "I find confirmation of this fact in the correspondence [the defendant] has been having with the young American, who gave herself to him under such strange circumstances." The audience laughed again during the prosecution's closing argument, when Bréville claimed not to understand how Pranzini possibly could have stomached having sex with older women like Marie Regnault. "I hesitate to believe it, too," he told the jurors. "I do not know how he could have liked ladies in their fifties; but I would like to suggest, as per the young American, that they loved his muscles."[55]

Edith read her private words in New York's newspapers and learned that Parisians were laughing at them—as the words themselves were being used to convict the man she loved. She also learned some hard truths about that man who had captured her heart. She read of Enrico Pranzini's many liaisons with older women, and of the ongoing relationship he'd had with one client in particular, Antoinette Sabatier, whose time with Pranzini had overlapped with the time when Edith still lived in Paris.[56]

The stories must have been devastating to her—and humiliating, too, even though no one actually knew who the mysterious banker's daughter was. If Edith started acting strangely in the final months of 1887, it almost certainly was *not* "without apparent reason," as her father's attorney asserted. Indeed, not only did Edith have her privacy violated, her ego bruised, and her heart crushed but she also had to read about what the American press dubbed the "Pranzini Skin Scandal" in the weeks that followed the public beheading of her lover on August 31, 1887.[57]

The *New York Herald*'s correspondent put the crowd that gathered to watch Enrico Pranzini be executed on Paris's Place de la Roquette at 20,000. A correspondent for the *London Daily News* gave his readers a far more conservative estimate of 2,500, but that's because he counted only the people who were ticket-holders to the event. The *Herald*'s correspondent included the "jeering gamins"—street urchins—who had climbed up into trees around the execution square so that they could catch a glimpse of the condemned man's head "rolling into the basket."[58]

Following the execution Pranzini's corpse was taken to the Medical School of Paris and turned over to the faculty there. This was a common practice in the nineteenth century; medical scientists in Europe and the United States would regularly dissect the bodies of criminals, often in the presence of journalists, searching for some physical indication of a biological propensity for criminality. In the case of Enrico Pranzini, his identity as an exotic "Oriental," combined with the sexual prowess he had exhibited by earning a living as a gigolo, made the probing of his body particularly interesting to members of the press.

One French journalist acknowledged with no sense of shame that

Pranzini's naked body constituted "a beauty of incomparable forms." He went on to marvel that someone who possessed such an elegant body could also be capable of committing such a heinous crime. "As my gaze fell upon this superb being that lay there," the journalist confessed, "I thought of that troubling passage from Renan's *Marcus Aurelius* about how 'beauty was equal to virtue.'" Ernest Renan was a French philosopher and historian. Five years earlier he'd criticized Christian stoics for failing to recognize that beauty and virtue were gifts from God that often went hand in hand. In Enrico Pranzini, however, great beauty was able to exist in the absence of virtue, which is why the journalist was troubled by Renan's observation. Another, less poetic reporter informed his readers that "one of [Pranzini's] organs, so to speak, has become legendary" and claimed that doctors had needed a bigger-than-usual jar to preserve the condemned man's penis.[59]

There was nothing about what happened to Pranzini's body that sent up red flags when French journalists reported on the dissection in the days that followed his execution. In fact American newspapers found the dissection so boring, they didn't even bother to report on it—at least not at first. Two weeks after Edith Drake's former lover was beheaded, however, Georges Grison, the journalist who'd compiled a transcript of the trial, got a disturbing scoop; he wrote about it for the Parisian daily *Le Figaro*. Grison had learned that three high-ranking detectives in Paris's police department had taken *souvenirs* from Pranzini's dissection—or rather, they'd taken some material that they then used to make souvenirs. That material was skin from Enrico Pranzini's body.[60]

At first Parisians thought the story was a canard. According to Grison, the men had had the skin tanned and turned into calling-card purses—an action that was simply too bizarre and uncivilized to have happened in a modern and refined city like Paris. Soon, however, one of the men mentioned in Grison's story admitted that the purses were real, and that they had, in fact, been made from Pranzini. The response was immediate and intense: Parisians were disgusted and horrified. Public opinion was "violently upset," in the words of one French newspaper. "This is the first scandal of its kind—ever," another paper observed, hoping to redeem the city by emphasizing the utterly exceptional nature of what the three detectives had done.[61]

Six years earlier, while workers were putting the finishing touches on the Ames Brothers monument in Albany County, Wyoming, a similar human skin–tanning incident had occurred out there. In 1881 an outlaw named George "Big Nose" Parrot (his nickname seems to have been only a description, not an anti-Semitic slur) was lynched after he stole several cattle and murdered a private detective who worked for the Union Pacific Railroad. Two doctors named Thomas Maghee and John Osborne took possession of his body afterward, ostensibly to look for physical markers of Parrot's criminality. The physicians took skin from the lynched man's thighs and chest and sent the swatches down to Denver to be tanned. Osborne then turned the human leather into a pair of shoes.[62]

Osborne wore those shoes to his inauguration as Wyoming's first Democratic governor in 1893. In 1995 tests confirmed that the leather the shoes were made from is, in fact, human. In the wilds of late nineteenth-century Wyoming, human skin–tanning just wasn't a big deal—certainly not grotesque enough to create a scandal for any politician to have to deal with. In the cultivated salons of Paris, however, what happened to Pranzini's corpse was repulsive, the kind of behavior one would find among "the Redskins who fashion belts from the hair of the *petits blancs* they've scalped," according to *Le Figaro*. When the Catholic newspaper *La Croix* reported that Paris's chief of police, Marie-François Goron, had accepted one of the calling-card purses made from Enrico Pranzini's skin as a gift—a decision that amounted to an "act of cannibalism," in the paper's estimation—the scandal that followed was sweeping. It ultimately destroyed the careers of several politicians who were connected to the police department, including that of Jules Grévy, who resigned from his post as president of France's Third Republic in December of 1887.[63]

In the United States, several newspapers picked up the story of the "ghastly trophies" that were made from Pranzini's skin, and Edith Drake learned what happened to that "magnificent" body she'd admired so much. It was during the months and years that followed that she started obsessively writing to the actor Francis Wilson and submitting inappropriate jokes to the *New York Evening World*. She also started wandering into the reading room of the Marlborough Hotel—a venue traditionally reserved for men—and regaling the patrons there with wild and nonsensical stories, claiming on one occasion that she desperately needed to get to Lexington, Kentucky, in order to avoid being arrested.[64]

When James Monroe Drake finally sought the advice of his attorney, it was because he believed Edith had become dangerous. She "crept into my room one night to murder me," he finally admitted to the *New York World* in 1899, six years after the story of his daughter's marriage had captured the press's attention. "Her nerve failed her, and she told me afterward. As a matter of self-protection I had my bedroom doors heavily bolted at night." There were times when his daughter was "gone for days in a ragged condition in the parks without food, and we passed many sleepless nights in anxiety."[65]

After she ran away from her father and his efforts to have her committed, Edith lived with her husband for nearly four years in a boardinghouse in Harlem, "not in prosperous circumstances," according to one reporter who checked up on her in 1896. In the fall of 1897, Edith Drake McGibney showed up on Wall Street, "standing as if dazed and confused in front of the United States Treasury Building." She was taken into police custody, and her older brother, Herbert Drake, eventually brought her home to their parents, who were both in their seventies by that point. Efforts to locate her husband were unsuccessful, and a survey of her neighbors in Harlem suggested she may have been living by herself for months.[66]

This time James Monroe Drake's efforts to have his daughter committed were successful. He got Charles Henry Truax, a state judge with Knickerbocker roots who was listed in Moses King's *Handbook of Notable New Yorkers*, to order that Edith be committed to the Middletown State Homeopathic Hospital for the Insane in Orange County, New York. Edith tried to run away again when the order came down, but police arrested her. On the morning of October 23, 1897, two doctors arrived at the precinct where she was being held and took her to their facility.[67]

Edith remained at the Middletown Hospital for at least three years. At some point in the fall of 1899, she briefly left the state-run facility to be cared for by doctors at a private sanitarium in Goshen, New York. Called the Interpines Sanitarium, it was similar, in some respects, to the Spring Hill House for Nervous Invalids where Gus Hemenway spent thirteen years, in that the doctor who ran it, Frederick Seward, believed that rest was the best treatment for nervous disorders.[68] Edith didn't seem to get much rest, however, during her brief stay at the Interpines. While she was there, she wrote a letter to the *New York World* in which she complained about Dr. Seward, claiming he had called her "scheming and erratic." "The mere fact of me being held under commitment would account for any disturbance of my mind," Edith insisted. By June 1900 she was back at the Middletown State Homeopathic Hospital for the Insane, listed in census records as one of the residents.[69]

By 1904—the year she penned her advice to America's housewives about how to keep their husbands happy—Edith was in Newport, Rhode Island. "A woman slightly under middle age, richly gowned, stopped a policeman on Bellevue avenue yesterday," several newspapers reported. She was "recognized by a chance pedestrian as Edith Drake McGibney." The woman "asked if there was a law to prevent her father from kidnapping her. She also spoke of a husband from whom she said she was anxious to be divorced." The news coverage reminded readers that "the Drake family was for years prominent in Newport society and entertained lavishly in Red Cross cottage, their luxurious home here." Edith wasn't staying at Red Cross Cottage, however; she was living in a "cheap boarding house in one of the poorest quarters of the city." Additionally, reporters had learned that "for some time she has been haunting the telegraph offices, claiming to be a newspaper correspondent and endeavoring to send dispatches."[70]

Edith was once again taken into police custody. The incident seems to have been the last straw for her eighty-one-year-old father, who arrived in Newport two days later, "white-haired, broken-hearted, and anxious."[71]

It was after this incident that Herbert and Bertha Drake arranged for their sister to be sent far away from the family. By June 1906 Edith was married to John Dudley Sargent and living with him on his homestead along Jackson Lake at the base of the Teton Mountains. For the next seven years, Herbert and Bertha would pay Jack to keep Edith out there—in a place that was as far away from the prying eyes of the press as one could ever hope to get in the early years of the twentieth century.[72]

6

The Cable Railway Grab

It was a Monday afternoon in early January when Robert Ray Hamilton and Evangeline Steele walked into the Market Street Methodist Episcopal Church in Paterson, New Jersey, and asked the pastor there to marry them. They didn't belong to the congregation. Eva had no formal religious affiliation at all, and Ray's religiosity, like that of all Hamiltons and Rays, was Anglican, not Methodist. When he went to worship services (which wasn't nearly often enough, according to his Aunt Nathalie), Ray attended the Church of the Holy Apostles in New York City. It was built on land his mother's parents had donated to the Episcopal Diocese of New York in the 1840s, after the historic Trinity parish where Alexander and Eliza Hamilton were buried was no longer big enough to serve the needs of New York's Episcopalians.[1]

Reverend Edson W. Burr later testified he had never met Ray and Eva before the couple walked into his office and asked him to marry them. He honored their request anyway, joining thirty-seven-year-old Robert Ray Hamilton and twenty-eight-year-old Evangeline Lydia Steele in matrimony on January 7, 1889. Burr's wife, Josephine, and his secretary, Harriett Hill, stood as witnesses. We are left to wonder whether Ray noticed or commented on the mild irony of the good reverend's last name. Burr was, in fact, related to the man who had killed Ray Hamilton's great-grandfather, but the connection was distant. Edson was descended from Benjamin Burr, who was born in England and settled in Connecticut sometime in the late 1630s. Aaron, the man who shot Alexander Hamilton in 1804, was descended from Jehu Burr, Benjamin's older brother.[2]

It's not clear why Ray and Eva chose to be married in Paterson. Neither of them lived there. Eva did own property in nearby Passaic, however; she'd purchased it the previous April, and Ray, who specialized in real estate law, had helped her file the paperwork. He'd also financed the purchase. During Eva's trial, Ray testified he'd given her $1,500 (the equivalent of more than $42,000 today) to acquire the land.[3]

He also testified he met his daughter, Beatrice Ray Hamilton, for the first time a day or two before he got married. She was born in early December in Elmira, New York. That was where Eva had gone for the final three months of her pregnancy. Before that Eva had spent the spring and summer months in England with a friend named Joshua Mann, who went by the nickname "Dotty." Ray told the court he and Eva left Beatrice Ray with Dotty Mann's mother, Anna Swinton, when they traveled to Paterson to be married.[4]

The wedding was definitely not something the couple had spent a lot of time planning. Ray's family didn't even find out about it until seven months later—just a few weeks, actually, before the stabbing in Atlantic City that made Eva Hamilton famous. "I heard last night from my Father of your marriage and that I am an uncle," Ray's younger brother, Schuyler Hamilton Jr., wrote on August 7, 1889. The letter was a departure from Young Schuyler's usual habits. As Ray's father observed, "Schuyler hates writing as most folks hate dying." But Ray's unexpected marriage at the age of thirty-eight (which is how old he was by the time his family found out about it) was a pretty big deal to his younger brother. Schuyler Jr. had been married for nearly thirteen years by that point; he had welcomed three children into the world, losing one shortly after her birth, and had a fourth child on the way. Ray's little brother was anxious to meet his new sister-in-law and niece, whom he was convinced "will find a tender spot in my heart for her." He encouraged Ray to send him photographs of Eva and Beatrice Ray. "I am glad to hear that the lady is handsome and the baby is sweet and pretty," Young Schuyler wrote, not anticipating that, in less than three weeks' time, his handsome new sister-in-law would grab a Mexican dagger that had belonged to his father and plunge it into the abdomen of an Irish wet nurse.[5]

"Your letter announcing Ray's marriage was a great surprise to me, and I delayed writing to you until you had returned [to New York]," Ray's aunt, Charlotte Hamilton, wrote to her brother on August 11, 1889. Schuyler Sr. had met Eva for the first time two weeks earlier, and he'd taken it upon himself to share the news of his son's marriage with the family. Charlotte was the sister who'd maintained a meaningful connection with Robert

P. Hamilton, the mysteriously ostracized son of John Church Hamilton who moved to Nicaragua and was disinherited by his father. Confronting awkward family situations and working to relieve the tension seems to have been a role Charlotte willingly assumed in the Hamilton family. Not long after she was in touch with Schuyler Sr. and had learned that he was "pleased" with Eva and the infant, she sent her brother some baby clothes she hoped he would pass along to Eva the next time he saw her. Charlotte would have sent the gift to Eva and Ray directly, but she didn't know what address to use. Ray had been moving around in recent months, spending a lot of time in California and New Jersey. "I do not understand why he should leave New York and reside elsewhere," Charlotte confided to her brother, "but when I see him in the autumn, I hope he will tell me all about it."[6]

Aunt Charlotte wasn't the only one who was confused by Ray's peregrinations. The torchbearer for the next generation of Hamiltons had been out of touch with all of his family members for many months before his father announced he'd gotten married. When the story of Mary Ann Donnelly's stabbing appeared in the newspapers on the morning of August 27, Ray's uncommunicativeness and his prolonged absence suddenly made a lot more sense. "Reading in today's paper the accounts of the tragic events in Atlantic City," his Aunt Nathalie wrote to him, "I understand your long silence. You must have been suffering horribly & I pity you with all my heart." Young Schuyler's wife, Gertrude, also dashed off a note to Ray on the day the story broke. "You always have my affection & sympathy," she assured her brother-in-law. "I hope it will not be long before you return to your own people . . . who have always loved you & have never had any thing but your welfare & happiness at heart."[7]

We can only guess at how the family understood Ray's behavior prior to August 27, 1889. After they knew about Eva—but before the young mother had stabbed her daughter's wet nurse—they may have concluded his silence was an effort to punish his father. Schuyler Hamilton Sr. had gotten married three years earlier after being a widower for nineteen years, to a woman who was several years younger than Ray. "It is not known whether the sons approve of the father's step," the *New York World* reported after the marriage was announced. Ray and his younger brother had not attended the wedding.[8]

The surviving correspondence between Schuyler Hamilton Sr. and his first-born son does suggest Louise Frances Allen Paine Cavanaugh Hamilton (Schuyler Sr. was her third husband . . .) was not one of Ray's favorite people. "My wife always feels hurt that you fail to mention her or send her some such thing as respects or kindly regards," the general wrote to his son on August 23, 1889.[9] Four days later the nation learned that Ray's young stepmother was not the most complicated female relationship he had in his life. His wife, Evangeline Steele, would prove to be far more complicated.

Before they learned he was married, Ray's family members may have thought his travels and silence had something to do with a difficult turn his political career took during the early weeks of 1889. The New York State House, where he served, was a cesspool of corruption, debased by kickbacks, graft, patronage, and the financial shenanigans of figures like William Tweed, the "boss" of Tammany Hall. Tammany was a private political club that got Democratic leaders elected to office by cultivating the loyalty of New York's large, expanding, and primarily Catholic immigrant population. In an age before Franklin Roosevelt's "New Deal," when there were few government-run programs to protect people from the effects of their poverty, a promise to give a man a job—or pay for his brother's funeral—could go a long way toward influencing that man's vote.[10]

"If I said that the legislature at Albany was a school of vice [and] a fountain of political debauchery . . . I could fill an entire volume with illustrations of my charges," the Anglo-Irish journalist E. L. Godkin wrote.[11] Godkin was the founder of the political magazine the *Nation*. He considered New York's assembly to be the most corrupt state legislature in the country—which was not an insignificant distinction, given that Godkin believed *all* state legislatures were dens of malfeasance and jobbery to a greater or lesser degree. The cause of this universal corruption, Godkin claimed, was the fact that elected officials received salaries in the United States, unlike in the United Kingdom, where lawmakers served without compensation, because it was a mark of distinction.

"In England, the non-payment of members of the legislature excludes poor men from it," Godkin observed in 1868. "The social distinction conferred by a seat in [Parliament] attracts rich men who are not accessible to pecuniary bribes." Thirty years later Godkin was still singing this jejune tune about the moral purity of the rich when he explained to British readers that "the legislatures [in America] are mainly composed of very poor men," and that "the result is that the country is filled with stories of scandals after every adjournment."[12]

New York's assembly was particularly vulnerable to corruption because there was so much money to be taken from businesses and people in New York City. There was money to be taken whenever a barkeep or builder wanted a license to sell liquor or construct a new tenement house. There was money to be taken whenever a telephone or cable car company wanted a right-of-way to construct the lines it needed for its communication or transportation services. Once poor men got themselves elected to state office, "the temptation to use their great power for the extortion of money from rich men . . . is great," E. L. Godkin asserted.[13] His conviction that poor people were the problem in politics may have been the reason Godkin's magazine singled out Robert Ray Hamilton for a backhanded compliment in 1888. The heir to Robert and Cornelia Ray's fortune, after all, didn't need to rely on graft to enjoy a bottle of fine wine every night and several memberships in exclusive hunt clubs.

Claiming to be relaying the thoughts of an attorney from New York City who'd caught Ray "enjoying one of his spells of ceiling study" (i.e., sleeping) during an important legislative session in Albany, the *Nation* quoted its unnamed source as saying, "Look at Mr. Hamilton and see what a man can do, just by being honest." According to the attorney, Ray wasn't a very good lawyer. "Why, if I went into court with the poorest case known to law and he had the best, I'd expect to beat him," the young attorney bragged. "Yet up here, he's a great man and has a big reputation . . . simply by being honest."[14]

It was faint praise, to be sure—but it was also true. The soft-spoken lawmaker from Manhattan's Eleventh District who came from a famous family and walked with a slight limp wasn't among the brightest attorneys practicing in Gilded Age New York. But he definitely had a reputation—in the Empire State and beyond—for being among the most honest.

"The *Evening Post* said you had been beaten, but I have not yet heard particulars," the Harvard historian Henry Adams wrote to his good friend

Henry Cabot Lodge in November 1881, after Lodge had lost his seat in Massachusetts's House of Representatives. "Every man who has looked on at the game has been struck by the remarkable way in which politics deteriorate the moral tone of everyone who mixes with them," the descendant of two U.S. presidents observed. Adams's friend should be grateful he'd lost; if he'd stayed in politics and managed somehow not to be infected by the corruption, impotence was the most Lodge could have hoped to achieve. "I could give a list as long as the Athenaeum Catalogue," Adams told him, "from my two brothers, John and Brooks, down to Willy Astor, Ham Fish, and Robert Ray Hamilton. They all try to be honest, and then are tripped up by the dishonest; or they try to be dishonest (i.e., 'practical politicians') and degrade their own natures."[15]

Ray was part of a cohort of young Republicans in New York's legislature known as the "Reform Seven." Tammany referred to them as a "sort of 'I-am-holier-than-thou' group." They included Ray's law partner, Hamilton Fish, who would serve twelve terms in the state assembly before moving on to the U.S. House of Representatives. There was a recent widower in the group who didn't stay in the assembly for very long, but he and Ray bonded over a shared enthusiasm for hunting and fishing. His name was Theodore Roosevelt. And the Reform Seven included Ernest Howard Crosby, an attorney and devout vegetarian who filled Roosevelt's seat in the assembly after T.R. briefly left politics following the death of his wife.[16]

The Reform Seven each had pet projects they took on in the 1880s, some more glamorous than others. Crosby was a big advocate for animal rights, and he often went after the streetcar companies in New York for the way they treated their horses. Teddy Roosevelt spent his brief stint in the New York Assembly focused on the problem of prostitution, specifically on the blind eye New York City's police officers frequently turned to it in exchange for cash payments. Ray's interests tended to be less sexy, but they were no less concerned with the problem of corruption. He put together a set of ethics rules that were meant to restrict the private financial dealings of men who served in state government. He introduced legislation that was designed to make it more difficult for men who had failed to graduate from dental school to receive a license to practice dentistry anyway. He also oversaw an investigation into a cost overrun on repairs to the governor's mansion. The project had cost $160,000 more than was budgeted for, an overrun of more than $4.5 million today. Ray's report stopped short of accusing New York's Democratic governor of outright fraud, but it did insist the overrun was "irregular and contrary to the spirit and purpose" of the original budget allocation.[17]

Robert Ray Hamilton and Ernest Howard Crosby frequently collaborated on legislative crusades. Two issues of particular interest fueled their partnership: they wanted the mayor of New York City to have what was known as "home rule" over the schools, police, firefighters, and sewage and transportation services in Manhattan and parts of the Bronx; and they wanted the entire state of New York to adopt what was known as the "Australian ballot" in all of its elections.[18]

Prior to the 1890s, most states didn't assume the costs of printing or distributing ballots. Ballots were printed by local chapters of the various political parties, often in the newspapers the political parties sponsored. Voters cut the ballots out of the paper and brought them to the polls. The ballots printed by a party contained the names of all of the party's candidates for every single office that was open during a particular election—and *only* the names of that party's candidates. This made it impossible for voters who used these ballots to split their tickets. The ballots were also printed in different colors, supposedly so illiterate voters could easily recognize which ballots supported the candidates from the party of their choice. These colors made it difficult, however, for voters to cast their ballots secretly, since everyone at the poll could see that a man was dropping a red ballot or a ballot with a bright pink border on it into the box. The lack of secrecy made it easier for party strongmen to ensure voters cast the ballots they'd been paid to cast.[19]

Ray Hamilton, Ernest Crosby, and other (mostly Republican) reformers wanted the state to assume responsibility for printing and distributing ballots. This idea, which was first adopted in the English-speaking world in 1857 in Southern Australia, was the only way to ensure that voters had the freedom to select the candidates they really wanted, because all of those candidates' names would be available to voters on a single ballot, and no one would be able to determine which candidates the voters had selected. Many powerful people in the United States had invested a lot of time and money into designing campaign strategies that relied upon the old way of printing and distributing ballots, however. The Australian ballot, therefore, didn't attract a lot of attention in the United States at first, although it had been adopted in England, Canada, Belgium, Luxenbourg, and Italy by 1875.[20]

The first American state to propose adopting the Australian ballot was Michigan, in 1885. The measure failed. Two years later Ray Hamilton proposed that New York adopt the Australian ballot. After some tweaking by Ernest Howard Crosby, his bill managed to pass. The legislation was vetoed by the state's Democratic governor, however, and advocates of ballot reform in New York were forced to settle for a compromise known as the "paster ballot." Political parties would still have the responsibility of printing and distributing ballots, but if voters wanted to, they could scratch out the name of any candidate on a party's ballot and paste in the name of an oppositional candidate instead. In this way voters could conceivably split their tickets, although they would appear to be casting a party ballot when they actually voted at the polls.[21]

It was a defeat for Robert Ray Hamilton, but it probably wasn't the defeat his family members blamed for his mysterious travels and absence from their lives (before they knew about Evangeline Steele, that is). The development they probably looked to was a defeat that had been personally embarrassing to the lawmaker. Not only had Ray hitched his wagon to a bill that failed but he'd also alienated many of his constituents and traditional allies in the process, and he'd abandoned his well-known commitment to home rule for New York City as a way to combat corruption.

Home rule is an issue that continues to vex New Yorkers. "Albany to City: Drop Dead" was the headline the *New York Times* gave its article on home rule in 2018. "Regardless of where you stand on banning plastic bags, regulating speeding cars near schools, or how to fix the subways," the *Times*'s urban affairs correspondent wrote, "most New York City residents are probably asking the same question: Why are those decisions made in Albany by the governor and the state Legislature, instead of in City Hall by the mayor and the City Council?"[22]

The answer has to do with a provision in New York's constitution known as "Article IX." Its origins lie in changes made to the constitution in 1894, shortly after Ray Hamilton's time in the legislature. Article IX gives local officials control over matters pertaining to "property, affairs or government" within the boundaries of their particular municipalities (provided they don't do anything that conflicts with state law), unless someone in Albany asserts that the matter is one touching upon a "substantial state interest." If that happens local leaders need the state's approval before they can proceed. As New York State's largest city by far—and its primary economic engine—New York City has often found its affairs identified by lawmakers as ones of "substantial state interest." Municipalities in New York, in other words, have had some version of home rule since 1894; in practice, however, officials in the Big Apple have not been able to make good on that promise to the extent that their colleagues in smaller cities and towns have.[23]

Prior to 1894 there was no guarantee of home rule in New York's state constitution. This meant there were things local leaders wanted to do in their hometowns that they couldn't do without the cooperation of lawmakers in Albany. It also meant there were things the state could do within the confines of a municipality, regardless of whether the people living there actually wanted the things to be done.

For many years state and local leaders rarely clashed. In the first half of the nineteenth century, there was no reason, really, for anyone in Albany to pay close attention to what was happening on the local level. Not until after the Civil War was there a "rich source of spoils" in Manhattan and Brooklyn for state lawmakers to tap. "Until the government organized large forces for police protection, fire protection and sanitation, it was of no great advantage, either financially or politically, to control the appointment or remuneration of city employees," one early twentieth-century legal scholar observed. "The great industrial expansion subsequent to the Civil War created legislative prizes beyond the dreams of an avaricious legislator a generation earlier."[24]

It's difficult for modern-day Americans to appreciate just how rapidly cities in the Northeast grew during the first few decades that followed the Civil War. Brooklyn's population was six times bigger in 1880 than it had been in 1850. In Philadelphia, the population ballooned from 112,000 to 847,000 residents in that same time. Almost all of this growth was a consequence of migration, some of it from the domestic countryside and most of it from abroad.[25]

The growth put pressure on municipal authorities to provide adequate housing and schools, along with sanitation, police, fire, and transportation services to thousands of new people every year. Recall that the decades following the Civil War had been a boom time for Washington County, Maine, in part because cities in the Northeast needed so much lumber to construct housing for their new residents. As E. L. Godkin rightly observed (even if his faith in rich people was naive), state lawmakers wanted a piece of the action that came with such a massive expansion of a city's infrastructure, especially if those lawmakers represented upstate districts where the populations were dwindling because everyone born there was moving to the Big City.

To that end lawmakers in Albany insisted on controlling the appointments to dozens of offices in New York City and Brooklyn that licensed, regulated, franchised, and disciplined all of the people and private companies working within the cities' public safety, health, housing, educational, and transportation sectors. Every one of these offices was an opportunity for some of the money circulating in New York City to find its way into the pocket of a legislator from Cooperstown or Oneonta.

Republican reformers like Robert Ray Hamilton and Ernest Howard Crosby assailed the state capital's control over local appointments in New York City. As the two men explained to a group of teetotaling Baptists who'd gathered at Delmonico's Restaurant in December 1887 (pointedly "eschewing the haggis and champagne," the *New York Times*'s reporter drolly noted), patronage was "an immoral system" that would continue to fester so long as the city's mayors did not have "the power of removing from office those who have betrayed their trust."[26]

One of the more notoriously corrupt offices in Gilded Age New York was the Rapid Transit Commission, created by state lawmakers in 1875 and tasked with modernizing New York City's antiquated transportation system. Throughout much of the nineteenth century, horse-drawn street cars were the primary way people got around New York. It was a messy, smelly, and inefficient system, and you didn't have to be a vegetarian like Ernest Howard Crosby to recognize it was also extremely cruel to the horses fated to be a part of it.[27]

A typical urban horse produces as much as thirty pounds of manure every single day. In 1880 Manhattan and Brooklyn had roughly 175,000 horses within their city limits, 22,000 of them just pulling streetcars. That meant sanitation workers had to remove more than two and a half tons of horse poop from the cities' streets every day, and on most days, the workers failed to keep up. When it rained ladies were forced to drag their hems though currents of liquid manure that streamed down the cities' streets; during dry spells residents often complained about the "pulverized horse dung" that made its way into their eyes, noses, and throats. Once a horse found itself hitched to an urban streetcar, it could look forward to a life expectancy of about two years—and given the way most draft horses were whipped and starved, death probably didn't come soon enough. Veterinarians recommended that urban horses be shod with rubber-padded shoes so that they wouldn't slip on the slick cobbles or macadam whenever it rained, but few transit companies bothered. A horse that faltered and injured itself was usually shot dead in the street, its body left there until sanitation workers got around to removing it. In 1880 alone workers hauled more than fifteen thousand dead horses off of Manhattan's streets.[28]

"I envy no man his gains obtained by the cruel sufferings of a dumb, speechless servant," Henry Bergh wrote to "Commodore" Cornelius Vanderbilt in 1868, less than two years after Bergh had founded the American Society for the Prevention of Cruelty to Animals. Vanderbilt's company had a franchise—approved by Albany—that allowed it to operate several of the horse-drawn rail routes in New York City. Bergh had recently discovered one of Vanderbilt's horses, still alive, covered in seeping sores and lying in an icy gutter.[29]

The move to steam-powered cable cars was a step in the right direction, hygienically and morally—at least according to Charles P. Shaw, an attorney who represented the New York Cable Railway Company. That company received a charter in 1884 from the Rapid Transit Commission to develop an extensive system of cable car routes for New York City, along the lines of what San Francisco and Chicago had adopted in 1873 and 1878, respectively. "No golden shower ever fell with greater profusion of benefits to this City than will be ensured by [the charter's] application," Shaw told a panel of judges in 1885, when the right of the Rapid Transit

Commission to award such a charter was challenged in court. The New York Cable Railway Company would provide the city's residents with "a practical system of intramural transit . . . at once elegant, commodious, adequate, cheap, noiseless, and in every way pleasant," and it would do so "without the *faeculent* voidings incident to the use of animal power."[30]

It was a ringing endorsement of a form of transportation technology that had already been embraced by cities not just in the United States, but around the world. Sydney, Australia; Beirut, Lebanon; Lisbon, Portugal; Edinburgh, Scotland; London, England; and Toronto, Canada, all had cable rail lines either in place or in the process of being built by 1885, when Charles Shaw made his case in court.[31] In New York, however, there was a formidable challenge to the prospect of bringing this technology to commuters: many wealthy New Yorkers who lived along the routes the New York Cable Railway Company planned to build didn't want their streets cluttered with loud and sometimes dangerous cable cars.

Their safety concerns weren't unfounded. Early on, especially, it was easier to get a horse to stop whenever a clueless pedestrian stepped in front of a moving streetcar than it was to unhook the car from a perpetually moving cable line. Nevertheless, these well-heeled New Yorkers had other, less altruistic motives. They didn't want their neighborhoods to become more accessible to the riffraff living downtown. They also didn't want to have to sell any of their property, which some of them would have to do in order for the new lines to be built.[32]

The Rapid Transit Commission gave the New York Cable Railway Company the right to build twenty-one new rail lines throughout the city without requiring the company to present its route maps to the public first. When the company's plans were finally revealed, the uproar among New York's elite residents was nearly instantaneous. Engineers wanted to cover Manhattan Island with seventy-six miles' worth of new rail, some of it running right through Central Park, which had only recently been completed, and some of it running through Gramercy Park, a charmingly treed and discreetly fenced oasis with two acres of carefully cultivated gardens and impeccably groomed crushed-stone paths that to this day is still private property, owned and maintained by the people living in the area around East Twentieth Street and Irving Place and accessible only to them.[33]

Wealthy New Yorkers in the late nineteenth century did exactly what they do today—they sued, alleging that the Rapid Transit Commission had violated the Transportation Act of 1884, which had been passed just a few months before the New York Cable Railway Company received its franchise. That law seemed to require transportation officials to get the permission of at least half of the people whose property would be affected by a new rail line before awarding a franchise to anyone. It took a few years, but New York's State Court of Appeals ultimately agreed with that interpretation of the law, and so the railway company's allies in the state legislature moved to change the law.[34] It was a shameless maneuver, led by lawmakers who were almost certainly in the pocket of the New York Cable Railway Company. Ray Hamilton's reform-minded partner, Ernest Howard Crosby, was outraged.

"Is it possible that the gentlemen have hid their heads in the sand like an ostrich and do not know what the world is saying about them?" Crosby asked rhetorically when two of his Tammany-tainted colleagues in the assembly, Milo Baker of Steuben County and George Greene of Orange County, endorsed a bill in May 1887 that would have completely legalized the New York Cable Railway Company's franchise. Crosby, it should be noted, was an ardent supporter of animal rights. There was no love lost between him and the horse-drawn rail companies that lawyers for the New York Cable Railway Company claimed (with some merit) were the real forces behind the opposition to the company's franchise. Ernest Howard Crosby would have gladly gotten rid of New York's horse-based transportation system. But he didn't want to do it in a way that seemed to reward corruption, and he definitely didn't want to do it in a way that involved having Albany shove one more thing down the throats of powerless New Yorkers.

"Mr. Greene has asked why we should not pass this bill," Crosby told his colleagues in the assembly. "I will give him the best reason in the world. The people of New York don't want it. . . . We don't want railroads in every street. We don't want them in Lexington-Avenue or Gramercy Park or in little narrow streets like Catherine-Street." New York City already had more than one hundred miles' worth of horse-drawn rail line, Crosby informed his colleagues, "and we are asked now to accept as a gift seventy or eighty miles more." A far better option would be the expansion of elevated train lines, a few of which had already been built in the city, or the development of an extensive network of underground rail, along the lines of what New York City did, eventually, adopt in the early twentieth century.[35]

Ernest Crosby's anger hit its mark. The bill that would have legalized the New York Cable Railway Company's charter from the Rapid Transit Commission failed.[36] New York City's elected leaders still didn't have the power to remove any Albany-appointed official who failed to respect the wishes of the city's residents. But when it came to the issue of cable cars, lawmakers in Albany had heard the voice of the people (the rich ones, at least) who lived on Manhattan Island.

Alas, the cable railway interests did not give up so easily. In December 1888—a year and a half after Ernest Howard Crosby had delivered his withering speech before the New York State Assembly; almost a year to the day after he and Robert Ray Hamilton had spoken to those teeto-taling Baptists at Delmonico's about the importance of home rule; and just three weeks before Ray Hamilton secretly married Evangeline Steele in Paterson, New Jersey—"the Cable Railway Grab came up again in the legislature," the *New York Times* reported. But this time, "to the aston-ishment of his constituents, Mr. Hamilton was earnest in the support of the bill."[37]

Not only did Ray support the bill, but he was also the one who intro-duced it. This new effort to legalize the Cable Railway Company's franchise was different from the earlier version, in that it required the company to kick a larger portion of its profits back to the city. New York's residents were not fooled by the change, however, particularly the ones who lived in Ray Hamilton's Murray Hill district, which would have been heavily altered by the company's plans. These constituents were astounded to learn that their representative suddenly supported an idea he had voted against just eighteen months earlier. They banded together and passed a resolution formally censuring Robert Ray Hamilton for having favored the interests of a private company "against those of the people of his district and of the city on matters of great importance."[38]

Ray's Republican colleagues were stunned, as well. They couldn't understand why he'd cast his lot with a bunch of rough-and-tumble Tammany Democrats. The original bill that would have legalized the company's charter had been introduced by John Shea, a Jesuit-trained, first-generation Irish American Democrat from the Fordham section of the Bronx. He hardly constituted the kind of company a person like Robert Ray Hamilton would normally keep. Shea's critics described him as "one of the most unscrupulous and dangerous men in the New York delegation." According to one former lawmaker, his "power to work harm" was held in check "only by the utter distrust with which the decent members of the assembly regard him." Yet, in December 1888, when a new proposal to revive the New York Cable Railway Company's franchise came up in the assembly, it was because Robert Ray Hamilton, who was known *specifically* for his decency, had joined Shea in introducing the bill.[39]

It was a strange move that alarmed and dismayed many of Ray's friends and political allies. Six years earlier, in 1882, Ray and several other young and idealistic attorneys "from the most prominent families of the city" had gathered in Teddy Roosevelt's living room to found an organization they called the "City Reform Club." Its members pledged to root out corruption in New York's government, independent of party.[40] The group published a yearly evaluation of every state lawmaker's record, and although most of the club's members were Republicans, the evaluators pledged to use the same standards for everyone when making their assessments.

In 1888, after Ray's effort to get New York to adopt the Australian ballot had failed, the City Reform Club praised him, calling him an "honest, conscientious, and vigilant representative" who was "one of the best New York City men in the Assembly." Less than two years later, following the Cable Railway Grab, the City Reform Club's evaluators turned on their founding member. They pronounced Ray's actions "worthy of the most disreputable member of the Assembly," and they chastised him for setting such a shockingly poor example for others. "When members of the legislature of Mr. Hamilton's education, character, and experience undertake to mislead a legislative body in regard to a measure of such importance," the evaluators wrote, "there is small cause for wonder that members of less reputation find it quite proper to follow so eminent a guide."[41]

The Cable Railway Grab was probably what Ray's father, brother, aunts, and sister-in-law looked to when trying to understand why he had been out of touch with them for so many months in 1889—at least until they learned about Eva, Nurse Donnelly, and Baby Beatrice Ray. After the fracas in Atlantic City, not only did Ray's family members believe they had a better understanding of his silence but his political allies in New York also thought they understood why he had mysteriously supported a bill that would have covered his district with miles of unwanted rail lines. "By many people to whom Mr. Hamilton's conduct in the Legislature last Winter was inexplicable, this revelation is regarded almost as a complete explanation," the *New York Times* reported a few days after Eva had stabbed Mary Ann Donnelly. Ray's "personal demeanor" had "undergone a change" that winter, according to his friends; he became "quieter than ever, inclined to melancholy, and seemed ever burdened by something that never left him." If the esteemed lawmaker who represented the next generation of Hamilton family values had gotten a young woman of modest (and possibly immoral) means pregnant, "the knowledge could have been brought to bear as a powerful means of influencing his action toward any measure," especially if the information had "become known to the men who control legislation at Albany."[42]

Mary Ann Donnelly survived. Following Eva's trial she took a job at a dime museum in lower Manhattan, earning $150 a week, according to the *New York World*—a little more than $4,200 today—regaling patrons with stories about not only the stabbing but also the relationship her employer had had with Evangeline Steele. Donnelly shared the stage with Steve Brodie, a "sort of half-witted fellow" who'd famously taken a dive off the Brooklyn Bridge three years earlier to win a bet. He was only the second person to try this stunt in the bridge's then-short history, and the first one to survive.

"What a commentary is this upon the morbid characteristics of human nature," the *New York World* judgmentally observed when informing its readers that Beatrice Ray Hamilton's wet nurse was "now a dime museum freak"—as if the paper's own coverage had had nothing to do with the popularity of an exhibit featuring a simple-minded bridge jumper and an Irish immigrant who'd had the good fortune to be stabbed by the wife of a Founding Father's great-grandson. The manager of the museum was "not to blame" for the lowbrow and sensationalist tone of the exhibit; he was just "a product of the public," the newspaper insisted. But the *World* was not about to accept responsibility, either. "Those who patronize dime museums and enjoy looking at Steve Brodies . . . Nurse Donnellys, and such creatures," the paper proclaimed, "are alone responsible."[43]

But if visitors to the Globe Museum thought Mary Ann Donnelly had something to say about Ray Hamilton's marriage, it was only because newspapers like the *New York World* had told them she did. "It seems that the nurse for some fancied grievance . . . betrayed her mistress and told Mr. Hamilton of the relations existing between his wife and a young man named 'Josh' Mann," the paper reported one day after Eva had attacked Mary Ann Donnelly. Mann was the person Eva had traveled to England with a few months before Beatrice Ray Hamilton was born. He went by the nickname "Dotty," and, according to the *New York World*, he and his mother, Anna Swinton, had been living near Ray and Eva in Atlantic City for at least a month before the young mother stabbed her daughter's wet nurse. The *World* told its readers that Dotty Mann was known to people along the boardwalk as Eva's "brother," and Mrs. Swinton was known to them as Baby Beatrice's "grandma."[44]

The *New York Times* told a different story, however. Its correspondent hadn't encountered anyone in Atlantic City who thought Dotty Mann was Eva's brother—most especially not Ray. According to the *Times*, Ray had had no idea who Mann was until a few days before the stabbing. He'd noticed him on the boardwalk in Atlantic City, and "remembering having seen him in New-York and at nearly every point in his six months' trip throughout the West," the lawmaker became determined to "keep a close watch on him." Ray hired a private investigator, and after that investigator told him Mann had "met Mrs. Hamilton at a beer garden," the lawmaker flew into a rage. "His indignation and terrible temper overcame him," the *New York Times* reported. "Grabbing [Eva] by the neck, he said, 'You are my wife and you remain here. Let Mann take care of himself.'"[45]

So who was Dotty Mann? Was he Eva's brother? Or was he Eva's friend? Did Ray learn something about him from Nurse Donnelly? Or did he learn something about him from a private investigator? To clear up the confusion, the *New York Evening World* sent an army of reporters to West Fifteenth Street in New York City, where Ray and Eva lived in a brownstone known as the "Marshall Flats." What the reporters discovered there only added to the confusion. They learned that Dotty Mann and Mrs. Swinton lived on the same street, in a building just a few doors down from Ray and Eva. A "strong and vicious pull" of the doorbell's cord at that building "brought a gray-haired old man, a short-cut-haired young man, a good-looking middle-aged woman [who was probably about thirty, judging from the way the *Evening World* applied that term to ladies], a younger woman and a baby to the door." The crew turned out to be a "mine of information."[46]

"I always knew that Mrs. Mann was a bad lot," the middle-aged woman volunteered about Eva, immediately raising the eyebrows of the reporters in the room. When one reporter gently corrected her by using the name "Mrs. Hamilton," the woman sniffed with obvious disregard for the distinction. "She went by the name of Mann," the woman insisted. "But Mann or Hamilton, she was a devil. The high and mighty ways of her and the curses she used were enough to provoke a saint."[47]

Eva's frequent use of profanity was confirmed by a woman the reporters encountered at the Marshall Flats. That building's janitor was a "taciturn colored man who was not disposed to say anything about his former tenants." While one of the reporters "kept him in conversation in the hallway," however, "another slipped down in the basement to see his wife." She knew all about Ray and Eva and was more than willing to talk.[48]

"While they lived here, I only knew them as Mr. and Mrs. Mann," the janitor's wife informed the *Evening World*—a revelation that at least explained why the paper's reporters had found the name "E.C. Mann, written in a feminine hand" on the mailbox associated with the Hamiltons' six-room flat. "Mr. Mann" was a "famous politician," in the woman's words, who "used to come down here from Albany on Fridays and remain until Monday mornings." Mrs. Mann was a woman to be avoided, if at all possible. "Her profanity was something terrible," the janitor's wife observed, "and she was a morphine fiend."[49]

On the days when Mr. Mann was in Albany, his wife was often visited by a man who was "stoop-shouldered," according to the janitor's wife. To her this man seemed much older than he was. "His head hung low," she told reporters, "as if he lived years ago and was only struggling through the world now." This description was a close match to the description of

Dotty Mann given by the good-looking middle-aged woman who lived down the street. She described him as a "quiet sort of man with round shoulders who always held his head down as if he were thinking about something." If there were any lingering doubts in the minds of the *Evening World*'s readers about who Eva's frequent visitor was, the newspaper provided them with one final observation from the janitor's wife: "I heard her call him 'Josh' two or three times," the woman recalled about Eva, before her husband came downstairs and gruffly chastised her for "for talking about what you know nothing about."[50]

Ray and Eva were both taken into custody on the day of the assault. They spent the night in separate cells at the Atlantic County jail in Hamilton Township, New Jersey, named (of course) for Ray's great-grandfather when it was created by an act of the state legislature in 1813. The next morning, when the couple appeared in court, Ray was released on a $600 bond. Eva was charged with felonious assault and returned to custody.[51]

The sheriff for Atlantic County brought a nurse in from a nearby hospital to watch Baby Beatrice during the night her parents spent in jail. The infant slept at Noll Cottage, the inn in Atlantic City where the stabbing took place. "The little one was cooing and grinning in great glee over the funny-looking nursing bottle she was given," a reporter from the *Philadelphia Times* relayed. News outlets in that city had taken a great interest in the Hamilton-Donnelly stabbing, given how many Philadelphians visited the South Jersey coast during the summer. The proprietress of Noll Cottage, Elizabeth Rupp, was herself from Philadelphia; she lived there during the off-season when she wasn't running the inn.[52]

It wasn't long before newspapers in New York and Pennsylvania weren't the only ones featuring stories about what Eva had done. Thanks to the Associated Press, readers in Decatur, Illinois; Nashville, Tennessee; Newton, Kansas; Sacramento, California; Kansas City, Missouri; Lincoln, Nebraska; Muscatine, Iowa; Madison, Wisconsin; Salt Lake City, Utah; El Paso, Texas; New Orleans, Louisiana; Raleigh, North Carolina; and Bismarck, North Dakota, were all able to read about what had happened in Atlantic City, New Jersey (just to give a *small* sampling of the communities that elected to run stories about Eva and Ray).[53]

Even as far away as Victoria, Australia, the scandal was interesting enough to attract the attention of news editors. "One of the most noted families in the United States is that of the Hamiltons," a New York–based correspondent for the *Melbourne Age* explained, as one might explain the mystique of the Kennedy family to a foreign audience today. After giving readers a primer on who Alexander Hamilton was, the writer went on to say Ray Hamilton had been "prominent in local politics for at least ten years" and "was a 'holy terror' whenever anything came up that had the smell of corruption about it" (except, of course, for the Cable Railway Grab, which the writer failed to note). For this reason it was a complete shock to everyone when it turned out "the incorruptible politician was married, or at all events was posing as the husband of a woman who, in a fit of passion, stabbed with a dagger, not with a prosaic meat knife, the nurse of her infant."[54]

The situation must have been terribly humiliating to Ray. After he got out of jail, he arranged for Elizabeth Rupp to bring his infant daughter to her home in Philadelphia. He'd hoped to do this without attracting the attention of the press, but word of Baby Beatrice's location soon got out. "There are a great many people coming to see Baby," Rupp wrote to Ray in frustration in early October, a few weeks after Eva had been convicted and sent to the state penitentiary in Trenton. "Yesterday, the manager of the dime museum was here & wanted to know if they could have the Baby & I referred him to you, as I do not think it a fit place for a baby."[55]

Ray was living in Manhattan by this point with his stepcousin, Charles Peabody. "I learned last night that you were staying at Charlie's & made up my mind to come around and see you this morning," his good friend and hunting companion Casimir de Rahm Moore wrote during the first week of Eva's trial. Moore's grandfather Clement Clarke Moore was the author of *A Visit from St. Nicholas* (known better to readers today as *The Night before Christmas*). "I think, however, that you have so much trouble on your mind now, that it might be a relief to enjoy all the quiet you can. I therefore write that you may know that I sympathize with you in your trouble, which I trust will soon be over."[56]

Moore's sentiments were echoed in dozens of letters Ray received from friends and colleagues, none whom knew he had gotten married until they read about the stabbing in the papers. "I have not been able to get your troubles out of my mind," U.S. representative Ira Davenport wrote on August 28, 1889. "I want you to know that you can count on me as one of those friends, of whom you will learn there are many, whom you can depend on, through evil as well as good."[57]

Fordham Morris told Ray he felt "confident that you intend & wish to do the honorable & gentlemanly thing" with regard to Eva. The lawmaker from Westchester County wasn't sure Ray ought to be following his instincts on this one, however. "You should call on your friends & best well wishers for advice," Morris cautioned his friend. "Should you in any way want a helping hand from me . . . that the world may see and know that you are not ostracized by your friends, command me."[58]

From his summer cottage in Warwick Neck, Rhode Island, U.S. senator Frank Hiscock wrote that he understood "words hardly render substantial aid." Nevertheless, he believed "they can at least convey the knowledge that you are not forgotten." Ray had a "great army of friends all over New York State," the senator assured him, and they were all convinced that "our friend Hamilton will not be overwhelmed by this misfortune."[59]

Curiously, these letters are not part of the Hamilton Family Papers in Columbia University's archives. The papers of Ray's paternal grandfather, John Church Hamilton, are at Columbia, as are those of the nation's first treasury secretary, who graduated from the school in 1778. The papers of Ray's father and brother (the two Schuylers), while less extensive, are at Columbia, as well. The files from Ray's law firm, however, and all of the letters he received following the stabbing in Atlantic City, are housed forty blocks south, at the New York Historical Society, in a collection that does not bear the Hamilton family name.

The collection supposedly contains the personal documents of Ray's maternal grandfather, Robert Ray, although there is very little pertaining to Robert Ray among these papers. The ephemera from the Nurse Donnelly scandal are by far the greatest part of the collection. It's as if the person who gave the papers to the historical society could not bear to destroy them—being a Hamilton, perhaps, and having a strong sense of the importance of letters like these to future generations' understanding of history. Clearly, however, the person did not want to make it easy for anyone to find them, and for many decades, the strategy he or she devised worked. Until the internet came along, and it became possible to type the name "Robert Ray Hamilton" into a search engine and have the New York Historical Society's description of the collection pop up, you had to already know Ray's papers were there, under his grandfather's last name, in order to find them. Before the internet their existence was basically forgotten.

Ray received letters from hundreds of people in the wake of the stabbing, most of whom he did not know. He'd become a "celebrity": a term that used to apply only to the condition of being celebrated or honored, as one would speak of the "celebrity" of a playwright like Shakespeare or a general like George Washington. In the mid-nineteenth century, however, around the time Ray was born in 1851, English-speaking writers started using the word to describe not the condition, but the people who found themselves in it—the men and women (and sometimes even children) who basked in the light of the press or had gotten caught in the media's snare.[60]

A few of the people who wrote to Ray had a passing acquaintance with him. They'd met him at a hotel or convention, perhaps, or been introduced to him at dinner by a mutual friend. "There is in my memory a most pleasant recollection of meeting you a year ago in Saratoga," John Roberts wrote to Ray on August 28, 1889. "This slight acquaintance with which I was privileged on that occasion would hardly give me the right to speak with you personally," he apologized. "I have, however, for a number of years had my eye upon you and have held you not only in highest esteem, but have given to you a large place in the affairs of the future."[61]

Roberts was the assistant editor of the *Northern Christian Advocate*, a newspaper published by the Methodist Episcopal Church. He wanted Ray to know that the scandal had had no impact on his estimation of the lawmaker. "Please do not disappoint us who have looked to you for the perfection of Hamiltonian superiority over circumstance," Roberts pleaded. "Remember that the world is kind to those who do not shrink, and that the Good Lord is with those who put their trust in him."[62]

Roberts's heartfelt words were probably very gratifying to Ray. They weren't typical, however, of the sentiments sent to him by people who didn't know him. The vast majority of strangers who wrote to Ray had some kind of agenda, and often that agenda involved money.

"Will you please help a poor orphan girl with a few dollars," Alice Lonsborough wrote from Lowell, Massachusetts, in a letter that was fairly typical of the ones asking for cash. "My parents are dead . . . I have no home & no one to help me. I work in one of the Cotton mills in Lowell. My pay is small. $3.36 per week."[63]

Lonsborough did little to convince Ray to give her money, other than point to the obvious. "I am in need of a hat, dress, shoes & cloak for the winter," she told him. "You are rich & have plenty to spare." A few people did attempt to offer Ray something in return for the money they sought, however. Captain Elmer Deakyne of Gladstone, New Jersey, suggested he and Ray buy an $8,000 steamer together that they could then rent to companies trading in the Chesapeake Bay. He predicted they could clear $2,000 each by the end of the first year. Deakyne's contribution to the partnership would have to be his familiarity with "coastal piloting," however, "as to be frank be with you, I have not the means to purchase a steamer."[64]

One unhappy woman wrote to Ray with a very different kind of investment opportunity. "Mary J. Webster," as she called herself, claimed she had been "raised by one of the best families in N.H." She and her husband had left New England several years earlier and moved to Florida, because her husband's uncle was "a prominent citizen here—has been governor of this state for four years." At first life was wonderful. But then Mary's husband started drinking. He'd "ruined" them financially and taken to abusing her. "I am almost disheartened and tired of life," Mary told Ray, "but if I could find a friend who could assist me with a thousand dollars, I could do quite a millinery business successfully."[65]

Mary may have been telling the truth about her entrepreneurial prospects. The ladies' millinery industry was booming in the late nineteenth century, and Florida was a fantastic place to be designing women's hats; it was where all the snowy egrets whose feathers adorned the most fashionable ladies' headgear could be found. The drastic depletion of the snowy egret population in Florida eventually led to the founding of the National Audubon Society, which began its life as the Massachusetts Audubon Society, after Gus Hemenway Jr.'s wife, Harriet, became concerned about what the hat industry was doing to the ibis and tern populations along Cape Cod.[66]

Mary J. Webster was looking for more than just a thousand dollars from Robert Ray Hamilton, however. "It is with much reservedness and hesitantness," she told him, "that I say I feel I could brighten and make your life happy as your wife." The lonely woman told Ray she was "gentle and agreeable in manners, honest, virtuous, and sensible." She had "traveled over Europe" and "always been accustomed to good, American society." Now, however, she was desperate. "Nothing on earth but my deplorable condition prompts me to do all in my power to release myself from the position I am so unfortunate to be bound to."[67]

Unlike Sally Hemenway or her granddaughter, Alice Sargent, Mary J. Webster didn't have the fortitude to get a divorce entirely on her own. "I could get a bill of divorcement at any time I should apply to the court for it," she assured Ray, but she didn't feel she could do so without "a helping hand." "I shall not give you my real name at present," the miserable woman told the disgraced lawmaker, but she promised him she was a "church-member of good standing in this place." She also promised she wasn't hard on the eyes. "I am a very nice looking lady," Mary told Ray, "tall, well developed, black hair, blue eyes, fair complexion, with color and expressive features—but express sorrow in every feature at present."[68]

One of Ray's admirers (there were more than thirty of them . . .) didn't need to describe herself to him. She included a photograph with her letter, one that had the name and address of the studio that produced it scratched out, since the admirer wished to remain anonymous, at least for the time being. "I again take the liberty of writing you since seeing your picture in today's Journal," the correspondent wrote in her second letter to Ray. She lamented the "dirty scheme" Eva had "dragged" him into and promised she would "devote my life to you . . . if you intend to give this woman up." "I feel jealous to think a woman who had led such a low life could and did get the chance of such a man as you," the writer confessed, clearly having read some of the unflattering profiles of Eva in the press. "When this is all over and you need the friendship and sympathy of some true, high-minded woman, you can privately put [a] personal [ad] in some Sunday's World, and I will send my address where to write and you can see me." She signed her letter, "Your Unknown Ardent Admirer."[69]

Three of the letters written by strangers came from people who shared Ray's last name. They all expressed regret about what had happened to the storied name, and one of them—a lonely, childless woman in her seventies who had recently lost her husband—sought to claim Ray as a relation. She opened her letter with a quote from Shakespeare's *Troilus and Cressida*: "One touch of nature makes the whole world kin."[70]

One rather bizarre writer told Ray she'd be able to "break [Eva's] temper," if he simply turned his wife over to her for a few months. "They call my power Woman Tamer," Renee E. Roi bragged. "I have taken wimmen [*sic*] that drank and no person could do anything with them, and in less than three months have them reformed & they have never been other than good, pure wimmen since." Madame Roi would not discuss her methods with Ray, other than to say they involved having Eva move into her home in Binghamton, New York. "Now Mr. Hamilton, don't think me a fraud. I am sincere & am as proud as can be & don't want the world to know my charms over a female," the self-described "French widow" wrote. Strangely, she then supplied Ray with her measurements: "I weigh about 139—measure 20 waist, shoulders 41—bust 36. Height five six." She was "healthy," she assured him, had "no habits of any kind," and had "a perfect knowledge of woman through & through."[71]

Renee Roi was one of nearly a dozen people who wrote to Ray, convinced that they knew how to reform individuals who'd gone astray. Most of these writers were interested in reforming Ray, however, rather than Eva. "Robert, is there a Ray of Hope, apart from Me," one writer asked, before providing the lawmaker with a list of verses from the Gospel of Matthew that seemed to apply to his situation. "Eternity. Where will you spend it? Hell or Heaven?" asked another, before going on to describe the two roads Ray's life could follow from that point forward: "The Narrow Road," which led to "Happiness, Life, and Eternal Glory," or "The Broad Road," which was "crowded by those who forsake God, who do iniquity and serve the devil."[72]

One writer describing herself as "a Sunday school girl" who wanted to "lead some brother to Jesus" sent Ray several pamphlets on Reformed theology. "If what the papers said was true, that your life was in danger and you were spared," she told him, "then perhaps God saved you for Himself as you may not have been ready to go if your Name was not written in God's Book of Life." The postmark on the writer's envelope indicated she lived in Portland, Maine. Her minister was not local, however. She was a follower of the Chicago-based evangelist Dwight L. Moody, who'd become an international sensation by that point, preaching to crowds as big as thirty thousand in the United States, Great Britain, and Canada.[73]

Moody began his evangelization efforts as a spokesman for the YMCA. He eventually went on to found his own school, the Moody Bible Institute, which continues to award theology degrees today. "Someone asked Mr. Moody where to get a good wife," the anonymous writer from Portland told Ray about one of the revivals she'd attended, "and he said in the church or Sunday School, not in [a] Theater or Ballroom." Closing out her letter, she exhorted Ray to "please come to Jesus" before telling him, "I will pray for you, as you may not have a praying mother."[74]

As amusing—or dismaying—as these dispatches are, they don't represent the vast majority of letters Ray received from strangers after his wife stabbed his daughter's wet nurse. Most of the letters that came to him were not about money or love or God or business—or some kind of mysterious boot camp for drunken and ill-tempered women. They were about one topic, over and over again: Ray's infant daughter, Beatrice Ray Hamilton. What was going to happen to her, now that her mother was in jail?

More than two hundred people wrote to Ray in the weeks following the stabbing, offering to take care of the little baby girl. Some of these people imagined they would offer her a foster family. She would remain Ray's daughter, but be raised in their homes for a fee. "I would take great care of the little Darling & guard it well if you would let me bring it to Canada," Sarah Nash wrote from Perry Station, Ontario. "If we can come to terms, I have no doubt but that I can begin my duties immediately."[75]

Sarah Crawford of Media, Pennsylvania, was more specific in her offer. "If you can give me $2,000, $1,000 to be placed at interest for [Beatrice] when she grows to be a Woman, $500 to pay for clothing & educating her, & the other $500 to be mine," she told Ray, "I should use every endeavor to raise her to be an honest, upright woman." Crawford did have one stipulation, however. "I do not want my husband to know her true name, lest he should become prejudiced and not love her as he should."[76]

A number of writers expressed concern about Beatrice Ray's notoriety. They worried that their lives would not be normal if word got out that the child living with them was the daughter of Robert and Eva Hamilton. "I would like her called by a totally different name during her stay with me," Margaret Schuyler explained when she offered to care for Ray's daughter while he attended his wife's trial. Mrs. G. Webster of Brooklyn, New York, told Ray she knew a couple who wanted to adopt his daughter but insisted that "they must positively be assured that no one would know except the one or two parties necessary & unless it could be so arranged, they would not consider it." This fear of unwanted publicity was echoed by Mrs. John C. Livingston, whose infant had died the previous May. She, too, wanted to adopt Beatrice Ray, but "I should not like my name to appear so that it could get into the papers . . . I know that I would be run to death by reporters!"[77]

All of the letters Ray received about his daughter conveyed some combination of loss and hope and professed great concern for the little girl's welfare—except for one. This one letter, like so many others, was anonymous, sent to Ray by "A Friend." The writer harbored no ill will toward Beatrice, of course—but she also made it clear the infant was not the person she was most concerned about. The person she was most concerned about was Ray.

"[I] refrain from giving you my name, as I keep a respectful home," the writer began. She wanted Ray to understand, however, that she was not entirely unknown to him. After reading about the incident in Atlantic City, she'd written to him "in justice to you as I know you and have opened my door for you on more than one occasion." The reason the writer knew Ray was that she knew Eva. The two of them were friends—or at the very least they had been friendly at one point in time. The writer knew Eva well enough to remember when Ray first began associating with her. "I think you are the person from Albany who came twice a week," she recalled. "You were tall and I think a little lame."

The writer wanted Ray to know Eva was not to be trusted. "She allways [sic] said her ambition was to get a hold on you," the writer told the lawmaker. "I could tell you of a man she was bleeding at the same time she was you, but my advice is get your hand out of the Lion's mouth as easy as you can."[78]

Beatrice, of course, was the way Eva had gotten her "hold" on Ray. The writer had something very important to tell Alexander Hamilton's great-grandson about that little girl, however: surprise, surprise—she wasn't his. Surprise, even greater surprise—she wasn't Eva's, either. "You say [Eva] is the mother of that child," the mysterious friend wrote. "But [Eva] never in her life had a child, for she told me the doctors have told her she could not have one as there is something the matter with her womb."[79]

If Ray stopped to think about it, the writer told him, he would realize this news made a great deal of sense. Eva had had a rather wild life before she met Robert Ray Hamilton—a truth the writer knew Ray was privy to. If Eva couldn't conceive, "the no. [number] of men she has been staying with would make the difference." "It would be an easy thing after a while for a woman to make a man believe she is 3 months gone," the writer continued, and to insist that "to hide her shame," her lover had to "send her away for 6 or 7 months, and then for her [to] return and bring a young baby back and say it was hers."[80]

This scenario was exactly what had happened in the run-up to Beatrice Ray's birth. Eva had left for England in late May, about six months before she claimed her daughter was born. She returned to the States in August and then spent the fall in Elmira, before returning to New York City in January with an infant she said had been born in December. After seeing that infant, Ray had decided to marry her.

Beatrice Ray Hamilton, it turned out, was not actually a Hamilton. Beatrice Ray Hamilton was not even a Steele. So then whose daughter was she? On this point the mysterious writer gave Ray no information. It wasn't hard to fathom, however, how a woman like Evangeline Steele could have gotten her hands on an infant to pawn off on Ray as his. When it came to a quandary like that, the monstrous poverty of the Gilded Age was more than able to provide.

Baby Waifs

The wheels of justice moved fast in the New Jersey Pine Barrens. It took Atlantic County prosecutors less than three weeks to convict Eva Hamilton. On September 19, 1889, she was sentenced to two years in prison, but in a scheme that was later investigated by the New Jersey State Senate, she managed to get a pardon from Governor Leon Abbett about a year into her sentence. Eva got the pardon after she dumped the attorney she'd been using and gave a $1,000 retainer (the equivalent of about $28,000 today) to William Heppenheimer, an attorney who'd been recommended to her by the governor himself. Conveniently, Heppenheimer also happened to be the newly elected speaker of the New Jersey Assembly and an officer in the state's Democratic Party.[1]

Getting her marriage to Robert Ray Hamilton annulled proved to be far more expensive and time-consuming than Eva's conviction and pardon combined. Eva didn't want the marriage annulled, of course. She insisted she loved her husband, who was bringing in close to $60,000 a year, between his annuity and law practice. But Ray wanted the marriage dissolved—especially after a bevy of embarrassing tidbits came to light during Eva's assault trial, including the fact that the mysterious "friend" who'd written to Ray about Beatrice Ray Hamilton was correct: the little girl was neither his nor Eva's biological daughter. She was a baby Eva had purchased in order to trick Ray into marrying her.[2]

The first hint that there might have been something unusual about Beatrice's origins surfaced before Eva's trial even began. A New York–based correspondent for the *Chicago Tribune* was intrigued by the figure of Mrs. Swinton, Josh Mann's mother. Several papers in New York and Philadelphia had said she was the widow of a paleontologist for the Smithsonian Institution named F. J. Swinton, but the *Tribune*'s correspondent wanted to know more. He (or possibly she) dug deeper and discovered that Anna Swinton was the daughter of a prominent brick manufacturer in Baltimore named Joshua Dryden. He'd served with distinction during the War of 1812, been a member of Baltimore's city council for several years, and died at the age of eighty-six in 1879.[3]

"Representing that she owned an interest in the estate of her father," the *Tribune* reported, Anna Swinton had "borrowed large sums of money" from several banks in Pennsylvania and Maryland in the mid-1880s. Unbeknownst to these banks, Swinton had already spent her entire share of her father's estate. In an effort to get out of debt, she ran "a confidence game in Philadelphia" for a number of years. She also "ran a baby farm during part of this time, and the place had a bad reputation."[4]

Baby farms were an artifact of a dark time in America's history when there were few orphanages and thousands of babies born every year to women who were too poor, too young, too sick, or too unmarried to care for them. Infant abandonment had been a problem in America's cities going all the way back to the colonial days. This was why Ray Hamilton's great-grandmother had "established the first private orphanage in New York City," as fans of Lin-Manuel Miranda's famous musical know. Eliza sings that line about the Orphan Asylum of New York at the end of *Hamilton*, in a song that asks audience members to consider "Who Lives, Who Dies, Who Tells Your Story."[5]

Originally located in Greenwich Village, the Orphan Asylum was funded entirely with private donations. It served a pressing need that was not being met by city and state lawmakers, since public health officials worried they would only encourage "habits of infidelity, immorality, and dissoluteness" among women if they took on the responsibility of caring for abandoned children.[6]

In the 1850s, however, with hundreds of desperately poor immigrants coming into New York every week, the practice of infant abandonment rapidly became a problem that was too pervasive, egregious, and tragic for elected leaders to ignore. In 1858 police officers turned 386 infants—more than 1 per day—over to officials at the New York City Almshouse, after they found the babies abandoned in various locations. The following year, they turned another 367 infants over to the facility for the same reason.[7]

Almshouses were terrible places for children, especially infants who had not yet built up immune systems to fight the diseases that ran rampant wherever poor people gathered. In 1868 one physician working in New York's almshouse claimed that the mortality rate among the abandoned infants he saw there had "always been eighty-five percent." The one exception to this grim rule was in 1866; that year, the doctor reported, "not an infant survived."[8]

When it came to pressuring lawmakers to do something about the situation, the taste the yellow press had for shocking and gruesome stories proved to be quite helpful. One reformer recalled in 1879 that "accounts of newborn infants found in open lots, the public docks, and not infrequently in the most thickly populated streets of our city" were what had finally pushed public health officials to act.[9] Alas, the solution these officials adopted was only slightly better than their previous policy of ignoring the problem altogether.

Their solution was to pay women to care for infants in their homes. Sometimes this worked out well. Elizabeth Rupp, the innkeeper in Atlantic City who cared for Beatrice Ray Hamilton after Eva stabbed Nurse Donnelly, was a part-time "baby farmer" in Philadelphia, just like Anna Swinton. When she wasn't managing the inn, Rupp was paid by the Commonwealth of Pennsylvania to take care of infants, and her reputation for providing this kind of care was good enough that Ray felt comfortable handing his "daughter" over to Rupp following Eva's arrest.[10]

Often, however, infants went missing once they were sent out to baby farms. Sometimes this was because they died of natural causes, and the women caring for them wanted to continue to collect payments from the state, so they didn't report the deaths. It's shocking, really, how poor the record-keeping on human lives was in the nineteenth century.

Other times the infants sent to baby farms died because of neglect. Life among the poor was a perpetual battle in the Gilded Age, and it was not uncommon for women—especially ones whose husbands had left them or died—to take infants into their homes and then use the money they got from the state to feed their own children. In one particularly notorious incident, a baby farmer in New York named Mary Cullough was found to have three filthy and nearly starved infants in her apartment when police raided the place after a man Mary worked for claimed she had stolen from him.[11]

"Murder of the Innocents" was the headline the *New York Tribune* gave the story about the raid. In a narrative that is disturbing and grave, even in the absence of judicious punctuation editing, readers learned that the babies Mary Cullough had in her charge "had not the strength to cry! Not even if pinched! They were motionless with exhaustion! Their limbs were shrunk to an inch diameter, and their hands looked like bird's claws!" One of the babies, "in the agonies of starvation, had sucked its arm to an unnatural shape! They had evidently been drugged! Their eyes were idiotic and ghastly!"[12]

The director of New York's almshouse insisted the *Tribune*'s coverage was unfair, since the infants brought to him were practically dead upon arrival. "We have many children brought here who are constitution-ally diseased," Washington Smith told a reporter for the *Tribune*. "Many of them are almost perfectly destroyed with scrofula or with syphilis from their parents; so that when you take them up into your hands you have nothing but a putrefying mass of sores."[13] Such children had little hope of surviving, regardless of where or to whom public health officials sent them.

Sometimes infants disappeared from baby farms not because they had starved or succumbed to illness, but because they'd been sold. Many infants never even made it to baby farms, because they weren't left in public places to be found by police; rather, they were sold by midwives or doctors shortly after they came out of the womb. The hundreds of letters Ray received from people looking to adopt Beatrice Ray testified to the fact that there was a real market for unwanted infants. In fact, Nellie Bly had taken a trip into the dark underworld of infant-trafficking about a year before Beatrice Ray Hamilton was born.

Bly's objective was "to find out what becomes of all the baby waifs" born in New York City. "Not the little ones who are cordially welcomed by proud parents, happy grandparents and a large circle of loving relatives," she explained, "but the many hundreds of babies whose coming is greeted with grief and whose unhappy mothers hide their lives in shame."[14]

She began by taking a look at the medical advertisements in her own newspaper, the *New York World*. Recall that many traditional newspapers refused to accept such ads, because the services the ads promoted were sometimes morally fraught. Finding several that were "suggestive," Bly arranged to visit a "Dr. Hawker" on West Thirteenth Street. She didn't tell her readers what it was, specifically, about the language in Hawker's ad that caught her eye, but she did explain that during the course of her investigation, she came to understand that "fully eight out of every ten [people] who advertised medicated, vapor, electric, or any sort of baths were in the habit of taking children for money."[15]

"The floor was nicely carpeted," Bly observed when describing Dr. Hawker's office to her readers. "The chairs, desk, and medicine case all helped to lend the air to the office of a well-to-do physician." The unconventional nature of Dr. Hawker's services soon became apparent, however, after Bly told him she had "a baby I want to dispose of." Without batting an eye, the doctor asked her how old the infant was and whether it was a boy or a girl.[16]

Bly was strangely unprepared for the question. She quickly told him the child was a girl who was almost six months old—making the rest of the details up as she went along, because "I hadn't thought of this before." Dr. Hawker was disappointed. He lamented the baby's age and gender, explaining it was easier to dispose of infants right after they'd been born and that girls were "hard to get rid of."

He asked Bly about the baby's complexion—a question that was almost certainly designed to determine if Bly had given birth to a mixed-race child. She told him the baby's skin tone was "neither dark nor fair." Dr. Hawker assured her that for a $25 fee, he could arrange to have the baby taken care of. "It is done daily," he told her, before adding that the transaction would be easier if she were willing to "make a full surrender." That meant "you give up the child and never know where it goes or anything more about it."[17]

Bly pressed Dr. Hawker to tell her what might become of her daughter if she elected to give the girl up. "After a mother makes full surrender of a babe," he informed her, "she has no way to tell what becomes of it." The baby "may be ill-treated or reared in the wrong manner," he admitted bluntly, but there wasn't much he could do to prevent that, as the people who purchased babies were usually loath to provide details about who they were. "I don't know as much about them as I do you at this moment," Dr. Hawker told the reporter who was quite deliberately obscuring her identity. "Many of the women come veiled, and we never even see their faces. If satisfied, they take the babe, pay their fee, jump into a carriage and drive no one knows where."[18]

For her next interview, Bly visited a woman named "Mrs. Conradsen" who lived on West Fifteenth Street. This time Bly pretended she was looking to get rid of a five-month-old boy. The price Mrs. Conradsen quoted her was considerably less than the one Dr. Hawker had given, confirming his assertion that boys were easier to dispose of. "It seems odd for you to keep the child for so long," the baby broker observed with what may have been a small amount of suspicion. "I always advertise them in about a day after they are born. I do not charge anything for placing babies when they are born here, but as yours was not, I will have to charge you $10 for my trouble."[19]

Mrs. Conradsen told Nellie Bly she was a doctor who ran a clinic for women in her home. The fact that Bly denied her the same honorific she gave to Dr. Hawker when constructing pseudonyms for all of her interview subjects says much about the battles female physicians still faced, nearly forty years after Elizabeth Blackwell became the first woman to graduate from a U.S. medical school in 1849. "My house is never empty. I have only one room unoccupied now," Mrs. Conradsen informed Bly. Among the services she offered her pregnant patients were "massages and electric baths," the latter being a terrifying-sounding therapy that is actually quite safe, if done correctly; it's used in Japan and parts of India today to treat a variety of rheumatic diseases and nervous system disorders.[20]

Mrs. Conradsen offered services to her female patients that were designed to bring them some degree of comfort. This fact suggests she was not the monster many journalists and public health officials depicted baby-brokers as being. To be sure, the black market in infants was densely populated with unscrupulous people whose sole purpose was to make money. It was also populated with trained medical profes-sionals, however—many of them women—who rightly saw themselves as helping people and saving lives when they distributed contraceptives, performed abortions, and yes, sometimes even sold babies.[21]

Still, Mrs. Conradsen had no idea why people wanted the babies she had to sell, and for that reason alone, Nellie Bly was not going to give her a sympathetic rendering on the pages of the *New York World*. "I have known women to get babies repeatedly, but I don't know what for," the physician told the reporter. She occasionally worked with baby farmers, and "no, I do not suppose the best care is taken of babies" she sent to such homes. "What can one expect of a woman who may have twelve to care for?" Mrs. Conradsen asked rhetorically. "When they die, they are buried as the woman's child, and no questions are asked."

Nellie Bly found it strange to think babies could just die, and no one would ever ask any questions. When she visited her next baby-seller, a midwife named "Mrs. Stone," she point-blank asked the woman what happened to infants who died in her care. "Is it difficult to obtain a burial permit?" Bly wanted to know. "No, it is very easy," Mrs. Stone answered. "We always retain a physician who never asks any questions, but writes out the burial permit according to our instructions. We never give the correct name, but assume any we wish."[22]

One such physician was a man named William Kemp, who played a very important role in Eva Hamilton's assault trial and in the marriage annulment lawsuit that followed. He'd been practicing medicine for more than twenty years by the time he met Evangeline Steele in New York in 1885. He testified under oath that when he met her, she'd introduced herself to him as "Mrs. Brill." By October 1888, however, he'd come to know her as "Mrs. Joshua Mann." In December 1888 Eva asked Dr. Kemp to make a house call. "I was called in professionally to attend a sick baby," the physician testified. "It was an adopted baby, she told me." Ray's attorney, Elihu Root, asked Kemp for more details about the infant's health as part of his effort to get Ray's marriage to Eva annulled. "It died subsequently," the doctor told him, "sometime about January 4, 1889."[23]

Three days later Ray Hamilton married Evangeline Steele in Paterson, New Jersey. At his wife's trial, Ray told the court he'd met his infant daughter for the first time a day or two before he and Eva were married— meaning Ray met Beatrice Ray Hamilton *after* the baby Dr. Kemp had attended had died.[24]

The *Chicago Tribune*'s article about Anna Swinton's baby farm came out on the morning of August 30, 1889. It was picked up later that afternoon by several newspapers in New York and Pennsylvania, and the following day, an anonymous woman identifying herself to Ray as "A Friend" put pen to paper and warned him that Eva wasn't able to conceive because there was "something the matter with her womb."[25]

"A Friend" must not have done a good job of hiding her identity. Perhaps it was her admission that she had hosted Ray a number of times in her home that gave it away—but, whatever the reason, Ray was able to figure out who she was. During the first week of September, he traveled to Reading, Pennsylvania, with a New York police officer named Thomas Byrnes. They checked into a hotel under assumed names, but a local reporter figured out who they were. That reporter published a story in Reading's newspaper that alleged Ray had met with a woman who gave him "evidence which convinced him that he was not the father of the child which his wife had palmed off upon him."[26]

The paper didn't identify the woman, other than to say "she is a near relative of a prominent manufacturer of this city."[27] Ray's letter-writer, however, was almost certainly Mary Bowman Jennings. We know this, because her husband, C. H. Jennings, wrote to Ray shortly after the story in the Reading newspaper was published. His letter is among the hundreds that someone tried to hide in a collection that bears Ray's maternal grandfather's name.

Cortez Hicks Jennings was a "multi-millionaire lumber king," according to his obituary from 1920. He was originally from Towanda, Pennsylvania, the same tiny town along the North Branch of the Susquehanna River where Evangeline Steele apprenticed as a milliner when she was fifteen years old. Jennings's wife, Mary Bowman, was from Towanda, as well. He was born in 1855, and she was born 1866—meaning one or both of them probably knew Eva, as Eva fell smack-dab in the middle, age-wise, between the husband and wife.[28]

"If my wife was the one who gave you the first information [about Eva and Beatrice]," Jennings wrote to Ray on September 9, 1889, "I would not have her retract that grand & brave deed, knowing what the result has been for you." Nevertheless, Jennings was deeply concerned his wife's identity might be discovered by the press. "There is not one man in a thousand, much less a woman, that would have dared to speak out at such a time as this," he insisted, enclosing a clipping from the Reading newspaper in the envelope with his letter. "I trust you will appreciate her brave deed and see that her honor and good name is [sic] most unquestionably protected."[29]

As Jennings knew, a reporter for the *New York Herald* had already gotten dangerously close to identifying his wife under slightly different circumstances. The journalist had done some investigating after Anna Swinton's background as a baby farmer came to light. He'd discovered that a mysterious woman named "Mrs. Jennings" had visited Swinton two or three times in December 1888 and January 1889. On one of those occasions, Swinton's landlord had come by to collect the rent and found Mrs. Jennings there with Swinton and an infant. "I heard the baby cry when I went upstairs," the landlord recalled. "That's the only way I ever knew that there was a baby there."[30]

C. H. Jennings included the *Herald*'s article with his letter to Ray, along with the clipping from the newspaper in Reading. He didn't deny that his wife knew Anna Swinton, but he also didn't tell Ray how Mary knew her. He said his wife had given Swinton $5 during the final days of 1888, by way of explaining her presence in Swinton's apartment. But he insisted the money had been a "loan" and that when his wife had visited Swinton to give her this loan, "at this call there was no baby."[31]

The story was almost certainly a lie. At her trial Eva refused to answer when she was asked whether she'd purchased Beatrice Ray Hamilton. She did tell the court, however, that Anna Swinton dabbled in the baby-selling business. "She told me a Mrs. Jennings wanted her to buy a baby," Eva testified, "that Mrs. Jennings offered her $500 for the right kind."[32]

According to the Census of 1900, Cortez Hicks Jennings and his wife had two children: a son named Paul, who was born in 1891, and a daughter named Sarah, who was born in 1888.[33] The year Sarah was born was the year Mary Jennings visited Anna Swinton at her apartment in New York City—where a crying baby may or may not have been present—and "loaned" her $5.

Beatrice Ray Hamilton wasn't just *a* baby Evangeline Steele purchased to trick Ray Hamilton into marrying her—she was the *fourth* baby. The first baby died a day or two before Ray and Eva were married. Dr. William Kemp signed that infant's death certificate, attributing her passing at ten days old to "maternal malnourishment." The certificate listed the child's name as "Alice Mann" and her parents' names as "George and Alice Mann." "Mann," of course, was the surname William Kemp said Eva had been using by the time he visited her apartment to examine the sick baby. "George" and "Alice" were the first names of Eva's brother and sister-in-law.[34]

One week after Ray and Eva were legally wed, then, the infant Ray said he'd met for the first time right before he got married died, as well. Ray was in Albany when it happened. This time a Dr. Charles Gilbert signed the death certificate. The infant's name was listed as "Ethel Parsons," and her parents were named as "Walter and Lydia Parsons." "Lydia" was Eva's middle name and the first name of her adoptive mother in Pennsylvania. "Walter Parsons" was the name of the man she told Nellie Bly she'd married in 1877, when she was sixteen years old.[35]

In a sworn statement, Dr. Gilbert claimed Eva and Mrs. Swinton had told him the baby was worth a great deal of money. They "urged him to do his utmost to save it," Gilbert's attorney told the court at Eva's trial. "Mrs. Swinton said a large moneyed estate depended upon its life, and it would be worth $100,000" if it lived.[36]

After she was arrested and charged with conspiring to steal from Ray, Anna Swinton told police Eva went into a panic when the second baby died. She and Swinton rushed out and spent $10 on a third baby while Ray was still in Albany. A day later, however, Eva decided the child's hair color was "too dreadfully different" from the hair color of the second baby who'd passed away—the one her new husband had already seen. "Ray will be sure to notice the difference between them," Eva reportedly told Mrs. Swinton. She sent Swinton out to return the baby and get a fourth one. In addition to having to pay another $10 to get that fourth baby, Swinton also had to give the midwife who'd sold her the third infant $5 to take the child back.[37]

There were two other doctors who played important roles in the trials that followed Eva's stabbing of Mary Ann Donnelly. One was a physician named Royal Wells Amidon who practiced in New York City. He testified that he was called to an apartment on West Thirteenth Street in January 1888—a full year before Ray and Eva were married—to treat a patient there named J. J. Mann. The patient had been "thrown from a carriage" a few years earlier, according to the doctor, and had been "mentally unstable" ever since. Amidon testified that Mann had two people caring for him during this visit. One was "a middle aged or rather old woman." The other (to use the doctor's annoyingly misplaced modifier) was a "woman whom I was introduced to as his wife." When Ray's attorney, Elihu Root, asked Amidon to clarify whether the woman who was introduced to him as Josh Mann's wife was there in the courtroom, the doctor pointed to Eva Hamilton and said, "At the time I saw her, her hair was of a different color, but I should say it was the same woman." When pressed for more details, Amidon explained that in January 1888, Eva's hair had been an "artificial color," and she had been "a blonde."[38]

The fourth physician who sealed Eva's fate was Dr. Burnett Morse. He practiced not in New York City, but in Elmira, the town just a few miles north of the Pennsylvania border where Eva had gone after she returned from Europe, having spent the summer there with Josh Mann. Elmira was where she claimed she'd given birth to Beatrice Ray Hamilton in December 1888. Morse told the court this claim was a "gigantic falsehood." He testified that when he treated Eva for indigestion in November 1888, she "was not in an interesting condition and it was impossible that she should have been delivered of a child." Morse also told the court that when Eva was his patient, he knew her and her summer traveling companion as "Mr. and Mrs. Mann."[39]

Needless to say, newspaper editors were giddy about these revelations. The *Brooklyn Daily Eagle* called Beatrice Ray a "Bogus Baby," while the *New York Times* referred to the revelations as a "Villainous Conspiracy." The *New York Tribune* delighted its readers with details of Anna Swinton's arrest, describing how police had followed her to a baby farm on West Twenty-Ninth Street, where they arrested her and then lay in wait for her son. Reportedly, Dotty Mann was "considerably under the influence of liquor" when police took him into custody. The *New York Evening World* called Eva a "Syren" and marveled that Ray, "who was not regarded as a 'marrying man'" and "was, even to his intimates, socially a quiet bachelor," had fallen for her scheme. Pulitzer's newspaper was the first to use the "B" word when describing the revelations, informing its readers that the "evidence of bigamy" presented at Eva's trial "is likely to free the Assemblyman from his pseudo wife."[40]

The substance and tone of the coverage in New York's papers was echoed in newspapers across the country. Readers in St. Paul, Minnesota, learned that Eva was a "Cyprian," a slang term for a prostitute. In Fort Worth, Texas, residents were told that Ray looked "pale and haggard" at Eva's trial and that he "gave his testimony in an almost inaudible voice." The *Salt Lake City Herald* reported that Ray was determined to "take the best care of the infant he supposed until now was his own." The paper told its Mormon readers that Alexander Hamilton's great-grandson believed he had an obligation to provide for the abandoned child. "What can I do?" he reportedly said to a friend. "I must take care of [the baby] for the present. It can't be thrown away in a field and left there."[41]

During the arraignment for Anna Swinton and Dotty Mann, reporters learned Ray had given Eva quite a bit of money before they were married. Swinton and Mann were arraigned at "the Tombs," a notorious prison and courthouse that had been built on top of a pond that served as New York's primary source of drinking water for nearly two centuries. The Collect Pond became dirty and polluted, thanks to all of the slaughterhouses and tanneries that sprang up around it. In 1811, therefore, city officials decided to drain it and fill it with dirt, eventually building a road on top of the channel that engineers constructed to empty the water from the Collect Pond into the Hudson River. Today, that east-west thoroughfare is known as "Canal Street."

Because the Collect Pond was spring-fed, the area remained muggy and mosquito-ridden even after it was drained. In 1838, when city officials were looking for a place to build a new prison, that's where they chose to put it, not having much respect for the idea that people who've been arrested are "innocent until proven guilty," a notion that wasn't enshrined in American jurisprudence until six years after Anna Swinton and Josh Mann were taken into custody.[42]

The detention center was dank, and it began to sink into the ground a few years after it was built. The Tombs was the prison where Herman Melville's character Bartleby the Scrivener went to die. Mark Twain had two of his characters end up there, as well, in the novel he wrote with

Charles Dudley Warner, *The Gilded Age: A Tale of Today*. When Charles Dickens visited the Tombs in 1842, the author of *Oliver Twist* was shocked to find something so draconian in a new and progressive country like the United States. "Such indecent and disgusting dungeons as these cells," he famously proclaimed, "would bring disgrace upon the most despotic empire in the world!"[43]

The fetid prison Charles Dickens encountered in 1842 was the same facility Robert Ray Hamilton reported to in September 1889, when the wealthy lawmaker from an esteemed—if somewhat battered—American family was called before a judge and asked to explain the nature of his relationship with a group of lowly and ignoble con artists. In a series of answers that were surprisingly laconic, given how justified Ray would have been in seeking the punishment of the people who'd manipulated him, Alexander Hamilton's great-grandson told Judge Edward Hogan he'd interacted with Anna Swinton just a handful of times before he and Eva traveled to southern New Jersey to leave the infant he thought was his daughter with her, so that the couple could continue on to Paterson to be married.

The first time Ray met Mrs. Swinton, he said, was in 1887. Eva had been the one who made the introduction. "I think I said nothing beyond, 'How do you do,'" Ray recalled of the meeting, offering no information about why Eva had introduced him to Swinton or where the introduction had taken place. The second time he met Dotty Mann's mother was in the summer of 1888, when Eva was in Europe with Dotty and supposedly pregnant with Ray's child. Swinton came by his office and asked him for $30 so she could pay her rent. "I told her that she had no claim upon me," Ray told the court, "and I invited her to leave my office."[44]

The lawmaker said he met Eva for the first time in 1885, in a house on West Forty-Third or Forty-Fourth Street—he couldn't remember which. He also couldn't remember the name of the person who owned the house or why he had been there in the first place. When Anna Swinton's lawyer asked him to describe the "character of the house," Assistant District Attorney William Jerome objected, and Ray was not required to answer. Newspapers would later claim Ray had met Eva at what was known as a "French ball." These were masked parties, typically "invitation only," at which wealthy New Yorkers—men and women alike—would mingle with scantily clad prostitutes and men dressed in drag. "Husbands and wives often go," one observer said of these balls (which Nellie Bly also did an exposé on), but "generally with somebody else's wives and husbands."[45]

Ray admitted he'd had "intimate relations" with Eva prior to December 1888, when Beatrice Ray Hamilton was born, and that these relations had gone on for "three or four years." He also told Judge Hogan, however, that he had seen Eva "not so often" during this time, since he spent every week in Albany, and that he didn't know where she lived—even though he'd been married to her for eight months and had just returned from spending two months with her in California.[46]

That Ray was being less than candid about the nature of his relationship with Eva seems obvious now, and it probably seemed obvious then to Judge Hogan. Ray, however, came from a class of Americans whose privacy enjoyed a certain degree of protection under the rules of decorum—rules that weren't always followed by the publishers of newspapers, but were highly respected by judges, who also benefited from them. Hogan, therefore, did not press Ray for more details about how he knew Eva.

Ray did tell the court that shortly after he met the woman who became his wife, he started giving her money. He said that at first, he gave Eva just a few hundred dollars here and there. Before long, however, the sums Ray was giving her exceeded $1,000. At one point he even took a check he'd received from a client for $3,250 (the equivalent of about $93,000 today) and endorsed it over to her. He estimated that, on average, he gave Eva about $6,000 a year before they were married; in the eight months since they'd become husband and wife, the amount he'd given her was "scarcely less than $10,000."[47]

Ray gave Eva $1,000 in the spring of 1888 so she could travel to Europe with Josh Mann, an individual the lawmaker said he didn't know very well, but whom he understood to be important to the woman who was going to give birth to his child. Shortly after Josh and Eva returned from Europe, Josh went missing. Ray told the court he and Eva visited Anna Swinton together in September, hoping she would be able to tell them where her son was. This visit meant Ray had seen Eva during the third trimester of her supposed pregnancy—yet the lawmaker still had no idea his companion was not actually with child.

When Swinton couldn't help them, Ray hired a private detective to track Josh down. That investigator eventually found him after speaking to the owners of several liquor stores on Sixth Avenue that Josh was known to frequent. "Eva was anxious about him and seemed much worried," Ray told the court, by way explaining his decision to hire the detective.[48] After Josh was found, he and Eva absconded to Elmira.

Ray didn't see Dotty Mann again, then, until August 1889, when the lawmaker and his bride returned from California and took an apartment in Atlantic City. Josh was there in the oceanside town with Mrs. Swinton, and he and Ray had several conversations with one another—meaning the New York Times had gotten the story wrong when it reported Ray had hired a private investigator to find out who Josh Mann was. "At Atlantic City, he talked of the child as mine," Ray told the court about the conversations he'd had with Dotty Mann. Anna Swinton spoke of Beatrice Ray as his child, too. "She said I ought to be proud of such a nice baby and so on," Ray recalled.[49]

At the arraignment Inspector Byrnes told the court about the evidence he'd gathered in Reading, Pennsylvania, from the anonymous woman who wrote to Ray and was probably Mary Jennings. The transcript of his testimony has not survived, but according to the Brooklyn Daily Eagle, Byrnes told Judge Hogan the evidence was "strong."

The paper also reported that Byrnes told the judge some tidbits Josh Mann had shared with him after he was arrested. According to Byrnes, Josh claimed Eva had shown him a copy of Ray's will, "leaving all of the property to the daughter, with Eva to have sole charge of it until the daughter came of age." Eva had also made a rather disturbing remark to Josh while she had the will in her hand. "Now Dotty, you know Ray is very reckless; he got thrown from his horse once and broke his leg," Inspector Byrnes told Judge Hogan that Josh Mann had told him Eva had said. (Suffice it to say that even in 1889, this testimony would have been thrown out as "hearsay," had the proceedings been an actual trial. They weren't a trial, however; they were an arraignment.) "Something is liable to happen to him any time. If he dies, I will marry you and we will have his money."[50]

Inspector Byrnes told the court Anna Swinton had confessed to having purchased the second, third, and fourth babies for Eva. "The first one . . . she claimed to believe was the child of a friend of Ray's who had got a friend in trouble," Byrnes explained. Swinton brought police to the baby farms where she'd purchased the three other infants, and Byrnes said he was confident they'd identified the woman who sold Swinton "the last child, the present Beatrice Hamilton."

There was one other element to Swinton's confession that Byrnes wanted the court to know. "Mrs. Swinton also said to me . . . 'If you get me talking, I'll make a big scandal,'" he told the judge in front of Ray. "'If Ray Hamilton prosecutes me, I'll make it hot for him.'" ADA Jerome objected to this testimony, and Byrnes was "not allowed to tell what more she said on this point," according to the *Daily Eagle*. The paper's correspondent pressed the officer for more information when he left the courtroom, but Byrnes "would not tell the reporter afterward."[51]

As it turned out, Anna Swinton didn't have to make good on her threat, since Ray dropped the larceny charges he'd filed against her and her son. He also declined to press charges against Eva—suggesting, again, that there may have been more to the story than Ray was letting on. He paid a doctor in Atlantic City to give Mary Ann Donnelly his undivided attention, so that the nurse would be sure to survive, and Eva would not be charged with murder. "It was your request that I should give her special attention and do everything possible to save her life, as it was a very serious case, and much depended upon her recovery," Dr. George Crosby reminded Ray in October 1889, when he sent the lawmaker a bill for $310.[52]

Ray was also very supportive of Eva during her trial. His testimony was "strongly in his wife's favor at almost every point," according to newspaper accounts. It was Nurse Donnelly, Ray insisted, who had been the aggressor, not his wife. "She used fearfully abusive language," he told the court. "She said, 'You—; God—you. I'll kill you. Let me at her!'" Ray admitted to the court that on the morning of the stabbing, he and his wife had been arguing because Ray wanted a divorce. He didn't explain why he wanted his marriage to end, but he did testify he had offered to give his wife $5,000 a year in alimony for the rest of her life. She'd refused the offer—not because she wanted to preserve the marriage, but because she wanted more.[53]

In retrospect Eva probably should have taken Ray up on his offer. The evidence brought to light during her trial strongly suggested the entire marriage was a fraud. Ray might be able to get out of it without having to pay her a dime. The day after Eva was convicted of felonious assault, Ray filed the paperwork to have his marriage annulled. Those proceedings were the only legal action he ever took against Evangeline Steele, however, in spite of the embarrassing and expensive nature of the con she had pulled on him.[54]

Ray wanted to get away from all of it as fast he could. He resigned from his position in the assembly. The Cable Railway Grab had already alienated many of his constituents, and the developments with Eva seemed to signal the end of his political career.[55] He still had a substantial income from his law practice with Hamilton Fish—but Ray also had a $40,000 annuity from his maternal grandfather, along with a number of properties he co-owned and rented out with his aunt, Nathalie Ray Baylies. Ray didn't *need* to work, in other words—and he also didn't need to stay in New York.

The summer after he'd graduated from law school in 1874, Ray visited his friend George Bird Grinnell in the Montana Territory. Grinnell was working as a zoologist on a government-funded expedition into Yellowstone, which, two years earlier, had become America's first national park. Grinnell developed a deep conservationist ethos as a consequence of that experience and went on to edit the outdoor magazine *Forest and Stream*, which aimed to get people out of the cities and into the woods, so that they would develop an understanding of why natural landscapes like Yellowstone's needed to be protected.[56]

Hunting—regulated and restricted, of course—became a strategic component of Grinnell's efforts to get Americans to care about the American West. It was a strategy his friend, Ray Hamilton, embraced, as well. By the time the scandal with Eva broke, fifteen years after that first trip he made to Montana, Ray had become the owner of an extensive gun collection, three professionally trained bird dogs, and several memberships in exclusive hunt clubs.[57]

After Eva went to prison, the disgraced lawmaker decided he wanted to return to the America West. Late fall wasn't a good time to be heading to the Rockies or Great Plains, so he stayed in New York with his friend and stepcousin, Charles Peabody, until the following spring. When Ray finally did head west, however, he did not return to Montana. That state was filling up fast with people from the East Coast, and much like John Dudley Sargent, Robert Ray Hamilton wanted to leave the East Coast behind.

Between 1880 and 1890, Montana's population increased by nearly 240 percent. The same edition of the *New York Herald* that told readers Anna Swinton was being kept in the Tombs had also featured an article about all the "land grabbing in Montana" that was happening in anticipation of the completion of the St. Paul–Manitoba Railway Line (later known as the "Great Northern"). The railroad was "offering the inducement of rapid settlement" in Big Sky Country, and Ray didn't want to be anywhere near it.[58]

The destination he chose, therefore, was not Montana, but Wyoming—a brand-new state where the White population was less than half the size of Montana's, and where the number of women (a group Ray probably wasn't feeling terribly charitable toward . . .) was so small, men in the territorial legislature had actually given them an unrestricted right to vote and hold office, the hope being that the ability to have civil rights would encourage more women to migrate to the state.

There were fewer than sixty-three thousand people living in Wyoming in 1890. That meant the ninety-eight thousand square miles that made up the Equality State had nine thousand fewer people living within them than did the sixty square blocks that made up Ray Hamilton's assembly district in the Murray Hill section of Manhattan.[59] Wyoming seemed like the perfect place for a man's humiliations to be forgotten.

This collectible postcard was given to consumers "compliments of the Warren Thread Company, Worcester, Mass.," ca. 1890. Evelyn Way Kendall Collection, Smithsonian National Air and Space Museum (NASM 9A14616).

John Dudley Sargent wrote the words "Compliments of Hamilton + Sargent"
on the back of a photograph of his ranch in 1891. He planned to turn the
photograph into postcards. American Heritage Center, University of Wyoming.

Robert Ray Hamilton during his first year in the New York
State Assembly, 1882. Rijksmuseum, Amsterdam.

This photo of Evangeline Steele appeared in newspapers
across the country after she died in 1904. It is the only known
photo of Eva. *Butte Miner*, December 15, 1904.

Jack Sargent's maternal uncle, Augustus Hemenway Sr.
He was thought by many people to be the richest man in America
when he died in 1876. Phillips Library, Peabody Essex Museum.

John Dudley Sargent and his second wife, Edith Drake, shortly after they were married in 1906. American Heritage Center, University of Wyoming.

Enrico Pranzini's mugshot following his arrest in March 1887. Wikimedia Commons, Préfecture de Police, Paris, Identité Judiciaire.

Daniel C. Nowlin was one of several settlers in Jackson
who traveled to Marymere in the spring of 1897. D. C.
Nowlin Collection, Wyoming State Archives.

Jack Sargent's arraignment in 1899, after he was arrested for murder. His daughter, Catherine Winthrop Sargent, sits on his lap. American Heritage Center, University of Wyoming.

The back of a photograph of Catherine Winthrop Sargent, where
Jack noted she had "Her father's features" and "Her gt. grandfather's
insight of human nature." Courtesy of Celeste Havener.

Edith, wearing her hat, poses with engineers from the Minidoka dam
project in 1911. American Heritage Center, University of Wyoming.

Edith's long-dead "violin tree" has been propped up by
people managing the biological research center on what
used to be Jack Sargent's homestead. Author photo.

The view in 2018 from Edith's violin tree. Author photo.

Monument on the Hamilton Family plot in Green-Wood Cemetery,
Brooklyn. Ray is not actually buried here. Author photo.

Hamilton Fountain in Riverside Park, New York City. Author photo.

```
een lynched by a mob
His (meaning thereby
rgent, a prominent
s Foundry.
y this plaintiff)
  intimate companion XXX
 was a mystery in the
ing thereby this plain-
n) that was never sat-
eby that this plain-
his actual relations
```

Stenographer's rendering of the article that prompted
Jack to sue the *New York Herald*—with three Xs next to the
phrase "intimate companion." Author photo.

Catherine Winthrop Sargent in 1960 with her daughter, Cathy Fessel,
who shared her mother's titian hair color. Courtesy of Bill Fessel.

Katharine Beatrice Hamilton Costello, standing next to her daughter,
Beatrice "Mike" Costello Seacrest, on Mike's wedding day in 1944.
Courtesy of Kent Hamilton Seacrest and Ann Seacrest.

8

Cowpunching

John Dudley Sargent was seventeen years old when he got off the train in Cheyenne. Ten years younger than Ray Hamilton, he had neither the lawmaker's wealth nor his education when he arrived in Wyoming—but he also didn't have Ray's public humiliation. The humiliation Jack felt was personal, confined to the realm of his wealthy and historically significant family. He went west not because he was trying to hide from the press, but because he was tired of being sidelined and passed around by family members, especially his father, whose return to Machias after being gone for fourteen years may have been the biggest reason Jack decided to leave New England.[1] The circumstances compelling Jack's migration were different from those of Ray, but both men came to Wyoming with the same hope: they wanted to be liberated from their East Coast burdens by the freedom the West seemed to offer.

The southeastern corner of Wyoming Jack initially migrated to was still a frontier in 1879, a transitional zone of settlement, far away from the dense populations and technological and commercial infrastructures that were then the marks of modernity, but also connected to those infrastructures in important ways, making the frontier different from the vast swath of wilderness that lay west of it, where seminomadic tribes like the Bannock, Crow, and Shoshone Indians lived and the trappings of the modern age had not yet reached.

Cheyenne was the territorial capital when Jack arrived. The town had been founded in 1867 by the Union Pacific Railroad, back when the region was still a part of the Dakota Territory. Eight months after the UP opened its offices in Cheyenne, Congress decided to create the Wyoming Territory out of land that had previously been grouped with the Dakota, Utah, and Idaho territories. The Transcontinental Railroad promised to improve transportation by leaps and bounds, but in 1868 Yankton, the capital of

Dakota, was still unconnected to that railroad, and it was slightly more than five hundred miles away from Cheyenne. The area that became the Wyoming Territory had fewer than nine thousand non-Indigenous people living within it in 1870, two-thirds of them scattered in tent cities and mining towns like Laramie and South Pass City that were even farther away from Yankton than Cheyenne. In an "uncivilized" territory, famous—still—for its lawlessness, it just didn't make sense to have lawmakers be so far away from the people they were supposed to govern.[2]

By the time Jack arrived, Cheyenne had nearly 3,500 residents and had eclipsed Yankton in size. Not only that, but eight of the town's residents were millionaires, giving Cheyenne one of the highest per capita incomes in the world in 1880.[3] The Union Pacific Railroad was important to the town's growth and economic success, but it wasn't the only source of Cheyenne's wealth. The other source was Americans' gustatory sensibilities—and the fact that they had developed a taste for beef.

As with so much of what happened in the 1860s and 1870s, the trend could be traced to the recent Civil War. Newspaper accounts of hogs that had rooted through battlefields across the South, consuming human remains, soured many Americans on pork, the meat that had previously dominated the plates of those who could regularly afford to eat animal protein. Thanks to savvy advertisers, urbanites were getting used to the idea of eating beef that had been slaughtered in the Midwest and shipped in refrigerated boxcars to cities in the Northeast. The thick-cut, marbled ribeye we now call a "Delmonico steak" was popularized in the 1870s by the restaurant that would later hold a dinner for J. P. Morgan and Jay Gould on the same night Ray Hamilton and Teddy Roosevelt gathered across the street to celebrate the centennial of the British army's departure from New York. The animals that became Delmonico steaks were slaughtered in Chicago or St. Louis and butchered in New York or Boston, but they were born in Texas and fattened in Montana and Wyoming. And in 1872 Cheyenne became home to the trade group that represented the interests of the men who profited from their lives.[4]

The Wyoming Stock Growers' Association was founded by a collection of cattlemen who wanted to press their industry's interests with federal and territorial lawmakers. Cheyenne was where they had their headquarters, not only because it was the capital of Wyoming but also because it was near the Goodnight-Loving Trail that cowboys used to drive wild "longhorn" cattle up from western Texas and into the plains of eastern Wyoming and Montana. There the animals could spend the summer months getting fat off of forty million acres of buffalo grass, blue grama, and western wheatgrass that had become available for open-range ranching, after the Blackfeet, Crows, Arapahos, and Cheyennes were forced onto reservations by the federal government in the late 1860s.[5]

Longhorns were the wild descendants of cattle that had been brought to the New World by the Spanish in the sixteenth and seventeenth centuries. Their population had boomed in Texas during the 1860s, when the settlers who normally would have captured them were off fighting the Civil War. If you could wrangle a longhorn in Texas, he was yours to keep for free. If you could get him up to Montana or Wyoming to graze cheaply on federal land, he became worth $4 to you (or about $110 in today's money). If you could then get him to Chicago or St. Louis to be slaughtered, and to New York or Boston to be butchered and cooked, that animal from Texas you'd spent no money to claim and little money to feed had a value of $40 to $50, which in 1879 was the equivalent of between $1,100 and $1,300 today.[6]

For the massive money-making potential of the longhorns in Texas to be realized, however, the cattlemen arranging for them to be captured needed to know they would always have free access to what had been "Indian territory" for grazing, and that the railroads they needed to get their fattened cattle to slaughterhouses and markets in the East would always be available for their use. They wanted to know that rustlers would be pursued and punished (remember poor George "Big Nose" Parrot, who was turned into shoes). And the men who were invested in the biggest cattle operations also wanted to know that competition from small-time operators for access to Wyoming's grass and water would be kept to a minimum. This was why the owners of the big cattle companies formed the Wyoming Stock Growers Association and made Cheyenne their headquarters.[7] The location gave them access to lawmakers not only in Wyoming but also in Washington DC.

Cheyenne was right on the line the U.S. Census Bureau still believed separated the "civilized" part of the United States from the part that was "wilderness," and the town leaned heavily toward the civilized side of that line. When Jack Sargent arrived, Cheyenne had wooden sidewalks, solid brick buildings, six churches, two daily newspapers, and a school. It also had a police department and a train depot. Thanks to that depot, a cattleman who needed to meet with a senator or congressman could get to Washington DC in fewer than four days. Fifteen years earlier that journey would have required three uncomfortable weeks in a stagecoach, just to get to a train depot in St. Louis.[8]

By the time the Wyoming Stock Growers Association was founded in 1872, cattlemen could also send messages to anyone in the District of Columbia in a matter of minutes, thanks to the transcontinental telegraph, to which Cheyenne had been connected since 1867. The year before John Dudley Sargent arrived, Wyoming's capital even got its first telephone line. "Cheyenne has gone crazy over its telephone," J. W. Hayford, editor of the *Laramie Sentinel*, jealously remarked in February 1878. "Mr. Arnett, proprietor of the telephone at Cheyenne, proposes to place our city in telephonic communication with the Magic City," Hayford told his readers. "Then the Cheyenne boys can talk to their Laramie girls without paying car fare."[9]

Hayford's sarcasm belied his deep interest in the new technology. When Laramie finally got its first telephone line in 1881, J. W. Hayford made sure it went straight from the post office to his house. It would be another quarter century before the technology was good enough to carry the human voice from Wyoming to New York or the District of Columbia. Until 1906 the thousand miles that lay between Cheyenne and Chicago were about as far as the human voice could travel without being overwhelmed by static.[10] Still, the territorial capital that newspaper editors like J. W. Hayford called the "Magic City of the Plains" was not a backwater in 1879, when Jack Sargent arrived. It existed on the edge of the wilderness, but it was also strongly connected to the East Coast, where names like "Hamilton" and "Sargent" had a lot of power—and sometimes carried a lot of baggage.

Jack didn't stay in Cheyenne for long. Nearly a century and a half after he left New England for the first time, his grandson Bill Fessel recalled hearing stories about the years Jack spent working as a cowboy before he got married and had a family. Fessel heard these stories from his mother, Catherine Winthrop Sargent, the daughter Jack named after his distant Puritan ancestor. The second-youngest of Jack's five children, she was the one who spent the most time with him, living with her father on his ranch in Wyoming for several years after all of her siblings were gone. "She always called him 'John Sargent,' never 'my father' or 'your grandfather,'" Fessel recalled in 2018 from his home in Haines, Oregon. "He told her a bit about his early years in the West, driving cattle from Ogallala, Nebraska, to Tongue River, Wyoming. From what I understand, that experience really prepared John Sargent for his life in the Tetons."[11]

The cattle Jack "punched" would have been driven to Ogallala from southern Texas, along a trail cowboys started using in 1876 known as the "Great Western." Ogallala, Nebraska, was a railroad town on the South Platte River, about thirty miles northeast of the Colorado border. It had 114 residents in 1880, the first full year Jack spent in the American West. The town was known to many as the "Gomorrah of the Cattle Trail," thanks to the entertainment options it offered the lonely cowboys who regularly passed through it. According to writer Andy Adams, whose 1903 novel, *The Log of a Cowboy*, is set along the same route Jack would have followed from Nebraska to Tongue River, Ogallala had "half a hundred buildings in it" in 1882, and all of them were "without a church spire."[12]

The cattle were driven to Ogallala so that some of them could be loaded onto trains and shipped to Chicago or St. Louis for slaughter. Most of the steers who made it to Nebraska were too thin at that point to be sent to the stockyards, however. If they hadn't been too skinny to be tasty when they were rounded up in Texas, they were certainly too skinny by the time they got to Nebraska. A thousand-mile walk was bound to make any animal tough.

That's why the cattle needed young men like Jack Sargent to take them to a lush grazing area along the Tongue River, about fifteen miles north of Sheridan, Wyoming. In 1861, the year Jack was born, this grazing area had been the location of a massive gathering of Cheyennes, Arapahos, and Dakota Sioux. "Camp criers had to change mounts several times before making a complete circle around the entire encampment," according to one Native historian who is familiar with the oral histories of the tribes. The Indians had gathered to launch an assault against the Crows, whose hunting grounds—in the early 1860s, at least—had not been as devastated by White settlement as the grounds of their aggressors. Twenty years later, when Jack and the cattle he punched arrived, the Cheyennes, Arapahos, Sioux, *and* Crows were all living on tightly defined reservations that had been established by the U.S. government. Little hunting could occur on these reservations, since most of the game were gone.[13]

Not a lot is known about Jack Sargent's early years in Wyoming, not even by his grandson Bill Fessel. Bill's very existence, however, attests to the fact that the churchless entertainment options available to Jack in Ogallala weren't enticing (or debilitating) enough to keep him from getting married and having children. He got married in February 1885, at the age of twenty-four, to a local girl from Machias, Maine, named Adelaide Crane. Their first child, Charles Hemenway Sargent, was born in December in Connecticut. Jack was spending that winter working for Addie's father, Leander Crane, who manufactured Franklin stoves and had a distribution warehouse in New Haven. Crane's business was the reason Jack could afford to heat his lodge in the Tetons with several of these cast iron furnaces—a mark of gentility in the wilds of Wyoming that caused some settlers in Jackson Hole to conclude he was a "remittance man."[14]

Addie gave birth to the couple's second child, Mary, in Cheyenne, in August 1887. According to scraps of an autobiography Jack started to write when he was in his late thirties, the year Mary was born was the year "I decided to come [to Wyoming] for life." He spent the early months of 1887 working for the Union Pacific Railroad, and then shortly after his daughter was born, he and his family left Cheyenne. Jack's pocket was full of the money he'd earned from the UP, plus $700 his cousin Gus had given him for the journey.[15]

Jack, Addie, and their two young children set out for western Wyoming, spending "nearly four months in a prairie schooner" with "a balky pony team" on the Oregon Trail. Mapped out by fur traders in the early nineteenth century—and following paths Native Americans had been using for generations—the trail began in Independence, Missouri, and split in southern Idaho, taking some pioneers to Oregon and others to northern California. Jack and Addie took a spur off the trail at South Pass City known as the "Lander Road." That brought them to the settlement of Big Piney, Wyoming, in December 1887.[16]

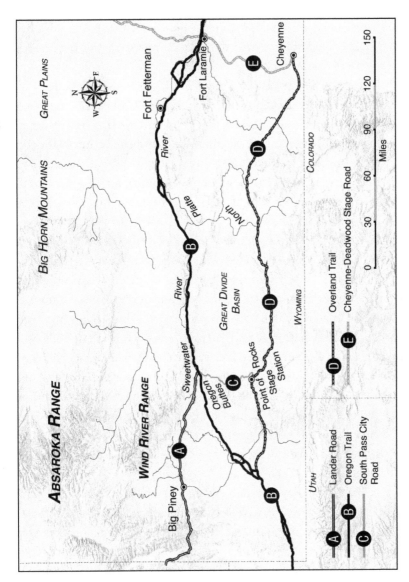

Pioneer trails across Wyoming. Map created by Mark Moore.

The South Pass was incredibly important to pioneers looking to make it to the West Coast. It's a trough, about thirty-five miles wide, north to south, that's situated along the Continental Divide. The reason it's called the "South Pass" is that it's 350 miles south of the trail Merriweather Lewis took through the aptly named Bitterroot Mountains in 1806, when returning from the Pacific Northwest, where he and his partner, William Clark, had gone, hoping to find the shortest route possible between the Missouri and Columbia Rivers.

North of the South Pass lies the Wind River Range of the Rockies; south of the South Pass lie the Oregon Buttes. What makes the trough so special is that it's unbelievably flat. Pioneers traveling from Missouri would have gained more than six thousand feet in elevation by the time they got to the Continental Divide, but they'd have done all that climbing over the course of more than eight hundred miles, making much of the elevation change barely perceptible. At the Continental Divide, then, they might have faced a towering wall, three thousand to seven thousand feet high, depending upon where they were when they got to the Divide, if it weren't for the South Pass. That's how many feet above the plains the Rocky Mountains rise, from the Sangre de Cristo Mountains in northern New Mexico to the Canadian Rockies in British Columbia.

There's a "break" in that wall, however, that the Sweetwater River runs through, and depending upon where you are in the thirty-five-mile-wide trough that is the South Pass, the elevation change you experience as you travel east to west through it might be as little as four hundred feet over the course of more than thirteen miles. The last two hundred of those feet are actually downhill.[17] Once a runner gets her red blood cell count adjusted to being at seven thousand feet above sea level, a race through the South Pass could be one of the easiest half-marathons she runs in her life.

It shouldn't have taken Jack and Addie four months to get from Cheyenne to Big Piney. They were definitely going at a leisurely pace. We know that the family spent a few weeks at Fort Fetterman, about 140 miles north of Cheyenne. It was enough time for them to rack up a $52 hotel bill and write a fraudulent check for it, prompting the proprietor there to have the sheriff issue arrest warrants for John and Adelaide Sargent. The bounced check must have been a misunderstanding; Jack had plenty of money at that point, and the few surviving letters we have from Addie suggest she was the sort of woman who would have been mortified to know there was an arrest warrant in her name.[18]

The couple probably didn't know about the warrants, however. Unless they returned to Fort Fetterman—which they seem not to have done, since the warrants were never delivered—there'd have been no way for them to know they were wanted by the law. Sure, there were telegraph lines in the region, but that didn't mean there was a central database where law enforcement officials could share information about people who should be arrested. The way information like that was shared was through the distribution of those "WANTED" posters you'll often see in movies and television shows about the Wild West, and in an age of cattle thievery and train robberies (Billy the Kid had been killed just a few years earlier, and Butch Cassidy was about to rob his first bank), Jack and Addie's alleged crime wasn't egregious enough to make it onto a poster.

Why Jack and Addie went to Fort Fetterman in the first place isn't clear. It wasn't the most direct route out of Cheyenne to the Oregon Trail, and the Oregon Trail wasn't the most direct route from Cheyenne to the South Pass. Jack and Addie could have taken the Overland Trail to the Point of Rocks Stage Station and then taken the South Pass City Road north, to connect with the Lander Road that would bring them to Big Piney. The Overland Trail was used by stagecoach companies and contractors with the U.S. Postal Service in the 1860s. By 1887 it wasn't being used for mail delivery anymore, thanks to the Union Pacific Railroad. But it was still used by travelers who didn't want to take the train or couldn't afford to. Indeed, in some sense, it could be said that the Overland Trail is still being used by travelers today, since most of the original trail through Wyoming is now Interstate 80.[19]

Fort Fetterman was along the path Jack would have followed during his cowboy days, however, back when he was driving cattle from Ogallala to Tongue River. In fact, when he and Addie got married in Maine in 1885, Jack's official address was listed on the paperwork as "Ft. Fetterman, Wyoming Ter." His reasons for going there first, therefore, may have simple: the new husband may have wanted to show his bride some of the world he'd inhabited before he married her. The vast and rolling, tree-less, but verdant landscape would have been unlike anything Adelaide Crane had ever seen—or probably could have imagined—while growing upon along the craggy shoreline of eastern Maine.[20]

Why Jack chose to take his family through the South Pass in late fall is much more of a mystery. The average daytime temperature at South Pass City in November is 34°F. In and of itself, that isn't terribly unpleasant, especially if it's sunny, but again, the area is treeless and flat. Daily wind speeds there can be as high as twenty miles per hour. That means Jack and his family (not to mention their "balky pony team") could have experienced wind-chill temperatures in the low twenties during the day. At night, these temperatures could have been even lower.[21] Why, then, did Jack dally so long at Fort Fetterman, when he could have been through the South Pass by late September or early October?

The reason may have had something to do with those criminals who found their visages on "WANTED" posters. It may also have had something to do with the fact that even though the U.S. Army was working hard to get the Indigenous people of Wyoming onto reservations, not all of those people were cooperating with the army's efforts—and some of them were quite angry about what the U.S. government was doing to them.

The Overland Trail that Jack didn't take had a reputation for being subject to raids by Indians and outlaws, primarily because it was used by stagecoaches, which tended to carry politically connected easterners who were in Wyoming on temporary business, usually to visit a mine. These people carried a lot of cash, and their political and economic prominence meant they had many reasons to believe they might be targeted by Native warriors who were unhappy with the U.S. government. The Overland Trail's reputation for violence may have been the reason Jack avoided it, in addition to his desire to show his wife where he had spent his cowboy days. He may have chosen, then, to travel with his family through some of the most sparsely populated parts of the Oregon Trail when it was cold, because he hoped outlaws and Indians alike would choose to stay home when the wind was raging and the temperatures were dropping.

The reputation the Overland Trail had for being inordinately dangerous was exaggerated. Pioneer guides singled the trail out for scalpings, and the surviving narratives of people who traveled this route do frequently mention rumors of Indian violence that were heard from other travelers. But the Indian violence experienced on the Overland Trail by the people keeping these narratives was actually no worse or more frequent than that experienced by other pioneers keeping other narratives on other trails.[22] It's not that the Overland Trail wasn't violent; it's that its reputation for violence was overblown. The trail was actually no more violent than the Oregon trail Jack chose to take with his family.

If Jack stayed away from the Overland Trail because he believed it was more dangerous than other trails, that may have been the first time in his life he made a decision involving his family that was based upon faulty information about Native Americans. It would not be the last time, however.

Eight years after he arrived in the Tetons, Jack Sargent decided to spend nine months away from his homestead because of rumors he'd heard about the Bannock Indians. The Bannocks were said to be planning a retaliatory raid on White settlers in Jackson Hole in the summer of 1895.

The rumors were completely false, and Jack didn't actually need to spend that much time away from home. Because he did, however, his ability to file a patent claim on the land he'd staked out as his homestead was thrown into serious jeopardy. That development prompted Jack to make another decision involving his family—and this decision, then, cost his wife and unborn child their lives.

9

One of God's Garden Spots

The piece of earth in Wyoming that John Dudley Sargent laid claim to is so exquisitely beautiful, first-time visitors may have to remind themselves to breathe as they stand amid the canary yellow balsamroot and amethyst-colored lupines that decorate the shores of Jackson Lake in the summertime and stare across the water at the massive cathedral of mountains looming on the other side.

The lake is fed by the Snake River, and it's thirty-nine feet higher today than it was when Jack moved his family to the area in 1890. This makes for an extraordinarily dramatic effect, as nine perpetually snow-capped peaks—each of them nearly ten million years old and composed of metamorphic rock that's been in the region for more than two and a half billion years—rise up out of the water, five and six thousand feet high, in an audacious challenge to the importance and meaning you thought your precious and consequential human life had before you saw the Tetons.[1]

The range is about forty miles long, north to south, and ten miles wide, east to west. Even before the U.S. Reclamation Service built a dam along the Snake River, bringing the shoreline of Jackson Lake right up to the foot of Mount Moran, the mountains didn't give climbers much of an opportunity to adjust to their verticality. Whether you approach them from the west in Idaho, or the east in Jackson Hole, you come to the base of the Tetons from a remarkably flat plain. On the Wyoming side, that plain is covered with silvery, blueish-green sagebrush that smells like a combination of camphor and spearmint on a warm, rainy day. On the Idaho side, it's covered with bright green potato fields that farmers are able to cultivate there only because of a federal irrigation project that created five reservoirs along the Snake River between 1904 and 1939, including the now greatly expanded Jackson Lake, which engineers dammed for the first time in 1907.[2]

"Unspeakable grandeur" was how an army lieutenant named Gustavus Doane described the range when he visited Jackson Hole for the first time in November 1876, three years before Jack was old enough to leave his native Maine. "There are no foothills to the Tetons," Doane marveled about the "twenty-two summits in a line" he could see from his camp near the southern end of the range. "They rise up in rugged majesty from the rock-strewn plain."[3]

Six years before he explored the Tetons, Doane led an army expedition into the geyser-riddled landscape north of the range that Americans soon started calling the "New Wonderland." His assignment was to create an accurate map of the region around Yellowstone Lake. Doane's report to Congress consisted of more than just maps, however; it was filled with vivid details about the marvels he encountered. "No figure of imagination, no description of enchantment can equal in imagery the vistas of these great basins," he wrote about the thermal pools that glowed like iridescent abalone shells in what is now called the Midway Geyser Basin of Yellowstone National Park. "We had all heard fabulous stories of this region and were somewhat skeptical as to appearances . . . then conviction was forced upon us."[4]

Doane's words played a critical role in the campaign to get Congress to create Yellowstone National Park in 1872. That's why the army ordered him to explore the Snake River four years later, from its origins in northwestern Wyoming to its confluence with the Columbia River in southeastern Washington. Several scientific, political, and military leaders wanted to see Yellowstone's boundaries expanded almost as soon as the park was created. One of those leaders was Lieutenant General Philip Sheridan, who oversaw the army's operations in the vast swath of territory between the Missouri River and the Rocky Mountains. When he ordered Doane to explore the area south and west of the park, Sheridan hoped the army lieutenant with a flair for describing the landscape would be able to do for the Snake River what he had done for the Grand Prismatic Spring, the largest thermal pool and the most-photographed feature today in America's oldest national park.[5]

Doane didn't disappoint, at least as far as the vividness of his observations was concerned. "The soft light floods the great expanse of the valley," he wrote about the plain between the Gros Ventre and Teton Mountains that early fur trappers had named after one of their own, a trapper from Virginia named David Jackson. A full moon illuminated "the winding silvery river and the resplendent, deeply carved mountain walls" during one "glorious night" Doane spent at the base of a densely forested mountain he called Upper Gros Ventre Butte. That night impressed upon him "a vision of glittering, glaciated rock" that he felt certain would remain with him for rest of his life.[6]

Alas, the lieutenant's descriptions did not hit their mark this time. America's lawmakers were not moved by his reports to protect the Tetons from development. Slightly more than seven years after Gustavus Doane ended his exploration of the Snake River (he never did make it to Washington; a series of unfortunate events forced him to return to Montana shortly after he reached Idaho), the first White settlers—with all their ravenous cattle and sheep—moved into Jackson's Hole.[7]

Embarrassment was why Congress created Yellowstone National Park. European visitors had been criticizing Americans for more than four decades by the time the park was founded; they believed the young country was doing a terrible job of protecting its most awe-inspiring features from the ravages of capitalism. Niagara Falls was a particular source of European criticism. No less than Alexis de Tocqueville had predicted the glory of Niagara Falls would be destroyed in his lifetime, and that the almost pathological obsession Americans had with making money would be to blame.[8]

Tocqueville visited the falls in August 1831, during his famous tour of the United States that led to the publication of *Democracy in America*, a flawed but remarkably insightful evaluation of American culture in which the French aristocrat concluded he knew of "no other country where the love of money has taken a stronger hold on the affections of men." Tocqueville was blown away by the Horseshoe Falls. "The whole river formed a crystal arch almost impenetrable to the rays of the sun," he wrote to his mother about the largest of the three waterfalls at the southern end of Niagara Gorge. "Surrounding me was a damp darkness and a feeling of destruction and chaos that truly had something fearsome about it." The young man wanted his mother to experience this feeling, too. He warned her, therefore, to get to the United States as soon as she could. "If you delay, your Niagara will have been spoiled for you," he predicted with great confidence. "I don't give the Americans ten years to establish a saw or flour mill at the base of the cataract."[9]

Tocqueville wasn't being a horrible son when he told his mother he wanted her to experience a force that was "fearsome." He was expressing his admiration for an aesthetic quality European intellectuals and artists had long extolled, known as the "sublime." Things that were sublime were not merely beautiful; in fact, some thinkers, such as the Anglo-Irish philosopher Edmund Burke, believed that "beauty" and "sublimity" could not coexist in the same object or scene, because beauty was a comforting aesthetic, while sublimity could be quite disconcerting.

Things that were sublime often caused the observer to feel vulnerable, inconsequential, or obscure. They produced "an unnatural tension and certain violent emotions of the nerves," according to Burke. Beauty was about peace, but sublimity was about power, and an appreciation of the sublime required an observer to give himself over to that power. "I say, altogether it takes away language as well as thought," John Quincy Adams observed about Niagara Falls in 1843, a few days after he had visited the gorge for his first and only time. "In this enraptured condition, one is almost capable of prophesying—standing, as it were, in a trance, unable to speak."[10]

One could not appreciate the sublime and seek to control it at the same time. Europeans supposedly understood this truth and knew how to relinquish control whenever they encountered features on the landscape that were compelling enough to be sublime. Americans, however, were businessmen and entrepreneurs. A few of them knew how to give themselves over to the sublime, as the nation's sixth president proved. But for the most part, *control* was what Americans sought when it came to the landscape, because control was what gave them the opportunity to make money.

Control—not an appreciation of the landscape's "sublime" qualities— was what officials in New York had sought when they built a canal and drained the Collect Pond into the Hudson River. It was what Gus Hemenway and his brother, William, had sought when they timbered the forests of northeastern Maine. Control over the landscape was what the Union Pacific Railroad attempted to gain, when it laid track across the plains and dug deep into Wyoming's earth, searching for coal. And control was what the U.S. Army wanted to achieve when its soldiers slaughtered Cheyenne and Arapaho Indians who refused to respect the property rights of White farmers who were, themselves, seeking to gain control over the landscape through their agriculture.

To be sure, John Quincy Adams wasn't the only American capable of basking in the sublimity of nature and allowing himself to be humbled by it. The falls were America's most popular tourist destination by 1840, in no small part because many Americans craved an experience they believed would "take away the power of speech by its grandeur and sublimity." That experience even had a name by the mid-nineteenth century: one who gave herself or himself over to the sublimity of the falls was said to have been "Niagarized." It was a feeling one young visitor described as being a bit like having the river go "sounding through all one's soul, and heart, and mind, commingling with all one's ideas and impressions, and uniting itself with all one's innermost ideas and fancies."[11]

But hundreds of tourists looking to be "Niagarized" only added to the profit-making potential of the falls. Tocqueville hadn't gotten it quite right when he predicted that American businessmen would put a sawmill at the base of the falls, but developers did purchase much of the land within viewing distance of the natural wonder. They built hotels and put up high fences, charging visitors expensive entrance fees for a glimpse of the raging Niagara River as it tumbled over that famously wide ledge of dolomitic limestone.[12]

Margaret Fuller, who worked as an editor and a foreign correspondent for the *New York Tribune*, wasn't terribly concerned by the trend. Seemingly oblivious to the class implications of what was happening, she thought only about the aesthetic impact the structures could be having upon the scene, and she was confident the river could handle it. "People complain about the buildings at Niagara, and fear to see it further deformed," she observed in her wildly popular travelogue, *Summer on the Lakes*, published in 1844. "I cannot sympathize with the apprehension: the spectacle is capable to swallow up all such objects; they are not seen in the great whole, more than an earthworm in a wide field."[13]

Fuller's European counterparts, however, were not so blasé about the threat that commercial development posed to Niagara's sublimity. "'Tis a pity that such ground was not reserved as sacred in perpetuum," one English journalist observed in 1833, lamenting that Niagara's forests "were not allowed to luxuriate in all their wild and savage beauty about a spot where the works of man will ever appear paltry." Another British journalist told his readers the hotels around the falls were "destined to become a positive nuisance." He wished "it were provided by law that no building should be erected within sight of any little plot of ground immediately adjoining the cataract." In a dig that probably should have been aimed more at the Canadians than the Americans, given the current state of the two sides of the river, this reporter went on to predict that "in another twenty years, [we] may see the whole amphitheater filled with grog-shops, humbug museums, etc., etc."[14]

The criticisms weighed on America's leaders. The country had no castles or Roman ruins to point to when asserting its cultural bona fides to the world. It had no great philosophers, poets, artists, or musicians, either—or at least none who'd been recognized as such, at home or abroad, in the early decades of the nineteenth century.

Culturally America was suffering from an inferiority complex when Alexis de Tocqueville levied his charges, one that Ralph Waldo Emerson gave voice to in 1837, when he told a group of Harvard students it was time for the "sluggard intellect of this continent" to "look from under its iron lids and fill the postponed expectation of the world with something better than the exertions of mechanical skill." Inventors like Peter Smith had already shown the world that Americans could be great engineers. Recall that Smith invented the iron-framed printing press in 1821, and that his nephew, Richard Hoe, would go on to invent the "lightning press" less than a decade after Emerson delivered his lecture. It was time for Americans to make original contributions to the *cultural* realm—the realm of art and ideas. "Our long apprenticeship to the learning of other lands draws to a close," Emerson announced in a speech Oliver Wendell Holmes would later call America's "intellectual Declaration of Independence."[15]

Writers and artists took Emerson up on his challenge. In the mid-nineteenth century, America began to develop a literary tradition, thanks to novelists and short-story writers like Nathaniel Hawthorne and Herman Melville, poets like John Greenleaf Whittier, Henry Wadsworth Longfellow, and Emily Dickinson, and essayists like Bronson Alcott, Frederick Douglass, Margaret Fuller, and Henry David Thoreau. The country started to develop an artistic tradition, as well, thanks to painters like Thomas Cole, Albert Bierstadt, and Susie Barstow.

But all of these painters—and nearly all of these writers—looked to the same source of inspiration when laying the foundation for America's cultural heritage: the country's unspoiled natural landscape. The United States didn't have an Abbatiale du Mont Saint Michel to inspire anyone (that's the medieval monastery in Normandy, France, that inspired the pointillist painter Paul Signac and the impressionist composer Claude Debussy; it's also where many of the *Harry Potter* movies were filmed). America did have Mount Katahdin in Maine, however—the beginning (or end) of the Appalachian Trail today, where Henry David Thoreau once experienced the "inexpressible tenderness and immortal life of the grim forest."[16] There was no Hadrian's wall in America, but there was the Hudson River Valley, which inspired a whole movement in painting known as the Hudson River School.

America's *natural* history was fueling its *cultural* history. That natural history was under threat, however. By 1879 Frederick Law Olmsted could tell a group of New York state regulators that the sublimity of Niagara Falls had been completely eclipsed by "rope-walking, diving, brass bands, fireworks, and various 'side shows.'"[17] Americans' "love of money" (not to mention their poor taste) was destroying not only their country's landscape but its cultural potential, as well.

The "discovery" of Yellowstone's geysers and mudpots presented a new opportunity for America's landscape to be spoiled. Human beings had known about the thermal wonders in the northwest corner of Wyoming for centuries, of course, by the time America's first national park was founded in 1872. If the French trappers who passed through the region in the eighteenth century realized the ground they were walking on was seething with hydrothermal activity underneath, they left no written record of it. The Indigenous Americans living in the region almost certainly knew there was something special about Yellowstone, however. Their name for the South Fork of the Shoshone River translated loosely to "Stinking Waters," a reference to the odorous sulfur found in the hot springs near the river.[18]

It wasn't until the nineteenth century that the first non-Indigenous American encountered Yellowstone's thermal marvels. That person was an explorer from Virginia named John Colter who joined Lewis and Clark on their Corps of Discovery expedition to the Pacific Northwest. After the group had reached their destination and begun their journey back to St. Louis in 1806, Colter went off on his own, intending to meet up with the Crow nation, whose hunting grounds were along what is now the Montana-Wyoming border. Being an American, John Colter figured he could do some trading and make some money.

Historians have long debated what route Colter took through Wyoming, since he left no written record of his journey. He did tell stories about the wild things he saw, however, and those stories eventually made their way to Washington Irving, who joked in 1837 about the "hidden fires, smoking pits, noxious streams, and all-pervading 'smell of brimstone'" John Colter supposedly encountered when he was west of the Missouri River. Irving's skepticism was shared by many Americans at the time. Most people didn't believe the wonders Colter claimed to have seen were real; his stories about bubbling mud and streams of hot water that shot hundreds of feet into the air were just too fabulous to be believed.[19]

That's why Ferdinand Hayden took an artist with him when he set out to explore Yellowstone one year after Gustavus Doane returned from his map-making expedition into the region. Doane's report to Congress had confirmed much of what John Colter said, but not everyone is capable of being moved by the written word. Even the editors of the *New York Times*—who worked with words for a living—had to admit that the official report submitted by Doane "reads like the realization of a child's fairy tale." Some people (many people, perhaps) need pictures, in addition to words, before they will believe something is real.[20]

Hayden recognized the importance of images, thanks to a banker from Philadelphia named Jay Cooke. Cooke had helped to finance the Civil War, providing the government with nearly $5 million in loans it used to transport, equip, and pay the Union's soldiers.[21] Cooke was also heavily invested in the Northern Pacific Railroad, which was chartered by Congress in 1864 but didn't lay its first mile of track until 1870, when Jay Cooke's money got involved.

The NP started in Minnesota, at the southwestern tip of Lake Superior. The plan was to have the railroad run along the southern edges of North Dakota and Montana, before skipping across the Idaho panhandle and heading into Washington State. Congress wanted to ship commodities like wheat and lumber between the Great Lakes and Puget Sound.[22] After Gustavus Doane and his colleagues got back from their Yellowstone expedition, however, Jay Cooke saw the potential of using the Northern Pacific Railroad to ship one other commodity across the northern tier of the western United States: tourists.

Tourism—or the possibility of it—was the reason Jay Cooke asked Ferdinand Hayden to take with him a thirty-four-year-old self-taught artist from Philadelphia named Thomas Moran when Hayden set out on the first federally financed geological survey of Yellowstone. Describing the finely boned Moran as a "rare genius," Cooke's secretary insisted it wasn't his employer's intention to "burden you with more people than you can attend to." Nevertheless, the banker believed Moran would be a "very desirable addition to your expedition," and he knew that having an artist in the party would be "a great accommodation to our [banking] house and the [rail]road."[23]

Thomas Moran's paintings, Gustavus Doane's words, and the black-and-white photographs of a Civil War veteran in his late twenties named William Henry Jackson, whom Ferdinand Hayden also invited along, came together to create a powerful force in defense of the exquisite and unique landscape in northwestern Wyoming. Moran made watercolor sketches of thirty sites during the forty days he spent with the Hayden expedition. He worked closely with Jackson when determining what to sketch, as his paintings—which had all of the light and grandeur of the Hudson River School that had strongly influenced him—were meant to complement the less dramatic, if more substantive, photographs of William Henry Jackson, whose ability to capture the sweeping depths of the landscape was limited by the lenses and light metering technology available in the field of photography at the time.[24]

Moran's watercolors of the Upper and Lower Geyser Basins, the water-falls at Sulphur Mountain, and the peaks in the Lower Yellowstone Range were reproduced in color on the pages of *Scribner's* magazine, using chromolithographic technology that had been available in the United States since the 1840s. *Scribner's* also ran an essay by Nathaniel Pitt Langford, a banker-turned-prospector-turned-explorer from New York who'd moved to Montana in the early 1860s in search of gold and joined Gustavus Doane on his earlier expedition into Yellowstone in 1870.

Langford's essay was derived from lectures he'd delivered across the Northeast in 1871. Those lectures, just like Moran's paintings, were financed by Jay Cooke, which is why Langford ended each evening by observing there was "one thing wanting to render this remarkable region accessible" to the American people. That "one thing," of course, was the completion of "the N.P.R.R., by means of which the traveler . . . will be able to reach this region from the Atlantic seaboard within three days and see all the wonders I have here described."[25]

Jay Cooke's strategy worked. Thomas Moran's paintings "convinced everyone who saw them that the regions where such wonders existed should be preserved for the people forever," according to Hiram Chittenden, an engineer who helped to construct the Grand Loop Road, which is now used by more than four million tourists in Yellowstone every year. The American people wanted the marvels Thomas Moran had painted to be protected, and their representatives in Washington responded accordingly.[26]

There was a precedent for doing what Congress did when it founded the world's first national park. In June 1864, a few weeks after nearly ninety thousand Americans had died in Ulysses S. Grant's failed campaign to take the Confederate capital of Richmond, Abraham Lincoln signed the Yosemite Valley Grant Act into law. The legislation gave the valley it was named after to the state of California, along with a grove of giant sequoias situated about sixteen miles to the south, "upon the express conditions that the premises shall be held for public use, resort, and recreation." Federal lawmakers didn't want businessmen like the ones who had descended upon Niagara Falls to stake a claim to the best views of El Capitan or Half Dome and charge exorbitant fees to anyone wanting to experience their sublimity.[27]

It quickly became apparent, however, that the young state of California was ill-equipped to preserve the integrity of the Yosemite Valley. It could prevent savvy businessmen from blocking off the best views, but opening the state park up to "resort and recreation" meant that politically connected developers were able to indiscriminately clear forests in order to build hotels and then bring in destructive livestock to feed and transport tourists. The state had no resources for policing the giant sequoia forests it had been tasked with protecting. The trees, themselves, were relatively useless to lumbermen; they were so large and brittle, they shattered when they hit the ground after being felled. Within California's sequoia groves, however, many smaller, sugar pine trees grew (sugar pines are actually the tallest pine trees in the world, but compared to a giant sequoia, they're "small"). Throughout the 1860s loggers illegally chopped down hundreds of sequoias in an effort to get at these more valuable pines.[28]

California's inability to protect Yosemite was one of the reasons Congress decided to place Yellowstone under federal care. The other reason was that Wyoming was just a territory in 1872, as were Idaho and Montana; there was no "state" for the New Wonderland to be given to.

Under the provisions of the Yellowstone National Park Protection Act, the Department of the Interior was tasked with ensuring that the New Wonderland remained a "pleasuring ground for the benefit and enjoyment of the people" (meaning all of the people—not just the ones who were willing and able to pay a high fee). Interior officials were also charged with protecting "from injury or spoliation . . . all timber, mineral deposits, natural curiosities, or wonders" within the park, and they were required to work "against the wanton destruction of the fish and game found within said park, and against their capture or destruction for the purposes of merchandise or profit." The secretary of the interior could grant conditional leases to private developers, so buildings could be constructed "for the accommodation of visitors." The sites for these hotels, however, would have to be carefully chosen with the Interior Department's conservationist responsibilities kept firmly in mind. The same held for any roads or bridle paths that might be constructed within the park.[29]

One week after Congress passed the act to create Yellowstone National Park, E. L. Godkin—the editor of the Nation who was convinced the problem with American politics was that poor people could afford to serve in the state legislatures—praised the move. "It is the general principle which is chiefly commendable in the act of Congress setting aside the Yellowstone region as a national park," Godkin wrote, suggesting that his contempt for the poor may have extended only to their lawmaking capabilities and not to their capacity to appreciate the sublime. "It will help confirm the national possession of the Yo Semite, and it may in time lead us to rescue Niagara from its present, degrading surroundings."[30]

It would be quite some time before lower-income Americans could afford to take in the marvels of Yellowstone National Park, even with Congress's guarantee that the land would never fall into private hands. A visit to Old Faithful was—and still is—a substantial financial commitment. That's why African Americans, who tend to have less disposable income than other demographic groups, are underrepresented in the country's national parks. The Obama administration tried to address this problem in 2015, when it created the "Every Kid in a Park" program. That program continues to give a free annual park pass to any fourth grader whose family requests one. Nearly a decade into the program, however, African Americans still make up less than 2 percent of the visitors to America's national parks, and that's because the $80 fee for an annual park pass isn't really the problem. Finding the time and money to *get there* is the hurdle.[31]

It was the same for most Americans in the years immediately following Yellowstone's creation. Jay Cooke's banking house collapsed during the Panic of 1873, a financial crisis that was precipitated by rampant speculation in railroad stocks (facilitated by short-sellers like Edith Drake's father). The Northern Pacific Railroad had laid track no farther west than Bismarck, North Dakota, by the time Cooke's bank failed. This made it difficult, if not impossible, for people from New York or Boston to get to Yellowstone National Park.[32]

Fewer than five hundred tourists a year visited the park during the first five years of its existence—a remarkably large number, actually, given that the only options for getting to Yellowstone were an 834-mile-long voyage out of Bismarck along the Missouri River that took a minimum of two weeks and still required an additional two days on a stagecoach;

or a 438-mile-long stagecoach journey from the Union Pacific Railroad's station in Corrine, Utah, that took four days and passed through some very hostile territory. One traveler reported losing $400 in 1875 (the equivalent of about $9,000 today) when his stage was held up by outlaws along this route.

The overland journey from Utah cost thirteen cents a mile—unless a passenger had more than twenty-five pounds in baggage, which he or she almost certainly did. A Saratoga Ladies' half-trunk, one of the more popular models for short-term travel in the 1870s, weighed thirty-two pounds, empty. With excess baggage the price of a stage trip went up to 23.5 cents per mile. In today's money that overland ride from Utah to Yellowstone cost about $2,300, not counting the price of the train ticket to Corrine.[33]

It would be another six years, following the collapse of Jay Cooke's bank, before construction on the Northern Pacific Railroad could resume. When the NP finally started transporting passengers to a station just eight miles away from the park's entrance in the summer of 1883, the company's investors were not inclined to make the tickets cheap. At nearly $140 roundtrip, a ride from Washington DC to Cinnabar, Montana, like the one President Chester Arthur took three months before he celebrated Evacuation Day at Delmonico's with Jay Gould, cost the equivalent of about $3,800 today.[34]

Still, a surprising number of Americans were able to afford a trip to Yellowstone after the completion of the Northern Pacific Railroad. Recall that there was no federal income tax at this point in time. Middle-class salaries went farther in the late nineteenth century than they do today—even if infants like Beatrice Ray Hamilton were underwriting those trips to the New Wonderland by being the casualties of a society that had little funding to help the poor.

"To-day I am in the Yellowstone Park, and I wish I were dead," Rudyard Kipling wrote in his journal in 1889, overwhelmed by the sheer number of people who'd decided to visit the park at the same time he did. "The train halted at Cinnabar station, and we were decanted, a howling crowd of us, into stages." The twenty-three-year-old British writer, who'd been raised in India and was no stranger to crowds, asked his driver if the throng were typical. "You've struck one of Rayment's excursion parties—that's all," the driver assured him, referring to one of the concessioners who led trips into the park. The author of *The Man Who Would Be King* didn't have a high opinion of "Mister Rayment" or his clients. "He collects masses of Down Easters from the New England states and hurls them across the continent and into the Yellowstone Park," Kipling observed disdainfully. "It is not the ghastly vulgarity . . . and ignorance of the men that revolts me, so much as the display of these same qualities in the women folk."[35]

Five years before Rudyard Kipling visited Yellowstone National Park, a private company with close ties to the Northern Pacific Railroad constructed a hotel near the Mammoth Hot Springs, a grotesque geothermal feature in the northern part of the park that proves Edmund Burke was correct when he insisted the sublime and the beautiful were not one and the same. Kipling believed the white and rust-colored travertine terraces that change their form daily as acidic hot springs bring two tons of calcium carbonate to the earth's surface looked like "a huge yellow barn." It was a disappointingly prosaic description (Kipling *really* did not like Yellowstone . . .) that failed to capture what it's like to be in the presence of the Mammoth Hot Springs in almost every way—except, perhaps, for their smell.[36]

The National Hotel had room for eight hundred guests and was modern and luxurious by any standard, let alone the standards of a region that had been more than four hundred miles away from the nearest train station just one year before construction on the establishment began. The hotel had four wings, three floors of private rooms, a dining hall, a gentlemen's library, a ladies' parlor, a Steinway piano, and a kitchen that could accommodate up to fifteen cooks—enough to serve meals to five thousand people. The hotel's carpeted hallways were heated with large Franklin stoves like the ones Jack Sargent's father-in-law sold in Connecticut, and the common rooms were wired with electric arc lamps that got their energy from an in-house electromagnetic generator known as a "Dynamo."[37]

Staying at the National Hotel was an opulent experience. Not everyone who could afford to get to Yellowstone, however, could also afford to spend the night reading by the light of an arc lamp. For those whose funds were more modest, there was a different kind of accommodation available: camping.

Thomas Wentworth Higginson, the Unitarian promoter of Muscular Christianity who exhorted America's businessmen to join him at the gym, was a great believer in the physical and spiritual benefits of spending a few nights under the stars. "I have never slept more delightfully than in our tent last night," he wrote to his mother about a six-day trip he and his congregants took to Maine's Mount Katahdin. "The freedom of the woods descends deeper and deeper into us, and . . . all of us are better and stronger than when we started."[38]

The year was 1855, and retreating into the woods for the purpose of recreation, rather than migration or exploration, was still a relatively new activity. For most of America's history, the woods had been a fearsome place—and not in the way Alexis de Tocqueville used the term when he wrote to his mother about Niagara Falls. There was nothing sublime about the prospect of getting attacked by Indians or eaten by wolves.[39] The fact that Higginson and his party felt safe going into the Maine woods to find themselves said much about the extent to which the New England wilderness had been subdued by the mid-nineteenth century.

It also said much about the talents of Higginson's guide, "a noble youth of twenty-three, an Indian in figure, strength, and quietness." Choosing the right guide was "the most important of all considerations to one about to visit the wilderness," according to William Murray, whose handbook on camping, *Adventures in the Wilderness; or Camp-Life in the Adirondacks*, was published in 1869. The book is widely believed to be the origin of the word "vacation," since Murray wanted his readers to "vacate" the confines of a walled and roofed domicile while they were on holiday.[40]

Like Thomas Wentworth Higginson, William Murray was a devotee of Muscular Christianity. He believed physical exercise could cure a variety of illnesses in men. "To such as are afflicted with that dire parent of ills, dyspepsia, or have lurking in their systems consumptive tendencies, I most earnestly recommend a month's experience among the pines," Murray wrote. It was essential one go into the pines with the right guide, however. "With an ignorant guide, you will starve," he warned. "With a lazy one, you will lose your temper." The worst kind of guide was the "witty" kind. "He inundates the camp with gab. If you chance to have company, he is continually thrusting himself impertinently forward. He is possessed from head to foot with the idea that he is *smart*."[41]

By the mid-1870s, travel books were devoting entire sections to the pleasures and benefits of "camping out." The *New York Times* reported on city residents who chose to spend their holidays not in fancy hotels, but "along streams and by the banks of lakes," sleeping "on spruce boughs," so they could "look up at the stars if they wake during the night." Christian men hoping to beef up their faith weren't the only ones leading campers into the woods. "Camping parties comprised wholly or in part of women are quite the thing, this summer," the *Brooklyn Times Union* reported in 1888, in a story about three groups of women who had chosen to spend time together, outside, in the Catskills and along the beaches of Long Island. The article detailed the kind of clothing any woman looking to emulate these ladies would need to acquire: "Garibaldi blouse with sailor collar opening away from the throat; loose sleeves; and a straight, undraped skirt, light, full, and as short as the general sentiment of the camping party will allow."[42] It was a perfect description of the outfit Edith Sargent donned several years later, when she posed with her violin in front of Mount Moran.

The company that had arranged vacations for those vulgar "Down Easters" Rudyard Kipling encountered was the Raymond and Whitcomb Travel Agency, based in Boston. It was one of several that worked with local guides, cooks, suppliers, and drivers to offer all-inclusive camping excursions into Yellowstone National Park. All a camper had to do was show up—the cooking, cleaning, and tent-pitching were done by someone else. A few of these local guides eventually formed their own companies. One such guide was William Wallace Wylie, whose firm, the Wylie Permanent Camping Company, was licensed by the federal government to set up campsites at several exclusive locations within the park.[43]

Wylie had moved to Montana in 1878 to be a school principal. One year later, while returning to Bozeman from a trip to Iowa to retrieve his wife, he saw a herd of twenty thousand bison crossing the Missouri River. After that, William Wylie never wanted to be confined to a classroom or office again.

It was one of the last times anyone in the United States witnessed a sight like that. Railroad companies had started letting passengers shoot bison from moving trains ten years earlier, since herds as large as the one Wylie encountered represented a real hazard to locomotives as they barreled cross the plains. Cattle barons like the one John Dudley Sargent worked for also encouraged the slaughter. Bison, after all, ate the juicy grasses these barons needed to fatten their livestock. The fact that Indigenous populations on the plains depended upon the bison for their survival gave an added incentive to the military to kill the animals. The result was that by 1883, a population in the northern plains that had numbered more than five million just twenty years earlier was whittled down to no more than three hundred creatures.[44]

Wylie and his employees met their clients at the Cinnabar station, near Yellowstone's northern entrance. A typical tour consisted of six full days in the park and an additional half day of travel between the park and the train station. The cost was $35 per person, which included not just the food, tents, guides, and travel between the park and the station, but also an afternoon of boating on Yellowstone Lake. In contrast, just five days at the National Hotel cost $50 per person, and although this fee included meals and the travel between the hotel and the train station, tourists who wanted to explore Yellowstone Lake or take a guided tour of the park had to pay extra.[45]

William Wallace Wylie had found a niche. He'd identified a population that had the money to get to Yellowstone, but couldn't afford to live in the lap of luxury once they got there. These people didn't mind roughing it a bit, if it meant they could afford to see Old Faithful—just so long as they didn't have to pitch their own tents or kill their own meals. They were, after all, on vacation.

But what about people who *did* want to kill their own meals? People for whom the game animals in the American West, more so than the geysers and mudpots, were the primary attraction? People who didn't want to sleep in a tent, perhaps—and could afford not to do so—but also didn't want to stay in a fancy, electrified hotel with eight hundred other people?

Hunting in Yellowstone National Park was outlawed by Congress in 1894. Everyone in the region knew the move was coming long before it happened, however, and the territorial legislature in Wyoming had insisted as early as 1884 that, in the absence of federal restrictions, its game laws applied to all the wildlife in the park.[46] Building a business around hunting in America's first national park would have been a fool's errand, no matter how attractive the park's big game might have been to eastern sportsmen.

Yellowstone's boundaries were not infinite, however—and Wyoming's elk and deer had no idea where those boundaries were. There was a stunning area just a few miles south of the park where hunting was perfectly legal, and where beauty and sublimity were so intimately intertwined that Edith Drake Sargent called the area "one of God's garden spots" when she wrote to the editor of the *Los Angeles Times* to condemn that paper's coverage of her husband's death.[47]

By 1890 thousands of people were visiting Yellowstone National Park every year, and John Dudley Sargent figured that more than a few of them would want to take in the glory of the Tetons, as well—if only they had a place to stay. Robert Ray Hamilton figured that many of the wealthy men he knew from hunt clubs in New York and Michigan would find the area around Jack Sargent's homestead to be an absolute paradise, situated as it was at the northern edge of a valley that was fifty-five miles long and thirteen miles wide and had just twenty-nine people settled within it (including Ray Hamilton and the five members of the Sargent family).[48]

It was fortuitous, in many ways, that the two men met one another when they did. Jack's land and Ray's connections, Jack's ideas and Ray's inheritance: together they added up to the kind of business proposition Alexis de Tocqueville would have considered quintessentially "American." And because Gustavus Doane's reports to Congress about the "glittering, glaciated rock" he'd seen near Jackson Lake had failed to convince lawmakers to expand Yellowstone's boundaries into Jackson Hole, Ray and Jack didn't have to ask anyone for permission to do anything.

There is no surviving evidence *anywhere* that indicates how Ray Hamilton knew Jack Sargent or when and where the two men met for the first time. Years after they were both dead, people in Jackson Hole claimed that Ray and Jack had met in college—but that information is wrong.[49] Jack didn't go to college, and he and Ray were also nearly eleven years apart in age. Ray was the older of the two.

Not a single one of the hundreds of letters Ray received from friends, family, and colleagues in the days and weeks after the Atlantic City stabbing bore John Dudley Sargent's name, even though Ray knew Jack well enough to travel to Wyoming and move in with him and his family less than a year after Eva had stabbed Mary Ann Donnelly. On Jack's side just four surviving documents indicate he knew Ray Hamilton at all (not counting the extensive press coverage their partnership received). All of these documents have dates that were *after* Ray had moved in with the Sargent family.

The most recent document is a haphazard budget Jack drew up in pencil shortly before he died in June 1913. In it he noted the various revenue sources he'd relied upon during his two and a half decades in Wyoming, and one of those sources was Ray. He gave Jack $6,000 when he moved into the Sargent family's home along the shores of Jackson Lake in late May or early June 1890. It was the equivalent of more than $170,000 today.[50]

The second document establishing Jack's relationship with Ray is a letter Jack wrote in February 1906 to Secretary of State Elihu Root, who'd been Ray's attorney during the annulment proceedings against Eva. Jack was having trouble validating his homestead application for the land in the Tetons he'd been living on for the last sixteen years. "In June of 1891, I went from my home on Jackson Lake, Wyoming, to New York at General Hamilton's request, and met you," Jack wrote to the secretary of state by way of introduction. He then enclosed some of the correspondence he'd received from the Department of the Interior, suggesting he'd failed to meet the requirements of the Homestead Act. "With my wife and five children, I fully complied with the Homestead Law," Jack assured the secretary of state. "Can you save my home for me, my daughter, and my betrothed wife?" The daughter he spoke of was thirteen-year-old Catherine Winthrop Sargent, the only one of his five children who still lived with him by 1906. Jack's "betrothed wife" was Edith Drake.[51]

The third document indicating that Jack knew Ray is a letter Jack wrote to the commanding officer in charge of the U.S. Calvary unit stationed in Yellowstone in August 1890. In that letter, Jack spoke of a $500 reward Ray Hamilton had posted to help officials deal with the problem of elk poaching within the park. Hunting had not yet been banned in Yellowstone, but it was heavily restricted, and hunters were flagrantly violating those restrictions because park officials had few resources for enforcing them. Ray hoped to make enforcement easier by giving people an incentive to tattle.[52]

The final document is a black-and-white photograph of the ranch where Ray and Jack lived. The photograph was taken in the spring of 1891. On the back of it, Jack wrote the words, "Compliments of Hamilton + Sargent—Marymere," the final word being the name he'd given the lodge, in honor of his oldest daughter, Mary Sargent.[53]

Ray's decision to move in with Jack and Addie was unusual, given how small their quarters were, not to mention how young their children were—their only son, Hemenway, was five; Mary was three; and Martha was two. Catherine Winthrop and Adelaide, the youngest of the five Sargent children, had not yet been born. The Sargents' house may actually have been a dugout at this point, rather than a cabin. They were yet not living in the ten-room lodge that would later be built, where one of the rooms was specifically set aside as Ray's—and referred to as such by Jack for the rest of Jack's life.[54]

We don't know why Ray decided to move in with the Sargents or how the plan was hatched, but we do know the arrangement was not unprecedented in Ray's life. He'd never done anything like it before, but he knew someone who had: his mysteriously ostracized uncle, Robert P. Hamilton, whom he met in August 1883, when he traveled to New Orleans to give Robert P. a one-time payment from John Church Hamilton's estate that John Church had not wanted Robert P. to have.

Remember that Ray's uncle lived in Central America, and that he struck up a correspondence with his sister, Charlotte, after she wrote to him in 1874 to inform him their mother had died. It had been twenty years since Robert P. Hamilton left New York, and during that time, he'd had only cursory exchanges with his older brother, Schuyler—Ray's father—about financial matters involving the family. Nothing personal was ever shared between the two brothers. When Charlotte wrote to him, therefore, and included a gentle lie about how their father had sent him his love, Robert P. Hamilton eagerly interpreted the letter—perhaps incorrectly—as an invitation to fill his sister in on his life.

"I am very well and quite comfortable as far as living is concerned," he told her. "I am living about fifteen miles from Wounta with an old friend of some fifteen years standing whom I was acquainted with in

San Juan." The friend's name was Joseph Mills. He was British and ran a rubber-exporting business along the Mosquito Coast. "We lead a very quiet life, fishing and hunting when business is not brisk," Robert P. wrote to his sister. "I am, from long intimacy, quite at home with him and his wife. We have a small garden, cattle, hogs, &c, and buy everything that can be obtained to contribute to personal comfort, but luxuries . . . are very scarce."[55]

The trio lived a pretty isolated life together along the banks of the Prinzipolka River. "We have no society except one another and are desirous of visits from a captain or stranger, the residents of the coast not being what we can call 'society,'" Robert P. wrote. The amusements he and the Millses had at their disposal were pretty limited. "We seldom get any reading matter," he informed his sister. The mail delivery system in Nicaragua was not reliable enough to support a magazine or newspaper subscription. "The weather is extremely warm now," he wrote in March. "This month we are very much molested by yellow flies, which scarcely allow one to write, as they bite sharply and are regular blood suckers." Still, in spite of the heat, the insects, the isolation, and the lack of reading materials or luxury items, Robert P. Hamilton wanted his sister to know he was happy in Central America. "Where there is no law, there is more respect for individual rights as far as the person is concerned," he explained to Charlotte. "Few insults are given us."[56]

It was an extraordinary letter for what it subtly implied—namely, that there was something unconventional about the relationship Robert P. Hamilton had with Mr. and Mrs. Mills, something that might have engendered insults in a country like the United States, where laws and customs were better policed than they were in Nicaragua and a person's privacy was less respected.

We are left to wonder how Charlotte Hamilton responded to her brother's revelations about his life, as her reply to him has not survived the test of time. Robert P. continued to write to her over the years, however, mostly about the financial troubles Joseph Mills was experiencing as the rubber market in Central America declined.

Jack needed the income, and Ray wanted the conversation. Jack wanted to build a reputation for himself, one that was independent from that of all the Brahmins and newly rich entrepreneurs he was related to in New England, and Ray needed to rehabilitate the reputation he already had. These needs and desires are why the two men decided to construct a lodge at the base of the Teton Mountains and equip that lodge with luxuries—books, rugs, cigars, Franklin stoves, a wine collection, a piano—that would attract wealthy visitors to Jackson Lake from Yellowstone National Park.[57]

Ray believed that the storm his marriage had kicked up would eventually pass. The press would lose interest in him once he'd moved west, beyond what he still thought of in 1890 as the frontier. The scandal with Eva and Baby Beatrice would eventually be forgotten. Thanks to the letters he'd received from friends and former colleagues, he knew he was still deeply respected by many people in New York. There was no reason for him to hide, therefore, from anyone who wasn't a reporter. He didn't need to sit passively in the Tetons and wait for some "stranger" or "captain" to stop by for a visit, the way his uncle was doing on the Mosquito Coast. Ray Hamilton could actively solicit visits from friends and acquaintances.

A month or two after he moved in with Jack and Addie, Ray wrote to his good friends Gilbert Speir and Casimir de Rahm Moore and invited them to come out to Wyoming in late summer or early fall for a visit. Cas Moore was one of the people who wrote to Ray immediately after news of the stabbing in Atlantic City broke, the one whose grandfather wrote *The Night before Christmas*. Gil Speir was a friend from Columbia University. He and Ray frequently traveled to Michigan together, where Ray was a shareholder in the Monroe Marsh Company, an exclusive hunt club founded in 1881 that had just twenty-five members.[58]

Hunt clubs became popular in the late nineteenth century, as a growing number of men who enjoyed the challenge of leaving their urban environs and going into the woods to stalk animals for sport started to worry the populations their hobbies depended upon might be disappearing, thanks to human encroachment upon the land. In 1888 two men Ray knew well founded a hunt club in New York called the Boone and Crockett Club, which continues to exist today (although it is now headquartered in Montana, rather than the Big Apple). The club promotes wildlife conservation and ethical hunting practices, emphasizing the obligation of hunters to forswear devices like traps or floodlights that might give them an unfair advantage over their wild prey.[59]

One of the Boone and Crockett Club's founders rather famously refused to kill a bear he'd been given an unfair advantage over after his guide used dogs to corner the animal in a Mississippi forest and then conked it over the head, tying it to a tree. The hunter who refused to kill the trapped bear was Ray's former colleague in the New York State Assembly Teddy Roosevelt—whose fairmindedness made headlines across the country and inspired the creation of the "teddy bear."[60]

The other founder of the Boone and Crockett Club was George Grinnell, the friend Ray Hamilton had visited in Montana shortly after he graduated from law school in 1874. As a child Grinnell attended a school in Manhattan that was run by Lucy Audubon, whose husband, John James Audubon, was the ornithologist Harriet Hemenway (i.e., Cousin Gus's wife) named her bird conservation society after. Lucy Audubon taught Grinnell that hunting could encourage human beings to respect and protect wild animals. Her husband, after all, had killed at least one member of the four hundred bird species he painted over the course of his life, and sometimes he killed dozens.[61]

New York was where George Grinnell became a conservationist and a hunter. It was in the West, however, that he turned his eye away from birds and toward big game. Specifically, it was those bison that had so impressed William Wylie that concerned Grinnell the most. He became obsessed with their declining numbers after he went on a buffalo hunt with some Pawnee Indians in 1873. After searching for days before finally finding a herd, Grinnell realized that the "shaggy, brown beasts" were doomed to extinction "unless some action on the subject is speedily taken."[62]

The Boone and Crockett Club's goals reflected Grinnell's disgust at what had happened to the bison population. The club was made up of "men of intelligence and education" who had "killed one or more variety of North American large game with a rifle." Proof that a man had killed a large, wild animal was actually required before he could join the club. Every member also had to have a "high social standing" that would enable him to "wield a great influence for good in matters of game protection."

Members agreed to use their resources to "work for the preservation of the large game of this country" and "promote travel and exploration in the wild and unknown, or partially known portions of the country."[63]

Few areas were more wild or unknown in 1888 than the northwest corner of Wyoming where Ray Hamilton retreated after Evangeline Steele used a purchased baby to trick him into marrying her and then stabbed that baby's wet nurse with a dagger his father had acquired during the Mexican War. When Ray and Jack arranged for several Swedish carpenters from Idaho to come over to their side of the Tetons in June 1890 to build a lodge on Jack's property that was bigger than any other domicile in Jackson Hole at the time, it was because Ray knew that members of the Boone and Crockett Club would be astounded by the sublimity of the Teton range and want to come back to the area time and again.[64]

"The scenery around the lake is magnificent and full of game," Ray wrote to Gil Speir on July 14, 1890. "A week ago I rode up to within fifty yards of a bunch of cow elk lying in some trees. I had my rifle on one of them when I saw she had a fawn, and I concluded I would not shoot, although we wanted the meat." The area where John Dudley Sargent had settled with his family was teeming with so much wildlife that sometimes Ray encountered animals even when he wasn't looking for them. "Coming down from the ranch one day, Sargent had a shot at a moose, but missed him," Ray informed his friend. "I was right beside him, but had no gun. [The moose] was a beauty; as black as a bear, and with immense horns, and he looked bigger than a horse."[65]

If Gil Speir visited Ray in Wyoming, he would almost certainly return to New York qualified to join the Boone and Crockett Club. "You must be sure to come out," Ray told him. "You will have a first rate time and be sure to kill an elk, and perhaps a bear." Ray believed his friend would probably want to do some camping, but because, even in July, Ray had occasionally awakened to "hoar frost on the blankets" after he'd spent a night outside, he wanted Gil to know other accommodations would soon be available. "I am building a log house which will be finished about August 1st. [I] have six ponies and a colt who swims rivers and generally behaves as if he is the biggest horse in the bunch."[66]

Gil took Ray up on his invitation. He and Cas Moore left New York City on the morning of August 29 and arrived at the Utah and Northern Railroad's Market Lake Station in Idaho three days later, on the afternoon of September 1. They took a stage coach to Rexburg, Idaho, which was about twenty-five miles away from the station, and then rode horses over the mountains, through the Teton Pass (which is now a seventeen-mile-long highway, as gorgeous as it is intimidating, known at wyo-22), and down to the Snake River, on the eastern side of the range. The rest of their 150-mile-long journey from the train station was done on foot. They followed the Snake River to its confluence with Jackson Lake, and arrived at the lake's southern shore on the afternoon of September 5, 1890.[67]

That's where Gilbert Speir and Casimer de Rahm Moore met John Dudley Sargent, possibly for the first time. He was alone when he met them. Jack's assignment had been grim when he'd left his wife and children the day before to meet the two New Yorkers. His job was to tell the pair that Ray Hamilton's body had been found floating in the Snake River three days earlier, on the day they set out to cross the Teton Mountains on horseback. Judging from the condition of their friend's bloated and fish-eaten corpse, Ray had probably died a couple of days before Gil and Cas even left New York.[68]

10

Final Resting Places

It took ten days for America's newspapers to get a hold of the story. Twenty-five years earlier it would have taken several weeks for news of what had happened to reach the East Coast. Thirty years earlier the press might never had learned what happened to Robert Ray Hamilton at all.

Casimer Moore and Gilbert Speir borrowed two of Ray's horses and traveled a hundred miles north, up to and through Yellowstone National Park, to get to the nearest telegraph office at the National Hotel. There they sent Cas's wife a telegram, telling her Ray had drowned. Harriet Moore passed the terrible news along to Ray's brother on September 12, one week after Cas and Gil had learned their friend was gone. The Hamiltons kept the information to themselves. Two days after they'd learned of Ray's demise, however, James Oliver Green walked into the offices of the *Daily Independent* in Helena, Montana, and told reporters there what had happened. The *Daily Independent* ran Green's story the next morning, and by that evening, newsboys in Boston and New York were shouting headlines about the tragedy.[1]

J. O. Green was one of the men who'd found Ray's body in the Snake River. A physician by training, he was, ironically, the son of Norvin Green, president of the Western Union Company that had a near monopoly on telegraphy services in the United States and was the reason, really, there was never any chance Ray was going to be able to escape the clutches of the press by going west.[2] The disgraced former lawmaker's best shot at having his humiliation be forgotten was not to hide, but to become so boring that the press lost interest in him—and dying unexpectedly in the Snake River was not a good way for Ray's story to become boring.

"The strange part of the affair is that thus far, not a word of news about it has appeared in the newspaper," the *Daily Independent* remarked, its editors clearly impressed with themselves for having gotten the scoop.

"As will be remembered, Hamilton was the leading figure in the biggest social scandal in New York in recent years."

According to the paper, James Oliver Green had been on a hunting trip, following the course of the Snake River, when his party happened upon John Dudley Sargent's homestead and learned from Addie that Ray had left a few days earlier and not returned. The paper's story wasn't quite right. Green later testified that he had first learned of Ray's disappearance after he and his friends encountered a search party in the woods. The *Daily Independent* was correct, however, when it said Addie was the first person to sound the alarm about Ray. Jack wasn't home on the day Ray left; he was on the other side of the Tetons in Idaho, purchasing household supplies and gathering the mail.[3]

Green and his friends had no interest in joining the search at first. The doctor recognized Ray's name when the men in the party shared it with him; he told a judge he thought he might even have met Ray on "one or two occasions, but I cannot state so positively." Green's wife, Amelia, was the daughter of Abram Hewitt, New York's mayor at the time of the Cable Railway Grab. It's likely Green did, in fact, meet Ray at some point before the two men made their way to Wyoming. It's not surprising, however, that they did not become friends. Not only was J. O. Green a Democrat and Ray a Republican, but Green's father-in-law had also worked hard during his term as mayor to get New York invested in an underground transit system like one the city of London had. Abram Hewitt was deeply opposed to any expansion of New York's cable railway system—and Ray, of course, had inexplicably endorsed such an expansion at the start of Hewitt's second year in office.[4]

Green knew who Ray was, but he wasn't willing to abandon his plans to kill a bear in order to find him. Three days later, however, when two men from the search party approached his campfire and told him Ray was still missing, the doctor agreed to join the search. "They told me that his horse and dog had been found," Green later recalled. The discovery was a clear sign Ray had not had trouble finding game and chosen to stay in the woods longer than he'd told Addie he would. Something had gone wrong. His horse's saddle was badly twisted by the weight of a dead antelope Ray had tied to it. The antelope was partially eaten, probably by the dog.

A few hours after J. O. Green joined the search, Ray Hamilton's body was found "lying face downwards, with the arms and legs extended" in a pool that had been formed in the Snake River. "There were two deer pine trees uprooted and fallen into the water and held across the current by the roots still in the bank," Green recalled. "It occurred to me that if the body were in that pool, it would be naturally caught by the branches of these trees." Three members of the search party jumped into the water and wrapped a rope under Ray's arms, so that they could pull his corpse from the river. Green insisted on examining the body "to satisfy myself whether a crime had been committed." He found that none of Ray's personal items had been removed from his pockets, and "there was no sign of violence, nor wound of any kind to be seen."[5]

Among the items found on Ray were "several letters, some of them from his attorneys, concerning the divorce suit now pending," the *Daily Independent* reported. At least one of the letters concerned "the closing up of his business affairs in the east." A pocket watch was found on his body, as well. The watch had stopped working a little after 9:30, even though it was still wound, suggesting it had been damaged by exposure to the water and "indicating that he might have been drowned at that hour."[6]

It was a sad and undignified end to a life that had promised to liberate the Hamilton family from a string of ignominies that hobbled three—and now four—generations of Hamilton men. The *Daily Independent* told its readers it sent a courtesy telegram to Schuyler Hamilton Sr. before going to press with the story, just to make sure he knew his son was dead. "While the family was informed of the affair, it seems that the eastern papers have learned nothing of it," the paper noted, reminding its readers for a second time that it had been the one to break the latest development in the story of Eva and Ray.[7]

The *New York Evening World* was interested in more than just courtesy. When it went to press with the story, the newspaper insisted on getting a formal statement from Ray's father. He told them he hadn't seen his son since May. "He came to bid me good-bye, and set out for Idaho the next day, where he bought a ranch which he was fitting up as an outfitting place for tourists and hunters," Schuyler Sr. disclosed, revealing a certain lack of clarity on the part of the father about where his son had actually been for the last three months of his life. Schuyler Sr. refused to speculate on whether Ray's drowning had been an accident. "I am now waiting for more definitive information," he told the paper, before asking that he and his family be left alone to mourn. "General Hamilton would not discuss his son's marital troubles," the *Evening World* grumbled, "nor say whether he would renew the suit for the annulment of his [son's] marriage." The status of Ray's marriage had not been settled by the time he died. His annulment lawsuit wasn't even scheduled to go before a judge until that November. It was entirely possible, the *Evening World* observed, that "Evangeline, now in Trenton State Prison, and Baby Beatrice shall come into the magnificent patrimony of Robert Ray Hamilton."[8]

From the Hamilton family's perspective, the situation was a mess. Ray couldn't have died at a more inconvenient time. Under New York State law, his widow—if he had one—was entitled to one-third of his estate, which, in addition to several properties he jointly owned with his aunt, Nathalie Ray Baylies, included the $40,000 annuity set aside for him by his maternal grandfather. That annuity would revert entirely to Aunt Nathalie only if Ray had no legal spouse when he died. If he did one-third of his annuity would go to his widow until the day of her death.

The entitlement was known as a "dower right," and nearly every state in the union had one. Well into the nineteenth century, women could not legally own property in many states once they married; everything they owned became the property of their husbands. Husbands were not permitted to disinherit their wives, however, no matter how nasty or unpleasant the marriage may have been. A man was free to leave much more than one-third of his estate to his wife, but he could not leave less. Additionally, creditors could not stake a claim to a widow's dower right. The thinking behind the law was that one-third of a man's estate was enough to guarantee that most widows got back the property they had brought into their marriages. A dower right also ensured that a widow was not left needlessly destitute after her only source of income had died.[9]

Eva stood to come into a boatload of money if Ray's family could not get her marriage to the deceased former lawmaker dissolved. The Hamiltons and Rays, therefore, spared no expense in their effort to prove not only that Ray had married Eva only because he thought the baby she'd purchased was his but also that Eva could not legally enter into a marital union with Ray, because she was already married to Josh Mann.

Of the two arguments, the one about Eva's bigamy had the most potential to block her access to Ray's estate. "Unless Eva Steele had a husband living at the time of her marriage to Robert Ray Hamilton," one prominent divorce attorney told the *New York World*, she and Ray were legally wed at the time of his death, "no matter how great the fraud by which that marriage was brought about." Eva's fraud was grounds for an annulment while both parties were still alive—and indeed, Abe Hummel, the attorney advising the *World*, fully believed that Ray would have succeeded in getting his marriage dissolved, had he not drowned. But even if "fraud and conspiracy of a most damnable kind were proven . . . and the judge was about dipping his pen in the ink for the purpose of writing a decree annulling the marriage," Hummel advised, "the woman would remain [the man's] wife in the sight of the law and retain her dower right . . . [if] before the judge had time to affix his signature, the husband should die."[10]

The list of witnesses Ray's attorney, Elihu Root, brought forward to prove that Evangeline Steele was a bigamist was five pages long. It included her brother, William, and his wife, Alice. William testified that his sister had introduced Josh Mann to their father as "her husband" when she brought Mann to the Steele family's home in Bradford County, Pennsylvania, in 1885. William's wife, Alice, corroborated this story. "I had a conversation with her, with Evangeline, about her being married," Alice told the court. "She said she was married in Philadelphia. She didn't say what time or anything about that, for I didn't ask her."[11]

William Foyle also testified that Eva and Josh had presented themselves to him as husband and wife. Foyle was an attorney who'd defended Eva's brother, Joseph, against a larceny charge in 1888. He'd called Josh Mann to speak as a character witness on Joseph's behalf. "He testified upon the trial that he was married to Joseph Steele's sister," Foyle recalled. "He said he had been married about seven years."[12]

Additional witnesses included the proprietors of hotels where Josh and Eva had stayed over the years, checking in as "Mr. and Mrs. Mann," "J. J. Mann and wife," and the like. There was a traveling salesman who'd lived next door to Mrs. Swinton in Philadelphia in the mid-1880s; he said he knew Eva as Swinton's daughter-in-law. The bookkeeper at the Union Dime Savings Bank in New York also testified Eva had had an account at the bank since 1886 under the name "Eva L. Mann." He brought the paperwork on that account to the court as proof, including several transactions in 1889, the year Eva married Ray, during which she transferred more than $3,000 to an account bearing the name of "Joshua J. Mann." And then, of course, there was William Kemp, the doctor who'd tried to help the first purchased baby who died. He testified that when he'd attended Eva in October 1888, she was going by the name "Mrs. Mann."[13]

The case was going well for the Hamiltons and Rays. A judge ruled in November 1890 that Eva was not legally married to Ray, and he allowed the family to move forward with the probating of Ray's estate.[14] Eva appealed that decision, but the testimony against her was damning, and it seemed likely she would lose her case again—until February 1891, when the story of Ray's unexpected death in Wyoming took a bizarre turn that had the potential to delay his family's efforts at settling his estate.

People started claiming that Ray was still alive. One man identifying himself as A. O. Howard told a reporter for the *Philadelphia Times* that he'd gone to college with Ray, although no one in the classes of 1871, 1872, or 1873 at Columbia had that last name (not that the reporter bothered to check). Howard said Ray was in Australia, "beginning life anew there, under an assumed name." He showed the reporter a letter Ray had supposedly sent him from San Francisco in October 1890, saying the former lawmaker had "apprised me of his intention of going to Japan, and thence to Sydney, New South Wales." Howard refused to allow the reporter to read the correspondence, however, insisting the letter was "of a personal nature" and that letting someone from the press read it "would result in no good to [Ray.]"[15]

One would think Howard's refusal to substantiate his claim would have been enough to convince the reporter to end his article there. Recall the mantra Theodore Dreiser encountered when he visited the offices of the *New York World*: "*Accuracy! Accuracy! Accuracy!*"[16] The *Philadelphia Times*, however, did not hold itself to that standard. Rather than ending its article with Howard's refusal to let the reporter read his letter, the paper allowed the man to go on and make bigger, even more controversial claims about Robert Ray Hamilton. These claims were picked up by newspapers in at least thirteen other states, including New York.

Ray and Eva had hosted wild parties in Albany during Ray's time in the state assembly, according to A. O. Howard. "There were frequently disgraceful orgies enacted there," he reported, "and much champagne was drunk." Eva had become "acquainted with many State secrets" at these parties, ones that would "humble to the dust the heads of many New Yorkers who now stand before the world as emblems of morality and virtue." This was why Ray had married her—to keep her quiet. Following her conviction, however, Eva had "threatened to make things hot for [Ray] and certain others high in New York politics as soon as she was released from the New Jersey State Prison." This was why Ray had faked his death and fled the country. "He would not bring disgrace upon those he esteemed," Howard claimed, "if any sacrifice to prevent it were possible."[17]

The story was almost certainly a fabrication, manufactured by one of Eva's attorneys, in all likelihood. It was over the top, even by the standards of yellow journalism. Nevertheless, the tale was powerful, and it resonated with readers. Worse than that, it inspired copycats.

Henry Strong came forward in June 1891 and claimed he had seen Ray a few weeks earlier in Yellowstone National Park. He'd recognized Ray's face and voice because he'd lived in Albany in 1889, the lawmaker's final year in office, and had often turned out to hear him speak. "I was particularly interested in Mr. Hamilton because he was the only Republican from New York City," Strong explained—incorrectly. There were four other Manhattan Republicans in the assembly along with Ray, including Ernest Howard Crosby, Ray's partner and collaborator until the Cable Railway Grab messed up that alliance (and possibly that friendship).[18]

Strong said he'd been in California "and started home three weeks ago by way of the Northern Pacific. At Yankton, [South Dakota,] I stopped off and took the stage route into the Yellowstone Park to see what it was like." He'd spent about a week there, staying in a hotel. While he was passing through that hotel's lobby, he saw Ray Hamilton. "I could have recognized him by his voice if I hadn't seen him at all," Strong asserted, but because no one else seemed to know who Ray was, he said nothing to the disgraced former lawmaker. "I thought if he wanted to remain unknown, it was none of my business."[19]

This time the paper breaking the story had the decency, at least, to cast doubt on Strong's claim and to refuse to allow him to allege anything more controversial than what he'd already said. "Mr. Strong looks like an honest farmer and talks like a man who knows what he is about," the *New York Herald* conceded, "but he is a little out of range in his geography. The Northern Pacific Railway doesn't run through Yankton, and that place is a long distance from the park."[20] Nevertheless, Strong's allegation (never mind Howard's . . .) was enough to complicate the efforts of Ray's family to block Eva's access to his money. If Ray were still alive, his family members had no standing to push to have his marriage annulled; only he could do that. So long as he was alive, Ray was also financially responsible for his wife's bills.

Schuyler Hamilton Sr., therefore, made some requests. He asked three of the Swedish carpenters from Idaho who'd been building the lodge at Jackson Lake to come to New York and testify about his son's death. He also asked Ray's business partner to come east and tell a judge what, exactly, had happened in the days before and after Ray's body was found in the Snake River. This was the visit John Dudley Sargent would later refer to, when he wrote to Elihu Root, asking the secretary of state for help with his homestead application and reminding the secretary that "in June of 1891, I went from my home on Jackson Lake, Wyoming, to New York at General Hamilton's request, and met you."[21]

John Dudley Sargent's letter to Schuyler Hamilton Jr. was direct. "Dear Sir," Jack began. "On Saturday, Aug. 23, while I was at Kamtuck Post-Office, Idaho, for our mail and freight for the ranch, your brother, Robert Ray Hamilton, was accidentally drowned in [the] Snake River, about six miles below the outlet of Mary Mere."[22]

Jack's letter went on to explain how he believed the accident happened. "As you will see from the map inclosed [sic], he had to ford the Snake River below the lake," he told Young Schuyler. "He forded all right, headed down Friday, staid [sic] at the south camp that night, and started back Saturday night with an antelope head, skins, and hams tied on his saddle." Jack knew that Ray had made it to the south camp—known to locals as "South Landing"—because Ray had left him a note there, realizing Jack would spend the night in the camp's wooden lean-to on his way back from Idaho.[23] The lean-to was one of several that settlers and soldiers had constructed throughout the region, to be used by any traveler who needed temporary shelter. Gil and Cas, in fact, had spent the night at South Landing on their way to Marymere, not knowing that their friend had written his last note ever there a little more than a week before they arrived.

It was after Ray spent the night at South Landing, Jack believed, that he made his fatal mistake. "Mrs. Sargent tried to persuade him not to go," the Mainer told Young Schuyler, by way of subtly suggesting that Ray should not have attempted to navigate the woods on his own. He'd arrived in Wyoming just three months earlier, after all. Thanks to snowmelt and rainfall, the character of the Snake River could be radically different from one month to the next. Seven men before Ray had drowned that same year, all of them because they'd underestimated the power of the Snake, which had not yet been enfeebled by a dam.[24]

"He went into the river at night, above the ford, in about the worst place he could have struck," Jack informed Schuyler. "It seems that his spurs tangled up in the grass in the bottom of the river." Ray's spurs were a "California" style that had unusually large rowels and two-piece heel bands that made them fashionable but difficult to remove. They'd been a gift from Jack.[25]

"He was brought up here in the boat today and buried close to our house, on a spot overlooking Mary Mere and the Teton Mountains," John Dudley Sargent told Schuyler Hamilton Jr., hoping this description of Ray's final resting place would bring some comfort to the Hamilton family. "He once told me he would rather be buried here, should anything happen. I know he was going to change his residence and make this his home."[26]

Jack wanted Young Schuyler to know he and Addie were heart-broken by the loss of Ray. "Although we have known him but a short time, we grieve him from the bottom of our hearts," he wrote. "In sorrow and respect, I am faithfully yours, John D. Sargent."[27]

Jack's letter was the reason Schuyler Hamilton Sr. asked him to come to New York and testify about his son's death. That testimony was covered by newspapers across the country, making Jack a public figure for the first time in his life. Unlike Robert Ray Hamilton—or, later, Edith Drake—John Dudley Sargent had attracted no press attention before he moved to Wyoming. Before Ray died there were just two references to him in any newspaper, both in 1885: the *Machias Union* announced that Jack had married Leander Crane's daughter, Adelaide, in February of that year, and the *Laramie Daily Boomerang* reported that he and his bride were staying at the Thornburgh Hotel there two months later. Other than these two obscure references, Jack was unknown to reporters prior to Ray's death. The humiliation he fled on the East Coast when he moved to Wyoming wasn't public, it was internal—a not-unfounded sense that he was unwanted by the only family he had in his life until he created his own.[28]

After Ray Hamilton died, John Dudley Sargent's name was mentioned in several nationally distributed articles about the drowning. They explained that Jack and Ray had been business partners, and that Jack was the one who'd identified Ray's body. These early articles focused primarily on J. O. Green, however, because his political and business connections were well known to reporters at the time.[29] Little was said about the man with the Brahmin last name until he came east to testify that Robert Ray Hamilton was dead—and then the interest of reporters was decidedly piqued.

"A tall, dark man wearing a soiled grey corduroy suit and a large light colored sombrero got off the Pennsylvania railroad express last night in Jersey City," the *New York Sun* reported on June 10, 1891. "He wore a hunting belt with field glasses slung in it. Everybody in the station noticed him as he walked down the platform leading a dog." "Mr. Sargent is a typical looking frontiersman," the *New York Herald* told its readers. "He is over six-feet high, is somewhat sparely built, but has every movement indicating a wiry, tough body, used to hardships and exposure."

Jack's eyes were "small and blue," and his face was dominated by "high cheek bones" and a "dark moustache." To the disappointment of reporters, he showed up at the law offices of Elihu Root a few days after his arrival in the city, wearing not a sombrero, but a "grey suit that made him look like any other citizen of New York." Reporters had been hoping he would don the "leggings of a frontiersman" for the important meeting. Jack did reveal some uncivilized qualities, however, when he gave his name to the front desk at the Park Avenue hotel where Schuyler Hamilton Sr. had rented a set of rooms for him. The dog the *Sun*'s reporter had observed in Jersey City was Ray's pointer, Jocko. Jack apparently believed he'd be able to bring the dog into the hotel with him. "Mr. Sargent has arrived with Hamilton's dog," a reporter for the *New York Tribune* who'd been stationed at the hotel gleefully reported. The dog was quickly taken into custody by a servant from General Hamilton's household who was summoned by the hotel to deal with the faux pas.[30]

Jack Sargent's sartorial decisions were a disappointment to reporters, but his testimony was not. For more than an hour, he answered questions that were fired at him by Eva's attorney, who was looking to discredit him. "You say that the body identified by you as Mr. Hamilton was not badly decomposed," Charles Fuller observed several minutes into the session. Yet "Dr. Green, who saw it before you did, swears that it must have been in the water ten days; that it was so badly decomposed that recognition was impossible; that the upper lip and mustache were eaten away by fish and turtles; that the body had swollen as much as it could swell without bursting; and that the flesh had turned purple." How, Fuller intended to ask, could Jack possibly have determined that the body J. O. Green found in the Snake River was Ray's?[31]

The lawyer didn't have a chance to ask the question, however, because he was interrupted. "Did he swear to that?" Jack Sargent asked, "springing to his feet excitedly," according to a published excerpt of the exchange. A court official instructed Jack to sit down, and Fuller replied that Green had, in fact, "sworn to" his description of the body. "If Dr. Green testified as you say, he testified to an untruth," Jack angrily told the lawyer. "The decomposition was trifling, and the change no more than what you would expect in a man who had been drown. The fishes had not destroyed his features. Something had drawn his upper lip, so that his front teeth might be seen, but no one who knew him in life could make a mistake."[32]

Fuller moved on to ask Jack several questions about the dates and circumstances involved. When did Ray leave the homestead? When did Jack learn he had not returned? When did Cas Moore and Gil Speir arrive? Had they seen the body? Why not? What was found on the body when it was pulled from the river? After these questions were asked and answered, Fuller returned to the condition of Ray's corpse, questioning once again how Jack possibly could have identified it, given its rotting, bloated, and fish-eaten condition. "When Mr. Fuller again went into details about certain conditions of the man's features, Mr. Sargent turned his head away and declined to speak more on the subject," the *Pittsburgh Dispatch* reported. "He shed a few tears, and it was some moment before he recovered his composure."[33]

It was a surprisingly deep response, given that Jack had known Ray "but a short time," according to the letter he'd sent to Schuyler Hamilton Jr. After he stopped crying, Jack told Charles Fuller he had come to New York to "stop the trash in the newspapers about Mr. Hamilton's not being dead." It was time to "put a stop to the ridiculous talk," Jack declared. Robert Ray Hamilton was gone. "It would be to my interest to find him alive, if only I could."[34]

Jack's testimony, along with that of the Swedish carpenters, should have been enough to put the question of whether Ray was actually dead to rest. One carpenter, Roman Sepert, testified he'd seen the former lawmaker "every day in August until the twenty-second day," when Ray left to go on his final hunt. Sepert recognized the body pulled from the river "by the hair, mustache, general cast of features, and clothes it had on," which were the same clothes Ray had been wearing "when I saw him go away— corduroy pants and vest and a light summer coat." Another carpenter, Christian Aeschenbacher, said he'd made the coffin Robert Ray Hamilton was buried in. He claimed he "knew Mr. Hamilton very well in his lifetime," and that he was "certain that it was his body that I helped to bury about the twenty-eighth day of August, 1890."[35]

Still, the rumors persisted—partially because Eva Hamilton's lawyers had an interest in keeping them alive, and partially because newspaper editors across the country did. Finally, in the fall of 1891, Charles Anderson Dana of the *New York Sun* decided it was time for his paper to create a pseudoevent. He knew he could manufacture a story for his reporters to cover, if he could just convince the Hamilton family to have the body that was buried on John Dudley Sargent's homestead exhumed.

"In 1891, the *Sun* . . . sent my father into Jackson's Hole, Wyo, to dig up the drown body of Robert Ray Hamilton," Raymond Spears recalled in 1934. Spears's father was John Randolph Spears, a journalist who'd worked for the *Sun* from 1882 to 1896 and covered a number of sensational stories during that time, including one that involved a family feud most Americans had never heard of until Spears wrote about it for the *New York Sun*. The feud attracted his attention after several members of the Hatfield family in West Virginia surrounded the cabin of Randolph McCoy in Kentucky and set fire to it while the McCoys were still inside.[36]

J. R. Spears began his article about the examination of Ray Hamilton's bones by reminding his readers of the Atlantic City scandal. He then told them it was "not without reason" that some people had begun to question whether Ray was actually dead. "The story of his death, when broken to his father, did not fall apparently like an overwhelming blow," Spears observed. The "briefest possible announcement" of Ray's death had been made by the family, and Ray's funeral had not been held until October 6, nearly a month after the Hamiltons learned of his death.[37]

Added to this list of suspicious behaviors was the fact that "seven other men had been drowned in the Snake River that year." In light of that gruesome statistic, "people in the East" had begun "to wonder whether one of these seven bodies had been dressed in Hamilton's clothes and passed off to the public as that of the body of the legislator." John Randolph Spears himself had begun to suspect that Ray might not be dead. When he arrived at the Market Lake train station in Idaho, he talked to a number of locals there about the case, including Roman Sepert, one of the carpenters who'd testified to Ray's death. "When asked to describe the body, [Sepert] said among other things that the upper front teeth had been filled with gold in a most conspicuous fashion," Spears reported. "In fact, the upper front teeth of Robert Ray Hamilton were large and noticeably perfect."[38]

To put an end to the uncertainty (which the *Sun* had helped to stoke), John Randolph Spears assembled a team that consisted of a coroner and an "experienced surgeon" from Idaho. Together the men set out for Marymere on the morning of October 1, 1891. Spears's story about their "adventures in crossing the plains and Teton Pass in a blinding snowstorm" would later be criticized by a number of the *Sun*'s competitors as a cynical stunt. The *Illustrated American* accused Spears and Charles Dana of engaging in behavior that was "inexpressibly distressing to Mr. Hamilton's family and friends." For the rest of his career, however, J. R. Spears would defend his reporting on Robert Ray Hamilton. "My paper cheerfully spent a large sum of money to get *all* the facts in the case," he recalled several years after Ray had died. "The life of a reporter employed by a reputable newspaper is passed in a persistent and usually success-ful search for truth."[39]

It took Spears and his team a week to get to Jack Sargent's homestead. Finally, on the morning of October 9, they were able to open the grave in question, and the body within it was "carefully examined for such marks as would identify it, if it were really the body of Robert Ray Hamilton." In his official report, Dr. W. A. Hocker noted that he'd found several gold and silver fillings in the lower teeth of the body in the grave, and that one of the body's lower molars had been removed. "Partner Sargent said that these teeth had been filled and the one extracted by a dentist in New York during the month of May preceding Hamilton's death," Spears reported—revealing a surprisingly intimate understanding of Ray's per-sonal health on the part of Jack. "He probably told the truth, for he had a memorandum book in which were noted in Hamilton's hand the charges made by the dentist."[40]

Dr. Hocker also "found the left tibia had been fractured about the middle, and the leg [was] a little shorter as a result of the fracture." This discovery seemed to be irrefutable evidence that the body was, in fact, that of Robert Ray Hamilton. Ray had had a serious accident while riding his horse in Central Park when he was a teenager. He'd "fractured his left leg below the knee," John Randolph Spears explained. The injury had "kept him in Presbyterian hospital for eleven weeks. When this fracture healed, the growth of the bone formed a prominent projection on the front of the shin."[41]

Officials in Uinta County, Wyoming, declared that Robert Ray Ham-ilton had accidentally drowned in the Snake River on August 23, 1890. Now that he knew the body in the grave was Ray's, John Randolph Spears was indignant. "Here lay the body of one who had served his constitu-ents well in the Assembly, and who was, moreover, a great-grandson of one of the most distinguished statesmen," the reporter wrote. And "it was crowded into a box too shallow to allow the feet to remain upright." Spears continued: "Overwhelmed by the disgrace into which he had fallen, Robert Ray Hamilton sought seclusion and peace in the wildest regions of the Rocky Mountains." On "an evil day" he'd tried to cross "the treacherous south fork of the Snake River," and "a life marred only by one great mistake went out in the night."[42]

"Strangers found his body, and those who could not know his worth knocked a few rough boards together for a coffin," Spears angrily declared. "Without a tear or a prayer," these strangers "dumped [Hamilton's body] into a hole in a desolate hillside, under the shadow of the barren, forbidding Tetons—and there it was allowed to remain, marked only by rough-pine head and footboards, on which someone scrawled with a lead pencil a tribute of praise that, when viewed in the light of the facts, is an exasperating mockery."[43]

It was a bitter description of Ray's burial place that made for fantastic copy. John Randolph Spears must not have been in Elihu Root's office four months earlier, however, when Jack Sargent met with Eva Hamilton's attorney. If he'd been there, Spears would have known that what he wrote about the disregard everyone in Wyoming supposedly had for Ray Hamilton's life and death was simply not true.

Ray's bones weren't going back into that grave at Marymere, regardless of what Jack Sargent said he had told him about where he wanted his final resting place to be. Ray was coming home to New York.

Green-Wood Cemetery in Brooklyn was the third "garden cemetery" to open in the United States. The first was Mount Auburn, in Cambridge, Massachusetts. Before Green-Wood, Mount Auburn, and Mount Hope Cemetery in Bangor, Maine, started receiving bodies in the 1830s, most Americans didn't even use the word "cemetery" to describe where their ancestors were buried. "Graveyard" and "burial ground" were the terms typically used.[44]

Christopher Wren, the architect who designed St. Paul's Cathedral in London, was one of the first people in western Europe to call for burial grounds to be moved away from churchyards to more expansive "suburban" locations. When Queen Anne called for fifty new churches to be built in London in 1708, Wren told a friend he believed none of the plans should include a graveyard, since the constant upturning of dirt had increased moisture levels within many of London's older churches, causing mold to grow along the stone walls. "It shall be enquired, where then shall be the burials," the architect wrote. "I answer, in Cemeteries seated in the out-skirts of town . . . where the Dead need not be disturbed by the Pleasure of the Sexton, or piled four or five upon one another, or bones thrown out to make room."[45]

Wren believed these suburban cemeteries should be places where families could relax and recreate. They ought to have "a Walkaround, and two cross Walks, decently planted with Yew trees," so that people would want to visit them. Stopping by a dead relative's grave, after all, would no longer be something people could easily do after church services, if Wren's ideas were realized. As it was, even when graves didn't require much effort to be visited, many Anglo-Americans in the eighteenth century did not enjoy calling upon them. "I have a most settled enmity to all ceremonies for the dead," the Reverend William Bentley of Salem, Massachusetts, confessed in 1804, expressing a sentiment that was surprisingly common among men of the cloth at the time. "Let their memories live, but let their ashes be forgotten."[46]

It would be a hundred years before Christopher Wren's ideas about cemetery placement and design gained any traction in Europe, and even then, it was in Paris, not London, where his ideas were realized first. In the United States, one of the earliest advocates of garden cemeteries was Jacob Bigelow, the friend who visited Gus Hemenway Sr. at the Spring Hill House for Nervous Invalids in 1862 and reported back to Gus's wife, Mary, that the businessman's "memory did not retain impressions." Bigelow was a doctor who believed that Boston's crowded burial grounds were starting to become health hazards, or what he more colorfully called "receptacles for putrefying matter and hotbeds of miasmata." The germ theory of disease hadn't yet taken root in the medical community, but Bigelow understood that where dead bodies congregated, disease rates tended to be higher.[47]

In 1822, in the midst of a yellow fever epidemic, several Boston churches petitioned city officials to allow them to bury bodies in their basements, since they were running out of room in their graveyards. That was when Jacob Bigelow decided it was time to act. He called for a moratorium on burials within the city limits and recommended the creation of a new burial ground on the outskirts of town. Boston's officials weren't willing to fund his idea, so in 1825, Bigelow started raising private money. Five years later he purchased a seventy-acre farm along the Charles River, not far from Harvard's campus, and engaged the Massachusetts Horticultural Society to do some minor landscaping that would enhance the beauty of the area's towering poplar trees.[48]

When Mount Auburn Cemetery opened in 1831, many European visitors saw it as a sign that American culture was not completely beyond redemption. Scottish travel writer Basil Hall called it "one of the prettiest burial places I ever saw." There was much in the United States that failed to impress him, but the example Hall saw in Cambridge of how Americans treated their dead left him feeling ashamed. Compared to Mount Auburn, the "soppy churchyard" in his native Dunglass, Scotland, was a place where "mourners sink ankle deep in a rank and offensive mould, mixed with broken bones and fragments of coffins." The English actress Fanny Kemble found that Mount Auburn's winding gravel paths and thick tree canopy made the cemetery feel "like a pleasure garden, instead of a place of graves." Carl David Ardwefson, a travel writer from Sweden, declared in 1832 that "a glance at this beautiful cemetery almost excites a wish to die."[49]

Mount Auburn—and the Green-Wood cemetery in Brooklyn that opened seven years after it—served as models for dozens of garden cemeteries that opened across the United States and Canada in the mid-nineteenth century: Oak Woods in Chicago; Forest Home in Milwaukee; Mount Hermon in Quebec City; Beechwood in Ottawa; Laurel Hill in Philadelphia; Crown Hill in Indianapolis; Cave Hill in Louisville; and Oak Hill in Washington DC—just to name a few. These cemeteries were more than simply places for people to bury their dead. In an age before the "parks movement" that inspired Young Gus Hemenway Jr., garden cemeteries were oases for urbanites, places where they could go to escape the increasingly congested and loud conditions of the city. People used to picnic and take carriage rides through these cemeteries, honoring the dead by celebrating life. To this day it's still possible to stand in some parts of Green-Wood

Cemetery in the summertime and have the only sounds you hear be that of katydids and rustling beech trees, even though you are in the middle of the most populous borough in the most populous city in the United States of America.

Schuyler Hamilton Sr. bought his family's plot in Green-Wood in 1867 so that he could bury his beloved wife, Cornelia, there. Eight years later he buried his seventeen-year-old son there, as well. Charles, the youngest of the three Hamilton boys, is in a space just to the east of his mother. In May 1899 Schuyler Jr., Ray's brother, arranged to have his second wife, Jane Mercer Hamilton, buried in the plot, which is big enough to hold a total of nine bodies. Jane died tragically after overdosing on morphine in the middle of a violent thunderstorm. Four years later Young Schuyler arranged to have his eighty-one-year-old father buried in the plot. And four years after that, in 1907, Young Schuyler's third wife, Emma, arranged for him to be buried in the plot next to his brother, Charles, in the space farthest removed from the remains of Jane.[50]

Robert Ray Hamilton is not buried in the Hamilton family plot. If you visit the cemetery today, however, you might make the mistake of thinking he's there, because a granite monument towering over the plot tells you he is. "ROBERT RAY HAMILTON, ELDEST SON OF SCHUYLER AND CORNELIA HAMILTON," an inscription on one of the monument's eight, pentagon-shaped panels reads. "BORN, N.Y., MARCH 18, 1851. DIED, WYOMING TY., AUG. 23, 1893."

The year of Ray's death is wrong. So is Wyoming's listed status as a territory; it became a state about six weeks before Ray died in August 1890. The inscription wasn't carved onto the monument until 1909, many years after Ray's death and after both of his parents, his aunt, Nathalie Ray Baylies, and his only two siblings were all dead. Schuyler Jr.'s third wife, Emma, arranged for Ray's information to be added to the monument about a year and a half after her husband died. Emma Gray Hamilton never knew her brother-in-law. That's probably why she got the date of Ray's death wrong. Ray died twelve years before Emma married Schuyler Jr. The only sister-in-law he ever knew was Gertrude Van

Cortlandt Hamilton, who wrote to him in sympathy when the scandal with Eva first broke. Gertrude divorced Young Schuyler in 1894.[51]

Ray *is* buried in Green-Wood Cemetery, however. His father insisted on bringing his remains there after they were disinterred. Schuyler Sr. arranged to have his son buried with his maternal grandfather in the Ray family vault, which is dug into a hillside in the heart of Green-Wood Cemetery, nowhere near the Hamilton family plot. There's a sarcophagus on top of the hill. It bears the name of Ray's maternal grandfather, Robert Ray. There's a small tombstone on the hill, as well, that bears the name of Ray's maternal uncle, Richard Cornelius Ray, Schuyler Hamilton Sr.'s aide-de-camp who died in Mississippi while fighting in the Civil War. It was his death that prompted Schuyler Sr. to ask thirteen-year-old Ray to consider dropping the "Hamilton" name, so that his maternal grandfather's name would continue.[52]

The sarcophagus and the tombstone are the only markers on the hill. There is no indication, in other words, that Ray Hamilton's bones are there in the Ray family vault. Only the records of Green-Wood cemetery tell the story of where Ray's remains ended up, and as recently as 2019, the computerized version of those records didn't tell visitors how to find him. You had to go to the paper records to determine where Ray was buried, since Green-Wood's computer database didn't include his name. That database includes his name now.[53]

Clearly, the Hamiltons didn't want him found. Several reporters had learned his remains were being sent from Wyoming to New York, and because they knew the Hamilton family had a plot in the city's first garden cemetery, they accurately predicted Green-Wood was where Ray was going.[54] To avoid having his final resting place become a destination for gawkers, Ray's family members hid him with his maternal grandfather—just as someone did with his personal papers, housed at the New York Historical Society under his grandfather's name.

Ray's death was now certain. Eva, however, remained a problem. Elihu Root did a great job of showing that she and Josh Mann had presented themselves to dozens of people over the years as husband and wife, but there was one piece of evidence Root lacked: a certificate, saying Eva and Josh had been legally wed. Eva's attorney, Charles Fuller, had a certificate. It said Eva had married Robert Ray Hamilton. Fuller also had the Reverend Edson Burr on his side. He testified he'd performed a marriage ceremony for Eva and Ray in Paterson, New Jersey, in January 1889.[55]

In spite of this significant hole in Elihu Root's argument, the New York State Supreme Court rejected Eva's appeal and ruled that her marriage to Ray was not valid. The deceased lawmaker's executors soon found, however, that the decision was not enough for them to proceed with the probating of their charge's estate. The absence of a marriage certificate clearly showing Eva had not been free to marry Ray Hamilton made the private companies insuring Ray's life and property nervous; they refused to sign his policies over to his executors without Eva's signature. Edmund Baylies and Gilbert Speir, therefore, offered Eva a deal. If she signed the forms they needed her to sign, they would give her a one-time payment of $10,000 to add to the $28,000 she already had sitting in her bank account, thanks to payments Ray had made to her while he was alive. In modern-day terms, Eva would be walking away from her marriage to Ray with slightly more than $1 million in cash, plus the clothing, jewelry, and property in Passaic he'd purchased for her, which she'd be allowed to keep.[56]

Eva took the deal. After getting out of jail, she lay low for several months but then went on to star in a play called *All a Mistake* that was written for her by a friend and produced by a theater in Boonton, New Jersey. Two hundred fifty people showed up for the one-night-only performance, which was billed as featuring the talents of "Mrs. Robert Ray Hamilton, undoubtedly the most famous woman in the land." "The plot of the play follows incidents known to the public, but it follows them in a distorted way," one critic wrote. "Eva Mann is made out to be a heroine and a martyr. Robert Ray Hamilton is a weak, but noble-hearted man of the world, and both are victims of the wiles of a character who is supposed to be Josh Mann." Another critic found Eva's performance underwhelming. "Considering the fact that she never acted before on the stage, her poses and her stage walk are quite good," the critic wrote. "But when it comes to reading the lines, Eva Mann is not there at all . . . [she] expressed tremendous passion in her gestures, while her voice had about as little excitement in it as a glass of rain water."[57]

In 1893, after a judge had Josh Mann committed to an asylum, ostensibly because his brain injury and drinking habits had rendered him incapable of caring for himself, Eva married an Englishman named Archie Gaul. Using the surname "Hilton," the Gauls briefly ran a boarding house for actors in New York City before moving to England in the late 1890s. Eva returned to the United States, then—alone—sometime during the early years of the twentieth century. According to the *New York Evening World*, "she developed signs of heart failure" in November 1904 and slipped into a coma before the paramedics could get her to the charity ward of St. Vincent's Hospital. She died in that ward at the age of forty-seven on November 22. "A sister living in Pennsylvania has been notified," the paper reported, referring to Alice Steele as Eva's sister, rather than her sister-in-law, as so many newspapers had mistakenly done when the scandal in Atlantic City first made headlines sixteen years earlier.[58]

It was an ignoble end to a life that had been led undeniably, if understandably, ignobly. But Eva's death was not the final chapter in the story of Eva and Ray. There was one other life that had been touched by that stabbing in Atlantic City in August 1889. During all of these developments— Ray's move to Wyoming; his death in the Snake River; his disinterment by the *New York Sun*; Eva's challenge to his estate—where had the infant that so many people from across the United States and Canada wanted to adopt been growing up? Whatever happened to Baby Beatrice Ray?

Like Cures Like

The campus that used to be the Middletown State Homeopathic Hospital for the Insane lies about seventy miles northwest of midtown Manhattan, just up the road from a low-income housing complex and a recreational dog park. Most of the red brick buildings on the hospital's campus have been burned by arsonists or razed by municipal authorities in the years since the hospital closed.[1] Of the structures that remain, many are boarded up and covered with colorful graffiti and Virginia creeper vines. Maple and oak saplings grow out of their gutters and shoot up through cracks in their dilapidated cement staircases.

The hospital is where Edith Drake's family sent her after police found her "dazed and confused" in front of the United States Treasury building in the fall of 1897. It closed in 2006, after a decades-long push by state medical authorities to get mentally ill patients out of institutions and into smaller, more residential facilities. At its height in the 1960s, Middletown treated more than 3,600 residential patients for a variety of addictions and mental illnesses.[2]

After it closed all of the hospital's records dating back to its opening in 1874 were transferred to the New York State Archives in Albany. That archive now stores twenty-two volumes of case files on patients who were admitted to the Middletown hospital between 1874 and 1898, the year after Edith arrived. These records include questions that were asked of patients upon their admittance, along with the answers; details about the incidents that led to the patients' being admitted to the facility, voluntarily or involuntarily; descriptions of the patients' symptoms; and examination notes about treatments that were tried on the patients and the progress (or lack thereof) the patients made during their time at the facility.[3]

Somewhere in these volumes, there's an explanation of what Edith Drake was struggling with when she arrived in Middletown, New York.

The explanation is undoubtedly a product of its time, meaning it might not accord with our modern-day understandings of mental illness—what it is, what it isn't, and how to treat it. But at least the explanation is something put forward by people who had Edith's welfare as their concern and goal. The descriptions of her behavior hidden in these volumes were written by people who wanted to help her, not by people looking to use her antics to sell newspapers.

The patient case files in Albany could allow for a sensitive and sophisticated profile of Edith Drake to be constructed, one that is more respectful of her struggles than the *New York Sun*'s stories about how she danced in the street in front of Francis Wilson's house ever were. The profile would also be deeper and more nuanced than the modern-day tales known to locals and graduate students in Jackson Hole about how Edith liked to climb trees naked, so she could play her violin and gobble peanuts.[4]

The state of New York, however, considers mental health privacy to be a right that belongs to all human beings, alive or dead. Under the provisions of the Health Insurance Portability and Accountability Act, passed by Congress in 1996, a patient's medical records are sealed—available to doctors, family members, and law enforcement agents only under a set of very tightly defined circumstances—until fifty years after the patient has died. After that the information can be used by researchers, even if those researchers aren't related to the patient or working in a medical or law enforcement field.[5]

HIPAA does not trump state laws with higher standards, however, and Chapter 27, Article 33, Section 13 of New York State's Mental Hygiene Law, passed in 1972, places no statute of limitations on a New Yorker's privacy when it comes to his or her mental health. The law states simply that all information "tending to identify patients or clients" within the state's mental health system "shall not be a public record," regardless of how long ago the patients' time within the system was. Any historian looking to use the files to construct a profile of Edith Drake will be denied, therefore, until or unless New York's Mental Hygiene Law is changed.[6]

The law is well intentioned, and its consequences have probably been mostly good (even if the law does perpetuate the notion that there is something uniquely and deservedly stigmatizing about mental illness). Nevertheless, the American Psychiatric Association recognizes the importance of opening mental health archives up to historians. In 2019 the organization awarded its prestigious Benjamin Rush Award to King Davis, a senior research fellow at the University of Texas, for his work on the Central State Hospital Archives Project. That project has located, restored, catalogued, and digitized more than eight hundred thousand documents and thirty-six thousand photographs and slides kept by the Central Lunatic Asylum for Colored Insane. The facility opened in Petersburg, Virginia, in 1870 and was the first psychiatric hospital founded for Black patients in the United States.

A review of the documents makes it clear that the hospital was founded to alleviate White fears of Black people who were no longer fettered by slavery, not to help African Americans who suffered from neurological disorders or mental illnesses. "What struck me the most," King Davis has said about the records, "is that in many instances, the cause of [the patients'] mental illness was freedom: the [supposed] inability of Black people to manage freedom." In one particularly telling intake interview, doctors determined that a forty-five-year-old man named Isham Thomas was "insane" because "he claims that he is not a human being, because he says he has not been allowed to vote." Gems like this are the reason King Davis has worked to make intake interviews like Isham Thomas's a part of the public record. "We must recognize how important this information is and make it a part of the curricula in programs in social work, psychology, nursing, psychiatry, and medicine," Davis has argued. The leaders of the American Psychiatric Association agree.[7]

The hospital in Middletown opened at a time when America's physicians—and the elected officials they advised—were committed to the idea that asylums were the best way to help people recover from four main categories of mental illness, any or all of which could have been something Edith Drake struggled with: *mania*, which included not just hyperactivity or euphoria but also delusions; *melancholia*, which we think of today as depression; *catatonia*, which manifested in a variety of ways, ranging from an inability to eat or perform basic hygiene functions, to repetitive motion or complete paralysis; and *dementia*, which included not just memory issues but also impaired problem-solving skills and hallucinations.

Prior to the mid-nineteenth century, as is the case today, the thinking was that residential facilities—homes, rather than institutions—were the best environments for the mentally ill. Officials strove to place people who were commonly said to be "insane" with relatives or neighbors, often providing a stipend to help family or friends care for a mentally ill patient. Institutions existed, but they were almshouses, not hospitals. They weren't devoted to helping the insane; they were devoted to helping the poor (who, not infrequently, had mental health challenges).[8]

In the 1850s, about a decade before Gus Hemenway Sr. checked himself into a private sanitarium in Connecticut, things began to change. Psychiatrists (who were known then as "alienists," the idea being that mentally ill patients were "alienated" in some way from their true selves) started to believe that institutions rather than homes were the best way to help their patients.[9] This change had a lot to do with their growing sense that modern life was the reason people were sick.

"Insanity is a part of the price we pay for civilization," Edward Jarvis wrote from his medical office in Dorchester, Massachusetts, in 1851. "The causes of the one increase with the developments and results of the other." It was a "well-established fact," according to Pliny Earle, "that there is a constant parallelism between the progress of society, and the increase of mental disorders." "While in aboriginal races and people insanity is comparatively unknown," Earle noted (clearly having spent no time at all with Indigenous patients), "it prevails with greatest frequency in nations with the highest culture and refinement." He told his students at the Berkshire Medical College in Pittsfield, Massachusetts, that "it may, indeed, seriously be asked, whether the condition of highest culture in society is worth the penalties which it costs."[10]

Edward Jarvis and Pliny Earle shared the thinking of S. Weir Mitchell that technology, or, more specifically, the rapid change that came with technology, was making Americans sick. Recall that Mitchell believed the "racing speed which the telegraph and railway have introduced into commercial life" was to blame for the sleep disorders and digestive issues he was seeing among his White, middle-class patients.[11]

Jarvis and Earle thought that change was only part of problem, however. The other part of the problem was *choice*. Thanks to democracy and capitalism, White middle-class Americans had been given an array of choices—about careers and toothpaste and politicians and marriage and schools. These choices were only getting more complicated as the nineteenth century progressed, and they were making people crazy. "In this country where no son is necessarily confined to the work or employment of his father, but all the fields of labor, of profit, or of honor are open to whomsoever will put on the harness," Edward Jarvis observed, "the ambition of some leads them to aim at that which they cannot reach, to strive for more than they can grasp . . . and they end in frequent disappointment." The condition, Jarvis believed, was an unavoidable consequence of the freedom and fluidity offered to (some) Americans by a culture that claimed "all men" were "created equal," even as some men were clearly born smarter, faster, or stronger than others. "Where people are overborne by despotic government, or where men are born in castes and die without overstepping their native condition," Jarvis wrote, "these undue mental excitements and struggles do not happen." The doctor wasn't advocating a return to despotism, of course—but it was a fact, he said, that as "the manifold ways of life are opened to all, the danger of misapplication of the cerebral forces and the mental powers increases, and men may think and act indiscreetly and become insane."[12]

Isaac Ray agreed. An alienist who helped to found the discipline of forensic psychology, Ray believed America's democratic impulses had created a culture in which "we question everything." Earlier generations had been satisfied with "taking their opinions on trust," especially when it came to "subjects which once were supposed to be confined to the province of the learned." By 1863, however, everyone had become an expert—resulting in an environment of confusion and instability that was making people sick. "Subjects that once were supposed to be confined to the learned, and even by them approached with a modest distrust in their abilities," Ray wrote, "are now discussed by an order of minds that disdain the trammels of logic, and care little for the established principles of science."[13] It was a defensive and elitist observation about a supposed cause of illness that seemed destined to age poorly—until the twenty-first century, when blogs and YouTube videos presented significant and unnecessary challenges to epidemiologists working to control a global pandemic among a fiercely democratic group of people.

By the mid-nineteenth century, American alienists were suspicious of ministers, who sometimes raised the enthusiasm levels of their congregants struggling with mental illness. They were suspicious of schoolteachers and college professors, who sometimes cultivated an unhealthy sense of competition between and among students. And they were suspicious of parents, who sometimes damaged their children through neglect or overindulgence—the latter being the more damaging mistake of the two, according to Ray, since it encouraged children to see life "not as a field of discipline and improvement, but as a scene of inexhaustible opportunities for fulfilling hope and gratifying desire." This mindset caused children to become adults who reeled "under the first stroke of disappointment . . . and thus it is than many a man becomes insane."[14]

Thus it was that many a woman became insane, as well. Throughout the nineteenth century, women were thought to be far more vulnerable than men to the dictates of their passions. Anger, sadness, jealousy, selfishness, and desire were believed to be the passions that exerted the greatest natural influences on the mind of a woman. The less trained and more indulged a young girl's mind was, the greater her chances of becoming a slave to her passions and developing a mental illness later in life.[15]

"Be kind to women, for their whole existence centres in their sexual sphere," one alienist who practiced in upstate New York advised his colleagues in 1885. "Wherever there is that predisposition, insanity may break out at any period in their life." When S. Weir Mitchell was asked whether the time he'd spent working with "the petty moral deformities of nervous feminine natures" had lessened his esteem for women, the doctor adamantly replied, "Surely, no!" With what he undoubtedly believed was genuine respect, Mitchell explained that the moral deformities he encountered in his female patients were "due to educational errors"—upbringings that had failed to teach women not to tell dirty jokes in newspapers, perhaps; or not to dance in the street in front of actors' houses; or not to fall in love with exotic and sensual polyglots who'd lived in faraway cities like Constantinople and Bombay. "No group of men interprets, comprehends, and sympathizes with woman as do physicians," Mitchell insisted. A woman's doctor knew "how near to disorder and how close to misfortune she is brought by the very peculiarities of her nature."[16]

Because there were so many outside factors contributing to the development of insanity, American physicians started pushing lawmakers in the mid-nineteenth century to move mentally ill patients out of homes and into more controlled environments, where the factors that facilitated or exacerbated mania, melancholia, catatonia, and dementia could be managed and sometimes even kept at bay. In an asylum choices would be limited. Routines would be implemented. Sights and sounds would be muted or softened. The pace would be slowed. And passions and competitive impulses would be discouraged rather than cultivated and indulged. In 1810 the number of institutions in the United States that catered to the mentally ill could be counted on one hand; by 1860 twenty-eight of the thirty-eight states in the country had at least one publicly funded hospital that treated the insane, and many—like New York—had several.[17]

Medical professionals put a great deal of thought into the design of these facilities. Because the idea was to protect patients from certain forces at work in society, asylums should be built on the outskirts of town, according to one handbook on hospital design, far enough away that patients would be able to take walks, undisturbed, in a tranquil and rural environment, preferably one that accommodated a wide view of the landscape, unobstructed by trees, and protected patients "from the gaze and impertinent curiosity of visitors."[18]

The handbook was written by Thomas Kirkbride, founder of the American Psychiatric Association. Kirkbride believed that an "abundant supply of good water" was essential to any decent mental hospital, since "the very extensive use of baths is among the most important means of treatment." He wanted all hospitals to have a ratio of one doctor to no more 250 patients. And he insisted that no building, "however beautiful its exterior may appear," should ever be constructed without running the plan by a board of physicians first. "So different from ordinary buildings or other public structures are hospitals for the insane," Kirkbride explained, "that it is hardly possible for an architect, however skillful . . . to furnish such an institution with all the conveniences and arrangements indispensable for the proper treatment and care of its patients." "Everything repulsive and prison-like should be avoided," Kirkbride stressed, "and even the means of effecting the proper degree of security should be masked."[19]

Insane asylums were not meant to be prisons or places of punishment (segregated institutions like the Central Lunatic Asylum in Virginia excepted). The effect designers were going for was not "creepy" or "terrifying"—words that are often used today to describe the dozens of abandoned asylums dotting the landscape in the United States.[20] These hospitals for the mentally ill were meant to be "asylums" in the truest sense of the word: places of refuge for patients who were persecuted by the power of their own minds.

Certainly asylums were abused by people who had ulterior motives— not just White people who were afraid of Black people, but also husbands who didn't want to be married anymore and sometimes used the liberal power that various state laws gave them to have their wives institutionalized.[21] The work of reporters like Nellie Bly also makes it clear that not everyone had the requisite patience and empathy to work with mentally ill patients.

But facilities like the Middletown State Homeopathic Hospital for the Insane proliferated in the 1860s and 1870s because of hope. They were supposed to be more than just places where troubled people like Edith Drake could be "put away" by family members, out of sight and out of mind. Doctors pushed for asylums to be built because they believed that mentally ill patients could actually be helped. In a sign of just how much care and attention went into creating these facilities, architects were specifically told by physicians to pay special attention to the placement of all windows, "so that every possible advantage may be derived from the views," and "the prevailing winds of summer may also be made to minister to the comfort of the inmates."[22]

The fact that Edith Drake was committed to the Middletown hospital suggests her family cared about her and planned on being involved in her treatment to some degree. Had her family not been involved, Edith would have been committed to the state hospital on Ward's Island in the East River, near Queens and the South Bronx. That's the hospital the New York State Care Act had designated as the treatment facility for all mentally ill Manhattanites who were committed against their will. Edith ended up at the hospital in Middletown only because someone had specifically requested she be sent there.

The Care Act was passed by the state legislature in 1890, a few months after Ray Hamilton resigned from his position in the assembly. It broke New York up into several districts, and each district was assigned a state-financed hospital that would care for all of the involuntarily committed patients living within the district. The legislature also created a Lunacy Commission, which sought to provide a greater degree of regulation over facilities working with the mentally ill. The move was prompted not only by Nellie Bly's coverage of the treatment patients received at the Women's Lunatic Asylum on Blackwell's Island but also by reports of cruelties at other institutions in the state, such as the Buffalo Asylum for the Insane, where a patient named John Turney was kicked in the stomach and choked with a towel until "they had to blow in his mouth to restore consciousness," according to the *New York Times*.[23]

Administrators at the Middletown hospital resisted some of the provisions in the New York State Care Act. Specifically, they didn't like that the law forced them to give priority to patients from Orange, Dutchess, and Ulster Counties. This mandate failed to appreciate the special nature of Middletown's "homeopathic" approach to mental illness, because it required the hospital to accept patients even if those patients had no knowledge of or interest in the field of homeopathy. In so doing the law all but ensured that there would be times when Middletown didn't have enough beds for patients from other parts of the state whose families understood what homeopathy was and wanted to take that kind of approach to their illness.[24]

Today the word "homeopathy" elicits eyerolls from traditionally trained medical professionals, many of whom see the foul-smelling tinctures and bitter-tasting teas associated with the discipline as quackery. In the nineteenth century, too, some doctors disparaged the discipline. When he wasn't writing novels about Boston Brahmins, Oliver Wendell Holmes worked as a physician. In 1842 he told the Boston Society for the Diffusion of Knowledge that homeopathy was "a mingled mass of perverse ingenuity" that relied upon the "imbecile credulity" of its patients. He predicted that it would disappear from the annals of respectable medicine, surviving only among unscrupulous practitioners "who wring their bread from the cold grasp of disease and death, in the hovels of ignorant poverty."[25]

Holmes's evaluation of homeopathy was controversial at the time. As the decades progressed, however, more doctors joined him in questioning its medical legitimacy. In 1893, the year Edith Drake married Samuel McGibney, students from the University of Pennsylvania's medical school in Philadelphia refused to march in a parade with their peers from the nearby Hahnemann Medical College because that school's curriculum was homeopathic. To suggest there was any parity between the two schools' curricula was "a danger to health and dignity," according to one Penn student, who turned out for the parade along Chestnut Street in late October only so he could join his peers on the sidewalk in shouting, "Sugar Pill! Sugar Pill! Never cured and never will!"[26]

The boycott was a move to "freeze the homeopaths out," according to the *Philadelphia Inquirer*, which reported on a "secret agreement" between Penn's students and the students at Jefferson Medical College to withdraw from the parade. Administrators at both schools were a bit embarrassed when news of the agreement got out. They didn't teach homeopathy themselves, but they had enough respect for their colleagues who did to lie about why their students were engaged in the boycott. "They have not withdrawn from the parade on account of Hahnemann," one administrator told the *Philadelphia Times*, "but simply because they are afraid of catching cold."[27]

The tenets of homeopathy were put forward in the late eighteenth century by a German physician named Samuel Hahnemann (hence the name of the school in Philadelphia). Hahnemann was not guided by the scientific method, an approach to the creation of knowledge that relies upon testing and observation for its understanding of the natural world.[28] His ideas were reasoned philosophically from the "principle of similarity" that had characterized medicine in the days of Hippocrates. According to that principle, every part of the human body had a corresponding element in the natural world that held the key to that body part's healing. The way to know which element corresponded to which body part was to look for physical similarities: walnuts, for instance, which look a little like the human brain, or certain kinds of beans, which resemble kidneys.

Samuel Hahnemann didn't teach that walnuts and beans could cure migraines and nephritis; he did rely, however, on the principle of similarity to formulate his idea that "like cures like." The word "homeopathy" itself is derived from the Greek words for "similar" and "suffering." Hahnemann believed that substances that trigger certain symptoms in healthy people could be used to treat illnesses that produced the same or similar symptoms in unhealthy people. The idea was that a patient's symptoms were the body's attempt to expel some noxious, foreign substance. Facilitating or exacerbating the symptoms, therefore—while momentarily unpleasant—would accelerate the healing.

Onions, for example, which cause healthy people to cry and sniffle, could be used to treat patients whose eyes were watering and noses were running because they had contracted a head cold or were allergic to ragweed. Jesuits' bark—that stuff Gus Hemenway's company harvested in Chile—could be used to accentuate the abdominal cramps and heart palpitations associated with malaria, because tea made from the bark of a cinchona tree produces diarrhea and a rapid heart rate in healthy people who consume it in excessive quantities.[29]

As the saying goes, even a broken clock is right twice a day. Samuel Hahnemann did hit the mark on using Jesuits' bark to treat malaria; his understanding of *why* the quinine-rich substance worked was simply wrong. Many of Hahnemann's theories, in fact, are laughable today, and even modern-day homeopathic practitioners tend not to rely upon most of them anymore. They do retain Hahnemann's faith in the healing power of natural substances, however, and often insist that the modern-day pharmaceutical industry is more about patents and pocketbooks than it is about human health. They also retain his emphasis on the importance of paying attention to symptoms, instead of just trying to eliminate them or cover them up with drugs.[30]

That emphasis on talking to patients about their symptoms and seeing symptoms as a tool when it comes to healing is the reason homeopathy continued to enjoy a certain degree of respect in the realm of mental health, even at a time when its prestige in other specialties was declining. Homeopathic alienists were still respected enough in 1870 to convince state lawmakers to fund an entire asylum devoted to homeopathy in Middletown, New York. By 1897, the year Edith Drake was committed, Middletown's hospital had become one of fifty-three institutions in seventeen states—eight of them supported primarily or exclusively by tax dollars—that used homeopathic methods when treating the mentally ill. Homeopathic alienists were also respected enough to get an exemption to the New York State Care Act less than a year after the law was passed. That exemption allowed them to receive patients like Edith at their facility, even though she wasn't from one of the counties assigned to the hospital by the state.[31]

Without a sense of what Edith's diagnosis was, it is impossible to know what kind of treatment she received. We do know that the Middletown hospital occasionally used straitjackets and other forms of restraint on its patients. Such aggressive measures were something doctors there rarely adopted, however. One physician, in fact, who worked at the Middletown hospital for several years believed that restraints were "substitutes for forbearance and watchful attention," and that his colleagues at nonhomeopathic institutions were far too willing to resort to them whenever patients became difficult. "It may seem presumptuous to criticize the treatment advised by those who have made the care of the insane the work of a life time," Samuel Worcester wrote in 1881, "but while I am willing to acknowledge that there are times when the use of restraint may be necessary, and of benefit to the patient, I also contend that the use of restraint, as it now prevails in most hospitals, is excessive and injurious to the patient."[32]

Samuel Worcester was particularly critical of those "baths" Thomas Kirkbride had said were "among the most important means of treatment" at any well-ordered asylum. The baths patients received at these facilities were not the baths you'll see discussed today on websites devoted to "wellness" or the phenomenon of "self-care." There were no lotions made of honey and vanilla or fizzing cubes of Epsom salt and patchouli oil. In a description that probably sounds familiar to any American who is old enough to remember the United States' war in Iraq, Worcester noted with dismay that during some baths, a "patient's hands and feet are tied and sometimes a gag is inserted in the mouth. He is then placed on the bottom of a bathtub upon his back, his face directly under the faucet. . . .

The faucet is then opened, and the water rushing through falls directly on and into the patient's face, filling his nostrils and mouth, producing all the sensation of suffocation by drowning."[33]

Worcester called for an "absolute" end to such tactics, and to any form of restraint that was used more for the benefit of employees at an asylum than for the benefit of patients. If a patient were unruly, the solution was not to put him in a straitjacket or subject him to waterboarding; it was to place him in seclusion for limited and closely monitored periods of time, ideally no more than half an hour at a stretch. "If our superintendents were required to keep for inspection an accurate record of every instance of use of restraint, seclusion, or use of the bath," Worcester asked, nearly a decade before the creation of the Lunacy Commission to monitor mental health professionals, "is it probable that they would consider it necessary to use them as often as is now the case?"[34]

The Middletown hospital's homeopathic commitment to avoiding aggressive therapeutic treatments may have been the reason Edith Drake's family elected to have her sent there. In the case of mania, homeopaths didn't strap patients into bed or confine them in canvas straitjackets; instead, they used heavy wet sheets (similar, in many ways, to those weighted blankets being touted by "lifestyle experts" on morning news programs today) to calm patients down. In the case of melancholia, doctors administered small amounts of Aurum metallicum (i.e., gold) orally to their patients, the expectation being that the weight of the gold would mirror the weight of the anxiety, sadness, or guilt being felt by someone who was depressed (gold, at least, is a nonreactive element, and so doctors weren't poisoning anyone when they fed it to their patients; they were simply increasing the value of their stool). In the case of hysteria—a variety of mania that was believed to be the exclusive province of women—physicians applied low levels of electrical impulses to their patients' muscles, in an effort to mimic the internal contractions that were thought to be the cause of heart palpitations and hyperventilation.[35]

Whatever the treatment Edith Drake received was, it didn't work. We don't know when exactly she left the hospital, but we do know that by 1904 she was taken into custody by police in Newport, Rhode Island, after they found her wandering along Bellevue Avenue, "richly gowned," speaking in an incoherent manner, and once again attracting the attention of reporters. It was after this incident that her brother, Herbert, and sister, Bertha, paid a man named John Dudley Sargent $7,700 (the equivalent today of about $220,000) to take her to his homestead in northwestern Wyoming and marry her.

Jack and Edith could get hitched, because they were both single by 1905. Edith's divorce from Samuel McGibney was finalized that year, and Jack's wife, Adelaide Crane, whom he'd known since they both were children, had died in April 1897, a few months before Edith was committed to the asylum in Middletown. The circumstances surrounding Addie's death were tragic and mysterious, and they remain a part of the lore in Jackson Hole today.[36]

Marymere

The Swedish carpenters who built Ray Hamilton's first coffin and testified in court that he was the one they had buried at Marymere finished the job they'd started before the former lawmaker died. The ten-room lodge Ray and Jack envisioned managing together would later be described by a paying guest as a "very commodious and well-built house," made of "perfectly hewed" logs and "furnished elegantly." Jack Sargent moved into the lodge with his family about a month after Ray died. The Sargents didn't stay for long, however. That winter Jack and his family moved to New York, where Jack spent four months working for his cousin, Gus Hemenway Jr. Ray had put up most of the money to have the lodge built, but the Hamilton family never expressed any interest in laying claim to the building or to the sublime piece of property it sat on.[1]

In the years that followed, Jack and his family would continue to leave Marymere during the winter months, since the days in northwestern Wyoming are short at that time of year; the snowfalls are measured in feet, rather than inches; and the winds off Jackson Lake can make the single-digit temperatures that dominate the nights feel more like twenty degrees below zero. Even before "winter" formally set in, life in the region could sometimes be a challenge. In surviving excerpts of an autobiography he was working on before he died, Jack recalled having to move his family to the western side of the Tetons in October 1892, a month earlier than usual, because the weather conditions on his homestead had become dangerously unpredictable. Some days still felt like summer, while others were consumed by snowstorms. "There were five of us to move across the Tetons before we could get to the Railway," Jack recalled, "three children from four to eight years old, their mother, and the writer." Nowhere in the narrative does he mention that his wife was pregnant, but a few weeks later, on November 14, 1892, the couple's fourth child, Catherine Winthrop Sargent, was born in Salt Lake City.[2]

Jack did the move in three separate trips. His household included not only Addie and the children but also a Mormon girl from Idaho whom Jack had hired to assist his wife with the housekeeping. Five horses, three of which had belonged to Ray, weren't enough to move the entire family and everything they needed to spend five months away from home all at once.

He went over the mountains with his wife and eight-year-old son first, "leaving the other two children with the hired girl at the ranch." For his journey with Addie and Hemenway, Jack took three saddle horses and a pack horse. He put together an outfit that consisted of a tent, several heavy, woolen blankets, and "a weeks rations of Elk meat, flour, sugar, dried fruit, baking powder, salt, pepper, bacon, and matches." The route they took to Idaho was an old Indian pass that reached a height of 8,520 feet above sea level and was later called "Horse Thief Pass" by the writer Owen Wister, when his famous novel about a nameless Wyoming cowboy known only as "The Virginian" was published in 1902. "Our route was the seldom travelled Conant Trail," Jack recalled, which was about fifteen miles long and crossed the Tetons six miles north of the head of Jackson Lake.[3]

Jack didn't take any tent poles with him on this trip. He'd done the journey over the Conant Pass often enough to have a set of poles "stacked away . . . in a little grassy park" at the base of the mountains, a day's ride from his ranch. The family made it to the apex of the trail, where they enjoyed "a panoramic view of half the state of Idaho," on the second day of their journey. After they came down off the western side of the mountains, they happened upon a settler from "an Idaho Hamlet that was our destination before going to the Railway." The settler was chopping hay in a meadow, and he agreed to take Addie and Hemenway with him when he returned home the next day. Mother and son would wait for the rest of the family to join them in St. Anthony, a tiny settlement about twenty miles away from the train that would take them to Utah.[4]

Jack spent the night with his family and the settler, and the following morning, he made his way back up over the Conant Pass, "driving the horses before me in the narrow trail, single file at a trot whenever the ground would permit." Jack Sargent had inherited his great-grandmother's need for speed. The landscape he experienced along the rocky Conant Trail would have been very different from the landscape Sally Hemenway experienced along the Atlantic coast on that manic day seven decades earlier, when she'd trotted for six hours across Washington County, Maine, so she could pick raspberries and turn them into wine and jam that same afternoon. But Jack, like his grandmother, liked to do things fast—even when he was a mile and a half above sea level. He arrived at his homestead on the other side of the Tetons by sundown, having done the journey in half the time it took him when he'd been traveling with Addie and Hemenway.[5]

The next day Jack put his older daughter, Mary, and the hired servant girl into a wagon and took them and the family's supplies for the winter up into the southern part of Yellowstone National Park. The trail he chose was the Fall River Pass, which was "passable for wagons, but not a smooth road." The absence of any good road connecting Marymere to the park would prove to be a constant source of frustration to Jack as he sought to make a living off of tourism in the region. What Jack did with Mary and his servant, once they got to Yellowstone, is unclear. His narrative says only that after that, "I was alone with my four-year-old daughter Martha at the ranch."[6]

Jack and Martha spent three nights together while Jack did what needed to be done to close the lodge up for the winter. Years later his second-youngest daughter, Catherine Winthrop, would recall that her father always left an elk carcass on the kitchen table whenever the family made these winter retreats, so that the children's cat, Tom, could feed off it while his owners were gone.[7]

On their second evening together, as a big snowstorm loomed, Jack and Martha were visited by several soldiers from Yellowstone who'd been out conducting surveys in the southwestern corner of the park. "We all enjoyed the comfort of the big ranch fireplace that evening while the snow steadily fell outside," Jack recalled. One of the soldiers in the party, Captain George Anderson, had recently become the superintendent of Yellowstone National Park. In the years before the National Park Service was founded in 1916, the U.S. Army managed Yellowstone for the Department of the Interior. Jack would later write to Captain

Anderson to complain about the elk poaching both men knew was happening in the park.[8]

After the soldiers left, Jack prepared to go back up over the Conant Pass one last time, "to join the others in Idaho, and then go on into Salt Lake City for the winter." There was a foot of snow on the ground at his ranch. He knew that meant there'd be three feet or more up along the pass. "Martha, the 'baby,' was going across in midwinter weather," Jack marveled, "and her mother and brother had crossed in beautiful Indian Summer weather, less than a week earlier! It can do that in the Teton Mountains sometimes."[9]

Jack's biggest concern as he prepared for the journey was that little Martha would get cold while she sat by herself on top of a horse. In reading over his recollections, it's impossible to miss that Jack's children were important to him. He didn't leave much for historians to sink their teeth into, and what little material there is is disjointed and incomplete. Reminiscences about family picnics that took place in the 1890s are followed by grievances against Jack's uncle Gus for taking UT 36 away from his grandfather in the 1870s. These grievances, in turn, are followed by a description of a hike Jack did over the Conant Pass in 1906 with a mysterious companion identified only as "L," who may have been Lou Joy, a rancher originally from upstate New York who was one of the few friends Jack Sargent had in Wyoming.[10] Even these jumbled scraps, however, make it clear that fatherhood mattered to Jack. His own father had been mostly absent from his life, and Jack had left New England in part because no one else in his birth family had wanted to take permanent responsibility for him after his mother and grandfather died. That experience may have made the family he created for himself in Wyoming all the more precious to him.

As a sign of his affection, Jack named five islands in Jackson Lake after each of his children. In one revealing vignette, he fondly recalled how the far end of the lake's biggest island (which he pointedly did *not* name after a child; Jack knew better than to do something foolish like that . . .) came to be christened "Ice Cream Point" by his son and daughters. It happened while the family spent a delightful day together on the island, celebrating the Fourth of July. "Big Island," as the land mass was diplomatically called, was two miles long and a mile wide in the days before the U.S. Reclamation Service dammed the Snake River. It was visible from the lodge, and in late June, the children had been able to see snow on a bluff at the northern end of the island. Jack promised if the snow were still there by Independence Day, he'd sail them all out to the island so they could use it to make ice cream.

"The day was very warm; grass green; the aspins [*sic*] and cotton woods along the shores of the island were all leaved out; and Cow Elk with their month-old calves [were] hiding from the midday sun all through the pine trees of the mid-island," Jack wrote about the day. The memory had to have been at least seven years old by the time he put pen to paper. A date at the bottom of the vignette indicates the memory was recorded in August 1903, and because the day at Ice Cream Point had included Addie, the latest year the Fourth of July picnic possibly could have happened was 1896. Jack's wife was gone by April 1897.

"The sun went down as they passed between Catherine and Martha Islands and with the sun the wind, so the Children's father rowed the remaining three miles home in the beautiful afterglow," Jack wrote, referring to himself in the third person. He rowed "to the sweet music of old songs on a lake of azure, darkening to black, as the night shadows fell and stars came out and were reflected in the now jet-black water, while the Evening star hung like a lamp from Heavens Portal in an after-glow of fading, but slowly fading gold, over the crest of the Cascade Peak on the west shore of the lake directly opposite the Children's home."[11]

It was a memory that revealed more than just the fact that Jack Sargent loved his children. The man from Machias, Maine—whose personal library included the romantic works of James Fenimore Cooper, Robert Louis Stevenson, and Emily Dickinson—also had a poetic soul.[12]

Jack wrapped four-year-old Martha in multiple layers of wool until she was "very fat and all ready for anything outside" and put her into a saddle on "a thoroughly safe old-time pony." Together they set out for the train station in Market Lake, Idaho. The pair didn't spend their first night in the "grassy park" at the base of the Teton range where Jack had stashed his tent poles and camped with Addie and Hemenway the week before, however. Father and daughter had gotten a late start, and so, not long after they crossed the Snake River at the head of Jackson Lake, Jack "chose an old spot of Beaver Dicks where I knew he had his lodge poles cached." He set up his tipi, spread blankets within it, and was soon "cooking things inside, [on] a fire in the centre of the lodge."[13]

"Beaver Dick" was Richard Leigh, a barely literate but surprisingly prolific trapper, originally from Manchester, England, who'd settled in the Tetons in the early 1860s, when hardly any White people were living in the region. Ferdinand Hayden's team named Leigh Lake in what is now Grand Teton National Park after Beaver Dick, and they named nearby Jenny Lake after his Shoshone wife. Richard Leigh kept a diary about his life in the Snake River Valley. It's difficult to decipher sometimes because of his spelling and punctuation (and also because of his habit of not using an "h" to start words that begin with that letter—a reflection, perhaps, of his Mancunian accent). The diary has been important, however, to historians looking to understand what life was like for people living along America's last frontier.[14]

In one particularly heartbreaking entry from June 1878, Beaver Dick admitted to himself (and to anyone he thought might one day read his words) that a recent visit to a trade post along the North Fork of the Snake River (known today as "Henry's Fork") had left him feeling depressed. "I had not beene thare since August 1876[,] when I took my famley with me to do some trading and a pleshur trip for them," he explained. The wife of a shopkeeper at the post had recently had a baby, and the woman was too sick to nurse the infant. Even though Jenny Leigh was preg-nant, she was still nursing her fifth child, Elizabeth, and so she shared her breast milk with the shopkeeper's son. "He is a fine boy now[.] I nursed and played with him plenty this time wile thare," Beaver Dick fondly recalled.

Later that night, however, "after going to bed[,] my mind run a grate deele about my wife and that child[,] so that I could not sleep[,] and I must tell the truth[,] I [h]ad wet eyes that night." The sad man vowed to bring a three-year-old filly he owned with him the next time he visited the post, so that he could give it to the boy. "I intended braking it for my youngest daughter before she died," he explained in plaintive words. Baby Elizabeth had succumbed to small pox two years earlier, not long after she'd visited the trade post with her family. All four of her older siblings had succumbed, as well, as had their mother and the infant Jenny Leigh gave birth to two weeks before she died.[15]

Life could be cruel along America's last frontier—and fathers like Beaver Dick Leigh and John Dudley Sargent made themselves vulnerable to those cruelties by loving their wives and children.

Jack and his daughter reached the apex of the Conant Trail on their second day. They ended up having to camp there, and because no one—including Jack—had stashed any tent poles at nearly nine thousand feet, they had only "a fir tree and sky for our roof" that second night they spent on the trail. It was a risky decision, especially given that it had snowed most of the day, and "by the time we reached the top of the pass, [we] could not see 30 yards." Jack had no choice, however. They'd been delayed during their ascent by the loss of Martha's mitten—or, rather, by the utter devastation the four-year-old girl must have felt upon realizing she'd lost her mitten. Jack doesn't say that Martha's tears were the reason for the delay, but they are the likeliest explanation for his decision to backtrack after they got to the top of the pass and head a quarter of a mile down the trail, through three feet of snow, to retrieve the mitten. There are other ways to keep a child's hand warm, after all. At no point in his narrative does Jack complain about having to do this; he states simply that "it was a black mitten, so [it was] easily recovered in all that snow." Any parent who has been in a similar situation knows his irritation, however—and also understands why leaving the mitten behind was never an option.[16]

On their third day, Jack and Martha made it down into the Idaho prairie, where it was once again Indian summer. After traveling about ten miles, they came upon a farmhouse. "There was a woman standing in the door of the house holding a baby," Jack recalled. In a sign of just how isolated he and his family were, the baby was the "first one Martha had ever seen. Pointing at it with her hand, she laughed and said, 'Oh! Daddy! See the live doll.'" The farmhouse also had pigs running in the yard. "She'd never seen them before, either. Pulling her feet up out of the stirrups, she said: 'They'll bite my toes! Daddy, what are they?'"

Finally, on the fourth day, father and daughter made it to St. Anthony, where Addie, Hemenway, and Mary were waiting for them. Jack proudly noted that Martha had "landed with both mittens," while "her sister lost both of hers on the first day out from the ranch in the wagon with the woman she was the charge of." "Martha now thinks this was the best camping experience ever," Jack wryly observed—his only hint at ever having been annoyed by his daughter for the lost mitten.[17]

The family left for Salt Lake City two days later. They stayed there until early April. When they returned to the ranch, there was still quite a bit of snow on the ground, but young Martha Sargent no longer confused babies with dolls. She'd had plenty of opportunity to play with an infant since her camping experience with her father. Catherine Winthrop Sargent, Jack and Addie's fourth child, was now five months old.

Jack knew where Beaver Dick had stashed his tent poles because he wasn't an outsider to Jackson Hole, even though he lived in the northernmost part of the valley, fifty miles away from the nearest settlement. He knew people in the area, and people knew him. Even so, the Sargents were pretty isolated.

The ranch did manage to host paying visitors from time to time, among them George Eastman of the Kodak Company and two of Andrew Carnegie's nephews. But children who were not Sargents were a rarity at Marymere. Decades after Jack had died, a woman who grew up in Jackson and knew Mary Sargent as a teenager told a historian for the National Park Service that she used to try to imitate Mary's accent, "broadening my As and leaving out the Rs." The effect Carrie Nesbit Dunn was going for was a classic "down east" accent, still found today among people in the easternmost counties of Maine (which are downwind and east of Boston as far as sailing goes—hence the region's term). Dunn's recollection was a sign of just how few people the Sargent children knew while they were growing up on the ranch. Even though Mary had spent most of her childhood in Wyoming, she sounded like her parents, who'd grown up in Washington County, Maine.[18]

The ranch's isolation was something Jack had sought, partly because it gave him the freedom to create a life for himself that wasn't tied to his identity as a Sargent, a Dudley, a Winthrop, or a Hemenway, and partly because the isolation was what protected the sublimity of those towering peaks—the ones John Randolph Spears had disparaged as "barren" and "forbidding" in his article about Ray Hamilton's body but which Jack

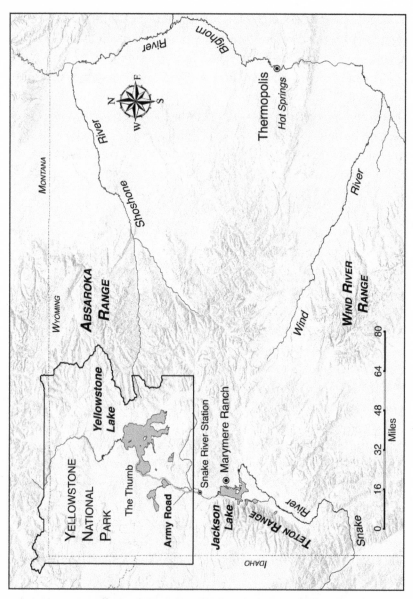

Marymere Ranch in relation to the Thumb on Yellowstone Lake and
the hot springs at Thermopolis. The state road from Thermopolis
to YNP was never built. Map created by Mark Moore.

described as "aflame with sunset colors or indescribable gorgeousness" during an evening he spent by himself at Marymere in the early years of the twentieth century.[19] The isolation had its benefits, which Jack clearly appreciated in a way John Randolph Spears did not. But once the Mainer started running a business on his homestead, the remoteness of the ranch's location presented some real challenges.

People couldn't *get* to Marymere—not easily, anyway. During the twenty-three years he spent in Jackson Hole, Jack wrote regularly to elected and appointed officials about two topics, and the absence of a road connecting Marymere to Yellowstone National Park was one of them. "I should like to take a contract for building part of the road down from the Thumb," Jack wrote to Superintendent George Anderson in June 1895, after he had learned that a road the U.S. Army Corps of Engineers was building from the West Thumb Geyser Basin to the southern boundary of the park had been delayed by the corps' inability to get enough soldiers to the region to finish the job. "There are plenty of qualified teams here," Jack assured Anderson. "I can get them on the ground quick."[20]

Later Jack wrote to Wyoming's governor, William Richards, nudging him about a proposal Richards had made to build a road that would connect Yellowstone's southern entrance to the hot springs at Thermopolis, about two hundred miles southeast of the park. Wyoming had recently acquired the rights to those therapeutic springs from the Shoshone. "What was done about your recommendation for a State Road from the Big Horn Hot Springs . . . to the southern line of the Nat'l Park?" Jack asked the governor in March 1896. Referring to the same army road he had written to George Anderson about, Jack observed that "a State Road as you recommended, connecting to this new Park Road, when completed, will give Wyoming the most picturesque drive into the Park and the shortest route to the great points of interest for Wyoming's people."[21]

A road from Thermopolis to the southern entrance of the park would also run right by Jack Sargent's homestead, which is exactly what he wanted. He was hoping, ultimately, to run a stage service down from Yellowstone to his lodge, so that visitors to the national park could easily add a stay in the Tetons to their itineraries.[22] Alas, the same wilderness that Jack had craved as part of his plan to reinvent himself—and Ray Hamilton had hoped would make it possible for his humiliation in New York to be forgotten—stymied Jack's efforts to make money off the sublimity of the Teton Range. The truth is there were other factors that probably would have made it difficult for him to thrive in the hospitality industry. Jack had a sometimes fragile emotional disposition, an inheritance from his great-grandmother Sally, who had passed it along to her son Gus, as well. Nevertheless, Jack needed roads in order for his scheme to have any chance of working. And sadly for him, the roads he needed weren't built until after his death.

The road within the park that Jack wrote to Superintendent Anderson about—the one from the geyser basin down to Yellowstone's southern boundary—was completed during his lifetime. It was a horrible road, however, and not one most tourists wanted to travel. One of the army's own engineers described it as a "disgrace to the Government," constructed in a "wretched condition" with "stumps left in the roadway for most of the distance."[23]

Equally important to Jack, the road extended only to the army's Snake River Station within the Yellowstone Timberland Reserve, a 1.2-million-acre buffer along the southern and eastern boundaries of the park that was created by President Benjamin Harrison in 1891 at the suggestion of General Philip Sheridan, who wanted to see Yellowstone National Park's boundaries expanded.

Unlike the park the timberland reserve was open to logging. Private companies no longer had the option of owning the land, since Harrison had put it into a public trust. They could lease acreage, however, and so long as they followed strict limits that were defined and enforced by the newly created Division of Forestry within the Department of Agriculture, timber barons could harvest trees from the reserve. For that reason, some people—such as Ray Hamilton's friend George Grinnell—hoped that the Yellowstone Timberland Reserve would eventually be folded into the park, where no commercial logging could ever take place.[24]

The Snake River Station where the federal road ended was fourteen miles away from Marymere. That meant Jack still had a transportation problem. The road he hoped Governor Richards would build from Thermopolis to the southern entrance of the park never did become a reality. It wasn't until 1917, four years after Jack died, that any usable road came within easy traveling distance of what had been his property. As a

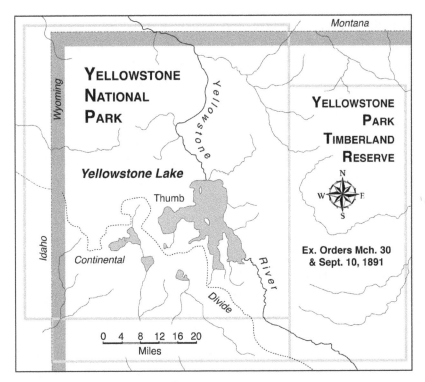

Boundaries of the Yellowstone Timberland Reserve,
created in 1891. Map created by Mark Moore.

consequence Marymere never saw the visitors—or the income—Ray and
Jack had imagined.[25]

Here, then, was the great irony of the plan Hamilton and Sargent had
hatched: the far-flung wilderness they had each gravitated toward with
the hope of starting their lives over was so wild and unsettled it kept
Jack from generating a reliable income from tourism in what is now the
fifth-most-visited national park in the United States. That wilderness
was not so wild and unsettled, however, that it could provide either man
with the autonomy or anonymity he needed to start over or be forgotten.
This truth was one Ray mercifully never lived to see. But it was a truth
that followed Jack for the rest of his life, after his wife, Adelaide Crane
Sargent, died in April 1897.

The other topic Jack wrote to officials about was poaching—particularly the poaching of elk, which irked him to no end. It had bothered Ray, as well. When he first arrived in Wyoming, Ray offered a $500 reward to anyone who helped the U.S. Army capture and prosecute big game poachers within Yellowstone National Park. The reward also applied to individuals who facilitated "the arrest and conviction of anyone breaking the Game laws of the State of Wyoming," according to Jack, a group that to his mind included not only White settlers who killed elk and bison for their tusks and hides but also Native Americans who "slaughter game by the wholesale and may do worse."[26]

Jack's evaluation of Indigenous hunting practices wasn't entirely accurate. The question of whether it's appropriate to use the word "slaughter" when describing the way Indians hunted is subject to some debate. Recent studies have suggested that even though White people who hunted from train cars were primarily responsible for the near extinction of the American Bison, the Indian practice of indiscriminately running entire herds over cliffs wasn't exactly helpful, especially after the railroads came along. Indigenous Americans had a relationship with the natural world that was different from the one White people brought into the North American interior with them, but that didn't mean the Native relationship left no mark on the environment or didn't privilege the needs of human beings over those of other animals.[27]

The question of whether Native Americans were violating Wyoming's game laws when they hunted, however, is not subject to debate. They were not—full stop. Statutes that were passed in the 1880s and 1890s by Wyoming's legislature limited *settlers* in terms of how much game they could legally take from the land and where they could take that game from. The Bannock and Sheepeater Indians who hunted in northwestern Wyoming didn't have to follow the state's rules when it came to hunting, however, because those rules did not apply to them.

The treaties the various tribes had entered into with the U.S. government were supposed to supersede any authority state officials might otherwise have had over Indigenous people living within the state's boundaries. The Treaty of Fort Bridger in particular gave the various bands of Shoshone and Bannock people "the right to hunt upon the unoccupied lands of the United States, so long as game may be found thereupon."[28] This meant the tribes in Wyoming were supposed to be able to continue their traditional hunting practices after they moved onto reservations, regardless of where the game led them or whether those traditional practices accorded with any limits state authorities might place on hunting.

Jack hated to see animals killed in large numbers, which may have been why he lumped the Bannocks in with the White "tusk-hunters" who killed thousands of elk each year not for the meat or even the hides, but for the two marble-sized canine teeth every elk has, vestiges of a prehistoric time when the creature is believed to have had tusks that protruded from its mouth, just like modern-day elephants. Bulls and cows alike have these teeth, which are made of solid ivory and sell for about $40 a pair today. They sold for at least that much back in the 1880s, when $40 had the modern-day buying power of about $1,000.

Their value stemmed from the fact that elk tusks had become extremely popular jewelry items among men who belonged to the ironically named Benevolent and Protective Order of Elks. The group began in New York City in 1867 as a private drinking club but quickly expanded, in terms of its geography and mission, to include 1,300 charity-oriented lodges with more than four hundred thousand all-White and all-male members by the turn of the twentieth century.[29]

The tusks were rounded, polished, and mounted in gold casings, so that Elks Club members could wear them on chains around their necks or suspend them from pins on their lapels. More than five thousand elk were killed for their tusks in Yellowstone in 1881, their carcasses left to rot—or sometimes laced with strychnine to serve as wolf bait. Five years later, when Captain Moses Harris became Yellowstone's superintendent, he assigned fifty soldiers to do regular patrols throughout the park, looking for poachers. The move did have an impact on the number of animals killed within the park that year, but the decrease was small, since poachers knew that military officials didn't have the resources to prosecute them, even if soldiers caught them. Harris's patrols also had an unfortunate and unintended side effect. "Fires which have been started intentionally may be attributed to unscrupulous hunters," Harris acknowledged, "who, being prevented from hunting in the Park, resort to this method of driving the game beyond the Park limits."[30]

John Dudley Sargent estimated that three-fourths of the settlers in Jackson Hole were "making a precarious living by killing bull elk for tusks." The failure of government officials to stop the slaughter infuriated him. Writing to the commissioner of the General Land Office in Washington DC about an alleged poacher named John Ferry, Jack claimed the man "has, on the word of his daughters, killed 13 elk since November last. I can swear they threw away last winter enough good, whole round steak to have amply fed their whole family." Ferry was killing the elk because he was a homesick immigrant. "He is now anxious to return to Germany, so his children tell mine, but can raise no money," Jack informed the commissioner. "That means he will in the meantime kill every elk he can for tusks." It was "a notorious fact hereabouts that Ferry has repeatedly and most willfully broken the game law." Nevertheless, he had never once been arrested, and "he openly swears at our State and our national laws, our park and reserves, our county, State, and Federal officials."[31]

Jack's letter to the General Land Office made it clear he was willing to name names. John Ferry wasn't the only poacher he ratted out. Over the years Jack named other settlers in Wyoming and Idaho when complaining about illegal hunting: Ed Sheffield, D. W. Spalding, Dave Dougherty, Bill Clarke, Samuel Gregory, Ed Jones, Herbert Whiteman, John Stadtler, Al and Charles Collins, Henry Moran, W. B. Rodgers, Dick Murray, Jim and Al Courtney, Billy Birch, Jack Kooch, Henry Spencer, and Charles Hodsick were all on his list. These men had violated not just state and federal game laws, according to Jack; some of them had also grazed livestock within the boundaries of the national park and settled within the timberland reserve *after* the reserve had been created, when the land there was no longer open to new homesteading.[32]

John Dudley Sargent made a lot of people in Jackson Hole angry when he told officials what they were up to. There was a reason Lou Joy was one of the few friends he had in Wyoming. Jack was a tattletale. He even tattled on soldiers sometimes, telling Captain Anderson he'd seen some "Buffalo soldiers"—that is, Black infantrymen who served in the American West after the Civil War—"pouring down 'rot gut' at the saloon on the meadow, as tho' they never expected to see whiskey again on earth."[33]

People in the area knew Jack, even though he lived in the northernmost part of the valley, fifty miles away from almost everyone else. But that didn't mean they liked him. He was a rich easterner—a "remittance man," in the estimation of those who did not come from families with money—who failed to play by the unwritten social rules of life along America's last frontier. "They have no use for me because I never visit them, and have told some plain facts about them," Jack explained in March 1897 in a letter he wrote to George Anderson about the people who lived in Jackson Hole.[34] He knew he wasn't liked by many of the locals—and he did not care.

Jack's letter suggests his tattling wasn't the only reason he had few friends. He also hadn't made much of an effort to acquire any friends in the years since Ray Hamilton died. "I never visit them" was how he had phrased it to George Anderson. On his trips to Idaho to get mail and supplies or to send his family to more hospitable climates for the winter, Jack could have taken the route along the southern part of Jackson Lake that Gil Speir and Cas Moore had taken during that fateful vacation in August 1890 when they learned their friend had drowned. In fact, when Jack first arrived in Jackson Hole, he *did* take that southern route along the Teton Pass that brought travelers close to the settlement of Jackson. Remember that Ray left him a note in the lean-to at South Landing the day before he died, since he knew that Jack would be coming through there on his trip back from Rexburg, Idaho.

After Ray was gone, however, Jack always went north in order to go west. He went over the Conant Pass, on a route that brought him to a remote place where Beaver Dick had stashed his tent poles and ensured Jack would never have to come anywhere near the settlers in Jackson, Wyoming—the people he had tattled on for poaching elk.

It was unusual for Jack to be writing to Captain Anderson from Marymere in March. The Sargents usually left their homestead in the wintertime, after all. They typically left in November and did not return until April.

Jack chose to spend the winter of 1896–97 at Marymere, however. His reasons for doing this will never be known for sure, since he left no document behind, explaining his decision. It seems likely, however, that he stayed at the lodge because the year before, he and his family had gotten stuck away from their homestead for much longer than Jack intended.

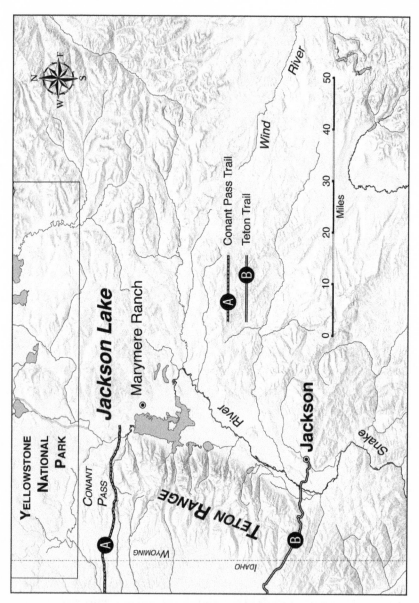

After Ray died Jack always took the Conant Pass Trail over the Tetons, avoiding the Teton Pass Trail, since it led into the town of Jackson. Map created by Mark Moore.

They were gone for nearly nine months, leaving Marymere in late July 1895 and not returning until mid-April 1896.

The reason the family spent so much time away from home was that the Bannock Indians were supposedly slaughtering White settlers in Jackson Hole during the summer of 1895 in a fight over Indigenous hunting rights.[35] The truth of the so-called Bannock War is that the Natives were the real victims of the violence, not the settlers. Not a single White person was killed throughout the entirety of the scare. That's not how the situation was portrayed by the press, however.

The tensions began after law enforcement officials in Jackson decided it was their responsibility to enforce the state's game laws among Wyoming's native people. They deputized more than twenty settlers in the spring of 1895 and instructed them to arrest any Indians they found hunting in the valley. In July several citizen-sheriffs arrested a party of Bannocks who were hunting in Hoback Canyon, about fifteen miles south of Jackson. When the Indians tried to escape, the settlers fired upon them, killing at least one and wounding several others.[36]

Rumors soon circulated that three hundred to four hundred Bannocks and Eastern Shoshones were organizing a retaliatory raid on Jackson Hole, and that "all mountain passes are in their control." The *Idaho States-man* reported on July 24 that "settlers have abandoned their crops and are moving their families out of the country," without explaining how the settlers were able to do this if the natives had commandeered all the mountain passes. Two days later the paper reported that "59 white people were killed by the Bannocks near Jackson's Hole, but there is no way to confirm the report and it is not believed," begging the question of why the paper elected to publish the charge at all.[37]

By July 27 newspapers across the country were reporting that dozens of settlers in Jackson Hole had been killed. "White Settlers Butchered in Massacre by Bloodthirsty Bannocks" was the headline the *San Francisco Chronicle* ran with. The *Chicago Tribune* chose "None Is Left Alive. Every White Man Slain." In New York the focus was on the fate of a group of geology students from Princeton University who'd arrived in Wyoming shortly before the deputized settlers fired upon the arrested Indians. The *Tribune* reported that the students had "fallen into the hands of the Bannock Indians," but two days later, the *Times* denied that report, insisting that "all fears for the safety of the Princeton students" had been put to rest "by the receipt of news direct from a member of the party." The *Sun* gave its readers a primer on the history of the tribe involved in the "troubles" that included the hair-raising if specious claim that "scalps and horses are the two things every Bannock is taught to crave."[38]

The stories were proof that in spite of what alienists believed, "hysteria" was not a malady confined to women. Many *men* participated in the rumor-mongering that resulted in the newspapers' inaccurate and inflammatory coverage. "William Ross of the firm of Ross, Grey, & Wyatt . . . reports everyone in Jackson's Hole killed this morning," the *Idaho Statesman* conveyed in a story that was picked up by newspapers in Colorado, Kansas, North Carolina, and New Jersey. An engineer for the Union Pacific Railroad named Robert Fitzpatrick told reporters that the Bannocks had killed a settler and his family near the confluence of the Salt and Snake Rivers, just to the east of Idaho's border with Wyoming. Thomas Teter, the government's agent at the Fort Hall reservation, claimed he'd been "reliably informed that there are from 200 to 300 [Indians] camped in the Fall River Valley." And the report that Indians had managed to take control of all of the mountain passes out of Jackson Hole was confirmed by none other than "Courier Sargent of Marymere," even as his wife told a reporter she was "confident that there has not been an Indian in Jackson's Hole all summer," and that "the scare was precipitated . . . by the cruelty of the Jackson's Hole posse deputized to arrest Indians found hunting in violation of the Wyoming law."[39]

The U.S. Army eventually marched into Jackson Hole. When the soldiers arrived, they found no Indians and no dead White people. Speaking about the affair a month later, Lieutenant General John Schofield insisted the dangers faced by Jackson's settlers had been "exaggerated." "There is no doubt that those frontier whites were the cause of the whole thing," he told the *New York Times*. "That country is one of the best hunting regions on the continent . . . and the whites wanted the whole game country to themselves."[40]

After it became clear that the Bannock War of 1895 was much ado about nothing, settlers in the region started pointing fingers, perhaps recognizing that they looked ridiculous to the rest of the country. Almost all of their fingers were pointed at John Dudley Sargent. Some of the blame was deserved. Jack had written to Ray's father about the uprising, and General Hamilton's military connections were the reason troops had been sent in.[41] But the misinformation Jack conveyed wasn't nearly as inflammatory as the misinformation spread by men like William Ross and Robert Fitzpatrick. All Jack had said was that Indians had captured the passes out of Jackson Hole; Ross and Fitzpatrick were the ones who'd claimed White people were being slaughtered. Jack was singled out for the blame not because his participation in the hysteria had been particularly egregious, but because the settlers in Jackson didn't like him. He was a tattletale and a remittance man.

Jack must have believed that the threat he spoke about was real, however. He left his ranch with his family in July, more than three months before he normally would have, during a summer when he should have been filing a patent on his homestead, something he was finally able to do now that he'd been living on the land for five years. If Jack were deliberately spreading false rumors in an effort to hurt the Bannocks (whose hunting of elk, admittedly, he did not like), it seems strange that he would have taken the dramatic step of removing his family from Marymere. That decision, after all, threw his eligibility to file a patent on his land into serious jeopardy.

The federal homestead laws required that settlers occupy the land they wanted to patent, a provision the government hoped would cut down on land speculation. For more than six months of every year, settlers had to continuously live on the homesteads they intended to claim. Leaving for five months, the way the Sargents normally did, was fine. Leaving for nine months, as they did from 1895 to 1896, was not.[42]

In many parts of the United States, federal officials might have been willing to turn a blind eye to the extended time Jack and his family spent away from Marymere, given the well-documented hysteria that had precipitated the move. But many powerful people were looking at the area around Jack's ranch with an eye toward putting it into the public trust— maybe even folding it into Yellowstone National Park. One of those people was a distant relation to Jack, though there's no evidence the two men knew one another. Charles Sprague Sargent was descended from Epes Sargent's first wife, Esther McCarty. He was the director of Harvard's Arnold Arboretum and the nation's leading expert on trees. Recall that

Sargent had teamed up with Frederick Law Olmsted and Jack's cousin, Gus Hemenway Jr. in the 1870s to create the "Emerald Necklace" in Boston.

C. S. Sargent was the chair of the National Forestry Commission, which the Department of the Interior had created in 1896 to assess the condition of the Yellowstone Timberland Reserve. Sargent determined that the five-year-old reserve was a conservationist success, and he recommended that another 829,440 acres in Wyoming be put into the public trust. The General Land Office followed his advice and created the Teton Forest Reserve on February 22, 1897. The land Jack and his family had been living on since the spring of 1890 was part of that new reserve.[43]

During the nine months Jack spent away from Marymere in 1895 and 1896, he was painfully aware of the interest the National Forestry Commission had in his land. He wrote to George Anderson about the situation shortly after he returned to his ranch, hoping Yellowstone's superintendent might be able to give him a sense of how likely it was that a new timberland reserve would be created. Unlike most people in the area, Jack was not adamantly opposed to the idea—so long as the change didn't happen until *after* he had staked a legal claim to the property along Jackson Lake that might eventually become a part of the reserve.[44]

Private property owners complicated the government's efforts to put land into a public trust. Jack Sargent knew that if they could do it, interior officials would deny his homestead application on the basis of the time he'd spent away from Marymere during the Bannock War, just to make it easier for them to turn the property into a timberland reserve, should the opportunity ever arise, as it subsequently did. When he returned to his ranch in April 1896, therefore—several months before Charles Sprague Sargent recommended that a new forest reserve be created—he didn't want to draw the government's attention to his existence; he wanted to quietly resettle on the land and eventually make a full-proof claim to it, which required him to start the clock over and wait another five years before applying for a patent.

This is probably why Jack elected to stay at Marymere with Addie and their children during the winter of 1896–97. He knew the winters along Jackson Lake were harsh, but he didn't want to get stuck someplace else for nine months ever again. What he didn't realize was that his decision to remain on the ranch would end up delaying his effort to patent his

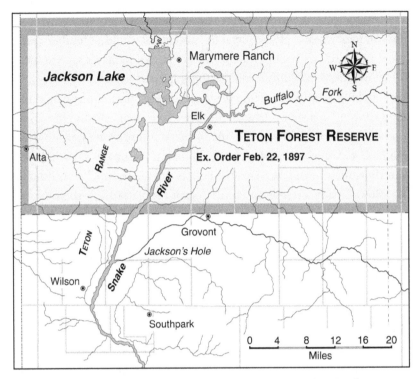

Boundaries of the Teton Forest Reserve, created in 1897. Jack's homestead was within the boundaries. Map created by Mark Moore.

homestead even longer. It would also permanently alter the course of John Dudley Sargent's life.

On February 22, 1897, the day the General Land Office created the Teton Forest Reserve, two soldiers who were a part of the U.S. Army's Sixth Cavalry Unit at the Snake River Station in the Yellowstone Timberland Reserve stopped by Marymere to look in on Jack and his family, whom no one had seen for nearly three months. According to Sergeant Hal Winslow, the visit was a routine wellness check—something the army did during the winter months for all of the people who'd elected to stay in Jackson Hole.

What Winslow and his colleague Jay Chandler encountered when they entered the Sargent home was far from routine, however. They had trouble getting into the lodge at first. Jack was highly suspicious of the two men when they arrived at the ranch and wouldn't let them past the threshold. "He seemed as though he wanted to take a shot at me," Winslow later recalled. After the soldiers convinced him they were only there to help, Jack let them into the lodge, where they found Addie alone in her room "in a very pitiful condition—so weak physically, she could not turn in bed." Addie asked one of the soldiers to get her a nurse, but Jack "disapproved of it . . . he said he didn't want any of them Jackson Hole doctors and nurses—that he was nurse enough," according to Winslow. Finally, after some coaxing, Jack agreed to allow the soldiers to summon a midwife named Hattie Osborne from Jackson. She'd been up to the ranch three years earlier, in May 1894, when Addie gave birth to the family's fifth child, a daughter named Adelaide. According to Jack, Obsorne's assistance with his daughter's birth was the only reason he felt comfortable allowing her onto his property.[45]

The soldiers snowshoed down to Jackson, a journey that took them three full days. They weren't able to locate Hattie Osborne, however, and so when they returned to Marymere on March 4, they brought a woman named Laura Nowlin with them instead. Her husband, Daniel, was a prominent rancher in Jackson who would be elected to Wyoming's state legislature one year later. He joined his wife on the trip to Marymere, as did an attorney from Jackson named Will Simpson, whose son, Milward, and grandson, Alan, both went on to represent Wyoming in the U.S. Senate.[46]

Jack Sargent didn't like Will Simpson. He didn't like Laura and D. C. Nowlin, either; in fact, he called the couple "the two most infamous liars out of prison in Wyoming." Months after his wife had died in April 1897, Jack wrote to Wyoming's governor, blaming the trio for her death. He said he had allowed them to take Addie from Marymere in March 1897 only because they'd promised to put her on a train that would bring her back to Maine. "I candidly admit I wronged her and my daughters by living for seven years on my isolated ranch to get a wretched Homestead Claim," Jack wrote to Governor Richards. "She was an Eastern woman used to cultivation and refinement, and altho' in Wyoming all of our married life, she never liked the West and always wanted me to go East with her."[47]

For the rest of his life, Jack would regret allowing the Nowlins and Will Simpson to take Addie from his ranch. They didn't send her to Maine, as they had promised they would. Instead they "criminally procured an abortion on [her]," according to Jack. Addie "lived <u>ten days</u> after the abortion and murder of the undersigned's unborn child (<u>six months along</u>)," he angrily wrote to Wyoming's governor.[48] Jack referred to himself in the third person to give his letter the feel of a formal, legal charge. He was also probably desperate to distance himself from the tragic results of decisions he had made.

13

Little Girls

Will Simpson was the first person to go to the press with the story. In an article he wrote for the *News-Register* in Evanston, Wyoming, on April 2, 1897, Simpson accused John Dudley Sargent of being a "brute in human form" who "refused his dying wife medical treatment" and "prevent[ed] even his children from waiting upon their mother." He reminded the newspaper's readers that Jack was "known for his connection to the deceased Ray Hamilton, who lost his life in [the] Snake River some years since." He said Addie was from "a prominent and wealthy family in Maine," and that "stories have long been current of Sargent's arrogant and brutal nature and the insane delight with which he inflict[s] punishment upon his children." Until recently those stories had been "nothing but neighborhood gossip," since the "remote locality of Sargent's domicile and its long distance from the settlements" had kept the stories from being confirmed. But "four weeks ago, a couple of messengers arrived in the settlements, requesting someone to go at once to Sargent's, as Mrs. Sargent was dangerously ill." Since then Jack's failures as a husband and father had been more than just "neighborhood gossip." They were the truth.[1]

A party of concerned settlers from Jackson had snowshoed up to Marymere in early March, Simpson told his readers (without divulging that he'd been among the people in this party). They brought food and medical supplies, along with a toboggan, so that they could bring Addie into town if they determined her condition required it. "Upon arrival at the Sargent place, they were confronted with the puritan visage of Sargent and ordered off the premises with all the lordly presence of a diseased mind," Simpson reported—with no sense of irony, since he didn't know the man he'd accused of having the face of a Puritan was actually a direct descendent of several Calvinist governors of colonial Massachusetts. The party refused to leave, in spite of Jack's orders, and "proceeded against Sargent's protest to investigate." They found Addie lying on a couch inside the lodge, enervated, emaciated, and moaning in pain.[2]

"Inquiry developed the fact that during her long illness, no hand of pity, no heart of love had been held out to her by the brute who, fifteen years before, had sworn to love, honor, and protect her," Simpson wrote. The visitors removed Addie and her children from the lodge, taking them down to Jackson and sending word to her parents and brother in Maine. "Although her life now hangs upon the merest thread," Simpson told Evanston's readers, "it is sincerely hoped that kind treatment will bring her back to health, while living alone, the husband is left to the pangs of an accusing conscience."[3]

Will Simpson was an attorney. Three years earlier he'd convinced a jury in Lander, Wyoming, to send Butch Cassidy to jail for being an accessory to horse thievery. It was a bit like the tax evasion strategy Mabel Walker Willebrandt would eventually use against mobsters like Al Capone, in that law enforcement officials really wanted to get Cassidy for robbing banks, not purchasing stolen livestock. Still, the tactic resulted in Cassidy's incarceration for the very first time, suggesting that Will Simpson was a pretty clever lawyer.[4] Nevertheless, he may have missed his calling. The article he wrote for the *Evanston News-Register* had all the hallmarks of a successful piece of journalism in the late nineteenth century: dramatic language, incendiary and unsubstantiated charges, a sympathetic victim, a mildly famous perpetrator, and moral depravity. Not surprisingly, it was picked up by newspapers around the country.

The *Salt Lake City Herald*—the same paper that had published both installments of Nellie Bly's profile of "Mrs. Eva Hamilton"—was the first newspaper outside Wyoming to notify readers of the tragedy at Marymere. Lifting language directly from Will Simpson's piece in the *News-Register*, the *Herald*'s writer spoke of Jack's "arrogant and brutal nature" and the "insane delight" he took in punishing his children. Addie was dead by the time the article ran on April 11, but because she had been alive when Simpson's piece came out on April 3, readers in Utah learned Addie "may with good care recover, but it is doubtful."[5]

According to the *Herald*, Jack's children, "some of whom are grown, say that Sargent treated them and their mother in a terrible manner, not only whipping them, but he refused to give them food." None of the Sargent children was "grown." The oldest, Charles Hemenway, was a few months shy of his thirteenth birthday in the spring of 1897—a fact that Will Simpson had actually mentioned in his article for the *Evanston News-Register*. The *Herald*'s writer was a sloppy reader, however, who'd gotten the details wrong. Mistakes like that were "forgivable," so long as they were committed by "one who has in him at least the desire to represent the truth." Edwin Shuman had said as much three years earlier in his textbook *Steps into Journalism*.[6]

By summer any American who hadn't learned who John Dudley Sargent was in 1891, when he'd traveled to New York with a dog to testify in Elihu Root's office about Robert Ray Hamilton's death, had a second chance to get to know him, when newspapers from Los Angeles, California, to Machias, Maine, reported he'd murdered his wife on their remote homestead in Wyoming and then fled the state, after settlers there threatened to lynch him. Readers in Waterloo, Iowa; Muncie, Indiana; Woodstock, Vermont; and Wilmington, North Carolina, learned that Jack was "the man who was the partner of Robert Ray Hamilton, whose drowning in [the] Snake River . . . was regarded as a most mysterious affair at the time." They read that Addie wasn't merely ill, but was actually "suffering from broken bones caused by being beaten by Sargent" when she arrived at the home of D. C. and Laura Nowlin in March 1897. And they read that in the time that had passed since Addie's death, "intimations have been thrown out that [Sargent] knew more of Hamilton's death than has developed."[7]

From that point forward—the summer of 1897 until well into the third decade of the twenty-first century—John Dudley Sargent would be known as a "fiend" and a "torturer."[8] He was a Wyoming homesteader who had abused his children and killed his wife. He was also the man who had murdered the great-grandson of Alexander Hamilton.

The year 1897 was an important one for the little girl known as Beatrice Ray Hamilton, as well. It was the year Ray's executors realized they didn't have enough money to fund the annuity he'd created for her shortly before he moved to Wyoming.[9]

Ray created the annuity when he revised his will. "I give and devise to the child, my adopted daughter, christened Beatrice Ray at Atlantic City in August 1889, an annuity of twelve hundred dollars a year," he wrote in March 1890, more than six months after the world had learned of Eva's treachery. It wasn't a lot of money; in modern-day terms, it came to about $34,000. But again, it was set aside for Beatrice in Ray's will—meaning that if she received it, it was only because the child who'd been born into a kind of poverty that was so abject, it had resulted in her being *sold* was now truly without parents, not even ones who'd been tricked into taking responsibility for her. The inheritance Ray left her was large enough to ensure Beatrice would never be poor. She would never have the kind of life she had actually been born to inherit.[10]

Ray also didn't intend for her to collect the annuity until many years down the road, after he had spent decades paying for Beatrice to grow up. Whether he had any intention of bringing the girl to Wyoming is not known; none of the paperwork he left behind with his lawyers suggests this was ever his plan. But certainly he didn't plan on dying in the Snake River at the age of thirty-nine, right after he had invited his best friends to come all the way out to Wyoming to visit him and stay in the lodge he was looking forward to having completed. In the weeks after his death, some reporters speculated Ray's drowning had been a suicide, but that's very unlikely. Ray intended to live, and he intended to pay for Beatrice's upbringing while he was doing so. He arranged for a lawyer to provide Elizabeth Rupp in Philadelphia with a regular stipend to care for Beatrice. According to Mrs. Rupp, Ray also sent Beatrice "two small turquoise pins and two picture books" for Christmas in 1889.[11] He may not have loved the little girl, but he had no intention of abandoning her.

After Ray died his executors retrieved two-year-old Beatrice from Mrs. Rupp and gave her to Ray's brother, Schuyler Jr., and his wife, Gertrude. The couple arranged for a nanny named Mary Nevins to care for the little girl in their home until 1894, when they divorced.[12] The separation was contentious. Young Schuyler Hamilton, it turned out, was a philanderer and a financial screw-up. He actually owed his brother $50,000 when Ray died. The loan was due to be repaid in February 1891, and if Schuyler didn't have the funds to reimburse Ray, the loan's conditions required him to sell two properties he owned in Manhattan so that he could do so.

Ray's executors elected not to pursue Schuyler for the money after they learned he was heavily mortgaged on the buildings he was supposed to sell. Schuyler Jr. ended up declaring bankruptcy anyway.[13]

Gertrude Van Cortlandt Hamilton didn't want her ex-husband to have custody of their three children. A nasty, expensive, and drawn-out legal battle ensued, and it was during the years of that battle—sometime between 1894 and 1897, when Ray's executors determined they didn't have the money to fund Beatrice's annuity—that Gertrude gave Ray's daughter to a woman named Jane McCrystal to care for. McCrystal had another name she went by: Sister Teresa Vincent. She was the director of the Foundling Hospital, an orphanage on 68th Street and Lexington Avenue that was run by the Sisters of Charity of Saint Vincent de Paul.[14]

Ray's executors had run out of money fighting Eva's efforts to assert a dower right. They had no income from his law practice to draw upon, since Ray was no longer accepting clients. They didn't have the $40,000 annuity he'd been getting from his grandfather, either; that went to Ray's aunt, Nathalie Ray Baylies, after he died. Eva might have gotten one-third of it, had the courts ruled she was Ray's legal wife. But there was never any chance Ray's estate would continue to receive annual payments from the estate of his grandfather. The annuity was for the entirety of Ray's natural life, which was now over.

Ray's executors sold two properties he owned in Brooklyn in an effort to fund Beatrice's annuity. The properties were not in good condition, however, and Ray had recently mortgaged one of them (presumably to finance Eva's lifestyle, and maybe to fund the loan he'd given his brother, as well). The sale brought in just $24,000, and to fund the full annuity, Ray's executors needed at least $40,000.[15] They decided, therefore, to sell a property Ray owned in Manhattan, to make up the difference.

The problem was that Ray didn't own the property all by himself. He co-owned it with his mother's sister, and Aunt Nathalie didn't want Ray's estate to sell his share. She was opposed to having any part of the property pass out of the family's hands, since it had been purchased by her grandfather Nathaniel Prime years before he slit his throat. Aunt Nathalie could have bought Ray's share herself, allowing Beatrice's annuity to be funded while keeping the property in the family. She had plenty of money, after all: her own annuity from her father, and now Ray's annuity, as well. But Aunt Nathalie didn't do that. Instead, she sued Ray's estate—because the fact of the matter was that her gripe with Ray's executors was about more than just the lot on the corner of Broadway and Spring Street her grandfather had purchased back in 1824. Nathalie Ray Baylies disapproved of the annuity her nephew had left Beatrice Ray Hamilton, because, in spite of her name, the little girl was neither a Ray, nor a Hamilton.

Dinner at the Baylies residence must have been delightfully awkward that Thanksgiving. One of the executors Aunt Nathalie sued was Ray's cousin: her own son, Edmund Baylies. He and his coexecutor, Gil Speir, hired an attorney named George Ellis to represent Beatrice, who was not yet nine years old. Ellis's assignment was to convince a judge that Beatrice's annuity was a "first charge" on Ray's estate—meaning it was an obligation his executors were bound to meet before all others, so long as his estate continued to possess anything of value.

Ed Baylies was motivated purely by a desire to be a good executor, and not by any personal affinity for the little girl at the center of Ray's drama (a fact that may have saved his relationship with his mother). Ray had actually wanted Ed to be Beatrice's guardian. He said as much in his will, but Ed elected not to take on that responsibility after he realized he didn't have to. He told the judge overseeing his mother's lawsuit that he'd contacted authorities in New York and New Jersey to determine whether Ray had ever legally adopted Beatrice. "So far as I could learn," Ed told the court, "no formal adoption took place anywhere, and so I did not take out letters of guardianship." He recognized that his cousin had fully intended for Beatrice's financial needs to be taken care of, and he was determined to do whatever was necessary to make that happen. But other than the will, there was no legal document establishing Ray's parental responsibilities to Beatrice, and Ed was not about to do anything he wasn't legally obliged to do. "I have only acted . . . in so far as the said will casts certain duties upon me as executor in reference to said child," he explained to the judge (and to his mother).[16]

Ray hadn't adopted Beatrice, but the referee tasked with reviewing the case and making a recommendation to the judge believed he thought of Beatrice as his daughter. Hamilton Odell was struck by the fact that Ray had given Beatrice "his mother's family name, as well as his own." He saw this decision as proof that even after Eva's scam was revealed, Ray thought "the infant Beatrice Ray Hamilton was his child with all the obligations of maintenance, education, and life-long support which such relation implies." "The conclusion is irresistible," Odell told Justice Henry Gildersleeve, "that Hamilton intended this annuity as a first charge on his whole estate." Gildersleeve took Odell's evaluation under advisement and ruled on May 12, 1898, that Ed Baylies and Gil Speir could sell Ray's share of the building on the corner of Broadway and Spring Street and use the money to fund Beatrice Ray Hamilton's annuity.[17]

Eight months later a four-judge panel overturned that decision. The problem for Beatrice was that her father had specifically identified his property holdings in Brooklyn—not Manhattan—as the intended funding source for her annuity. The $1,200 she was supposed to receive was "to be paid to her by my executors in monthly installments during her natural life," Ray wrote in his will, "and I hereby charge the same upon my property in the city of Brooklyn." "The testator was a lawyer," Justice P. J. Van Brunt noted in the appellate court's decision. "He drew his own will and probably knew what he intended to do with his property." Van Brunt believed that Ray thought of Beatrice as his daughter, regardless of what Aunt Nathalie thought of the little girl's status within the family. However, "in consequence of litigations arising after his death, which he had no reason to anticipate," Ray's estate had been emptied of the funds it needed to take care of Beatrice the way her father had intended. "The fact that Robert Ray Hamilton made this annuity a charge upon specific real estate is an evidence that it was his intention that his other real estate should not be incumbered with any such charge," Justice Van Brunt wrote. The property in Manhattan was off the table, as far as Beatrice's annuity was concerned.[18]

By the time this decision came down, Ed Baylies and Gil Speir had already sold Ray's share of the building on Broadway and Spring Street. Disgusted with the entire situation, Aunt Nathalie sold her share of the building, as well. Ray's estate walked away from the sale with $131,250—more than enough money to fund Beatrice's annuity. None of it could be used to achieve that end, however. After the costs of Aunt Nathalie's lawsuit were settled, the remaining funds went to Schuyler Jr.'s children, who were also named as heirs in Ray's will.[19]

Beatrice Ray Hamilton wasn't penniless, at least. Her father's executors still had about $24,000 they could use to set up an annuity for her. Depending upon the year, that investment might yield between $650 and $750: the equivalent in the early years of the twentieth century of between $15,000 and $20,000 today. Again, it wasn't a fortune, but it would keep Beatrice out of the poorhouse. It might also help to get her adopted—something hundreds of people across the United States and Canada had said they wanted to do, back when Beatrice was still an infant. By January 1899, however, she was eleven years old and decidedly less adoptable, sans an annuity.

The orphanage where Beatrice lived after Gertrude and Young Schuyler divorced had opened its doors in 1869. The Sisters of Charity ran it out of a brownstone at first, placing a bassinette in the house's vestibule so mothers could turn their infants over to the nuns anonymously, usually in the middle of the night. By the time Beatrice moved into the orphanage in the mid-1890s, it was located on a modern campus on the Upper East Side of Manhattan that took up an entire square block. The New York Foundling Hospital, as it came to be called, provided medical care and nursing services to pregnant women and new mothers, regardless of their marital status. It had a team of pediatricians who catered to children living at the orphanage and beyond. And starting in 1881, it also offered daytime childcare services to women who had jobs outside of the home, making it one of the very first "day cares" in the United States.[20]

Because the Sisters allowed mothers to remain anonymous (something most Protestant orphanages refused to do), many women stuck around to nurse the infants they gave up. This had an astonishingly positive impact on the survival rate of the babies brought to the New York Foundling Hospital. While most orphanages had infant mortality rates in excess of 80 percent, three-quarters of the babies brought to the New York Foundling in the 1880s survived.[21]

It wasn't unusual for a child to spend two years or more at the Foundling; extended stays, however, were not the nuns' goal. In 1897, the year Sr. Teresa Vincent named herself as Beatrice's guardian in Nathalie Ray Baylies's lawsuit, more than 40 percent of the children living in the orphanage in January were gone by October 1. Some of these children, undoubtedly, had died, but most of them had been given to families.[22]

Years before the Sisters of Charity started accepting babies in bassinettes, the thinking on how best to address the needs of orphans, especially orphans over the age of six, had started to change in the United States. The trajectory these changes followed was opposite to the trajectory followed by the professional thinking on mental health. Alienists believed that the best way to help mentally ill patients was to get them *into* institutions, while child welfare advocates believed that the best way to help abandoned or parentless children was to get them *out*.

Charles Loring Brace was primarily responsible for this change in thinking. Trained as a Congregationalist minister, Brace withdrew from Union Theological Seminary and abruptly left New York in February 1850 at the age of twenty-four, after his favorite sister, Emma, died unexpectedly. He traveled aimlessly in Europe for nearly two years and briefly spent time in a Hungarian prison, after royal officials there accused him of spreading seditious literature. Europe had been rocked three years earlier by a series of violent social revolutions (recall that this violence had played a role in Gandolfo Pranzini's decision to leave Tuscany and raise his son, Enrico, in Egypt). The Austrian and Russian authorities who'd recently regained control of the cities of Buda and Pest were suspicious of Americans like Brace, because Americans represented a threat to monarchical power simply by being a thriving example of self-rule.[23]

Charles Loring Brace returned to New York in 1852, deeply moved by the conversations about poverty he'd had with the revolutionaries he encountered in prison. The city he returned to was experiencing its own anxieties about the social instability that accompanies pervasive and wretched poverty. Shortly before Brace left New York—at the high point of the violent revolutions in Europe—a group of mostly Irish immigrants had rioted in front of the Astor Place Opera House, a theater about four blocks east of Washington Square Park. The Opera House catered to wealthy theatergoers, and in May 1849, it brought a famous British actor to New York to play Macbeth. That actor, Charles Macready, had cultivated a rivalry with a popular American actor named Edwin Forrest, who was scheduled to play Macbeth that same week at the Broadway Theater, where the tickets were inexpensive and the performances enjoyed a reliable following among working-class New Yorkers.

It's hard to imagine today that anyone could be provoked to riot over a theater performance (especially one involving Shakespeare). But prior to 2020, it was also hard to imagine anyone would ever throw a punch at a school board meeting over a mask mandate in the midst of a deadly pandemic. Cultural identity is a powerful force when it is rightly or wrongly perceived as being threatened or ridiculed. Remember how angry and defensive Henry Cabot Lodge was when he realized the status of Brahmin families like his own was being undermined by a new class of businessmen with different values, beliefs, and goals. When a group of people perceives they are losing power or being denied power altogether because of who they are—the way they talk, the things they eat, the beliefs they hold, the occupations they fill—that group gets angry. This anger can be extremely productive. It can also render the group's members vulnerable to the manipulative rhetoric of self-interested actors.[24]

Irish immigrants in New York hated the British (though they were apparently willing to give the Bard a pass, so long as Edwin Forrest was the one playing Macbeth). This hatred was the reason they continued to celebrate Evacuation Day well into the 1880s, after most New Yorkers had forgotten all about the holiday. Several Tammany politicians saw an opportunity in the Forrest-Macready rivalry and the poverty and anti-Anglo sentiment that fueled it. They organized a demonstration against Macready's performance in an effort to embarrass the Whig party in charge of New York's government. When police officers fired on the crowd, they killed thirty-one protesters and injured another forty-eight. More than two hundred police and guardsmen were also injured.[25]

It was no coincidence that when Charles Loring Brace founded the Children's Aid Society in 1853, he chose the second floor of Clinton Hall, the building on Lafayette Street that had previously been known as the Astor Place Opera House (which New Yorkers had started calling the "DisAster Place Opera House"), as the society's headquarters. Brace believed that the social instability embodied in the Astor Place Riot began with the twenty thousand children who were living poor and unsupervised lives on the streets of New York.[26]

The city did have a municipal orphanage. The New York Juvenile Asylum had opened its doors two years earlier, in 1851. But Brace believed that institutions were not the best environment for children to be raised in. They were too impersonal. They frequently brought otherwise decent children into the orbits of bullies and malefactors. And they were premised upon a very pessimistic understanding of human nature, one that saw children as miscreants who needed to have their delinquency disciplined out of them, rather than creatures of God who were capable of virtue, if only that virtue were nurtured and encouraged.[27]

Children needed to be with families. This was the animating philosophy of the Children's Aid Society, which launched what it called its "Emigration Plan" in October 1854, when forty-five children who'd been living on the streets of New York traveled to Michigan with one of the society's agents and gathered in a Presbyterian church about twenty-five miles north of South Bend, Indiana, so farmers there could meet the children and decide to take one or two of them home. By the end the week, all but eight of the forty-five children had found homes with Michigan farm families. By 1929, the last year the society implemented its Emigration Plan, more than one hundred thousand children from New York had found homes with families in every state except Arizona, thanks to the Children's Aid Society. Another 150,000 more were similarly adopted or fostered, after other orphanages and child welfare associations—including, eventually, the New York Juvenile Asylum—adopted Charles Loring Brace's approach.[28]

Today the phenomenon Brace initiated is known as the "Orphan Train Movement," though no one at the time ever called it that. The term "Orphan Train" became popular in 1978, after CBS News aired a series about the history of adoption in the United States called *The Orphan Trains*.[29]

The Sisters of Charity did use a similar term, however, when speaking about the adoption and fostering system they developed in the 1870s. The Foundling Hospital sent what the nuns called "Baby Trains" or "Mercy Trains" out to Catholic communities in Louisiana and the Midwest, so that orphans could be raised by families in uncongested environments. That the families accepting these children be Catholic was a requirement the nuns were unwilling to compromise on. The Sisters of Charity never sent children out to a church or community center so that arbitrary farmers could decide whether they wanted to bring any of the children home. Each child who left New York on a Mercy Train was destined to live with a specific family who had been picked out for him or her by a network of priests, nuns, and lay volunteers whom the Sisters worked with in parishes throughout the country.[30]

The Sisters of Charity had founded the New York Orphan Asylum because they viewed what Charles Loring Brace was doing as a threat. Half of New York City's population was Catholic by 1865, thanks to the massive wave of desperately poor immigrants who had come into the city from Ireland in the 1840s and 1850s.[31] The vast majority of babies being abandoned on docks and street corners were born to Catholic mothers; the odds are high, in fact, that the woman who gave birth to Beatrice Ray Hamilton was a Catholic.

When these children became the charge of the Children's Aid Society—or any one of the numerous privately funded child welfare organizations founded by Protestants in the early nineteenth century—retaining and maintaining the children's Catholic identity was not a priority. In fact, sometimes eliminating that religious identity and replacing it with some variety of Protestantism was an unabashed goal.[32] When the Sisters of Charity founded their orphanage, therefore, they saw themselves as saving more than just the *bodies* of the children they took in; the nuns believed they were also saving the children's *souls*.

After Beatrice Ray Hamilton lost her appeal in the case her great-aunt brought against her, she disappeared entirely from the public record. The census of 1900 does not list her as being among the "inmates" at the New York Foundling Hospital. Indeed, Beatrice Ray Hamilton isn't listed in *any* census that was taken *anywhere* in the United States in 1900. There were thirty-nine "Beatrice Hamiltons" living in the country that year, and not one of them was Ray's daughter.[33]

No marriage certificate was ever filed in her name; no death certificate was ever filed, either. If Beatrice Ray Hamilton and her tiny annuity were placed on a Mercy Train and sent to live with a Catholic family in Louisiana or the Midwest, her last name would have changed when that family adopted her. That, in turn, would have resulted in her being lost forever to anyone who wasn't directly descended from her and didn't know her full story. Unlike some of the other aid organizations that shipped children out of New York on orphan trains, the New York Founding Hospital has not agreed to make its records available to the public.[34] If Beatrice Ray Hamilton were adopted by a family in the Midwest, the records of that adoption are sitting on a shelf at the New York Historical Society—organized, labeled, and as inaccessible to the public as Edith Drake's medical records in Albany.

Something happens when you're researching a person's life that all biographers need to be careful about: the tendency to become so invested in your subject's life that you lose the ability to confront his or her flaws. "Most biographies tend to be written in affection and love," Leon Edel acknowledged in 1984, after his biography of Henry James had won the Pulitzer Prize. "If there ensues an emotional involvement on the part of the biographer, he or she must be reminded that love is blind." Without such a reminder, Edel warned, biographers run the risk of creating "retouchings, erasure of wrinkles, and even alterations of character and personality."[35]

Adelaide Crane Sargent's voice is nearly absent from this story. She kept no great cache of correspondence from her family and friends that could be tucked away in a deliberately misidentified collection at a regional historical society, the way Robert Ray Hamilton did. She wrote no goofy essays about marriage or irate letters to the editor about Irish revolutionaries, the way Edith Drake did. And she attempted no autobiography, the way her husband did.

We do know that life could not have been easy for Addie in Wyoming. When she gave birth to her youngest daughter at the ranch in 1894, she was lucky she didn't have any complications, since the nearest doctor was nearly 150 miles away. Jack usually hired a Mormon girl from Idaho to help his wife with the housekeeping, but the bulk of the responsibility for feeding and clothing the five Sargent children would have fallen on Addie's shoulders. Caring for Marymere's occasional guests would have been her responsibility, as well. The lodge those Swedish carpenters built was luxurious by Jackson Hole's standards, but it was primitive by the standards of Addie's native New England. It had no indoor plumbing, and although we can't say for sure that the house Addie grew up in had running water, we do know that plumbed houses were being constructed in Washington County, Maine, as early as the 1850s, nearly a decade before she was born.[36] Leander Crane's income as a stove manufacturer almost certainly made it possible for him to raise his family in a house that had the most modern conveniences available.

Marymere's infrequent guests were usually hunters and soldiers, which meant they were almost always men. Other than her daughters and the servant girl Jack hired, Addie would have had very little female companionship during the months she spent on the ranch. In September 1896 she apparently worried that a recent illness might keep her from seeing Captain George Anderson's sister, who was briefly in the area for a visit. "Please tell Miss Anderson that Mrs. Sargent . . . is on the mend and says she will be on her feet again Monday," Jack wrote to Yellowstone's superintendent, telling Anderson his wife was anxious to meet the young woman, since she rarely had an opportunity for "feminine conversation."[37]

The only words we have from Addie are those she shared with a reporter in the midst of the Bannock War about how she felt the entire affair had been provoked by the cruelty of Jackson Hole's White residents. There are also two letters she sent to her father in Machias, Maine, less than a year before she died. Those letters make it clear her husband was right when he told Wyoming's governor he had done his wife a disservice by keeping her in the American West. Addie was desperately unhappy in Wyoming—and with Jack—and she wanted to go home.

It wasn't just that *she* was unhappy. Her children were unhappy, too. "I want to ask a favor of you, and I do not want you to grant it unless it be favorable to all," she wrote to Leander Crane in August 1896. "I would like to send Hemenway home to you this fall, if I can get the money to send him. The child is unhappy here. His father is too strict with him. In fact, he abuses him. He has to work beyond his strength, and I cannot endure to see it." Addie took full responsibility for her decision to disregard her father's advice and marry Jack. "You know I never complain," she told Leander Crane, "and I have always made the best of everything, on account of it being my own will that has made me suffer what I have. But father, I am unhappy and have been for a long time."[38]

Addie and her husband didn't agree "about how the children should be raised." "He does not consider my happiness at all, and I have about decided that I do not have to stand it much longer," she told her father. "The only thing that keeps me with him is the children. I would not leave one of them with him. Sometimes he says he wishes we were all dead or in Machias, but then I know that if I were to say I was going, he would not let me have them." "He seems to love them," she wrote in closing, "but does not know how to care for them."[39]

It was a very different rendering of Jack's relationship with his children from the one he conveyed in that poetic story about Ice Cream Point or his endearing description of Martha's "best camping experience" along the Conant Trail. Jack's tales about his children, written years after the events had happened, may have been a bit of revisionist history. If they weren't, and the happy stories about ice cream and camping were true, then the father of five must have undergone a dramatic transformation in the years that passed between Martha's lost mitten in 1892 and Addie's death in 1897—one that made his wife and son miserable.

Addie's second letter to her father was written while the soldiers from the Snake River Station were there in the lodge with her. When the soldiers left Marymere to head to Jackson for help, they took the letter with them and mailed it for Addie. "Dear Father, I am very sick. Have not been out of bed for a month, suffering so much pain all the time," she wrote on February 26, 1897. "Do not know what is the trouble. Nearest doctor is 150 miles away, so entirely out of the question." The soldiers from Yellowstone would be "going down to the Hole tomorrow to bring a woman . . . to take care of me," she told her father. Her husband was worried about how he was going to pay for the woman's services. "Father, I must have something done for me, or I cannot live," Addie wrote. "I thought that, perhaps, among you down home, you could let me have money to pay her. Uncle James, perhaps, can—and there is Mr. Sargent."[40]

Addie closed her letter to her father with an observation that suggested she knew how sick she was, even if she didn't fully understand why. "I thought I ought to let you know the circumstances," she told him, "for if anything happens to me, you would think I did wrong not to let you know." It was the last bit of correspondence Leander Crane ever received from his daughter. On March 30, 1897, Adelaide Crane Sargent "expelled a putrid foetus from [her] uterus," in the words of a physician named J. M. Woodburn, who'd been called in from Idaho by Daniel and Laura Nowlin to attend her. Eight days later, at the age of thirty-two, she died.[41]

Addie's letters and the physician's description of her death are in a collection of depositions housed in a musty, dimly lit, and seemingly chaotic (though actually tightly organized) archive on the northwest corner of Chambers and Centre Streets in New York City. Files are shoved into accordion folders and stacked on shelves running from floor to ceiling along the walls of the seventh floor of the Surrogate's Courthouse. There's a seldom-used door on the west side of the building that leads to a tiny alley, just two blocks long, called Elk Street. It used to be called Elm Street, but city officials renamed it in 1939 to honor the Benevolent and Protective Order of Elks, which met for the first time in a boarding-house on the street in 1867.[42]

Addie's letters were included in a deposition that an attorney in Machias, Maine, took from her father in January 1899. Dr. Woodburn's testimony about her death is part of a deposition he gave to an attorney in Victor, Idaho, that same month. The two depositions were forwarded to a court in New York, along with depositions taken from several people in Wyoming, including Will Simpson, Laura and D. C. Nowlin, and Hal Winslow, one of the soldiers who encountered the Sargent family in February 1897. The testimonies were requested by lawyers representing Joseph Pulitzer and James Gordon Bennett Jr. in two $10,000 libel lawsuits John Dudley Sargent brought against them, after their newspapers published inflammatory articles about him and what supposedly happened at Marymere in the spring of 1897.[43]

The now brittle and browned pages are folded and bundled in random order. A pink cloth string that's tied around them is the only thing keeping them together. Some of the pages consist of questions that lawyers in New York wanted to have answered—what are formally known as "interrogatories." Other pages consist only of answers that were recorded by disinterested attorneys in Wyoming, Idaho, and Maine. Some of the stand-alone answers give an indication of what the questions were, and others do not:

1. My name is D. C. Nowlin, I am forty-one years of age. I reside in Jackson, Uinta County, Wyoming, and am a ranchman by occupation.
2. I do.
3. I first made his acquaintance in the winter of 1880 and 1881.
4. I did.
5. He was living at a ranch known as the "Marymere Ranch" near the head of Jackson Lake, in Uinta County, in the state of Wyoming.

Because the pages are in random order, you'll sometimes encounter a set of answers before the interrogatories associated with those answers as you make your way through the packet. The uncontextualized replies are harmless enough at first. But, as you continue reading, a picture of what those settlers from Jackson encountered at Marymere emerges—and the effect is chilling. It becomes impossible for any biographer to continue to see Jack as a poetic soul who loved his family and was maligned by gossips who thought of him as a remittance man and resented his efforts to protect Wyoming's elk population.

There are, for instance, the answers of D. C. Nowlin:

30. Their supplies were very scanty, except as to meat and a moderate supply of flour, but they were entirely out of coffee and sugar, and were wanting in a supply of medicines ordinarily carried by a ranchman. The children were very poorly clad indeed, not enough clothing to protect them against the climate, and some of the little girls were wearing cloth moccasins that Mrs. Sargent had made early in the fall, and their underclothing had been made of flour sacks.
31. They were not, in my opinion.
32. Actual observation.
33. It was cold.
34. Well, I should say that by the time we arrived there, the temperature was about zero.[44]

There are the answers of Will Simpson:

31. Yes.

32. Plenty of them—both talk and rumor.

33. The further statements of both Mary Sargent and Hemenway Sargent, children of John D. Sargent, of the gross abuses and cruelties of Sargent to their mother, his wife, during her lifetime, such as the fact that [when] Sargent started for Jackson in November AD 1896, he attempted to take two of the younger children with him; that Mrs. Sargent pled with him not to take the baby on such a long, cold trip; that he grabbed the baby and the other child from their mother and put them in the cart and started off to Jackson; that Mrs. Sargent ran after him and that Sargent whipped up the horse and ran over her with both horse and cart, and that their mother never got out of bed afterwards.[45]

And there are the answers of Laura Nowlin:

102. I knoweth not.

103. Not to my knowledge.

104. On our ranch, not far from the house.

105. No, he was not.

106. Mrs. Sargent told me a few days after I had arrived at Mary Mere ranch that Mr. Sargent had had sexual intercourse with her, forcebly [sic] and against her will, while she was sick in bed and helpless; that Mr. Sargent would make such proposals to her and that she at such times felt like scratching his eyes out.[46]

The picture that emerges from these sworn testimonies is horrifying. The man who had carefully packed "flour, sugar, dried fruit, baking powder, salt, pepper, bacon, and matches" for a five-day-long trip over the Conant Pass with his wife and son in 1892 had hardly any food in his house in 1897. The father who had trudged through three feet of snow to retrieve his daughter's mitten now had that same daughter walking around shoeless in the middle of a Wyoming winter when the temperatures had dropped to single digits. The husband who had taken his new wife on a circuitous route through eastern Wyoming so he could show her the stunning and unusual landscape there and give her a sense of the world he had inhabited before he married her had run over his wife with a horse-drawn cart and raped her while she lay in bed, trying to recover from her injuries.

When the settlers from Jackson arrived, only one of the five Franklin stoves in the lodge had been lit. The stove was in Addie's room, and the small amount of heat it kicked out "failed to keep water from freezing in the children's rooms," according to Laura Nowlin. There was no fire in the fireplace Jack and Martha had sat in front of five years earlier, watching the snow fall while they visited with George Anderson and his team of soldiers from Yellowstone National Park. There was no fire in the cook stove, either—although other than elk meat, there really wasn't any food in the lodge to be cooked.[47]

"When we arrived, there was not a stick of wood except what was in the one Franklin," D. C. Nowlin recalled. "But the boy, Heminway [sic], I think he was about twelve years old, was out after fuel upon snow shoes." The snow was about four feet deep, in Nowlin's estimation. "He had to chop down trees with a dull ax and pull the fuel up a steep hill from 100 to 200 yards on a sled."[48]

D. C. Nowlin, Will Simpson, and the other men from Jackson who had joined them spent the next few days hauling a supply of wood to the lodge and cutting it into sizes that were appropriate for the stoves and fireplace. Laura Nowlin washed the children's clothing and prepared the food the settlers had brought for the family, while Hattie Osborne, the midwife who had helped deliver the Sargents' youngest child, tended to Addie. Osborne had been unavailable when the Yellowstone soldiers first arrived in Jackson, but she traveled to Marymere with two other settlers, William Miller and Henry Steltz, a few days later.

Addie's condition deteriorated. At one point, she was unable to speak, and believing she would soon die, D. C. Nowlin walked into the lodge's main room to alert Jack. "[He] was asleep," Nowlin recalled. "I waked him myself and apprised him of his wife's condition and asked him to come into his wife's room." Jack sat with Addie for a couple of hours. "Sargent seemed to be somewhat affected," Nowlin testified. He "told his wife he had 'been a brute' to her. He asked her if he 'had not been a brute,' and she nodded he had." Addie eventually recovered her ability to speak, and after exchanging a few words with her, Jack left the room.

"I observed Mr. Sargent's conduct toward his wife and had observed it previous to this conversation," D. C. Nowlin told the attorney taking his deposition, "and to speak mildly, he was very indifferent as to her condition, sometimes not coming near her room for twenty-four hours."[49]

It's possible the settlers from Jackson were lying—or, if not lying, then exaggerating or misinterpreting the things they saw and heard at Marymere. Jack was not well liked in the valley, after all, and he and Will Simpson had had an argument with one another at the Jackson post office (which was also Simpson's home) a few months earlier, in November 1896. The argument had been about politics—specifically, the reelection bid of Representative Frank Mondell. Jack was a supporter of Mondell, but many people in the valley, including Will Simpson, were unhappy with the congressman's stance on the question of Yellowstone's expansion. Mondell thought the Tetons should be folded into the national park. Jack thought they should, too (so long as his homestead rights were respected). Will Simpson adamantly opposed the idea.[50]

But while Jack disagreed with Simpson on one hot-button issue, he completely agreed with D. C. Nowlin on another. Nowlin was a conservationist. One of the first things he did when he got into the Wyoming State Legislature in 1898 was draft laws that limited the hunting of game animals to seasons. He also created a "game warden" for the state who was tasked with ensuring those hunting seasons were respected. When the state's first game warden, Albert Nelson, resigned in 1902, D. C. Nowlin took over the position himself, holding it for eight years. He started requiring licenses to hunt and used the fees generated from those licenses to fund the enforcement of Wyoming's game laws. He also helped to create what is now an unmistakable feature on the landscape around Jackson, Wyoming: the National Elk Refuge. It's a twenty-five-thousand-acre protected habitat that visitors have to pass by as they travel between Jackson and Grand Teton National Park. Every winter, approximately 7,500 elk migrate to the refuge, which is maintained by the U.S. Fish and Wildlife Service. The first superintendent of the National Elk Refuge when it opened in 1912 was none other than Daniel Nowlin.[51]

Nowlin's testimony about what he encountered at Marymere when he arrived at the ranch in early March 1897 was almost certainly the truth. John D. Sargent was not in his right mind. In the parlance of the day, he had gone "insane." The demons that haunted the Hemenway side of his family made their appearance that winter when he chose to stay on his isolated homestead with his family. Had those demons provoked Jack to run over his wife with a horse and cart? It's hard to say. Will Simpson, after all, was passing along a story that had been relayed to him by children, and because Simpson didn't like Jack, the story is one he may have been overly primed to believe. Something did happen to Addie, however, to cause her to miscarry a child she'd conceived in July or August 1896. Dr. Woodburn estimated that her fetus was more than seven months along when she expelled it from her womb, and that it had been dead within her for six to ten days.[52]

Had Jack had sexual intercourse with his wife against her will? Probably. It's a very serious charge for Addie and Laura Nowlin to have made, after all. It's doubtful Jack saw the action as "rape," however. Indeed, Addie and Laura Nowlin may not have seen it as "rape," either, even as they condemned Jack for it. The rape laws in every American state exempted husbands until 1975, when Nebraska made it illegal for one married partner to have forced sexual relations with another. Not until 1993 did every state in the union have a statute outlawing marital rape.[53]

One thing is undeniable, and that is that Jack's family was not adequately prepared to stay at Marymere for the winter. It's unconscionable that there was no firewood at the ranch in March. If he'd planned to stay for the entire year, Jack should have started putting cords of wood away as soon as he returned to the ranch in April 1896, after being gone for nine months because of the Bannock War. He'd been living in the American West for seventeen years by this point. Although he didn't usually spend his winters at Marymere, he knew what the weather was like there; he knew how cold it could get and how much snow could fall. Jack's decision to keep his family at Marymere for the winter without an adequate supply of fuel was tantamount to murder—or, at the very least, manslaughter. It's extraordinary, really, that Addie and her unborn child were the only ones who died.

The settlers from Jackson stayed at Marymere for about three weeks, and when the weather finally permitted it, they loaded Addie onto a toboggan and took her to the Nowlins' ranch in the southern part of the valley. The trip took three days. Will Simpson hiked ahead of the group so he could get to Jackson first and arrange for Dr. Woodburn to come over from Idaho. D. C. Nowlin later testified that he, Simpson, and William Miller paid Woodburn's fees, which were $200, but that Leander Crane eventually reimbursed them.[54]

The settlers brought the Sargent children with them when they left Marymere—or rather, they brought four of the five Sargent children with them. For reasons that are entirely unexplained in all of the depositions taken from people who were in a position to know, Catherine Winthrop Sargent was allowed to stay with her father when the settlers brought her siblings down to Jackson. She was left with Jack, in spite of the fact that Addie had told Leander Crane she "would not leave <u>one</u>" of her children with her husband. The fact that Catherine Winthrop stayed at Marymere might never have even been revealed, except that Laura Nowlin mentioned it when Joseph Pulitzer's attorneys asked her if Addie had ever expressed an interest in seeing her husband after she left the ranch. "I once found her crying and asked her if she wanted to see her little girl, Catherine, and she said yes," Laura Nowlin replied. "I said we might send someone for the little girl, but she said it would be too much trouble. 'But,' she said, 'I do not want to see John. I never want to see him again as long as I live.'"[55]

Shortly after Addie told Laura Nowlin she wanted to see Catherine Winthrop, D. C. Nowlin and Will Simpson headed back up to Jack's lodge. They brought his twelve-year-old son, Charles Hemenway, with them, and together the trio retrieved Hemenway's four-year-old sister. Jack's children were parceled out among the settlers in Jackson while Daniel Nowlin waited to hear from the Crane and Sargent families about what should be done with them. Will Simpson's mother, Margaret, took ten-year-old Mary, while Simpson and his wife took nine-year-old Martha. The Nowlins took two-year-old Adelaide, and Hemenway went to live with a settler named John Emery. After Addie died Catherine Winthrop went to live with a couple named Charles and Maria Allen.[56]

Before Addie died, however, Catherine Winthrop briefly lived with the Nowlins. They were the ones who asked Dr. Benjamin Jones to come over from Idaho Falls to take a look at her. He, too, was required to submit a deposition in Jack's libel lawsuit against Joseph Pulitzer and James Gordon Bennett Jr. Jones's uncontextualized answers are the first pages in the packet of depositions tied together with pink string at the Surrogate's Courthouse in New York City—the first words from the case that a researcher encounters, after everything she has read up until that point about Jack Sargent has suggested he was a misunderstood figure, unfairly scorned by people who were too eager to find the worst in him, and a devoted father who sought to give his children the love he had been denied as a child:

> To the tenth interrogatory—he sayeth, it was.
> To the eleventh interrogatory—he sayeth, five or six years old.
> To the twelfth interrogatory—he sayeth, I exposed to view the external genital organs and made an inspection of the parts.
> To the thirteenth interrogatory—he sayeth, the condition showed that the bruising had been done some time previous to the examination.
> To the fourteenth interrogatory—he sayeth, it was swollen, bruised and inflamed.
> To the fifteenth interrogatory—he sayeth, yes.[57]

The warrants for Jack Sargent's arrest were issued on June 2, 1897. The first warrant was for "murder in the second degree." The second warrant was for "assault with an intent to commit rape on a female under the age of eighteen." The warrants were not delivered, however, because John Dudley Sargent had fled the state.[58]

14

Katharine and Catherine

Kent Seacrest and Ann Raschke met in 1972, during their freshman year at the University of Nebraska. She was the daughter of a small business owner from Watertown, South Dakota. He came from a family of newspaper publishers in Lincoln, Nebraska. Kent's great-grandfather purchased the *Lincoln Evening News* in 1897. For nearly one hundred years, generations of Seacrest men forged careers in the news industry, starting out in the circulation department or the advertising division and working their way up to the editorial desk. From 1958 until 1986, Kent's father, Joseph Rushton Seacrest, edited what was then known as the *Lincoln Journal*. Kent chose a different path, however. He became an attorney, specializing in real estate law.[1]

In 1991 Kent and Ann went on a fly-fishing trip in the Bridger-Teton National Forest near Moran, Wyoming. They fell in love with the region, and by 2003 they were able to purchase a cabin there along the Buffalo Fork, about fourteen miles east of where that meandering tributary, famous for its fly-fishing, empties into the Snake River.

During their first summer in the cabin, the Seacrests brought Kent's mother to see the place. "Mike" Seacrest was a well-known figure in Nebraska: she was president of the Nebraska Art Association and a fundraiser for Lincoln's Sheldon Museum of Art. Throughout the 1970s and 1980s, Mike also cohosted a show on Nebraska Public Television called *Grand Generations* that explored the stories of older men and women living in the Cornhusker State. At its high point, *Grand Generations* had nearly seventy thousand viewers.[2]

"Mike" wasn't Kent's mother's real first name. It was a nickname her husband gave her in the 1940s, not long after the couple met at the Philadelphia Navy Yard in the midst of World War II. Joe Seacrest called his future wife Mike because growing up in Nebraska, he'd learned to pronounce her real name differently from the way she pronounced it, and no matter how hard he tried, he just couldn't seem to break himself of the habit. The source of Joe's troubles was Beatrice, Nebraska, a city in the southeastern corner of the state, about four miles east of the very first homestead claim. The name is shibboleth. Locals pronounce it "Bee-at-triss."[3]

"You know, my grandfather drowned not far from here," Beatrice "Mike" Seacrest told her son and daughter-in-law during that first summer the family spent in their cabin in Wyoming. "He drowned in the Snake River, somewhere near the Buffalo Fork." Kent Hamilton Seacrest had always known his great-grandfather died young, when his mother's mother was still a baby. He'd also always known he was a descendant of Alexander Hamilton. Kent hadn't realized, however, that his great-grandfather had drowned. On that day in 2003, he also had no reason to think that his great-grandfather's death had anything to do with his grandmother's decision to change her name. Kent and Mike Seacrest both assumed that's just what you did when you converted—that Beatrice Ray Hamilton became Katharine Beatrice Hamilton because she became a Catholic.[4]

The *Lincoln Evening News* didn't cover the story of what happened at Marymere Ranch in the spring of 1897 until two years later, when Jack returned to Wyoming to face the charges against him. By that time the canard about how Jack had been implicated in Ray Hamilton's death was a standard and unquestioned part of the story.

"John D. Sargent of New York, who was suspected in the murder of Robert Ray Hamilton . . . and now stands charged with the murder of his wife and criminally assaulting his 4-year-old-daughter at Jackson in March of 1897 has been released from custody, owing to his mental condition," the *Evening News* reported in a story with the headline "Sargent Goes Insane." The Nebraska newspaper told its readers Ray had been "a wealthy New York club man." It explained that Jack had fled following his wife's death, but "returned to Wyoming last summer to face the charges against him." He was released from jail to await his trial because "while he was bound over to the district court on the charge of murder, he brooded over his troubles so much that he was fast becoming a physical wreck, and his release from jail was ordered to prevent a complete breakdown."[5]

The *Evening News* got Jack's home state wrong; it said he was from New York, not Maine. The information about how he was "suspected" of murdering Ray Hamilton was wrong, too—or at the very least highly misleading, in that it implied the suspicions dated back to the time of Ray's death nine years earlier, when in fact no such suspicion had ever been cast Jack's way until after Addie died. The rest of the story was correct, however. Jack did return to Wyoming in August 1899. He was arrested on October 14 and formally charged with second-degree murder. He was released from prison, then, on December 11, after his "brooding" convinced the court to let him out on a $2,000 bond.[6]

What the *Lincoln Evening News* failed to tell its readers is what Jack had been brooding about, or why the only charge he'd been bound over to the district court on was murder; the child rape charge never became an official part of his arrest. It turned out Jack was brooding about his daughters, Mary and Catherine Winthrop, ages twelve and seven. When he'd returned to Wyoming, he had both girls with him. After he was arrested, he arranged for the girls to be sent to a school in Utah that he and Addie used to enroll their children in during the winter months. While he sat in prison, Jack worried about how he was going to pay the tuition. "Your petitioner is wholly without means to pay for their care and maintenance," he wrote in his application for bail. His cousin Gus Hemenway had stopped "grubstaking" him money. "If the defendant is released on his own recognizance," Jack continued, referring to himself in the third person as he often did when writing to officials, "he can and will earn sufficient money for the support of said children and will be and appear for trial at the next term of this court to abide by the decision there-of."[7]

When Jack Sargent left Wyoming in May 1897, it was because he was in danger of being lynched after word of what Dr. Jones had discovered about his daughter got out to the settlers in Jackson Hole. "I heard considerable talk from most every resident in the valley," Will Simpson recalled in his deposition. "Most all expressed themselves to the effect that Sargent needed hanging." Some newspapers even reported that Jack *had* been hanged. On July 24, 1897, in an article filed from Machias, the *New York Herald* told its readers "a report just received here from Wyoming states that John D. Sargent of this place has been lynched by a mob in the region near Jackson's Hole." The *Herald* eventually corrected its report. The threat the paper had described was real, however. Settlers in Jackson, Wyoming, wanted to do to Jack what settlers in Rawlins, Wyoming, had done to George "Big Nose" Parrot ten years earlier.[8]

That's why he fled. Jack Sargent was afraid for his life. It wasn't that he was worried about being tried for the murder of his wife and the attempted rape of his daughter. He knew he was innocent, and he firmly believed his innocence would be apparent in any trial—*if* he got to have one. "He said that he knew he was guilty of enough things, but that they had charged him with things he did not do," Hal Winslow recalled of the three days Jack spent at the Snake River Station before he left Wyoming. "Sargent told me he was afraid of them people, that they were after him and would lynch him if they caught him."[9]

Why, then, had Jack brought Catherine Winthrop with him when he returned to Wyoming? The little girl could only serve as a reminder of the heinous charge against him. And how did he even get custody of her? All five children were sent back east to live with relatives after Jack left Marymere. According to Martha Sargent's daughter, Barbara Titus, the Cranes and Sargents of Washington County, Maine, found the Wyoming side of their family to be very strange at first. "One of the family stories is that all four girls arrived in Maine following their mother's death wearing necklaces of elks' teeth set in gold nuggets," Titus recounted in 1978.[10]

D. C. Nowlin had told Leander Crane and Henry Sargent all about the things that happened at Marymere. "It is very proper that this whole matter be thoroughly ventilated," he wrote in July 1897. "Such action may be the means of giving J. D. Sargent what he has always deserved: that is, exact justice."[11] Why had Jack's father and father-in-law allowed him to have Catherine Winthrop, given the horrible truth Nowlin had revealed to them? And what happened to the arrest warrant for child rape? Why was Jack not bound over to the district court in Wyoming, on *that* charge?

The article in the *Lincoln Evening News* does not say. None of the coverage of Jack's return to Wyoming answered these questions, actually—even though Mary and Catherine Winthrop were there with Jack at his preliminary hearing following his arrest in October 1899. There's a photograph of that hearing, in fact, in which Catherine Winthrop Sargent is sitting *on her father's lap*, with the county sheriff and the justice of the peace at the table with them.[12] The scenario is utterly bizarre, given what Dr. Benjamin Jones discovered about Catherine Winthrop and the child rape charge that was levied against Jack in June 1897.

The reporters writing about Jack's arrest thought it was important to remind readers of his connection to Robert Ray Hamilton nine years earlier. They also thought it was important to remind them he had "gained some notoriety in 1895 by sending East reports of an Indian massacre which led to sending a military expedition into the Jackson's Hole country on a fruitless errand."[13] Not one reporter, however, thought it might be important to explain why Jack had custody of his daughter, if he'd sexually molested her.

Not only was Jack able to bring Catherine Winthrop to Wyoming but he was also able to bring her almost everywhere he went during the two years he was on the run from the law out west. After she grew up and got married—twice, since her first husband died of tuberculosis at the age of thirty-six in 1921—Catherine Winthrop Sargent spoke to her youngest child, Bill Fessel, about the time she spent away from Marymere between 1897 and 1899. She told him she and her father had lived in New York and Machias during those years, and that they took "a sea voyage to Valparaiso, Chile," which has to have been so Jack could work for his cousin Gus's company, although Catherine Winthrop didn't seem to understand that this was the reason she spent some of her childhood in South America. Until recently, in fact, Bill Fessel had never even heard the name Augustus Hemenway, and he feels certain his mother had no idea her father was the grand-nephew of one of the richest men in America. She also didn't know how Adelaide Crane Sargent died and went to her own grave in 1990 at the age of ninety-eight believing it was the journey down to Jackson on a toboggan that had killed the ailing woman.[14]

Catherine Winthrop Sargent enjoyed the time she spent with her father while he was on the run from the law. "She told me that those two years, and then also the two and a half years that she and John Sargent were alone at the ranch after Mary got married [in 1902] were the happiest and most memorable times of her childhood," Bill Fessel recalls. But then, in 1906, things changed at Marymere. Jack got married to Edith Drake. "My mother did not get along with her stepmother," Bill says. "She found her odd."[15]

The census of 1900 lists "Katharine Beatrice Hamilton" as a resident and student at Mount St. Joseph's Academy, a Catholic bordering school in Philadelphia. She was enrolled at the school in 1899 by Gertrude Van Cortlandt Hamilton. Before that she'd attended what she told her daughter was a "convent school" in New York City.[16]

"Your mother had an outstanding background," Charles Costello wrote to his children—Ray Hamilton Costello, Beatrice Hamilton Costello Seacrest, and Charles Francis Costello—in April 1952, a few months after their mother, Katharine, had died at the age of sixty-three. Charles mistakenly thought that his wife's father had been killed after he was "violently thrown from a horse on his ranch in Arizona." He believed that her mother had died shortly after giving birth. Charles correctly knew Katharine was a Hamilton, however. "She was a lineal descendant of Alexander Hamilton," he told his children. "The Hamiltons have for almost two centuries occupied a position in the inner circle of the so-called high society of New York City."[17]

Charles didn't know that his wife's connection to Alexander Hamilton wasn't biological—which means he didn't know his wife was a purchased baby. Mike Seacrest didn't know her mother had been purchased and adopted, either (though she did know her grandfather had died in Wyoming, not Arizona). "We all thought the connection was biological," Ann Seacrest recalled from her home in the Bridger-Teton National Forest in the summer of 2021. "It wasn't until a few years ago, when I started looking at old newspapers online that we discovered any of this."[18]

Ann and Kent Seacrest think it's possible that Katharine herself did not know the full story of her connection to Alexander Hamilton, that she didn't realize she began her life as a baby who was purchased by a grifter and used to trick the great-grandson of the nation's first treasury secretary. "When Katharine was alive, you couldn't easily find old newspaper stories, the way I did," Ann observes. "You had to go to a library and pull the papers up on microfilm. You had to know what issues to look for and what you were looking for. You couldn't just do a search on a name."[19]

If no one ever told Katharine Beatrice Hamilton the truth of her story, she may not have known it. She may not have understood that the reason she was encouraged to change her name when she converted to Catholicism was that she had become famous as Beatrice Ray Hamilton, the little girl at the center of a society scandal whom people across the United States and Canada had wanted to adopt. The nuns who cared for her may have encouraged Beatrice Ray to think of the name change as a way to honor Mother Katharine Drexel, an heiress from Philadelphia who'd founded a religious order (and was subsequently canonized) a few years before Beatrice converted.[20] Note the unusual way in which both women spelled their name: "Katharine" not just with a "K" but also with an "A."

Like many of the abandoned and parentless children who were cared for at the New York Foundling Hospital, Ray's daughter was sent to live with a good Catholic family outside of the city. Between the ages of eleven and eighteen, when she wasn't away at school, Katharine Beatrice Hamilton lived with George and Sarah McNichols and their six children in Pennsylvania. Sarah's maiden name was McCrystal. She had five older siblings, including a sister, Jane, who grew up to become a nun. When Jane McCrystal took the habit, she changed her name to Sr. Teresa Vincent. Shortly thereafter she started caring for infants who'd been abandoned in a bassinet she left in the vestibule of the house on East Twelfth Street in New York that she shared with her fellow Sisters of Charity.[21]

Robert Ray Hamilton's daughter, in other words, hadn't ended up on just any old Mercy Train when she left New York. The train the Sisters put her on took her—and the small annuity she'd inherited from her adopted father—straight into the arms of the family of the Foundling Hospital's cofounder.

Catherine Winthrop Sargent went to boarding school, too. When she was ten years old, she started traveling east every fall. Initially she attended Kemper Hall, an Episcopal school for girls in Kenosha, Wisconsin. Later, when she was in the eighth grade, she started attending the Smead School for Girls in Toledo, Ohio.[22]

"She hated the flat, monotonous Midwest countryside," her son, Bill Fessel, recalls. "Her schoolmates teased her at first. One young lady made fun of her red hair. I suspect my mother didn't have the strongest social skills. I remember she said that she had no playmates on John Sargent's ranch, and that her cat was her one companion."[23]

Catherine Winthrop Sargent had a benefactor. Her name was Ellen Linn, and she was a prominent socialite from Chicago whose father owned a paper mill in the western suburbs. Nellie Linn belonged to the exclusive "Monday morning reading group" that Frances Glessner hosted in her mansion on Prairie Avenue that had been designed by H. H. Richardson. Nellie also knew Jane Addams and served on the finance committee for Addams's famous settlement experiment, Hull House.[24]

In August 1902 Nellie and her husband, William, visited Yellowstone National Park. In spite of the absence of a good road, they eventually made their way down to John Dudley Sargent's ranch. The couple had four children, the youngest of whom, Dorothy, was a few months older than Catherine Winthrop. Nellie was struck by how shy Jack's daughter was, compared to her own, and she attributed that shyness to the girl's isolation on her father's ranch. "She convinced John Sargent that [my mother] needed some time in the East to continue her schooling and develop some social skills," Bill Fessel says.[25]

Jack was reluctant to let his daughter go at first, since it would mean he'd be alone on the ranch. Mary, who'd come back to Wyoming with him because the humidity in Maine made it difficult for her to breathe, had gotten married several months earlier (at the age of fifteen) and moved in with some settlers her father did not like. Jack finally agreed to Nellie's plan, however, and Catherine Winthrop left Marymere with the Linns in early October 1902. She returned to her father's ranch every spring and stayed with him the entire summer, until he married Edith Drake. After that Catherine Winthrop made her visits to the ranch as short as possible.[26]

Bill Fessel says his mother told him Jack was not her biological father. "John Sargent told her that her father was an old friend and rancher in a remote part of southern Wyoming or northern Colorado," Bill recalls of the conversation he had with his mother when he was a teenager. "When his wife died in childbirth, [the friend] was terribly distraught and had no idea what to do with a little girl. By coincidence Adelaide Sargent had just been delivered of a stillborn child. It seemed only logical for the Sargents to take the youngster and raise [her] as their own." Bill says he "later received corroboration of this account from an unexpected source." That source was Nellie Linn's son, Howard. It was 1951, and Bill was a college student in upstate New York. He was heading out west to spend the summer working for the U.S. Forest Service, an experience he ultimately turned into a career. His mother recommended he get in touch with Howard Linn when he changed trains in Chicago. "She said that she knew him when she was a child—that she vacationed with him and his family sometimes in their house in Lake Geneva, Wisconsin," Bill recalls.[27]

Howard Linn met the young man for lunch at the University Club on Michigan Avenue. At some point in the conversation, "he asked me if I was familiar with the story of my mother's parents and the circumstances of her birth." When Bill told him he was not, Linn said his own mother, Nellie, had been "a dear friend" of Catherine Winthrop Sargent's birth mother. He then told Bill a story about a cowboy whose wife had died in childbirth that was similar to the one Bill's mother had told him, adding that Catherine Winthrop was born in Salt Lake City, which is also where her biological mother died.[28]

It's understandable that Bill Fessel believes this story, given that he heard it from two different people. "If I had just heard it from [my mother], I might have reason for suspicion that it might be just a handy cover-up for a past misdeed on Sargent's part," Bill admits. But "the supporting information from Howard Linn gives me some reason for confidence that it is true."[29] Nevertheless, there are also reasons to think the story *isn't* true—or not completely true.

First, there are the birth records from Salt Lake City, Utah, which clearly list "Catherine Winthrop Sargent" as having been born to "Adelaide Crane Sargent" and "John D. Sargent, ranchman" on November 14, 1892. Of course the rules governing vital statistics were fast and loose back then; parents weren't even required to record the birth of a child in Utah until 1909. Jack and Addie easily could have assumed responsibility for the newborn daughter of Jack's cowboy friend and then walked into the county clerk's office and claimed her as their own. Recall that late October 1892 was when Jack took his family over the Conant Trail so that they could spend the winter in Salt Lake City, and at no point in his narrative about that trip did Jack indicate that his wife was pregnant.[30]

But then there are the death records from Salt Lake City. Jack and Addie Sargent told the county clerk they were Catherine Winthrop's parents on December 5, 1892—twenty days after the baby girl was born. In that time four women of child-bearing age died in Salt Lake City: Abbie Little, who was twenty-seven; Margaret Wilcox, who was twenty-six; Martha Holman, who was forty-six; and Agnes Davis, who was twenty-one. Holman and Wilcox both died of a "chronic disease," ruling out pregnancy as the cause of their deaths. Agnes Davis died on November 22 from "shock shown after labor." She had been "sick for four days," indicating she must have given birth on November 18. Next to her name in the death records, however, is a listing for "Flossie Davis," an infant who died when she was two days old. Catherine Winthrop Sargent, in other words, could not have been Agnes's daughter, because the baby Agnes gave birth to died, as well.[31]

That leaves Abbie Little, who died of a "heart clot accompanying pulmonary edema" at the Manitou Hotel in Salt Lake City on November 14, 1892, the same day Catherine Winthrop Sargent was born. The record of Abbie's death does not say she died in childbirth, but pulmonary edema is frequently the cause of death in women who have developed preeclampsia, a pregnancy complication characterized by high blood pressure that can still be fatal today.[32] If there is any truth to the stories Bill Fessel heard about how Adelaide Crane Sargent was not his mother's birth mother, Abbie Little was almost certainly the woman who gave birth to Catherine Winthrop Sargent.

So then who was Abbie Little? Her parents, Richard and Ruth Hopkins, were Mormon settlers in the Bear Lake Valley of southeastern Idaho. Skirmishes between these settlers and Shoshone and Bannock Indians in the 1860s were what led to the creation of the Fort Hall Reservation, where the Bannocks were living in 1895, when newspapers claimed—incorrectly—that they were slaughtering White settlers in Jackson Hole. One is left to wonder how (or *if*) the daughter of two scrappy Mormon pioneers from rural Idaho became the "dear friend" of a Windy City socialite who was raised by a wealthy paper industrialist and grew up to discuss literature in a mansion designed by H. H. Richardson.[33]

Sometime in 1885 Abigail Hopkins married Frederick Little, a real estate agent who'd earned his business degree from the University of Deseret (now the University of Utah). He was the son of Feramorz Little, whose mother, Susannah, was the older sister of Brigham Young, the second president of the Church of Jesus Christ of Latter-day Saints. Feramorz was the mayor of Salt Lake City from 1876 until 1882. Abbie and Frederick Little had a daughter named Cora in July 1889. She was three years old when her mother died. After Abbie's death Frederick and Cora moved in with Frederick's mother, Annie. It's not clear how long Frederick stayed in his mother's household, but by 1900, when the census was taken, ten-year-old Cora Little was still living with her grandmother.[34]

The husband of Catherine Winthrop Sargent's birth mother, in other words, was not a cowboy from southern Wyoming or northern Colorado. He was a college-educated businessman from a prominent Mormon family. More important, he wasn't a man who was afraid to raise a little girl on his own after his wife died—nor was he a man who even *needed* to raise a little girl on his own after his wife died, thanks to the help of his mother.

Frederick Little may have been unwilling to raise the baby his wife gave birth to on November 14, 1892, however, if that baby were not his. And if Abbie Little had gotten pregnant with someone else's child, that might also explain why she was living in a hotel on the day she gave birth and died, in a city where her husband was a residential real estate broker and her father-in-law had been the mayor.

If the father of Abbie's child were John Dudley Sargent (who spent his winters in Salt Lake City and would have been there in February 1891, when Abbie Little conceived), that might explain why Will Simpson and Laura and D. C. Nowlin didn't take Catherine Winthrop with them when they left Marymere Ranch in April 1897 with all of the other Sargent children. If Jack didn't want his daughter to go with the group, Addie wouldn't have had a claim that entitled her to deny him that right.

Jack's infidelity would also explain words he wrote on the back of a photograph that Catherine Winthrop sent him shortly after she arrived at the Episcopal school in Wisconsin where Nellie Linn enrolled her. The photograph is a portrait of Catherine Winthrop. On the back of it Jack wrote, "From my Daughter, Born Nov. 1892." He recorded the address of her school in Wisconsin. And then he added the words, "Her father's features. Her gt. grandfather's insight of human nature."[35]

When Bill Fessel was shown this photograph in the fall of 2018 and asked how Jack Sargent—who was, of course, raised by his grandfather—possibly could have known anything at all about Catherine Winthrop Sargent's great-grandfather if she were not his biological child, Bill paused. He stared at the words and thought for a moment. "Well," he replied, "this really would suggest she was his, wouldn't it?"[36]

On August 16, 1904, five years after he had returned to Wyoming to face the charges against him, John Dudley Sargent finally applied for a patent on his homestead along Jackson Lake. He had been living there continuously since his return, with the exception of those few weeks he spent in jail before he was released on bail. The lodge Jack returned to was missing some of the furnishings it had had before he left. Hattie Osborne, the midwife who'd attended Addie, sued him while he was gone for services rendered, and in his absence, a court had allowed Osborne to take several blankets and pieces of furniture from Jack's lodge. She took the black walnut piano he'd paid to have shipped over the Teton Mountains, thus earning himself a reputation for being a "remittance man."

The piano was worth $200 (not counting what it cost to ship it), which was far more than what Osborne had sued Jack for. Jack was particularly angered over the loss of the musical instrument. After a grand jury in Jackson failed to indict him for murder, he wrote to Wyoming's governor to complain that D. C. Nowlin, Will Simpson, and Hattie Osborne had broken into his lodge and stolen the piano from him.[37]

Just as Jack had anticipated back in 1896, the Department of the Interior balked at his homestead application. Marymere—or what Jack had started calling "Pine Tree Ranch" after Mary angered him by marrying into a settler family he didn't like—was now smack-dab in the middle of a timberland reserve. Federal officials didn't want anyone owning property there. One can almost envision the alarm on the clerk's face in the

U.S. Land Office in Evanston once he realized where Jack Sargent's ranch was. Two days after Jack filed his patent, the clerk furiously scribbled the following words onto the front of his application: "All of this Township reserved by Proclamation of February 22, 1897, for Teton Forest Reserve & also withdrawn by Ex. Order, May 22, 1902."[38]

Knowing that federal officials were going to be unhappy about his application, Jack asked two men who were among the few friends he had in Jackson Hole to sign statements in front of an attorney, stating they knew Jack had been living on the land long before it became a part of the timberland reserve. James Uhl and Emile Wolff both swore their friend had "settled on said land in 1890; that he has resided continuously on said land since that date, except as stated in his application or affidavit; that he has made bona fide improvements on said land; and that said improvements consist of a log house, 70x20 ft., with ten rooms; a stable, Boathouse, Garden, corral, and 2 miles of private road." In his own sworn statement, Jack acknowledged he had been away from his ranch for an extended period in 1895 "because of the Bannock Indian troubles," and from June 1897 to August 1899 "because of my wife's death and circumstances beyond my control."[39]

The initial response from Washington was to say that the government's representatives in Wyoming had "erred" in allowing Jack to submit his homestead application, "on account of the withdrawal of the land for forestry Purposes." Additionally, Jack's ranch sat on land that had been identified in 1902 by the recently created U.S. Reclamation Service as "a potential site for a federal water development project" (i.e., the dam that ultimately raised the level of Jackson Lake by thirty-nine feet). Until the government decided whether it wanted to follow through on that project, the land was off-limits to homesteaders.[40]

Jack appealed that decision, arguing that his residency at Pine Tree Ranch pre-dated the founding of the Forest Reserve by seven years and the creation of the U.S. Reclamation Service by twelve years. He wasn't squatting on federal land, he argued; he was just seeking to make the last fourteen years of his life official.[41]

The government responded by sending an officer from the U.S. Forest Service out to Jack's property. Reading over the report filed by that officer—a man with the ironic name of C. W. Woods—it's hard not to see the government as a bit thuggish, even if you're someone who applauds the scope and reach of federal regulation. Woods's report concluded that Jack had "taken [his] land for speculation, not a home." He flat-out lied in his description of the property. Woods claimed that the improvements on it consisted only of a chicken coop and a "little garden with a very small amount of vegetables." He made no mention of the lodge where Jack had lived with his wife and five children—the lodge that had hosted Andrew Carnegie's nephews and William and Nellie Linn. He made no mention of the boathouse, the stable, the corral, or the road. When asked whether Jack had met the improvement requirements of the Homestead Act, Woods wrote simply, "He has not."[42]

Jack was distraught. He contacted an attorney in Evanston who told him it was going to be hard to secure his patent. "Don't think for a moment that it is an easy task, for it is not," R. S. Spence warned him. "You not only have the Department [of the Interior] against you, but the forest officers, also." Nevertheless, Spence believed he could help Jack. "I will take hold of the case and work it for all it is worth, and I am usually successful," he told him in December of 1905. Spence's talents did not come cheap, however. His starting fee was $200, and Jack didn't have that kind of money. The guests who stayed at his ranch paid him $10 a day, but he never had a consistent stream of paying visitors. His family used to be a reliable source of income, but they'd cut him off after the fiasco in 1897. Gus Hemenway Jr. didn't think it was good for Jack to be in Wyoming, and he wasn't going to pay for him to be out there anymore.[43]

That's probably why Jack chose to marry Edith Drake. How exactly he knew her isn't known, though Jack claimed to have met Edith for the first time in New York in 1899. Edith was a patient at the Interpines Sanitarium in Goshen that year, so it's unlikely (but not impossible) that Jack actually met her. He may have crossed paths with her older brother, Herbert Drake, who ultimately paid Jack a total of $7,700 to take Edith to Wyoming and marry her, so that newspapers in Boston and New York would finally leave her alone.[44]

Jack hired R. S. Spence in July 1906, one month after he and Edith were married in Victor, Idaho. He also wrote letters to anyone he thought might be able to help him: Representative Frank Mondell of Wyoming; Representative Franklin Brooks of Colorado; Secretary of the Interior

Ethan Hitchcock; and Secretary of State Elihu Root, who had been Ray Hamilton's attorney and remembered Jack well enough to write to the commissioner of the General Land Office on his behalf, asking the commissioner to look into the situation. Jack even wrote to the president of the United States, Theodore Roosevelt, asking him to intercede. In his appeal he told the president he was living in Wyoming with his daughter, who "would be the chief sufferer if I lost my home," and his wife, "whose life has been [as] full of sorrow and wrong as my own." He acknowledged that some of the bureaucratic difficulties he was encountering were his own fault, since he hadn't filed his homestead claim before the Teton Forest Reserve was created, but he ended his letter by asking the president bluntly, "Should jealousy and prejudice and technicalities now deprive me of my just rights?"[45]

Shortly after Elihu Root wrote to the General Land Office, Ethan Hitchcock of the Department of the Interior offered Jack a compromise. The government still didn't want him to have the property. "The lands are upon the shores of Jackson Lake and are required for use for the reclamation purposes in connection with the Minidoka [dam] Project," Hitchcock explained to Jack's attorney in November 1906. "Had a patent [been] issued, the land would be subject to appropriation by the United States by proceedings of eminent domain, in case the entryman refused to sell." Hitchcock acknowledged, however, that Jack had "fully complied . . . with the [Homestead] law as to settlement, residence, and cultivation" of the land. He offered, therefore, to pay Jack for his ranch.[46]

At this point Jack's loyalty to Wyoming representative Frank Mondell paid off. Recall that Modell's reelection bid had been the source of an argument Jack had with Will Simpson in 1896. That argument may (or may not) have made Simpson a little too eager to believe the stories Mary and Hemenway Sargent told him about how Jack had run over their mother with a cart.

In December 1906 Mondell brought a resolution forward in the U.S. House of Representatives: HR 20086, "authorizing and directing the Secretary of the Interior to issue patent to John D. Sargent for lands embraced in his homestead entry." In explaining his reasons for the resolution, Mondell wrote: "I am personally acquainted with the homestead entry of John D. Sargent, having visited his homestead in 1894. At that time he had lived upon his place nearly four years with his family and had a good substantial house and other buildings and improvements." Because the congressman had been to Jack's ranch and knew where the property was in relation to the lake, he told the secretary of the interior that "I cannot believe that any portion of [the property] will be reached by any water stored by storage works contemplated on Jackson Lake." It would be "a very great injustice," Mondell concluded, "to deprive this man of his lands after he had lived on them thirteen years before the reclamation Act was passed."[47]

On January 17, 1907, Secretary of the Interior Ethan Hitchcock instructed the General Land Office to give John Dudley Sargent his homestead patent.[48] The sublime property at the base of the Teton Mountains that Edith thought of as "one of God's garden spots" was finally his.

Jack and Edith could now focus on building a life together in Wyoming. But the eccentricities that had dominated Edith's personality in New York did not disappear simply because she was living at a much higher altitude. She soon developed a reputation in Jackson Hole for being "solidly out of her mind," according to Hilda Stadler, a German immigrant who worked as a cook at Pine Tree Ranch during the years when Edith was there. Jack's wife was said to wander his homestead in the summertime, naked except for a pair of booties, playing her violin. Sometimes, the stories claimed, she would hug trees and cry. Not long after Jack and Edith were married, rumors began to circulate that Edith "had been in a sanitarium in Flatbush, N.Y., and her mentality was the cause." Those same rumors claimed with a striking degree of accuracy that Jack was being paid by her family to take care of her.[49]

Interestingly, no one in Jackson Hole ever seemed to figure out that Jack's new wife, Edith, was the same "Edith" who had lost her virginity more than twenty years earlier to a notorious and exotic gigolo named Enrico Pranzini, who was beheaded in Paris for murdering three people and then skinned and turned into calling-card purses, ultimately provoking the resignation of the president of the Third Republic of France. No one on the East or West Coast ever made the connection, either— not even when Edith wrote to newspapers in New York and Los Angeles about Jack's death. Her family probably had the patriarchy to thank for that small favor, rather than the frontier. Once she got married "Mrs. McGibney" became "Mrs. Sargent," and her past was finally forgotten.

Edith's "mentality," to use Hilda Stadler's word, was seen by people in Jackson Hole as bizarre but harmless—charming, even, at times. The engineers who worked on the Minidoka dam project viewed Edith as a kind of "mascot" and posed for a picture with her in 1911. The men are all dressed in conservative slacks and button-down shirts, while Edith stands in the middle of the group, much shorter than everyone else, wearing a buckskin coat and a cap with a feather sticking out of it.[50]

The hat was something she donned fairly regularly. Three years earlier, in the summer of 1908, an art history professor from Wisconsin named John MacHarg had encountered Edith, Jack, and "Katie," whom he described as Jack's "daughter of seventeen by a former mate," while camping in Yellowstone National Park. The Sargents were the "most unusual people I ever saw," MacHarg wrote in his diary. "All used exceedingly good English. Mrs. S. especially spoke with a sweet, almost fascinating accent." Edith's appearance was "hard," however—quite different from that of the "handsome brunette" reporters had described years earlier, when she'd married Samuel McGibney. MacHarg believed she looked "more like a savage Indian than a civilized woman in appearance." Her hair, he wrote, "was partly held in place by an old fez with an eagle feather in it."[51]

Jack's hair was "banged all around, heavy and gray. He talked incessantly," according to MacHarg. The professor "wished for a phonograph" so he could record the homesteader's pattern of speech. MacHarg and his party offered to have the Sargents stay with them in their tents, but the family refused, sleeping on their own outside instead. They did sit around a campfire with the group, drinking tea and eating pieces of meat they carried around in a box. "Mr. S. ate incredible quantities of ham and drank tea from a can until I feared for his life," MacHarg wrote. "Mrs. S. smoked cigarettes and sat in uncouth attitudes. She looked like a hag—but o, her voice! It would grace a drawing room!"[52]

Jack and Edith spent quite a bit of time together during the summer months, camping around Yellowstone—enough time to be annoyed by some of the "improvements" the Army Corps of Engineers was making to the park. "May two of the eighty odd million who are supposed to own the Park find fault with the closets 27 paces from the Apollinaris Spring—and those on the banks of DeLacy Creek?" Jack wrote to the park's superintendent in August 1907 about a set of public toilets that had recently been installed near two of the park's more popular natural features. "Mrs. Sargent was indignant in both cases. Surely there is enough ground on the lower side of the road, well screened by green timber, opposite and <u>below</u> the Apollinaris Springs for these unsightly, unsanitary closets!"[53]

Jack's reputation for being cantankerous on his good days—and deranged and violent on his worst—never disappeared, in spite of a grand jury's failure to find enough evidence to indict him for murdering his first wife. Many people in Jackson Hole believed he subjected Edith to the same fits of violence he had reportedly unleashed upon Addie, and it's not beyond the realm of possibility that he did. Addie was desperately unhappy with Jack, after all, and it's undeniable that he had a dark side. After Jack died in 1913, Edith told his attorney he'd taken her beloved violin away from her and sold it against her wishes. "I am trying hard to keep out of the hospital," she wrote plaintively to J. W. Sammon in the fall of 1913, following her husband's death. "My husband, John D. Sargent, having sold my old fiddle for $125.00, I am helpless to earn money till I can buy another."[54]

Yet Jack and Edith did seem to enjoy one another's company. It's hard to ever get a sense of what goes on in a marriage, of course—even when the marriage is your own. It's even harder when you're an outsider, looking at a marriage from a distance of more than one hundred years, through a primitive spyglass that consists of a few jokes, letters, and random thoughts that the husband and wife you're considering recorded in the margins of books they read out loud to one another during the long winter nights they spent at the base of the Teton Mountains.

Nevertheless, Jack and Edith do seem to have been a decent match. They were both voracious readers. They both loved music. Jack referred to Edith as "Dearest" in the few surviving letters he wrote to her. And Edith had wisdom and experience she shared with Jack during those periods when her husband exhibited the signs of what she told the *New York Times* was "melancholia." "Take this from me," she wrote to Jack in an undated note. "Dry, high air [is the] worst thing for insomnia—causes insanity." She instructed him to "fill your kettle; [put it] on a <u>hot stove</u>, & let it steam good and <u>hard</u>." The humidified air, she told him, "will put you right to sleep! Save yourself <u>now</u>, for <u>my sake</u>, & do what I tell you. Concentration of mind & sound sleep afterward in [a] <u>damp atmosphere</u> will make you young again, as it has your wife!" She gave Jack a copy of William Penn's *Some Fruits of Solitude*, claiming—correctly—that it had helped Robert Louis Stevenson deal with his feelings of melancholy. Edith further advised her husband to "fix your mind on work, <u>not persons</u>, and <u>enjoy your</u> leisure. Work hard, rest hard, & sleep sound!"[55]

Edith shared this homeopathic advice during a period in 1913 when she was away from her husband, visiting her sister, Bertha Drake Sparguer, in San Diego, California. Edith stayed on the West Coast for several months. Jack spent most of that time alone at Pine Tree Ranch, but he did travel to California in February 1913, to see not only his wife but also his son. Charles Hemenway Sargent had been twelve years old when he left Marymere in 1897, the same age Jack had been when his mother and grandfather died. He spent the rest of his childhood in Maine, and there is no evidence he ever returned to Wyoming after his mother's death. There's no surviving correspondence between him and his father, but clearly the young man did write to Jack at some point, because Jack knew Hemenway had joined the U.S. Navy and was stationed at the Thirty-Second Street Naval Station in San Diego in 1913. He and Edith saw Hemenway there.[56]

The trip to California was not a good one for Jack. He got some bad news while he was out there, something he wrote about to his wife later that spring, after he'd returned to Wyoming and was at Pine Tree Ranch by himself. "Edith, Dearest," he wrote in cryptic and forlorn tones, "day and night, I do long for the old Ocean." Jack was "too head and body tired to do any business." He told Edith it was because he "never got over the night shock" he'd experienced on the "corner of Monroe & 42nd Sts., San Diego" while he was in California visiting her. Jack's letter doesn't say what he saw or heard on that corner, but his words suggest Edith knew what he was talking about. He called the experience "the straw that broke the camel's back." He told his wife, "I reckon mother must take care of me now," referring to Alice Hemenway Sargent, who'd been dead for nearly forty years.[57]

Sometime between June 27 and July 1, 1913, while Edith was still with her sister in California, John Dudley Sargent placed a record on his Victrola—the same instrument Edith had played her violin next to a few a years earlier, when she'd posed for that dramatic and quirky photograph Sumner Matteson took in front of Mount Moran. Jack had become an agent for the Victor Talking Machine Company in western Wyoming and eastern Idaho. Hoping to bring in some additional income, he used to play records on his Victrola at the post office in Moran, believing that people who experienced the marvels of that machine would lay down $17.50 (the equivalent today of about $500) to buy one for themselves. What Jack failed to understand was that most settlers in Wyoming didn't have that kind of cash. He never convinced anyone to buy a record player.

The song Jack chose was a German lied, an orchestration by Tchaikovsky of a poem by Goethe that had been recorded by a contralto named Elsie Baker one year earlier, in May of 1912: "Nur wer die Sehnsucht kennt/Weiß was Ich liede" (Only those who know longing know what sorrow I sing).

Jack sat down in a chair next to the fireplace where he and his daughter, Martha, had watched the snow fall with several soldiers from Yellowstone National Park twenty years earlier. He tied one end of a string to the trigger of his shotgun, tied the other end to his big toe, placed the gun's barrel in his mouth, and pulled the trigger. His body was found a week later, after he failed to show up at the post office in Moran where he usually showed off his Victrola. John Dudley Sargent was fifty-four years old.[58]

We'll never know what Jack learned on that night in San Diego that gave him such a shock, nor can we ever know if what he learned had anything to do with his decision to kill himself. We do know, however, that Hemenway Sargent had had something significant happen in his own life shortly before Jack traveled to California, and it's possible the young sailor told his father about that event: in December 1912 Jack's twenty-seven-year-old son, Charles Hemenway Sargent, got married. His new wife was Catherine Winthrop Sargent—Jack's twenty-year-old daughter.[59]

Family Matters

Edith Sargent claimed that Jack had sold her violin against her wishes in a series of desperate letters she wrote to his attorney, trying to stake a claim to Pine Tree Ranch. Jack had wanted Catherine Winthrop Sargent to have his homestead. He'd used the property as collateral, however, on a $1,300 loan he took from a bank in Denver in 1905. That action threw his ability to leave the property to anyone into serious question.[1]

But Edith knew what a dower right was (even if she mistakenly thought it was to half, rather than a third of her husband's estate). She came from New York, after all, where a quarter century earlier, Evangeline Steele had famously attempted to assert a dower right to everything Robert Ray Hamilton owned. Edith knew that thanks to the right of dower, no will or creditor could ever deny a wife—a legal wife, anyway—ownership of at least part of her deceased husband's estate.

"The estate must belong to me—or half of it, at least," she wrote to Jack's attorney, J. W. Sammon, in November 1913. She asserted her ownership on the basis of "the legacy of five thousand dollars left to me by my father, of which sum I never got a dollar." Edith's plan was to sell the homestead. "I have an offer to rent, with option to buy from an old friend of my husband's," she told Sammon. The income generated from the sale would allow her to be "independent of any aid," and that, in turn, might keep her out of the hospital, since it would mitigate the stress she'd been experiencing since her husband died. "My nerves are in very bad shape, and I am in a forlorn condition," Edith wrote, revealing some awareness of the precarious nature of her own mental state.[2]

But J. W. Sammon had bad news for his client's wife. The state that gave women the right to vote thirty years before the passage of the Nineteenth Amendment (which still lay seven years in the future) didn't have a dower right. "Our law provides that the wife of the deceased shall be entitled to certain items of the personal property only," Sammon explained. Edith could have the "bed and bedding and other household goods" if she wanted them; Sammon would auction them off if she didn't, to pay the costs of settling Jack's estate. But unless the deed was in Edith's name—which it was not—no part of Pine Tree Ranch was hers.[3] That's just how they did things in the Equality State.

The name on the deed was that of Edith's brother, Herbert Drake—who, along with their sister, Bertha, had sent Edith to Wyoming in the first place. He'd been out to Pine Tree Ranch in early May to visit Jack and knew that his brother-in-law had "suffered from insomnia, loneliness, & carelessness as to food" during the last few months of his life. According to Drake, Jack's loan from 1905 had come due and he was in danger of losing his ranch. "I then paid off the mortgage," Drake explained to county officials, "and they—his wife and he—voluntarily deeded the property to me."[4]

Edith claimed that Jack had forced her to sign the ranch over to her brother. No one believed her, though, given her well-known eccentricities. County officials tried to contact Catherine Winthrop Sargent, since she was Jack's intended heir, but they were unable to find her. Eventually, they determined the property belonged to Herbert Drake. He had no real interest in it, however—other than keeping it away from his mentally unstable sister—and so he didn't bother to pay the property taxes on it. In 1918, less than one year after a road connecting Pine Tree Ranch to Yellowstone National Park was finally completed, county officials sold the sublime homestead along the shores of Jackson Lake for the value of the taxes Drake owed on it, which was about $600.[5]

The ranch remained in private hands for the next fifty-eight years, serving as a summer home for wealthy easterners—first, for an executive from the Hoover Vacuum Cleaner Company named William Johnson, and then for one of the heirs to the Eagle Pencil fortune, Alfred Berol. Grand Teton National Park, which was created by President Calvin Coolidge in 1929, grew up around the ranch.

Finally, in 1976, the children of Alfred and Madeleine Berol sold the property that John Dudley Sargent had wanted his daughter to have to the National Park Service. The price was $3.3 million. Today the value of the sale would be about $14.8 million—nearly $4 million more than the adjusted value of the disagreement Jack's grandfather had had with his Uncle Gus back in 1874. That disagreement, of course, was what had provoked John Dudley Sargent to move to Wyoming in the first place.[6]

Edith Sargent spent the next thirty-three years in and out psychiatric hospitals, living for the longest period at the Hudson River State Hospital in Poughkeepsie, New York, the town where her great-grandfather Samuel Neilson, the Irish patriot, had died of yellow fever in 1803. Edith herself died in Manhattan on June 24, 1947, at the age of eighty-one.[7] No newspaper reported her death.

Edith's name did eventually make its way back into the *New York Times*, however. It was 1989, and Mikhail Gorbachev was bringing glasnost to the Soviet Union. In the spirt of that new openness to the West, he'd sent his foreign minister, Eduard Shevardnadze, to the United States to meet with Secretary of State James Baker. "Mr. Baker . . . told friends that he chose Jackson Hole because he wanted to share with the Russians one of the garden spots of the earth," the *Times* reported, using words that were strikingly similar to the ones Edith had used seventy-six years earlier to describe her husband's ranch. That ranch was where Shevardnadze and Baker had their summit.

For three days in September 1989, they met in the lodge Alfred Berol had constructed on what used to be Jack Sargent's homestead. The two men discussed the fragility of human existence in the nuclear age as they walked through the very woods Edith had once explored—reportedly naked—with her violin. "The transience of humans here is reflected in a poem by Edith Sargent, a pioneer settler from New York," the *Times*'s reporter Timothy Egan told his readers. "In her poem, titled 'The Grand Teton,' she wrote:

> The ages pass and men die fast
> But still the Tetons stood
> In stately silence to the last
> Wrought by no human hands."[8]

County officials in Wyoming weren't able to locate Catherine Winthrop Sargent, because she didn't want to be found. After she graduated from the Smead School for Girls in 1910, she didn't return to Pine Tree Ranch, although her son, Bill Fessel, thinks a fire that swept through northwestern Wyoming probably had more to do with her unwillingness to return to the region than her dislike of Edith did. "She vowed she would never go there again, because she thought the place had been unalterably ruined," Bill says.[9]

Catherine Winthrop did return to the American West, if not to Wyoming. After she graduated from high school, she moved to Salt Lake City, where she worked as a domestic in the home of Malcolm and Elizabeth Keyser, a businessman and his wife. We know she was with the family, not because she ever told her son she was there, but because in April 1911, newspapers across the state reported she had been arrested and charged with stealing $700 in personal property from her employers.[10]

"The girl . . . appears to have a mania for taking anything she sees," the *Salt Lake City Tribune* reported, noting that some of what Catherine Winthrop had taken, while valuable to the family, had little to no resale value—photographs that belonged to Malcom Keyser, for example, and several pairs of men's socks. Catherine Winthrop made a "full confession" after she was arrested, admitting she had stolen photographs from a family she'd worked for in Idaho as well. Elizabeth Keyser took this confession to heart and agreed not only to drop the charges against her young employee but also to rehire her. She was particularly moved when nineteen-year-old Catherine Winthrop revealed that her mother had been "murdered" in Jackson Hole by several settlers who hated her father.[11]

It was in Salt Lake City that Catherine Winthrop and Charles Hemenway became reacquainted with one another. It's not clear if Hemenway made the effort to find his sister all on his own, or if members of the Sargent and Crane families in Maine had asked him to look for her. Either way Catherine Winthrop Sargent had been out of touch with her family on the East Coast for quite some time before the reunion took place.[12]

"The Crane family firmly believed that John Dudley was her father, but Adelaide was not her mother," Martha Sargent's daughter, Barbara Titus, recalled in 1978. "My mother brought me up on stories of the Tetons and her happy childhood there, but she always said she had one brother and only two sisters, Mary and Adelaide." It wasn't until Barbara was a teenager "that one of my Crane aunts told me about Catherine, merely mentioning the fact that my mother should have told me that she had three sisters, Mary, Adelaide, and red-headed Catherine." The hyphenated adjective was a literal description of Catherine Winthrop, whose natural hair color was the dark shade of red described as "titian" by Lucy Maud Montgomery and Carolyn Keene in their famous books about a lovable and loquacious orphan named Anne Shirley and a tenacious teenaged sleuth named Nancy Drew.[13] The description was also a snide commentary on Catherine Winthrop Sargent's status within the Crane family, however: in Maine, Jack's daughter was a "red-headed stepchild."

During the years of their marriage, Hemenway and Catherine Winthrop Sargent lived in an apartment on Riverside Drive in New York City, although Hemenway was often away from home because he worked for the navy. Bill says his mother had no contact with her father after she got married in December 1912. She claimed to have been too busy in 1913, preparing for the birth of her first child, to "digest the news relayed through members of the family that John Sargent had died by his own hand."[14]

It couldn't have been *just* from family members that Catherine Winthrop learned of her father's death, however. Jack's suicide was heralded by every major newspaper in New York, thanks to his association with Robert Ray Hamilton a quarter century earlier. "Hamilton's Chum Himself a Suicide," was the front-page headline the *New York Times* ran on July 26, 1913, when it told its readers John Dudley Sargent was "formerly the closest friend" of Robert Ray Hamilton and claimed he was "suspected of killing the unfortunate New Yorker." The *New York Sun* spoke of a "Third Fatality at Hamilton Lodge," reminding readers of Jack's supposed involvement in not just Ray's death, but his first wife's, as well. The *New York Tribune* echoed this invocation of Ray and Addie. Sparing no details, it told readers Jack's "face [was] almost unrecognizable" when he was found, thanks to the bullet that had "shattered his skull."[15]

Hemenway and Catherine Winthrop had five children together, three of whom—Alice, Charles, and Dorothy—made it to adulthood. Hemenway briefly left the navy and worked for the New York Central Railroad around the time his son was born in 1915. During World War I he rejoined the service, and in 1920 he was given command of the USS *Arethusa*, a steam tanker that was commissioned in 1898 at the Philadelphia Navy Yard, the place where Katharine Beatrice Hamilton's daughter, Beatrice Hamilton Costello, would later meet her husband, Joe Seacrest.[16]

In 1921 Hemenway agreed to allow his sister, Mary, onto his boat so she could catch a ride down to South Carolina from Boston. It was a violation of military policy, and Hemenway was investigated for doing it. The fact that he had allowed a civilian onto his ship was the least of his problems, however. Mary had told someone on the ship that their lieutenant commander was married to his sister, and the navy was preparing a court martial.[17]

The person Mary spoke to was a sailor named G. D. Stowman. He's the one who leveled the charge of incest against his commander. To support this charge, Stowman gave the navy a letter he received from Mary in December 1921, several weeks after she'd told him her siblings were married. That letter is now stored at the National Archives in Washington DC.

"I just had 2 letters from my Bro[ther], saying you had reported him for having me on his boat and other charges which I made to you," Mary Sargent wrote. "Well, it was all true . . . and it was your duty to report him." She went on to say her brother was "very wrong" to have married Catherine Winthrop, "especially with his bold way of saying he was right living with his sister and having children." She told the sailor Hemenway had recently informed her he was ill. "He writes he spits blood and is very weake [sic] and may not live long. But he better be dead than live the life he has been." She offered to help the navy in its investigation. "I don't believe in doing anyone harm and I could of [sic] been Hemenway's best friend," Mary wrote, except that his "boldness just disgusted me." "Catherine should be careful also," Mary warned. "To make trouble, she liyed [sic] about me. I am sick of it and I am willing to put her and him also where they can't keep bring[ing] children into the world."

Mary told G. D. Stowman that Catherine Winthrop "looks like me." Her father, she said, "never told me she wasn't [my sister]," and Hemenway "knows she is his sister and will have to prove she is not." "I think she and he are both crazy," Mary observed in her letter's closing. "They must be."[18]

The U.S. Navy ultimately dropped its investigation of Charles Hemenway Sargent, because what Mary didn't realize when she penned her letter to G. D. Stowman on December 21, 1921, was that her brother was already dead. He'd died at the age of thirty-six on-board the USS *Arethusa* three days earlier. His cause of death was tuberculosis—the same thing that had killed his grandmother Alice Hemenway Sargent when she was thirty-four and his father was twelve.[19]

A few days before he died, Charles Hemenway Sargent wrote to his wife from Fall River, Massachusetts, where his ship was to be docked for the next few weeks. "Catherine, I am in awful shape and have been for a long time," he told her. "I fear my lungs are badly affected . . . I am having hemorrhages and spitting blood." He hadn't gone to see a doctor, because the Christmas holiday was coming up, and he worried he would be quarantined. "If my lungs show the least sign of trouble," he explained, "I will be sent to a hospital either in California or Colorado, and they must either cure me or keep me there until I die." Hemenway assured his wife he wasn't going to die. But he didn't want to be locked up in a hospital for Christmas, when he could be down in New York with Catherine Winthrop and their children.[20]

Mary's charges against him had soured Hemenway Sargent on his birth family, and he didn't want any of them to visit for the holidays. "I will always suffer to think that there is such a thing in the world as a man not being able to trust his sister," he wrote. He told Catherine Winthrop he was going to call Martha, who lived in Cambridge, Massachusetts, and tell her not to come to New York for Christmas. "I really don't care about having any of them with us," he wrote. "Adelaide is rather nice, but I know she loves what she gets from me more than she really cares for me, and I don't believe she would stick with me in trouble." Martha, he said, "would not help me one bit if I asked her to, and I feel that she would talk a lot if she could about us." His sisters, he told his wife, were "a little envious of you. You have more than others. You should see how they live."[21]

"Please write to me," Hemenway wrote. "I must hear from you in every port, or else I feel badly. Regardless of what you have said about me at times, I love you and consider you the best and finest lady in the world." He closed his final letter to his wife with the words "Love to you all, Charley."[22]

Catherine Winthrop Sargent did not stay in touch with her family in Maine after her husband and brother died. Bill Fessel knows all about the unusual circumstances surrounding his mother's first marriage—but again, he grew up believing there was no biological connection between his mother and the man he refers to as her "first husband." He claims Mary and Martha, whom he never knew, threatened to have his mother's children taken away from her not long after Hemenway was gone. "That's the main reason she cut off contact," he says. "I don't think she liked the way they treated her when she was married to her first husband, but she might not have cut off relations if they hadn't threatened her that way."[23]

When he died on March 24, 1927, Jack's absentee father, Henry Sargent, left one-fifth of his estate to Catherine Winthrop Sargent, identified in his will as having been his "granddaughter." He gave Mary, Martha, and Adelaide one-fifth each, as well, and then he divided the remaining fifth of his estate evenly among his three "great-grandchildren," named in his will as Alice, Charles, and Dorothy Sargent and identified as having been the "children of Hemenway Sargent, grandson, deceased." Whatever thoughts Henry Sargent may have had about the marriage of his grandchildren, those thoughts did not lead him to disown anyone.[24]

After Catherine Winthrop Sargent accepted her share of her grandfather's estate and signed off on the shares that were left to her children, she never interacted with her siblings again. She'd moved on with her life since her husband's death, fallen in love with William C. Fessel, and was one-month pregnant when Henry Sargent died. She gave birth to Catherine Virginia Fessel in December 1927. A few years later, Bill came along.

Bill says he had a great relationship with his mother. He says his father died when he was young, and that after his sister, Catherine Virginia, moved out of the house, it was just the two of them, Bill and Catherine Winthrop, living together in upstate New York. When Bill was in his teens, his mother started to fret "that all her children had grown up Easterners." In the summer of 1948, she took Bill and Catherine Virginia to Wyoming. "We hiked many of the trails in the southern part of the Tetons and soaked up the history and heritage of the land," Bill recalls. "She was greatly relieved to find that contrary to what she had heard years before, the Tetons had not burned in the great fires of 1910."[25]

That summer they were in Wyoming, Bill's mother took him and his sister to John Dudley Sargent's homestead, which by this point belonged to Alfred and Madeleine Berol and was managed by a caretaker named Slim Lawrence. The lodge that Ray and Jack had arranged to have built was gone; on Berol's instructions, Lawrence had torn it down and burned it a few years earlier.

The trio encountered Lawrence as they were leaving. He chatted with them about the place, having no idea who Bill's mother was, as she had introduced herself to him as "Mrs. Winthrop" and said simply that she had some family who used to live in the area. Slim Lawrence told her the name "Winthrop" sounded vaguely familiar, but he apparently made no connection.

"They talked about the Sargent children," Bill recalls. "They both knew that Adelaide had died in childbirth years before. He told her that Mary and Martha were still living, but that Catherine had died." Bill says he was puzzled when he heard that. He almost started laughing, but sensing his mother had her reasons for not fully identifying herself to the man, he kept his reaction to himself. "Later [my mother] told me emphatically that she felt no trust in any of the people in Jackson Hole, who she felt were mostly the descendants of the settlers that John Sargent had despised."[26]

That summer proved to be formative for Bill Fessel. He grew up to work for the U.S. Forest Service—the same arm of government that had tried in the early years of the twentieth century to deny his grandfather his homestead patent. In the 1960s and 1970s, Bill was a district ranger, preparing timber sales in the Siuslaw National Forest near Corvallis, Oregon. A full century had passed since Gus and William Hemenway had had their costly disagreement about the management of UT 36 in Washington County, Maine, and at least one member of the Hemenway family was still working in the timber industry.[27]

There are some ironies on Robert Ray Hamilton's side of the story, as well. Not only did his granddaughter, Beatrice "Mike" Hamilton Costello, marry into a newspaper family and spend part of her adult life working in the news industry herself, but his great-grandson, Kent Hamilton Seacrest, became a real estate attorney, which was Ray's legal specialty. That's why he was able to help Eva buy that land in Passaic, New Jersey, shortly before they got married.

Sipping wine one summer evening in 2021 as he sat on his deck in the Bridger-Teton National Forest, Kent Seacrest chatted about the shockingly high mortality rates experienced by abandoned infants in the Gilded Age, and the reality that if his grandmother had not been purchased by Evangeline Steele and used to trick Robert Ray Hamilton, she almost certainly would have died. "I guess I do owe my existence to that deception," Kent conceded quietly, noting with a slight smile how extraordinary it is that any of us exists at all.[28]

He wasn't going to be plagued by this realization, however. Ray, Eva—even his grandmother Katharine Beatrice Hamilton Costello, who died a year before Kent was born—were all strangers to him. "And in the end," Kent Hamilton Seacrest observed matter-of-factly, "aren't all of our lives determined to some degree by the decisions made by strangers?"[29]

Epilogue
Strings

In his will Ray left $10,000 to the City of New York so that the Parks Commission could build a fountain in his honor.[1] It was the sort of thing you did in the Gilded Age when you came from a wealthy and historically prominent family and had served your city well. Sure, some of Ray's constituents were upset about his support of a public transit system that made it easier for the riffraff to get into Manhattan's Eleventh District. But Ray hadn't planned on dying so soon after the Cable Railway Grab. He thought for sure all of the anger and humiliation staining his political career would be forgotten after he'd spent some time in Wyoming.

The fountain is on Riverside Drive at Seventy-Sixth Street. It was designed by Warren and Wetmore, the architectural firm that designed Grand Central Terminal and the chapel in Green-Wood Cemetery, where Ray's bones were hidden with those of his maternal grandfather. Made from Tennessee marble, the fountain was integrated into a retaining wall along the eastern boundary at the southern end of Riverside Park.[2] It's about fifteen feet wide and eleven and a half feet tall, with a giant eagle at the top, spreading its wings in full glory.[3]

The base of the monument is a water trough, designed to be used by the horses that were once ubiquitous on New York's streets. Henry Bergh, founder of the ASPCA, had started calling for public troughs to be built in the 1870s, but city officials were slow to respond to his entreaties. New York's animal fountains were small, dirty, and few in number, and the water piped to them was frequently shut off whenever lawmakers tussled over budgets. Ray's will didn't specify that the memorial needed to benefit horses, but it probably isn't a coincidence that his fountain provided a service to the animals that were so important to Ernest Howard Crosby, his friend whom he'd alienated with the Cable Railway Grab.[4]

Along the outside of the trough, the words "Bequeathed to the people of New York by Robert Ray Hamilton" can be seen—*if* you know to look for them. "You want granite, not marble," a friend's mother once advised me as we strolled through Rose Hill Cemetery in Macon, Georgia, one of the dozens of garden cemeteries built in the United States in the mid-nineteenth century.[5] Many of the marble headstones we were looking at had become worn and difficult to read. The Tennessee marble Warren and Wetmore's architects favored in almost all of their designs is gorgeous. It has a pinkish-grey tone and polishes easily. Alas, it also hasn't held up well to the rigors of acid rain.

A large sign next to the fountain tells passers-by that Ray was "the great-grandson of Alexander Hamilton." It informs them he went to Columbia College and Law School and that he served in the state legislature. "Not long before his death in a hunting accident," the sign reads, "he was involved in a public scandal involving Eva Mann, whom he had secretly married, and who had used this alliance to raid his substantial financial holdings."

The sign is exactly what Ray's family members worried about when they read his will. They didn't want the fountain to be built. In 1891 nine members of the Hamilton family, including Ray's father, petitioned New York's mayor and aldermen, asking them not to set aside any land for the memorial. "We, the nearest relations and most interested in the family of the said deceased," they wrote, "respectfully, but earnestly request and desire for the honor of all concerned, past history and the present, that no permission be given for the erection of any such structure whatsoever."[6]

It was one more example of how humiliated Ray's family members were by what had happened with Eva. First they hid his bones. Then they hid his papers. Then they tried to block a very specific last wish Ray had expressed in his will, all because they believed the Hamilton family's "honor" had somehow been violated by the scandal.

It's a reaction that has always struck me as a little extreme, even by the standards of the day—especially given that the stabbing in Atlantic City had followed a long string of scandals in the Hamilton family. The Hamiltons should have been used to scandal by that point.

Also, Ray was the *victim* of the scam, not the perpetrator. He had done right by Eva in marrying her, back when he thought Beatrice Ray was his child. Even if Eva had been a high-end prostitute, as some newspapers suggested, Ray certainly wasn't the first or only "society man" to pay for sex or to attend a French ball. He wasn't the first man to get a woman pregnant outside of marriage, either. Remember that Inspector Byrnes told a judge in 1889 that Anna Swinton had told him she thought the first baby Eva had "was the child of a friend of Ray's who had got a friend in trouble."[7]

But if Eva's first baby had belonged to one of Ray's friends, surely he would have known that. Why would Ray ever have thought Beatrice Ray Hamilton was his?

This brings us to a handful of letters hidden away in that collection at the New York Historical Society—the one that doesn't bear the Hamilton family name. Two of the letters in that collection were written by Eva. Neither has a date, although one says it was written on a "Thursday." Both letters were written at a time when Ray was in Albany.

In the first letter, Eva complains about money and tells him to send her more. "I have to pay my bills," she tells him, "& I must have a little chang[e] for myself." In the second letter, she angrily demands that he come home to New York. "My dear Husband, what is the reason you do not come home to me, your poor wife?" Eva begins. "I am not going to be treated in this way any longer," she tells him, before threatening to sue him for divorce. And then Eva drops the bomb—the reason she wants Ray to come home: "Nettie Ray Hamilton, the baby, is dead."[8]

Nettie Ray Hamilton? *Who was Nettie Ray Hamilton?*

She has to have been one of the babies who died—the second one, probably, since Eva refers to herself as Ray's "wife," and she didn't marry Ray until a few days after the first baby, the one Dr. William Kemp attended, had succumbed to malnutrition.

Ray *knew*, in other words. Maybe he didn't know exactly how many babies were involved, but he knew that the baby who became Kent Seacrest's grandmother—the infant found "propped up on the bed" in the room where Mary Ann Donnelly was stabbed—was not his.[9] He knew she was not Eva's, either. Why, then, did he pretend he thought otherwise? Why did he marry Evangeline Steele?

Recall that Anna Swinton told Inspector Byrnes, "If Ray Hamilton prosecutes me, I'll make it hot for him," and that Ray dropped the larceny charges against her after that threat was revealed at the Tombs. Recall also that after the scandal broke, Ray's friends told the *New York Times* his "personal demeanor" had "undergone a change" recently, and that he had become "quieter than ever, inclined to melancholy." The *Times* theorized someone was blackmailing Ray, and that this was the reason he had endorsed the Cable Railway Grab. Recall also that the *New York World* said Ray was "not regarded as a 'marrying man,'" and that he "was even to his intimates, socially a quiet bachelor."[10]

There are four other mysterious letters in the hidden collection at the New York Historical Society. The collective tone of these letters is undeniably flirtatious. The first letter is short and seems innocent enough. It isn't dated, but it arrived in an envelope marked "Personal and Important" that bears a postmark of August 29, 1889—two days after the news of the stabbing in Atlantic City broke. "Hoping the coming year will bring only happiness to you," the writer says plainly enough, signing off as "Your sincere friend." A fistful of dried and pressed flowers—more than 130 years old by this point, but unmistakably pansies—is tucked in with the note.[11]

"Did you receive the note I sent you from 'Asbury Park'?" the letter writer asks a couple of weeks later, on September 16. "Not hearing from you, I thought perhaps the wind had blown you away, as it very nearly did poor little me." "Will you be in the city this winter?" the letter continues. "I hope so. Have you forgotten the walk we enjoyed before leaving for the summer? I hope the 'Prospect' is good for many more." "Do write an old friend, who will be so happy to hear from you," the correspondent concludes, underling the words "so happy" three times before signing off again as "your sincere friend."[12]

In the third letter, dated October 4, the writer frets about possibly having offended Ray with the familiar tone of the previous piece of correspondence. "Not having received an answer to my last note to you, I am afraid that in it, I may have said something, and believe me it was the last thing I would have thought of doing, wounding your feelings in any way." "If I have been in fault, forgive me," the writer pleads, "and believe it was all due to my earnestness."[13]

In the fourth letter, dated October 21, the flirtatiousness is back. "Are you still angry with me?" the writer coyly asks, and then follows that question with two equally rhetorical questions. "Don't you think a day off would do you good? I do. And why not let us go on a little trip over to Prospect Park this Saturday morning, and if you say so, lunch there and enjoy a jolly walk?" "If I am ever to be forgiven, answer my letter at my city address," the correspondent instructs Ray, "and don't write again down here, as I may not go after the mail myself." This time the writer chooses to sign off not as Ray's "sincere friend" but as "Semper Idem"—in Latin, "Always Constant" or "Forever the Same."[14]

"Always Constant" was the personal motto of Queen Elizabeth I. She adopted it early in her reign, by way of denying the charge, maintained by the pope, that in breaking with the Catholic Church, she had broken with a seamless line of faith that went all the way back to the time of Christ. The Protestant Church of England, Elizabeth insisted, was the embodiment of Christ's true principles; it was the extension of his mission and the Church that had always been the same. Queen Elizabeth used the word "eadem" in her motto, however—"semper eadem"—because that's the word in Latin for female things that are constant.[15] The word for male things that are constant is "idem," the word Ray's correspondent elected to use.

Parks like Prospect Park in Brooklyn were some of the safest places for gay men to gather in late nineteenth- and early twentieth-century New York. Two men who were picnicking in the Long Meadow or bird-watching along the Lullwater Trail didn't stand out among the hundreds of couples, families, and friends who used the park every day. Parks were what one historian has called a "point of entry into the rest of the gay world" for men who were new to New York or new to their identities as gay men. They were a place, out in the open, where men could go to look for the signals—the glances, the gestures—that would allow them to access the city's hidden gay subculture. More so than some of New York's other parks, Prospect Park was known to be the place where the city's older, more conventional gay men gathered—the ones who had careers and owned their own homes and often had families.[16]

It would be another quarter century beyond Ray's death before the word "pansy" became a nasty and pejorative term for a man who was a homosexual. There is almost always some habit, practice, or trend that precedes an innovation in slang, however, and long before the word "pansy" became an insult, men who dressed in drag at French balls like the one Ray reportedly met Eva at would give flowers to the straight men (or seemingly straight men) who were open-minded enough to show up at these balls. Pansies—like the ones Semper Idem included in his first letter to Ray—and carnations that had been dyed green were the flowers most commonly used.[17]

The Anglo-Irish playwright Oscar Wilde was primarily responsible for the association of the green carnation with homosexual subculture. Wilde exhorted the men who attended the 1892 London premier of his play *Lady Windermere's Fan* to wear a green carnation on their lapels when they showed up at the theater, the way one of his characters would be doing on stage. Many of the gay men who were a part of Wilde's inner circle did just that.[18]

The turn Wilde's career took shortly after the debut of that play serves as an important reminder of why no man who was the great-grandson of one of the nation's Founders ever could have been openly gay in the 1890s, especially if he wanted to have a public career. Less than a year after Ray Hamilton died, Oscar Wilde began an indiscreet affair with a young man named Alfred Douglas, who was the son of a Scottish nobleman. That nobleman, the Marquess of Queensbury, accused Wilde of being a "sodomite," and the celebrated playwright sued—a bit too confident, perhaps, in the power of his fame.

Queensbury and his attorneys threatened to have several men who'd had sex with Oscar Wilde testify, since the truthfulness of an allegation had been a defense against libel in British law since 1843. Wilde dropped his case, but shortly afterward he was arrested and charged with gross indecency. At the trial an attorney for the prosecution read a poem Alfred Douglas had written about his lover. That poem is the origin of the phrase, "the love that dare not speak its name."

Oscar Wilde was convicted and given the maximum sentence of two years of hard labor, a punishment the judge in the case believed was "inadequate." Before announcing the sentence, Judge Alfred Wills accused Wilde of being "dead to all sense of shame" and claimed the playwright had been "at the center of a circle of extensive corruption of the most hideous kind."[19]

Wilde emerged from prison in 1897, frail, sickly, financially broke, and partially deaf, thanks to an eardrum injury he had suffered while he was incarcerated (probably the result of a beating). He died three years later at the age of forty-six, reportedly having converted to Catholicism.[20]

I don't know for sure that Ray was gay, but I strongly suspect he was. If he were gay and someone powerful had found out about it (remember that Eva was politically connected enough to get a pardon from New Jersey's Democratic governor), that would explain a lot. It would explain why Ray married Eva, when he knew Beatrice Ray was not his child. It would explain why his friends said he had become withdrawn and depressed shortly before he married her. It would explain why his family's humiliation was so extreme. It might even explain why he supported the Cable Railway Grab, when his constituents were opposed to it; his friend and ally in the state legislature Ernest Howard Crosby hated it; and he, himself, had voted against it a year and a half earlier. And of course it would explain the flirtatious tone of those four letters from Semper Idem.

It might also explain the libel lawsuits Jack Sargent brought against James Gordon Bennett of the *New York Herald* and Joseph Pulitzer of the *New York World* in 1897. So many inflammatory things were written about Jack after his wife's death that it would be hard to guess which article or articles had angered him enough to take the step of suing. Was it the stories about how he had beaten Addie and broken her bones, when the doctor who examined her before she died had found no injuries of that kind? Or was it the stories about how he was suspected of killing Ray Hamilton, when no one had hinted at that possibility until nine years later (though papers at the time *had* reported that Jack broke down in tears when an attorney representing Evangeline Steele badgered him with gruesome descriptions of Ray's bloated and fish-eaten corpse)? Or maybe it was the stories about how he had assaulted his four-year-old daughter, when the arrest warrant for him on that charge was mysteriously abandoned, and no grand jury was ever even asked to consider the charge?

Fortunately, a court stenographer thought to type up a copy of the article in the *Herald* that had set Jack off. We don't know what the article in the *World* was, but as far as James Gordon Bennett Jr. was concerned, the article that had angered Jack enough to sue was the one that came out on July 24, 1897, alleging he had been lynched in Jackson Hole. The stenographer's rather clumsy reproduction of the article reads as follows:

Machias, Me. (meaning thereby Machias, in the state of Maine), July 23, 1897.—A report just received here from Wyoming states that John D. Sargent (meaning thereby this plaintiff) of this place has been lynched by a mob in the region near Jackson's Hole. His (meaning thereby this plaintiff's) father is Henry Sargent, a prominent citizen and proprietor of the Machias Foundry.[21]

It was a rather odd allegation for Jack to have gotten angry about. The charge was easy enough to disprove, after all, and it wasn't one he would ever have to worry about having whispered behind his back, since the mere fact that Jack still had a back was proof enough the article was wrong. Also, the *Herald* printed a retraction six days later, clarifying that Jack had not, in fact, been lynched.

But the July 24 article continued:

John D. Sargent (meaning thereby this plaintiff) was Robert Ray Hamilton's friend and intimate companion [when] the Wyo. tragedy occurred. There was a mystery in the relations of the two young men (meaning thereby this plaintiff and the said Robert Ray Hamilton) that was never satisfactorily cleared up (meaning thereby that this plaintiff had concealed evidence showing his actual relations with the said Hamilton).

At some point in the last 125 years, on the stenographer's official, typed rendering of the article at the heart of Jack's lawsuit against James Gordon Bennett, someone scrawled three tiny Xs in pencil next to the words "intimate companion": xxx.[22]

I will never know who it was. I feel confident, however, that I was the first person to look at these court records in more than a century when I found them in the Surrogate's Courthouse in New York City in February 2019. The only people who have paid as much attention to Jack Sargent's life as I have are Kenneth and Lenore Diem. Kenneth was first director of the biological research center on what used to be Marymere Ranch—

the one that hosts graduate students who enjoy hunting for Edith's violin tree.[23] The Diems collected hundreds of documents about the history of the property, and without the work they did (which included interviews with people who knew Jack Sargent and are now deceased), I never would have been able to write this book. Nevertheless, the Diems had no idea Jack had sued James Gordon Bennett for libel.

If Ray were gay, and there were rumors in New York or Wyoming to that effect, that might explain why *this* article, with *that* second paragraph and *those* two words, was enough to provoke Jack to sue. Recall the context the *New York Times* gave to Edith's letter in August of 1913, when she wrote to that paper's editor to complain about how it had covered Jack's suicide: "The stories to which Mrs. Sargent objects originated among ranchers in Jackson's Hole who did not like Sargent and Hamilton," the *Times* told its readers. The words "intimate companion," on their own, might not have implied that Ray's relationship with Jack was sexual. But combined with "stories" that had originated among ranchers who didn't like Ray and Jack, they could have.

Jack dropped his lawsuits against Pulitzer and Bennett after those damning depositions taken from settlers in Jackson were passed along to attorneys in New York City. This brings us to one final set of loose strings in this story: What exactly happened at Marymere in the winter 1896–97? Did Jack Sargent kill his wife? And why was he allowed to have custody of a little girl who had clearly been sexually abused? As with the questions that linger in Ray's story, I cannot say for sure. But I, for one, don't think Jack murdered Addie.

This conclusion is one that may meet with some resistance in Jackson Hole. The American West is still a place fueled by myths—just google "Sacajawea's burial site" or "where Butch Cassidy died" if you need any proof of this assertion. In the years since his death, Jack Sargent has become a rather monstrous figure to those who pride themselves on knowing something about the human history of Jackson Hole.[24] Some of these people may be reluctant to give up their monster.

Still, I don't think Jack murdered his wife. I do think there were times when he was not a good husband to her, however. And I think he was very hard on his only son. Remember that the greatest source of Addie's unhappiness was the way Jack treated Hemenway. I also think it's fair to say Jack played a role in his wife's death, even if he didn't actually kill her. I'm not willing to use the word "blame" to describe this role, however, since Jack seems to have struggled with mental illness.

I think John Dudley Sargent lost his grip on reality during the winter of 1896–97. His pregnant wife was running a massive fever, thanks to a fetus that was rotting within her, and his kids were running around with no shoes on in the middle of a Wyoming winter. Yet Jack did nothing about it. Indeed, he exhibited a certain degree of paranoid resistance to the efforts of people who wanted to help him. This is not the response of a sane man. It is not the response of even a sane monster. I think Jack fell victim to a serious, if not formally recognized psychological phenomenon known as "cabin fever," and his wife and unborn child died because of it.

In the years that followed, Jack's perspective became increasingly divorced from reality. He kept spending money, even though he had no consistent source of income—buying another piano to replace the one that was taken from him; investing in a business that tried to sell expensive, phonographic equipment to cash-poor settlers who could not afford it; and taking trips to California with his second wife. Jack nearly drowned in March 1913 while he was in Long Beach with Edith. The newspaper article about his near-drowning didn't refer to him as "John Sargent," however; the article called him "John Hemenway," because that was the name he started going by some time around 1912. He even had fancy stationery printed up with that name on it.[25]

In the late 1970s, his granddaughter, Barbara Titus, told Kenneth and Lenore Diem that Jack's father had rejected him after the winter of 1896–97 and refused to talk to him ever again. It's not like Henry Sargent had really been much of a presence in Jack's life to begin with, but the rejection still probably hurt. At some point, Jack decided to make the rejection a two-way street. He changed his name—the name he had researched and published a genealogy on, and the name that connected him to New England's "Brahmin" history through that great-great-great-grandmother he'd named his daughter after, Catherine Winthrop Sargent. He even told his lawyer at one point that Henry Sargent was not his real father. His real father, he claimed, was some guy named Jerome Talbot who lived in Machias, Maine.[26]

Of course, increasing mental instability may explain why Jack started pretending he wasn't a Sargent, but it doesn't explain why he had custody of his daughter after the winter of 1896–97, if he'd sexually assaulted her. This is another mystery I cannot definitively explain. I have my thoughts, however, and I offer them up cautiously, knowing that writing biography can sometimes be a blinding act of love:

I don't believe Jack molested Catherine Winthrop. I think his son, Charles Hemenway, was the one who did it—probably when he went back to the lodge with Will Simpson and D. C. Nowlin to retrieve the little girl.

The Sargent children were incredibly isolated from people their own age. Mary Sargent sounded like she'd grown up in Maine, because her parents from Washington County were the only people she saw during most months of the year. Charles Hemenway Sargent was a boy on the verge of puberty—maybe a boy in the midst of puberty—who had no girls in his life except his sisters. Very few studies have been done on the prevalence or causes of sibling incest in the United States (that's how taboo the topic is). But one study conducted in 2014 found that out of 2,885 randomly selected college students (1,821 women and 1,064 men), 137 of them said they had participated in sibling incest, defined as any kind of sexual contact, up to and including intercourse. That's nearly 5 percent of the people in the survey. And only thirty-eight of these people said the sexual contact had been coerced. The study found that the incest usually began when both participants were young (under the age of fifteen), and it identified several factors within the family that were associated with the incest, among them, familial isolation and an emotionally abusive or distant parent.[27]

If Jack convinced his family members in Maine that this was what had happened, that would explain why they allowed him to take Catherine Winthrop away from Maine—to New York, and then to Chile, and finally back to Wyoming. If he convinced law enforcement officials in Wyoming that this was what had happened, that would explain why he was not arrested for attempted child rape, even though a warrant for his arrest on that charge had been issued two years earlier. And if Jack had made it his life's mission to keep his son and daughter separate from one another after the winter of 1896–97, that would explain why he killed himself a few months after he learned that Charles Hemenway and Catherine Winthrop had wed.

As I was winding up my interview with Bill Fessel in Haines, Oregon, on a rainy day in the fall of 2018, he said something unexpected. The cottonwood trees around his house had lost most of their leaves, but they still had enough yellow foliage to stand out against the purple-gray sky. We had just finished discussing the fact that his mother had married a man who was, at the very least, her legal brother—and probably her biological brother, as well. "You know, my mother remained Catherine Winthrop Sargent her entire life," Bill told me. I didn't understand what he meant by that, and so I asked him for clarification. He explained that his mother never took his father's last name, Fessel. "It was embarrassing to me growing up, I'll admit," Bill said. "This was the 1930s. Women didn't do that kind of thing. No one I knew had a mother with a different last name than her husband."[28]

I asked Bill why he thought his mother had kept her maiden name, anticipating he'd say it had something to do with her appreciation of the historical heritage that came with it—an appreciation her father had had at one point in his life, as well. "Well, of course, it was the name of her first husband," Bill said to me. "And I think my mother really loved her first husband."[29]

This powerful and unembarrassed observation reminded me, once again, of how complicated human beings can be.

I wrote this book for a number of reasons. First, I'd be less than honest if I didn't admit the process of discovery thrilled me sometimes. Parts of this story were a real mystery, and I was determined to figure out as much of the mystery as I could. That's what the act of writing was for me, really: figuring it out.

I am also a teacher of history. I want people to know more about the past and to understand the extent to which the institutions, values, landscapes, practices, and laws that animate our lives today and seem to be stable, abiding, and immutable had to *become*. When I have gone off on tangents about the number of horses that died on New York City's streets, or the disgust people felt at the thought of eating refrigerated meat, or the seething anti-Catholicism that Harvard's administrators have had to deal with when negotiating the terms of the Dudleian lectures, it has been because all of these tangents testify to the fact that our world today had to become what it is. This simple truth means the institutions and habits that are intensely important to us now because they bring order to our world and direction to our lives—the values we use to judge ourselves and one another as we navigate this time in history we have each been fated to have—will *change*.

Which brings me to my third reason for writing this book: we are living in a very contentious time. I am always quick to point out to my students that they're wrong when they say, "America has never been more polarized than it is now." "I think we were more polarized in, say, July 1861," I tell them, reminding them of the First Battle of Bull Run (or "First Manassas," as southerners call it—more than a century and a half later, and we still can't agree on even that!). It's true, however, that American culture is pretty polarized right now—and that that polarization is exhausting, debilitating, and dangerous.

There are many factors fueling the polarization, not the least of them being the inequity, injustice, and hypocrisy that have persisted in American society for the last four hundred years. But the internet sure hasn't been helping matters.

We have become very quick, as a culture, to use the internet to identify and condemn transgressions, large and small, and the people who have committed them—those who have violated the norms of our communities or those who have simply failed to echo or embody these norms. And once we have identified the transgressors and condemned them through the internet, their transgressions endure. They can be easily discovered five, ten, even twenty years later and feel brand-new to the people discovering them, obscuring the complexity of human beings, hindering the work of redemption, and maybe even rendering redemption impossible.

There's a phrase social commentators have come up with to describe what has been lost in this internet age. They call it "the right to be forgotten." Supporters of this right say people have a "fundamental need to determine the development of their lives in an autonomous way, without being perpetually or periodically stigmatized as a consequence of a specific action performed in the past." To that end they have pushed regulators—successfully in Europe—to require that internet search engines give people the ability to "opt out." Europeans can now request that companies like Google, Bing, and Yahoo render certain web pages inaccessible to their search capacities because those pages contain information that is embarrassing to the person making the request: details on a lawsuit the person lost because he was a selfish and boorish neighbor, for instance, or a bar fight he was arrested for initiating when he was uncontrollably drunk; video of the person using a racial slur when she was an ignorant fifteen-year-old, desperate to seem cool, or coverage of a tasteless, insensitive, and ill-conceived joke she tweeted and now deeply regrets.[30]

In talking about this book with one of my undergraduate students (I'm going to name her here: Anna Zeitz, who has wisdom beyond her years), it occurred to us both that when we speak about the right to be forgotten, what we are really talking about is the desire to be *forgiven*—forgiven for our transgressions and the question of what forgiveness demands of us all. One thing I think it demands is a recognition of that truth history is well equipped to teach us: The truth that things change. Values change. Habits change. Laws change. Landscapes change. And people change.

Forgiveness also requires us to recognize that even in the midst of all this change, some elements of human nature are semper idem. Always constant. Forever the same. The passions and ignorance often fueling the transgressions the internet lays bare are not new, and they are not foreign. They live within us all.

The twentieth-century French Catholic historian Yves Congar once said that a knowledge of history has the potential to cultivate "a way of being and seeing oneself truly."[31] Done right, Congar seems to have been saying, a knowledge of history has the potential to breed humility, as we are brought to recognize ourselves in the failures and foibles of others who came before us. Humility, in turn, makes forgiveness possible.

I believe that the frontier, as a literal space or as a metaphorical construct, denies us the truth of who we are by working against the creation of historical knowledge. In that sense the closing of the frontier—be it the closing Ray, Jack, and Edith experienced at the dawn of the twentieth century or the closing we are witnessing now, in the digital age—should not be lamented, even if the casualties of these closings have sometimes been quite tragic. What has made the casualties tragic is not the closing of the frontier or the demise of our right to be forgotten. It has been our inability to see ourselves truly—a lesson that stories like those of Ray, Jack, and Edith have the potential to teach us.

Notes

Prologue

1. Jean L. Parsons, "The Shirtwaist: Changing the Commerce of Fashion," *Fashion, Style, and Popular Culture* 5 (January 2018): 8; Daniel Delis Hill, *As Seen in Vogue: A Century of American Fashion in Advertising* (Lubbock: Texas Tech University, 2004), 24.
2. "Wife Says Sargent Was Innocent Man," *New York Times*, August 17, 1913.
3. "Wife Says Sargent Was Innocent Man."
4. "Wife Says Sargent Was Innocent Man."
5. "Edith Drake's Lovers," *Boston Globe*, July 7, 1893.
6. "1800s Settler Drama Inspires 1-Act Opera," *Jackson Hole News and Guide*, June 16, 2010; "New Works Showcase," Brooklyn Academy of Music, accessed December 15, 2020, https://www.bam.org/newworksshowcase; Susan Springer Butler, *Scenic Routes and Byways: Yellowstone and Grand Teton National Parks* (Guilford CT: Morris, 2012), 266; Kendra Leah Fuller and Shannon Sullivan, *Images of America: Grand Teton National Park* (Charleston SC: Arcadia, 2014), 52; Bradley Mayhew and Carolyn McCarthy, *Lonely Planet's Yellowstone and Grand Teton National Parks* (New York: Hatchett, 2008), 17; "Signal Mountain," Teton Hiking Trails, accessed December 15, 2020, http://www.tetonhikingtrails.com/signal-mountain.htm.
7. "The Story of the Lady with the Violin: Music in the Tetons, JH Chamber of Commerce Fall Arts Festival 1989 Poster," Jackson Hole Historical Society (JHHS), 2220.0548002; Samantha Ford, "John Sargent Gravesite," JHHS, 2017.0459.007; Caroline Muller, "Mysterious Sargent Family Depicted in Festival Poster," *Jackson Hole News*, September 13, 1989; Richard Anderson, "Pettycoat Opens to Near-Full House," *Jackson Hole News*, July 5, 2000; "Previous Seasons," Off the Square Theater Company, accessed November 19, 2019, https://www.offsquare.org/previousseasons; Esther Allan, "Strange Music at Marry Mere," *Teton: The Magazine of Jackson Hole, Wyoming* 9 (1976): 17–18.
8. L. P. Hartley, *The Go-Between* (New York: New York Review of Books, 1953), 17.
9. Judge Kent is quoted in Richard Brookhiser, *Alexander Hamilton: American* (New York: Simon & Schuster, 1999), 206. The word "pathetic" had become

a pejorative term by 1925 (if not sooner). That was when H. L. Mencken used the word to describe William Jennings Bryan during the infamous "Scopes Monkey Trial" in Dayton, Tennessee. See H. L. Mencken, *A Religious Orgy in Tennessee: A Reporter's Account of the Scopes Monkey Trial*, ed. Art Winslow (New York: Melville House, 2006), 64, 83, 105–6, 109, 117.

10. Donald Worster, ed., *The Ends of the Earth: Perspectives on Environmental History* (New York: Cambridge University Press, 1988), 291; George Grinnell, "Their Last Refuge," *Forest and Stream* 19 (1882): 382–83; N. P. Langford, *Report of the Superintendent of the Yellowstone National Park for the Year 1872* (Washington DC: Government Printing Office, 1873), 4–6; Horace M. Albright, "Report on S.3427 and H.R.9917, Proposing Revision to the North, East, and South Boundary Lines of Yellowstone National Park," in *Hearings before the Committee on Public Lands and Surveys, United States Senate, Ninth Congress* (Washington DC: Government Printing Office, 1926), 177; Kiki Leigh Rydell and Mary Shivers Culpin, *Managing the "Matchless Wonders": A History of Administrative Development in Yellowstone National Park 1872–1965* (Yellowstone National Park WY: National Parks Service, 2006), 5.

11. Meg Leta Jones, *Ctrl + Z: The Right to Be Forgotten* (New York: New York University Press, 2018); Viktor Mayer-Schönberger, *Delete: The Virtue of Forgetting in the Digital Age* (Princeton NJ: Princeton University Press, 2011).

12. Robert P. Porter, *Compendium of the Eleventh Census: 1890, Part 1—Population* (Washington DC: Government Printing Office, 1892), xlviii.

13. Frederick Jackson Turner, *The Frontier in American History* (New York: Henry Holt, 1921). Turner first developed the thesis for this book in a lecture delivered to the American Historical Association in 1893.

14. Patricia Nelson Limerick, *The Legacy of Conquest: The Unbroken Past of the American West* (New York: W. W. Norton, 1987); Glenda Riley, "Frederick Jackson Turner Overlooked the Ladies," *Journal of the Early Republic* 13 (1993): 216–30; Megan Mondi, "'Connected and Unified'? A More Critical Look at Frederick Jackson Turner's America," *Constructing the Past* 7 (2006): 30–34; Thomas Doherty, "Review: *Hell or High Water*," *Cinéaste* 1 (Winter 2016): 44–45; Alex Trimball Young, "Settler Colonial Studies and/as the Transnational Western: Resistance and Representation in Academic Discourse and Cultural Production," *History of the Present* 11 (April 2021): 87–93.

15. Exhibit K1: letter from Robert Ray Hamilton to Gilbert Speir, July 14, 1890, and deposition of Gilbert M. Speir, taken March 10, 1891, Supreme Court, New York County, Pleadings, Reference No. 1889 H-67, Record Room, County Clerk of New York County (CCNY); *Supreme Court, General Term, First Department: In the Matter of Proving the Last Will and Testament of Robert Ray Hamilton,*

Deceased (New York: Livingston Middleditch, 1893), 243, 315–17; *A Description of the Western Resorts for Health and Pleasure, Reached Via Union Pacific Railway* (Omaha NE: Union Pacific, 1889), 49; *Sights and Scenes in Idaho and Montana for Tourists* (Omaha NE: Union Pacific, 1888), 2; Robert Strahorn, *The Resources and Attractions of the Idaho Territory* (Boise City ID: Idaho Legislature, 1881), 79–80, 82–84; George A. Crofutt, *Crofutt's Trans-Continental Tourist* (New York: George Croffutt, 1874), 34–40; Joshua D. Wolff, *Western Union and the Creation of the American Corporate Order, 1845–1893* (New York: Cambridge University Press, 2013), 1–10; Sandy Barnard, *I Go with Custer: The Life and Death of Reporter Mark Kellogg* (Bismark ND: Ast, 1996).

16. J. Martin Klotsch, "The Star Route Cases," *Mississippi Valley Historical Review* 22 (1935): 407–8; John Dudley Sargent to Captain George Anderson, October 22, 1896, Letters Received, Letter Box 13, S–Z, Yellowstone Heritage and Research Center (YHRC), Gardiner MT; John S. Gallagher and Alan H. Patera, *Wyoming Post Offices: 1850–1980* (Burtonsville MD: Depot, 1980), 5–16, 119–21; *United States Official Postal Guide, Revised and Published Monthly by the Authority of the Post Office Department* 23 (1901): 7, 850, and 12 (1890): 6.

17. Photo 65-2, Folder 10, Box 3, Collection No. 400007, Kenneth L. Diem and Lenore L. Diem Papers (Diem), American Heritage Center (AHC), University of Wyoming; Jennifer M. Black, "Exchange Cards: Advertising, Album Making, and the Commodification of Sentiment in the Gilded Age," *Winterthur Portfolio* 51, no. 1 (2017): 1–53, esp. 12.

18. John Daugherty, *A Place Called Jackson Hole: The Historic Resource Study of Grant Teton National Park* (Moose WY: Grand Teton Natural History Association, 1999), 185; Jackson Lake Lodge–Grand Teton Lodge Company, accessed November 16, 2019, https://www.gtlc.com/lodges/jackson-lake-lodge; "Visitation Numbers, 2020," National Parks Service, accessed September 22, 2021, https://www.nps.gov/aboutus/visitation-numbers.htm; "Mary Mere Ranch," advertisement included in John Dudley Sargent to Captain George Anderson, September 18, 1896, Letters Received, Letter Box 13, S–Z, YHRC.

1. Revolutionary Legacies

1. Maya Jasanoff, *Liberty's Exiles: American Loyalists in the Revolutionary World* (New York: Vintage, 2012), 5–6, 86; Ira Rosenwaike, *Population History of New York City* (Syracuse NY: Syracuse University Press, 1972), 14–15; Wallace Brown, *The Good Americans: The Loyalists in the American Revolution* (New York: William Morrow, 1969), 132; John Jay and John Corwallis Godley, *The Peace Negotiations of 1782–1783: As Newly Illustrated by Confidential Papers of Shelburne and Vergennes* (New York: Houghton Mifflin, 1888), 162.

2. George Templeton Strong, November 25, 1835, and November 26, 1836, in *The Diary of George Templeton Strong*, ed. Allan Nevins and Milton Halsey Thomas (New York: Macmillan, 1952), 1:6, 42.

3. Clifton Hood, "An Unusable Past: Urban Elites, New York City's Evacuation Day, and the Transformation of a Memory Culture," *Journal of Social History* 37, no. 4 (2004): 883–913; Jennifer Steenshorne, "Evacuation Day," in *The Best of New York Archives: Selections from the Magazine, 2001–2011*, ed. New York State Archives Partnership Trust (Albany: State University of New York Press, 2017), 83; "By the Mails," *Portland Advertiser and Gazette of Maine*, December 1, 1834.

4. "Evacuation Day Once a Glorious Holiday Here," *New York Times*, October 19, 1924; Robert Sullivan, *My American Revolution: Crossing the Delaware and 1-78* (New York: Farrar, Straus & Giroux, 2012), 180; James W. Baker, *Thanksgiving: The Biography of an American Holiday* (Durham: University of New Hampshire Press, 2010), 71; Catherine Quayle, "Oh, and Happy Evacuation Day," *PBS: Need to Know*, November 25, 2010, http://www.pbs.org/wnet/need-to -know/the-daily-need/oh-and-happy-evacuation-day/5411/.

5. Faith K. Pizor, "Preparations for the Centennial Exhibition of 1876," *Pennsylvania Magazine of History and Biography* 94 (April 1970): 213–32.

6. *Report of the Joint Committee on the Centennial Celebration of the Evacuation of New York by the British, November 26th, 1883* (New York: J. J. Little, 1885), i.

7. Carlos A. Schwantes, *Vision and Enterprise: Exploring the History of Phelps Dodge Corporation* (Tucson: University of Arizona Press, 2000), 25–79, 133–58; James Byrkit, "The Bisbee Deportation," in *American Labor in the Southwest: The First One Hundred Years*, ed. James C. Foster (Tucson: University of Arizona Press, 1982), 86–102; Henry Martyn Field, *The Story of the Atlantic Telegraph* (New York: Scribner's, 1892); Massimo Guarnieri, "The Conquest of the Atlantic," *IEEE Industrial Electronics Magazine* 8 (2014): 53–55, 67; Queen Victoria to James Buchanan and James Buchanan to Queen Victoria, August 16, 1858, in "Telegraph Supplement," *Harper's Weekly*, September 4, 1858. Field's first cable broke down about two months after Queen Victoria sent her message, and then the Civil War broke out, delaying its repair until the war was over.

8. Richard Cheek and Tom Gannon, *Newport Mansions: The Gilded Age* (Little Compton RI: Foremost, 1982), 7; "Sargent Portrait of Cornelius Vanderbilt, II Acquired, Returned to the Breakers," Preservation Society of Newport, July 7, 2009, https://www.newportmansions.org/press/press-releases/sargent -portrait-of-cornelius-vanderbilt-ii-acquired-returned-to-the-breakers; Marshall B. Davison and Elizabeth Stillinger, *The American Wing and the Metropolitan Museum of Art* (New York: Harrison House, 1985), 488.

9. *Joint Committee*, 3.
10. *Joint Committee*, 35, 178; Jeffrey Karl Ochsner, *H. H. Richardson: Complete Architectural Works* (Cambridge MA: MIT Press, 1982), 84, 114–15, 235–36, 325–26.
11. *Joint Committee*, 177–78.
12. *Joint Committee*, 177–78; Paul Freedman, *Ten Restaurants That Changed America* (New York: W. W. Norton, 2016), 3–48; Frank H. Goodyear, *A President in Yellowstone: The F. Jay Haynes Photographic Album of Chester Arthur's 1883 Expedition* (Norman: University of Oklahoma Press, 2013), 3–40.
13. Edward Kirkland, *Industry Comes of Age: Business, Labor, and Public Policy, 1869–1897* (New York: Quadrangle, 1961), 1–2; Axel Madsen: *John Jacob Astor: America's First Multi-Millionaire* (New York: Wiley, 2001), 166–67, 195–213, 244–54. All efforts in this book to provide estimates of the modern-day buying power of prices and incomes are derived from a table of Consumer Price Indexes put together by the Federal Reserve Bank of Minneapolis: https://www.minneapolisfed.org/about-us/monetary-policy/inflation-calculator/consumer-price-index-1800- (accessed August 21, 2023).
14. G. Edward White, *The Eastern Establishment and the Western Experience: The West of Frederic Remington, Theodore Roosevelt, and Owen Wister* (Austin: University of Texas Press, 1989), 12.
15. George Rogers Taylor, *The Transportation Revolution, 1815–1860* (New York: Routledge, 1951), 395; Henry Cabot Lodge, *Early Memories* (New York: Scribner's, 1913), 208.
16. David Nasaw, *Andrew Carnegie* (New York: Penguin, 2006), 106–7; Ron Chernow, *Titan: The Life of John D. Rockefeller, Sr.* (New York: Vintage, 1998), 11, 107, 181.
17. Lodge, *Early Memories*, 206–9; Rockefeller, quoted in Chernow, *Titan*, 3.
18. Oliver Wendell Holmes, *Elsie Venner* (New York: Routledge, 1862), 4; Brian K. Smith, *Classifying the Universe: The Ancient Indian Varna System and the Origins of Caste* (New York: Oxford University Press, 1994), 3. Holmes's novel was originally published in serial form in the *Atlantic Monthly* in 1860.
19. Holmes, *Elsie Venner*, 4, 9.
20. George J. Varney, "History of Winthrop, Maine," in *A Gazeteer of the State of Maine* (Boston: B. B. Russell, 1886), 599; Paul Dudley, *Town Records of Dudley, Massachusetts* (Pawtucket RI: Adam Sutcliffe, 1893).
21. Frederic Cople Jaher, "Nineteenth-Century Elites in Boston and New York," *Journal of Social History* 6 (1972): 36.
22. John Updike, "The Changeling," *New Yorker*, April 9, 2007; Yvonne Zipp, "In the House of Edith Wharton," *Christian Science Monitor*, May 15, 2007. The Wharton quote appears in White, *Eastern Establishment and the Western Experience*, 17.

23. *New York: Indelible Photographs* (New York: A. Witteman, 1891), 39; *Appleton's Dictionary of New York and Its Vicinity* (New York: Appleton's, 1879), 220 and (1892), 131, 220.

24. *Joint Committee*, 178; Raven D. Walker and Glenn A. Jones, "Consumer-Driven Depletion of the Northern Diamondback Terrapin in the Chesapeake Bay," *Marine and Coastal Fisheries: Dynamics, Management, and Ecosystem Science* 10, no. 1 (2018): 133, 139.

25. *Joint Committee*, 178; Richard Edwards, ed., *New York's Great Industries: Exchange and Commercial Review* (New York: Historical Publishing Company, 1884), 241, 277.

26. *Catalogue for Phipps Musical and Lyceum Bureau* (New York: n.p., 1892), 10; Robert Grau, *The Businessman in the Amusement World: A Volume of Progress in the Field of the Theater* (New York: Broadway, 1910), 189–91; Dawn Spring, "The Globalization of American Advertising and Brand Management: A Brief History of the J. Walter Thompson Company, Proctor and Gamble, and U.S. Foreign Policy," *Global Studies Journal* 5 (2013): 51–63.

27. Eric Homberger, *Mrs. Astor's New York: Money and Social Power in a Gilded Age* (New Haven CT: Yale University Press, 2002), 235–36.

28. Reneé Somers, *Edith Wharton as Spatial Activist and Analyst* (New York: Routledge, 2005), 26–27; Barbara Seward, "Dante's Mystic Rose," *Studies in Philology* 52, no. 4 (October 1955): 515–23; William Bryk, "The Father of the Four Hundred," *New York Sun*, August 9, 2005; Gary Sharnhorst and Tom Quirk, *Research Guide to American Literature: Realism and Regionalism, 1865–1914* (New York: Facts on File, 2005), 4:10; O. Henry, *The Four Million* (New York: Doubleday, 1906).

29. *Joint Committee*, 179; "A History of Schenectady during the Revolution, Individual Records of Service, Q to T," Schenectady Digital History Archive, accessed October 1, 2018, http://www.schenectadyhistory.org/resources /hanson/revwar_q_t.html; John Dos Passos, *The Men Who Made the Nation: Architects of the Young Republic* (New York: Doubleday, 1957), 480; "Albert Gallatin," in *Appleton's Cyclopaedia of American Biography* (New York: Appleton, 1900), 578–79; "Presidents Roosevelt Awarded Posthumous J.D.s," Columbia Law School, September 25, 2008, https://www.law.columbia.edu /media_inquiries/news_events/2008/september2008/roosevelt_jds.

30. *Joint Committee*, 179; John C. Hamilton, *Life of Alexander Hamilton: A History of the Republic of the United States of America* (Boston: Houghton, Osgood, 1879); "The Death List of a Day: John Church Hamilton," *New York Times*, July 26, 1882; Alexander Hamilton, *The Works of Alexander Hamilton, Comprising His Correspondence and His Official and Political Writings, Exclusive of the Federalist*, ed. John C. Hamilton (New York: J. F. Trow, 1851); "Alexander Hamilton,"

Sedalia Weekly Bazoo, July 23, 1878; "The Hamilton Family," *Des Moines Register*, July 27, 1879.

31. Ron Chernow, *Alexander Hamilton* (New York: Penguin, 2005), 362–418, 654–55.

32. J.F.B., "Actions for Breach of Promise of Marriage," *American Law Register* 20 (February 1872): 65–73; Harvard Law Review Association, "Statute Outlawing Breach-of-Promise Suits Does Not Bar Action Based on Fraudulent Promise to Marry," *Harvard Law Review* 70 (April 1957): 1098–100; "The Nemesis of the Hamiltons," *St. Louis Post-Dispatch*, September 27, 1903.

33. Alexander Hamilton of Heuvel, *Dramas and Poems* (New York: Dick & Fitzgerald, 1887); "Is General Hamilton Insane," *New York Times*, August 11, 1893.

34. "The Nemesis of the Hamiltons," *St. Louis Post-Dispatch*, September 27, 1903; John Lockwood Romer, *Historical Sketches of the Romer, Van Tassel, and Allied Families* (Buffalo NY: W. C. Gay, 1917), 122; Cuyler Reynolds, *Genealogical and Family History of Southern New York and the Hudson River Valley* (New York: Lewis Historical Publishing, 1914), 3:1386–87. The *Post-Dispatch* incorrectly reported John Cornelius Adrian Hamilton's name, giving him the middle initial "J."

35. Henry David Thoreau, *On the Duty of Civil Disobedience* (London: Simple Life, 1903), 12; Nicholas Lawrence, "Francis Parkman's 'The Oregon Trail' and the U.S.-Mexico War: Appropriations of Counter-Imperial Dissent," *Western American Literature* 43 (Winter 2009): 372–91; B. H. Gilley, "Tennessee Whigs and the Mexican War," *Tennessee Historical Quarterly* 40 (Spring 1981): 54.

36. "The Nemesis of the Hamiltons," *St. Louis Post-Dispatch*, September 27, 1903; Brown, *The Occupation of Mexico*, 11; Jack D. Welsh, *The Medical Histories of Union Generals* (Kent OH: Kent State Press, 1996), 148.

37. Reynolds, *Family History of Southern New York*, 1387; Sylvan J. Muldoon, *Alexander Hamilton's Pioneer Son: The Life and Times of Colonel William Stephen Hamilton, 1797–1850* (Harrisburg PA: Aurand, 1930), 9, 31–33, 37–43, 115–28, 142, 234, 239.

38. Reynolds, *Family History*, 1384; S. Shapiro, "Development of Birth Registration and Birth Statistics in the United States," *Population Studies* 4 (June 1950): 87; E. Wayne Carp, *Family Matters: Secrecy and Disclosure in the History of Adoption* (Cambridge MA: Harvard University Press, 1998), 45.

39. Robert P. Hamilton to Charlotte Augusta Hamilton, March 11, 1874, MS0546, Box 2, Hamilton Family Papers (HFP-Columbia), Columbia University Rare Book and Manuscript Library (CURBML).

40. Robert P. Hamilton to Charlotte Augusta Hamilton, February 10, 1875, Box 2, HFP-Columbia.

41. Robert P. Hamilton to Charlotte Augusta Hamilton, February 2, 1874, Box 2, HFP-Columbia.

42. "Mrs. Hamilton's Will," *New York Times*, February 27, 1883; "New York Dispatches," *Boston Globe*, February 27, 1883; William Gaston Hamilton to "Sisters," August 11, 1883, and to Charlotte Augusta Hamilton, August 23, 1883, Box 2, HFP-Columbia; "Mrs. Hamilton's Will," *New York Times*, February 27, 1883.

43. Mortgage Deed, Abraham Franklin and his wife, Ann; John Franklin and his wife, Charity, to Cornelius Ray, Matthew Clarkson, and Joshua Sands, trustees, December 9, 1807, in H. Croswell Tuttle, ed., *Abstracts of Farm Titles in the City of New York, Between 39th and 75th Streets, East of the Common Line* (New York: Spectator, 1877), 191; Barbara Broome Semans and Letetia Broome Schwartz, *Rebecca Lloyd: Their Descendants and Related Families, 18th to 21st Centuries* (Bloomington IN: Xlibris, 2009), 209–10; James O. Wettereau, "New Light on the First Bank of the United States," *Pennsylvania Magazine of History and Biography* 61 (July 1937): 263–85.

44. "Last Will and Testament of Nathaniel Prime," April 24, 1840, in Tuttle, *Abstracts*, 257–61; Edwin G. Burrows and Mike Wallace, *Gotham: A History of New York City to 1898* (New York: Oxford University Press, 1999), 445; Julius Shiskin, "An Application of Electronic Computers to Time-Series Analysis," *Analysts Journal* 11 (May 1955): 37.

45. George Templeton Strong, November 26, 1840, in *The Diary of George Templeton Strong*, 1:152.

46. "It Was Ray Hamilton," *New York Sun*, October 15, 1891; "Alexander Hamilton," *Sedalia Weekly Bazoo*, July 23, 1878; "From the State Capital," *Brooklyn Daily Eagle*, April 15, 1888; Robert Ray Hamilton, "Last Will and Testament," March 17, 1890, in *Baileys v. Hamilton et al., January 20th, 1899*, in *The New York Supplement, New York State Reporter, Containing the Decisions of Supreme and Lower Courts of Record of New York State* 55 (January 12–March 2, 1899): 391.

47. "Order of Exercises, 118th Commencement of Columbia College, June 26th, 1872" and "Minutes of the Class of Seventy-Two," 46, Folder 6, Box 1, UA #0126, Commencement Collection, 1758–, CURBML; Cindy S. Aron, *Working at Play: A History of Vacations in the United States* (New York: Oxford University Press, 1999), 46.

48. "Gotham Gossip," *New Orleans Times-Picayune*, April 19, 1881; "Married amid Flowers," *New York Times*, April 28, 1887; "The Davenport-Sharpe Wedding," *New York Tribune*, April 28, 1887; "Receiving French Visitors," *New York Tribune*, August 26, 1881; "Rough on Hamilton," *Buffalo Courier*, August 28, 1889; "Robert Ray Hamilton," *Buffalo Evening News*, August 29, 1889; New

York Genealogical and Biographical Society, "John Watts Russell," *New York Genealogical and Biographical Records* 11 (1880): 162; *The Union League of New York: Annual Report, March 1st, 1886* (New York: Club House, 1886), 3; "Rich Paintings and Glass: Decorations in the New Union League Club House," *New York Times*, February 16, 1881; Richard Alan Ryerson, *John Adams's Republic: The One, The Few, and the Many* (Baltimore MD: Johns Hopkins University Press, 2016), 28; *Conrad Edick Wright, Revolutionary Generation: Harvard Men and the Consequences of Independence* (Amherst: University of Massachusetts Press, 2005), 55.

49. Schuyler Hamilton to John Church Hamilton, July 25, 1864, Box 1, HFP-Columbia.

50. "General Hamilton Married," *Chicago Tribune*, July 15, 1886; "New York Supreme Court," *Brooklyn Daily Eagle*, April 10, 1899; "Hamilton's Infatuation," *Brooklyn Daily Eagle*, August 30, 1889; "Riverside Park: Robert Ray Hamilton Fountain," NYC Parks, accessed February 8, 2020, https://www.nycgovparks.org/parks/riverside-park/monuments/666; "A Sad Story's End," *Buffalo Evening Express*, September 18, 1890.

51. "Petition," April 4, 1891, in *Proceedings of the Board of Alderman of the City of New York, From April 7 to June 30, 1891* (New York: Martin B. Brown, 1891), 67–68; "Current Events," July 30, 1882, *The Literary Digest: A Repository of Contemporaneous Thought and Research* 5 (May–November 1892): 28.

2. Blueberries and Timber

1. Augustus Hemenway to Mary Hemenway, November 4, 1873, and October 15, 1874, Folder 12, Box 1, MHS 122, Hemenway Family Papers (HFP), Phillips Library, Peabody Essex Museum, Rowley MA; E. Robert Stevenson, ed., *Connecticut History Makers* (Waterbury CT: American Republican, 1938), 3:153; Peter R. Knights, *Yankee Destinies: The Lives of Ordinary Nineteenth-Century Bostonians* (Chapel Hill: University of North Carolina Press, 1991), 184–86. My assumption that the morning in July when Gus left Boston was "cool" is based on temperature data that Henry David Thoreau recorded in his journal for that month. See Henry David Thoreau, *Journal* 31 (February 15–July 22, 1860), 83, in *The Writings of Henry David Thoreau*, accessed October 21, 2023, https://thoreau.library.ucsb.edu/writings_journals31.html.

2. "Remarkable Career of Augustus Hemenway, of Boston—Insane for Thirteen Years and Again at His Desk," Folder 12, Box 1, HFP; Brian Black and Marcy Ladson, "Oil at 150: Energy Past and Future in Pennsylvania," *Pennsylvania Legacies* 10 (2010): 6–13; Richard White, *Railroaded: The Transcontinentals and the Making of Modern America* (New York: W. W. Norton, 2012); Massimo Guarnieri, "The Conquest of the Atlantic," *IEEE Industrial Electronics Maga-*

zine 8 (2014): 53–55, 67; Frank E. Comparato, *Chronicles of Genius and Folly: R. Hoe and Company and the Printing Press as a Service to Democracy* (Culver City CA: Labyrinthos, 1979), 3–23; Paul Starr, *The Creation of the Media: Political Origins of Modern Communications* (New York: Basic Books, 2004), 252; Loretta Fowler, "Arapaho and Cheyenne Perspectives: From the 1851 Treaty to the Sand Creek Massacre," *American Indian Quarterly* 39 (Fall 2015): 364–90; Jacob K. Friefeld, Mikal Brotnov Eckstrom, and Richard Edwards, "African-American Homesteader 'Colonies' in the Settling of the Great Plains," *Great Plains Quarterly* 39 (Winter 2019): 11–37.

3. "Remarkable Career of a Successful Merchant," *New York Sun*, June 29, 1876, and *Newark Advocate*, June 30, 1876.

4. Frederic A. Eustis, *Augustus Hemenway, 1805–1876: Builder of United States Trade with the West Coast of South America* (Salem MA: Peabody Museum, 1955), 3.

5. Sarah Upton Hemenway to Augustus Hemenway, October 12, 1818, Folder 1, Box 1, HFP.

6. Sarah Upton Hemenway to Augustus Hemenway, August 5, 1821, Folder 1, Box 1, HFP; Heather Smith Thomas, *Storey's Guide to Training Horses*, 3rd ed. (North Adams MA: Storey, 2019), 278.

7. Sarah Upton Hemenway to Augustus Hemenway, October 5, 1819, Folder 1, Box 1, HFP.

8. Eustis, *Augustus Hemenway*, 3–4.

9. Eustis, *Augustus Hemenway*, 4; *A Record of the Streets, Alleys, Places, Etc., of the City of Boston* (Boston: City of Boston Printing Department, 1910), 134; Madeline Bilis, "Why Boston's Brutalism Is Back in a Big Way," *Boston Magazine*, February 12, 2019; Sarah Upton Hemenway to Augustus Hemenway, October 19, 1818, and Eleazer A. Porter to Augustus Hemenway, October 11, 1820, Folders 1 and 3, Box 1, HFP.

10. Sarah Upton Hemenway to Augustus Hemenway, August 17, 1818; May 16, 1819; October 19, 1818; August 25, 1821; August 7, 1824; February 16, 1826; March 2, 1826; June 4, 1826, Folder 1, Box 1, HFP.

11. "Tragic Events in Which Maine People Were Concerned," *Belfast (ME) Republican Journal*, August 14, 1913; Mary S. Smith to John Dudley Sargent, February 22, 1889, Jackson Hole Historical Society and Museum (JHHSM), Jackson, Wyoming, 2002.532.001; Verba Lawrence, "Scrapbook," Folder Sargent, Box 7, Collection No. 400007, Kenneth L. Diem and Lenore L. Diem Papers (Diem), American Heritage Center (AHC), University of Wyoming; "United States Census, 1850," Lubec ME, Washington County, enumerated August 6, 1850, 64, Microfilm Publication M432, Record Group 29, National Archives and Records Administration (NARA); "United States

Census, 1880," Cambridge MA, Middlesex County, enumerated June 3, 1880, 208, Microfilm Publication T9, Record Group 29, NARA.

12. J. H. Baily to Trustees of A. Hemenway, February 12, 1869, Folder 1, Box 6, HFP; Last Will and Testament of Mrs. Sarah Hemenway, November 2, 1865, and Memo for the Division of the Estate of Mrs. Sarah Hemenway, March 15, 1879, Folders 1 and 2, Box 11, HFP; J. H. Bailey to the Trustees of Augustus Hemenway, December 9, 1878, Folder 8, Box 5, HFP; John R. Mullin, "Development of the Assabet Mills in Nineteenth Century Maynard," *Historical Journal of Massachusetts* 40 (1992): 64–88.

13. "Death of Augustus Hemenway," *Boston Globe*, June 19, 1876; "Cured by a Balloon: Singular Recovery of a Millionaire Madman," *Tennessean*, June 23, 1876; "Remarkable Career of a Successful Merchant," *Woodstock Sentinel*, January 6, 1876; "A Successful Merchant," *Ogden Junction*, July 1, 1876; Michael George Mulhall, *The English in South America* (London: Ed Stanford, 1878), 612. The *Globe* got it wrong when it called Augustus Hemenway "the wealthiest man in America"; Cornelius Vanderbilt's estate was worth more than twice as much as Hemenway's when he died in 1877. But Hemenway was definitely *one* of the wealthiest men in America—and probably the wealthiest man in Boston.

14. Gary B. Nash, *The Urban Crucible: The Northern Seaports and the Origins of the American Revolution* (Cambridge MA: Harvard University Press, 1979, 1986), 1–33.

15. Nash, *Urban Crucible*, 184–88, 224–32; Benjamin L. Carp, *Rebels Rising: Cities and the American Revolution* (New York: Oxford, 2007), 23–61, and *Defiance of the Patriots: The Boston Tea Party and the Making of America* (New Haven CT: Yale University Press: 2010), 106; Alvin Rabushka, *Taxation in Colonial America* (Princeton NJ: Princeton University Press, 2008), 749–96; Richardson Dilworth, *Cities in American Political History* (Thomas Oaks CA: CQ, 2011), 41–46; Thomas L. Purvis, *Almanacs of American Life: Colonial America to 1763* (New York: Facts on File, 1999), 81; Jacob M. Price, "The American Panorama of Atlantic Port Cities," in *Atlantic Port Cities: Economy, Culture, and Society, 1650–1850*, ed. Franklin W. Knight and Peggy K. Liss (Knoxville: University of Tennessee Press, 1991), 262–80.

16. Paul B. Trescott, "Federal-State Financial Relations, 1790–1860," *Journal of Economic History* 15 (September 1955): 229; E. James Ferguson, "Speculation in the Revolutionary Debt: The Ownership of Public Securities in Maryland, 1790," *Journal of Economic History* 14 (Winter 1954): 35–45; Leonard L. Richards, *Shays' Rebellion: The American Revolution's Final Battle* (Philadelphia: University of Pennsylvania Press, 2002), 4–22.

17. Thomas Urquart, *Up for Grabs: Timber Pirates, Lumber Barons, and the Battles over Maine's Public Lands* (Lanham MD: Down East, 2021), 6; Harlow Giles

Unger, *John Hancock: Merchant King and American Patriot* (New York: John Wiley & Sons, 2000), 33, 68; James Elliot Defebaugh, *History of the Lumber Industry of America* (Chicago: American Lumberman, 1907), 10; Lloyd C. Irland, "Rufus Putnam's Ghost: An Essay on Maine's Public Lands, 1783–1820," *Journal of Forest History* 30 (April 1986): 60–65.

18. Andrew Barton, Alan White, and Charles Cogbill, "Reconstructing the Past: Maine Forests, Then and Now," *Northern Woodlands* (Summer 2013): 40–47; "The Maine Forest: Information Sheet, Revised August 2009," Maine Forest Service, accessed February 1, 2020, https://www.maineforestry.net/the -maine-forest; "How Old Is Our Forest," Maine Tree Foundation, accessed on February 25, 2020, http://www.mainetreefoundation.org/forestfacts /How%20Old%20Is%20Our%20Forest.htm; "Land Acreage: Total by State, National Association of Foresters, 2004," Statemaster, accessed February 1, 2020, http://www.statemaster.com/graph/geo_lan_acr_tot-geography-land -acreage-total; Bill McKibben, "An Explosion of Green," *Atlantic*, April 1995, 70–72; Patrick Strauch, "Maine's Voices: Forest Products Industry Has Much to Celebrate," *Portland Press Herald*, October 21, 2019; Julia Bayly, "Never Forget, All Roads Are Private in the North Maine Woods," *Bangor Daily News*, May 13, 2017; Justin G. Sharaf, "Timberland and Taxes in Maine: Property and Federal Income Taxes," *Maine Law Review* 17 (1965): 227–51; Richard A. Hebert, *Modern Maine: Its Historic Background, People, and Resources* (New York: Lewis Historical Publishing Company, 1951), 2:92; Maine State Auditor's Office, "Unorganized Territory Annual Report Fiscal Year 2013," Maine. gov, accessed February 14, 2020, https://www.maine.gov/audit/documents /2013utreport.pdf; "2010 Census: Population Density Data (Text Version)," U.S. Census Bureau, accessed February 14, 2020, https://www.census.gov /data/tables/2010/dec/density-data-text.html; Matt Wickenheiser, "Census: Maine Most Rural State as Urban Centers Grow Nationwide," *Bangor Daily News*, March 26, 2012. Amazingly, most of Maine's trees have taken root naturally—meaning they have not been planted by the paper companies that own the trees and monitor their growth. Human behavior has influenced the kinds of trees that grow in Maine, however. For instance, spruce competes with fir, and the heavy harvesting of spruce in the early nineteenth century facilitated the spread of fir in Maine's northern woods.

19. Irland, "Rufas Putnam's Ghost," 60–65; Susan L. Danforth, "The First Official Maps of Maine and Massachusetts," *Imago Mundi* 35 (1983): 38; J. N. Larned, Charles Seymour, and Donald E. Smith, eds., *The New Larned History for Ready Reference, Reading, and Research* (Springfield MA: C. A. Nichols, 1924), 7:5388; James Elliot Defebaugh, *History of the Lumber Industry of America* (Chicago: American Lumberman, 1907), 10; Kenneth T. Palmer, G.

Thomas Taylor, Jean E. Lavigne, and Marcus A. LiBrizzi, *Maine Politics and Government* (Lincoln: University of Nebraska Press, 2009), 8–9; Urquart, *Up for Grabs*, ix–x, 7–19.

20. Executors' Inventory, Augustus Hemenway's Estate, filed June 8, 1877, Folder 11, Box 3, and Folders 9 and 10, Box 7, HFP; "Sargent's Lawyer Has Posthumous Letter," *Wyoming Tribune*, September 16, 1913.

21. Maine Department of Administrative and Financial Services, "Maine Population Outlook, 2016–2026," Maine.gov, accessed February 15, 2020, https://www.maine.gov/dafs/economist/sites/maine.gov.dafs.economist/files/inline-files/Maine%20Population%20Outlook%20to%202026.pdf, 3; A. J. Higgins, "Verizon Wireless Terminating Service for 2,000 Cellphone Customers in Washington County," *Bangor Daily News*, September 12, 2017; Jacqueline Weaver, "Cellular Service to Improve for Verizon Customers Downeast," *Ellsworth American*, November 30, 2015; Sarah Craighead, "Verizon's Rural Withdrawal Leaves More Questions than Answers," *Calais Advertiser*, September 22, 2017.

22. James Spielman and Charles Mitchell, "Windbreaks Protect Blueberries Downeast," *Soil and Water Conservation* 12 (May–June, 1991): 14; Jean Marie Laskus, *Hidden America: From Coalminers to Cowboys, an Extraordinary Exploration of the People Who Make This Country Work* (New York: Berkeley, 2012), 56–57; Christopher Cumo, *The Ongoing Columbia Exchange: Stories of Biological and Ecological Transfer in History* (Santa Barbara CA: ABC-CLIO, 2015), 29–30; Bob Duchesne, "Here Are 9 Things You Probably Don't Know about Maine's Wild Blueberries," *Bangor Daily News*, July 31, 2019; Nancy Heiser, "A Foliage Alternative," *Boston Globe*, September 9, 2011.

23. "Quick Facts: Washington County, Maine," U.S. Census Bureau, July 1, 2019, https://www.census.gov/quickfacts/washingtoncountymaine; Samuel Stebbins, "Poorest Counties in the U.S.: A State by State Look at Where Median Household Income Is Low," *USA Today*, January 25, 2019; "United States—Poverty Rate by County," Index Mundi, accessed February 26, 2020, https://www.indexmundi.com/facts/united-states/quick-facts/all-states/percent-of-people-of-all-ages-in-poverty#map; Ann Acheson, *Poverty in Maine: 2010* (Orono ME: Margaret Chase Smith Policy Center, University of Maine, 2010), 6, 8, 58–60; Jenna Russell, "In Maine, a Losing Battle for Health," *Boston Globe*, May 20, 2008; Hugh Cowperthwaite and Richard Clime, *Maine Seafood Study: A Look at the Integration of Maine Seafood into Food Distribution Systems* (Wiscasset ME: Coastal Enterprises, 2014), 5.

24. Johanna S. Billings, "Festival Celebrates Maine's Signature Fruit," *Ellsworth American*, August 7, 2019; National Parks Service, *National Register of Historic Places, 1966–1994* (Washington DC: Preservation, 1994), 317–18.

25. "Plan of Township 36, Middle Division," Land Office, Plangood 18a, 22, Maine State Archives (MSA), #209525.

26. "UT36, Middle Division, List of Lots and Owners Names," Land Office, Plangood 23, MSA; Irland, "Rufus Putnam's Ghost," 62; John Dudley, "A Story of the Unorganized Territories of Washington County," 101–2, unpublished manuscript prepared for the Washington County Council of Governments, March 2017, https://www.washingtoncountymaine.com/images/places /UTHistory.pdf; Ignatius Sargent to Charles Hemenway, September 1, 1878, Folder 6, Box 4, HFP; J. H. Bailey to Trustees of A. Hemenway, May 8, 1878, Folder 8, Box 5, HFP; "Sargent's Lawyer Has Posthumous Letter," *Wyoming Tribune*, September 16, 1913.

27. Bill Vasquez, "'An Era to Remember' Chronicles Time When Shipbuilding Was King Down East," *Bangor Daily News*, December 24, 1990; Augustus Hemenway to Mary Hemenway, December 15, 1842, Folder 4, Box 8, HFP; Estate of Augustus Hemenway Sr., September 11, 1875, Folder 10, Box 3, HFP; Samuel Eliot Morison, *The Maritime History of Massachusetts, 1783–1860* (Boston: Houghton Mifflin, 1921), 34, 271; Wessel, Duval & Company, *A Centennial Review of the Business Founded by Augustus Hemenway of Boston in 1825* (New York: privately printed, 1925), 5; Santiago Dod, "Stray Glimpses at the History of the Cuban Sugar Industry," *Louisiana Planter and Sugar Manufacturer* 27 (June 28, 1902): 419–21.

28. Estate of Augustus Hemenway Sr., Folder 10, Box 3, HFP; Charles Thomas Davis, *The Manufacture of Paper: Description of the Various Processes for the Fabrication, Coloring, and Finishing of Every Kind of Paper* (Philadelphia: Henry Carey Bairds, 1886), 57–59; Eustis, *Augustus Hemenway*, 102; A. J. Valente, "Changes in Print Paper in the 19th Century," in *Charleston Conference Proceedings, 2010: Anything Goes*, ed. Katina P. Strauch, Beth R. Bernhardt, and Leah H. Hinds (West Lafayette IN: Purdue University Press, 2011), 214.

29. McKibben, "Explosion of Green," 66.

30. John Adams Upton, *The Upton Memorial: A Genealogical Record of the Descendants of John Upton* (Bath ME: E. Upton & Son, 1874), 177; "Power of Attorney, Augustus Hemenway to C. P. Hemenway, Francis Bacon, and Thomas Tileston, March 6, 1860," Folder 2, Box 3, HFP; Eustis, *Augustus Hemenway*, 26, 87, 92; Jane Achen, Abrose O. Talisuna, Annette Erhart, Adoke Yeka, James K. Tibenderana, Frederick N. Baliraine, Philip J. Rosenthal, and Umberto D'Alessandro, "Quinine, an Old Anti-Malarial Drug in the Modern World: Role in the Treatment of Malaria," *Malaria Journal* 10 (2011): 144; *Catalogue of the Chilian [sic] Expedition at the Centenary of Philadelphia* (Valparaiso, Chile: Mercurio Printing, 1876), 28.

31. Last Will and Testament of Sarah Hemenway, November 2, 1865, Folder 1, Box 11, HFP; Eustis, *Augustus Hemenway*, 82–83; "Petition of William H. Hemenway and Another, for Authority to Erect and Maintain a Wharf in Machias River" (February 4, 1870), in *Journal of the Senate of Maine* (Augusta ME: Sprague, Owen & Nash, 1870), 159; George W. Drisko, *Narrative of the Town of Machias: The Old and the New, the Early and Late* (Machias ME: Press of the Republican, 1904), 237, 549; Work Projects Administration, *Ship Registers and Enrollments of Machias, Maine, 1780–1930* (Rockland ME: National Archives Project, 1942), 194–95, 233–34, 243–44, 291, 370, 424–25. William and Augustus were partial owners of several other schooners as well.

32. "Story of a Boston Merchant," *Newberry Weekly Herald*, March 15, 1876; "Local Department," *Natchez Daily Courier*, August 3, 1866; "Death of Augustus Hemenway," *Boston Globe*, June 19, 1876; "A Successful Merchant," *Ashtabula Weekly Telegraph*, March 24, 1876.

33. *Centennial Review*, 9.

34. Executors' Inventory—Augustus Hemenway's Estate, filed June 8, 1877, Index Number 9274, Folder 11, Box 3, HFP.

35. Eustis, *Augustus Hemenway*, xii–iii, 81, 102.

36. G. Edward White, *The Eastern Establishment and the Western Experience: The West of Frederic Remington, Theodore Roosevelt, and Owen Wister* (Austin: University of Texas Press, 1989), 12; "At Boston," *Daily National Democrat*, February 26, 1860; "The Wealth of Boston," *New York Herald*, August 24, 1870; "Miscellaneous," *Leavenworth Times*, July 24, 1867; "Mail Items," *Harrisburg Telegraph*, July 27, 1867; "Mail Gleanings," *Raleigh Weekly Progress*, August 1, 1867; "General Items," *Montana Post*, September 7, 1867.

37. "Story of a Boston Merchant," *Boston Herald*, March 14, 1876; *Newberry Weekly Herald*, March 15, 1876.

38. "Sargent's Lawyer Has Posthumous Letter," *Wyoming Tribune*, September 16, 1913.

39. Benjamin Rush, *An Inquiry into the Effects of Ardent Spirits upon the Human Body and Mind* (Boston: James Loring, 1823), 8–11, 13; Kathleen R. Merikangas and Cheryl Shea Gelernter, "Comorbidity for Alcoholism and Depression," *Psychiatric Clinics* 13 (1990): 613–32.

40. Augustus Hemenway to Mary Hemenway, September 14, 1874, Folder 12, Box 1, HFP.

41. Augustus Hemenway to Mary Hemenway, September 14, 1874, HFP.

42. "Sargent's Lawyer Has Posthumous Letter," *Wyoming Tribune*, September 16, 1913; Inventory, Book List, Estate of John D. Sargent, Lincoln County District Court, Probate, Docket 1, 21, August 4, 1913, Wyoming State Archives (WSA).

One of the books Jack had in his possession when he died was about how to write an autobiography.

43. "Sargent's Lawyer Has Posthumous Letter," *Wyoming Tribune*, September 16, 1913; Estate of William H. Hemenway, Record Book 27, 206, Washington County Probate Records (WCPR), Washington County Courthouse, Machias, Maine.

44. "A Successful Merchant: Remarkable Career of Augustus Hemenway of Boston," *Rochester Democrat and Chronicle*, June 21, 1876; Jacob Bigelow to Mary Hemenway, August 4, 1862, Folder 6, Box 8, HFP.

45. Philip T. Coolidge, *History of the Maine Woods* (Bangor ME: Furbush-Roberts, 1963), 123–35; Jeremy S. Wilson, "Nineteenth-Century Lumber Surveys for Bangor, Maine: Implications for Pre-European Forest Settlement Characteristics in Northern and Eastern Maine," *Journal of Forestry* 3 (2005): 219.

46. J. H. Bailey to the Trustees of Augustus Hemenway Sr., August 21, 1878, Folder 8, Box 5, HFP; "What People Talk About: August 5, 1878," *Boston Globe*, June 20, 1902; Andrew Gyory, *Closing the Gate: Race, Politics, and the Chinese Exclusion Act* (Chapel Hill: University of North Carolina Press, 1998), 111; Denis Kearny, *Speeches of Denis Kearney, Labor Champion* (New York: Jesse Haney, 1878).

47. Bailey to Trustees, Folder 8, Box 5, HFP; *Jeremiah Drummond, Maine Society of the Sons of the Revolution* (Portland ME: Lefavor Tower, 1903), 108.

48. J. H. Bailey to the Trustees of Augustus Hemenway, October 18, 1880, and November 13, 1880, Folder 8, Box 5, HFP; Drisko, *Narrative of the Town of Machias*, 237; "Finding Aid," 4, Ames Family Papers, Special Collections, Raymond H. Folder Library, University of Maine; Sheryl Cannady, "Library of Congress Adds 25 Films to National Film Registry," Library of Congress Press Release, December 17, 2002, https://www.loc.gov/item/prn-02-176/.

49. J. H. Bailey to the Trustees of Augustus Hemenway, October 18, 1880, HFP.

50. City of Hampden ME, "Archeological Phase 1 Survey: Turtle Head Cove, Parker and Stearns Sawmill Sites," by Rick Morris, March 2012, 5–6, https://www.hampdenmaine.gov/vertical/sites/%7B1FCAF0C4-5C5E-476D-A92E-1BED5B1F9E05%7D/uploads/Turtle_Head_Cove_Sawmill_Sites_sm.pdf; Defebaugh, *History of the Lumber Industry of America*, 29; Roy E. Appleman, "Timber Empire from the Public Domain," *Mississippi Valley Historical Review* 26 (1939): 194.

51. Andrew M. Barton, Alan S. White, and Charles B. Cogbill, *The Changing Nature of the Maine Woods* (Lebanon: University of New Hampshire Press, 2012), 125–26; James L. Huffman, "A History of Forest Policy in the United States," *Environmental Law* 8 (1978): 239–80; Lloyd C. Irland, "Maine's Forest Area, 1600–1995: Review of Available Estimates," in *Miscellaneous*

Publication 736 (Augusta: Agricultural & Forest Experiment Station, University of Maine, 1998), available at University of Maine Digital Commons, accessed April 1, 2020, https://digitalcommons.library.umaine.edu/cgi /viewcontent.cgi?article=1033&context=aes_miscpubs.

52. "Blueberry Fire," *Lewiston Journal*, June 28, 1885; Coolidge, *Maine Woods*, 131–32.

53. For these statistics I am deeply indebted to Jereme M. Frank of the Maine Forest Service, who put together a spread sheet for me, using forest inventory data from October 2019 that has been made available by the U.S. Forest Service. Frank used the U.S. Forest Service's "EVALIDator" tool to compile these statistics. It is available here: https://apps.fs.usda.gov/Evalidator /evalidator.jsp (accessed November 7, 2023).

54. Douglas M. Griffith and Carol L. Alerich, *Forest Statistics for Maine, 1995* (Radnor PA: U.S. Department of Agriculture, Forest Service, 1996), 1; "Lumber and Other Personal Property at Machias Maine," Executors' Inventory—Augustus Hemenway's Estate, filed June 8, 1877, Index Number 9274, Folder 11, Box 3, HFP.

55. J. H. Bailey to the Trustees of Augustus Hemenway, June 17 and June 19, 1880, Folder 8, Box 5, HFP.

56. "A Successful Merchant," *St. Louis Post-Dispatch*, June 22, 1876.

3. The Fourth Estate

1. Elizabeth M. Harris, *Printing Presses in the Graphic Arts Collection: Printing, Embossing, Stamping, and Duplicating Devices* (Washington DC: Smithsonian Institute, 1996), 24–25; Richard L. Bushman, *Joseph Smith and the Beginnings of Mormonism* (Urbana: University of Illinois Press, 1984), 107–13; Frank E. Comparato, *Chronicles of Genius and Folly: R. Hoe and Company and the Printing Press as a Service to Democracy* (Culver City CA: Labrynthos, 1979), 4–9, 16–17.

2. Rob Banham, "The Industrialization of the Book, 1800–1970," in *A Companion to the History of the Book*, ed. Simon Eliot and Jonathan Rose (Malden MA: Wiley Blackwell, 2007), 276; James T. Hamilton, *All the News That's Fit to Sell: How the Market Transforms Information into News* (Princeton NJ: Princeton University Press, 2004), 48.

3. Hamilton, *All the News*, 48; Michael Schudson, *Discovering the News: A Social History of Newspapers* (New York: Basic Books, 1978), 13–14; James L. Crouthamel and Andrew Jackson, "James Gordon Bennett, the *New York Herald*, and the Development of Sensationalism," *New York History* 54 (July 1973): 298; Harold A. Williams, *The Baltimore Sun: 1837–1987* (Baltimore MD: Johns Hopkins University Press, 1987), 35; "The New York Newspaper Press," *New*

York Herald, August 16, 1837; W. J. Gordon, "The Newspaper Printing Press of To-Day," *Leisure Hour* 39 (February 1890): 264.

4. Thomas Carlyle, *On Heroes, Hero-Worship, and the Heroic in History*, ed. David R. Sorenson and Brent E. Kinser (New Haven CT: Yale University Press, [1841] 2013), 139; Charles Mitchell, *Newspaper Press Directory* (London: C. Mitchell, 1857), 30; Tim Ross, Amanda Andrews, and Katherine Rushton, "News of the World Loses Adverts over Milly Dowler Scandal," *Telegraph*, July 5, 2011. Carlyle's idea, which he attributed to the eighteenth-century parliamentarian Edmund Burke, was that the British government consisted of the House of Lords, the House of Commons, and the Monarch—and then "yonder [in the press gallery] sits the fourth estate, more powerful than them all."

5. Schudson, *Discovering the News*, 14–31; Paul Starr, *The Creation of the Media: Political Origins of Modern Communications* (New York: Basic Books, 2004), 89–90, 131–36.

6. S. Elizabeth Bird and Robert W. Dardenne, "Myth, Chronicle, and Story: Exploring the Narrative Quality of News," in *Social Meanings of News*, ed. Dan Berkowitz (Thousand Oaks CA: Sage, 1997), 333–50; James Gordon Bennett, "Sketches of My Own Life," *New York Herald*, October 11, 1836.

7. Crouthamel and Jackson, "James Gordon Bennett," 299–300; *New York Herald*, May 11–15, 19, 22, and 28; June 17; July 11, 13, and 15; and August 4, 1835; Christina Snyder, *Great Crossings: Indians, Settlers, and Slaves in the Age of Jackson* (New York: Oxford University Press, 2017), 3–4, 8–9, 51–53.

8. Schudson, *Discovering the News*, 23.

9. See, for example, "The Result of the Great Whig Meeting," *New York Herald*, November 1, 1843; and "Great Clay Mass Meeting at Castle Garden," *New York Herald*, February 18, 1848.

10. Schudson, *Discovering the News*, 25; Jim Bach, "The Big Shift in Newspaper Revenue," *American Journalism Review*, February 27, 2014; Kristen Senz, "Why Paywalls Aren't Always the Answer for Newspapers," *Forbes*, August 1, 2019; Ken Doctor, "The Newsonomics of Crossover," Nieman Lab, March 2, 2012, https://www.niemanlab.org/2012/03/the-newsonomics-of-crossover/.

11. George S. Merriam, *Life and Times of Samuel Bowles* (New York: Century, 1885), 69–70; Gerald Ensley, "The Democrat, a Name—and Newspaper—with a Lot of History," *Tallahassee Democrat*, March 19, 2014; "Our Story: About the *Herald-Whig* and QMI," *Quincy Herald-Whig*, April 11, 2020; Michael F. Holt, *The Rise and Fall of the American Whig Party: Jacksonian Politics and the Onset of the Civil War* (New York: Oxford University Press, 1999); Ray Allen Billington, *The Protestant Crusade: A Story of the Origins of American Nativism* (New York: Macmillan, 1938), 408–9.

12. "A Pioneer in Journalism," *New York Times*, December 22, 1889. Abell's quote can be found in Brantz Mayer, *Baltimore: Past and Present, with Biographical Sketches of Its Representative Men* (Baltimore MD: Richardson & Bennett, 1871), 158.

13. Susan Strasser, *Satisfaction Guaranteed: The Making of the American Mass Market* (Washington DC: Smithsonian Institute, 1989), 18.

14. Schudson, *Discovering the News*, 19–21, 55–56; Starr, *Creation of the Media*, 135–36; Sanny Danna, "Classified Advertising," in *The Advertising Age Encyclopedia of Advertising*, ed. John McDonough and Karen Egolf (New York: Routledge, 2002), 325; Robert Seamans and Feng Zhu, "Responses to Entry in Multi-Sided Markets: The Impact of Craiglist on Local Papers," *Management Science* 60 (February 2014): 476–93; Janet Farrell Brodie, *Contraception and Abortion in Nineteenth-Century America* (Ithaca NY: Cornell University Press, 1995), 87; "Disgraceful Advertisements," *Boston Medical and Surgical Journal* 44 (May 1851): 265, reprinted in Andrea Tone, *Controlling Reproduction: An American History* (Lanham MD: SR, 1997), 100–101; Rebecca Onion, "19th-Century Classified Ads for Abortifacients and Contraceptives," *Slate*, August 6, 2014.

15. Frederic Hudson, *Journalism in the United States, from 1690–1872* (New York: Harper & Brothers, 1873), 460–61. The quotes all come from Hudson's reprinting of various editorials.

16. Hudson, *Journalism in the United States*, 461; Schudson, *Discovering the News*, 18–19, 55–56.

17. "State Laws Governing Early Voting," National Conference of State Legislatures, August 2, 2019, https://www.ncsl.org/research/elections-and-campaigns/early-voting-in-state-elections.aspx; Wendy Underhill, "Voter Identification Requirements/Voter ID Laws," National Conference of State Legislatures, February 24, 2020, https://www.ncsl.org/research/elections-and-campaigns/voter-id.aspx; "Felon Voting Rights," National Conference of State Legislatures, October 14, 2019, https://www.ncsl.org/research/elections-and-campaigns/felon-voting-rights.aspx; Jim Rutenberg, Jo Becker, Eric Lipton, Maggie Haberman, Jonathan Martin, Mathew Rosenberg, and Michael S. Schmidt, "77 Days: Trump's Campaign to Subvert the Election," *New York Times*, February 1, 2021.

18. Jacob Katz Cogan, "The Look Within: Property, Capacity, and Suffrage in Nineteenth-Century America," *Yale Law Review* 107 (November 1997): 476–77.

19. Arthur W. Bromage, "Literacy and the Electorate," *American Political Science Review* 24 (November 1930): 946–47; Alexis de Tocqueville, "On Relations between Associations and Newspapers," in *Democracy in America* (1835),

trans. Arthur Goldhammer (New York: Literary Classics of the United States, 2004), 2:600.

20. Bromage, "Literacy and the Electorate," 946.

21. John Logan, "Schooling and the Promotion of Literacy in Nineteenth-Century Ireland," *Irish Economic and Social History* 21 (1994): 76; Kevin Kenny, ed., *New Directions in Irish-American History* (Madison: University of Wisconsin Press, 2003), 5.

22. Stanley A. Renshon, *Allowing Non-Citizens to Vote in the United States: Why Not?* (Washington DC: Center for Immigration Studies, 2008), 7; Jamin B. Raskin, "Legal Aliens, Local Citizens: The Historical, Constitutional, and Theoretical Meaning of Alien Suffrage," *University of Pennsylvania Law Review* 141 (April 1993): 1391–470; Gerald M. Rosberg, "Aliens and Equal Protection: Why Not the Right to Vote?" *Michigan Law Review* 75 (April–May 1977): 1092–93; Stanley L. Engerman and Kenneth L. Sockoloff, "The Evolution of Suffrage Institutions in the New World," *Journal of Economic History* 65 (December 2005): 898; Chilton Williamson, *American Suffrage: From Property to Democracy, 1760–1860* (Princeton NJ: Princeton University Press, 1960), vii–iii; Bromage, "Literacy and the Electorate," 948–53; Thomas J. Misa, *A Nation of Steel: The Making of Modern America, 1865–1925* (Baltimore MD: Johns Hopkins University Press, 1995), 1–44.

23. Stephen D. Tucker, *History of R. Hoe & Company, 1834–1885* (Worcester MA: American Antiquarian Society, 1972); "Richard March Hoe," in *Appleton's Cyclopaedia of American Biography*, ed. J. G. Wilson and J. Fiske (New York: Appletons, 1892), 225–26.

24. Hamilton, *All the News*, 48; D. J. R. Bruckner, "Yelling 'Stop the Presses!' Didn't Happen Overnight," *New York Times*, November 20, 1995.

25. J. David Hacker, "A Census-Based Count of the Civil War Dead," *Civil War History* 57 (December 2011): 307–48; Guy Gugliotta, "New Estimate Raises Civil War Death Toll," *New York Times*, April 2, 2012.

26. Hazel Dicken-Garcia, *Journalistic Standards in Nineteenth-Century America* (Madison: University of Wisconsin Press, 1989), 56.

27. Hamilton, *All the News*, 49; David Mindich, "Edwin M. Stanton, the Inverted Pyramid, and Information Control," in *The Civil War and the Press*, ed. David B. Sachsman, S. Kitrell Rushing, and Debra Ridden van Tuyll (New Brunswick NJ: Transaction, 2000), 179–208. Although most of the AP's writers were employed by papers in New York, many southern publishers accepted articles from the AP, because they were written in a nonpartisan manner. Southern papers did eventually organize their own version of the AP, called the Press Association of the Confederate States of America, but the move was more about the South's desire to define its independence from the North

than it was about any perceived bias in the AP's reporting. See Ford Risley, "Wartime News over Southern Wires: The Confederate Press Association," in *Words and War: The Civil War and American Journalism*, ed. David B. Sachman, S. Kitrell Rushing, and Roy Morris Jr. (Indianapolis: Purdue University Press, 2008), 149–64.

28. Hamilton, *All the News*, 53.

29. Diana Tweed, Susan E. M. Selke, Donatien-Pascal Kamden, and David Shires, *Cartons, Crates, and Corrugated Board: Handbook of Paper and Wood Packaging Technology* (Lancaster PA: DEStech, 2015), 37–39; Strasser, *Satisfaction Guaranteed*, 31–32, 89–90; William Cronon, *Nature's Metropolis: Chicago and the Great West* (New York: W. W. Norton, 1991), 235–46; Drew Gilpin Faust, *This Republic of Suffering: Death and the American Civil War* (New York: Knopf, 2008), 92.

30. Strasser, *Satisfaction Guaranteed*, 4–5; Cronon, *Nature's Metropolis*, 235; Louis Franklin Swift and Arthur Van Vlissingen, *Yankee of the Yards: The Biography of Gustavus Franklin Swift* (Chicago: A. W. Shaw, 1927), 69.

31. Strasser, *Satisfaction Guaranteed*, 91; James B. Twitchell, *Twenty Ads That Shook the World* (New York: Three Rivers, 2000), 2. Since the end of the twentieth century, the typical American has been seeing three thousand to five thousand advertisements every single day.

32. Strasser, *Satisfaction Guaranteed*, 44–55, 163–202; Twitchell, *Twenty Ads*, 42; T. J. Jackson Lears, "From Salvation to Self-Realization: Advertising and the Therapeutic Roots of Consumer Culture, 1880–1930," *Advertising and Society Review* 1 (2000), doi:10.1353/asr.2000.0009; Mark Pendergast, *For God, Country, and Coca-Cola: The Definitive History of the Great American Soft Drink and the Company that Makes It* (New York: Basic Books, 1993), 101–3.

33. Schudson, *Discovering the News*, 93; Hamilton, *All the News*, 53.

34. W. Joseph Campbell, "Story of the Most Famous Seven Words in U.S. Journalism," BBC News, February 10, 2012.

35. John Tresch, "Extra! Extra! Poe Invents Science Fiction," in *The Cambridge Companion to Edgar Allen Poe*, ed. Kevin J. Hayes (New York: Cambridge, 2002), 113–32; W. Joseph Campbell, *Getting It Wrong: Debunking the Greatest Myths in American Journalism* (Berkeley: University of California Press, 2017), 9–25.

36. Daniel J. Boorstin, *The Image: A Guide to Pseudo Events in America* (New York: Atheneum, 1962), 11; "The Road to Ujiji," *New York Herald*, August 10, 1872.

37. Alice Gregory, "Nellie Bly's Lessons in Writing What You Want To," *New Yorker*, May 14, 2014; Karen Roggenkamp, *Narrating the News: New Journalism*

and *Literary Genre in Late Nineteenth-Century American Newspapers and Fiction* (Kent OH: Kent State University Press, 2005), 25–27.

38. "Experts Shed Light on David Livingstone Massacre Diary," BBC News, November 1, 2011, https://www.bbc.com/news/uk-scotland-edinburgh-east -fife-15536564.

39. Daniel Liebowitz and Charles Pearson, *The Last Expedition: Stanley's Mad Journey through the Congo* (New York: W. W. Norton, 2005); Martin Dugard, *Into Africa: The Epic Adventures of Stanley and Livingstone* (New York: Broadway, 2004), 308–9; Brooke Kroeger, *Nellie Bly: Daredevil, Reporter, Feminist* (New York: Random House, 1994), 96–98.

40. Schudson, *Discovering the News*, 68, 144–45, 212–13; Jack Shafer, "How the Byline Beast Was Born," Reuters, July 6, 2012.

41. Schudson, *Discovering the News*, 73; Keith Newlan, ed. *Theodore Dreiser Encyclopedia* (Westport CT: Greenwood, 2003), 63, 248; Karen Roggenkamp, "Jack London, War, and the Journalism That Acts," in *The Oxford Companion to Jack London*, ed. Jay Williams (New York: Oxford University Press, 2017), 129–43; James A. Jaap, "'Paul's Case' and Pittsburgh: Industry and Art in the Great Manufacturing Town," in *Willa Cather and the Arts*, ed. Guy J. Reynolds (Lincoln: University of Nebraska Press, 2020), 125–51.

42. Theodore Dreiser, *A History of Myself: Newspaper Days* (New York: Horace Liveright, 1922), 467, 483–85.

43. Edwin L. Shuman, *Steps into Journalism* (Evanston IL: Correspondence School of Journalism, 1894), 66.

44. Shuman, *Steps*, 122–23; Dreiser, *Newspaper Days*, 52.

45. Shuman, *Steps*, 122–23; "Mrs. McGibney Again Protests by Letter," *New York World*, September 23, 1899; John Brainard MacHarg, "Diary of a Trip through the Park in 1908," 52, Item 49, Box 2, Collection 430, File No. 917.87, Yellowstone Heritage and Research Center (YHRC); "John D. Sargent Insane," *Washington (DC) Evening Star*, December 27, 1899; "United States Census, 1870," Machias ME, Washington County, enumerated June 21, 1870, 2, Microfilm Publication M593, Record Group 29, National Archives and Records Administration (NARA); "Miscellaneous," *Leavenworth Times*, July 24, 1867; "Mail Items," *Harrisburg Telegraph*, July 27, 1867; "Mail Gleanings," *Raleigh Weekly Progress*, August 1, 1867; "General Items," *Montana Post*, September 7, 1867; "The Wealth of Boston," *New York Herald*, August 24, 1870.

46. "A Woman's Ready Dagger," *New York Times*, August 27, 1889; Dominick Mazzagetti, *The Jersey Shore: The Past, Present, and Future of a National Treasure* (New Brunswick NJ: Rutgers University Press, 2018), 67, 69–71; Cindy Sondik Aron, *Working at Play: A History of Vacations in the United States* (New York: Oxford University Press, 1999), 45–68.

47. "A Woman's Ready Dagger"; Nellie Bly, "Mrs. Eva Hamilton's Story," *New York World*, October 9, 1889.

48. "Cross-Examination of Evangeline L. Hamilton," in *Supreme Court, General Term, First Department: In the Matter of Proving the Last Will and Testament of Robert Ray Hamilton, Deceased, as a Will of Real and Personal Property, Case on Appeal* (New York: Evening Post Job Printing Office, 1893), 328–29; "Hamilton Tells of His Relations with Eva," *Brooklyn Daily Eagle*, September 7, 1889; "Mrs. Robert Ray Hamilton a Prisoner in Atlantic City," *New York Evening World*, August 27, 1889.

49. "A Woman's Ready Dagger"; "Mrs. Robert Ray Hamilton a Prisoner," *New York Evening World*, August 27, 1889; "Punishment Should Be Speedy," *New York Evening World*, November 7, 1889. Examples of articles that used the term "she-devil" include "She-Devils," *Buffalo Weekly Express*, July 18, 1890; "National Divorce Laws," *York Gazette*, February 20, 1889; "Wheeler and Collier," *Scranton Tribune*, October 17, 1889; "The Programme," *Pittsburgh Dispatch*, September 15, 1889; and Clement Scott, "Our Omnibus Box," *The Theater: A Monthly Review the Drama, Music, and the Fine Arts* 5 (January–June, 1885): 41.

50. "A Woman's Ready Dagger"; "Mrs. Robert Ray Hamilton a Prisoner."

51. "A Mad Infatuation," *New York Times*, August 28, 1889; "Hamilton's Syren," *New York Evening World*, August 28, 1889; "Mrs. Robert Ray Hamilton a Prisoner"; "More of the Woman's History," *Buffalo Evening News*, August 30, 1889; Christine V. Baird, "Neighborhood Snapshot: Waverly," *Newark Star-Ledger*, April 10, 2008.

52. "Fiction Outdone: Full Story of the Downfall of Robert Ray Hamilton," *Chattanooga Daily Times*, September 19, 1889, *Independence Weekly Star and Kansan*, November 8, 1889, *St. Joseph Weekly Gazette*, October 10, 1889, and *Montpelier Argus and Patriot*, October 2, 1889; "Testimony of Mrs. Alice Steele, January 12th, 1891," in *Supreme Court, General Term, First Department: In the Matter of Proving the Last Will and Testament of Robert Ray Hamilton, Deceased, as a Will of Real and Personal Property, Case on Appeal* (New York: Evening Post Job Printing House, 1893), 22.

53. "Guilty Mrs. Hamilton," *Atlanta Constitution*, September 20, 1889; "Telegraphic Summary, Etc.," *Baltimore Sun*, September 20, 1889.

54. "Mrs. Eva Hamilton's Story," *New York World*, October 9, 1889.

55. "Mrs. Eva Hamilton's Story"; "Record of Climatological Observations," National Oceanic and Atmospheric Administration, Atlantic City, Marina NJ, October 8, 1889, https://www.ncdc.noaa.gov/cdo-web/quickdata.

56. "Eva Ray Hamilton Dead," *Baltimore Sun*, December 7, 1904; "Eva Hamilton Dead," *Passaic Daily News*, December 7, 1904; "Passes from Earth without a Single Mourner," *San Francisco Call*, December 7, 1904.

57. "Mrs. Eva Hamilton's Story"; "Eva Ray Hamilton," *Salt Lake City Herald*, October 10, 1889; "United States Census, 1870," Colley Township PA, Sullivan County, enumerated July 14, 1870, 6, Microfilm Publication M593, Record Group 29, NARA. In its initial reporting, the *New York Times* described Eva as "a blonde, with large expressive eyes of gray." Papers in the United Kingdom also felt compelled to describe Eva as a "blonde woman whose beautiful form was writhing in a furious passion." See "Mrs. Hamilton in Prison," *New York Times*, August 31, 1889; and "Shocking Tragedy in High Life," *Blackburn Weekly Standard and Express*, August 31, 1889.

58. "Mrs. Eva Hamilton's Story."

59. "Mrs. Eva Hamilton's Story"; James Fisher, *Historical Dictionary of American Theater: Beginnings* (New York: Rowan & Littlefield, 2015), 172.

60. "Mrs. Eva Hamilton's Story."

61. "Mrs. Eva Hamilton's Story."

62. Charles Thomas Davis, *The Manufacture of Paper: Description of the Various Processes for the Fabrication, Coloring, and Finishing of Every Kind of Paper* (Philadelphia: Henry Carey Bairds, 1886), 57–59; Kitti Canepi, Becky Ryder, Michelle Sitko, and Catherine Weng, "Managing Microforms in the Digital Age," American Library Association, August 16, 2013, http://www.ala.org /alcts/resources/collect/serials/microforms.

63. "Mrs. Eva Hamilton's Story."

64. "Eva Ray Hamilton," *Salt Lake City Herald*, October 19, 1889.

4. Charity Begins at Home

1. John T. Morse Jr., "Memoir of Oliver Wendell Holmes, DCL," *Proceedings of the Massachusetts Historical Society* 11 (1897): 51; Winthrop Sargent, *Early Sargents of New England* (Boston: n.p., 1922), 46–47; William Richard Cutter, *Genealogical and Personal Memoirs Relating to the Families of Boston and Eastern Massachusetts* (New York: Lewis Historical Publishing, 1908), 1207; Henry Cabot Lodge, *Early Memories* (New York: Scribner's, 1913), 208.

2. Sargent, *Early Sargents*, 88; Larry Witham, *A City upon a Hill: How Sermons Changed the Course of American History* (New York: Harper One, 2007), 1–6; John Winthrop, "A Modell of Christian Charity" (1630), in *Collections of the Massachusetts Historical Society*, 3rd series (Boston: Charles C. Little & James Brown, 1838), 7:31–48; Ronald Reagan, "Election Eve Address: A Vision for America," November 3, 1980, and "Farewell Address to the Nation," January 11, 1989, Presidential Library and Museum Archives, https://www

.reaganlibrary.gov/11-3-80 and https://www.reaganlibrary.gov/research
/speeches/011189i.

3. Sargent, *Early Sargents*, 42; Pauline Maier, "The Pope at Harvard: The Dudleian Lectures, Anti-Catholicism, and the Politics of Protestantism," *Proceedings of the Massachusetts Historical Society* 97 (1985): 16–41; Heather
Gray, "Cushwa Center Director to Present Harvard's Dudleian Lecture Next
Week," Cushwa Center for the Study of American Catholicism, October 23,
2015, https://cushwa.nd.edu/news/kathleen-sprows-cummings-to-present
-harvards-dudleian-lecture-next-week/.

4. Sheila L. Skemp, *First Lady of Letters: Judith Sargent Murray and the Struggle for
Female Independence* (Philadelphia: University of Pennsylvania Press, 2009);
Richard C. Davis, *Encyclopedia of American Forest and Conservation History*
(New York: Macmillan, 1983), 2:783; John Daugherty, *A Place Called Jack-
son Hole: The Historic Resource Study of Grant Teton National Park* (Moose WY:
Grand Teton Natural History Association, 1999), 115; Lynn Cullen, *Mrs. Poe:
A Novel* (New York: Gallery, 2014); John May, *Poe and Fanny: A Novel* (Chapel
Hill NC: Plume, 2005); Evan Charteris, *John Sargent* (New York: Scribner's,
1927); Sargent, *Early Sargents of New England*, 31; "Sargent Portrait of Cornelius Vanderbilt II Acquired, Returned to the Breakers," Preservation Society
of Newport County, July 7, 2009, https://www.newportmansions.org/press
/press-releases/sargent-portrait-of-cornelius-vanderbilt-ii-acquired
-returned-to-the-breakers.

5. Mary S. Smith to John Dudley Sargent, February 22, 1889, and W. Otis Sargent to "Uncle," December 21, 1877, Jackson Hole Historical Society and
Museum (JHHSM), 2002.532.001 and 2002.533.001.

6. Mary S. Smith to John Dudley Sargent, February 22, 1889, and W. Otis Sargent to "Uncle," December 21, 1877, JHHSM; "United States Census, 1850,"
Lubec ME, Washington County, enumerated August 6, 1850, 64; "United
States Census, 1880," Cambridge MA, Middlesex County, enumerated June
3, 1880, 208; Kenneth L. Diem, Lenoir L. Diem, and William C. Lawrence,
*A Tale of Dough Gods, Bear Grease, Cantaloupe, and Sucker Oil: Marymere/Pine-
tree/Mae-Lou/AMK Ranch* (Moran WY: National Parks Service, 1986), 4; Ignatius Sargent, "Colonel Paul Dudley Sargent of Sullivan, Maine, and Family,"
Bangor Historical Magazine 7 (1887): 125–31.

7. Mary S. Smith to John Dudley Sargent, February 22, 1889, JHHSM; "Epes Sargent Dixwell," *Cambridge Chronicle*, December 9, 1899; Lodge, *Early Memories*, 81–82; G. Edward White, *Justice Oliver Wendell Holmes: Law and Inner Self*
(New York: Oxford University Press, 1993), 23–24, 103.

8. Mary S. Sargent to John Dudley Sargent, February 22, 1889, JHHSM; "Sargent's Lawyer Has Posthumous Letter," *Wyoming Tribune*, September 16, 1913;

Will of John Dudley Sargent, August 30, 1899, Estate of John D. Sargent, Lincoln County District Court, Probate, Docket 1, 21, August 4, 1913, Wyoming State Archives (wsa); *Great Register of the County of Sacramento, 1866–1898*, fhl Roll No. 977988, California State Library, Sacramento.

9. Mary S. Sargent to John Dudley Sargent, February 22, 1889, jhhsm; "United States Census, 1870," Machias me, Washington County, enumerated June 21, 1870, 3, Microfilm Publication m593, Record Group 29, National Archives and Records Administration (nara); Verba Lawrence, "Scrapbook," Folder Sargent, Box 7, Collection No. 400007, Kenneth L. Diem and Lenore L. Diem Papers (Diem), American Heritage Center (ahc), University of Wyoming; Birth Certificate for John Dudley Sargent, December 16, 1861, Certified by Martha A. Bagley, Clerk of Machias, Maine, May 25, 1978, jhhsm, 2002.536.001.

10. National Archives Project, Works Projects Administration, *Ship Registers and Enrollments of Machias, Maine, 1780–1930* (Rockland me: National Archives Project, 1942), 557, 653, 692, 710, 854.

11. Sargent, "Colonel Paul Dudley Sargent," 125; Martha Sargent Eaton to Ella Davis, February 20, 1964, Folder Sargent, Box 7, Diem, ahc.

12. "United States Census, 1880," Machias me, Washington County, enumerated June 11, 1880, 23, Microfilm Publication t9, Record Group 29, nara; Henry C. Sargent, Maine Infantry, Company C, Sixth Regiment, Military Service Branch, 1440, General Notation R & P 551257, Card Nos. 13528315, 13528410, 13528504, 13528612, 13529836, 36363143, nara.

13. "United States Census, 1850," Bangor me, Penobscot County, enumerated August 30, 1850, 94, Microfilm Publication m432, Record Group 29, nara; "Sargent's Lawyer Has Posthumous Letter," *Wyoming Tribune*, September 16, 1913; Will of John D. Sargent and "Estate of John D. Sargent," Lincoln County District Court, Probate, Docket 1, 21, August 4, 1913, wsa.

14. "Sargent's Lawyer Has Posthumous Letter"; Henry C. Sargent and Alice B. Hemenway, July 18, 1861, "Marriages Registered in the City of Boston for the Year Eighteen Hundred and Sixty-One," *Massachusetts Vital Records, 1840–1911*, 66, New England Historic Genealogical Society (nehgs), Boston ma; *Machias Union*, July 23, 1861; Gouvenor Morris, *The History of a Volunteer Regiment, Being a Succinct Account of the Organization, Services, and Adventures of the Sixth Regiment New York Volunteers Infantry* (New York: Veteran Volunteer, 1891), 77, 128–29; "Sixth Regiment, N.Y.S.V., Wilson's Zouaves," *New York Sunday Mercury*, October 16, 1861.

15. "Sargent's Lawyer Has Posthumous Letter"; Will of John D. Sargent, Lincoln County District Court, Probate, Docket 1, wsa; *Great Register of the County of Sacramento, 1866–1898*, fhl Roll No. 977988, California State Library, Sac-

ramento; Edward Lansing Wells, "Notes on the Winter of 1861–1862 in the Pacific Northwest," *Northwest Science* 21 (1947): 76–81; Jan Null and Joelle Hulbert, "California Washed Away: The Great Flood of 1862," *Weatherwise* 60 (January 2007): 26–30; "United States Census, 1870," Omaha City NE, Douglas County, enumerated September 7, 1870, 43, Microfilm Publication M593, Record Group 29, NARA. Henry Clay Sargent had left California by 1870, when the U.S. Census listed him as a "locomotive builder" living in Omaha, Nebraska.

16. "Sargent's Lawyer Has Posthumous Letter"; Will of John D. Sargent, Lincoln County, Docket 1, WSA; Alice B. Sargent, née Hemenway, "Deaths Registered in the City of Boston for the Year Eighteen Hundred and Seventy-Four," *Massachusetts Vital Records, 1840–1911*, NEHGS; Fames S. Pula, "'A Passion for Humanity': Founding the New England Hospital for Women and Children," *Polish Review* 57 (Summer 2021): 67–82.

17. "Sargent's Lawyer Has Posthumous Letter"; "Estate of John D. Sargent," Lincoln County, Docket 1, WSA; "Will of Elizabeth E. Tileston, November 14th, 1987," *Essex County, Massachusetts, Probate Records and Indexes, 1638–1916*, vol. 599, 39, Essex County Courthouse, Salem MA; "United States Census, 1850," Bangor ME, Penobscot County, enumerated August 30, 1850, 94; Machias ME, Washington County, enumerated July 30, 1850, 57; and Lynn MA, Essex County, enumerated September 11, 1850, Microfilm Publication M432, Record Group 29, NARA.

18. "Sargent's Lawyer Has Posthumous Letter"; "Estate of John D. Sargent," Lincoln County, Docket 1, WSA; "United States Census, 1860," Machias ME, Washington County, enumerated July 16, 1860, 73, Microfilm Publication M653, Record Group 29, NARA; J. Howard Tileston and E. Estelle Leese, July 7, 1862, "Marriages Registered in the City of Lynn for the Year Eighteen Hundred and Sixty-Two," *Massachusetts Vital Records, 1840–1911*, NEHGS; Estate of William H. Hemenway, January 5, 1875, Probate Court, Washington County, Maine, Index 1, 366; J. Howard Tileston and Alice J. Rice, October 14, 1850, "Marriages in the Town of Barre," in *Massachusetts Vital and Town Records, 1620–1988* (Provo UT: Holbrook Research Institute, 1989); Guardianship and Probate Papers, Jonathan H. Tileston, December 2, 1860–April 3, 1894, in *Probate Records, 1648–1924: Massachusetts Probate Court (Middlesex County)* (Provo: Genealogical Society of Utah, 1964–67).

19. Estate of Augustus Hemenway Sr., September 11, 1875, Folder 10, Box 3, MHS 122, Hemenway Family Papers (HFP), Philips Library, Peabody Essex Museum, Rowley MA; John Adams Vinton, *Genealogical Record of the Descendants of John Upton of North Reading, Mass* (Bath ME: E. Upton & Son, 1874), 177; "Samuel C. Hemenway," in *Maine, Fayleen Hutton Cemetery Collection*,

ca. *1780–1990* (Salt Lake City UT: Family Search, 2016); "Jane M. Hemenway," Maine Vital Records, 1892–1907, 04333-0084, Roll 26, Maine State Archives, Augusta; Verba Lawrence, "Scrapbook," Folder Sargent, Box 7, Diem, AHC.

20. Estate of Augustus Hemenway, Folder 10, Box 3, HFP.

21. Augustus Hemenway to Mary Tileston, November 11, 1838, Folder 5, Box 1, HFP.

22. Augustus Hemenway to Mary Tileston, November 11, 1838, HFP.

23. Augustus Hemenway to Mary Hemenway, September 14, 1874, Folder 12, Box 1, HFP.

24. Augustus Hemenway to Mary Hemenway, October 28, 1873, and October 29, 1873, Folder 12, Box 1, HFP.

25. Augustus Hemenway to Mary Hemenway, June 1, 1874; October 15, 1874; November 12, 1874; December 22, 1874; and December 3, 1875, Folder 12, Box 1, HFP; James H. Horner to Charles P. Hemenway, June 22, 1876, Folder 9, Box 3, HFP.

26. M. A. Porter to Mary Hemenway, October 26, 1873, Folder 6, Box 8, HFP.

27. E. P. Peabody to Mary Hemenway, n.d., Folder 6, Box 8, HFP; Philip F. Gura, *American Transcendentalism: A History* (New York: Hill & Wang, 2007), 7–9, 130. For more on Sophia Peabody, see Megan Marshall, *The Peabody Sisters: Three Women Who Ignited American Romanticism* (New York: Houghton Mifflin, 2006).

28. M. O. Paine to Augustus Hemenway, October 19, 1873, Folder 6, Box 8, HFP.

29. Mary Hemenway to Augustus Hemenway Jr., August 2, 1875, Folder 7, Box 8, HFP; Inventory, Book List, Estate of John D. Sargent, Lincoln County District Court, Probate, Docket 1, 21, August 4, 1913, WSA; "Sargent's Lawyer Has Posthumous Letter."

30. S. Weir Mitchell, *Wear and Tear, or Hints for the Overworked* (Philadelphia: J. B. Lippincott, 1871), 7–8.

31. Cindy S. Aron, *Working at Play: A History of Vacations in the United States* (New York: Oxford University Press, 1999), 47; "Warning: Reading This on a Smartphone May Cause Anxiety, Researchers Say," *Los Angeles Times*, June 7, 2019; Larry D. Rosen, "The Anxiety Epidemic: Our Smartphones May Be a Major Cause," *Psychology Today*, June 18, 2017; S. Weir Mitchell, *Wear and Tear, or Hints for the Overworked* (Philadelphia: J. B. Lippincott, 1871), 15, 18.

32. Mitchell, *Wear and Tear*, 15–16, 19.

33. Clifford Putney, *Muscular Christianity: Manhood and Sports in Protestant American, 1880–1920* (Cambridge MA: Harvard University Press, 2001), 3, 1–22, 45, 52, 56, 73–98; Charles D. Cashdollar, *A Spiritual Home: Life in British and American Reformed Congregations, 1830–1915* (University Park: Penn State University Press, 2000), 118.

34. "Gymnastics," *Atlantic*, March 1861, 283; Putney, *Muscular Christianity*, 46; "Exchanges," *University of Michigan Chronicle* 20 (December 15, 1888): 119.

35. "Mr. Thomas Hughes and His Address," *Harvard Advocate Supplement* 10 (October 14, 1870): ii; Thomas Hughes, *Vacation Rambles* (New York: Macmillan, 1895), 176; Albert Mallard Barnes, "Harvard College, Class of 1871, Secretary's Report," Wisconsin Historical Society, Madison, 1x83HZ1871; "Gymnasium Facts," *Harvard Crimson*, March 18, 1908; Burt Feintuch and David H. Watters, *The Encyclopedia of New England: The Culture and History of a Region* (New Haven CT: Yale University Press, 2005), 282.

36. "Gymnasium Facts"; Aaron J. Miller, "The Highest Court in the Building," *Harvard Crimson*, February 11, 2016.

37. Charles Sprague Sargent, "The First Fifty Years of Arnold Arboretum," *Journal of Arnold Arboretum* 3 (1921): 127–71; Jarret Izzo, "The Place and the Maker: Frederick Law Olmsted and His Boston Parks," *Elements* 4 (Fall 2007): 57–68.

38. Michael Holleran, *Boston's "Changeful Times": Origins of Preservation and Planning in America* (Baltimore MD: Johns Hopkins University Press, 1998), 113; Sargent, *Early Sargents of New England*, 32; Ignatius Sargent of Daniel, November 2, 1765, and Ignatius Sargent of Ignatius, February 2, 1800, "Baptisms, Marriages, and Deaths from Gloucester Church Records, 1703–1835," in *Massachusetts Town and Vital Records*; Christopher Klein, *The Boston Harbor Islands* (Lanham MD: Rowan & Littlefield, 2020), ix.

39. Holleran, *Boston's "Changeful Times,"* 110–15; Betsy Mason, "How Boston Made Itself Bigger," *National Geographic*, June 13, 2017, https://www.nationalgeographic.com/news/2017/06/Boston-landfill-maps-history.

40. Frederick Law Olmsted, "Public Parks and the Enlargement of Towns" (1870), in *Civilizing Americans' Cities: Writings on City Landscapes*, ed. S. B. Sutton (New York: De Capo, 1997), 81; Frederick Law Olmsted and Calvert Vaux, "Preliminary Report to the Commissioners for Laying out a Park in Brooklyn" (1866), in *Landscape into Cityscape: Frederick Law Olmsted's Plans for a Greater New York*, ed. Albert Fein (Ithaca NY: Cornell University Press, 1968), 97–98; Frederick Law Olmsted, "Yosemite and the Mariposa Grove: A Preliminary Report" (1865), in *The Papers of Frederick Law Olmsted*, vol. 5, *The California Years, 1863–1865*, ed. Victoria Post Ranney (Baltimore MD: Johns Hopkins University Press, 1990), 502.

41. "Sargent's Lawyer Has Posthumous Letter."

42. "Augustus Hemenway," *Boston Globe*, May 26, 1931; William Souder, "How Two Women Ended the Deadly Feather Trade," *Smithsonian Magazine*, March 2013; Karen Leggett, "The Bird Ladies of Boston," *New York Times*, November 12, 1995.

43. "United States Census, 1880," Machias ME, Washington County, enumerated June 11, 1880, 23, Microfilm Publication T9, Record Group 29, NARA.

44. Patricia Nelson Limerick, *The Legacy of Conquest: The Unbroken Past of the American West* (New York: W. W. Norton, 1987), 58.

45. Limerick, *Legacy of Conquest*, 1–133. Examples of treaties the U.S. government made—and then broke—with Plains Indians in the 1850s and 1860s include the "Treaty with the Blackfeet," October 15, 1855, in *Indian Affairs: Laws and Treaties*, ed. Charles J. Kappler (Washington DC: Government Printing Office, 1904), 2:736–38; "Treaty with the Apache," July 1, 1852, Avalon Project, Lillian Goldman Law Library, Yale University, https://avalon .law.yale.edu/19th_century/apa1852.asp; "Treaty with the Comanche, Kiowa, and Apache," July 27, 1853, Lillian Goldman Law Library, Yale University, https://avalon.law.yale.edu/19th_century/cokiap53.asp; "Treaty with the Cheyenne, Apache, and Arapaho," October 17, 1865, Lillian Goldman Law Library, Yale University, https://avalon.law.yale.edu/19th_century/apchar65 .asp; and the "Fort Laramie Treaty of 1868," Lillian Goldman Law Library, Yale University, https://avalon.law.yale.edu/19th_century/nt001.asp.

46. Greg Bradsher, "How the West Was Settled: The 150-Year-Old Homestead Act Lured Americans Looking for a New Life and New Opportunities," *Prologue* 40 (Winter 2012): 26–35; Douglas W. Allen, "Homesteading and Property Rights; Or 'How the West Was Really Won,'" *Journal of Law and Economics* 36 (April 1991): 1–23; R. Douglas Hurt, *The Dust Bowl: An Agricultural and Social History* (Chicago: Nelson-Hall, 1981), 17–32.

47. Bradsher, "How the West Was Settled," 27.

48. "Resident Population and Apportionment of the U.S. House of Representatives, 1789–2000: Maine," U.S. Census Bureau, accessed June 20, 2020, https://www.census.gov/dmd/www/resapport/states/maine.pdf.

49. Andrea Constantine Hawkes, *The Same Great Struggle: The History of the Vickery Family of Unity, Maine, 1634–1997* (Gardiner ME: Tillbury House, 2003), 110–87; Wayne E. Reilly, "Migration West Caused Maine's Population to Stagnate," *Bangor Daily News*, December 8, 2012; "Waldo County Young Men," *Belfast Republican Journal*, October 16, 1884; "Our Home Folks in the South and West," *Belfast Republican Journal*, February 24, 1887; "Letter from Montana Territory," *Belfast Republican Journal*, May 29, 1881; "The Montanians," *Atlantic Monthly*, June 1898, 738.

50. "Sargent's Lawyer Has Posthumous Letter"; "Personal Notes" and "Inventory and Appraisement," Estate of John D. Sargent, Lincoln County District Court, Probate, Docket 1, 21, August 4, 1913, WSA; Pamela Sheffield to Lenore Diem, December 1, 1985, Folder Sargent, Box 7, Diem, AHC; "Deposition of D. C. Nowlin, January 21st, 1899, Supreme Court, New York County" and

Adelaide Crane Sargent to Leander Crane, August 17, 1896, in "Deposition of Leander Crane, January 28th, 1899, Supreme Court, New York County," both in Commissions and Depositions, CD-S-50, Record Room, County Clerk of New York County (CCNY).

51. Mary Sears, personal interview with Elizabeth Hayden, Summer 1955, Folder Sargent, Box 7, Diem, AHC; "Testimony of Gilbert M. Speir, Jr.," in *Supreme Court, General Term, First Department: In the Matter of Proving the Last Will and Testament of Robert Ray Hamilton, Deceased, as a Will of Real and Personal Property, Case on Appeal* (New York: Evening Post Job Printing Office, 1893), 248; John Dudley Sargent, "Best Camping Experience," JHHSM, 2002.0546.001; "Henry B. Tremaine, President of the Aeolian Company, Honored by World Wide Observance of International Tribute Week," *Musical Observer* 21 (January 1922): 57; "The Pianola in Furthest Australia," *Country Life in America: A Magazine for the Home-Maker in the Country* 18 (May 1910): 128.

52. "Designs on Kansas," *Kansas Agitator*, November 29, 1901; "The Man and the Job," *Victoria Daily Times*, December 23, 1908; "Horses and Remittance Men," *Ottawa Citizen*, August 21, 1900; L. D. Bruckart, "The Remittance Man," *San Francisco Call*, July 19, 1908; Monica Rico, *Nature's Noblemen: Transatlantic Masculinities in the Nineteenth-Century American West* (New Haven CT: Yale University Press, 2013), 45–82.

53. Mary Sears, interview with Elizabeth Hayden, Folder Sargent, Box 7, Diem, ACH; "Sargent's Lawyer Has Posthumous Letter."

54. Herbert H. Drake to Carl Cook, Esq., August 1, 1913, Estate of John D. Sargent, WSA; "Won't Disown Edith," *Boston Globe*, July 7, 1893; "Romance of Edith Drake," *Kansas City Journal*, October 31, 1897; Slim Lawrence, personal interview with Elizabeth Hayden, n.d., JHHSM, 2002.0114.021; Barbara Titus to Lenore Diem, September 12, 1978; Barbara Titus, personal interview with Lenore and Kenneth Diem, December 8 and 9, 1982; and Hilda Stadler to Verba Lawrence, March 31, 1956, all Folder Sargent, Box 7, Diem, AHC.

5. Off with Their Heads

1. Woodall's Publication Corporation, *Woodall's Frontier West/Great Plains & Mountain Region Campground Guide* (Elkhart IN: G&G Media Group, 2007), 736; *Tracking Trains in Cheyenne*, Cheyenne Convention and Visitors' Bureau pamphlet, Cheyenne WY, 2019; "Coal Production and Number of Mines by State and Mine Type, 2019 and 2018," U.S. Energy Information Administration, accessed January 27, 2021, https://www.eia.gov/coal/annual/pdf/table1.pdf; "Coal Production and Mining," Wyoming State Geological Survey, accessed January 27, 2021, https://www.wsgs.wyo.gov/energy/coal-production-mining.aspx.

2. Richard White, *Railroaded: The Transcontinentals and the Making of Modern America* (New York: W. W. Norton, 2011), 17–19; Tony Horowitz, "The Horrific Sand Creek Massacre Will Be Forgotten No More," *Smithsonian Magazine*, December 2014, 50–57; Gregory F. Michno, *Battle at Sand Creek* (El Segundo CA: Upton & Sons, 2004), 241.

3. John McPhee, *Annals of the Former World* (New York: Farrar, Straus & Giroux, 1981), 308–20; Steve Lickteig, "Home on the Range, Present at the Creation," *Morning Edition*, NPR, April 29, 2002, https://www.npr.org/templates/story/story.php?storyId=1142515.

4. John Wright, "Secretary Norton Gives Cheyenne Railroad Depot National Historic Landmark Designation," U.S. Department of the Interior, March 3, 2006, https://www.doi.gov/sites/doi.gov/files/archive/news/archive/06_News_Releases/060303.htm.

5. J. H. Beers, *Representative Men and Old Families of Southeastern Massachusetts* (Chicago: J. H. Beers, 1912), 28; Oakes Angier Ames, *Oakes Ames: A Memoir* (Cambridge MA: Riverside, 1884), 1–55.

6. White, *Railroaded*, 63–66; Heather Cox Richardson, *West from Appomattox: The Reconstruction of America after the Civil War* (New Haven CT: Yale University Press, 2007), 146–37; Stephen E. Ambrose, *Nothing Like It in the World: The Men Who Built the Transcontinental Railroad 1863–1869* (New York: Touchstone, 2000), 92–93; Roy Hoopes, "It Was Bad Last Time, Too: The Crédit Mobilier Scandal of 1872," *American Heritage*, February–March 1991, 49; John Debo Galloway, *The Transcontinental Railroad* (New York: Simmons Boardman, 1950), 206.

7. Hoopes, "Bad Last Time, Too"; "The King of Frauds," *New York Sun*, September 4, 1872; Robert B. Mitchell, "Run from the Shadows: How the First Modern Washington Scandal Enveloped James Garfield," *American History*, December 2020, 49–57.

8. Oakes Ames, "Crédit Mobiler Scandal," *San Francisco Daily Evening Bulletin*, September 26, 1872.

9. Hoopes, "Bad Last Time, Too"; Robert B. Mitchell, "Buying 'Friends in This Congress': The Smoking Gun That Triggered a Political Scandal," *Washington Post*, July 18, 2017; Linda Charlton, "From the 'Whiskey Ring' to 'Teapot Dome' and On," *New York Times*, May 1, 1973; Irwin F. Fredman, "The Presidential Follies," *American Heritage*, September–October 1987; Kevin Johnson and Ledyard King, "Justice Department Launches Inquiry of Senators Who Sold Large Chunks of Stock before Coronavirus Market Slide," *USA Today*, March 30, 2020; Associated Press, "As Coronavirus Ravaged U.S. Economy, Georgia Sen. Perdue Saw an Opportunity," *Los Angeles Times*, November 25, 2020; Associated Press, "Republicans Concede Their Losses in Georgia Senate Races," *Washington Post*, January 9, 2021.

10. Mitchell, "Run from the Shadows," 57; B. L. Wick, "John I. Blair and His Associates in Railway Building in Iowa," in *Annals of Iowa*, ed. Edgar R. Harlan (Des Moines: Historical Department of Iowa, 1913), 494; H. Clay Williams, *Encyclopedia of Massachusetts of the Nineteenth Century* (Boston: Metropolitan Publishing & Engraving, 1883), 66–82; Folders 10–11, Box 3, MH 122, Hemenway Family Papers (HFP), Philips Library, Peabody Essex Museum, Rowley MA; "Morris Gray & Another, Trustees, vs. Augustus Hemenway & Others, January 21st, 1916," in *Massachusetts Reports: Cases Argued and Determined in the Supreme Judicial Court of Massachusetts, February, 1916–May, 1916*, ed. Henry Walton Swift (Boston: Little, Brown, 1916), 293–97; Ethan Carr, "Eastern Design in a Western Landscape: Olmsted, Richardson, and the Ames Monument," *SiteLINES: A Journal of Place* 10 (Spring 2015): 19–21.

11. "Oakes Ames' Legacy," Oakes Ames Memorial Hall, accessed January 29, 2021, https://www.oakesameshall.org/; William E. Burns, *Science and Technology in World History* (Santa Barbara CA: ABC-CLIO, 2020), 504; Edward Sherwood Meade, "The Great American Railway Systems: The Chesapeake and Ohio," *Railway World*, October 22, 1904, 1207; Thomas Fleming, *Lincoln's Other Dream* (Boston: New Word City, 2017).

12. Loretta Fowler, "Arapaho and Cheyenne Perspectives: From the 1851 Treaty to the Sand Creek Massacre," *American Indian Quarterly* 39 (Fall 2015): 364–90; Dee Brown, *Bury My Heart at Wounded Knee: An Indian History of the American West* (New York: Holt, 1970), 67–102; Jerome A. Greene, *Washita, the Southern Cheyenne, and the U.S. Army* (Norman: University of Oklahoma Press, 2004), 27; Stan Hoig, *The Peace Chiefs of the Cheyenne* (Norman: University of Oklahoma Press, 1980), 61; Danielle Murphy, "Tribal Territories on Father DeSmet's Map for the Fort Laramie Treaty of 1851," WyoHistory, Wyoming State Historical Society, accessed January 31, 2021, https://www.wyohistory.org/sites/default/files/desmetmap2.jpg; Theda Perdue and Michael D. Greene, *The Cherokee Removal: A Brief History with Documents* (Boston: Bedford, 1995), 18–21.

13. Williams, *Encyclopedia of Massachusetts*, 77.

14. White, *Railroaded*, 305–14; Maury Klein, *The Life and Legend of Jay Gould* (Baltimore MD: Johns Hopkins University Press, 1986), 42–294. The Jay Gould quote has been used by many historians, all of whom place it in 1886. Some publications in Gould's own time also attributed the quote to him. The exact circumstances under which Gould made the claim are unclear, however, and some historians say he used the term "laboring class," rather than "working class." See, for example, Paul Avrich, *The Haymarket Tragedy* (Princeton NJ: Princeton University Press, 1984), 97; Nell Irvin Painter, *Standing at Armageddon: The United States, 1877–1919* (New York: W. W.

Norton, 1987), 33; Philip S. Foner, *History of the Labor Movement in the United States* (New York: International Publishers, 1975), 2:50; "Finding Ourselves Out," *The Eagle and the Serpent: A Journal of Egoistic Philosophy and Sociology*, February 12, 1893, 101.

15. Edwin G. Burrow and Mike Wallace, *Gotham: A History of New York City to 1898* (New York: Oxford University Press, 1998), 445; Ronald E. Shaw, *Canals for a Nation: The Canal Era in the United States, 1790–1860* (Lexington: University Press of Kentucky, 1990).

16. Tom Wolfe, *The Bonfire of the Vanities* (New York: Bantam, 1987), 236.

17. James J. Hill, *The National Cyclopaedia of American Biography* (New York: James T. White, 1906), 13:482; Edwin Lefèvre, *Reminiscences of a Stock Operator*, illus. ed. (Hoboken NJ: Wiley, [1923] 2005), 245; Edward J. Renehan Jr., *Commodore: The Life of Cornelius Vanderbilt* (New York: Basic Books, 2007), 264–65.

18. Lefèvre, *Reminiscences*, viii, 244–51; Matthew Hale Smith, *Twenty Years among the Bulls and Bears of Wall Street* (Hartford CT: J. B. Burr, 1871), 245–51; "The Convertible Bonds: How Jacob Little Manipulated Matters Years Ago," *New York Times*, February 23, 1882; Rafael Nam, "So What Is Short Selling? An Explainer," NPR, January 28, 2021, https://www.npr.org/2021/01/28/961619848/so-what-is-short-selling-an-explainer.

19. Hill, *National Cyclopaedia*, 482; "Private Bankers," *The Banker's Magazine and Statistical Registrar*, July 1864, 79; "Financial," *New York Sun*, August 15, 1887; "About Home," *Newport Daily News*, March 5, 1872; "Newport Cottages Ready," *New York Times*, June 16, 1879.

20. Charles Willing, "Interesting History of Red Cross Avenue," *Newport Mercury*, August 18, 1933; Manuel Gaytero, *A Guide to Narragansett Bay: Newport, Narragansett Pier, Block Island, Watch Hill, Rocky Point, Silver Spring, and All the Famous Resorts along the Shore* (Providence RI: J. A. & R. A. Reid, 1878), 74; Terrence Gavan, *The Barons of Newport* (Sarasota FL: Pineapple, 1998), 11; Joan Marter, ed., *The Grove Encyclopedia of American Art* (New York: Oxford University Press, 2011), 1:67; *Memorial Biographies of the New England Historic Genealogical Society* (Boston: New England Historic Genealogical Society, 1905), 6:419; Sean Flynn, "How Many People Visit the Cliffwalk Each Year," *Newport Daily News*, November 27, 2018.

21. "United States Census, 1880," Castleton NY, Richmond County, enumerated June 10, 1880, 29, Microfilm Publication T9, Record Group 29, National Archives and Records Administration (NARA); Ira K. Morris, *Morris' Memorial History of Staten Island, New York* (New York: Memorial, 1898), 1:104–8; James J. Hill, *The National Cyclopaedia of American Biography* (New York: James T. White, 1906), 13:482; Moses King, *King's Handbook of New York City* (New

York: Bartlett, 1892); *Notable New Yorkers, 1896–1899* (New York: Bartlett, 1899), 3–4, 214.

22. King, *Handbook*, 560; "Moses King Dead," *Boston Globe*, June 13, 1909; "Help Wanted—Females," *New York Times*, September 22, 1894.

23. King, *Handbook*, 290, 372, 401, 418, 550–51; Vincent Sheean, "Vincent Sheean on Oscar Hammerstein I," *Music Journal* 14 (October 1956): 30.

24. King, *Handbook*, 85, 131; "The Only Four Hundred. Ward M'Allister Gives Out the Official List," *New York Times*, February 16, 1892.

25. "United States Census, 1880," Castleton NY, Richmond County, enumerated June 10, 1880, 29, Microfilm Publication T9, Record Group 29, NARA; Hill, *National Cyclopaedia*, 482; "Died: MacAdam," *New York Times*, August 11, 1887; Richard Balls, "Surgeon's Report Reopens Debate on Tone," *Irish Times*, February 14, 1997.

26. Joshua J. Mark, "'A Planet of Light and Heat': Samuel Nielson and the Northern Star," *History Ireland* 23 (November–December 2015): 22–25; Tracey Tully and Stacey Stowe, "The Wealthy Flee Coronavirus. Vacation Towns Respond: Stay Away," *New York Times*, March 25, 2020; Justin Farrell, "Where the Very Rich Fly to Hide: Wyoming's Jackson Hole Has Become a Redoubt against the Coronavirus," *New York Times*, April 15, 2020; Gene Balk, "Coronavirus Flight: As the Affluent Head to Washington Vacation Homes, Some Year-Rounders Worry," *Seattle Times*, April 11, 2020; Fritz Hahn, "For the First Time, the Pistol Used to Kill Alexander Hamilton Is on Public View in D.C.," *Washington Post*, May 25, 2018.

27. "An Irish and Yankee Daredevil," *Los Angeles Times*, August 26, 1913. Any connection Edith may have had to Sir Francis Drake, the famous sixteenth-century English sea captain, could not have been "lineal," as that Francis Drake had no sons or daughters. The name "Sir Francis" was not uncommon, however, among families named "Drake" in the eighteenth and nineteenth centuries. Edith may have been directly descended from *a* Sir Francis Drake but not *the* Sir Francis Drake.

28. Edith Drake, "Twenty Minutes of Grace," *New York Evening World*, August 7, 1888.

29. "The Crab-Tree," in *Merry Songs and Ballads, Prior to the Year 1800*, ed. James A. Famer (New York: Privately Printed for Subscribers Only, 1896), 4:109; Gordon Williams, *A Dictionary of Sexual Language and Imagery in Shakespearean and Stuart Literature* (Highlands NJ: Athlone, 1994), 2:978.

30. Edith Sargent, "Planting a Garden," Jackson Hole Historical Society (JHHSM), 2002.530.002.

31. "All the Rage Now," *Leavenworth Times*, May 2, 1894; "Her Mind Effected," *St. Paul Globe*, February 21, 1904; "New Mystery Baffles Newport," *Buffalo Sunday Morning News*, December 4, 1904; "Banker's Daughter Becomes

Bohemian," *Salt Lake Telegram*, December 15, 1904; "Banker's Daughter Lives in Slums," *St. Paul Globe*, February 21, 1904; Inventory, Book List,
Estate of John D. Sargent, Lincoln County District Court, Probate, Docket 1,
21, August 4, 1913, Wyoming State Archives (wsa).

32. "Her Marriage Certificate," *New York Sun*, July 8, 1893; "Edith Drake's
Romance," *Buffalo Courier*, July 9, 1893; "She Is a Banker's Child," *New York
World*, July 6, 1893; "Francis Wilson, Manager: The Career of 'The Oolah' and
Its Coming Tour in the Country," *New York Times*, October 6, 1889.

33. John Dudley Sargent to Theodore Roosevelt (i.e., "The President"), November 1, 1906, Final Homestead Entry (fhe) Nos. 1024 and 1632, Letter No.
182354, 36428, Bureau of Land Management Field Office, Lander wy.

34. Edith Drake McGibney, "Cynical Plea for a Restless Man," *St. Louis Post-
Dispatch*, July 10, 1904.

35. Drake McGibney, "Cynical Plea for a Restless Man"; Janet Burns, "Mil-
lennials Are Having Less Sex than Other Generations," *Forbes*, August 16,
2016; Christopher Ingraham, "The Share of Americans Not Having Sex Has
Reached a Record High," *Washington Post*, March 29, 2019; Magdalene J.
Taylor, "Have More Sex, Please," *New York Times*, February 13, 2023.

36. McGibney, "Cynical Plea," *St. Louis Post-Dispatch*, July 10, 1904.

37. John D. Sargent and Edith A. Drake, Record No. 29513, Marriage Records,
Book 30, 53, Uinta County, wsa; "Rich Edith Not Too Young," *Boston Globe*,
July 5, 1893.

38. "United States Census, 1910," Manhattan ny, New York County, enumer-
ated May 6, 1910, 17b, Microfilm Publication t624, Record Group 29, nara;
"Edith's Certificate," *Portage (wi) Daily Democrat*, July 11, 1893; "Married
Good and Tight," *Boston Globe*, July 8, 1893.

39. "Edith's Certificate," *Portage Daily Democrat*, July 11, 1893.

40. "Married Good and Tight"; "A Banker's Daughter Missing," *Atlanta Constitu-
tion*, July 6, 1893; "Edith Drake's Lovers," *Boston Globe*, July 7, 1893; "All the
Rage Now"; "Miss Edith Drake Missing," *Indianapolis Journal*, July 6, 1893;
"Edith Plays Hide and Seek," *New York Evening World*, July 7, 1893.

41. "Her Secret Wedding," *New York Evening World*, July 11, 1893.

42. "She Is a Banker's Child."

43. "Her Secret Wedding."

44. "Edith Drake's Lovers."

45. "Edith Drake's Lovers"; Aaron Freundschuh, *The Courtesan and the Gigolo:
The Murders in the Rue Montaigne and the Dark Side of Empire in Nineteenth-
Century Paris* (Stanford ca: Stanford University Press, 2017), 155.

46. "Mystery of a Murder," *New York Herald*, March 26, 1887; G. Macé, *La Police
Parisienne: Le Service De La Sureté* (Paris: G. Charpentier, 1885); G. Macé, *My*

First Crime (London: Vizetelly, 1886); G. Macé, *My First Crime* (Chicago: M. A. Donohue, 1887); G. Macé, *My First Crime* (Chicago: Rand, McNally, 1887).

47. "Mystery of a Murder"; Freundschuh, *Courtesan and the Gigolo*, 76.

48. Freundschuh, *Courtesan and the Gigolo*, 5. It is no coincidence that the main character in Paul Schrader's film from 1980, *American Gigolo*, is named Julian.

49. Freundschuh, *Courtesan and the Gigolo*, 7, 106–15, 150.

50. Freundschuh, *Courtesan and the Gigolo*, 155–56; Georges Grison, *Le procès Pranzini: compte rendu complex des débats* (Paris: La Librairie Illustré, 1888), 10, 173, 260–61; "The Pranzini Trial: Peculiar Features of the Notorious Triple Murder," *Chicago Daily Inter Ocean*, July 31, 1887; "The Pranzini Trial," *San Francisco Daily Evening Bulletin*, August 5, 1887; "Old World News: Paris Gossip," *St. Louis Globe-Democrat*, July 10, 1887; "A French Trial," *Galveston Daily News*, July 28, 1887.

51. "The Pranzini Case," *New York Times*, July 28, 1887; "Fair Women His Prey," *St. Louis Post-Dispatch*, July 26, 1887; "Pranzini's Grand Dame Correspondent," *New York Times*, August 14, 1887.

52. Edwin L. Shuman, *Steps into Journalism* (Evanston IL: Correspondence School of Journalism, 1894), 52; "Don Juan No. 2," *New York Journal*, August 6, 1887, and *St. Paul Globe*, August 7, 1887.

53. "Miss Drake Had a Mercenary Lover," *St. Louis Globe-Democrat*, July 6, 1893; "United States Census, 1880," Castleton NY, Richmond County, enumerated June 10, 1880, 29, Microfilm Publication T9, Record Group 29, NARA; Grison, *Le procès Pranzini*, 10–11.

54. Grison, *Le procès Pranzini*, 11–12; "Don Juan No. 2"; Freundschuh, *Courtesan and the Gigolo*, 155.

55. Freundschuh, *Courtesan and the Gigolo*, 146; Grison, *Le procès Pranzini*, 259, 277.

56. Freundschuh, *Courtesan and the Gigolo*, 163.

57. "The Pranzini Scandal," *Philadelphia Times*, September 25, 1887; "Execution of Pranzini," *London Daily News*, September 1, 1887.

58. "His Head Off," *St. Louis Globe-Democrat*, August 31, 1887; "Execution of Pranzini," *London Daily News*, September 1, 1887; "Execution of Pranzini," *Glasgow (Scotland) Herald*, September 1, 1887. The *Globe-Democrat* story includes a copyright by James Gordon Bennet, indicating that the correspondent who wrote it worked for the *New York Herald*.

59. Freundschuh, *Courtesan and the Gigolo*, 181, 189; Huges Le Roux, *L'enfer parisien* (Paris: Victor-Havard, 1888), 378; *La Lanterne*, September 2, 1887; Ernest Renan, *Marcus Aurelius*, trans. William G. Hutchison (London: Walter Scott, 1903), 275. For more on the dissection of criminals' bodies in Europe and the United States, see John Knott, "Popular Attitudes to Death and Dis-

section in Early Nineteenth-Century Britain," *Labour History* 49 (November 1985): 1–18; Rachel E. Bennett, *Capital Punishment and the Criminal Corpse in Scotland, 1740–1834* (New York: Palgrave Macmillan, 2017); Michael Arntfield, *Gothic Forensics: Criminal Investigation Procedure in Victorian Horror and Mystery* (New York: Palgrave Macmillan, 2016); and Courtney E. Thompson, *An Organ of Murder: Crime, Violence, and Phrenology in Nineteenth-Century America* (New Brunswick NJ: Rutgers University Press, 2021).

60. Freundschuh, *Courtesan and the Gigolo*, 186; *Le Figaro*, September 14, 1887.

61. Freundschuh, *Courtesan and the Gigolo*, 186; "Town Talk from Paris," *New York Times*, September 25, 1887; *Gazette Anectdotique, Littéraire, Artistique et Bibliograhique* 18 (September 30, 1887): 186–87; "La peau de Pranzini," *La Justice*, September 22, 1887.

62. "Big Nose George Pleads Guilty," *Carbon County Journal*, September 18, 1880; "The Elk Mountain Murder," *Carbon County Journal*, December 18, 1880; "Big Nose George Forcibly Taken from the Jail and Hung to a Telegraph Pole," *Carbon County Journal*, March 26, 1881, and July 28, 1916; "The Last of Big Nosed George," *Laramie Republican*, December 21, 1920; Dena Lynn Winslow, "'They Lynched Jim Cullen': Story and Myth on the Northern Maine Frontier," in *Lynching beyond Dixie: American Mob Violence outside the South*, ed. Michael J. Pfeifer (Champaign: University of Illinois Press, 2013), 234; Lori Van Pelt, "Big Nose George: A Grisly Frontier Tale," WyoHistory, accessed February 14, 2021, https://www.wyohistory.org/encyclopedia/big-nose-george-grisly-frontier-tale; "Parrot's Pieces Reunited," *Billings (MT) Gazette*, October 31, 1995.

63. Van Pelt, "Big Nose George"; "Solution," *Le Figaro*, September 24, 1887; *La Croix*, September 23, 1887; Freundschuh, *Courtesan and the Gigolo*, 190–95; "The Cause of Grévy's Fall: From Lucy Hopper's Paris Letter," *San Francisco Daily Evening Bulletin*, January 8, 1888. The direct cause of Grévy's resignation was his son-in-law's involvement in a corruption scandal. That scandal was exposed, however, only because Marie-François Goron was hoping to distract the press from the skin scandal, which is why commentators at the time drew a connection between the skin scandal and Grévy's resignation.

64. "Army of the French," *Chicago Tribune*, September 25, 1887; "Pranzini Scandal"; "Town Talk from Paris"; "Purses from Pranzini's Skin," *Chicago Daily Inter Ocean*, September 23, 1887; "Purse of Murderer's Skin," *Raleigh News and Observer*, September 3, 1887; "A Reminiscence of Pranzini," *Denver Rocky Mountain News*, September 23, 1887; "Made Purses of Pranzini's Skin," *St. Louis Globe-Democrat*, September 23, 1887; "Edith Plays Hide and Seek"; "Edith Drake Still Missing," *New York Evening World*, July 6, 1893.

65. "She Is a Banker's Child"; "Romance of Edith Drake," *Kansas City Journal*, October 31, 1897; "Mrs. McGibney again Protests by Letter," *New York World*, September 23, 1899.

66. "Wants to Play Comedy," *Boston Globe*, August 5, 1896; "Would Shine as a Star," *New York World*, August 5, 1896; "Stars in Three Months," *New York World*, May 31, 1896; "Romance of Edith Drake"; "Edith Drake Insane," *Philadelphia Times*, October 25, 1897; "Banker's Daughter Is Insane," *Chicago Chronicle*, October 24, 1897.

67. King, *Handbook of Notable New Yorkers*, 73; Clark Bell, "Memorial Tributes: Hon. Charles Henry Truax, A.M., L.L.D.," *Medico Legal Journal* 28 (1910–11): 4; "Mrs. McGibney's Insanity," *New York Times*, October 24, 1897; "Banker's Child Insane," *New York World*, October 24, 1897.

68. J. Matthew Gallman, *America's Joan of Arc: The Life of Anna Elizabeth Dickinson* (New York: Oxford University Press, 2006), 182–83.

69. "Mrs. M'Gibney again Protests By Letter"; "United States Census, 1900," Middletown NY, Orange County, enumerated June 9, 1900, 9, Microfilm Publication T623, Record Group 29, NARA.

70. "Banker's Daughter Lives in Slums," *St. Paul Globe*, February 21, 1904; "Mrs. McGibney Getting Busy," *Brooklyn Times Union*, February 24, 1904; "Pathetic Career of a Banker's Daughter," *San Francisco Examiner*, February 28, 1904; "Lives over a Meat Market," *Boston Globe*, May 1, 1904; "New Mystery Baffles Newport," *Chicago Tribune*, November 13, 1904.

71. "Banker's Daughter Lives in Slums."

72. John D. Sargent and Edith Drake, Record No. 29513, Marriage Records, Book 30, 53, Uinta County, WSA; "1907–1913: H.H.D and B.S.," Estate of John D. Sargent, No. 21, March 26, 1915, Lincoln County, WSA.

6. The Cable Railway Grab

1. "Solitary and Gloomy," *New York Times*, September 2, 1889; N. E. Baylies to Robert Ray Hamilton, September 18, 1889, MS 513, Folder 6, Box 2, Ray Family Papers (RFP), New York Historical Society (NYHS); Lucius A. Edelblute, *The History of the Church of the Holy Apostles (Protestant Episcopal), 1844–1944* (New York: Lucius A. Edelblute, 1949), 114; Matthew A. Postal, *Guide to New York City Landmarks* (New York: John Wiley & Sons, 2008), 72.

2. "Testimony of Edson W. Burr," in *Supreme Court, General Term, First Department: In the Matter of Proving the Last Will and Testament of Robert Ray Hamilton, Deceased, as a Will of Real and Personal Property, Case on Appeal* (New York: Evening Post Job Printing Office, 1893), 16–17, 267; Charles Burr Todd, *A General History of the Burr Family: With a Genealogical Record from 1193–1891*

(New York: Knickerbocker, 1891), xvi, 1, 131, 134, 136, 143, 156, 278, 281, 283, 288, 296, 332–39, 393.

3. Henry McDaniels to Robert Ray Hamilton, August 22, 1889, Folder 2, Box 2, RFP, NYHS; "His Sad Story," *Brooklyn Daily Eagle*, September 7, 1889.

4. "Testimony of Evangeline L. Hamilton" and "Proponent's Exhibit R," in *Supreme Court*, 119, 144, 151, 308; "His Sad Story"; RRH: Deeds and Business Papers, Folder 5, Box 2, RFP, NYHS; "Still in Jail," *New York Evening World*, August 29, 1889.

5. Schuyler Hamilton Jr. to Ray Hamilton, August 7, 1889, and Schuyler Hamilton Sr. to Robert Ray Hamilton, August 23, 1889, Folder 6, Box 2, RFP; *New York Evening Post*, April 12, 1877; Cuyler Reynolds, *Genealogical and Family History of Southern New York and the Hudson River Valley* (New York: Lewis Historical Publishing, 1914), 3:1388.

6. Charlotte Hamilton to Schuyler Hamilton Sr., August 11, 1889, and Charlotte Hamilton to Louise F. P. Hamilton, August 19, 1889, Folder 6, Box 2, RFP.

7. Nathalie Baylies to Robert Ray Hamilton, August 27, 1889, and Gertrude Hamilton to Robert Ray Hamilton, August 27, 1889, Folder 6, Box 2, RFP.

8. "Gen. Hamilton Married," *Chicago Tribune*, July 15, 1886. Schuyler Sr.'s second marriage ended in divorce in 1893, after his much younger wife tried, unsuccessfully, to have him declared mentally incompetent. See "Another Hamilton Scandal," *Brooklyn Daily Eagle*, August 11, 1893.

9. Schuyler Hamilton Sr. to Robert Ray Hamilton, August 23, 1889, Folder 6, Box 2, RFP.

10. Terry Golway, *Machine Made: Tammany Hall and the Creation of Modern American Politics* (New York: W. W. Norton, 2014), 105–44; Richard White, *The Republic for Which It Stands: The United States during Reconstruction and the Gilded Age, 1865–1896* (New York: Oxford University Press, 2017), 172–212, 552–88.

11. "The Assembly," *Kingston Daily Freeman*, November 7, 1888; Edwin L. Godkin, *Unforeseen Tendencies of Democracy* (Boston: Houghton Mifflin, 1898), 140–41.

12. Godkin, *Unforeseen Tendencies*, 141; E. L. Godkin, "Commercial Immorality and Political Corruption," *North American Review* 107 (July 1868): 255. England's MPs were not paid until 1911, when an Act of Parliament made it possible for them to receive a salary of £400.

13. Godkin, "Commercial Immorality and Political Corruption," 255.

14. "From the State Capital—Special to the Eagle from the Nation," *Brooklyn Daily Eagle*, April 15, 1888.

15. Henry Adams to Henry Cabot Lodge, November 15, 1881, in Henry Adams, *Letters of Henry Adams, 1868–1891*, ed. Worthington Chauncy Ford (Boston: Houghton Mifflin, 1930), 331.

16. "Correspondence," *Tammany Times*, November 4, 1901; "Hamilton Fish, 86, Dies in Aiken, SC," *New York Times*, January 15, 1936; David McCullough, *Mornings on Horseback* (New York: Simon & Schuster, 1981), 283; "In and about the City: An Immoral System—Mr. Crosby and Mr. Hamilton Demand Municiple Reform," *New York Times*, December 3, 1887; "Dr. Howard Crosby Dead," *New York Times*, March 30, 1891; H. W. Brands, *TR: The Last Romantic* (New York: Basic Books, 1997), 182.

17. Karen Iacobbo and Michael Iacobbo, *Vegetarian America: A History* (Westport CT: Prager, 2004), 143–47; *Report and Proceedings of the Senate Committee Appointed to Investigate the Police Department of the City of New York* (Albany NY: James B. Lyon, 1895), 3:2920–21; *The Clerk's Manual of Rules, Forms, and Laws for the Regulation of Business in the Senate and Assembly of the State of New York* (Albany NY: Weed, Parsons, 1890), 1; William Carr, "Dental Law in this State," *Odontographic Journal* 9 (April–October, 1888): 85; "Minority Report, April 13th, 1888," in *Documents of the Assembly of the State of New York, One Hundred and Eleventh Session* (Albany NY: Troy, 1888), 1–4; "Governor Hill Is All Right: Nothing Wrong about the Purchase of that Piano and Billiard Table," *Brooklyn Daily Eagle*, April 13, 1888.

18. "In and about the City"; "Correspondence"; Gerald Kurland, *Seth Low: The Reformer in an Urban and Industrial Age* (New York: Twayne, 1971), 25–49; "The State Legislature," *New York Times*, May 8, 1888; "Killed by the Assembly: The Cable Railway Scheme Frustrated," *New York Tribune*, May 19, 1887; "A Secret Vote and the State Distribution of Ballots," *Brooklyn Daily Eagle*, January 18, 1888; "The Ballot Reform Bill," *New York Times*, May 24, 1888.

19. Eldon Cobb Evans, *A History of the Australian Ballot System in the United States* (Chicago: University of Chicago Press, 1917), 6–7; Jerrold G. Rusk, "The Effect of the Australian Ballot Reform on Split-Ticket Voting, 1876–1908," *American Political Science Review* 64 (December 1970): 1220; John F. Reynolds and Richard L. McCormick, "Outlawing 'Treachery': Split Tickets and Ballot Laws in New York and New Jersey, 1880–1910," *Journal of American History* 72 (March 1986): 835–58.

20. Evans, *Australian Ballot*, 17–18.

21. Evans, *Australian Ballot*, 19–20; Charles T. Saxton, "Changes in the Ballot Law," *North American Review* 152 (June 1891): 753–56.

22. Sam Roberts, "How Albany Weighs Down City Hall," *New York Times*, September 9, 2018, and "Albany to City: Drop Dead," *New York Times*, September 7, 2018, https://www.nytimes.com/2018/09/07/nyregion/albany-to-city-drop-dead.html.

23. Jesse McKinely, "Why Can't New York City Govern Its Own Affairs," *New York Times*, July 25, 2018; James A. Coon, *Adopting Local Laws in New York State*

(Albany: New York State Department of State, [1998] 2023), 1–7; Joseph L. Weiner, "Municipal Home Rule in New York," *Columbia Law Review* 37 (April 1937): 557–81; James D. Cole, "Constitutional Home Rule in New York: 'The Ghost' of Home Rule," *St. John's Law Review* 59 (Summer 1985): 713–49. Initially, in 1894, mayors were simply given veto power over any measures enacted by Albany that effected their cities and towns. This power was expanded in the early decades of the twentieth century to include the right to initiate measures without Albany's approval—again, provided the measures don't touch on a state interest.

24. Weiner, "Municipal Home Rule," 559.

25. Kurland, *Seth Low*, 26; Michael P. McCarthy, "The Philadelphia Consolidation of 1854: A Reappraisal," *Pennsylvania Magazine of History and Biography* 110 (October 1986): 531–48. Brooklyn and Philadelphia also folded a handful of villages—such and Williamsburg and Kensington—into their jurisdictions during these decades.

26. Roberts, "Albany to City"; Kruland, *Seth Low*, 25–49; "In and about the City."

27. Weiner, "Municipal Home Rule in New York," 559; Brian J. Cudahy, "Street Railways," in *The Encyclopedia of New York State*, ed. Peter Eisenstadt (Syracuse NY: Syracuse University Press, 2005), 1493; John Anderson Miller, *Fares, Please! A Population History of Trolleys, Horse-Cars, Street-Cars, Buses, Elevateds, and Subways* (New York: Dover, 1947), 17–34; Charles P. Shaw, *Cable Railways vs. Horse Railroads for Intramural Transit in the City of New York: Concluding Argument* (New York: Martin B. Brown, 1885), 5.

28. Joel A. Tarr, "Urban Pollution—Many Long Years Ago," *American Heritage*, October 1971, https://www.americanheritage.com/urban-pollution-many -long-years-ago.

29. Quoted in Ernest Freeberg, *A Traitor to His Species: Henry Bergh and the Birth of the Animal Rights Movement* (New York: Basic Books, 2020), 47–48.

30. Shaw, *Cable Railways*, 6–7, 3.

31. "A London Tramway," "A Cable Road in Lisbon," and "Extent of the Cable Road System," *American Railroad Journal* 58 (April 1884–March 1885): 280, 343, 375.

32. Miller, *Fares, Please*, 47–48; Charles Windsor Cheape, "The Evolution of Urban Public Transit, 1880–1912" (PhD diss., Brandeis University, 1976), 43–44.

33. "The Cable Railroad Swindle," *New York Times*, April 4, 1884; "Many Routes Laid Out. Corporations Preparing to Gridiron the City with Street Railroads," *New York Times*, May 9, 1884; "State and Vicinity," *Evening Telegraph*, August 3, 1885; "Public Notice, December 3rd, 1885," *New York Sun*, December 11, 1885; Robin Finn, "That's Some Key," *New York Times*, September 28, 2012.

34. Cheape, "Evolution of Urban Public Transit," 61–62; "A Defeat for the Cable Company," *New York Times*, September 28, 1884; "New York Cable Railway," *Buffalo Commercial*, December 17, 1886; "Three Important Bills," *New York Tribune*, May 16, 1887; "Railroad Schemes, Old and New," *New York Evening World*, January 23, 1888; "In Re: the New York Cable Railway Co., 109 N.Y. 32 (1888)," March 20, 1888, NY Court of Appeals, Harvard Law School Case Law Access Project, accessed September 1, 2020, https://cite.case.law/ny/109/32/.

35. "Killed by the Assembly," *New York Tribune*, May 19, 1887; James Blaine Walker, *Fifty Years of Rapid Transit, 1864–1917* (New York: Law Printing Company, 1918).

36. "Killed by the Assembly."

37. "A Mad Infatuation: The Story of a Career Wrecked by a Wicked Woman," *New York Times*, August 28, 1889.

38. "Mad Infatuation"; "That Cable Railway Bill," *New York Times*, February 22, 1889; City Reform Club, *Record of Assemblymen and Senators from the City of New York, Compiled from Official Sources by the City Reform Club* (New York: Burgoyne's, 1890), 47.

39. City Reform Club, *Record of Assemblymen*, 43–44, 47, 65–66; Edwin G. Burrows and Mike Wallace, *Gotham: A History of New York City to 1898* (New York: Oxford University Press, 1999), 1002, 1019; "The Cantor Law Attacked: The Final Efforts of the Cable Company," *New York Tribune*, April 8, 1887.

40. Theodore Roosevelt, "Phases of State Legislation," in *Essays on Practical Politics* (New York: G. P. Putnam's Sons, 1888), 34; Richard Welling, "Theodore Roosevelt at Harvard: Some Personal Reminiscences," *Outlook* 126 (September–December 1920): 368; Joshua David Hawley, *Theodore Roosevelt: Preacher of Righteousness* (New Haven CT: Yale University Press, 2008), 52.

41. City Reform Club, *What Are You Going to Do about It? Third Annual Record of Assemblymen and Senators of the City of New York in the State Legislature* (New York: Burgoyne's, 1888), 61; City Reform Club, *Record of Assemblymen*, 47.

42. "Political Odds and Ends," *New York Times*, August 2, 1889; "Mad Infatuation."

43. "Now a Dime Museum Freak," *Chicago Tribune*, September 30, 1889; "Globe Museum: Advertisement," *New York Evening World*, October 9, 1889; "A Leap from the Bridge," *New York Times*, July 24, 1886; "Steve Brodie's Funeral," *New York Times*, February 7, 1901; Jasmine K. Williams, "Steve Brodie—Daredevil or Hoaxter," *New York Post*, November 5, 2007.

44. "Mrs. Robert Ray Hamilton a Prisoner at Atlantic City," *New York Evening World*, August 27, 1889.

45. "A Woman's Ready Dagger," *New York Times*, August 27, 1889.

46. "Mrs. Robert Ray Hamilton a Prisoner."

47. "Mrs. Robert Ray Hamilton a Prisoner."

48. "Mrs. Robert Ray Hamilton a Prisoner."

49. "Mrs. Robert Ray Hamilton a Prisoner."

50. "Mrs. Robert Ray Hamilton a Prisoner."

51. "Mrs. Robert Ray Hamilton a Prisoner."

52. "Mrs. Robert Ray Hamilton a Prisoner"; "In a Jersey Jail," *Philadelphia Times*, August 28, 1889; Viola L. Hutchinson, *The Origin of New Jersey Place Names* (Trenton: New Jersey Public Library Commission, 1945), 15.

53. "Murdered by His Wife," *Decatur Herald and Review*, August 27, 1889; "Held without Bail," *Nashville Daily American*, August 28, 1889; "Drinking Hard," *Newton Daily Republican*, August 30, 1889; "Mrs. Hamilton," *Sacramento Record-Union*, August 31, 1889; "A Deep and Dark Conspiracy," *Kansas City Star*, September 4, 1889; "The Hamilton Case," *Nebraska State Journal*, September 7, 1889; "He Was Her Dupe," *Muscatine Journal*, September 4, 1889; "By Telegraph," *Wisconsin State Journal*, August 27, 1889; "A Woman's Career," *Salt Lake Herald*, August 29, 1889; "The Hamilton Scandal," *El Paso Times*, September 4, 1889; "Hamilton Comes to His Senses," *New Orleans Times-Democrat*, September 6, 1889; "Robert Ray Hamilton Rescued," *Raleigh News-Observer*, September 6, 1889; "More Conclusive Evidence," *Bismarck Weekly Tribune*, September 13, 1889.

54. "Our New York Letter," *Melbourne Age*, November 2, 1889; Bill Shaffer, *The Scandalous Hamiltons* (New York: Kensington, 2022), 3.

55. Elizabeth Rupp to Robert Ray Hamilton, October 6, 1889, Folder 8, Box 2, RFP.

56. Charles A. Peabody to Robert Ray Hamilton, August 28, 1889, and Casimir deR. Moore to Robert Ray Hamilton, September 5, 1889, Folder 8, Box 2, RFP; "Ex-Judge Peabody Married," *New York Times*, February 4, 1881; Biographical Directory Company, *Biographical Directory of the State of New York, 1900* (New York: Park Row, 1900), 320; Thomas G. Evans, *Genealogical Record of the Saint Nicholas Society* (New York: Saint Nicholas Society, 1902), 42.

57. "Woman's Ready Dagger"; Ira Davenport to Robert Ray Hamilton, August 28, 1889, Folder 8, Box 2, RFP; Henry Hall, *America's Successful Men of Affairs* (New York: New York Tribune, 1896), 2:227–28. Davenport had left his position in the House of Representatives a few months earlier.

58. Fordham Morris to Robert Ray Hamilton, August 28, 1889, Folder 8, Box 2, RFP; "Report of the Committee of Privileges and Elections on the Contested Seat of Ambrose H. Purdy, Claimed by Fordham Morris, February 8, 1878," in *Documents of the Assembly of the State of New York—One Hundred First Session*, no. 52 (New York: Jerome B. Parmenter, 1878), 1–3.

59. Frank Hiscock to Robert Ray Hamilton, August 30, 1889, Folder 8, Box 2, RFP; "Ex-Senator Hiscock Dies in 80th Year," *New York Times*, June 19, 1914.

60. Brian Cowan, "Histories of Celebrity in Post-Revolutionary England," *Historical Social Research* 32 (2019): 84; "Celebrity," Oxford English Dictionary Online, accessed November 13, 2021, https://www.oed.com/oed2 /00035303; Miss Mulock [a.k.a. Dinah Maria Mulock], *The Ogilvies* (London: Macmillan, [1849] 1875), 22.

61. John F. Roberts to Robert Ray Hamilton, August 28, 1889, Folder 8, Box 2, RFP.

62. John F. Roberts to Robert Ray Hamilton, August 28, 1889, RFP.

63. Alice Lonsborough to Robert Ray Hamilton, August 1889, Folder 9, Box 2, RFP.

64. Lonsborough to RRH and E. H. DeaKyne to Robert Ray Hamilton, September 9, 1889, Folder 9, Box 2, RFP; "Laid to Rest," *Bridewater Courier-News*, June 9, 1938.

65. Mary J. Webster to Robert Ray Hamilton, September 30, 1889, Folder 9, Box 2, RFP.

66. Jack E. Davis, *The Gulf: The Making of an American Sea* (New York: W. W. Norton, 2017), 190–91, 207; Linton Weeks, "Hats Off to the Women Who Saved the Birds," NPR, June 15, 2015, https://www.npr.org/sections/npr -history-dept/2015/07/15/422860307/hats-off-to-women-who-saved-the -birds.

67. Mary J. Webster to Robert Ray Hamilton, September 30, 1889, Folder 9, Box 2, RFP.

68. Mary J. Webster to Robert Ray Hamilton, September 30, 1889, RFP.

69. "Your Unknown Ardent Admirer" to Robert Ray Hamilton, September 4, 1889, Folder 9, Box 2, RFP.

70. Malissa Hamilton Beitman to Robert Ray Hamilton, August 31, 1889, Folder 9, Box 2, RFP.

71. Madame Renee E. Roi to Robert Ray Hamilton, September 1, 1889, Folder 9, Box 2, RFP.

72. These letters do not have names or dates. They can be found in Folders 10 and 13, Box 2, RFP.

73. Folders 10 and 13, Box 2, RFP.

74. Folder 10, Box 2, RFP. Much has been written on Dwight L. Moody. One particularly good book is Bruce J. Evensen's *God's Man for the Gilded Age: D. L. Moody and the Rise of Mass Evangelism* (New York: Oxford University Press, 2003).

75. Sarah Nash to Robert Ray Hamilton, n.d., Folder 10, Box 2, RFP.

76. Sarah Crawford to Robert Ray Hamilton, September 29, 1889, Folder 9, Box 2, RFP.

77. Margaret E. Schuyler to Robert Ray Hamilton, August 29, 1889, and Mrs. John C. Livingston to Robert Ray Hamilton, September 30, 1889, Folder 8, Box 2, RFP; Mrs., G. Webster to Robert Ray Hamilton, n.d., Folder 9, Box 2, RFP.

78. "A Friend" to Robert Ray Hamilton, August 31, 1889, Folder 9, Box 2, RFP.

79. "A Friend" to Robert Ray Hamilton, August 31, 1889, RFP.

80. "A Friend" to Robert Ray Hamilton, August 31, 1889, RFP.

7. Baby Waifs

1. *Senate Investigation, 1895: Report of the Select Committee of the Senator of New Jersey Appointed February 13, 1895, to Inquire into the Charges of Extravagance in Furnishing the State House, and Certain Other Charges Touching the Conduct of Public Officials, Etc.* (Trenton NJ: MacCrellish & Quigley, 1895), xxvi–vii, 723–54; "Local Politics," *Jersey City News*, October 24, 1889; William E. Sackett, *New Jersey's First Citizens* (Paterson NJ: J. J. Scannell, 1917), 242–43; "Guilty Mrs. Hamilton," *Atlanta Constitution*, September 20, 1889; "Telegraphic Summary, Etc.," *Baltimore Sun*, September 20, 1889; "It Was Ray Hamilton," *New York Sun*, October 15, 1891.

2. "Mrs. Hamilton Answers," *Sunbury (PA) Northumberland County Democrat*, January 3, 1890; "A Bogus Baby," *Brooklyn Daily Eagle*, September 4, 1889; "Conspiracy Exposed," *Indianapolis Journal*, September 4, 1889.

3. "Hamilton's Syren," *New York World*, August 28, 1889; "Mrs. Hamilton in Jail," *New York Tribune*, August 28, 1899; "In a Jersey Jail," *Philadelphia Times*, August 28, 1889; "A Most Unsavory Crowd," *Chicago Tribune*, August 30, 1889; "United States Census, 1850," Manhattan NY, New York County, enumerated August 28, 1850, 289, Microfilm Publication M432, Record Group 29, National Archives and Records Administration (NARA); "United States Census, 1870," Albany NY, Albany County, enumerated September 1, 1870, 138, Microfilm Publication M593, Record Group 29, NARA; "United States Census, 1880," Philadelphia PA, Philadelphia County, enumerated June 5, 1880, 506, Microfilm Publication T9, Record Group 29, NARA.

4. "Most Unsavory Crowd"; "Mrs. Robert Ray Hamilton a Prisoner at Atlantic City," *New York Evening World*, August 27, 1889; "Death of Major Joshua Dryden," *Baltimore Sun*, February 17, 1879.

5. Lin-Manuel Miranda, Bill Sherman, and Alex Lacamoire, "Who Lives, Who Dies, Who Tells Your Story," *Hamilton*, by Lin-Manuel Miranda, 2015, https://genius.com/Original-broadway-cast-of-hamilton-who-lives-who -dies-who-tells-your-story-lyrics; "Guide to the Records of Graham Windham, 1804–2011," MS 2916, New York Historical Society Museum and Library (NYHS), New York.

6. Julie Miller, *Abandoned: Foundlings in Nineteenth-Century New York City* (New

York: New York University Press, 2008), 85; "Domestic Economy," *National Advocate*, June 6, 1820.

7. Miller, *Abandoned*, 7, 57, 95.

8. William P. Letchworth, "The Removal of Children from Almshouses in the State of New York," in *Proceedings of the National Conference of Charities and Correction*, ed. Isabel C. Barrows (Boston: George H. Ellis, 1894), 132–36; Job Lewis Smith, "Hindrances to the Successful Treatment of the Diseases of Infancy and Childhood," *Transactions of the New York State Medical Association* 13 (1896): 95; "Infant Hospital," in *Eighth Annual Report of the Commissioners of Public Charities and Correction, New York, for the Year 1967* (Albany NY: Van Benthuysen & Sons, 1868), 24; Robert P. Gaynes, *Germ Theory: Medical Pioneers in Infectious Diseases* (Washington DC: ASM, 2011), 143–234.

9. Miller, *Abandoned*, 57, 86, 131.

10. Elizabeth Rupp to E. R. Vollmer, September 24, 1889, MS 513, Folder 8, Box 2, Ray Family Papers (RFP), NYHS.

11. Miller, *Abandoned*, 117–24.

12. "Murder of the Innocents," *New York Tribune*, February 5, 1859.

13. Miller, *Abandoned*, 118–19; "Defense of the Governors," *New York Tribune*, February 9, 1859.

14. Nellie Bly, "What Becomes of Babies," *New York World*, November 6, 1887.

15. Bly, "What Becomes of Babies."

16. Bly, "What Becomes of Babies."

17. Bly, "What Becomes of Babies."

18. Bly, "What Becomes of Babies."

19. Bly, "What Becomes of Babies."

20. Bly, "What Becomes of Babies"; Regina Morantz, "Feminism, Professionalism, and Germs: The Thought of Mary Putnam Jacobi and Elizabeth Blackwell," *American Quarterly* 34 (1982): 461–78; C. J. Whitby, "Rheumatic Arthritis and Electrical Baths," *British Medical Journal* 2 (July 1854): 103; John Saunders, "Considering the Alternatives: Or, Who Is the Medicine Man?" in *Medical Humanities Companion: Treatment*, ed. Pekka Louhiala, Iona Heath, and John Saunders (New York: Radcliffe, 2014), 102; Chris Rowthorn, *Japan* (Franklin TN: Lonely Planet, 2000), 400.

21. Charlotte G. Borst and Kathleen W. Jones, "As Patients and Healers: The History of Women and Medicine," *OAH Magazine of History* 19 (September 2005): 23–26; Michael Thomson, "Women, Medicine, and Abortion in the Nineteenth Century," *Feminist Legal Studies* 3 (1995): 159–83; Leslie J. Reagan, *When Abortion Was a Crime: Women, Medicine, and Law in the United States, 1867–1973* (Berkeley: University of California Press, 1997); Janet Farrell Brodie, *Contraception and Abortion in Nineteenth-Century America* (Ithaca

NY: Cornell University Press, 1997); Nicola Beisel and Tamara Kay, "Abortion, Race, and Gender in Nineteenth-Century America," *American Sociological Review* 69 (August 2004): 498–518; Jennifer Wright, *Madame Restell: The Life, Death, and Resurrection of New York's Most Fabulous, Fearless, and Infamous Abortionist* (New York: Hatchette, 2023).

22. Bly, "What Becomes of Babies."

23. "A Villainous Conspiracy," *New York Times*, September 4, 1889; "Bogus Baby"; "Testimony of William M. Kemp," in *Supreme Court, General Term, First Department: In the Matter of Proving the Last Will and Testament of Robert Ray Hamilton, Deceased, as a Will of Real and Personal Property, Case on Appeal* (New York: Evening Post Printing Office, 1893), 33–35.

24. "Opening Statement of Root and Clark," in *Supreme Court, General Term*, 97; "His Sad Story," *Brooklyn Daily Eagle*, September 7, 1889.

25. "Atlantic City's Scandal," *Scranton Republican*, August 30, 1889; "A Caged Tigress," *Buffalo Express*, August 30, 1889; "The Hamilton Scandal," *Buffalo Courier*, August 30, 1889; "Nurse Donnelly Better," *Rochester Democrat and Chronicle*, August 30, 1889; "A Friend" to Robert Ray Hamilton, August 31, 1889, Folder 8, Box 2, RFP.

26. "The Evidence Produced in Reading," clipping from "A Reading Paper," and unsigned telegraph from Reading PA, September 5, 1889, Folders 9 and 14, Box 2, RFP.

27. "Evidence Produced in Reading," RFP.

28. "Lumber King Is Claimed by Death," *Scranton Republican*, September 18, 1920; "Mary B. Jennings Is Called by Death; Born in Towanda," *Sayre (PA) Evening Times*, November 3, 1947.

29. C. H. Jennings to Robert Ray Hamilton, September 9, 1889, Folder 9, Box 2, RFP.

30. "A Rascally Gang," undated clipping from the *New York Herald*, Folder 9, Box 2, RFP; "Casts of the Siren's Thralls," *New York Herald*, September 5, 1889.

31. C. H. Jenning to Robert Ray Hamilton, September 9, 1889, Folder 9, Box 2, RFP.

32. "She Confesses Her Sin," *San Francisco Examiner*, October 9, 1889; "Mrs. Hamilton Weeps," *Philadelphia Inquirer*, September 19, 1889.

33. "United States Census, 1900," Colley Township PA, Sullivan County, enumerated June 7, 1900, 10, Microfilm Publication T623, Record Group 29, NARA.

34. "Bogus Baby"; "Villainous Conspiracy"; "Not Hamilton's Child," *New York Tribune*, September 4, 1889; "In the Toils," *New York Evening World*, September 4, 1889; "Swindled by a Siren," *St. Paul Globe*, September 4, 1889; "Testimony of Alice Steele," in *Supreme Court, General Term, First Department: In the Matter of Proving the Last Will and Testament of Robert Ray Hamilton, Deceased*, 22; "Fiction Outdone: Full Story of the Downfall of Robert Ray Hamilton," *Chattanooga Daily Times*, September 19, 1889.

35. "Ethel Parsons, No. 592892, Death Certificate 1757, Soundex P628," in *Register of New York City Death Records*, microfilm (Salt Lake City: Genealogical Society of Utah, 2006).

36. "Bogus Baby"; "Villainous Conspiracy"; "Not Hamilton's Child"; "In the Toils"; "Testimony of Charles E. Gilbert," in *In Court of Appeals from Supreme Court, Saratoga County, James I. Wakefield v. William G. Fargo and John McB. Davidson* (New York: William J. Read, 1881), 67.

37. "Bogus Baby"; "Villainous Conspiracy."

38. "Testimony of Royal Wells Amidon" and "Testimony of Julia Evers," in *Supreme Court, General Term*, 58–59, 68.

39. "Bogus Baby"; "Robert R. Hamilton: He Deserts Forever the Woman Who Deceived Him," *Salt Lake City Herald*, September 6, 1889.

40. "Bogus Baby"; "Villainous Conspiracy"; "Not Hamilton's Child"; "Hamilton's Syren"; "In the Toils."

41. "Swindled by a Siren"; Jonathan Green, *The Vulgar Tongue: Green's History of Slang* (New York: Oxford University Press, 2015), 189–90; "Hamilton on the Stand," *Fort Worth Daily Gazette*, September 7, 1889; "Robert R. Hamilton," *Salt Lake City Herald*, September 6, 1889.

42. Patrick Bunyon, *All around the Town: Amazing Manhattan Facts and Curiosities* (New York: Fordham University Press, 2011), 105–7; Terry Williams and Trevor B. Milton, *The Con Men: Hustling in New York City* (New York: Columbia University Press, 2015), 114; James Brady Thayer, "The Presumption of Innocence in Criminal Cases," *Yale Law Review* 6 (March 1897): 185–212; François Quintard-Morénas, "The Presumption of Innocence in the French and Anglo-American Legal Traditions," *American Journal of Comparative Law* 58 (Winter 2010): 107–49.

43. Charles Dickens, *American Notes for General Circulation* (London: Chapman & Hall, 1850), 63; Jerome Meckier, *Innocent Abroad: Charles Dickens's American Engagements* (Lexington: University Press of Kentucky, 2014).

44. "His Sad Story," *Brooklyn Daily Eagle*, September 7, 1889.

45. "His Sad Story"; "Eva Mann Hilton," *St. Louis Post-Dispatch*, September 17, 1893; Nellie Bly, "Jolly at the French Ball," *New York World*, February 10, 1889; Timothy J. Gilfoyle, *City of Eros: New York City, Prostitution, and the Commercialization of Sex, 1790–1920* (New York: W. W. Norton, 1992), 323–26, 234.

46. "His Sad Story."

47. "A Mad Infatuation," *New York Times*, August 28, 1889; "His Sad Story"; "First District, Police Court," in *Corporation of the City of New York: Communication from the Comptroller, Transmitting the Financial Estimates, or Budget for the Year 1868* (New York: E. Jones, 1868), 127; "Ignorant of the Game: Assistant Dis-

trict Attorney Jerome's Luck with His First Case," *New York Times*, February 3, 1888; "City and Suburban News," *New York Times*, November 23, 1889.

48. "His Sad Story."

49. "Ray's Story," *New York Evening World*, September 6, 1889; "His Sad Story"; "Plotters Held," *New York Evening World*, September 7, 1889; "A Woman's Ready Dagger," *New York Times*, August 27, 1889.

50. "His Sad Story"; John H. Wigmore, "The History of the Hearsay Rule," *Harvard Law Review* 17 (May 1904): 437–58.

51. "His Sad Story."

52. George W. Crosby to Robert Ray Hamilton, October 7, 1889, Folder 11, Box 2, RFP.

53. "In Defence [*sic*] of the Woman Who Wronged Him," *New York Herald*, September 19, 1889; "Mrs. Hamilton on Trial," *New York Times*, September 19, 1889; "In Self Defense," *Philadelphia Times*, September 19, 1889.

54. "In Defence"; "Will Sue for Divorce from Eva," *Philadelphia Inquirer*, October 3, 1889; "Hamilton Wants a Divorce," *Los Angeles Times*, October 4, 1889; "Hamilton Sues for Divorce," *Omaha Daily Bee*, October 4, 1889; "Mrs. Hamilton Files Her Answer," *Rochester Democrat and Chronicle*, December 28, 1889; "Willing to Pay Eva's Lawyer," *New York Sun*, April 1, 1890.

55. "Mad Infatuation."

56. *Catalogue of Officers and Graduates of Columbia University* (New York: Columbia University Press, 1906), 383; "Man's Coat," National Museum of the American Indian, Washington DC, Catalogue Number 19/1253, Barcode 191253.000, accessed March 17, 2021, https://www.npg.si.edu/object/NMAI _204115?destination=edan-search/default_search%3Fpage%3D24721 %26edan_fq%255B0%255D%3Ddate%253A%25221870s%2522%26search _si%3D1; *Charter, Constitution, House Rules, and List of Officers and Members of the University Club, 1882–1883* (New York: Henry Bessey, 1883), 33; John Taliaferro, *Grinnell: America's Environmental Pioneer and His Restless Drive to Save the West* (New York: Liveright, 2019), 84–102.

57. Taliaferro, *Grinnell*, 84–102; Robert Ray Hamilton, "Last Will and Testament," March 17, 1890, "Baileys v. Hamilton, et al., January 20th, 1899," *The New York Supplement, New York State Reporter, Containing the Decisions of Supreme and Lower Courts of Record of New York State* 55 (January 12–March 2, 1899): 391.

58. "Population of Montana by Counties and Civil Divisions," *Census Bulletin* 33 (January 17, 1901): 1; "Hamilton Will Tell His Story To-Day" and "Land Grabbing in Montana," *New York Herald*, September 6, 1889; Ralph W. Hidy, Muriel E. Hidy, and Roy V. Scott, *The Great Northern Railway: A History* (Minneapolis: University of Minnesota Press, 2004), 56–60.

59. Sidney Fleming, "Solving the Suffrage Puzzle One Piece at a Time," *Annals of*

Wyoming 62 (Spring 1990): 22–68; Virginia Scharff, "Broadening the Battle-field: Conflict, Contingency, and the Mystery of Woman Suffrage in Wyoming, 1869," in *Civil War Wests: Testing the Limits of the United States*, ed. Adam Arenson and Andrew R. Graybill (Berkeley: University of California Press, 2015), 202–23; U.S. Census Bureau, *Report of the Population of the United States at the Eleventh Census*, part 1 (Washington DC: Government Printing Office, 1895), xiii, cciv; T. A. Larson, *History of Wyoming* (Lincoln: University of Nebraska Press, 1965), 580; *Brooklyn Daily Eagle Almanac, 1893* (Brooklyn NY: Brooklyn Daily Eagle Book & Job Department, 1893), 7:32; "The Assembly," *Kingston Daily Freeman*, November 7, 1888; James Miller, "Miller's New Map of the City of New-York," 1862, Library of Congress, Call Number G3804.N4 1862.M5, accessed March 18, 2021, https://www.loc.gov/item/2015591066/.

8. Cowpunching

1. "United States Census, 1880," Machias ME, Washington County, enumerated June 11, 1880, 23, Microfilm Publication T9, Record Group 29, National Archives and Records Administration (NARA).

2. Larson, *History of Wyoming*, 63–64, 580; Mark Hufstetler and Michael Bedeau, *South Dakota's Railroads: An Historic Context* (Pierre: South Dakota State Historic Preservation Office, 1998), 8.

3. "Historical Diennial Census Population for Wyoming Counties, Cities, and Towns," Wyoming State Economic Analysis Division, accessed March 19, 2021, http://eadiv.state.wy.us/demog_data/cntycity_hist.htm; Christian Montès, *American Capitals: A Historical Geography* (Chicago: University of Chicago Press, 2014), 151; Christopher Knowlton, *Cattle Kingdom: The Hidden History of the Cowboy West* (Boston: Houghton Mifflin Harcourt, 2017), xiv, 118.

4. Knowlton, *Cattle Kingdom*, 16–17, 112–13; Winston Groom, *Shiloh: 1862* (Washington DC: Smithsonian Institution, 2012), 338–39, 388; Drew Gilpin Faust, *This Republic of Suffering: Death and the American Civil War* (New York: Vintage, 2009), 73, 102, 217, 225.

5. Krys Holmes, Susan C. Dailey, and David Walter, *Montana: Stories of the Land* (Helena: Montana Historical Society, 2008), 150–51; Hannah Nordhaus, "Two Visions Collide amid Push to Restore Montana Plains," *National Geographic*, January 16, 2020.

6. Knowlton., *Cattle Kingdom*, xi, 16; Joshua Specht, "The Rise, Fall, and Rebirth of the Texas Longhorn: An Evolutionary History," *Environmental History* 21 (2016): 347–48.

7. Knowlton, *Cattle Kingdom*, 117, 216–22, 255–99; John W. Davis, *Wyoming Range War: The Infamous Invasion of Johnson County* (Norman: University of Oklahoma Press, 2010), 48–50, 86–88, 275–77.

8. Knowlton, *Cattle Kingdom*, 119; "Wyoming Digital Newspaper Collection," University of Wyoming Libraries, accessed March 19, 2021, https://wyomingnewspapers.org/?a=cl&cl=CLl&e=14-11-1878-14-11-1884--en-20 --1--img-txIN%7ctxCO%7ctxTA-------0--Cheyenne----; Ralph Moody, *Stagecoach Travel West* (Lincoln: University of Nebraska Press, 1967), 50–51.

9. Larson, *History of Wyoming*, 11; "Local Jots," *Laramie Sentinel*, February 15, 1868.

10. Larson, *History of Wyoming*, 199; Seth Shulman, *The Telephone Gambit: Chasing Alexander Graham Bell's Secret* (New York: W. W. Norton, 2015); Michael Riordan and Lillian Hodeson, *Crystal Fire: The Invention of the Transistor and the Birth of the Information Age* (New York: W. W. Norton, 1997), 57–59.

11. Bill Fessel to Kim Gromer, November 15, 1998, Folder Sargent, Box 7, Collection No. 4000007, Kenneth L. and Lenore L. Diem Papers (Diem), American Heritage Center (AHC), University of Wyoming; Bill Fessel to Maura Jane Farrelly, personal interview, October 28, 2018; Record of Births in Salt Lake City, Utah, 1890–1911, 67–68, Salt Lake County Digital Archives, Image No. 004121037_00138, accessed March 22, 2021, https://slco.org/archives/vital -records/Birth.aspx.

12. Knowlton, *Cattle Kingdom*, xi; Andy Adams, *The Log of a Cowboy: A Narrative of the Old Trail Days* (Boston: Houghton Mifflin, 1903), 258; Harvey L. Carter, "Retracing a Cattle Drive: Andy Adams's *The Log of a Cowboy*," *Arizona and the West* 23 (Winter 1981): 369.

13. Joseph Medicine Crow, *From the Heart of Crow Country: The Crow Indians' Own Stories* (Lincoln: University of Nebraska Press, 1992), 67–69; Dee Brown, *Bury My Heart at Wounded Knee: An Indian History of the American West* (New York: Holt, 1970), 37–272.

14. Kenneth L. Diem, Lenore L. Diem, and William C. Lawrence, *A Tale of Dough Gods, Bear Grease, Cantaloupe, and Sucker Oil: Marymere/Pinetree/Mae-Lou/ AMK Ranch* (Moran WY: National Parks Service, 1986), 4–5; Davide Clendinning to Kenneth Diem, November 15, 1985, Folder Sargent, Box 7, Diem, AHC; Edward E. Atwater, ed., *History of the City of New Haven to the Present Time* (New York: W. W. Munsell, 1887), 519.

15. "Sargent's Lawyer Has Posthumous Letter," *Wyoming Tribune*, September 16, 1913; Diem, Diem, and Lawrence, *Tale of Dough Gods*, 4–5.

16. "Sargent's Lawyer," *Wyoming Tribune*, September 16, 1913; John Dudley Sargent to Theodore Roosevelt (i.e., "The President"), November 1, 1906, Final Homestead Entry (FHE) Nos. 1024 and 1632, Letter No. 182354, 36428, Bureau of Land Management Field Office, Lander WY (BLM-Lander); "Wyoming Historic Trails, 1840–1900," Bureau of Land Management–Wyoming State Office, 2019, https://www.blm.gov/sites/blm.gov/files/documents/files /HistoricTrails_web.pdf.

17. Ken Steele, Deb D. Steele, and Mark P. Fisher, "South Pass: Gateway to the West," Geology of Wyoming, accessed March 24, 2021, https://www.geowyo .com/south-pass.html; Will Bagley, "South Pass," WyoHistory, accessed March 24, 2021, https://www.wyohistory.org/encyclopedia/south-pass; "High Plains Water Level Monitoring Study," U.S. Geological Survey Nebraska Water Science Center, accessed March 24, 2021, https://ne.water.usgs.gov/projects /HPA/hpa.html.

18. *U.S. vs. John Sargent and Addie Sargent*, U.S. Clerk of Court, Criminal, 1885–1887, Wyoming State Archives (wsa); Adelaide Crane Sargent to Leander Crane, August 17, 1896, and February 26, 1897, "Deposition of Leander Crane," Supreme Court, New York County, Commissions and Depositions, cd-s-50, Record Room, County Clerk of New York County (ccny).

19. Bagley, "South Pass."

20. "Married," *Machias Union*, February 24, 1885; Tom Lindmier, *Drybone: A History of Fort Fetterman, Wyoming* (Glendo wy: High Plains, 2002).

21. "South Pass City Monthly Climate Averages," World Weather Online, accessed March 24, 2021, https://www.worldweatheronline.com/south-pass -city-weather-averages/wyoming/us.aspx.

22. Glenda Riley, "The Specter of a Savage: Rumor and Alarmism on the Overland Trail," *Western Historical Quarterly* 15 (October 1984): 427–44.

9. One of God's Garden Spots

1. John Daugherty, *A Place Called Jackson Hole* (Moose wy: National Parks Service, 1999), 15, 298; Kevin R. Chamberlain, B. Ron Frost, and Carol D. Frost, "Precambrian Geological Evolution of the Teton Range, Western Wyoming," *Grand Teton National Park Report* 23 (1999): 86.

2. Daugherty, *Jackson Hole*, 14; Scott Stuntz, "Farming in Teton Valley, Heritage or Future?" *Teton Valley News*, June 11, 2014; Hugh T. Lovin, "Dreamers, Schemers, and Doers of Idaho Irrigation," *Agricultural History* 76 (Spring 2002): 232–43.

3. Daughtery, *Jackson Hole*, 71; G. C. Doane, "Expedition of 1876–1887," 1–7, unpublished manuscript, Grand Teton National Park Archives (grte), Moose wy. Gustavus Doan is a controversial figure today because of his involvement in the Marias River Massacre of the Piegan Blackfeet in 1870. The Department of the Interior recently changed the name of Mount Doane in Yellowstone to First Peoples Mountain. There is still a summit in Grand Teton, however—right across the water from Jack Sargent's homestead—named Doane Peak. See April Rubin, "Massacre Leader's Name Is Removed from Yellowstone Mountain," *New York Times*, June 13, 2022; and U.S. Department of the Interior, *Decisions of the United States Board of Geographical Names* (Washington dc: Government Printing Office, 1936), 18.

4. Rodger C. Henderson, "The Piikuni and the U.S. Army's Piegan Expedition," *Montana: The Magazine of Western History* 68 (April 2018): 52; Jessica Gerde, "Alice's Adventures in the New Wonderland," National Parks Service: Yellowstone, accessed April 19, 2021, https://www.nps.gov/yell/blogs/alices -adventures-in-the-new-wonderland-brochure.htm; Hiram Martin Chittenden, *The Yellowstone National Park, Historical and Descriptive* (Cincinnati: Stewart & Kidd, 1915), 338–39; William W. Belknap, *Letter from the Secretary of War, Communicating the Report of Lieutenant Gustavus C. Doane upon the So-Called Yellowstone Expedition of 1870*, February 24, 1871, Senate Documents, 41st Cong., Exdoc 51 (Washington DC: Government Printing Office, 1871), 9, 25; Edward Smith to the Commanding Officer, Fort Ellis, Montana Territory, October 4, 1876, in *Campfire Tales of Jackson Hole*, ed. G. Bryan Harry (Moose WY: Grand Teton Natural History Association, 1960), 11; Aubrey L. Haines, *Yellowstone National Park: Its Exploration and Establishment* (Washington DC: National Parks Service, 1974), 66, 68, 92, 104.

5. Haines, *Yellowstone National Park*, 98; Philip Sheridan, *Report of the Exploration of Parts of Idaho, Wyoming, and Montana in August and September, 1882* (Washington DC: Government Printing Office, 1882), 17–18; George Grinnell, "Their Last Refuge," *Forest and Stream* 19 (1882): 382–83; Eduard de Blaye, *Frommer's USA: 1993–1994* (Hoboken NJ: Prentice Hall, 1993), 688.

6. Daugherty, *Jackson Hole*, 71, 295; Doane, "Expedition of 1876–1877," 3–5.

7. Orestes St. John, "Report of the Geological Fieldwork of the Teton Division," in *Eleventh Annual Report of the United States Geological and Geographic Survey of the Territories Embracing Idaho and Wyoming, Being a Report of the Progress of the Exploration for the Year 1877*, ed. F. V. Hayden (Washington DC: Government Printing Office, 1879), 446–48. Today Upper Gros Ventre Butte is known as Blacktail Butte.

8. Alfred Runte, *National Parks: The American Experience* (New York: Taylor, [1979] 2010), 5–9.

9. Alexis de Tocqueville, *Democracy in America*, ed. Francis Bowen, trans. Henry Reeve (Cambridge MA: Sever & Francis, 1863), 1:64. The quotes from Tocqueville's letter to his mother are in André Jardin, *Tocqueville: A Biography*, trans. Lydia Davis and Robert Hemenway (New York: Farrar, Straus & Giroux, 1988), 133; and William Irwin, *The New Niagara: Tourism, Technology, and the Landscape of Niagara Falls, 1776–1917* (University Park: Penn State University Press, 1996), 19.

10. Edmund Burke, *The Sublime and the Beautiful* (Oxford: Oxford University, 1796), 55–58, 143; John Quincy Adams, "Speech on Niagara Falls," in *Anthology and Bibliography of Niagara Falls*, ed. Charles Mason Dow (Albany NY: J. B. Lyon, 1921), 1:234.

11. Adams, "Speech on Niagara Falls," 233; William R. Irwin, "The New Niagara: The Meaning of Niagara Falls in American Culture, from Discovery to 1920" (PhD diss., University of Virginia, 1991), 24, 26; Emmeline Stuart-Wortley, *Travels in the United States, Etc., during 1849 and 1850* (London: Richard Bentley, 1851), 1:25–26.

12. Runte, *National Parks*, 6.

13. Margaret Fuller, *Summer on the Lakes in 1843* (Boston: Little, Brown, 1844), 7.

14. Runte, *National Parks*, 7; Thomas Rolph, *A Brief Account, Together with Observations, Made during a Visit in the West Indies, and a Tour through the United States of America* (Dundas ON: Heyworth Hackstaff, 1836), 198.

15. Ralph Waldo Emerson, *The American Scholar* (New York: Laurentian, 1901), 2; Oliver Wendell Holmes, *Ralph Waldo Emerson* (Boston: Houghton Mifflin, 1884), 115.

16. Henry D. Thoreau, "Ktaadn," in *The Maine Woods* (Boston: Tickner & Fields, 1864), 41.

17. Frederick Law Olmsted and James T. Gardner, *Special Report of New York State Survey on the Preservation of the Scenery of Niagara Falls* (Albany NY: Charles Van Benthuysen and Sons, 1880), 28.

18. Larry Lahren, *Homeland: An Archaeologist's View of Yellowstone Country's Past* (Livingston MT: Cayuse, 2006), 161; Aubrey L. Haines, *The Yellowstone Story: Our First National Park* (Boulder: University of Colorado Press, 1999), 1:i, 4; Harry, *Campfire Tales*, 6–7.

19. Harry, *Campfire Tales*, 4–7; Washington Irving, *The Adventures of Captain Bonneville* (New York: John B. Alden, 1886), 143.

20. Haines, *Yellowstone National Park*, 21–23, 32–33, 101; "The Yellowstone Expedition," *New York Times*, October 14, 1870.

21. Ellis Paxon Oberholzer, "Jay Cooke, and the Financing of the Civil War," *Century* 73 (November 1906–April 1907): 283.

22. John Harnsberger, *Jay Cooke and Minnesota: The Formative Years of the Northern Pacific Railroad, 1868–1873* (New York: Arno, 1981), 200–201.

23. A. B. Nettleton to Ferdinand Hayden, June 7, 1871, quoted in Haines, *Yellowstone National Park*, 101. For more on Hayden's expedition, see Megan Kate Nelson, *Saving Yellowstone: Exploration and Preservation in Reconstruction America* (New York: Scribner, 2022), 45–63.

24. Runte, *National Parks*, 33–34; Ira H. Latour, "Ansel Adams, the Zone System, and the California School of Fine Arts," *History of Photography* 22, no. 2 (1998): 147–54. The technology that enabled Ansel Adams to capture his now-famous images of the Snake River would not be available for another sixty years.

25. N. P. Lanford, quoted in Haines, *Yellowstone National Park*, 94–95, 145–46; Harold Holzer, *Lincoln at Cooper Union: The Speech That Made Lincoln President* (New York: Simon & Schuster, 2005).

26. Haines, *Yellowstone National Park*, 93–97; Runte, *National Parks*, 35–38; Paul Schullery, *Myth and History in the Creation of Yellowstone National Park* (Lincoln NE: Bison, 2011); Hiram M. Chittenden, quoted in Nancy K. Anderson, *Thomas Moran* (New Haven CT: Yale University Press, 1997), 53; Mary Shivers Culpin, *The History of the Construction of the Road System in Yellowstone National Park, 1872–1966* (Lakewood CO: National Parks Service, 1994), 1:43–68; "Visitation Statistics: Yellowstone," National Park Service, accessed June 7, 2021, https://www.nps.gov/yell/planyourvisit/visitationstats.htm.

27. Gordon Rhea, "The Overland Campaign of 1864," American Battlefield Trust, Spring 2014, https://www.battlefields.org/learn/articles/overland -campaign-1864; Runte, *National Parks*, 39; "Yosemite Act, 1864," in *America's National Park System: The Critical Documents*, ed. Lary M. Dilsaver (Lanham MD: Rowman & Littlefield, 2016), 4.

28. Runte, *National Parks*, 50–51; Associated Press, "Tree Hunters Find Three of the Tallest Sugar Pines Known on Earth," *Washington Post*, February 3, 2021; Leo Hickman, "How a Giant Tree's Death Sparked the Conservation Movement 160 Years Ago," *Guardian*, June 27, 2013.

29. Robert M. Utley and Barry Mackintosh, *The Department of Everything Else: Highlights of Interior History* (Washington DC: U.S. Department of the Interior, 1989), 1–10; "An Act to Set Apart a Certain Tract of Land Lying near the Head-Waters of the Yellowstone River as a Public Park," March 1, 1872, in *The Statutes at Large and Proclamations of the United States of America, from March 1871 to March 1873*, ed. George P. Sanger (Boston: Little, Brown, 1873), 17:32–33.

30. "Notes," *Nation*, March 7, 1872.

31. David Scott and Kang Jae Jerry Lee, "People of Color and Their Constraints to National Parks Visitation," *George Wright Forum* 35 (Winter 2018): 73–82; Elaine Glusac, "Celebrating the National Park Centennial," *New York Times*, June 30, 2016.

32. Haines, *Yellowstone Story*, 1:179, 193–94; Christopher P. Mundun, "Jay Cooke: Banks, Railroads, and the Panic of 1873," *Pennsylvania Legacies* 11 (May 2011): 3–5; Catherine Hannah Davies, *Transatlantic Speculations: Globalization and the Panics of 1873* (New York: Columbia University Press, 2018), 79–81; Scott Reynolds Nelson, "A Storm of Cheap Goods: New American Commodities and the Panic of 1873," *Journal of the Gilded Age and Progressive Era* 10 (October 2011): 449–50.

33. Haines, *Yellowstone Story*, 1:193–96; Jim Cardoza, "Re: trunk weights, 1870s," email message to Maura Jane Farrelly, June 11, 2021.

34. Henry Jacob Winser, *The Yellowstone National Park: A Manual for Tourists* (New York: G. P. Putnam's Sons, 1883), 89–90.

35. Rudyard Kipling, *From Sea to Sea: Letters of Travel*, part 2 (New York: Charles Scribner's Son, 1899), 143.

36. Kipling, *From Sea to Sea*, 146.

37. Haines, *Yellowstone Story*, 1:272; Margaret Andrews Cruikshank and Lee H. Whittlesey, "A Lady's Trip to the Yellowstone, 1883: 'Earth Could Not Furnish Another Such Sight,'" *Montana: The Magazine of Western History* 39 (Winter 1989): 2–15; Ross Thomson, "Did the Telegraph Lead Electrification? Industry and Science in American Innovation," *Business and Economic History* 9 (2011): 18–19; W. Bernard Carlson, *Tesla: Inventor of the Electrical Age* (Princeton NJ: Princeton University Press, 2015), 34–59, 87; Dugald C. Jackson, "Charles Francis Brush," *Proceedings of the American Academy of Arts and Sciences* 69 (February 1935): 494–98; Charles Francis Bush, "Magneto Electric Machine," April 24, 1977, U.S. Patent Number 189997a, Google Patent Repository, https://patentimages.storage.googleapis.com/5a/2b/90/c1d27ce02782bb/US189997.pdf; Mark A. Lemley, "The Myth of the Sole Inventor," *Michigan Law Review* 110 (March 2012): 709–60.

38. Thomas Wentworth Higginson, "Gymnastics," *Atlantic*, March 1861, 284; Thomas Wentworth Higginson to Louisa Wentworth Storrow Higginson, September 8, 1855, in Higginson, *Letters and Journals of Thomas Wentworth Higginson, 1846–1906*, ed. Mary Thacher Higginson (Boston: Houghton Mifflin, 1921), 118.

39. Roderick Nash, *Wilderness and the American Mind* (New Haven CT: Yale University Press, 1967), 23–43.

40. Higginson, *Letters and Journals*, 119; William H. H. Murray, *Adventures in the Wilderness; or Camp-Life in the Adirondacks* (Boston: Fields, Osgood, 1869), 32–33; Tony Perrottet, "Where Was the Birthplace of the American Vacation?" *Smithsonian Magazine*, April 2013; David Strauss, "Toward a Consumer Culture: 'Adirondack Murray' and the Wilderness Vacation," *American Quarterly* 39 (Summer 1987): 270–86; Cindy S. Aron, *Working at Play: A History of Vacations in the United States* (New York: Oxford University Press, 1999), 158–61.

41. Murray, *Adventures in the Wilderness*, 11, 32–33.

42. Aron, *Working at Play*, 164–65; "Women Who Camp Out," *Brooklyn Times Union*, August 4, 1888.

43. Aron, *Working at Play*, 139; Annie Gilbert Coleman, "The Rise of the House of Leisure: Outdoor Guides, Practical Knowledge, and Industrialization," *Western Historical Quarterly* 42 (Winter 2011): 436–57; Joel Daehnke, *In the Work of their Hands in Their Prayer: Cultural Narrative and Redemption on the Amer-*

ican Frontiers, 1830–1930 (Athens: University of Ohio Press, 2003), 265n45; Aubrey Haines, *The Yellowstone Story: Our First National Park* (Yellowstone National Park wy: Yellowstone Library & Museum Association, 1977), 2:101, 131; Elizabeth A. Watry, *Women in Wonderland: Lives, Legends, and Legacies of Yellowstone National Park* (Helena MT: Riverbend, 2012), 91–95.

44. Elizabeth Ann Watry, "More than Mere Camps and Coaches: The Wylie Camping Company and the Development of a Middle-Class Leisure Ethic in Yellowstone National Park, 1883–1916" (master's thesis, Montana State University, 2010), 15–16, 31; Christopher Knowlton, *Cattle Kingdom: The Hidden History of the Cowboy West* (Boston: Houghton Mifflin Harcourt, 2017), 6–7; James H. Shaw, "How Many Bison Originally Populated Western Rangelands?" *Rangelands* 17 (October 1995): 148–50.

45. Watry, *Women in Wonderland*, 91.

46. Haines, *Yellowstone Story*, 2:64; Kenneth L. and Lenore L. Diem, *A Community of Scalawags, Renegades, Discharged Soldiers, and Predestined Stinkers: A History of Northern Jackson Hole and Yellowstone's Influence* (Moose wy: Grand Teton Natural History Association, 1998), 68.

47. "An Irish and Yankee Daredevil," *Los Angeles Times*, August 26, 1913.

48. Daugherty, *Place Called Jackson Hole*, 91.

49. Slim Lawrence, interview with Lenore L. Diem, July 20, 1878; "Notes in Sargent's book, *Some Fruits of Solitude*, by William Penn," in Verba Lawrence, "Scrapbook," 3, Folder Sargent, Box 7, Collection No. 400007, Kenneth L. Diem and Lenore L. Diem Papers (Diem), American Heritage Center (AHC), University of Wyoming.

50. Estate of John D. Sargent, Lincoln County District Court, Probate, Docket 1, 21, August 4, 1913, Wyoming State Archives (WSA).

51. John D. Sargent to Hon. Elihu Root, February 5, 1906, Item No. FC 1024, Records of the Bureau of Land Management, Record Group No. 49.9.29: Records of Wyoming Land Offices (Evanston), National Archives and Records Administration, Denver (NARAD).

52. John Dudley Sargent to "Commanding Officer, U.S. Calvary Stationed in Yellowstone Nat' Park Wyoming," August 22, 1890, Letterbox 7, S–Z and Letterbox 2, Item 3, Document 425, Yellowstone Heritage and Research Center (YHRC).

53. Photograph No. 62-2, Folder 8, Box 3, Diem, AHC; Mary Sargent Cunningham Sears, interview with Elizabeth Hayden, Summer 1955, Folder Sargent, Box 7, Diem, AHC.

54. Barbara E. Titus to Lenore Diem, September 12, 1978, Folder Sargent, Box 7, Diem, AHC; Folder 10, 61-s, Box 3.

55. Robert P. Hamilton to Charlotte Augusta Hamilton, March 11, 1874, Box 2,

Hamilton Family Papers (HFP-Columbia), Columbia University Rare Book and Manuscript Library.

56. Robert P. Hamilton to Charlotte Augusta Hamilton, March 11, 1874, HFP-Columbia.

57. W. C. Lawrence to Alexander Hamilton, January 19, 1957, Jackson Hole Historical Society and Museum (JHHSM), 2006.0646.001; William Simpson, interview with J. Pierce Cunningham, n.d.; Slim Lawrence, interview with Lenore Diem, July 20, 1978; and Pamela K. Sheffield to Lenore Diem, December 1, 1985, Folder Sargent, Box 7, Diem, AHC; S. N. Leek, *In the Mountains of Wyoming: A Diary Illustrated* (Cleveland OH: self-published, 1923), 112, Collection No. 3138, S. N. Leek Collection, AHC; Olaf B. Kongslie, "Surveys Continued to Yellostone [*sic*] Park. Meeting Roosevelt. From Gillettes [*sic*] Iron Trails," Subject File 392, 4, undated interview with unnamed subject but probably Hiram Chittenden, WPA Federal Writers Project Files, Wyoming State Archives (WSA).

58. Robert Ray Hamilton to Gilbert Speir, July 14, 1890, and July 29, 1890, Exhibit No. K1 and L1—Proponent's and "Will of Robert Ray Hamilton, March 17th, 1890," in *Supreme Court, General Term, First Department: In the Matter of Proving the Last Will and Testament of Robert Ray Hamilton, Deceased, as a Will of Real and Personal Property, Case on Appeal* (New York: Evening Post Job Printing House, 1893), 6, 315–19; Casimir deR. Moore to Robert Ray Hamilton, September 5, 1889, MS 513, Folder 8, Box 2, New York Historical Society (NYHS); "Personal," *Columbia Daily Spectator*, May 6, 1881; David L. Eby, "Monroe Marsh: Once and Unspoiled Nature Paradise," *Monroe (MI) News*, September 20, 2020.

59. Nels Paulson, "The Place of Hunters in Global Conservation Advocacy," *Conservation and Society* 10 (Winter 2012): 53–62; "Fair Chase Statement," Boone and Crockett Club, accessed June 28, 2021, https://www.boone-crockett.org/fair-chase-statement?area=huntingEthics.

60. Minor Ferris Buchanan, *Holt Collier: His Life, His Roosevelt Hunts, and the Origin of the Teddy Bear* (Jackson MS: Centennial, 2002).

61. John Taliaferro, *Grinnell: America's Environmental Pioneer and His Restless Drive to Save the West* (New York: Liveright, 2019), 22–37, 57–58, 168–69, 198–99, 204–7; Anne Raver, "The Dark Side of Audubon's Era, and His Work," *New York Times*, March 30, 1997.

62. Taliaferro, *Grinnell*, 63–66; "Buffalo Hunt with the Pawnees," *Forest and Stream*, December 25, 1873.

63. "Snap Shots" and "The Boone and Crockett Club," *Forest and Stream*, February 16, 1888, and January 17, 1889.

64. "Testimony of Gottlieb Bieri," in *Supreme Court, General Term*, 252.

65. Robert Ray Hamilton to Gilbert Speir, July 14, 1890, in *Supreme Court, General Term*, 316–17.

66. Robert Ray Hamilton to Gilbert Speir, July 14, 1890.

67. Gilbert Speir to Robert Ray Hamilton, August 26, 1890, Exhibit No. M1—Proponent's and "Testimony of Gilbert Speir, Jr.," in *Supreme Court, General Term*, 246–50, 320.

68. "Testimony of Casimir de Rahm Moore," in *Supreme Court, General Term*, 250–51.

10. Final Resting Places

1. "'Ray' Hamilton's End," *Helena Daily Independent*, September 15, 1890; "Eva a Widow," *New York Evening World*, September 15, 1890; "Solitary End," *Boston Globe*, September 15, 1890.

2. "Dr. Norvin Green's Death," *New York Times*, February 13, 1893; David Hochfelder, *The Telegraph in America, 1832–1920* (Baltimore MD: Johns Hopkins University Press, 2012).

3. "'Ray' Hamilton's End"; "Testimony of James O. Green," in *Supreme Court, General Term, First Department: In the Matter of Proving the Last Will and Testament of Robert Ray Hamilton, Deceased, as a Will of Real and Personal Property, Case on Appeal* (New York: Evening Post Job Printing House, 1893), 262–66; John D. Sargent to Schuyler Hamilton, September 2, 1890, in "Buried in Idaho," *New York Evening World*, September 16, 1890.

4. "Hewitt-Green," *Detroit Free Press*, November 16, 1886; Clifton Hood, *722 Miles: The Building of the Subways and How They Transformed New York* (Baltimore MD: Johns Hopkins University Press, 1993), 21–28.

5. "Testimony of James O. Green," in *Supreme Court, General Term*, 264.

6. "'Ray' Hamilton's End."

7. "'Ray' Hamilton's End"; S. N. Leek, "Sargent's Homestead on Jackson Lake," unpublished manuscript, Collection No. 3138, S. N. Leek Collection (Leek), American Heritage Center (AHC), University of Wyoming.

8. "Eva a Widow."

9. Rick Geddes and Paul J. Zak, "The Rule of One-Third," *Journal of Legal Studies* 31 (January 2002): 119–37; Sara L. Ziegler, "Uniformity and Conformity: Regionalism and the Adjudication of the Married Women's Property Acts," *Polity* 28 (Summer 1996): 472–77. By the mid-nineteenth century, New York had become one of the few states that did allow married women to own property. The Married Women's Property Act was passed there in 1849, in response to the agitations of people like Elizabeth Cady Stanton, Susan B. Anthony, and Lucretia Mott.

10. "Baby Beatrice Is Here," *New York World*, September 29, 1890; "'Abe' Hummel Dies in London," *New York Times*, January 24, 1926.

11. "Testimony of William T. Steele" and "Testimony of Mrs. Alice Steele," in *Supreme Court, General Term*, 20, 22.

12. "Testimony of William Foyle," in *Supreme Court, General Term*, 24, 26.

13. "Testimony of John S. Mingos," "Testimony of James N. Dixon," "Testimony of Mrs. Llewellyn Adams," "Testimony of Francis M. Leake," and "Testimony of William M. Kemp," in *Supreme Court, General Term*, 28, 46, 31–32, 34–38.

14. *Supreme Court, General Term*, 1.

15. "Hamilton Is Alive," *Philadelphia Times*, February 8, 1891; "Order of Exercises, 117th Commencement of Columbia College, June 28th, 1871" and "Order of Exercises, 118th Commencement of Columbia College, June 26th, 1872," Folder 6, Box 1, Commencement Collection, 1758–, UA #0126, Columbia University Rare Books and Records Library (CRBRL); *Catalogue of the Officer and Students of Columbia College for the Year 1872–1873* (New York: D. Van Nostrand, 1872), 15–16.

16. Theodore Dreiser, *A History of Myself: Newspaper Days* (New York: Horace Liveright, 1922), 467.

17. "Hamilton Is Alive."

18. "Is He Ray's Double?" *Elmira Gazette*, June 11, 1891; Edgar L. Murlin, ed., *The New York Red Book* (Albany NY: James B. Lyon, 1897), 507.

19. "Is He Ray's Double?"

20. "Is He Ray's Double?"; "Hamilton Still Alive," *San Francisco Examiner*, June 11, 1891.

21. "Testimony of Gottleib Bieri," "Testimony of Christian Aeschbacher," and "Testimony of Roman Sepert," in *Supreme Court, General Term*, 252–61; John D. Sargent to Hon. Elihu Root, February 5, 1906, Item No. FC 1024, Records of the Bureau of Land Management, Record Group No. 49.9.29: Records of Wyoming Land Offices (Evanston), National Archives and Records Administration, Denver (NARAD).

22. John D. Sargent to Schuyler Hamilton, September 2, 1890.

23. John D. Sargent to Schuyler Hamilton, September 2, 1890; U.S. Geological Survey, *Wyoming Geographic Names*, book 1 (Reston VA: USGS Office of Research and Technical Standards, 1980), 336.

24. John D. Sargent to Schuyler Hamilton, September 2, 1890; "Is He Ray's Double?"; Esther B. Allan, "History of Teton National Forest," 61, unpublished manuscript, 1973, available at U.S. Forest Service, Department of Agriculture, https://www.fs.usda.gov/Internet/FSE_DOCUMENTS/fseprd534131.pdf.

25. John D. Sargent to Schuyler Hamilton, September 2, 1890; "Ray Hamilton's Death," *New York World*, September 17, 1890; "Spurs," Oregon History Project, accessed July 17, 2021, https://www.oregonhistoryproject.org/articles /historical-records/spurs/#.YPRMRehKg2w.

26. John D. Sargent to Schuyler Hamilton, September 2, 1890.

27. John D. Sargent to Schuyler Hamilton, September 2, 1890.

28. "Marriages," *Machias Union*, February 22, 1885; "Personal," *Laramie Daily Boomerang*, April 29, 1885.

29. "Ray Hamilton's Death"; "Further Details," *St. Louis Post-Dispatch*, September 16, 1890; "Robert Ray Hamilton Dead," *Brooklyn Daily Eagle*, September 15, 1890; "It Was Hamilton's Body," *Pittsburgh Post*, September 17, 1890. There are dozens of articles that came out in mid-September 1890 that mention Jack Sargent's name while focusing on J. O. Green. These are just a handful of examples.

30. "Ray Hamilton's Partner Here," *New York Sun*, June 10, 1891; "Is He Ray's Double?"; "Hamilton Still Alive"; "He Says Ray Hamilton Is Drowned," *New York Tribune*, June 11, 1891.

31. "Ray Hamilton's Fate," *Pittsburgh Dispatch*, June 21, 1891; "Mr. Sargent Testifies," *New York Times*, June 21, 1891.

32. "Ray Hamilton's Fate."

33. "Ray Hamilton's Fate."

34. "Ray Hamilton's Fate"; "Mr. Sargent Testifies," *New York Times*, June 21, 1891.

35. "Testimony of Christian Aeschenbacher" and "Testimony of Roman Sepert," in *Supreme Court, General Term*, 257–58, 260.

36. "Statement of R. S. Spears, Conservation Director of American Trappers' Association, January 19, 1934," in *Hearing before the Special Committee on Conservation of Wild Life Resources, United States Senate, Seventy-Third Congress, Second Session on Grazing of Sheep on the Public Domain and the National Forests, January 27, 1934* (Washington DC: Government Printing Office, 1934), 174; "Raymond S. Spears, Short Story Writer," *New York Times*, January 27, 1950; "John Randolph Spears," in *New International Encyclopedia*, ed. Daniel Coit Gilman, Harry Thurston Peck, and Frank Moore Colby (New York: Dodd, Mead, 1905), 418; John Randolph Spears, *The Hatfields and the McCoys: The Dramatic Story of a Mountain Feud* (Bayside NY: A. J. Cornell, [1888] 2012); "A Mountain Feud," *New York Sun*, October 7, 1888.

37. "It Was Ray Hamilton," *New York Sun*, October 15, 1891.

38. "It Was Ray Hamilton."

39. "It Was Ray Hamilton."

40. "It Was Ray Hamilton."

41. "It Was Ray Hamilton."

42. "It Was Ray Hamilton"; "Current Comment," *Illustrated American*, October 31, 1891; John R. Spears, "In the Snake River Valley," *Chautauquan* 15 (June 1892): 299.

43. "It Was Ray Hamilton."

44. Stanley French, "The Cemetery as Cultural Institution: The Establishment of Mount Auburn and the 'Rural Cemetery' Movement," *American Quarterly* 26 (March 1974): 38.

45. Christopher Wren, "A Letter to a Friend from Christopher Wren in 1708 Concerning the Act of Parliament Passed to Erect Fifty New Additional Parish Churches in the City of London and Westminster," in *Sir Christopher Wren*, by Lena Milman (New York: Charles Scribner's Sons, 1908), 339–40.

46. Wren, "Letter to a Friend," 340; William Bentley, December 13, 1804, in *The Diary of William Bentley, D.D.* (Salem MA: Essex Institute, 1911), 3:127.

47. Jacob Bigelow to Mary Hemenway, August 4, 1862, Folder 6, Box 8, MHS 122, Hemenway Family Papers (HFP), Phillips Library, Peabody Essex Museum, Rowley MA; City of Boston, *Report on the Joint Special Committee on Intramural Internments* (Boston: n.p., 1879), 9; French, "Cemetery and Cultural Institution," 42.

48. French, "Cemetery as Cultural Institution," 44–45.

49. French, "Cemetery as Cultural Institution," 38; Basil Hall, *Travels in North American in 1827 and 1828* (Edinburgh: Adell, 1829), 2:201; Frances Anne Butler, *The Journal of Frances Anne Butler, Better Known as Fanny Kemble* (New York: R. Blom, [1835] 1970), 175–76; Carl David Afwedson, *The United States and Canada in 1832* (New York: Johnson Reprint, [1834] 1969), 1:211.

50. Schuyler Hamilton Jr. to Thomas Marchant, May 24, 1899, and March 18, 1903; Emma G. Hamilton and Alexandra S. Hamilton to Green-Wood Cemetery Association, April 16, 1907, Folder 19596, Green-Wood Cemetery Archives; "Hamilton-Mercer," *Baltimore Sun*, August 15, 1895; "The News Condensed," *New York Times*, May 4, 1899; "United States Census, 1910," Norwalk CT, enumerated April 16, 1910, 1A, Microfilm Publication T624, Record Group 29, National Archives and Records Administration (NARA); *Nathalie E. Baylies v. Schuyler Van Cortlandt Hamilton et al.*, in *Supreme Court—Appellate Division, First Department* (New York: Livingston Middleditch, 1898), 30–31.

51. Gertrude Hamilton to Robert Ray Hamilton, August 27, 1889, MS 513, Folder 6, Box 2, Ray Family Papers (RFP), New York Historical Society (NYHS); *Schuyler Hamilton, Jr. v. Gertrude VC Hamilton, otherwise known as the Baroness Raul de Graffenreid*, November 25, 1901, New York County Clerk Records Office (NYCC), WR-H-286; Emma G. Hamilton and Alexandra S. Hamilton, April 16, 1907, Folder 19596, Green-Wood Cemetery Archives.

52. Schuyler Hamilton to John Church Hamilton, July 25, 1864, MS 0546, Box 1, Hamilton Family Papers (HFP-Columbia), Columbia University Rare Book and Manuscript Library.

53. "Burial Search—Robert Ray Hamilton, Lot 17, Section 67," Green-Wood Cemetery, accessed October 17, 2023, https://www.green-wood.com/burial _results/index.php.

54. "Buried in Greenwood," *Brooklyn Daily Eagle*, July 27, 1892; "Robert Ray Hamilton: His Remains Brought from Wyoming and Reinterred in Green- wood," *Brooklyn Standard Union*, July 27, 1892; "Robert Ray Hamilton's Body," *Middletown (NY) Times-Press*, July 27, 1892.

55. "Testimony of Edson W. Burr," in *Supreme Court, General Term*, 16–17, 267.

56. "Eva Mann Bought Off with $10,000," *Chicago Inter Ocean*, July 7, 1894; "None of Hamilton's Money for Eva," *New York Times*, February 17, 1894; *The Scrap Book: First Section* (New York: Frank A. Munsey, 1907), 4:530; "Woman Wins," *Boston Post*, July 8, 1894; "The Notorious Eva Mann," *Wilkes-Barre (PA) Weekly Union Leader*, July 13, 1894.

57. "Eva at the Footlights," *Tunkhannock (PA) Republican*, September 4, 1891; "Eva at the Footlights," *Pottsville (PA) Republican*, September 2, 1891.

58. "Mann Said to Be Insane," *New York Times*, March 28, 1893; "Now Mrs. Hilton," *Detroit Free Press*, September 13, 1893; "War of the Gauls," *New York World*, December 14, 1893; "Eva Mann Again," *Boston Globe*, September 12, 1893; "Eva Ray Hamilton Again," *Boston Globe*, December 12, 1893; "Eva Hamilton Dies a Pauper," *New York Evening World*, December 7, 1904; "Fic- tion Outdone. Full Story of the Downfall of Robert Ray Hamilton," *Chatta- nooga Daily Times*, September 19, 1889, *Independence Weekly Star and Kansan*, November 8, 1889; *St. Joseph Weekly Gazette*, October 10, 1889; and *Montpelier Argus and Patriot*, October 2, 1889.

11. Like Cures Like

1. Richard J. Bayne, "New Future Looms for Middletown Psychiatric Center," *Middletown Times Herald-Record*, November 7, 2015; James Nani, "Mid- dletown Seeking $500,000 to Remove Debris from Psych Center Fire," *Middletown Times Herald-Record*, September 21, 2016; Rachel Ettlinger, "Ex- Middletown Psychiatric Center Site Seeing Better Days," *Middletown Times Herald-Record*, September 18, 2021.

2. "Mrs. McGibney's Insanity," *New York Times*, October 24, 1897; "Banker's Child Insane," *New York World*, October 24, 1897; Edward P. Dougherty, *Cen- tennial Chronicle: The Story of 100 Years of Middletown State Hospital* (Middle- town NY: Trumbull, 1974), 7, 9.

3. "Middletown State Homeopathic Hospital Patient Case Files," New York State Archives, Series No. 14231-01.

4. "Her Marriage Certificate," *New York Sun*, July 8, 1893; "The Story of the Lady with the Violin: Music in the Tetons, JH Chamber of Commerce Fall Arts Festival 1989 Poster," Jackson Hole Historical Society and Museum (JHHSM), 2002.0548002.

5. "Health Information of Deceased Individuals," U.S. Department of Health and Human Services, accessed August 14, 2021, https://www.hhs.gov/hipaa /for-professionals/privacy/guidance/health-information-of-deceased -individuals/index.html.

6. New York Mental Hygiene Law (1972), Chapter 27, Article 33.13: Clinical Records; Confidentiality, Section (c) and Paragraph 9.iii, New York State Senate, accessed August 14, 2021, https://www.nysenate.gov/legislation/laws /MHY/33.13; Kenneth L. Diem, Lenore L. Diem, and William C. Lawrence, *A Tale of Dough Gods, Bear Grease, Cantaloupe, and Sucker Oil: Marymere/Pinetree/ Mae-Lou/AMK Ranch* (Moran WY: National Parks Service, 1986), 31.

7. Tony Moore, "Rescuing History," *Heller Magazine* (Heller School at Brandeis University), December 19, 2019; Andrea Campetella, "King Davis' Quest to Preserve the Records of the Central Lunatic Asylum for Colored Insane in the Digital Age," *Utopian* (Steve Hicks School of Social Work at the University of Texas at Austin), September 16, 2019; Brit Peterson, "A Virginia Mental Institution for Black Patients, Opened after the Civil War, Yields a Trove of Disturbing Records," *Washington Post*, May 29, 2021; Adam Metcalf Reed, "Mental Death: Slavery, Madness, and State Violence in the United States" (PhD diss., University of California, Santa Cruz, 2014), 1; Wendy Gonaver, *The Peculiar Institution and the Making of Modern Psychiatry, 1840–1880* (Chapel Hill: University of North Carolina Press, 2019), 173–93.

8. David J. Rothman, *The Discovery of the Asylum: Social Order and Disorder in the New Republic* (New York: Little, Brown, 1971), 36–39, 109, 122–23; Ralph Slovenko, "The Transinstitutionalization of the Mentally Ill," *Ohio Northern Law Review* 29 (May 2003): 641.

9. Rothman, *Discovery of the Asylum*, 131.

10. Rothman, *Discovery of the Asylum*, 112; Pliny Earle, "Pyschologic Medicine: Its Importance as Part of the Medical Curriculum," *American Journal of Insanity* 24 (January 1868): 272; F. B. Sanborn, ed., *Memoirs of Pliny Earle, M.D.* (Boston: Damrell & Upham, 1898), 254.

11. S. Weir Mitchell, *Wear and Tear, or Hints for the Overworked* (Philadelphia: J. B. Lippincott, 1871), 7–8, 15, 18.

12. Rothman, *Discovery of the Asylum*, 115–19; Edward Jarvis, *Causes of Insanity: An Address Delivered before the Norfolk, Massachusetts, District Medical Society* (Boston: Vote of the Society, 1851), 15–16.

13. I. Ray, *Mental Hygiene* (Boston: Ticknor & Fields, 1863), 248.

14. Rothman, *Discovery of the Asylum*, 119–22; Ray, *Mental Hygiene*, 261–62.

15. Elaine Showalter, "Victorian Women and Insanity," *Victorian Studies* 23 (Winter 1980): 157–81.

16. S. Lilenthal, "What Is Insanity?" in *Transactions of the Thirty-Eighth Session of the American Institute of Homeopathy*, ed. J. C. Burgher (Pittsburgh PA: Steven & Foster, 1885), 581; S. Weir Mitchell, *Doctor and Patient* (Philadelphia: J. B. Lippincott, 1909), 10–11.

17. Rothman, *Discovery of the Asylum*, 130.

18. Thomas Kirkbride, *On the Construction, Organization, and General Arrangements for Hospitals for the Insane* (Philadelphia: n.p., 1854), 7.

19. Kirkbride, *On the Construction*, 7–12.

20. Jamie Davis, *Haunted Asylums, Prisons, and Sanitoriums: Inside the Abandoned Institutions for the Crazy, Criminal, and Quarantined* (Woodbury MN: Llewellyn, 2013).

21. Slovenko, "Transinstitutionalization of the Mentally Ill," 643–44.

22. Kirkbride, *On the Construction*, 12.

23. Ian Dowbiggen, "'Midnight Clerks and Daily Drudges': Hospital Psychiatry in New York States, 1890–1905," *Journal of the History of Medicine and Allied Sciences* 2 (April 1992): 130–52; Nellie Bly, *Ten Days in a Mad-House* (New York: Ian L. Munro, 1887); "Brutes in an Insane Asylum," *New York Times*, February 7, 1881.

24. "The Middletown Hospital," *New York Times*, April 19, 1891; Dowbiggen, "'Midnight Clerks and Daily Drudges,'" 133; Nancy Tomes, *A Generous Confidence: Thomas Story Kirkbride and the Art of Asylum-Keeping, 1840–1883* (New York: Cambridge University Press, 1984), 294–310.

25. Francis H. Krebs, "A Sketch of the History of Medicine," in *Twentieth Session of the American Institute of Homeopathy, Section 6: Report of the Bureau of Registration, Report and Statistics* (Boston: Alfred Mudge & Son, 1868), 8.

26. Natalie Grams, "Homeopathy—Where Is the Science?" *EMBO Reports* 20 (March 2019): 1–5; Naomi Rogers, "The Proper Place of Homeopathy: Hahnemann Medical College and Hospital in an Age of Scientific Medicine," *Pennsylvania Magazine of History and Biography* 108 (April 1984): 179; "Medical Students Decide to Parade," *Philadelphia Inquirer*, October 24, 1893; "Hahnemann's Hurrah," *Philadelphia Times*, October 29, 1893.

27. "Refuse to Follow Hahnemann's Lead," *Philadelphia Inquirer*, October 25, 1893; "Warring Collegians," *Philadelphia Times*, October 26, 1893.

28. Henry Dale, "Scientific Method in Medical Research," *British Medical Journal* 2 (November 25, 1950): 1185–86.

29. Grams, "Homeopathy," 1; Carol B. Perez and Patricia L. Tomsko, "Homeopathy and the Treatment of Mental Illness in the Nineteenth Century," *Hospital and Community Psychiatry* 45 (October 1994): 1030–31; "Malaria," Mayo Clinic, accessed August 30, 2021, https://www.mayoclinic.org/diseases -conditions/malaria/symptoms-causes/syc-20351184; A. M. Goldenberg and L. M. Wexford, "Quinine Overdose: Review of Toxicity and Treatment," *Clinical Cardiology* 11 (1988): 716–18.

30. Laura Josephson, *A Homeopathic Handbook of Natural Remedies: Safe and Effective Treatment of Common Ailments and Injuries* (New York: Villard, 2002); Stephen Cummings and Dana Ullman, *Everybody's Guide to Homeopathic Medicines: Safe and Effective Remedies for You and Your Family* (New York: Tarcher/ Penguin, 2004).

31. Perez and Tomsko, "Homeopathy," 1030–33; Charles Gatchell, ed., *American Institute of Homeopathy: Transactions of the Fifty-Eighth Session* (Chicago: Public Committee, 1902), 609–22; "The Middletown Hospital," *New York Times*, April 19, 1891.

32. Samuel Worcester, *Insanity and Its Treatment* (New York: Boericke & Tafel, 1882), 65–77, 443–45.

33. Rebecca Dancer and Jenn Barthole, "Relaxing Bath Products to Seriously Up Your Self-Care Game," *Shape*, August 4, 2020, https://www.shape.com /lifestyle/beauty-style/self-care-bath-products; Angela Conklin, "71 Self Care Bath Time Ideas," Pinterest, accessed August 31, 2021, https://www .pinterest.com/angelacconklin/self-care-bath-time/; Worcester, *Insanity and Its Treatment*, 444–45.

34. Worcester, *Insanity and Its Treatment*, 446; Bruce Boman, "Henry Fitzgerald Maudley: Our Forgotten Founder," *Australasian Psychiatry* 21 (May 2013): 435–41.

35. Gatchell, *American Institute of Homeopathy*, 621; Worcester, *Insanity and Its Treatment*, 124–25, 177, 378; Mili Godio, "The Best Weighted Blankets to Shop, According to Experts," NBC Today, April 1, 2022, updated January 13, 2023, https://www.nbcnews.com/select/shopping/best-weighted-blankets -ncna1293860.

36. "Banker's Daughter Lives in Slums," *St. Paul Globe*, February 21, 1904; "Mrs. McGibney Getting Busy," *Brooklyn Times Union*, February 24, 1904; "Pathetic Career of a Banker's Daughter," *San Francisco Examiner*, February 28, 1904; "Lives over a Meat Market," *Boston Globe*, May 1, 1904; "New Mystery Baffles Newport," *Chicago Tribune*, November 13, 1904; "1907–1913: H.H.D and B.S.," Estate of John D. Sargent, Docket 1, 21, March 26, 1915, Lincoln

County, Wyoming State Archives (wsa); Pearl J. Germann to Slim Lawrence, August 14, 1950, Folder Sargent, Box 7, Collection No. 4000007, Kenneth L. and Lenore L. Diem Papers (Diem), American Heritage Center (ahc), University of Wyoming; "United States Census, 1910," Borough of Manhattan, New York County, enumerated May 6, 1910, 17b, Microfilm Publication t624, Record Group 29, National Archives and Records Administration (nara); Diem, Diem, and Lawrence, *Tale of Dough Gods*, 4, 17–19.

12. Marymere

1. "1907–1913: R.R.H.," Estate of John D. Sargent, Docket 1, 21, March 26, 1915, Lincoln County, Wyoming State Archives (wsa); John D. Sargent, "Landbook Notes," Jackson Hole Historical Society and Museum (jhhsm), 2002.0548.001; "Murder or Accident," *Elmira (NY) Star-Gazette*, November 17, 1891; "Mr. Sargent and the Dog," *Rochester Democrat and Chronicle*, June 12, 1891; "Notes in Sargent's book, *Some Fruits of Solitude*, by William Penn," Verba Lawrence, "Scrapbook," 2, Folder Sargent, Box 7, Collection No. 4000007, Kenneth L. and Lenore L. Diem Papers (Diem), American Heritage Center (ahc), University of Wyoming.

2. Barbara Titus to Lenore Diem, November 20, 1978, and Barbara Titus, interview with Lenore and Kenneth Diem, December 8, 9, and 10, 1982, Folder Sargent, Box 7, Diem, ahc; John Dudley Sargent, "Best Camping Experience," jhhsm, 2002.0546.001; Record of Births in Salt Lake City, Utah, 1892, Birth No. 925, Image No. 004121037_00138, Salt Lake County Digital Archives, accessed November 1, 2021, https://www.slco.org/archives/vital-records/birth.aspx; "Monthly Weather Forecast and Climate, Moran, Wyoming," Weather Atlas, accessed September 30, 2021, https://www.weather-us.com/en/wyoming-usa/moran-climate.

3. Sargent, "Best Camping Experience," jhhsm; Earle F. Layser, "Conant Pass Trail: Known to but a Few," *Teton Valley Magazine*, October 13, 2015.

4. Sargent, "Best Camping Experience," jhhsm.

5. Sargent, "Best Camping Experience," jhhsm; Sarah Upton Hemenway to Augustus Hemenway, October 12, 1818, Folder 1, Box 1, mhs 122, Hemenway Family Papers (hfp), Phillips Library, Peabody Essex Museum, Rowley ma.

6. Sargent, "Best Camping Experience," jhhsm.

7. Sargent, "Best Camping Experience," jhhsm; Bill Fessel to Kim Gromer, November 15, 1998, Folder Sargent, Box 7, Diem, ahc.

8. Sargent, "Best Camping Experience," jhhsm; Liz Kearney, "Old Yellowstone: Before National Park Service, U.S. Army Managed Yellowstone," *Yellowstone Insider*, August 24, 2016.

9. Sargent, "Best Camping Experience," jhhsm.

10. John D. Sargent, "A Single Full Summer Day" and "Journal"; and Slim Law-rence to Lenore Diem, personal interview, August 20, 1980, all in Folder Sargent, Box 7, Diem, AHC; Esther B. Allan, "History of Teton National Forest," 51, unpublished manuscript, 1973, available at U.S. Forest Ser-vice, Department of Agriculture, https://www.fs.usda.gov/Internet/FSE _DOCUMENTS/fseprd534131.pdf; "United States Census, 1880," Oneida County, Trenton NY, enumerated June 5, 1880, 6B, Microfilm Publication T9, Record Group 29, National Archives and Records Administration (NARA); "United States Census, 1910," Uinta County, Wilson Precinct, enumerated May 12, 1910, 17B, Microfilm Publication T624, Record Group 29, NARA; Deposition of Hal M. Winslow, February 23, 1899, Supreme Court, New York County, CD-S-50, Record Room, County Clerk of New York County (CCNY).

11. Sargent, "Single Full Summer Day," AHC.

12. Inventory, Book List, Estate of John D. Sargent, WSA.

13. Sargent, "Best Camping Experience," JHHSM.

14. Jordan Norviel, "The Life of Richard Leigh (Beaver Dick) and the Teton Mountains," *Annals of Wyoming* 85 (Autumn 2013): 17–25; Steve Roberts, "Beaver Dick Leigh, Mountain Man of the Tetons," WyoHistory, accessed September 7, 2021, https://www.wyohistory.org/encyclopedia/beaver-dick -leigh-mountain-man-tetons; "Beaver Dick Leigh: Englishman in the Rocky Mountains," *Jackson Hole Historical Society and Museum Chronicle* 35 (Winter 2014–15): 1, 4–5; Theodore Roosevelt, "An Elk-Hunt at Two Ocean Pass," in *The Wilderness Hunter* (New York: Scribner's, 1923), 167.

15. Diary of Richard Leigh, June 14, 1878, Collection No. 10512, AHC.

16. Sargent, "Best Camping Experience," JHHSM.

17. Sargent, "Best Camping Experience," JHHSM.

18. George Eastman to Stephen Nelson Leek, April 1907, Box 6, Collection No. 03138, S. N. Leek Papers (Leek), AHC; Mary Sargent Sears to Elizabeth Hayden, personal interview, Summer 1955; Hilda Stadler to Verba and Slim Lawrence, n.d.; Slim Lawrence to Lenore Diem, personal interviews, July 20, 1978, and August 25, 1981; "Mother of Frances Judge" to Russell A. Apple, personal interview, December 1960, all in Folder Sargent, Box 7, Diem, AHC; "Murder or Accident," *Elmira (NY) Star-Gazette*, November 17, 1891; "Fran-ces Amelia Judge," *Courier: Newsmagazine of the National Parks Service*, Feb-ruary 1993; Frances Judge, "Second Life," *Atlantic Monthly*, November 1952; "United States Census, 1900," Uinta County, Elk Precinct, enumerated June 15, 1900, 8, Microfilm Publication T623, Record Group 29, NARA; "United States Census, 1910," Bannack Township, Beaverhead County MT, enumer-ated April 13, 1910, 1A, Microfilm Publication T624, Record Group 29, NARA; Colin Woodard, *The Lobster Coast: Rebels, Rusticators, and the Struggle for a For-*

gotten Frontier (New York: Viking, 2004), 32. Russell Apple of the NPS identifies his interview subject only as having been "Frances Judge's mother." Census records indicate that Judge's mother was Carrie Nesbit Dunn, who was born in Montana in 1887, the same year Mary Sargent was born, and moved to Jackson, Wyoming, some time before 1900. Russell Apple also mistakenly identifies Mary Sargent as "Margaret" in his notes from the interview with Carrie Nesbit Dunn. Dunn was definitely talking about Mary, however, as this part of the interview is about James Pierce Cunningham and his family, who were homesteaders near Jackson. Mary married James's son, Fred, in 1902, when she was fifteen years old. They divorced ten years later.

19. "It Was Ray Hamilton," *New York Sun*, October 15, 1891; Sargent, "Journal," ACH.

20. John Dudley Sargent to George S. Anderson, June 3, 1895, Letterbox 7, S–Z, Yellowstone Heritage and Research Center (YHRC). Jack also brought up the need for roads that would connect Marymere to the park and to the train station in Idaho in letters that he wrote to Anderson on May 5, 1892; June 16, 1892; July 29, 1892; and June 10, 1893.

21. John Dudley Sargent to William Richards, March 9, 1896, General Correspondence, R–S, Department of Commerce, WSA.

22. John Dudley Sargent to Major John Pritcher, June 8, 1907, and "First Indorsement [*sic*]," Office of the Superintendent of Yellowstone National Park, Major John Pritcher, acting superintendent, April 27, 1907, and May 8, 1907, in Letters Received, September 30, 1906–December 31, 1908, Bound Volume 238, 81, YHRC.

23. H. M. Chittenden to Brigadier General John M. Wilson, February 27, 1900, in *Roads in the Yellowstone National Park: Letter from the Acting Secretary of War . . . Together with Copies or Originals of all Reports Relating to the Present Condition and Appropriate Plans for the Development of the System of Roads in Yellowstone National Park* (Washington DC: Government Printing Office, 1900), 10; Kenneth L. Diem and Lenore L. Diem, *A Community of Scalawags, Renegades, Discharged Soldiers, and Predestined Stinkers: A History of Northern Jackson Hole and Yellowstone's Influence, 1872–1920* (Moose WY: Grand Teton Natural History Association, 1998), 19–22.

24. Gerald W. Williams, *The USDA Forest Service—The First Century* (Washington DC: USDA Forest Service, 2005), 8; Philip Sheridan, *Report of the Exploration of Parts of Idaho, Wyoming, and Montana in August and September, 1882* (Washington DC: Government Printing Office, 1882), 17–18; George Bird Grinnell, "Their Last Refuge," *Forest and Stream*, December 14, 1882.

25. John Daugherty, *A Place Called Jackson Hole* (Moose WY: National Parks Service, 1999), 194; L. L. Newton, "South Entrance Now Open to Yellowstone Park," *Jackson Hole Courier*, August 2, 1917.

26. John Dudley Sargent to "Commanding Officer, U.S. Calvary Stationed in Yellowstone Nat' Park Wyoming," August 22, 1890, Letterbox 7, S–Z, and Letterbox 2, Item 3, Document 425, YHRC.

27. Elliott West, *The Last Indian War: The Nez Perce Story* (New York: Oxford University Press, 2009), 259.

28. Brief of Amicus Curiae, Shoshone-Bannock Tribes of the Fort Hall Reservation, in *Clayvin B. Herrera v. State of Wyoming*, U.S. Supreme Court Docket 17-132, accessed October 2, 2021, https://www.supremecourt.gov/DocketPDF/17/17-532/63310/20180911132729339_17-532tsacShoshoneBannockTribes%20FINAL.pdf, 1n3; Jessica Gresko, "High Court Sides with Crow Tribe Member in Hunting Dispute," Associated Press, May 20, 2019; Diem and Diem, *Community of Scalawags*, 68; H. Barry Holt, "Can Indians Hunt in National Parks? Determinable Indian Treaty Rights and *United States v. Hicks*," *Environmental Law* 16 (Winter 1986): 207–54; John Clayton, "Who Gets to Hunt Wyoming's Elk? Tribal Hunting Rights, U.S. Law, and the Bannock 'War' of 1895," WyoHistory, accessed October 2, 2021, https://www.wyohistory.org/encyclopedia/who-gets-hunt-wyomings-elk-tribal-hunting-rights-us-law-and-bannock-war-1895. In spite of the unambiguous language of the Fort Bridger Treaty (1869), the Supreme Court ruled in 1896 (*Ward v. Race Horse*) that the tribal hunting rights established in the treaty were invalidated by Wyoming's statehood in 1890. The principles of that decision were repudiated 123 years later, when the court ruled that Clayvin Herrera, a citizen of the Crow Tribe, did not violate Wyoming's game laws when he killed several elk in the Big Horn National Forest (*Herrera v. Wyoming*, 2019).

29. Jim Zumbo, *Elk Hunting* (Chanhassen MN: Creative Publishing, 2000), 19; Charles Marble, "Fifty Years around Yellowstone National Park," unpublished manuscript, 1932, Folder Law II, Box 6, Diem, AHC; Charles Edward Ellis, *Authentic History of the Benevolent and Protective Order of Elks* (Chicago: Ellis, 1910), 450; Meade E. Detweiler, *An Account of the Origin and Early History of the Benevolent and Protective Order of Elks of the U.S.A.* (Harrisburg PA: Harrisburg Publishing Group, 1898), 6–9, 27; Frank L. Nelson, "The Secret Society 'Zoo,'" *Hampton Magazine* 27 (April 1912): 194; Robert Enstad, "Elks Open Doors to Blacks," *Chicago Tribune*, July 20, 1973; Annette John-Hall, "In Nationwide Vote, Elks OK Membership for Women," *Philadelphia Inquirer*, October 2, 1995.

30. Diem and Diem, *Community of Scalawags*, 67–70; Kim Viner, "From Slaughter to Law: Wyoming Protects Big Game—Slowly," WyoHistory, accessed October 2, 2021, https://www.wyohistory.org/encyclopedia/slaughter-law-wyoming-protects-big-game%E2%80%94slowly; "Elk Hunting," Wyo-

ming Fish and Game Department, accessed October 2, 2021, https://wgfd
.wyo.gov/Hunting/Hunt-Planner/Elk-Hunting.

31. J. D. Sargent to Hon. W. A. Richards, June 4, 1901, Folder Sargent, Box 7,
Diem, AHC.

32. I. A. Macrum to W. A. Richards, July 24, 1901; and John Dudley Sargent to
George Anderson, June 16, 1892; July 29, 1892; July 30, 1892, all in Folder
Sargent, Box 7, Diem, AHC; John Dudley Sargent to George Anderson, July 23,
1893, and "Veritas" (i.e., John Dudley Sargent) to George Anderson, September 5, 1895, Letterbox 7, S–Z, YHRC.

33. John Dudley to George Anderson, n.d., private collection of Celeste Havener,
Centennial WY; Charles K. Mills, *Harvest of Barren Regrets: The Army Career of
Frederick William Benteen, 1834–1898* (Lincoln: University of Nebraska Press,
2011), 332. The term "buffalo soldier" originated with Native Americans.
It isn't clear which tribe was the first to use it to refer to African American
soldiers, but the term is generally thought to be a reference to the texture
of Black soldiers' hair, which was said to be like that of the fur found on a
bison's head. By the 1890s the term was being applied to all Black soldiers,
but today it's embraced by the members of any army unit that traces its lineage to one of the five all-Black cavalry and infantry units founded in 1866,
regardless of the soldier's race.

34. John Dudley Sargent to George Anderson, March 7, 1893, Letterbox 7,
S–Z, YHRC; Pearl J. Germann to Slim Lawrence, August 14, 1950, JHHS,
2002.0528.001; Pamela K. Sheffield to Lenore Diem, December 1, 1985,
Folder Sargent, Box 7, Diem, AHC.

35. Affidavit of John D. Sargent, August 8, 1904, Homestead Entry (H.E.) No.
1632, 281, Bureau of Land Management Field Office (BLM-Lander), Lander WY.

36. Clayton, "Who Gets to Hunt Wyoming's Elk?"

37. "Situation in Wyoming," *Idaho Statesman*, July 24, 1897; "Some Alarming
Rumors," *Idaho Statesman*, July 26, 1897.

38. "White Settlers Butchered," *San Francisco Chronicle*, July 27, 1895; "None Is
Left Alive," *Chicago Tribune*, July 27, 1897; "Massacred: Reports of the Slaugh-
ter in Wyoming Confirmed," *Louisville Courier-Journal*, July 27, 1895; "Have
Indians Got Them?" *New York Tribune*, July 22, 1895; "Princeton Students
Safe" and "Bannocks Are Fighters," *New York Sun*, July 24, 1895.

39. "All Reported Killed," *Idaho Statesman*, July 27, 1895; "An Alleged Massa-
cre," *Aspen Daily Times*, July 27, 1895; "Excitement Is Intense," *Topeka State
Journal*, July 27, 1897; "An Indian Massacre," *Roxboro (NC) Courier*, July 31,
1895; "All Massacred," *Paterson Evening News*, July 27, 1895; "War in Earnest,"
Idaho Statesman, July 25, 1895; "None Is Left Alive"; "Settlers and Bannocks,"
Washington (DC) Examiner, August 21, 1895.

40. "Whites at Fault, He Thinks," *New York Times*, August 3, 1895.

41. "Indians Pouring In," *New York Evening World*, July 29, 1895; "A Ranch Owner's Appeal for Troops," *Allentown (PA) Morning Call*, July 30, 1895; "Another Battle Fought," *New York Times*, July 30, 1895; "Nobody Hurt," *Brooklyn Citizen*, July 29, 1895; "J. D. Sargent in Jail for Wife Murder," *New York World*, October 3, 1899.

42. Greg Bradsher, "How the West Was Settled: The 150-Year-Old Homestead Act Lured Americans Looking for a New Life and New Opportunities," *Prologue* 40 (Winter 2012): 27; W. A. Richards to Register and Receiver, May 7, 1906, H.E. 1632, BLM-Lander.

43. Gerald W. Williams and Char Miller, "'At the Creation': The National Forest Commission, 1896–1897," *Forest History Today*, Spring–Fall 2005, 32–41.

44. John Dudley Sargent to George Anderson, October 22, 1896, and June 12, 1897, Letterbox 7, S–Z, YHRC.

45. Depositions of Hal M. Winslow, February 2, 1899, and D. C. Nowlin, January 29, 1899, and promissory note, n.d., from John Dudley Sargent, CD-S-50, CCNY; John Dudley Sargent to William Richards, October 9, 1897, General Correspondence, R–S, Department of Commerce, WSA.

46. Julie Beck, "Two Boy Scouts Met in an Internment Camp, and Grew Up to Work in Congress," *Atlantic*, May 17, 2019.

47. John Dudley Sargent to William Richards, October 9, 1897, General Correspondence, R–S, Department of Commerce, WSA.

48. John Dudley Sargent to William Richards, October 18, 1897, WSA.

13. Little Girls

1. Deposition of William Simpson, January 20, 1899, Supreme Court, New York County, Commissions and Depositions, CD-S-50, Record Room, County Clerk of New York County (CCNY).

2. "Inhumane Treatment," *Evanston News-Register*, April 3, 1897.

3. "Inhumane Treatment."

4. Mac Blewer, "Butch Cassidy in Wyoming," WyoHistory, accessed October 8, 2021, https://www.wyohistory.org/encyclopedia/butch-cassidy-wyoming; Bill Bryson, *One Summer: America, 1927* (New York: Random House, 2013), 116–17; Dennis E. Hoffman, *Scarface Al and the Crime Crusaders: Chicago's Private War against Capone* (Carbondale: Southern Illinois University Press, 2010), 159–64.

5. "Brutality of a Human Fiend at Jackson's Hole," *Salt Lake City Herald*, April 11, 1897.

6. "Brutality of a Human Fiend"; Edwin L. Shuman, *Steps into Journalism* (Evanston IL: Correspondence School of Journalism, 1894), 122–23.

7. Deposition of William Simpson, CD-S-50, CCNY; "Will Be Lynched," *Los Angeles Evening Post-Record*, May 6, 1897; "John D. Sargent Lynched," *Waterloo (IA) Courier*, July 26, 1897; "John D. Sargent Lynched," *Muncie (IN) Daily Herald*, July 26, 1897; "Maine Man Lynched," *Pittsburgh Press*, July 24, 1897; "Was Not Lynched," *Dayton (OH) Herald*, July 30, 1897; "Maine Man Lynched," *Woodstock (VT) Spirit of the Age*, July 31, 1897; "Machias Man," *Fall River (MA) Daily Evening News*, August 5, 1897; "New Claim on Hamilton Ranch," *Kansas City Star*, August 1, 1897; "Was Not Lynched," *Wilmington (NC) Messenger*, August 6, 1897; "Sargent of Jackson's Hole," *Salt Lake City Herald*, July 7, 1897; "Afraid of Judge Lynch," *Anaconda (MT) Standard*, July 5, 1897.

8. "Insatiate Fiend," *Wichita (KS) Eagle*, January 14, 1900; "J. D. Sargent in Jail for Wife Murder," *New York Evening World*, October 31, 1899.

9. *Nathalie E. Baylies v. Schuyler Van Cortlandt Hamilton et al.*, June 9, 1897, in *Supreme Court—Appellate Division, First Department* (New York: Livingston Middleditch, 1898), 35.

10. Robert Ray Hamilton, "Last Will and Testament," March 17, 1890, in *Baileys v. Hamilton et al., January 20th, 1899*, in *The New York Supplement, New York State Reporter, Containing the Decisions of Supreme and Lower Courts of Record of New York State* 55 (January 12–March 2, 1899): 391.

11. "Mr. Hamilton's Fate," *Philadelphia Inquirer*, September 16, 1890; "Where the Tragedy Began," *New York World*, September 16, 1890; Elizabeth Rupp to Edward Vollmer, September 24, 1889, MS 513, Folder 7, Box 2, Ray Family Papers (RFP), New York Historical Society (NYHS); "Cared for the Baby," *New York Evening World*, September 15, 1889; "Baby Beatrice Is Here," *New York World*, September 29, 1890.

12. "Baby Beatrice Is Here"; "To Whom Does Beatrice Belong?" *New York Sun*, September 29, 1890.

13. "Where Baby Beatrice Is," *New York Sun*, October 3, 1890; *Gilbert M. Speir, Jr., and Edward L. Baylies v. Schuyler Hamilton, Jr. et al.*, Reference No. 1891, S-51, CCNY; "Bankruptcies: New York," *National Bankruptcy News*, December 1, 1898, 120; *First National Bank of Sing Sing v. Hamilton*, Supreme Court, General Term, First Department, March 16, 1894, in *The New York Supplement*, February 15–April 12, 1894 (St. Paul MN: West, 1894), 27:1029–30; Ann Seacrest to Maura Jane Farrelly, personal interview, Moran WY, July 21, 2021.

14. *Schuyler Hamilton, Jr. v. Gertrude VC Hamilton*, WR-H-286, CCNY; *Nathalie E. Baylies v. Schuyler Van Cortlandt Hamilton et al.*, June 9, 1897, in *Supreme Court—Appellate Division*, 36–37; Alfred M. Heston, *Absegami: Annals of Eyren Haven and Atlantic City, 1609–1904* (Camden NJ: Sinnickson, Chew & Sons, 1904), 153; "United States Census, 1880," New York Foundling Asylum, County of New York, State of New York, enumerated June n.d., 1880, by

Thomas McManus, Microfilm Publication T9, Record Group 29, National Archives and Records Administration (NARA); Diary of Sr. Teresa Vincent, August 17, 1869, MS 347, Folder 3, Box 51, Records of the New York Foundling Hospital, Series VI: Foundling Administrators, New York Historical Society (NYHS); Martin Gottlieb, *The Foundling: The Story of the New York Foundling Hospital* (New York: Lantern, 2001), 36.

15. *Nathalie E. Baylies v. Schuyler Van Cortlandt Hamilton et al.*, 91–92; "Hamilton's Infatuation," *Brooklyn Daily Eagle*, August 30, 1889; "Robert Ray Hamilton: His Real Estate Deals as an Unmarried Man," *Rochester (NY) Democrat and Chronicle*, August 31, 1889; C. Arthur Williams Jr., "Higher Interest Rates, Longer Lifetimes, and the Demand for Life Annuities," *Journal of Risk and Insurance* 53 (March 1986): 165.

16. *Nathalie E. Baylies v. Schuyler Van Cortlandt Hamilton et al.*; "Referee Report: Points of Infant Beatrice Ray Hamilton," in *Supreme Court—Appellate Division*, 85.

17. *Nathalie E. Baylies v. Schuyler Van Cortlandt Hamilton et al.*; "Referee Report: Points of Infant Beatrice Ray Hamilton," in *Supreme Court—Appellate Division*, 3–11, 18–19, 38, 63, 76, 80, 88–91, 108–9, 112.

18. *Nathalie E. Baylies v. Schuyler Van Cortlandt Hamilton et al.*, in *Reports of Cases Heard and Determined in the Appellate Division of the Supreme Court of the State of New York*, reported by Marcus T. Hun (Albany NY: Banks, 1899), 36:135–39; "Beatrice Hamilton Loses," *Brooklyn Standard Union*, January 21, 1899; "Will Lose the $1,200 a Year," *Boston Globe*, January 21, 1899.

19. *Nathalie E. Baylies v. Schuyler Van Cortlandt Hamilton et al.*, 9, 31, 108–9.

20. Stephen O'Connor, *Orphan Trains: The Story of Charles Loring Brace and the Children He Saved and Failed* (Chicago: University of Chicago Press, 2001), 172; Harley L. Lutz, "The Progress of State Income Tax Legislation since 1911," *American Economic Review* 10 (March 1920): 66–91; David C. Hammack, "Nonprofit Organizations, Philanthropy, and Civil Society," in *A Companion to the Gilded Age and Progressive Era*, ed. Christopher McKnight Nichols and Nancy C. Unger (Malden MA: Wiley Blackwell, 2017), 215–28; Karen M. Kennelly, "Women and Spirit," *American Catholic Studies* 121 (Summer 2010): 11.

21. Julie Miller, *Abandoned: Foundlings in Nineteenth-Century New York City* (New York: New York University Press, 2008), 135–36.

22. *Nathalie E. Baylies v. Schuyler Van Cortlandt Hamilton et al.*, in *Supreme Court—Appellate Division*, 37–38; *Annual Report of the State Board of Charities for the Year 1897* (Albany NY: Wynkoop, Hallenbeck, Crawford, 1898), 2:543.

23. O'Connor, *Orphan Trains*, 39, 57–62.

24. Richard Hofstadter, "The Paranoid Style of American Politics," *Harper's*, November 1964; Mark Lilla, *The Once and Future Liberal: After Identity Politics*

(New York: Harper, 2017); Dan T. Carter, *The Politics of Rage: George Wallace, the Origins of the New Conservatism, and the Transformation of American Politics* (Baton Rouge: Louisiana State University Press, 1995); Francis Fukuyama, *Identity: The Demand for Dignity and the Politics of Resentment* (New York: Farrar, Straus & Giroux, 2018); Thomas West, "The Rhetoric of Therapy and the Politics of Anger: From the Safe House to a Praxis of Shelter," *Rhetoric Review* 19 (Autumn 2000): 42–58; Ted Smyth, "Irish American Organizations and the Northern Ireland Conflict in the 1980s: Heightened Political Agency and Ethnic Vitality," *Journal of American Ethnic History* 39 (Winter 2020): 36–61; Kenan Malik, "The Rise of White Identity Politics," *Prospect*, August–September 2020, https://www.prospectmagazine.co.uk/magazine/white-identity-politics-black-lives-matter-race-kenan-malik.

25. O'Connor, *Orphan Trains*, 41–42, 77, 83–84; Edwin G. Burrows and Mike Wallace, *Gotham: A History of New York City to 1898* (New York: Oxford University Press, 1999), 761–66; Paul A. Gilge, "Astor Place Riots," in *The Encyclopedia of New York City*, ed. Kenneth T. Jackson (New Haven CT: Yale University Press, 1995), 1006–8.

26. O'Connor, *Orphan Trains*, 38, 83–84; Burrows and Wallace, *Gotham*, 765.

27. O'Connor, *Orphan Trains*, 155–56; "Our City Charities; the New York House of Refuge" and "Our City Charities; the New York Juvenile Asylum," *New York Times*, January 23, 1860, and January 31, 1860.

28. O'Connor, *Orphan Trains*, xiii, xvi–vii; *Twenty-Ninth Annual Report of the New York Juvenile Asylum to the Legislature of the State and the Common Council of the City of New York for the Year 1880* (New York: Trow's, 1881), 15.

29. O'Connor, *Orphan Trains*, xix–xx; Eileen Boris, "Reconstructing the 'Family': Women, Progressive Reform, and the Problem of Social Control," in *Gender, Class, Race, and Reform in the Progressive Era*, ed. Noralee Frankel and Nancy S. Dye (Lexington: University of Kentucky Press, 1991), 73–86.

30. O'Connor, *Orphan Trains*, 171–75; Dianne Creagh, "The Baby Trains: Catholic Foster Care and Western Migration, 1873–1929," *Journal of Social History* 46 (Fall 2012): 197–218.

31. O'Connor, *Orphan Trains*, 168.

32. Miller, *Abandoned*, 134.

33. Carolee Inskeep, *The New York Foundling Hospital: An Index to the Federal, State, and Local Census Records, 1870–1925* (Baltimore MD: Genealogical Publishing Company, 2004), 10; "All 1900 Federal Census Results for Beatrice Hamilton," Ancestry.com, accessed October 12, 2021, https://www.ancestry.com/search/collections/7602/?name=Beatrice_Hamilton&name_x=1_1&fh=0.

34. O'Connor, *Orphan Trains*, 149.

35. Leon Edel, *Writing Lives: Principia Biographica* (New York: W. W. Norton,

[1959] 1984), 4; and "Transference: The Biographer's Dilemma," *Biography* 7 (Fall 1984): 286.

36. R. L. C. George, "The History of Plumbing," *Plumbing Engineer*, March 2001, 45–53.

37. John Dudley Sargent to George S. Anderson, September 18, 1896, Letterbox 7, S–Z, Yellowstone Heritage and Research Center (YHRC). For more on the experiences women had in the West in the late nineteenth century, see Margaret Walsh, "Women's Place on the Frontier," *Journal of American Studies* 29 (August 1995): 241–55; Susan A. Hallgarth, "Women Settlers on the Frontier: Unwed, Unreluctant, Unrepentant," *Women's Studies Quarterly* 17 (Winter 1989): 23–34; Elizabeth Jameson, "Women as Workers, Women as Civilizers: True Womanhood in the American West," *Frontiers: A Journal of Women Studies* 7 (Fall 1984): 1–8; Isabella L. Bird, *A Lady's Life in the Rocky Mountains* (Mineoloa NY: Dover, [1882] 2003); and Henrietta Dennistoun Haultain, *With the Mounties in the Boot and Saddle Days: An Original Account of Life in the Early West*, ed. Gord Tolton (Fort Macleod AB: Riders of the Plains Commemorative Troop, 2005).

38. Adelaide Crane Sargent to Leander Crane, August 17, 1896, in Deposition of Leander Crane, January 28, 1899, CD-S-50, CCNY.

39. Adelaide Crane Sargent to Leander Crane, August 17, 1896, CCNY.

40. Adelaide Crane Sargent to Leander Crane, February 26, 1897, in Deposition of Leander Crane, January 28, 1899, CD-S-50, CCNY.

41. Adelaide Crane Sargent to Leander Crane, February 26, 1897; Deposition of J. M. Woodburn, January 23, 1899, both CD-S-50, CCNY.

42. "New Hall of Records Site; the Chambers Street Property Formally Selected," *New York Times*, April 3, 1897; Paul Goldberger, *The City Observed: New York: A Guide to the Architecture of Manhattan* (New York: Random House, 1979), 31; "Surrogate's Court (Hall of Records), First Floor Interior," Landmarks Preservation Commission, May 11, 1976, LP-0926, 5, accessed October 20, 2021, http://s-media.nyc.gov/agencies/lpc/lp/0926.pdf; James R. Nicholson, ed., *History of the Order of Elks, 1868–1988* (New York: BPOE, 1992), 12–13.

43. *John D. Sargent v. James Gordon Bennett*, December 24, 1897, PL-1898-S7, CCNY; *John D. Sargent v. Press Publishing Company*, January 11, 1899, CD-S-50, CCNY.

44. Deposition of D. C. Nowlin, January 21, 1899, CD-S-50, CCNY.

45. Deposition of William Simpson, January 20, 1899, CD-S-50, CCNY.

46. Deposition of Laura Nowlin, January 23, 1899, CD-S-50, CCNY.

47. Deposition of Laura Nowlin, January 23, 1899, and Deposition of D. C. Nowlin, January 21, 1899, CCNY.

48. Deposition D. C. Nowlin, January 21, 1899, CCNY.

49. Deposition of D. C. Nowlin, January 21, 1899; Deposition of Laura Nowlin, January 23, 1899; and Deposition of Hattie Osborne, January 24, 1899, CD-S-50, CCNY.

50. Deposition of William Simpson, January 20, 1899, CCNY; John Dudley Sargent to George Anderson, March 30, 1897, and June 12, 1897, Letterbox 7, S–Z, YHRC; Jean A. Mathison, "The Government Ranch in Jackson Hole: A History of the National Elk Refuge," 7, unpublished manuscript, April 1977, U.S. Fish and Wildlife Service, https://ecos.fws.gov/ServCat/DownloadFile /159964?Reference=108453; Annette Hein, "The Establishment of Grand Teton National Park," WyoHistory, accessed October 22, 2021, https://www .wyohistory.org/encyclopedia/establishment-grand-teton-national-park; Wm. L. Simpson, "Address," Teton Lodge, August 17, 1934, Folder 17, Box 82, Collection No. 00026, Milward L. Simpson Papers, 1887–1995, American Heritage Center (AHC), University of Wyoming.

51. Mathison, "Government Ranch," 9–11; "D. C. Nowlin Inducted into the Hall of Fame in 2004," Wyoming Fish and Game, accessed October 22, 2021, https://wgfd.wyo.gov/Get-Involved/Outdoor-Hall-of-Fame/D-C-Nowlin; "National Elk Refuge: Refuge Description," U.S. Fish and Wildlife Service, accessed October 22, 2021, https://www.fws.gov/nwrs/threecolumn.aspx?id =2147510282.

52. Deposition of J. M. Woodburn, January 23, 1899, CD-S-50, CCNY; *The State of Wyoming vs. John D. Sargent*, Third Judicial District, District Court, Uinta County, Docket 2, 199, Wyoming State Archives (WSA).

53. Lily Rothman, "When Spousal Rape First Became a Crime in the U.S.," *Time*, July 28, 2015; Joann M. Ross, "Making Marital Rape Visible: A History of American Legal and Social Movements, Criminalizing Rape in Marriage" (PhD diss., University of Nebraska–Lincoln, 2015).

54. Deposition of Laura Nowlin, January 23, 1899; Deposition of D. C. Nowlin, January 21, 1899, CCNY.

55. Deposition of Laura Nowlin, January 23, 1899, CCNY.

56. Deposition of Laura Nowlin, January 23, 1899, CCNY.

57. Deposition of B. F. Jones, January 20, 1899, CCNY.

58. Deposition of William Simpson, January 20, 1899, CCNY; Jackson JP Civil and Criminal Docket, 1892–1912, AS 1192, 44–50, 58, WSA; *State of Wyoming vs. John D. Sargent*, Third Judicial District, District Court, Uinta County, Docket 2, 199, WSA; Kenneth L. Diem, Lenore L. Diem, and William C. Lawrence, *A Tale of Dough Gods, Bear Grease, Cantaloupe, and Sucker Oil: Marymere/Pinetree/ Mae-Lou/AMK Ranch* (Moran WY: National Parks Service, 1986), 18.

14. Katharine and Catherine

1. "Seacrest Family Legacy Endures," *Lincoln Journal Star*, August 4, 1995; "The Seacrest Family," *Spirit of Nebraska: Pathway*, accessed October 24, 2021, https://nebraskaeducationonlocation.org/families/seacrest-family/; Jacques Steinberg, "Pulitzer to Be Acquired by Lee Enterprises," *New York Times*, February 1, 2005; Kent and Ann Seacrest to Maura Jane Farrelly, personal interview, Moran WY, July 21, 2021.

2. Don Walton, "'Mike' Seacrest Remembered as a Visionary," *Lincoln Journal Star*, December 28, 2017; David Meisenholder, "'Generations' Takes Its Message to All Ages," *Lincoln Star*, November 10, 1983.

3. Monica Davey, "Cities View Homesteads as a Source of Income," *New York Times*, July 25, 2010; Kent and Ann Seacrest, personal interview, Moran WY, July 21, 2021.

4. Kent and Ann Seacrest, personal interview, July 21, 2021; Charles Costello to Beatrice Hamilton Costello Seacrest, April 23, 1952, personal collection of Kent and Ann Seacrest; "United States Census, 1900," Mt. St. Joseph's Academy, Philadelphia PA, enumerated June 15, 1900, 53, Microfilm Publication T623, Record Group 29, National Archives and Records Administration (NARA).

5. "Sargent Goes Insane," *Lincoln Evening News*, December 27, 1899.

6. *State of Wyoming vs. John D. Sargent*, Third Judicial District, District Court, Uinta County, Docket 2, 199, Wyoming State Archives (WSA).

7. *State of Wyoming vs. John D. Sargent*, WSA; Barbara Titus to Lenore Diem, September 12, 1978, Folder Sargent, Box 7, Collection No. 4000007, Kenneth L. and Lenore L. Diem Papers (Diem), American Heritage Center (AHC), University of Wyoming.

8. Deposition of William Simpson, January 20, 1899, Supreme Court, New York County, Commissions and Depositions, CD-S-50, Record Room, County Clerk of New York County (CCNY); "White Man Lynched," *New York Herald* and *Buffalo Enquirer*, July 24, 1897; "Sargent Not Lynched," *New York Herald* and *Buffalo Enquirer*, July 30, 1897; "A Lynching at Jackson's Hole," *Salt Lake City Herald*, July 13, 1897; "Maine Man Lynched," *Pittsburgh Press*, July 24, 1897; "John D. Sargent Lynched," *Waterloo (IA) Courier* and *Muncie (IN) Daily Herald*, July 26, 1897; "Minor News Items," *Algona (IA) Republican*, July 28, 1897; "Ray Hamilton's Ranch," *Baltimore Sun*, July 28, 1897; "Romance of an Idaho Ranch," *San Francisco Chronicle*, July 28, 1897.

9. Deposition of Hal Winslow, February 23, 1899, CD-S-50, CCNY.

10. Barbara Titus to Lenore Diem, September 12, 1978, Folder Sargent, Box 7, Diem, AHC.

11. Deposition of D. C. Nowlin, January 21, 1899, CD-S-50, CCNY; D. C. Nowlin to Charles Sargent, July 7, 1897, Item No. H64-90, D. C. Nowlin Collection, WSA; Leander Crane to D. C. Nowlin, n.d., Jackson Hole Historical Society (JHHS), 2001.0033.001.

12. 23-S, Folder 10, Box 3, Diem, AHC.

13. "J. D. Sargent in Jail for Wife Murder," *New York World*, October 31, 1899.

14. Bill Fessell to Kim Gromer, November 15, 1998, Folder Sargent, Box 7, Diem, AHC; Bill Fessel to Maura Jane Farrelly, personal interview, Haines OR, October 28, 2018.

15. Bill Fessel to Kim Gromer, November 15, 1998, and Hilda Stadler to Verba and Slim Lawrence, December 27, 1964, Folder Sargent, Box 7, Diem, AHC; Bill Fessel, personal interview, October 28, 2018; Kenneth L. Diem, Lenore L. Diem, and William C. Lawrence, *A Tale of Dough Gods, Bear Grease, Cantaloupe, and Sucker Oil: Marymere/Pinetree/Mae-Lou/AMK Ranch* (Moran WY: National Parks Service, 1986), 20, 22.

16. "United States Census, 1900," Philadelphia County, Philadelphia PA, enumerated June 3, 1900, 23A, Microfilm Publication T623, Record Group 29, NARA; Kent and Ann Seacrest, personal interview, July 21, 2021.

17. Charles Costello to Beatrice Costello Seacrest, April 23, 1952, and Beatrice Costello Seacrest to Ann Raschke Seacrest, personal interview, 1977, personal collection of Ann Seacrest.

18. Ann Seacrest, personal interview, July 21, 2021.

19. Ann Seacrest, personal interview, July 21, 2021.

20. Anne M. Butler, *Across God's Frontiers: Catholic Sisters in the American West, 1850–1920* (Chapel Hill: University of North Carolina Press, 2012), 191–230. Katharine Drexel became a saint in 2000.

21. Charles Costello to Beatrice Costello Seacrest, April 23, 1952, personal collection of Ann Seacrest; "United States Census, 1880," Philadelphia County, Philadelphia PA, enumerated June 1, 1880, 17A, Microfilm Publication T9, Record Group 29, NARA; "United States Census, 1900," Philadelphia County, Philadelphia PA, enumerated June 3, 1900, 23A, Microfilm Publication T623, Record Group 29, NARA; "United States Census, 1850," Kensington Ward, Philadelphia PA, enumerated August 9, 1850, 34, Microfilm Publication M432, Record Group 29, NARA; *Nathalie E. Baylies v. Schuyler Van Cortlandt Hamilton et al.*, June 9, 1897, in *Supreme Court—Appellate Division, First Department* (New York: Livingston Middleditch Company, 1898), 36–37.

22. John Sillito and Sarah Langsdon, *Ogden* (Chicago: Arcadia, 2008), 31; John Magerus to Maura Jane Farrelly, personal email, October 26, 2018; Bill Fessel to Kim Gromer, November 15, 1998, Folder Sargent, Box 7, Diem, AHC; "Girl Confesses to Being a Thief," *Ogden (UT) Evening Standard*, April 13, 1911.

23. Bill Fessel, personal interview, October 28, 2018.

24. Bill Fessel to Kim Gromer, Folder Sargent, Box 7, Diem, AHC; Albert Nelson Marquis, *The Book of Chicagoans: A Biographical Dictionary of Leading Men of the City of Chicago* (Chicago: A. N. Marquis, 1911), 421; William Tyre, "The Monday Morning Reading Reading Class," Glessner House, accessed October 31, 2021, https://www.glessnerhouse.org/story-of-a-house/2019/11 /21/the-monday-morning-reading-class-part-i; *Juvenile Protective Association Annual Report* (Chicago: JPA, 1910), 5; Eileen Ford, "Private Initiative and Public Support: The Chicago Juvenile Protective Association," in *A Noble Experiment? The First 100 Years of the Cook County Juvenile Court, 1899–1999*, ed. Gwen Hoerr Jordan (Chicago: Chicago Bar Association, 1999), 30; Nellie Linn to Jane Addams, May 18, 1908, Collection No. JAP-PSC-P, Jane Addams Papers, Series 1, Swarthmore College; List of Jull-House Donors, March 18, 1910, Jane Addams Digital Edition, Swarthmore College, accessed October 31, 2021, https://digital.janeaddams.ramapo.edu/items/show/2764; "Lucy Blair to Become Bride," *Chicago Daily Tribune*, April 16, 1914.

25. Bill Fessel, personal interview, October 28, 2018.

26. Diem, Diem, and Lawrence, *Tale of Dough Gods*, 22; Barbara Titus to Lenore Diem, November 20, 1978; Bill Fessel to Kim Gromer, Folder Sargent, Box 7, Diem, AHC; Bill Fessel, personal interview, October 28, 2018.

27. Bill Fessel, personal interview, October 28, 2018; Bill Fessel to Kim Gromer, AHC.

28. Bill Fessel to Kim Gromer, AHC.

29. Bill Fessel to Kim Gromer, AHC.

30. Record of Births in Salt Lake City, Utah, 1892, Birth No. 925, Image No. 004121037_00138, Salt Lake County Digital Archives, accessed November 1, 2021, https://www.slco.org/archives/vital-records/birth.aspx; Megan Weiss to Maura Jane Farrelly, personal email, October 21, 2018; John Dudley Sargent, "Best Camping Experience," JHHS, 2002.0546.001.

31. Records of Deaths in Salt Lake City, Utah, 1892, Nos. 4473, 4482, 4498, and 4503, Image Nos. 004139830_00141 and 004139830_00133, Salt Lake County Digital Archives, accessed November 1, 2021, https://www.slco.org /archives/vital-records/showDeathRecords.aspx?folder=004139830& filename=004139830_00131&isLedger=Y and https://www.slco.org/archives /vital-records/showDeathRecords.aspx?folder=004139830&filename= 004139830_00133&isLedger=Y.

32. Death No. 4473, Records of Deaths in Salt Lake City, 1892; B. M. Sibai, B. C. Mabie, C. J. Harvey, and A. R. Gonzalez, "Pulmonary Edema in Severe Preeclampsia-Eclampsia: Analysis of Thirty-Seven Consecutive Cases," *American Journal of Obstetrics and Gynecology* 156 (May 1987): 1174–79.

33. Russell R. Rich, *Land of the Sky-Blue Water: A History of the L.D.S. Settlement of the Bear Lake Valley* (Provo UT: Brigham Young University Press, 1963), 19; "Captain Hopkins," *Salt Lake City Daily Tribune*, December 27, 1882; Jill K. Gill, "The Power and the Glory: Idaho's Religious History," in *Idaho's Place: A New History of the Gem State*, ed. Adam M. Sowards (Seattle: University of Washington Press, 2014), 112–13; Henry E. Stamm, *People of the Wind River: The Eastern Shoshones, 1825–1900* (Norman: University of Oklahoma Press, 1999), 46–51, 79–96; "Mortuary: Oliver M. Butler," *Chicago Inter Ocean*, December 20, 1888.

34. Almira Larkin White, *Genealogy of the Descendants of John White of Wenham and Lancaster, Massachusetts, 1638–1901* (Haverhill MA: Chase Brothers, 1900), 92, 101; "Frederick W. Little," *Salt Lake Tribune*, May 6, 1943; "Notice of Sale under Deed," *Salt Lake Herald*, April 15, 1894; Grethe Ballif Peterson, "University of Deseret," in *Encyclopedia of Mormonism*, ed. Daniel H. Ludlow (New York: Macmillan, 1992), 1:1498–99; "United States Census, 1860," Salt Lake City, Salt Lake Territory, enumerated August 1, 1860, 227, Microfilm Publication M653, Record Group 29, NARA; "United States Census, 1900," Salt Lake County, Salt Lake City UT, enumerated June 4, 1900, 3, Microfilm Publication T623, Record Group 29, NARA.

35. Celeste Havener, private collection, Centennial WY.

36. Bill Fessel, personal interview, October 28, 2018.

37. Receiver's receipt, John D. Sargent, August 16, 1904, and John D. Sargent, "Pine Tree Ranch," Homestead Entry (H.E.) No. 1632, Bureau of Land Management Field Office (BLM-Lander), Lander WY; Diem, Diem, and Lawrence, *Tale of Dough Gods*, 18; Mary Sargent Cunningham Sears, interview with Elizabeth Hayden, Summer 1954, Folder Sargent, Box 7, Diem, AHC; *Hattie E. Osborne v. John D. Sargent*, Jackson JP Civil and Criminal Docket, 1892–1912, 44–50, Acc. No. 26, M. L. Simpson Collection, WSA; Adelaide Crane Sargent to Leander Crane, August 17, 1896, in Deposition of Leander Crane, January 28, 1899, CD-S-50, CCNY.

38. Gerald W. Williams and Char Miller, "'At the Creation': The National Forest Commission, 1896–1897," *Forest History Today*, Spring–Fall 2005, 32–41; Homestead Application, August 18, 1904, H.E. 1632, BLM-Lander; Hilda Stadler to Verba and Slim Lawrence, December 27, 1964, and Mary Cunningham Gonzalez to Mrs. Frederick (Barbara) Titus, August 30, 1985, Folder Sargent, Box 7, Diem, AHC.

39. Affidavits of James H. Uhl, Emile Wolff, and John D. Sargent, August 8, 1904, Folder Sargent, Box 7, Diem, AHC.

40. W. A. Richards to Register and Receiver, Lander WY, November 22, 1905, Folder Sargent, Box 7, Diem, AHC.

41. John D. Sargent to U.S. Land Office, Evanston WY, February 6, 1906, and John D. Sargent to Thomas V. Davis, May 29, 1906, Folder Sargent, Box 7, Diem, AHC.

42. W. A. Richards to Register and Receiver, May 7, 1906, and Agricultural Settlement Report, C. W. Woods, October 27, 1904, Folder Sargent, Box 7, Diem, AHC; "Murder or Accident?" *Elmira (NY) Star-Gazette*, November 17, 1891.

43. R. S. Spence to John D. Sargent, December 10, 1905, H.E. 1632, BLM-Lander; Barbara Titus to Lenore Diem, September 12, 1978, Folder Sargent, Box 7, Diem, AHC; John D. Sargent to Superintendent Samuel Young, September 19, 1908, Letterbox 7, S–Z, Yellowstone Heritage and Research Center (YHRC).

44. John D. Sargent to U.S. Land Office, Evanston WY, February 6, 1906, and John D. Sargent to the President, "Adenta," November 1, 1906, H.E. 1632, BLM-Lander; "Mrs. M'Gibney again Protests by Letter," *New York World*, September 23, 1899; "1907–1913: H.H.D. and B.S.," Estate of John D. Sargent, Lincoln County District Court, Probate, Docket 1, 21, August 4, 1913, WSA.

45. R. S. Spence, "Appeal from the Decision of the Hon. Commissioner, of the General Land Office, Holding the Said Entry H.E. No. 1632 for Cancellation, Rendered May 7th, 1906," July 2, 1906; Frank Mondell to W. A. Richards, May 5, 1906; Franklin E. Brooks to W. A. Richards, April 28, 1906; John D. Sargent to the Honorable Secretary of the Interior, June 11, 1906; John D. Sargent to Elihu Root, February 5, 1906; Elihu Root to William A. Richards, December 26, 1906; and John D. Sargent to the President, November 1, 1906, all in H.E. 1632, BLM-Lander.

46. Ethan Hitchcock to John D. Sargent via R. S. Spence, November 16, 1906, H.E. 1632, BLM-Lander.

47. Frank Mondell to W. A. Richards, December 13, 1906; Frank Mondell to E. A. Hitchcock, December 29, 1906, H.E. 1632, BLM-Lander.

48. Ethan Hitchcock to W. A. Richards, January 17, 1907, H.E. 1632, BLM-Lander.

49. "The Story of the Lady with the Violin: Music in the Tetons, JH Chamber of Commerce Fall Arts Festival 1989 Poster," Jackson Hole Historical Society and Museum (JHHSM), 2220.0548002; William M. Millikin, "Jack All Alone," JHHSM, 2002.0543.001; Caroline Muller, "Mysterious Sargent Family Depicted in Festival Poster," *Jackson Hole News*, September 13, 1989; Esther Allan, "Strange Music at Marry Mere," *Teton: The Magazine of Jackson Hole, Wyoming* 9 (1976): 17–18; Pearl Germann to Slim Lawrence, August 14, 1950, and Hilda Stadler to Verba Lawrence, March 31, 1956, Folder Sargent, Box 7, Diem, AHC.

50. 83-s, Folder 8, Box 2, Diem, AHC.

51. Diary of John Brainard MacHarg, July 21, 1908, Folder 29, Box 3, Collection No. 430, Yellowstone National Park Research Library and Archives Collection (YNPRLA), Montana State University.

52. Diary of John Brainard MacHarg, July 21, 1908; "Neenah Woman Gives Relics to Museum," *Appleton (WI) Post-Crescent*, October 22, 1930.

53. John D. Sargent to S. B. Young, August 8, 1907, Letterbox 7, S–Z, YHRC.

54. Hilda Stadler to Verba Lawrence, March 31, 1956, Folder Sargent, Box 7, Diem, AHC; Pearl Germann to Slim Lawrence, August 19, 1950, JHHS, 2002.0528.001; Sargent to J. W. Sammon, October 17, 1913, and November 5, 1913, Estate of John D. Sargent, Lincoln County District Court, Probate, Docket 1, 21, August 4, 1913, WSA.

55. Edith Sargent to John D. Sargent, n.d.; Inventory, Book List, Estate of John D. Sargent, WSA; Pamela K. Sheffield to Lenore Diem, December 1, 1985, and John D. Sargent, "Journal," Folder Sargent, Box 7, Diem, AHC; Diem, Diem, and Lawrence, *Tale of Dough Gods*, 26, 31; Edmund Gosse, "Introduction," in *Some Fruits of Solitude*, by William Penn (Boston: H. M. Caldwell, 1903), 5–8; "Wife Says Sargent Was Innocent Man," *New York Times*, August 17, 1913.

56. Diem, Diem, and Lawrence, *Tale of Dough Gods*, 26, 31; John D. Sargent, note in *Some Fruits of Solitude*, n.p.; John D. Sargent to Edith Sargent, n.d., Estate of John D. Sargent, WSA; Barbara Titus to Lenore Diem, August 20, 1985, Folder Sargent, Box 7, Diem, AHC; "Picturesque Cattleman Hies Himself Away to His Ranch in the Mountains," *Long Beach (CA) Press-Telegram*, April 9, 1913; "Near Drowning," *Los Angeles Times*, March 9, 1913.

57. John D. Sargent to Edith Sargent, n.d., WSA.

58. Pamela K. Sheffield to Lenore Diem, December 1, 1985, Folder Sargent, Box 7, Diem, AHC; Diem, Diem, and Lawrence, *Tale of Dough Gods*, 26, 32; Elsie Baker, "Ye Who Have Yearned Alone," Library of Congress, accessed November 6, 2021, https://www.loc.gov/item/jukebox-131310/.

59. Bill Fessel, personal interview, Haines OR, October 28, 2018; Diem, Diem, and Lawrence, *Tale of Dough Gods*, 21–22.

15. Family Matters

1. Kenneth L. Diem, Lenore L. Diem, and William C. Lawrence, *A Tale of Dough Gods, Bear Grease, Cantaloupe, and Sucker Oil: Marymere/Pinetree/Mae-Lou/AMK Ranch* (Moran WY: National Parks Service, 1986), 29; Will of John D. Sargent, August 30, 1899, and Herbert Hamilton Drake to Carl Cook, August 1, 1913, Estate of John D. Sargent, Lincoln County District Court, Probate, Docket 1, 21, August 4, 1913, Wyoming State Archives (WSA); "Service by Publication," *Jackson Hole Courier*, May 7, 14, and 21, 1936.

2. Edith Sargent to J. W. Sammon, November 5, 1913, and October 17, 1913, Estate of John D. Sargent, WSA.

3. J. W. Sammon to Edith D. Sargent, June 24, 1914, and Statement of Claims Presented, Estate of John D. Sargent, WSA.

4. Herbert Hamilton Drake to Carl Cook, August 1, 1913, and "1907–1913: H.H.D and B.S.," Estate of John D. Sargent, WSA.

5. Edith Sargent to Public Administrator, October 1, 1913, Estate of John D. Sargent, WSA; "Service by Publication"; Diem, Diem, and Lawrence, *Tale of Dough Gods*, 29; Marion V. Allen to Lenore Diem, May 5, 1985, Folder Sargent, Box 7, Collection No. 4000007, Kenneth L. and Lenore L. Diem Papers (Diem), American Heritage Center (AHC), University of Wyoming.

6. Diem, Diem, and Lawrence, *Tale of Dough Gods*, 33–56; Robert Righter, *Crucible for Conservation: The Struggle for Grand Teton National Park* (Moose WY: Grand Teton Association, 2008).

7. Diem, Diem, and Lawrence, *Tale of Dough Gods*, 31; "United States Census, 1930," Hudson River State Hospital, Poughkeepsie NY, Dutchess County, enumerated April 8, 1930, 69, Sheet 12a, Microfilm Publication T626, Record Group 29, National Archives and Records Administration (NARA); "United States Census, 1880," Castleton NY, Richmond County, enumerated June 10, 1880, 29, Microfilm Publication T9, Record Group 29, NARA.

8. Timothy Egan, "Where the Elk and the Diplomats Roam," *New York Times*, September 22, 1989; Dan Oberdorfer, "Soviets Might Present Major Proposals at Talks," *Washington Post*, September 17, 1989.

9. Bill Fessel to Kim Gromer, November 15, 1998, Folder Sargent, Box 7, Diem, AHC.

10. Bill Fessel to Kim Gromer, November 15, 1998, AHC; "Girl Confesses to Being a Thief," *Salt Lake City Tribune*, April 13, 1911; John S. McCormick, *Historic Buildings of Downtown Salt Lake City* (Salt Lake City: Utah State Historical Society, 1982), 142.

11. "Girl Confesses to Being a Thief"; "Trusted Domestic Robs Employers, Now in Jail," *Salt Lake City Tribune*, April 13, 1911; "Gives Girl New Chance in Life," *Salt Lake City Tribune*, April 17, 1911.

12. Bill Fessel to Maura Jane Farrelly, personal interview, Haines OR, October 28, 2018.

13. Barbara Titus to Lenore Diem, September 12, 1978, and August 10, 1977, Folder Sargent, Box 7, Diem, AHC; Bill Fessel, personal interview, October 28, 2018; Irene Gammel, *Looking for Anne of Green Gables: The Story of L. M. Montgomery and her Literary Classic* (New York: St. Martin's, 2008), 172; Melanie Rehak, *Girl Sleuth: Nancy Drew and the Women Who Created Her* (New York: Harcourt, 2005), 260, 292. The idea for Nancy Drew originated with a man named Edward Stratemeyer, but the character was created by a group of female writers who wrote under the collective name of "Carolyn Keene."

14. Bill Fessel to Kim Gromer, November 15, 1998, AHC.

15. "Hamilton's Chum Himself a Suicide," *New York Times*, July 16, 1913; "A Third Fatality at Ray Hamilton Lodge," *New York Sun*, July 26, 1913; "Third Death Mystery at Hamilton Lodge," *New York Tribune*, July 26, 1913. Examples of articles on the West Coast include "Recluse Puts End to His Life," *Spokane Spokesman-Review*, July 27, 1913; "Ends His Life in House of Mystery," *Tacoma Daily Ledger*, July 27, 1913; and "Writes Strange Letter," *Los Angeles Times*, July 31, 1913.

16. Bill Fessel to Kim Gromer, November 15, 1998; Ruth Crane to Louisa Crane, March 18, 1920; and Charles Hemenway Sargent to Catherine Winthrop Sargent, December 17, 1921, all in Folder Sargent, Box 7, Diem, AHC; James L. Moody, ed., *Dictionary of American Naval Fighting Ships*, vol. 1, part A (Washington DC: Naval Historical Center, 1991), 360.

17. J. G. Ward to the Judge General, Navy Department Bureau of Investigation, January 30, 1922, and E. B. Fenner to the Judge Advocate General, February 4, 1922, File No. 26283-4277:1, Stack 11w3, Row 14, Compartment 3, General Correspondence: Record Group 80, NARA.

18. Mary Sargent Curtis to Mr. Stowman, December 21, 1921, and G. D. Stowman to Admiral Rodman, January 26, 1922, File No. 26283-4277:1, Stack 11w3, Row 14, Compartment 3, Record Group 80, NARA.

19. E. B. Fenner to the Judge Advocate General, February 4, 1922, File No. 26283-4277:1, Stack 11w3, Row 14, Compartment 3, Record Group 80, NARA; Barbara Titus to Lenore Diem, August 20, 1985, Folder Sargent, Box 7, Diem, AHC.

20. Charles Hemenway Sargent to Catherine Winthrop Sargent, n.d., and December 17, 1921, Folder Sargent, Box 7, Diem, AHC.

21. Charles Hemenway Sargent to Catherine Winthrop Sargent, n.d., and December 17, 1921, AHC.

22. Charles Hemenway Sargent to Catherine Winthrop Sargent, n.d., and December 17, 1921, AHC.

23. Bill Fessel, personal interview, October 28, 2018.

24. Estate of Henry C. Sargent, Index 5, 563, Washington County Probate Records, Washington County Courthouse, Machias ME.

25. Bill Fessel, personal interview, October 28, 2018; Bill Fessel to Kim Gromer, November 15, 1998, AHC.

26. Bill Fessel to Kim Gromer, November 15, 1998, AHC.

27. Bill Fessel, personal interview, October 28, 2018.

28. Bill Fessel, personal interview, October 28, 2018.

29. Kent Seacrest to Maura Jane Farrelly, personal interview, Moran WY, July 21, 2021.

Epilogue

1. Will of Robert Ray Hamilton, *Baylies v. Hamilton*, in *The New York Supplement* (Albany NY: W. C. Little, 1899), 55:391.

2. Alexandra Kathryn Mosca, *Green-Wood Cemetery* (San Francisco: Arcadia, 2008), 24; "Hamilton Fountain," Riverside Park Conservancy, accessed November 10, 2021, https://riversideparknyc.org/places/hamilton-fountain/.

3. I say the fountain is eleven and a half feet tall because in May 2022 I asked a ten-year-old girl riding her bicycle in front of the fountain to estimate its height, and that's the height she gave me. Her name was Renee, and I got her grandfather's permission to cite her here. I told her I would do so—hi, Renee!

4. Arnold Arluke and Robert Bogdan, *Beauty and the Beast: Human-Animal Relations as Revealed in Real Photo Postcards, 1905–1935* (Syracuse NY: Syracuse University Press, 2010), 126; "S.P.C.A. Offers Prize," *New York Tribune*, September 1, 1903.

5. Thank you, Clyde Austin, for that wonderful day and memory.

6. *Proceedings of the Board of Alderman of the City of New York* (New York: Martin B. Brown, 1891), 202:67–68; "Let Him Be Forgotten," *New York Times*, April 22, 1891.

7. "His Sad Story," *Brooklyn Daily Eagle*, September 7, 1889.

8. Eva Hamilton to Robert Ray Hamilton, n.d., MS 513, Folder 9, Box 2, Ray Family Papers (RFP), New York Historical Society (NYHS).

9. "A Woman's Ready Dagger," *New York Times*, August 27, 1889.

10. "His Sad Story"; "A Mad Infatuation," *New York Times*, August 28, 1889; "Hamilton's Syren," *New York Evening World*, August 28, 1889.

11. "Your sincere old friend" to Robert Ray Hamilton, n.d. (but probably August 29, 1889), MS 515, Folder 9, Box 2, RFP, NYHS.

12. Your sincere friend to Robert Ray Hamilton, September 16, 1889, Folder 9, Box 2, RFP.

13. "A Sincere Friend" to Robert Ray Hamilton, October 4, 1889, Folder 9, Box 2, RFP.

14. "Semper Idem" to Robert Ray Hamilton, October 21, 1889, Folder 9, Box 2, RFP.

15. Maureen Waller, *Sovereign Ladies: Sex, Sacrifice, and Power—The Six Reigning Queens of England* (New York: St. Martin's, 2006), 220.

16. George Chauncey, *Gay New York: Gender, Urban Culture, and the Making of the Gay Male World, 1890–1940* (New York: Basic Books, [1994] 2008), 180–82.

17. Chauncey, *Gay New York*, 291–95, 301–30; Sarah Prager, "Four Flowering Plants That Have Been Decidedly Queered," JStor Daily, January 29, 2020, https://daily.jstor.org/four-flowering-plants-decidedly-queered/.

18. Karl Beckson, "Oscar Wilde and the Green Carnation," *English Literature in Transition, 1880–1920* 43 (September 2000): 387–97.

19. Merlin Holland, *The Real Trial of Oscar Wilde* (New York: Perennial, 2003); Richard Ellmann, *Oscar Wilde* (New York: Knopf, 1988), 435–526; Frank Harris, *Oscar Wilde: His Life and Confessions* (New York: Frank Harris, 1916), 1:318–19.

20. Ellmann, *Oscar Wilde*, 527–85; Leanne Grech, *Oscar Wilde's Aesthetic Education* (London: Palgrave Macmillan, 2019), 35.

21. *John D. Sargent v. James Gordon Bennett*, December 24, 1897, Supreme Court, New York County, PL-1898-S7, Record Room, County Clerk of New York County (CCNY).

22. *John D. Sargent v. James Gordon Bennett*, December 24, 1897.

23. Kenneth L. Diem, Lenore L. Diem, and William C. Lawrence, *A Tale of Dough Gods, Bear Grease, Cantaloupe, and Sucker Oil: Marymere/Pinetree/Mae-Lou/AMK Ranch* (Moran WY: National Parks Service, 1986).

24. Nathalie Massip, "When Western History Tried to Reinvent Itself: Revisionism, Controversy, and the Reception of the New Western History," *Western Historical Quarterly* 52 (Spring 2021): 59–85; Mike Mackey, *Inventing History in the American West: The Romance and Myths of Grace Raymond Hebard* (Powell WY: Western History, 2005); Michael Rutter, *Myths and Mysteries of the Old West* (Guilford CT: Two Dot, 2017); Robert B. Betts, *Along the Ramparts of the Tetons* (Boulder: Colorado Associated University Press, 1978), 150–53; John Daugherty, *A Place Called Jackson Hole* (Moose WY: National Parks Service, 1999), 96.

25. Narrative of John Hemenway, Pine Tree Ranch, and Inventory and Appraisal, Estate of John D. Sargent, Lincoln County District Court, Probate, Docket 1, 21, August 4, 1913, Wyoming State Archives (WSA); "Breakers Rescue," *Long Beach Press-Telegraph*, March 10, 1913.

26. Will of John D. Sargent, Estate of John D. Sargent, WSA; Barbara Titus to Lenore Diem, November 20, 1978, Folder Sargent, Box 7, Collection No. 4000007, Kenneth L. and Lenore L. Diem Papers (Diem), American Heritage Center (AHC), University of Wyoming.

27. Karen Griffee, Sam Swindell, Stephen L. O'Keefe, Sandra S. Stroebel, Keith W. Beard, Shih Ya-Kuo, and Walter Stroup, "Etiological Risk Factors for Sibling Incest: Data from Anonymous, Computer-Assisted Self Interview," *Sexual Abuse: A Journal of Research and Treatment* 28 (2016): 620–59; Mary J. Phillips-Green, "Sibling Incest," *Family Journal: Counseling and Therapy for Couples and Families* 10 (April 2002): 195–202; Paul Okami, Richard Olmsted, and Paul R. Abramson, "Sexual Experiences in Early Childhood: 18-Year Longitudinal Data from the UCLA Family Lifestyles Project," *Journal of Sex Research* 34 (September 1997): 339–47.

28. Bill Fessel to Maura Jane Farrelly, personal interview, Haines OR, October 28, 2018.

29. Bill Fessel, personal interview, October 28, 2018.

30. Alessandro Mantelero, "The EU Proposal for the General Data Protection Regulation and the Roots of the 'Right to Be Forgotten,'" *Computer Law and Security Review* 29 (June 2013): 229–35; David Streitfeld, "European Court Lets Users Erase Records on Web," *New York Times*, May 13, 2014; Dan Levin, "A Racial Slur, a Viral Video, and a Reckoning," *New York Times*, December 26, 2020; Jon Ronson, "How One Stupid Tweet Blew Up Justine Sacco's Life," *New York Times*, February 12, 2015.

31. Yves Congar, "Church History as a Branch of Theology," trans. Jonathan Cavanagh, *Concilium* 7 (1970): 88.

Index

cattle, 23, 34, 59, 116, 166, 168-69, 173, 178, 192

celebrity, 63, 106, 140

census. *See* U.S. Census Bureau

Central Lunatic Asylum for Colored Insane, 224, 229

Central Pacific Railroad, 92–93

Central Park, 85, 130, 214

Central State Hospital Archives Project, 224

Chamber of Commerce (Jackson WY), 4

Chamber of Commerce (New York City), 14

Chandler, Jay, 257

Charles River, 217

Cherokee people, 97

Chesapeake Bay, 141

Cheyenne people, 29, 88, 96–97, 167, 169–70, 180

Chicago Globe, 63

Chicago Tribune, 147–48, 153, 253

Children's Aid Society, 269–71

Chile, 38–39, 81, 237, 287, 323

Chinese laborers, 43, 98

Chinn, Julia. *See* Johnson, Julia Chinn

Chittenden, Hiram, 185

Chivington, John, 96–97

Church of Jesus Christ of Latter-day Saints, 48, 158, 237, 272, 292–93

Church of the Holy Apostles, 119

City Reform Club, 133

"city upon a hill" speech, 72

Civil War, 12, 27, 32, 35, 76, 96, 183–84, 219; and consumer culture, 15, 53, 58–59, 166–67; industrial expansion after, 37, 126–27; and newspapers, 57–59

Clark, William, 87, 172, 183

Clay, Henry, 52

Cleveland, Grover, 101

Cliff Walk (Newport RI), 13

Clinton Hall. *See* Astor Place Opera House

"closing of the American frontier." *See* Frontier Thesis

coal, 92, 98, 110, 180

Cochrane, Elizabeth. *See* Bly, Nellie

Cole, Thomas, 182

Collect Pond, 158, 179

Colorado, 92, 290, 293, 296–97, 303, 309

Colter, John, 183

Columbia River, 172, 177

Columbia University, 11, 21, 24, 26, 139, 197, 206, 314

Comanche people, 88

Conant Trail, 237–39, 242, 251

Confederate Army, 88, 185

Congar, Yves, 326

Congo. *See* Democratic Republic of the Congo

Congregationalism, 268

Connecticut, 17, 29, 90, 119, 170, 189, 225

Conradsen, Mrs. (baby broker), 152–53

Constitution. *See* New York State Constitution; U.S. Constitution

Continental Congress, 13, 21

Continental Divide, 171–72

Cooke, Jay, 183–85, 187–88

Cooper, James Fenimore, 240

Copley Square, 14

copper, 38

Cornhusker State. *See* Nebraska

corpse-skinning, 2, 10, 115–16, 167

Corps of Discovery, 183. *See also* Clark, William; Lewis, Meriwether

Costello, Beatrice Hamilton. *See* Seacrest, Beatrice "Mike" Costello

Foundling. *See* New York Foundling Hospital

The Four Hundred, 20, 27

The Four Million (O. Henry), 20

Fourth Estate, 49

Foyle, William, 205

France, 49, 81, 104, 109–15, 182, 298

Franklin, Benjamin, 70

Franklin, James, 70

Franklin stoves, 90, 170, 189, 197, 278

Fraunces Tavern, 11

French balls, 159, 315, 317–18

frontier, 3, 7–10, 29, 83, 90–91, 165–67, 197, 241–42, 251, 254, 299, 326–27

Frontier Thesis, 7–8

Fuller, Charles, 211–12, 220

Fuller, Margaret, 180, 182

Gallatin, Albert, 21

Gallatin, Horatio, 21

game laws, 192, 248, 250, 253, 279. *See also* hunting

garden cemeteries, 215–17, 314

Garfield, James, 95

Garibaldi blouse, 1, 191

Garrison, William Lloyd, 37

gasoline, 16

Gaul, Archie, 221

Gaul, Eva. *See* Steele, Evangeline

Georgia, 58–59, 97, 314

Germany, 19, 48, 250

germ theory of disease, 216

geyser basins, 177, 182, 185, 245–46

Gilbert, Charles E., 156

The Gilded Age (Twain and Warner), 12, 158–59

Gildersleeve, Henry, 266

Glessner House, 290

Globe Museum. *See* dime museums

Godkin, Edwin Lawrence, 122–23, 128, 186–87

gold, 78, 88, 93, 185, 213–14, 234, 249, 286

Goodnight-Loving Trail, 167

Gould, Jay, 14–15, 98–99, 166, 188

Gramercy Park, 130–31

Grand Central Terminal, 313

Grand Generations (television show), 283

Grand Loop Road, 185

Grand Prismatic Spring, 177

Grand Teton Lodge Company, 9

Grand Teton National Park, 3, 89, 241, 279, 304

Grant, Ulysses S., 185

grass, 37, 167

Gray, Emma. *See* Hamilton, Emma Gray

Great Northern Railroad, 164

Green, Amelia, 202–3

Green, James Oliver, 201–3, 210–11

Green, Norvin, 201

Greene, George, 131

Green-Wood Cemetery, 215, 217–18. *See also* garden cemeteries

Gremeret, Annette, 109–10, 112

Gremeret, Marie, 109–10, 112

Grévy, Jules, 116

Grinnell, George Bird, 163, 198, 246

Grison, Georges, 112–13, 115

Gros Ventre Mountains, 1, 177

Gros Ventre people, 88

guillotine, 109, 114

gymnasiums, 84–85

Hahnemann, Samuel, 231–32

Hahnemann Medical College, 231. *See also* homeopathy

Half Dome, 185–86. *See also* Yosemite Valley

Hall, Basil, 217

Hatfield family, 213
hats. *See* millinery industry
Hawker, Dr. (baby broker), 151–52
Hawthorne, Nathaniel, 82, 182
Hayden, Ferdinand, 183–85, 241
Hayford, J. W., 168
Hearst, William Randolph, 60–61
Helena Daily Independent, 201–3
Hemenway, Alice. *See* Sargent, Alice
   Hemenway
Hemenway, Amy, 77, 79, 81–82
Hemenway, Augustus, Jr., 53, 83–85,
   90–91, 170, 285
Hemenway, Augustus, Sr., 29–30, 33,
   35, 41–46, 78–79, 81–83
Hemenway, Caroline Vinton, 78–79
Hemenway, Charles, 79
Hemenway, Charles Porter, 30, 32,
   38–39, 78
Hemenway, Edith, 77, 82
Hemenway, Harriet Lawrence, 87, 141–
   42, 198
Hemenway, John, 322. *See also* Sar-
   gent, John Dudley
Hemenway, Martha, 79
Hemenway, Mary Tileston, 31, 39, 41–
   42, 77–78, 80–82
Hemenway, Samuel, Jr., 31, 79
Hemenway, Samuel, Sr., 30–31
Hemenway, Sarah "Sally" Upton, 30–
   31, 32, 38, 43, 47, 75–79, 142, 238,
   246
Hemenway, William, 31–32, 35–45,
   76–80, 179, 311
Hemenway Gymnasium. *See*
   gymnasiums
Henry, O. *See* O. Henry
Henry's Fork, 241
Heppenheimer, William C., 147
Hewitt, Abram, 202

Hewitt, Amelia. *See* Green, Amelia
Higginson, Thomas Wentworth, 84,
   189–90
Hill, Harriet, 119
Hiltons. *See* Gaul, Archie
Hinduism, 17
HIPAA, 223
Hippocrates, 231
Hiscock, Frank, 139
A History of New York (Irving), 18
Hitchcock, Ethan, 297–98
Hocker, W. A., 214
Hoe, Richard, 48, 54, 56, 181
Hoe, Robert, 48
Hoe Cylinder Press, 29, 49–50, 54,
   56–57, 181
Hoffman House, 63–64
Hogan, Edward, 159–60
hogs, 166, 196, 242
Holman, Martha, 292
Holmes, Amelia. *See* Sargent, Amelia
   Holmes
Holmes, Oliver Wendell, Sr., 17, 72,
   181–82, 230–31
Holyoke, Edward Augustus, 30
homeopathy, 230–33
home rule (New York City), 125–28,
   132
Homestead Acts, 29, 88–89, 194, 294,
   298
homosexuality, 316–19
Honduras, 24
Hoover Vacuum Cleaner Company,
   304
Hopkins, Richard, 292
Hopkins, Ruth, 292
horses, 16, 31, 124, 128–31, 161, 199,
   202, 214, 237–38, 314, 325
Horseshoe Falls. *See* Niagara Falls
Horse Thief Pass. *See* Conant Trail

hotels: Brunswick, 14–15, 18–20, 25, 28, 72, 93; Manitou, 292–93; Marlborough, 116–17; National, 189, 192; Thornburgh, 210

Howard, A. O., 206–8

Hudson River, 18–19, 158, 179, 182

Hudson River School, 182, 184

Hudson River State Hospital, 305

Hughes, Thomas, 84. *See also* Muscular Christianity

Hull House, 290

Hummel, Abe, 205

Hungary, 268

hunting, 5, 15, 47, 91, 124, 138, 163, 192–94, 202, 248–50, 279; and hunt clubs, 197–99; Indigenous, 170, 183, 248–49, 253–55. *See also* poaching

hysteria, 234, 254–55. *See also* mental illness

Ice Cream Point. *See* Big Island

Idaho, 176, 208–9, 239–40, 296–97

Idaho Statesman, 253–54

Illinois, 14, 23, 137; Chicago, 29, 58–59, 84, 129, 144, 166–69, 217, 290–91

Illustrated American, 214

immigrants: Bohemian, 98; Chinese, 43, 98; Danish, 98; Irish, 12, 43, 55–56, 65, 71, 98, 102–3, 120, 122, 133, 268–69, 271; Italian, 109–11, 268; Swedish, 98, 199, 208, 212, 236, 272

incest, 2, 10, 302, 307–9, 323–24

income tax, 35, 188

India, 111, 227

Indiana, 217, 262, 270

Indigenous Americans, 8, 86–88, 92, 96, 165, 169–70, 174–75, 180, 182–

83, 190, 198, 225, 248–49, 253–55, 292. *See also specific Indigenous groups*

infant trafficking, 146, 147–48, 150–53

"innocent until proven guilty" concept, 158

internet, 7, 52, 139–40, 288–89, 325–26

Interpines Sanitarium, 117–18, 296

Interstate 80, 92, 98, 173

Iowa, 137, 191, 262

Ireland, 43, 55–56, 98, 102, 271. *See also* immigrants

Irving, Washington, 18, 183

Italy, 110, 126, 268

Ivory (soap), 19

ivory (tusks), 248–50, 286

Jackson, David E., 178

Jackson, William Henry, 184

Jackson Lake, 9, 89–91, 104, 118, 193, 197, 199, 200, 208, 236–37, 251, 256, 276, 304

Jackson Lake Dam (Minidoka), 176, 209, 239–40, 295, 297–99

James, Henry, 272

Jarvis, Edward, 225–26

Jefferson Medical College, 231

Jennings, Cortz Hicks, 154–55

Jennings, Mary "Mollie" Bowman, 144–45, 154–55

Jennings, Paul, 155

Jennings, Sarah, 155

Jenny Lake, 241

Jerome, William T., 159, 161

Jesuits' bark, 38–39, 232

Johnson, Andrew, 21

Johnson, Julia Chinn, 51

Johnson, Richard M., 51–52

Johnson, William, 304

Lodge, Henry Cabot, 15–17, 72, 75,
124, 269
Loeffler, Kelly, 117
London, Jack, 63
Long Island, 26, 107, 191
Lonsborough, Alice, 141
Lord & Thomas, 59
Los Angeles Times, 103, 105, 193
Louisiana, 25, 37, 190, 270–71
Louisiana Purchase, 87
loyalists, 11
Lualaba River, 84
lumber. *See* timber industry
Lunacy Commission (New York),
230, 234
lynching, 116, 262, 285–86, 320

MacAdam, Jane, 102
MacAdam, Mary. *See* Drake, Mary
MacAdam
Macbeth (Shakespeare), 268–69
Macé, Gustav, 109–10
MacHarg, John, 299
Machias River, 33, 37
Machias Union, 210
Macready, Charles, 268–69
Madison Square, 14
Maghee, Thomas, 116
Maine: Machias, 6, 32, 41, 43–46, 75–
77, 87, 90, 273–75, 286–87, 320;
Washington County, 35–37, 128,
243, 273, 286, 311, 322
Mammoth Hot Springs, 189
mania, 224, 228, 234. *See also* mental
illness
Manifest Destiny, 87
Mann, Eva. *See* Steele, Evangeline
Mann, "George and Alice," 156–57
Mann, Joshua "Dotty," 120, 135–37,
147, 153, 156–61, 205–6, 219–21

manufacturing, 25, 53, 60
Marquess of Queensbury. *See* Doug-
las, John
Marshall Flats, 136–37
Martha Island, 240
Maryland, 33, 58–59, 148
Marymere, naming and renaming of,
195, 294
Massachusetts Horticultural Society, 217
Massachusetts jurisdiction in Maine,
30, 33–35
Massachusetts Medical Society, 30
Matteson, Sumner, 6, 302
McAllister, Ward, 20, 27, 100–101
McCarty, Henry. *See* Billy the Kid
McCoy, Judy, 99
McCoy, Sherman, 99
McCoy family, 213
McCrystal, Sarah. *See* McNichols,
George; McNichols, Sarah
McCrystal, Teresa Vincent (a.k.a.
Jane), 264, 289
McGibney, Edith. *See* Sargent, Edith
Drake
McGibney, Jessie, 107
McGibney, John, 107
McGibney, Samuel, 106–8, 117–18
McNichols, George, 289
McNichols, Sarah, 289
meat, 59–60, 166
melancholia, 1, 104, 224, 228, 234,
300–301. *See also* mental illness
Melville, Herman, 158, 182
Mental Hygiene Law (New York), 223
mental illness: and African Ameri-
cans, 224; changes in understand-
ing of, 223–29; and democracy,
226; and exercise, 84; and home-
opathy, 230, 232–33; and men, 83;
and modernity, 225; and poverty,